Art across Time

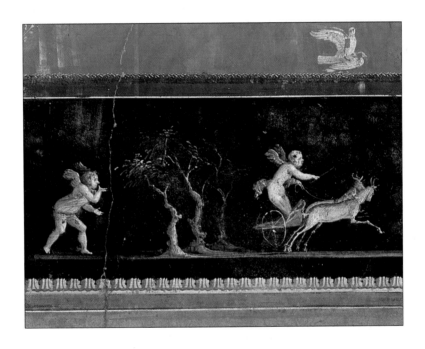

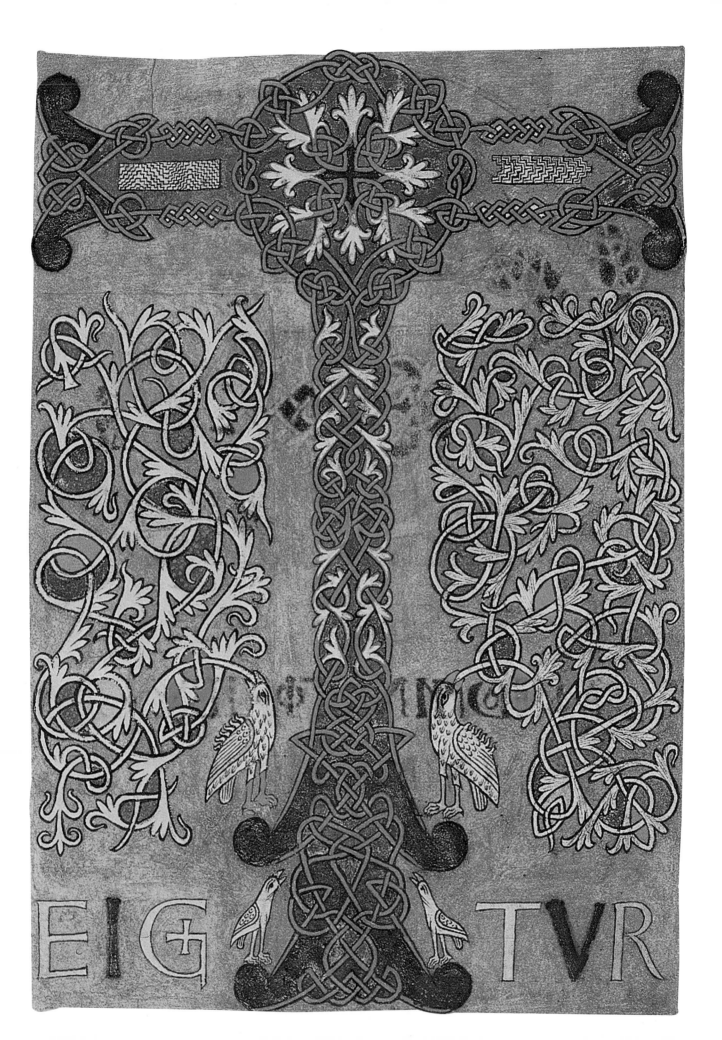

Art across Time

VOLUME I

PREHISTORY TO THE FOURTEENTH CENTURY

LAURIE SCHNEIDER ADAMS

John Jay College and the Graduate Center
City University of New York

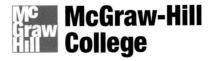 **McGraw-Hill College**

Boston   Burr Ridge, IL   Dubuque, IA   Madison, WI   New York   San Francisco   St. Louis
Bangkok   Bogotá   Caracas   Lisbon   London   Madrid   Mexico City   Milan   New Delhi
Seoul   Singapore   Sydney   Taipei   Toronto

*To the Memory of Howard McP. Davis
and Rudolf Wittkower*

McGraw-Hill College

A Division of The **McGraw·Hill** Companies

Art across Time

Copyright © 1999 by Laurie Schneider Adams. Printed in the
United States of America. Except as permitted under the United
States Copyright Act of 1976, no part of this publication may be
reproduced or distributed in any form or by any means, or
stored in a data base or retrieval system, without the prior
written permission of the publisher.

This book is printed on acid-free paper.

2 3 4 5 6 7 8 9 0   DOW/DOW   9 3 2 1 0 9

ISBN 0–697–27479–9 (volume 1)

Editorial director: Phillip A. Butcher
Executive editor: Cynthia Ward
Developmental editor: Allison McNamara
Marketing manager: David Patterson
Project manager: Denise Santor-Mitzit
Production supervisor: Scott Hamilton
Photo research coordinator: Keri Johnson
Cover designer: Michael Warrell
Supplement coordinator: Bethany J. Stubbe
Repro house: Articolor, Verona, Italy
Typesetter: Fakenham Photosetting, Norfolk, U.K.
Printer: R. R. Donnelley & Sons Company

This book was designed and produced by
CALMANN & KING LTD
71 Great Russell Street, London WC1B 3BN

Senior managing editor: Richard Mason
Designers: Ian Hunt and Linda Henley
Picture researcher: Callie Kendall
Maps by Advanced Illustration

Library of Congress Cataloging-in-Publication Data

Adams, Laurie.
    Art across time / Laurie Schneider Adams.
      p.   cm.
      ISBN 0-697-27478-0 (one vol. ed.) 0-697-27479-9 (v. 1)
  0-697-27480-2 (v. 2)
      Includes bibliographical references and index.
      1. Art -- History. I. Title.
  N5300.A3   1999
  709dc—21   98-38707

Cover: Casa del Bracciale d'Oro, Pompeii (detail). Courtesy of Art
Resource, New York.
Halftitle: Casa del Bracciale d'Oro, Pompeii (detail). Courtesy of Art
Resource, New York.
Frontispiece: Initial from the sacramentary of Saint-Sauveur de Figeac,
11th century. Ms. Lat. 2293, fol. 19v. Courtesy of Bibliothèque
Nationale, Paris/AKG, London.
Back cover: *Buddha Preaching the Law,* Cave 17, Dunhuang Province,
China, early 8th century. Courtesy of British Museum, London.

http://www.mhhe.com

Contents

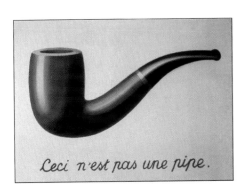

Ceci n'est pas une pipe.

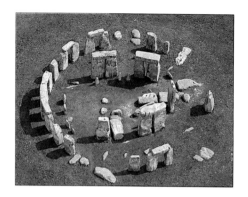

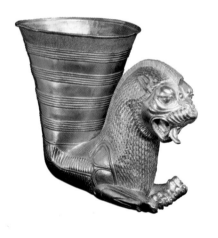

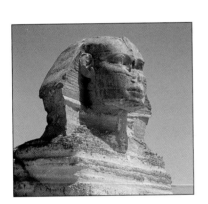

4

Ancient Egypt 76

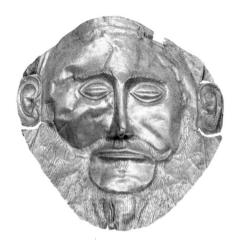

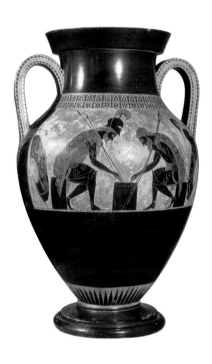

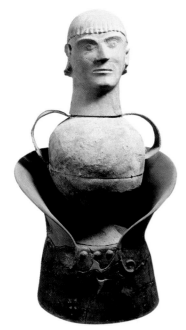

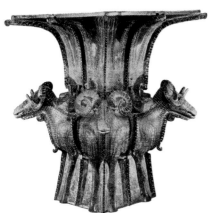

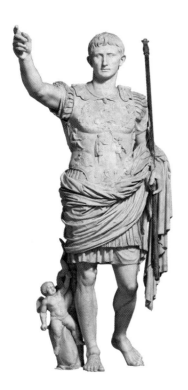

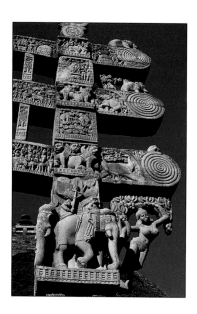

9

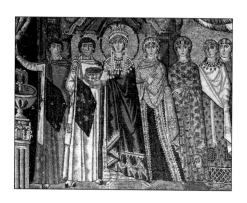

Early Christian and Byzantine Art 271

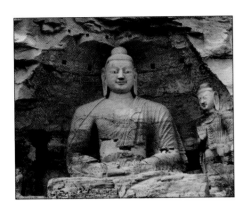

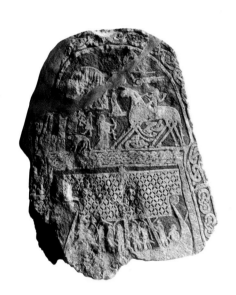

10

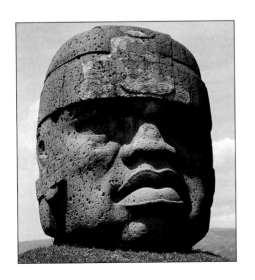

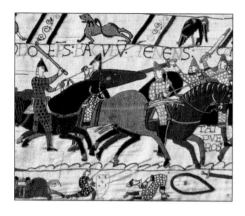

11

Romanesque Art 362

12

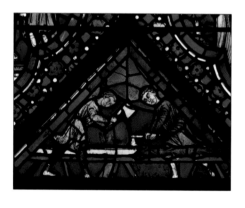

Gothic Art 388

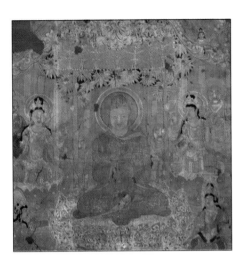

13

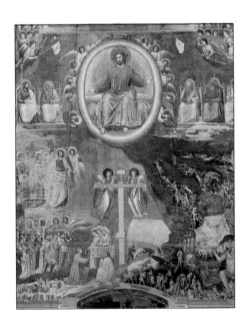

Timelines

Maps

Preface

We are bombarded with images from birth and tend to assume that we understand their meaning. But the paradoxical fact is that, although children read pictures before words, a picture is more complex than a word—hence the proverbial "a picture is worth a thousand words." One aim of *Art across Time* is therefore to introduce readers to the complexity of images, while also surveying the history of those images. Context is a particular area of concern, for works of art lose much of their meaning if separated from the time and place in which they were created. Context also includes questions of function, patronage, and the character and talent of the individual artist.

The complexity of the visual arts has led to different approaches to reading images. Throughout the text, therefore, there are discussions of methodology, and there is a brief survey of the modern methodologies of art historical interpretation in Chapter 1. Van Eyck's *Arnolfini Wedding Portrait* is considered from various methodological viewpoints in Chapter 14 (Volume II), as is Manet's *A Bar at the Folies-Bergère* in Chapter 23 (Volume II).

While comprehensive, *Art across Time* avoids an encyclopedic approach to art history and attempts instead a more manageable narrative that is suitable for a one-year survey course. Certain key works and artists are given more attention than in some books, while other works and artists are omitted entirely. An effort is made to present the history of art as a dynamic narrative grounded in scholarship, a narrative that is a dialogue between modern viewers and their past.

"Windows on the World"

Sections entitled "Windows on the World" provide an introduction to certain non-Western cultures and their art. They are intended to highlight specific periods within cultures, particularly when they are thematically related to, or have significantly influenced, Western art. Some of the Windows—such as Aboriginal rock paintings in the chapter on prehistory (Chapter 2) and Japanese woodblock prints in the chapter on Impressionism (Volume II, Chapter 23)—are within Western chapters. Others—for example those dealing with the Indus Valley Civilization, Olmec culture, and the Far East—are placed chronologically between Western chapters. These Windows offer a sense of the range of world art and remind readers that the history of Western art is only one of the many art historical narratives. These narratives reflect the differences, as well as the similarities, between cultures, and emphasize the complexity of the visual arts by taking Western readers far afield from their accustomed territory and exposing them to unfamiliar ways of thinking about the arts. Like the European artists of the early twentieth century who collected African and Oceanic sculpture in search of new, non-Classical ways of representing the human figure, so viewers who encounter such works for the first time are encouraged to stretch their own limits of seeing and understanding.

Boxes

Within chapters, readers will find "boxes" that encapsulate background information necessary for the study of art. These boxes take students aside, without interrupting the flow of the text, to explain media and techniques, as well as the different philosophies of art from Plato to Marx, Burke to Freud, and Winckelmann to Greenberg. Significant works of literature related to the arts are also covered: epics such as *Gilgamesh*, the *Iliad* and the *Odyssey*, the *Edda,* and *Beowulf,* as well as excerpts of Romantic, Dada, and contemporary poetry. A few of the boxes show artists quoting from their predecessors—Horace Pippin quoting Edward Hicks, for example, and Bob Thompson quoting Lucas Cranach and Paul Gauguin. This helps to establish personal artistic genealogies within the broader narrative of art history.

Illustration Program

The illustrations in *Art across Time* are in a consistently large format, which encourages careful looking. Most of the paintings are reproduced in color, and the percentage of color is higher than in any other survey text presently on the market. Two shades of black are used for the black-and-white illustrations, resulting in greater tonal density, and all illustrations are printed on a five-color press for optimal quality. Occasionally, more than one view of a sculpture or a building is illustrated to give readers a sense of its three-dimensional reality. Architectural discussions are enhanced with labeled plans, sections, and axonometric diagrams. Many of the picture captions include anecdotes or biographical information about the artists; these are intended to encourage readers to identify with painters, sculptors, and architects, and they also provide a sense of the role of artists in society. Maps both define geographical context and indicate the changing of national boundaries over time.

Other Pedagogical Features

Languages as well as the visual arts have a history, and the etymology of many art historical terms are therefore provided. This reinforces the meanings of words and reveals their continuity through time. In the chapter on ancient Greece, transcriptions of terms and proper names are given according to Greek spelling, with certain exceptions in deference to convention: Acropolis, Euclid, Socrates, and Laocoön, all of which would have a "k" rather than a "c" in Greek. Likewise, Roman names and terms are given according to Latin transcription. The first time an art historical term appears in the text, it is highlighted in bold to indicate that it is also defined in the glossary at the back of the book.

At the end of each chapter, a chronological timeline of the works illustrated is useful for review purposes. This lists contemporary developments in other fields as well as cross-cultural artistic developments, and it contains selected images for review.

Acknowledgments

Many people have been extremely generous with their time and expertise during the preparation of this text. John Adams has helped on all phases of the book's development. Marlene Park was especially helpful during the formative stages of the one-volume text; others who have offered useful comments and saved me from egregious errors include Paul Barolsky, Hugh Baron, James Beck, Allison Coudert, Jack Flam, Sidney Geist, Mona Hadler, Arnold Jacobs, Donna and Carroll Janis, Carla Lord, Maria Grazia Pernis, Elizabeth Simpson, Leo Steinberg, Rose-Carol Washton Long, and Mark Zucker. Steve Arbury has read the text several times.

For invaluable assistance with the chapters on antiquity, I am indebted to Larissa Bonfante, Professor of Classics at New York University; Ellen Davis, Associate Professor of Art and Archaeology at Queens College, CUNY; and Oscar White Muscarella of the Department of Ancient Near Eastern Art at the Metropolitan Museum of Art, New York.

For assistance with illustrations, I have to thank, among others, ACA Galleries, Warren Adelson, Margaret Aspinwall, Christo and Jeanne-Claude, Anita Duquette, Georgia de Havenon, the Flavin Institute, Duane Hanson, M. Knoedler and Co., Inc., Thomas Messer, John Perkins, Jim Romano, Irving Sandler, Sidney Janis Gallery, Ronald Feldman Gallery, Robert Miller Gallery, Pace Gallery, and Allan Stone Gallery.

I would like to thank the following readers of the proposal and/or manuscript whose advice has shaped the finished book in many positive ways: Jeffrey C. Anderson, George Washington University; Charlene Villaseñor Black, University of New Mexico; Bill Bryant, Northwestern State University; Kathleen Burke-Kelly, Glendale Community College; Deborah H. Cibelli, Youngstown State University; Andrew L. Cohen, University of Central Arkansas; Ann Glenn Crowe, Virginia Commonwealth University; Jeffrey Dalton, University of North Texas; Carol E. Damian, Florida International University; Kevin Dean, Ringling School of Art and Design; Mark S. Deka, Edinboro University of Pennsylvania; Michael H. Duffy, East Carolina University; Martha Dunkelman, Canisius College; James Farmer, Virginia Commonwealth University; Dorothy B. Fletcher, Emory University; Phyllis Floyd, Michigan State University; Elizabeth L. Flynn-Chapman, Longwood College; Norman Gambill, South Dakota State University; Larry Gleeson, University of North Texas; Thomas Hardy, Northern Virginia Community College; Sandra C. Haynes, Pasadena City College; Felix Heap, Boise State University; Michael Heinlen, University of North Texas; Sandra J. Jordan, University of Montevallo; Ellen Kosmer, Worcester State College; Kathryn Kramer, Purdue University, West Lafayette; Nancy LaPaglia, Daley College; Cynthia Lawrence, Temple University; Carla Lord, Kean College of New Jersey; Brian Madigan, Wayne State University; Susan Madigan, Michigan State University; Richard Mann, San Francisco State University; Virginia Marquardt, Marist College; Julia I. Miller, California State University, Long Beach; Joanne Mannell Noel, Montana State University; Christina J. Riggs, Boston Museum of Fine Arts; Howard Rodee, University of New Mexico; Adrienne Michel Sager, Madison Area Technical College; Patricia B. Sanders, San Jose State University; Fred T. Smith, Kent State University; Stephen Smithers, Indiana State University; Elizabeth Tebow, Northern Virginia Community College; J. N. Thompson, San Jose State University; Robert Tracy, University of Nevada, Las Vegas; Barry Wind, University of Wisconsin, Milwaukee; Astri Wright, University of Victoria.

I would also like to thank Sabra Maya Feldman, whose editing on Volume I was very helpful, and the team at McGraw-Hill: Allison McNamara, Kari Grimsby, David Patterson, Anne Sachs, Scott Hamilton, Michael Warrell, and Denise Santor-Mitzit, and especially executive editor Cynthia Ward, who oversaw the entire management of the project. At Calmann & King, I am grateful for the work of Richard Mason, who supervised the editing process and art program with great skill and good humor, picture researcher Callie Kendall, designers Ian Hunt and Linda Henley, editor Nell Graville, editorial director Lee Ripley Greenfield, and production director Judy Rasmussen.

Laurie Schneider Adams
New York, 1998

1

Why Do We Study the History of Art?

We study the arts and their history because they teach us about our own creative expressions and those of our past. Studying the history of art is one way of exploring human cultures—both ancient and modern—that have not developed written documents. For example, the prevalence of animals in the prehistoric cave paintings of western Europe reveals the importance of animals in those societies. Female figurines with over-sized breasts and hips express the wish to reproduce and ensure the survival of the species. Prehistoric structures, whether oriented toward earth or sky, provide insights into the beliefs of early cultures. If such objects had not been preserved, we would know far less about ancient cultures than we now do.

We would also know less about ourselves, for art is a window onto human thought and emotion. For example, van Gogh's self-portraits are explicitly autobiographical. From what is known about his life, he was sustained by his art. In figure **1.1** he depicts himself behind a painting that we do not see, even though we might suspect that it, too, is a self-portrait. For there are several elements in the

visible painting that assert the artist's presence. Van Gogh's self-image predominates; he holds a set of brushes and a palette of unformed paint composed of the same colors used in the picture. At the center of the palette is an intense orange, the distinctive color of his beard, as well as of his name (Vincent) and the date ('88), with which he simultaneously signs both the painting we see and the painting we do not see.

The Western Tradition

"Western art" is the product of a group of cultures that have historically been thought of as sharing common traditions. Some of these cultures, such as that of medieval France, developed in the western hemisphere, but others, such as that of ancient Babylon (in modern Iraq), did not. Likewise, some cultures that were geographically western, such as that of the Maya (in modern Mexico and Central America), have not traditionally been considered part of the West. This book follows the conventional (Western) usage of the terms "Western" and "non-Western": the Western world comprises North America and Europe, as well as ancient Egypt and the ancient Near East, while the non-Western world comprises all areas and traditions outside those boundaries. It is important, however, to be aware that these categories are based as much on ideas about culture as on geography.

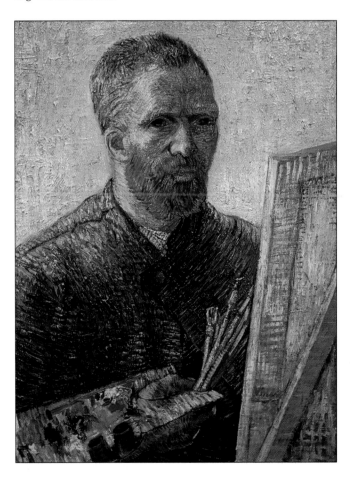

1.1 Vincent van Gogh, *Self-portrait Before his Easel*, 1888. Oil on canvas, 25¾ in × 19⅞ in (65.5 × 50.5 cm). Rijksmuseum, Amsterdam. Vincent van Gogh Foundation.

The arts exemplify the variety of creative expression from one culture to the next. This book surveys the major periods and styles of Western art (see Box), with certain highlights of non-Western art included to give readers a sense of differences—as well as similarities—in works of art around the world.

In the West, the major visual arts fall into three broad categories: pictures, sculpture, and architecture. Pictures (from the Latin *pingo*, meaning "I paint") are two-dimensional images (from the Latin *imago*, meaning "likeness") with height and width, and are usually flat. Pictures are not only paintings, however: they include mosaics, stained glass, tapestries, drawings, prints, and photographs.

Sculptures (from the Latin *sculpere*, meaning "to carve"), unlike pictures, are three-dimensional: besides height and width, they have depth. Sculptures have traditionally been made of a variety of materials such as stone, metal, wood, and clay. More modern materials include glass, plastics, cloth, string, wire, television monitors, and even animal carcasses.

Architecture, which literally means "high (*archi*) building (*tecture*)," is the most utilitarian of the three categories. Buildings are designed to enclose and order space for specific purposes. They often contain pictures and sculptures, as well as other forms of visual art. Some ancient Egyptian tombs, for example, were filled with statues of the deceased. Many churches are decorated with sculptures, paintings, mosaics, and stained-glass windows illustrating the lives of Christ and the saints. Buddhist caves and temples contain sculptures and paintings representing events in the life of the Buddha.

The Artistic Impulse

Art is a vital and persistent aspect of human experience. But where does the artistic impulse originate? We can see that it is inborn by observing children, who make pictures, sculptures, and model buildings before learning to read or write. Children trace images in dirt, build snowmen and sandcastles, and decorate just about anything from their own faces to the walls of their houses. All are efforts to impose order on disorder and to create form from form-lessness. Although it may be difficult to relate an Egyptian pyramid or a Greek temple to a child's sandcastle or toy tower, all express the natural impulse to build.

In the adult world, creating art is a continuation and development of the child's inborn impulse to play. This is clear from the statements of artists themselves: Picasso said that he was unable to learn math, because every time he looked at the number 7 he thought he saw an upside-down nose. The self-taught American artist Horace Pippin described his impulse to attach drawings to words when learning to spell. But the art created by adults takes on different meanings, which are cultural as well as individual.

One powerful motive for making art is the wish to leave behind after death something of value by which to be remembered. The work of art symbolically prolongs the artist's existence. This parallels the pervasive feeling that by having children one is ensuring genealogical continuity into the future. Several artists have made such a connection. In an anecdote about Giotto, the fourteenth-century Italian artist, the poet Dante asks Giotto why his children are so ugly and his paintings so beautiful; Giotto replies that he paints by the light of day and reproduces in the darkness of night. According to his biographers, Michelangelo said that he had no human children because his works were his children. The twentieth-century Swiss artist Paul Klee also referred to his pictures as children, and equated artistic genius with procreation. His German contemporary Joseph Albers cited this traditional connection between creation and procreation in relation to paint itself: he described a mixed color (see "The Language of Art," p. 17) as the offspring of the two original colors, and compared it to a child who combines the genes of two parents.

Related to the role of art as a memorial is the wish to preserve one's likeness after death. Artists are often commissioned to paint **portraits**, or representations of specific people. They also make self-portraits. "Painting makes absent men present and the dead seem alive," wrote Leon Battista Alberti, the fifteenth-century Italian humanist. "I paint to preserve the likeness of men after their death," wrote Albrecht Dürer in sixteenth-century Germany. Even as early as the Neolithic era (in western Europe c. 6000/ 4000–2000 B.C. (see Box) and the seventh millennium in the Near East), skulls were modeled into faces with plaster, and shells were inserted into the eye sockets. In ancient Egypt, a pharaoh's features were painted on the outside of his mummy case so that his *ka*, or soul, could recognize him. The Mycenaeans made gold death masks of their kings, and the Romans preserved the images of their ancestors by carving marble portraits from wax death masks.

Chronology

The Christian calendar, traditionally used in the West, is followed throughout this book. Other religions, such as Hinduism, Buddhism, Islam, and Judaism, have different dating systems.

Dates before the birth of Christ are followed by the letters B.C., an abbreviation for "before Christ." Dates after his birth are denoted by the letters A.D., from the Latin *anno Domini*, meaning "in the year of our Lord." The newer terms B.C.E. ("before the common era"; equivalent to B.C.) and C.E. ("common era"; equivalent to A.D.) are considered more religiously neutral. There is no year 0, so A.D. 1 immediately follows 1 B.C. If neither B.C. nor A.D. accompanies a date, A.D. is understood. When dates are approximate or tentative, they are preceded by "c.," an abbreviation for the Latin *circa*, meaning "around."

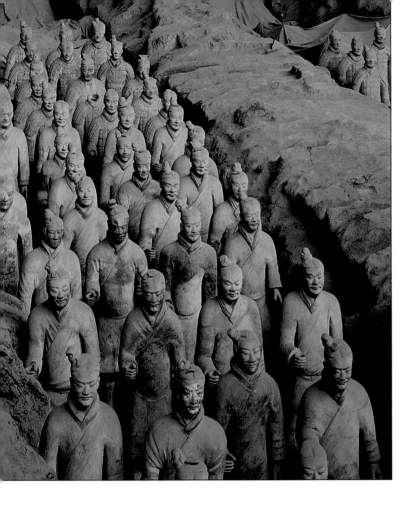

It is not only the features of an individual that are valued as an extension of self after death. A **patron**, someone who commissions (sponsors) works of art, often ordered more monumental tributes. For example, the Egyptian pharaohs spent years planning and overseeing the construction of their pyramids, not only in the belief that such monumental tombs would guarantee their existence in the afterlife, but also as a statement of their power while on earth. In ancient China, the Emperor Qin was buried with a "bodyguard" of several thousand lifesized **terracotta** statues of warriors, as well as chariots and horses (fig. **1.2**). Their function was literally to guard his body in the afterlife.

In fifth-century-B.C. Athens, the Parthenon was built to house a colossal sculpture of the patron goddess Athena and, at the same time, to embody the intellectual and creative achievements of Athenian civilization. Over two thousand years later, Louis XIV, King of France, built his magnificent palace at Versailles as a monument to his political power, to his reign, and to the glory of France. And in the same period in India, the Mughal emperor Shah Jahan commissioned the Taj Mahal as a memorial to his wife (fig. **1.3**).

1.2 Bodyguard of the Emperor Qin, terracotta warriors, Qin Dynasty (221–206 B.C.), *in situ*. Lintong, Shaanxi Province, China.

1.3 Taj Mahal, Agra, India, 1632–48.

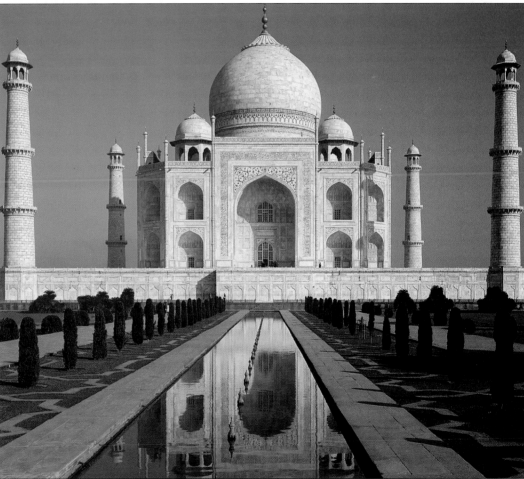

The Values of Art

Works of art are valued not only by artists and patrons, but also by entire cultures. In fact, the periods of history that we tend to identify as the high points of human achievement are those in which art was most highly valued and encouraged. In ancient Egypt, the pharaohs initiated building activity on a grand scale. They presided over the construction of palaces and temples in addition to pyramids, and commissioned vast quantities of sculptures and paintings. In fifth-century-B.C. Athens, the cradle of democracy, artists created many important works of sculpture, paintings, and buildings; their crowning achievement was the Parthenon (see p. 169).

During the Gothic era in Europe (c. 1200–1400), a significant part of the economic activity of every cathedral town revolved around the construction of its cathedral, the production of sculpture, and the manufacture of stained-glass windows. In medieval India the construction of a Hindu temple served similar economic purposes, the largest temples supporting permanent communities of artists and other temple-workers. The fourteenth- and fifteenth-century banking families of Italy spent enormous amounts of money on art to adorn public spaces, churches, chapels, and private palaces.

Today institutions, as well as individuals, continue to fund works of art, and there is a flourishing art market throughout the world. More people than ever before buy and enjoy art—often as an investment—and the auctioning of art has become an international business. Art theft is also international in scale, and the usual motive is money. Well-known stolen works may be difficult to fence, and thus are often held for ransom. The outrage that a community feels when some works of art disappear (or are vandalized) reflects their cultural importance. Various ways in which art is valued are explored below.

Material Value

Works of art may be valued because they are made of a precious material. Gold, for example, was used in Egyptian art to represent divinity and the sun. These associations recur in Christian art, which reserved gold for the background of religious icons (the word **icon** is derived from the Greek *eikon*, meaning "image") and for haloes on divine figures. During the Middle Ages in Europe, ancient Greek bronze statues were not valued for their esthetic character (their beauty), nor for what they might have revealed about Greek culture. Instead, their value lay in the fact that they could be melted down and re-formed into weapons. Through the centuries art objects have been stolen and plundered, in disregard of their cultural, religious, or artistic significance, simply because of the value of their materials. Even the monumental cult statue of Athena in the Parthenon disappeared without a trace, presumably because of the value of the gold and ivory from which it was made.

Intrinsic Value

A work of art may contain valuable material, but that is not the primary basis on which its quality is judged. Its intrinsic value depends largely on the general assessment of the artist who created it, and on its own esthetic character. The *Mona Lisa*, for example, is made of relatively modest materials—paint and wood—but it is a priceless object nonetheless, and arguably the Western world's most famous image. Leonardo da Vinci, who painted it around 1503 in Italy, was acknowledged as a genius in his own day, and his work has stood the test of time. The paintings of the late nineteenth-century Dutch painter Vincent van Gogh have also endured, although he was ignored in his lifetime. It was not until after his death that the esthetic value of his work was widely recognized. In the 1980s one of van Gogh's paintings was bought by a Japanese collector for $80 million. Intrinsic value is not always apparent, and in fact it varies in different times and places, as we can see in the changing assessment of van Gogh's works. "Is it art?" is a familiar question, which expresses the difficulty of defining "art" and of recognizing the esthetic value of an object (see Box).

Religious Value

One of the traditional ways in which art has been valued is in terms of its religious significance. Paintings and sculptures depicting gods and goddesses make their images accessible. Such buildings as the Mesopotamian **ziggurat** (stepped tower), temples in many cultures, and Christian churches have served as symbolic dwellings of the gods, relating worshipers to their deities. Tombs express belief in an afterlife. During the European Middle Ages, art often served an educational function. One important way of communicating Bible stories and legends of the saints to a largely illiterate population was through the sculptures, paintings, mosaics, wall-hangings, and stained-glass windows in churches. Beyond its didactic (teaching) function, the religious significance of a work of art may be so great that entire groups of people identify with the object. The value of such a work is highlighted when it is taken away. In 1973, the Afo-a-Kom—a sacred figure embodying the soul of an African village in Cameroon—disappeared. The villagers reportedly fell into a depression when they discovered that their statue was missing. The subsequent reappearance of the Afo-a-Kom in the window of a New York art gallery caused an international scandal that subsided only after the statue was returned to its African home.

Nationalistic Value

Works of art have nationalistic value inasmuch as they express the pride and accomplishment of a particular culture. Nationalistic sentiment was a primary aspect of the richly carved triumphal arches of ancient Rome because they were gateways for returning military victors. Today,

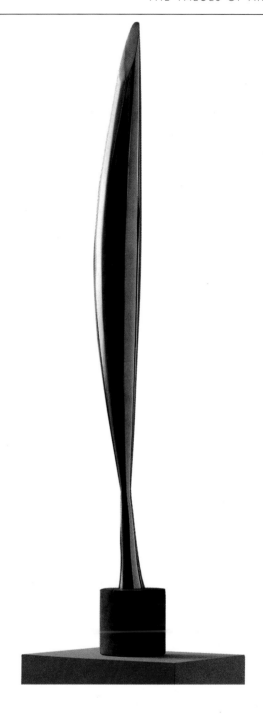

1.4 Constantin Brancusi, *Bird in Space*, 1928. Bronze, unique cast, 54 × 8½ × 6½ in (137.2 × 21.6 × 16.5 cm). Museum of Modern Art, New York. Given anonymously. Photograph © 1999 The Museum of Modern Art. Brancusi objected to the view of his work as abstract. In a statement published shortly after his death in 1957, he declared: "They are imbeciles who call my work abstract; that which they call abstract is the most realist, because what is real is not the exterior form but the idea, the essence of things."

Brancusi's *Bird*: Manufactured Metal or a Work of Art?

A trial held in New York City in 1927 illustrates just how hard it can be to agree on what constitutes "art." Edward Steichen, a prominent American photographer, had purchased a bronze sculpture entitled *Bird in Space* (fig. **1.4**) from the Romanian artist Constantin Brancusi, who was living in France. Steichen imported the sculpture to the United States, whose laws do not require payment of customs duty on original works of art as long as they are declared to customs on entering the country. But when the customs official saw the *Bird*, he balked. It was not art, he said: it was "manufactured metal." Steichen's protests fell on deaf ears. The sculpture was admitted into the United States under the category of "Kitchen Utensils and Hospital Supplies," which meant that Steichen had to pay $600 in import duty.

Later, with the financial backing of Gertrude Vanderbilt Whitney, an American sculptor and patron of the arts, Steichen appealed the ruling of the customs official. The ensuing trial received a great deal of publicity. Witnesses discussed whether the *Bird* was a bird at all, whether the artist could make it a bird by calling it one, whether it could be said to have characteristics of "birdness," and so on. The conservative witnesses refused to accept the work as a bird because it lacked certain biological attributes, such as wings and tail feathers. The more progressive witnesses pointed out that it had birdlike qualities: upward movement and a sense of spatial freedom. The court decided in favor of the plaintiff. The *Bird* was declared a work of art, and Steichen got his money back. In today's market, a Brancusi *Bird* would sell for millions of dollars.

as in the past, statues of national heroes stand in parks and public squares in cities throughout the world.

Sometimes the nationalistic value of art is related to its religious value. In such cases, rulers take advantage of the patriotism of their subjects to impose a new religious system, and to enhance its appeal through the arts. In the fourth century, under the Roman emperor Constantine, art was used to reinforce the establishment of Christianity as well as imperial power. Centuries earlier, the Indian emperor Ashoka had commissioned monuments throughout his realm to proclaim his conversion to Buddhism. Both Constantine and Ashoka patronized the arts in the service of revolutionary developments in politics and religion.

Works of art need not represent national figures, or even national or religious themes, to have nationalistic value. In 1945, at the end of World War II, the Dutch authorities arrested an art dealer, Han van Meegeren, for treason. They accused him of having sold a painting by the great seventeenth-century Dutch artist Jan Vermeer to Hermann Goering, the Nazi Reichsmarschall and Hitler's most loyal supporter. When van Meegeren's case went to trial, he lashed out at the court: "Fools!" he cried, "I painted it myself." What he had sold to the Nazis was actually his own forgery, and he proved it by painting another "Vermeer" under supervision while in prison. It would have been treason to sell Vermeer's paintings, which are considered national treasures, to the German enemy.

Another expression of the nationalistic value of art can be seen in recent exhibitions made possible by shifts in world politics. Since the end of the Cold War between communist eastern Europe and the West, Russia has been sending works of art from its museums for temporary exhibitions in the United States. In such circumstances, the traveling works become a kind of diplomatic currency, improving relations between nations.

The nationalistic value of certain works of art has frequently made them spoils of war. When ancient Babylon was defeated by the Elamites in 1170 B.C., the victors stole the statue of Marduk, the chief Babylonian god, together with the Law Code of Hammurabi (see fig. 3.22). In the early nineteenth century, when Napoleon's armies overran Europe, they plundered thousands of works of art that are now part of the French national art collection in the Musée du Louvre, in Paris.

When the nineteenth-century German archaeologist Heinrich Schliemann excavated ancient Troy, in modern Turkey, he removed a hoard of gold from the site and brought it to Germany. During World War II, the Russians invaded Germany and took the treasure to Russia. They later denied any knowledge of its whereabouts, admitting only in 1994 that they had it. The issue that then arose was who owned the gold—Turkey, Germany, or Russia. The Turks argued that it was theirs by right of origin, the Germans claimed that they had excavated and essentially "discovered" it, and the Russians pointed out that they had won the war (which Germany had started). At the time of writing the case is unresolved, and the hoard remains in Russia.

The nationalistic value of art can be so great that countries whose works have been taken go to considerable lengths to recover them. Thus, at the end of World War II, the Allied Army assigned a special division to recover the vast numbers of artworks stolen by the Nazis. A United States army taskforce discovered Hermann Goering's two personal hoards of stolen art in Bavaria, one in a medieval castle and the other in a bomb-proof tunnel in nearby mountains. The taskforce arrived just in time, for Goering had equipped an "art train" with thermostatic temperature control to take "his" collection to safety. At the Nuremberg war trials, Goering claimed that his intentions had been purely honorable: he was protecting the art from air raids.

Another example of the nationalistic value of art can be seen in the case of the Elgin Marbles. In the early nineteenth century, when Athens was under Turkish rule, Thomas Bruce, 7th Earl of Elgin, obtained permission from Turkey to remove sculptures from the Parthenon and other buildings on the Acropolis. At huge personal expense (£75,000), Lord Elgin sent the sculptures by boat to England. The first shipment sank, but the remainder of the works reached their destination in 1816 and the British Museum in London purchased the sculptures for only £35,000. The Elgin Marbles, also known as the Parthenon Marbles, are still in the British Museum, where they are a tourist attraction and are studied by scholars. For years,

the Greeks have been pressing for the return of the sculptures, but the British have refused. This kind of situation is a product of historical circumstance. Although Lord Elgin broke no laws, and probably saved the sculptures from considerable damage, he is seen by many Greeks as having looted their cultural heritage.

Modern legislation in some countries is designed to avoid similar problems by restricting or banning the export of national treasures. International cooperation agreements attempt to protect cultural property and archaeological heritage worldwide.

Psychological Value

Another symbolic value of art is psychological. Our reactions to art span virtually the entire range of human emotion. They include pleasure, fright, amusement, avoidance, and outrage.

One of the psychological aspects of art is its ability to attract and repel us, and this is not necessarily a function of whether or not we find a particular image esthetically pleasing. People can become attached to a work of art, as Leonardo was to his *Mona Lisa*. Instead of delivering it to the patron, Leonardo kept the painting until his death. Conversely, one may wish to destroy certain works because they arouse anger. In London in the early twentieth century, a suffragette slashed Velázquez's *Rokeby Venus* because she was offended by what she considered to be its sexist representation of a woman. During the French Revolution of 1789, mobs protesting the injustices of the royal family destroyed statues and paintings of earlier kings and queens. In 1989 and 1990, when eastern Europe began to rebel against communism, the protesters tore down statues of their former leaders. Such examples illustrate intense responses to the symbolic power of art.

Art and Illusion

Before considering illusion and the arts, it is necessary to point out that when we think of illusion in connection with an image, we usually assume that the image is true to life, or naturalistic (cf. **naturalism**). This is often, but not always, the case. With certain exceptions, such as some Judaic and Islamic art, Western art was mainly representational until the twentieth century. **Representational**, or **figurative**, art depicts recognizable natural forms or created objects (see "Stylistic Terminology," p. 23). When the subjects of representational pictures and sculptures are so convincingly portrayed that they may be mistaken for the real thing, they are said to be illusionistic (cf. **illusionism**). Where the artist's purpose is to fool the eye, the effect is described by the French term **trompe-l'oeil**.

The deceptive nature of pictorial illusion was simply but eloquently stated by the Belgian Surrealist painter René Magritte in *The Betrayal of Images* (see Box). This work is a convincing (although not a *trompe-l'oeil*) rendition of a pipe. Directly below the image, Magritte reminds the

Images and Words

Artists express themselves through a visual language which has pictorial, sculptural, and architectural rather than verbal elements. As a result, no amount of description can replace the direct experience of viewing art. The artist's language consists of formal elements—line, shape, space, color, light, dark, and so forth (see "The Language of Art," p. 17)—whereas discussion about art is in words. Imagine, for example, if the words in Magritte's *The Betrayal of Images* (fig. **1.5**) read "This is a pipe" (*Ceci est une pipe*) instead of "This is not a pipe" (*Ceci n'est pas une pipe*), or even only "Pipe." Although we might receive the same meaning of "pipeness" from both the word and the image, our experience of the verbal description would be quite different from our experience of its subject.

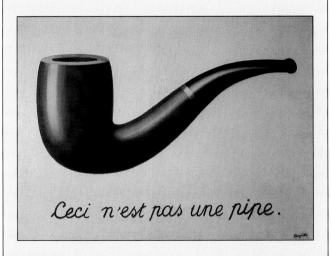

1.5 René Magritte, *The Betrayal of Images* ("This is Not a Pipe"), 1928. Oil on canvas, 23½ × 28½ in (55 × 72 cm). Los Angeles County Museum of Art, California.

viewer that in fact it is not a pipe at all—"Ceci n'est pas une pipe" ("This is not a pipe") is Magritte's explicit message. To the extent that observers are convinced by the image, they have been betrayed. Even though Magritte was right about the illusion falling short of reality, the observer nevertheless enjoys having been fooled.

The pleasure produced by *trompe-l'oeil* images is reflected in many anecdotes, perhaps not literally true but illustrations of underlying truths. For example, the ancient Greek artist Zeuxis was said to have painted grapes so realistically that birds pecked at them. In the Renaissance, a favorite story recounted that the painter Cimabue was so deceived by Giotto's realism that he tried to brush off a fly that Giotto had painted on a figure's nose. The twentieth-century American sculptor Duane Hanson was a master of *trompe-l'oeil*. He used synthetic materials to create statues which look so alive that it is not unusual for people to approach and speak to them.

In these examples of illusion and *trompe-l'oeil*, artists produce only a temporary deception. But such may not always be the case. For instance, the Latin poet Ovid relates the tale of the sculptor Pygmalion, who was not sure whether his own statue was real. Disillusioned by the infidelities of women, Pygmalion turned to art and fashioned a beautiful girl, Galatea, out of ivory. He dressed her, brought her jewels and flowers. He undressed her and took her to bed. During a feast of Venus (the Roman goddess of love and beauty), Pygmalion prayed for a wife as lovely as his *Galatea*. Venus granted his wish by bringing the statue to life.

Traditions Equating Artists with Gods

The fine line between reality and illusion, and the fact that gods are said to create reality while artists create illusion, have given rise to traditions equating artists with gods. Both are seen as creators, the former making replicas of nature and the latter making nature itself. Alberti referred to the artist as an *alter deus*, Latin for "other god," and Dürer said that artists create as God did. Leonardo wrote in his *Notebooks* that artists are God's grandsons and that painting, the grandchild of nature, is related to God. Giorgio Vasari, the Italian Renaissance biographer of artists, called Michelangelo "divine," a reflection of the notion of divine inspiration. The nineteenth-century American painter James McNeill Whistler declared that artists are "chosen by the gods."

Artists have been compared with gods, and gods have been represented as artists. In ancient Babylonian texts, God is described as the architect of the world. In the Middle Ages, God is sometimes depicted as an architect drawing the universe with a compass (fig. **1.6**). Legends in

1.6 *God as Architect (God Drawing the Universe with a Compass)*, from the *Bible moralisée*, Reims, France, fol. 1v, mid-13th century. Illumination, 8⅓ in (21.2 cm) wide. Österreichische Nationalbibliothek, Vienna.

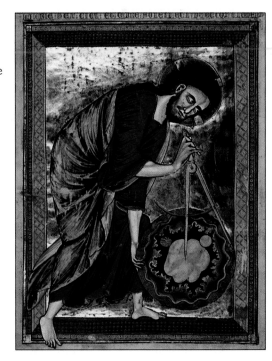

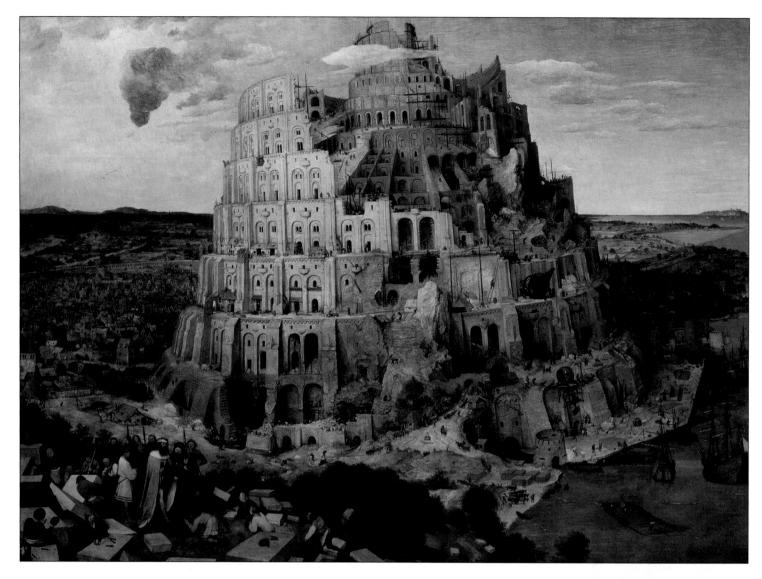

1.7 Pieter Bruegel the Elder, *The Tower of Babel*, 1563. Tempera on panel, 3 ft 9 in × 5 ft 1 in (1.14 × 1.55 m). Kunsthistorisches Museum, Vienna.

the Apocrypha, the unofficial books of the Bible, portray Christ as a sculptor who made clay birds and breathed life into them. Legends such as these are in the tradition of the supreme and omnipotent male artist-as-genius, and they reflect the fact that the original meaning of "genius" was "divinity."

The comparison of artists with gods, especially when artists make lifelike work, has inspired legends of rivalry between these two types of creator. Even when the work itself is not lifelike, the artist may risk incurring divine anger. For example, the Old Testament account of the Tower of Babel illustrates the dangers of building too high and rivaling God by invading the heavens. God reacted by confounding the speech of the builders, so that they seemed to each other to be "babbling" incomprehensibly. They scattered across the earth, forming different language groups. In the sixteenth-century painting by the Flemish artist Pieter Bruegel the Elder (fig. **1.7**), the Tower

of Babel seems about to cave in from within, although it does not actually do so. Bruegel's tower is thus a metaphor for the collapsed ambition of the builders. A related story is told by the Roman historian Pliny: the emperor Nero angered the god Jupiter by erecting a colossal statue of himself. Jupiter destroyed the image of the presumptuous mortal with a thunderbolt.

Some legends endow sculptors and painters with the power to create living figures without divine intervention. In Greek mythology, the sculptor Daedalos was reputed to have made lifelike statues that could walk and talk. Prometheus, on the other hand, was not satisfied with merely lifelike works: he wanted to create life itself. Since the ancient Greeks believed that human beings were made of earth (the body) and fire (the soul), Prometheus knew that he needed more than clay to create living figures. He therefore stole fire from the gods, and they punished him with eternal torture.

Art and Identification

Reflections and Shadows: Legends of How Art Began

Belief in the power of images extends beyond the work of human hands. In many societies, not only certain works of art but also reflections and shadows are thought to embody the spirit of an animal, or the soul of a person. Ancient traditions trace the origin of image-making to drawing a line around a reflected image or shadow. Alberti recalled the myth of Narcissus—a Greek youth who fell in love with his own image in a pool of water—and compared the art of painting to the reflection. The Roman writer Quintilian, on the other hand, identified the first painting as a line traced around a shadow. A Buddhist tradition recounts that the Buddha was unable to find an artist who could paint his portrait. As a last resort, he had an outline drawn around his shadow and filled it in with color himself.

A Greek legend attributes the origin of portraiture to a young woman of Corinth, who traced the shadow of her lover's face cast on the wall by lamplight. Her father, a potter, filled in the outline with clay, which he then fired. This story became particularly popular during the Romantic period in Europe and has been memorialized in *The Corinthian Maid* (fig. **1.8**) by the English painter, Joseph Wright of Derby. Legends such as this indicate that works of art are inspired not only by the impulse to create form, but also by the discovery or recognition of forms that already exist, and the wish to capture and preserve them.

Image Magic

People in many cultures believe that harm done to an image of someone will hurt the actual person. In sixteenth-century England, Queen Elizabeth I's advisers summoned a famous astrologer to counteract witchcraft when they discovered a wax effigy of the queen stuck through with pins.

Sometimes, usually in cultures without strong traditions of figural art, people fear that pictures of themselves may embody—and snatch away—their souls. Many nineteenth-century Native Americans objected to having their portraits painted. One of the outsiders who did so was the artist George Catlin, whose memoirs record suspicious and occasionally violent reactions. Even today, with media images permeating so much of the globe, people in remote areas may resist being photographed for fear of losing themselves. In fact, the very language we use to describe photography reflects this phenomenon: we "take" pictures and "capture" our subjects on film.

Portraits can also create very strong impressions. The nineteenth-century English art critic John Ruskin fell in love with an image on two separate occasions. He became

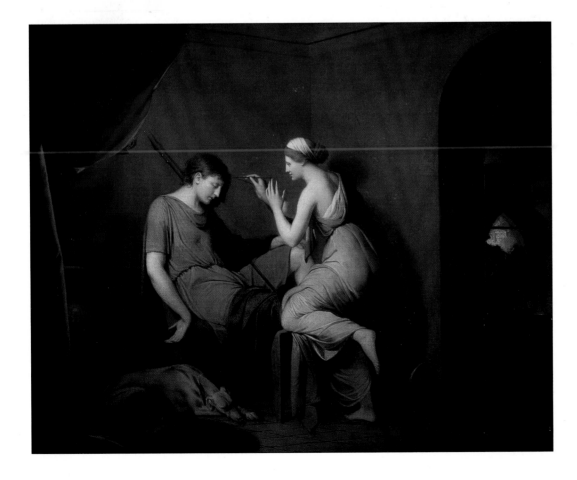

1.8 Joseph Wright of Derby, *The Corinthian Maid*, 1782–4. Oil on canvas, 41⅞ × 51½ in (1.06 × 1.30 m). National Gallery of Art, Washington, D.C. Paul Mellon Collection.

so enamored with the marble tomb effigy of Ilaria del Caretto in Lucca, Italy, that he wrote letters home to his parents describing the statue as if it were a living girl. Later, when Ruskin was in an even more delusional state, he persuaded the Accademia, a museum in Venice, to lend him a painting of Saint Ursula by the sixteenth-century artist Carpaccio. Ruskin kept it in his room for six months and became convinced that he had been reunited with his former fiancée, a young Irish girl named Rose la Touche, whom he merged in his mind with the painted saint. A less extreme form of the identification of a woman with an image concerns Whistler's famous portrait of his mother (fig. **1.9**). "Yes," he replied when complimented on the picture. "One does like to make one's mummy just as nice as possible."

The ability to identify with images, and the sense that a replica may actually contain the soul of what it represents, has sometimes led to an avoidance of images. Certain religions prohibit their adherents from making pictures and statues of their god(s) or of human figures in sacred contexts. In Judaism, the making of figurative images is expressly forbidden in the second Commandment: "Thou shalt not make unto thee any graven image, or any likeness of any thing that is in heaven above, or that is in the earth beneath, or that is in the water under the earth" (Exodus 20:4). Before receiving these instructions, the Israelites had been worshiping a golden calf, which Moses destroyed when he brought them the Commandments. Years later, the prophet Jeremiah declared both the point-lessness and the dangers of worshiping objects instead of God the Creator.

In Islam, as in Judaism, the human figure is generally avoided in religious art. The founder of Islam, the prophet Muhammad, condemned those who would dare to imitate God's work by making figurative art. As a result, Islamic art developed its characteristic emphasis on complex patterns.

During the Iconoclastic Controversy in the eighth and ninth centuries, Christians argued vehemently over the potential dangers of creating any images of holy figures. Like the Jews, Christians wishing to destroy existing images and to prohibit new ones believed that such works of art would lead to idolatry, or worship of the image itself rather than what it stood for.

A different interpretation of this connection between images and gods can be seen in Hindu beliefs about religious sculpture, which is intensely figurative. Hindu statues are considered available for their associated deities to inhabit. Because they are thought capable of changing their outer appearances in order to become manifest and comprehensible to human worshipers, the gods can enter sculptures that have the appropriate forms. Hindu sculpture is thus conceived of as a sacred vessel for the divine presence.

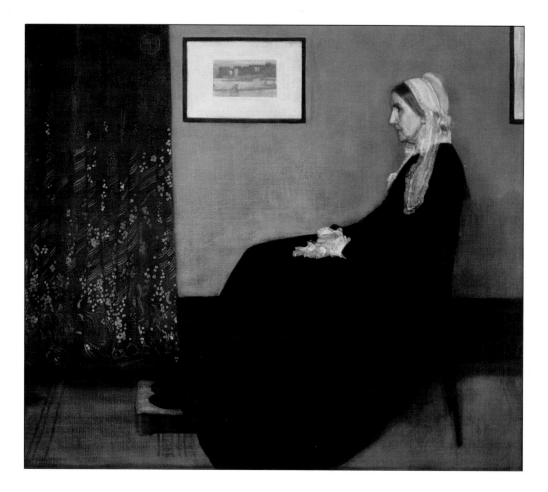

1.9 James Abbott McNeill Whistler, *Arrangement in Black and Gray (Portrait of the Artist's Mother)*, 1871. Oil on canvas, 4 ft 9 in × 5 ft 4½ in (1.45 × 1.64 m). Musée d'Orsay, Paris.

In the modern era, as societies have become increasingly technological, traditional imagery seems to have lost some of its magic power. But art still engages us. A peaceful **landscape** painting, for example, provides a respite from everyday tensions as we contemplate its rolling hills or distant horizon. A **still life** depicting fruit in a bowl reminds us of the beauty inherent in objects we take for granted. And it remains true that abstract works of art containing no recognizable objects or figures can involve us in the rhythms of their shapes, the movements of their lines, and the moods of their colors. Large public sculptures, many of which are **nonrepresentational**, mark our social spaces and humanize them. Architecture, too, defines and enriches our environment. In addition, contemporary images, many in electronic media, exert power over us in both obvious and subtle ways by drawing on our image-making traditions. Movies and television affect our tastes and esthetic judgments. Advertising images influence our decisions—what we buy and which candidates we vote for. Computer-based art is one of the fastest growing art fields. Such modern media use certain traditional techniques of image-making to convey their messages.

Architecture

As is true of pictorial and sculptural images, architecture evokes a response by identification. A building may seem inviting or forbidding, gracious or imposing, depending on how its appearance strikes the viewer. One might think of a country cottage as welcoming and picturesque, or of a haunted house as endowed with the spirits of former inhabitants who inflict mischief on trespassers.

Architecture is more functional, or utilitarian, than pictures and sculptures. Usually the very design of a building conforms to the purpose for which it was built. The criterion for a successful building is not only whether it looks good, but also whether it fulfills its function well. A hospital, for example, may be esthetically pleasing, but its ultimate test is whether it serves the patients and medical staff adequately. A medieval castle was not only a place to live, it was also a fortress requiring defensive features such as a moat, towers, small windows, and thick walls.

Beyond function, the next most important consideration in architecture is its use of space. The scale (size) of buildings and the fact that, with very few exceptions, they can enclose us make our response to them significantly different from our reactions to either pictures or sculptures. Pictures convey only the illusion of space. Sculptures occupy actual, three-dimensional space, although the observer generally remains on the outside of that space looking in.

In the ancient world many buildings, such as Egyptian pyramids and Greek temples, were intended to be experienced either exclusively or primarily from the outside. A Buddhist **stupa** had a solid core, and therefore no interior at all. Its hemispherical shape represented the Buddha's original burial mound, which became a symbol of the cosmos. Worshipers enter the sacred space surrounding a stupa through a gateway marking the transition from the ordinary to the spiritual world. They walk around the perimeter of the stupa in a ritual **circumambulation** that reiterates the Buddha's own spiritual journey. When religious structures do have interiors, access to their inner sanctuaries is frequently restricted. Psychologically as well as esthetically, therefore, our response to architecture is incomplete until we have experienced it physically. Because such an experience involves time and motion as well as vision, it is particularly challenging to describe architecture through words and pictures.

The experience of architectural space appears in everyday language. We speak of "insiders" and "outsiders," of being "in on" something, and of being "out of it." The significance of "in" and "out" recurs in certain traditional architectural arrangements. In parts of the ancient world the innermost room of a temple, its sanctuary, was considered the most sacred, the "holy of holies" which only a high priest or priestess could enter. Likewise, an appointment with a VIP is often held in an inner room which is generally closed to the public at large. Access is typically through a series of doors, so that in popular speech we say of people who have influence that they can "open doors."

Our identification with the experience of being inside begins before birth. Unborn children exist in the enclosed space of their mother's womb, where they are provided with protection, nourishment, and warmth. This biological reality has resulted in a traditional association between women and architecture. The inner sanctum of Hindu temples, for example, is called a **garbha griha**, meaning "womb chamber." In medieval Christianity, the intuitive relationship between motherhood and architecture gave rise to a popular metaphor. This equated the Virgin Mary (as mother of Christ) with the Church building itself. This metaphor is given visual form in Jan van Eyck's fifteenth-century painting *The Virgin in a Church* (fig. **1.10**). Here Mary is enlarged in relation to the architecture, identifying her with the Church as the house of God. Van Eyck portrays an intimacy between the Virgin and Christ that evokes both the natural closeness of mother and child and the spiritual union between the human and the divine.

This union is an important aspect of the sense of space in religious architecture. For example, Gothic cathedrals, such as the one in van Eyck's picture, contain several references to it. The vast interior spaces of such buildings are awe-inspiring, making worshipers feel small compared to an all-encompassing God. The upward movement of the interior space, together with the tall towers and spires on either side of the entrance, echo the Christian belief that paradise is up in the heavens. The rounded spaces of certain other places of worship, such as the domed ceilings of some mosques, likewise symbolize the dome of heaven. In a sense, then, these religious buildings stand as a kind of transitional space between earth and sky, between our limited time on earth and beliefs about infinite time, or eternity.

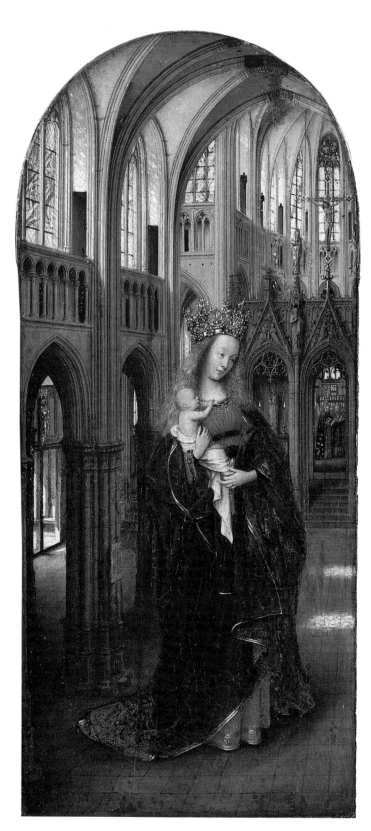

1.10 Jan van Eyck, *The Virgin in a Church*, c. 1410–25. Oil on panel, 12¼ × 5½ in (31 × 14 cm). Gemäldegalerie, Staatliche Museen, Berlin. It is thought that, given the narrowness of this picture, it may originally have been part of a **diptych**—a work of art consisting of two panels—in which case the other section is lost.

Just as we respond emotionally and physically to the open and closed spaces of architecture, so our metaphors indicate our concern for the structural security of our buildings. "A house of cards" or a "castle in the air" denotes instability and irrational thinking. Since buildings are constructed from the bottom up, a house built on a "firm foundation" can symbolize stability, even rational thinking, forethought, and advance planning. In the initial stages of a building's conception, the architect makes a plan. Called a **ground plan**, or floor plan, it is a detailed drawing of each story of the structure indicating where walls and other architectural elements are located. Although in everyday speech we use the term "to plan" in a figurative sense, unless the architect constructs a literal and well-thought-out plan, the building, like a weak argument, will not stand up.

Identification with images and spaces is as old as the human race, and it persists in everyday language. From the beginning of human history, pictures, sculptures, and buildings have been endowed with various kinds of literal and symbolic value related to personal experience and shared beliefs. Works of art are created and enjoyed as expressions of basic and universal human concerns.

Art Collecting

In antiquity, art was valued as booty taken from conquered peoples. In ancient Egypt, Babylon, China, and India, looted art was exhibited in temples and palaces to enhance the power of rulers and priests. Even today, the value of art as military booty has not been entirely eliminated. Since 1992, when the National Museum in Kabul, Afghanistan, was hit by rockets, looting soldiers have pillaged the collection. Afghanistan's location made it a crossroads of trade for thousands of years, and this was reflected in unique objects from many different cultures that have now disappeared. Experts believe that some of these thefts were "commissioned" by Middle and Far Eastern agents working for unscrupulous collectors.

These cultures have a long history of royal and aristocratic art collecting. In Europe, art collecting for the intrinsic value of the works began considerably later, in Hellenistic Greece (323–31 B.C.). Romans plundered Greek art, and also had a thriving industry copying Greek art, which was collected, especially by emperors. During the Middle Ages, the Christian Church was the main collector of art in Europe.

Interest in collecting ancient art revived in the West during the Renaissance, and continued in royal families for several centuries. Some of these royal collections became the basis for major museums—in the late eighteenth century, the Louvre was opened in Paris, and the Russian and British royal collections were opened to the public in the early nineteenth century. By that time more and more private individuals collected art, and since then dealers, auction houses, museums, and the media have further expanded collecting.

Archaeology and Art History

The works of art illustrated in this book are the subject of two academic fields: archaeology and art history. Archaeology (from the Greek *archaios*, meaning "old" or "beginning," and *logos*, meaning "word") is literally a study of beginnings. The value of such study was expressed by the German author Wolfgang von Goethe in 1819 as follows:

He who'd know what life's about
Three millennia must appraise;
Else he'll go in fear and doubt,
Unenlightened all his days.[1]

A related sentiment was expressed by Sigmund Freud when he declared that "only a good for nothing is not interested in his past."

The primary aim of the archaeologist is the reconstruction of history from the physical remains of past cultures. These remains are not confined to the arts, but can be anything from bone fragments and debris, safety pins and frying pans, to entire water-supply systems of buried cities. Unvandalized graves protected from the elements and hidden from the view of potential plunderers yield some of the best evidence. On occasion, cities such as Pompeii and Herculaneum in southern Italy are discovered relatively intact, providing a remarkable glimpse of the past. In its early days in the nineteenth century, archaeology was largely the province of amateur explorers and collectors of antiquities. There was little or no concern for preserving the cultural or historical context of the finds.

Today archaeology is more scientific and professional, calling on many other disciplines to assist with analyzing its discoveries by material, stylistic type, function, and date, as well as in preserving them (see Box). Ecology, for

The Archaeological Dig

Archaeologists locate buried cultures by observing anomalies in topography such as earth mounds, traces of roads, and the geological disposition of rocks and minerals. Aerial photography is particularly helpful for this purpose. The location chosen for excavation is known as the site. Typically each site has a director, a trained archaeologist who oversees the excavation. Under the director are various supervisors, staffers, and volunteers. Architectural drawings are made to record the remains of buildings and reconstruct their original plans. Finds are photographed, drawn, catalogued, and analyzed by specialists. A conservator advises on preserving objects. A foreman hires and oversees local workers as well as attending to necessities such as food, water, and medical supplies.

Archaeological Dating Techniques

The role of archaeology in studying prehistoric periods (i.e. those for which no contemporary written records exist) is crucial. Central to archaeological methods is the establishment of time sequences for events and objects. During the twentieth century a number of techniques have been developed for establishing the age of ancient objects and the chronology of prehistoric events.

Through **stratigraphy**, or the geological study of the layers (strata) of the earth, objects deposited in these layers can be dated. Stratigraphy rests on the principle—known as the Law of Superposition—that, in the absence of external factors, older (earlier) materials in an archaeological deposit are found lower than newer (later) materials. By careful excavation and meticulous record-keeping, archaeologists are able to relate objects to each other both vertically (to determine their relative chronology) and horizontally (for clues to cultural patterns within individual periods).

Seriation, another method of fixing relative dates, is based on the reconstruction of changes in style or type that can be observed in archaeological artifacts (e.g. tools, ceramics) over time. For instance, in any group of examples of a particular kind of object, the percentage of the total is small at the start of its production phase, increases as the object becomes popular and widely used, and decreases through its phases of declining popularity and eventual disuse.

Dendrochronology, or tree-ring dating, is the study of information contained in the annual growth layers of trees. It was discovered in 1917 that trees in any particular area have identical sequences of wide and narrow rings, each ring corresponding to one year's growth. This natural phenomenon has allowed archaeologists to reconstruct historic and prehistoric ring sequences and to assign accurate dates to prehistoric sites. Dendrochronology is valuable in areas such as North America and Europe where there is an abundance of wood and charcoal remains, but is of less value elsewhere.

Radiocarbon dating, which was first developed in 1952, provides a method of determining the precise age of carbonized wood and other organic materials such as antler, bone, and shell. Each living organism has a trace of radiocarbon (C-14) which begins to decay when death occurs. By measuring the residual C-14 content of an object it is possible to establish, within fairly narrow limits, its actual age.

Archaeometry involves the application of analytical techniques from the physical sciences and engineering to archaeological materials. Its interdisciplinary nature requires close cooperation between the archaeologists and experts in various fields in dating objects. The work of the archaeometrist is facilitated by computer analysis, with its potential for storing vast amounts of data.

example, elucidates aspects of the natural environment, some of which can be used for dating. Statistics indicating population size and growth in a particular culture can clarify its development and longevity. Other fields that contribute to archaeology include chemistry, physics, computer science, linguistics (where there is evidence of writing), sociology, anthropology, and art history.

Art history is the study of the history of the visual arts. It should be distinguished from art appreciation, which is primarily about esthetics. Philosophers in both East and West have discussed the nature of esthetics since antiquity. While art history has a venerable tradition in China, it did not become an academic discipline in the West until the nineteenth century. Art history in the West has traditionally dealt with the analysis of individual works of art and their grouping into larger categories of style. Art historians recognize that many factors contribute to the production of a work, including its culture (time and place), artist, patron, medium, and function. Art history is used by archaeologists as well as other scholars studying everyday life, religious practices, means of warfare, and so forth. Stylistic analysis of works of art helps archaeologists date layers of cultures, and is of great importance to cultural and economic historians in determining patterns of trade.

The Methodologies of Art History

The complexity of images has led to the development of various interpretative approaches. Principal among these so-called methodologies of art historical analysis are formalism, iconography and iconology, Marxism, feminism, biography and autobiography, semiology, deconstruction, and psychoanalysis.

Formalism

Chronologically, the earliest codified methodology is **formalism**, which grew out of the nineteenth-century esthetic of "Art for Art's Sake"—artistic activity as an end in itself. Adherents of pure formalism view works of art independently of their context, function, and content. They respond to the formal elements and to the esthetic effect that the arrangement of those elements creates. Two philosophers, Plato in ancient Greece and Immanuel Kant in eighteenth-century Germany, can be seen as precursors of formalist methodology. They believed in an ideal, essential beauty that transcends time and place. Other formalist writers on art did relate changes in artistic style to cultural change.

This approach was demonstrated by the Swiss art historian Heinrich Wölfflin, considered one of the founders of modern art history. In his *Principles of Art History*, first published in German in 1915, he demonstrated the formal consistency of Renaissance and Baroque styles.

In order to grasp the effect of formal elements, let us take as an example Brancusi's *Bird in Space* (see fig. 1.4). Imagine how different it would look lying in a horizontal plane. A large part of the effect of the work depends on its verticality. But it also has curved outlines, sleek proportions, and a highly reflective bronze surface. Its golden color might remind one of the sun and thus reinforce the association of birds and sky. Imagine if the *Bird* were made of another material (Brancusi did make some white marble *Birds*): its esthetic effect would be very different.

Even more radical an idea: what if the texture of the *Bird* were furry instead of hard and smooth? Consider, for example, the *Fur-covered Cup, Saucer, and Spoon* of 1936 (fig. **1.11**) by the Swiss artist Meret Oppenheim. When we experience the formal qualities of texture in these two sculptures, we respond to the *Bird* from a distance, as if it were suspended in space, as the title indicates. But the *Cup* evokes an immediate tactile response because we think of drinking from it, of touching it to our lips, and its furry texture repels us. At the same time, however, the *Cup* amuses us because of its contradictory nature. Whereas our line of vision soars vertically *with* the *Bird*, we instinctively withdraw *from* the *Cup*.

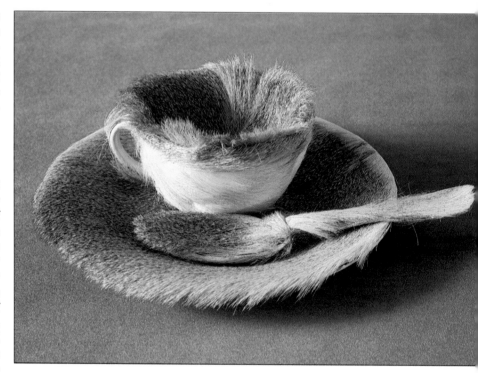

1.11 Meret Oppenheim, *Fur-covered Cup, Saucer, and Spoon (Le Déjeuner en Fourrure)*, 1936. Cup 4⅜ in (10.9 cm) diameter; saucer 9⅜ in (23.7 cm) diameter; spoon 8 in (20.2 cm) long; overall height 2⅞ in (7.3 cm). Museum of Modern Art, New York. Photograph © 1999 Museum of Modern Art.

Iconography and Iconology

In contrast to formalism, the **iconographic** method emphasizes content over form in individual works of art. The term itself denotes the "writing" (*graphe* in Greek) of an image (from the Greek *eikon*), and implies that a written text underlies an image. In Bruegel's *Tower of Babel* (see fig. 1.7) the biblical text is Genesis 11:6, in which God becomes alarmed at the height of the tower. He fears that the builders will invade his territory and threaten his authority. The iconographic elements of Bruegel's picture include the tower, as well as the figures and other objects depicted. The actual tower referred to in the Bible was probably a ziggurat commissioned by King Nebuchadnezzar of ancient Babylon, who is depicted with his royal entourage at the lower left of the picture. He has apparently come to review the progress of the work, which—according to the text—is about to stop. Bruegel shows this by the downward pull at the center of the tower that makes it seem about to cave in. He also refers to God's fear that the tower will reach into the heavens by painting a small, white cloud overlapping the top of the tower. The cloud thus heightens dramatic tension by referring to the divine retribution that will follow. Recognizing the symbolic importance of this iconographic detail significantly enriches our understanding of the work as a whole.

Iconology refers to the interpretation or rationale of a group of works, which is called a **program**. In a Gothic cathedral, for example, an iconographic approach would consider the textual basis for a single statue or scene in a stained-glass window. Iconology, on the other hand, would consider the choice and arrangement of subjects represented in the entire cathedral, and explore their interrelationships.

Marxism

The Marxist approach to art history derives from the writings of Karl Marx, the nineteenth-century German social scientist and philosopher whose ideas were developed into the political doctrines of socialism and communism. Marx himself, influenced by the Industrial Revolution, was interested in the process of making art and its exploitation by the ruling classes. He contrasted the workers (proletariat) who create art with the property-owning classes (the bourgeoisie) who exploit the workers, and believed that this distinction led to the alienation of artists from their own productions. Marxist art historians, and those influenced by Marxism, study the relationship of art to the economic factors (e.g. cost and availability of materials) operating within its social context. They analyze patronage in relation to political and economic systems. Marxists study form and content not for their own sake, but for the social messages they convey and for evidence of the manipulation of art by the ruling class to enhance its own power.

A Marxist reading of the message of Bruegel's *Tower* might associate the builders with the proletariat and God with the bourgeoisie. In between is Nebuchadnezzar who, because he is a king, is not punished as the workers are. It is they who assume the brunt of God's anger; their language is confounded and they are scattered across the earth, whereas Nebuchadnezzar continues to rule his empire. Bruegel emphasizes the greater importance of Nebuchadnezzar in relation to the workers by his larger size, his upright stance, and his royal following. The workers are not only much smaller, but some kneel before the king.

Feminism

Feminist methodology assumes that the making of art, as well as its iconography and its reception by viewers, is influenced by gender. Like Marxists, feminists are opposed to pure formalism on the grounds that it ignores the message conveyed by content. Feminist art historians have pointed out ways in which women have been discriminated against by the male-dominated art world. They have noted, for example, that before the 1970s the leading art history textbooks did not include female artists. Through their research, they have also done a great deal to establish the importance of women's contributions to art history as both artists and patrons—rescuing significant figures from obscurity as well as broadening our sense of the role of art in society. Feminists take issue with traditional definitions of art and notions of artistic genius, both of which have historically tended to exclude women. The fact that traditionally it has been difficult for women to receive the same training in art as men, due in part to family obligations and the demands of motherhood and partly to social taboos, is an issue which the feminists have done much to illuminate.

Taking the example of this introductory chapter, a feminist might point out that of seventeen illustrations of works of art only one is by a woman (Meret Oppenheim, see fig. 1.11). Furthermore, its subject is related to the woman's traditional role as the maker and server of food in the household. At the same time, the work is a visual joke constructed by a woman that combines female sexuality with the oral activity of eating and drinking. The "household" character of the *Cup* contrasts with the "divine" character of *God as Architect* (*God Drawing the Universe with a Compass*) (fig. 1.6). As depicted in the chapter, the male figures are gods, kings, soldiers, and workers, whereas female figures (except *The Corinthian Maid*, fig. 1.8) are mothers.

Biography and Autobiography

Biographical and autobiographical approaches to art history interpret works as expressions of their artists' lives and personalities. These methods have the longest history, beginning with the mythic associations of gods and artists described above. Epic heroes such as Gilgamesh and Aeneas are credited with the architectural activity of building walls and founding cities. The anecdotes of Pliny the Elder about ancient Greek artists have a more historical character, which was revived in fourteenth-century Italy. Vasari's *Lives of the Artists*, written in the sixteenth century, covers artists from the late thirteenth century up to his own time and concludes with his own autobiography. From the fifteenth century on, the genre of biography and autobiography of artists has expanded into various literary forms—for example, sonnets (Michelangelo), memoirs (Vigée-Lebrun), journals (Delacroix), letters (van Gogh), and, more recently, films and taped interviews.

The biographical method emphasizes the notion of authorship, and can be used to interpret iconography using the artist's life as an underlying "text." This being said, there are certain standard conventions in artists' biographies and autobiographies which are remarkably consistent and which show up in quite divergent social and historical contexts. These conventions parallel artists with gods, especially in the ability to create illusion. They also include episodes in which an older artist recognizes talent in a child destined to become great, the renunciation of one's art (or even suicide) when confronted with the work of superior artists, sibling rivalry between artists, artists who are rescued from danger by their talent, and women as muses for (male) artists.

Whistler's portrait of his mother (fig. 1.9) obviously has autobiographical meaning. By placing his own etchings on the wall beside her, he relates her dour personality to his black-and-white drawings and etchings, rather than to his more colorful paintings. Vincent van Gogh's *Self-portrait Before his Easel* (1888) in figure 1.1 is one of many self-portraits that reflect the artist's inner conflicts through the dynamic tension of line and color. In works such as these it is possible to apply the biographical method because the artist's identity is known, and because he makes aspects of himself manifest in his imagery. When works are entirely anonymous, such as Emperor Qin's "bodyguard" (fig. 1.2), biographical readings in terms of the artist(s) are more difficult, although they may sometimes be applied to the patron.

Semiology

Semiology—the science of signs—takes issue with the biographical method and with much of formalism. It has come to include elements of structuralism, poststructuralism, and deconstruction. Structuralism developed from a branch of language study called structural linguistics in the late nineteenth and early twentieth centuries as an attempt to identify universal and meaningful patterns in various cultural expressions. There are several structuralist approaches to art, but in general they diverge from the equation of artists with gods, from the Platonic notion of art as *mimesis* (making exact copies of nature), and from the view that the meaning of a work is conveyed exclusively by its author.

In the structural linguistics of the Swiss scholar Ferdinand de Saussure, a "sign" is composed of "signifier" and "signified." The former is the sound or written element (such as the four letters p-i-p-e) and the latter is the concept of what the signifier refers to (in this case a pipe). A central feature of this theory is that the relation between signifier and signified is entirely arbitrary. Saussure insists on that point specifically to counter the notion that there is an ideal essence of a thing (as stated by Plato and Kant). He is also arguing against the tradition of a "linguistic equivalent." The notion of linguistic equivalents derived from the belief that, in the original language spoken by Adam and Eve, words naturally matched the essence of what they referred to, so that signifier and signified *were* naturally related to each other. Even before Adam and Eve, the logocentric (word-centered) Judaic God had created the world through language: "Let there be light" made light, and "Let there be darkness" made darkness. The New Testament Gospel of John (1:1) takes up this notion again, opening with "In the beginning was the Word."

For certain semioticians, however, some relation between signifier and signified is allowed. These would agree that Magritte's painted pipe is closer to the idea of pipeness than the four letters *p-i-p-e*. But most semioticians prefer to base stylistic categories on signs rather than on formal elements. For example, Magritte's pipe and Oppenheim's cup do not resemble each other formally, and yet both have been related to Dada and Surrealism. Their similarities do not lie in shared formal elements, but rather in their ability to evoke surprise by disrupting expectations. We do not expect to read a denial of the "pipeness" of a convincing image of a pipe written by the very artist who painted it. Nor do we expect fur-covered cups and spoons, because the fur interferes with their function. The unexpected—and humorous—qualities of the pipe and the cup could be considered signs of certain twentieth-century developments in imagery. Another element shared by these two works is the twentieth-century primacy of everyday objects, which can also be considered a sign.

Deconstruction

The analytical method known as deconstruction is most often associated with Jacques Derrida, a French poststructuralist philosopher who writes about art as well as written texts. Derrida's deconstruction opens up meanings rather than fixing them within structural patterns. But he shares with the structuralists the idea that works have no ultimate meanings conferred by their authors.

Derrida's technique for opening up meanings is to question assumptions about works. Whistler's mother (see fig. 1.9), for example, seems to be sitting for her portrait, but we have no proof from the painting itself that she ever did so. Whistler could have painted her from a photograph or from memory, in which case our initial assumption about the circumstances of the work's creation would be basically untrue, even though the portrait is a remarkably "truthful" rendering of a puritanical woman.

Derrida also opens up the Western tendency to binary pairing: right/left, positive/negative, male/female, and so forth. He notes that one of a pair evokes its other half and plays on the relationship of presence and absence. Since a pair of parents is a biological given, where, a Derridean might ask, is Whistler's father? In the pairing of father and mother, the present parent evokes the absent parent. There is, in Whistler's painting, no reference to his father, only to himself via the etchings hanging on the wall. The absent father, the present mother, the etchings of the son—the combination invites speculation about their relationships: was the son trying to displace the father? Such psychological considerations lead us to the psychoanalytic methodologies.

Psychoanalysis

The branch of psychology known as psychoanalysis was originated by the Austrian neurologist Sigmund Freud in the late nineteenth century. Like art history, psychoanalysis deals with imagery, history, and individual creativity. Like archaeology, it reconstructs the past and interprets its relevance to the present. The imagery examined by psychoanalysts is found in dreams, jokes, slips of the tongue, and neurotic symptoms, and it reveals the unconscious mind (which, like a buried city, is a repository of the past). In a work of art, personal imagery is reworked into a new form that "speaks" to a cultural audience. It thus becomes part of a history of style (and, for semioticians, of signs).

Psychoanalysis has been applied to art in different ways, and according to different theories. In 1910 Freud published the first psychobiography of an artist, in which he explored the personality of Leonardo da Vinci through his iconography and his working methods. For Freud, the cornerstone of psychoanalysis was the Oedipus complex, which refers to various aspects of children's relationships to their parents. In the case of a boy, the Oedipus complex includes his wish for a romance with his mother and the resulting elimination of his father. The Oedipus complex of a girl is more complicated because her first love object is her mother and she is expected to grow up and love a man.

As we have seen, the Oedipus complex can be applied to Whistler's painting of his mother. An oedipal reading of that work is enriched by the fact that it contains an **underpainting** of a baby. An oedipal reading of Brancusi's *Bird* would have to consider the artist's relationship to his peasant father, an ignorant and abusive man who would have preferred his son to have been born a girl. In that light, the sculpture has been interpreted as a phallic self-image, declaring its triumph over gravity and outshining the sun. With *Bird in Space*, Brancusi symbolically "defeats" his father and "stands up" for himself as a creator.

According to classical psychoanalysis, works of art are "sublimations of instinct" through which instinctual energy is transformed by work and talent into esthetic form. The ability to sublimate is one of the main differences between humans and animals, and it is necessary for creative development in any field. Because art is expressive, it reveals aspects of the artist who creates it, of the patron who funds it, and of the culture in which it is produced.

The Language of Art
Form

The overall form of a work of art refers to the visual elements of its **composition**, arrangement, or structure. Within this overall form are individual forms. The individual forms in a still life, for example, might include a table, a bowl, apples, and a jug of wine. The forms in a building could include its walls, doors, windows, roof, as well as any architectural ornament and the site surrounding it.

Plane

A **plane** is a flat surface having a direction in space. Brancusi's *Bird* (fig. 1.4) rises in a vertical plane, Magritte's pipe (fig. 1.5) lies in a horizontal plane, and the figure of God in *God Drawing the Universe with a Compass* (fig. 1.6) bends over to create two diagonal planes.

Line

A line is the path traced by a moving point. For the artist, the moving point is the tip of the brush, pen, crayon, or whatever instrument is used to create an image on a surface. In geometry, a line has no width or volume; its only quality is inherent in its location, a straight line being defined as the shortest distance between two points. In the language of art, however, a line can have many qualities, depending on how it is drawn (fig. **1.12**). A vertical line seems to stand stiffly at attention, a horizontal line lies down, and a diagonal seems to be falling over. Zigzags have an aggressive, sharp quality, whereas a wavy line is more graceful and, like a curve, more naturally associated with the outline of the human body. Parallel lines are balanced and harmonious, implying an endless, continuous movement, while perpendicular, converging, and intersecting lines meet and create a sense of force and counterforce. The thin line (a) seems delicate, unassertive, even weak. The thick one (b) seems aggressive, forceful, strong. The undulating line (c) suggests calmness, like the surface of a calm sea, whereas the more irregularly wavy line (d) implies the reverse. The angular line (e) climbs upward like the edge of a rocky mountain. (Westerners understand (e) as going up and (f) as going down, as we read from left to right.)

Expressive Qualities of Line Many of the lines in figure 1.12 are familiar from geometry and can therefore be described formally. But the formal qualities of line also convey an expressive character because we identify them with our bodies and our experience of nature. By analogy with a straight line being the shortest distance between two points, a person who follows a straight, clear line in thought or action is believed to have a sense of purpose. "Straight" is associated with rightness, honesty, and truth, while "crooked"—whether referring to a line or a person's character—denotes the opposite. We speak of a "line of work," a phrase adopted by the former television program *What's my Line?* When a baseball player hits a line drive, the bat connects firmly with the ball, and a "hardliner" takes a strong position on an issue.

It is especially easy to see the expressive impact of lines in the configuration of the face (fig. **1.13**). In (a), the upward curves create a happy face, and the downward curves of (b) create a sad one. These characteristics of upward and downward curves actually correspond to the emotions as expressed in natural physiognomy. And they are reflected in language when we speak of people having "ups and downs" or of events being "uppers" or "downers."

Alexander Calder's (1898–1976) illustration (fig. **1.14**) merges the linear quality of the written word with the pictorial quality of what the word represents. The curve of the *c* outlines the face, a dot stands for the eye, and a slight diagonal of white in the curve suggests the mouth. The large *A* comprises the body, feet, and tail, while the tiny *t* completes the word, without interfering with reading the ensemble as *cat*. The figure seems to be walking, because the left diagonal of the *A* is lower than the right

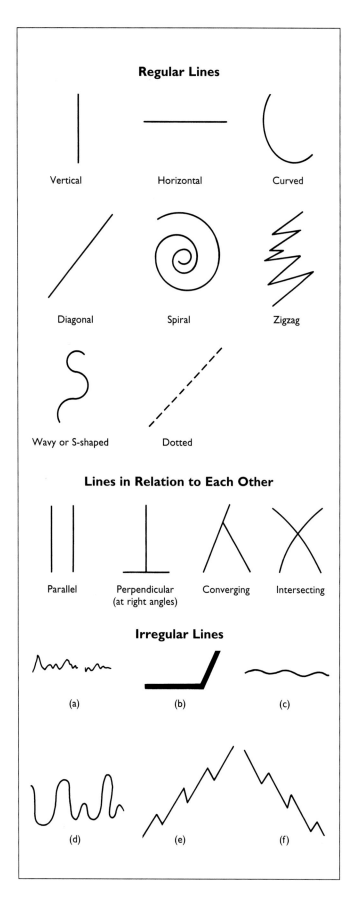

1.12 Lines.

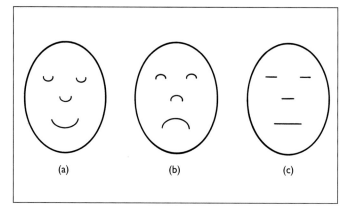

1.13 Lines used to create facial expressions.

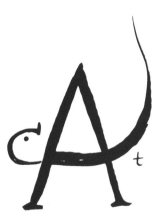

1.14 Alexander Calder, *Cat*, 1976. 22 × 30 in (55.88 × 76.2 cm).

one, and the short horizontals at the base of the *A* suggest feet. Not only is this cat a self-image—*C A* are the artist's initials reversed—but it defies the semiotic argument that signifier (*c–a–t*) and signified (the mental image of a cat) have no natural relation to each other.

The importance of the line in the artist's vocabulary is illustrated by an account of two ancient Greek painters, Apelles, who was Alexander the Great's portraitist, and his contemporary Protogenes. Apelles traveled to Rhodes to see Protogenes' work, but when he arrived at the studio, Protogenes was away. The old woman in charge of the studio asked Apelles to leave his name. Instead, Apelles took up a brush and painted a line of color on a panel prepared for painting. "Say it was this person," Apelles instructed the old woman.

When Protogenes returned and saw the line, he recognized that only Apelles could have painted it so well. In response, Protogenes painted a second, and finer, line on top of Apelles' line. Apelles returned and added a third line of color, leaving no more room on the original line. When Protogenes returned a second time, he admitted defeat and went to look for Apelles.

Protogenes decided to leave the panel to posterity as something for artists to marvel at. Later it was exhibited in Rome, where it impressed viewers for its nearly invisible lines on a vast surface. To many artists, the panel seemed a blank space, and for that it was esteemed over other famous works. After his encounter with Protogenes, it was said that Apelles never let a day go by without drawing at least one line. This incident was the origin of an ancient proverb, "No day without a line."

Lines enclosing space create shapes. Shapes are another basic unit, or formal element, used by artists. There are regular and irregular shapes. Regular ones are geometric and have specific names. Irregular shapes are also called "biomorphs," or biomorphic (from the Greek *bios,* "life," and *morphe,* "shape"), because they seem to move like living, organic matter (fig. **1.15**).

Shape

Expressive Qualities of Shape Like lines, shapes can be used by artists to convey ideas and emotions. Open shapes create a greater sense of movement than closed shapes (see fig. 1.15). Similarly, we speak of open and closed minds; open minds allow for a flow of ideas, flexibility, and the willingness to entertain new possibilities. Closed minds, on the other hand, are not susceptible to new ideas.

Specific shapes can evoke associations with everyday experience. Squares, for example, are symbols of reliability, stability, and symmetry. To call people "foursquare" means that they are forthright and unequivocal, that they confront things "squarely." If something is "all square," a certain equity or evenness is implied; a "square meal" refers to both the amount and content of the food. When the term "brick" is applied to people, it means that they are good-natured and reliable. Too much rectangularity, on the other hand, may imply dullness or monotony—

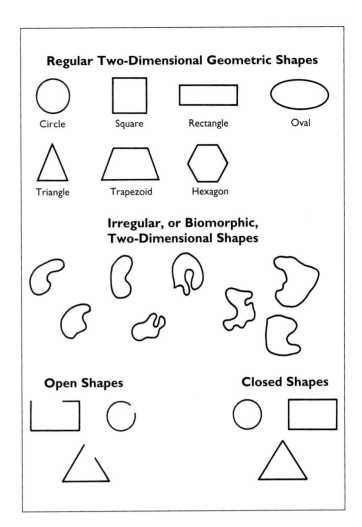

1.15 Shapes.

to call someone "a square" suggests over-conservatism or conventionality.

The circle has had a special significance for artists since the Neolithic era. In the Roman period, the circle was considered a divine shape and thus most suitable for temples. This view persisted in the Middle Ages and the Renaissance, when the circle was considered to be the ideal church plan—even though such buildings were rarely constructed.

The appeal of the circle's perfection is illustrated by a Renaissance anecdote about Giotto. As the story goes, the pope's messengers scoured Italy to find the best living artist. When a messenger arrived at Giotto's studio and asked for a sample of his work, the artist took up a piece of paper and a brush. He held out his arm stiffly, as if to make a compass of his whole body, and drew a circle. When the puzzled messenger asked the meaning of his action, Giotto told him to take the picture to the pope, who would understand. As soon as the pope saw Giotto's "O," he recognized his genius and summoned him to Rome. From that anecdote came the expression, "You are more stupid than Giotto's 'O.'"

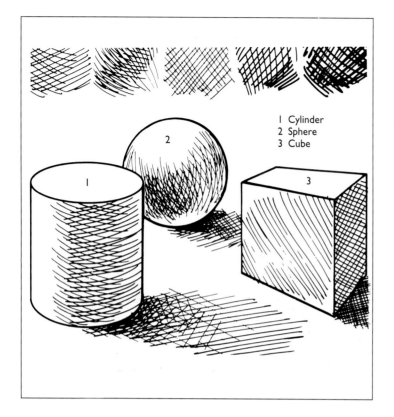

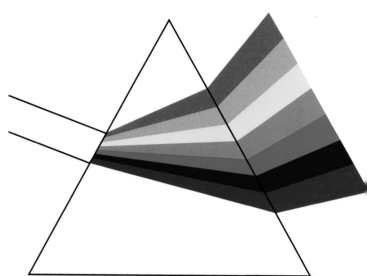

1.17 The visible spectrum has seven principal colors—red, orange, yellow, green, blue, indigo (or blue-violet), and violet—that blend together in a continuum. Beyond the ends is a range of other colors, starting with infrared and ultraviolet, which are invisible to the human eye. If all the colors of the spectrum are recombined, white light is again reproduced.

1.16 Drawing of solid shapes showing hatching and cross-hatching. The lines inside the objects create the illusion that they are solid, and also suggest that there is a source of light coming from the upper left and shining down on the objects. Such lines are called modeling lines.

Even though lines are two-dimensional, the use of **modeling** lines to form **hatching** or **cross-hatching** (fig. **1.16**) creates the illusion of mass and volume, making a shape appear three-dimensional. Hatching and cross-hatching can also suggest shade or **shading** (the gradual transition from light to dark), on the side of an object that is turned away from a light source.

Light and Color

The technical definition of light is electromagnetic energy of certain wavelengths which, when it strikes the retina of the eye, produces visual sensations. The absence, or opposite, of light is dark.

Rays of light having certain wavelengths create the sensation of color, which can be demonstrated by passing a beam of light through a prism (fig. **1.17**). This breaks the light down into its constituent **hues**. Red, yellow, and blue are the three **primary colors** because they cannot be produced by mixing any other colors. A combination of two primary colors produces a **secondary color**: yellow and blue make green, red and blue make purple, yellow and red make orange.

The **color wheel** (fig. **1.18**) illustrates the relationships between the various colors. The farther away hues are, the less they have in common, and the higher their contrast.

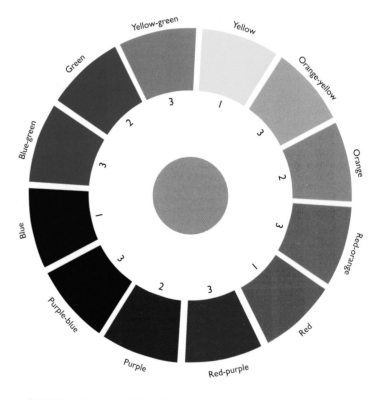

1.18 The color wheel. Note that the three primary colors—red, yellow, and blue—are equally spaced around the circumference. They are separated by their secondary colors. Between each primary color and its two secondary colors are their related tertiaries, giving a total of twelve hues on the rim of the wheel.

Hues directly opposite each other on the wheel (red and green, for example) are the most contrasting and are known as **complementary colors**. They are often juxtaposed when a strong, eye-catching contrast is desired. Mixing two complementary hues, on the other hand, has a neutralizing effect and lessens the intensity of each. This can be seen in figure 1.18 as you look across the wheel from red to green. The red's intensity decreases, and the gray circle in the center represents a "stand-off" between all the complementary colors.

The relative lightness or darkness of an object is its **value**, which is a function of the amount of light reflected from its surface. Gray is darker in value than white, but lighter in value than black. The value scale in figure **1.19**

provides an absolute value for different shades. But, in fact, our visual perceptions are more relative than absolute and are "colored" by the context in which we perceive something. For example, in figure **1.20** the band across the center is of a uniform shade of medium gray (i.e. it has the same value throughout). However, when seen alongside the darker gray on the right it looks lighter, and vice versa on the left. Artists are constantly aware of the absolute values of the shades with which they are working and of the effect of juxtaposing different colors.

Value is characteristic of both **achromatic** works of art—those with no color, consisting of black, white, and shades of gray—and of **chromatic** ones (from the Greek *chroma*, meaning "color"). On a scale of color values (fig.

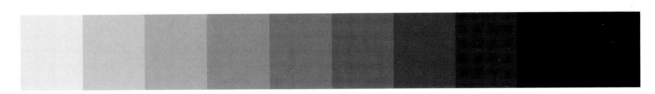

1.19 This ten-step value scale breaks the various shades from white to black into ten gradations. The choice of ten is somewhat arbitrary because there are many more values between pure white and pure black. Nevertheless, it illustrates the principle of value gradations.

1.20 The juxtaposition of objects with different tonal values produces a **contrast.** Objects from opposite ends of the value scale create a very high or strong contrast; the simplest example is the juxtaposition of black and white.

1.21), yellow reflects a relatively large amount of light, approximately equivalent to "high light" on the neutral scale, whereas blue is equivalent to "high dark." The normal value of each color indicates the amount of light it reflects at its maximum intensity. The addition of white or black would alter its value (i.e. make it lighter or darker) but not its hue. The addition of one color to another would change not only the values of the two colors but also their hues.

Intensity, which is also called **saturation**, refers to the relative brightness or dullness of a color. Dark red (red mixed with black) is darker in value, but less intense than pink (red mixed with white). There are four methods of changing the intensity of colors. The first is to add white. Adding white to pure red creates light red or pink, which is lighter in value and less intense. If black is added, the result is darker in value and less intense. If gray of the same value as the red is added, the result is less intense but retains the same value. These three methods are illustrated in figure 1.22. The fourth way of changing a color's intensity is to add its complementary hue. For example, when green (a secondary color composed of the primaries yellow and blue) is added to red, gray is produced as a consequence of the balance between the three primaries. If red is the dominant color in the mixture, the result is a grayish red; if green is dominant, the product is a grayish green. In any event, the result is a color less intense and more neutral than the original.

1.21 A color value scale. The central row contains a range of neutrals from white to black; the rows above and below match the twelve colors from the color wheel with the neutrals in terms of the amount of light reflected from each.

Expressive Qualities of Color Just as lines and shapes have expressive qualities, so too do colors. Artists select colors for their effect. Certain ones appear to have intrinsic qualities. Bright or warm colors convey a feeling of gaiety and happiness. Red, orange, and yellow are generally considered warm, perhaps because of their associations with fire and the sun. It has been verified by psychological tests that the color red tends to produce feelings of happiness. Blue and any other hue containing blue—green, violet, blue-green—are considered cool, possibly because of their association with the sky and water. They produce feelings of sadness and pessimism.

Colors can also have symbolic significance and suggest abstract qualities. A single color, such as red, can have multiple meanings. It can symbolize danger, as when one waves a red flag in front of a bull. But to "roll out the red carpet" means to welcome someone in an extravagant way, and we speak of a "red letter day" when something particularly exciting has occurred. Yellow can be associated with cowardice, white with purity, and purple with luxury, wealth, and royalty. We might call people "green with envy," "purple with rage," or "in a brown study" if they are quietly gloomy.

Texture

Texture is the quality conveyed by the surface of an object. This may be an actual surface, or a simulated or represented surface. The surface of Oppenheim's *Fur-covered Cup* (see fig. 1.11), for example, is actually furry, but the heavy cloth dress of Whistler's mother is simulated by means of its shaded surface (see fig. 1.9).

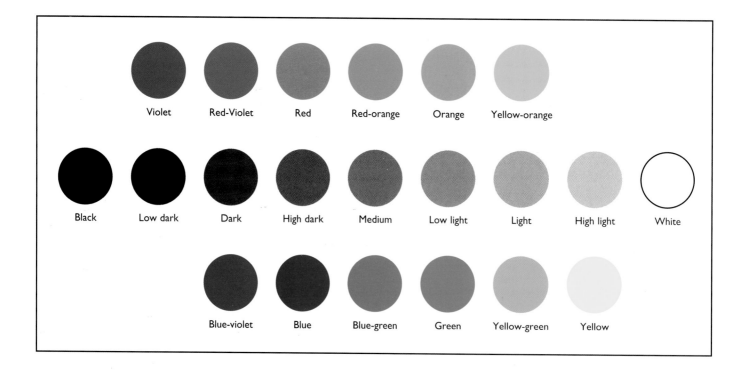

| Violet | Red-Violet | Red | Red-orange | Orange | Yellow-orange |

| Black | Low dark | Dark | High dark | Medium | Low light | Light | High light | White |

| Blue-violet | Blue | Blue-green | Green | Yellow-green | Yellow |

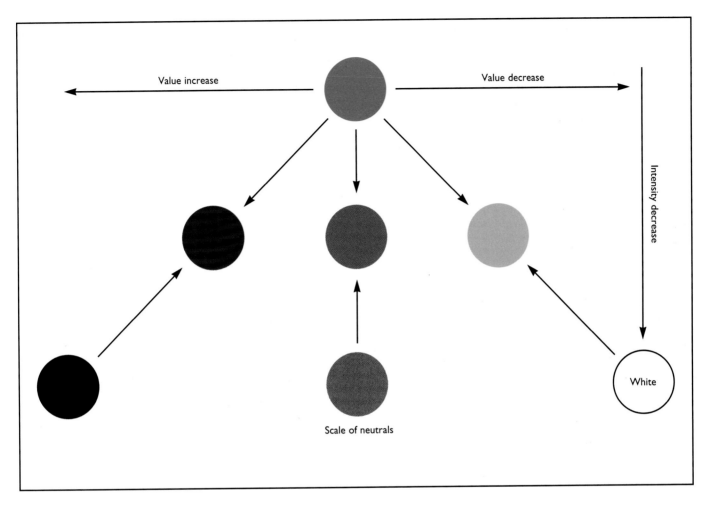

I.22 Changes of intensity.

Stylistic Terminology

Subject matter refers to the actual elements represented in a work of art, such as figures and objects or lines and colors. **Content** refers to the themes, values, or ideas in a work of art, as distinct from its form. The following terms are used to describe **representational**, or **figurative**, works of art which depict their subject-matter so that it is relatively recognizable:

- **naturalistic**: depicting figures and objects more or less as we see them. Often used interchangeably with "realistic."
- **realistic**: depicting figures and objects to resemble their actual appearances, rather than in a distorted or abstract way.
- **illusionistic**: depicting figures, objects, and the space they occupy so convincingly that the appearance of reality is achieved.

Note that an image may be representational without being realistic. Figures **1.23–1.26** are recognizable as images of a cow and are therefore representational, but only figures 1.23–1.25 can be considered relatively naturalistic.

If an image is representational but is not especially faithful to its subject, it may be described as:

- **idealized**: depicting an object according to an accepted standard of beauty.
- **stylized**: depicting certain features as nonorganic surface elements rather than naturalistically or realistically.
- **romanticized**: depicting its subject in a nostalgic, emotional, fanciful, and/or mysterious way.

If the subject-matter of a work has little or no relationship to observable reality, it may be called:

- **nonrepresentational** or **nonfigurative**: the opposite of representational or figurative, implying that the work does not depict (or claim to depict) real figures or objects.
- **abstract**: describes forms that do not accurately depict real objects. The artist may be attempting to convey the essence of an object rather than its actual appearance. Note that the subject-matter may be recognizable (making the work representational), but in a non-naturalistic form.

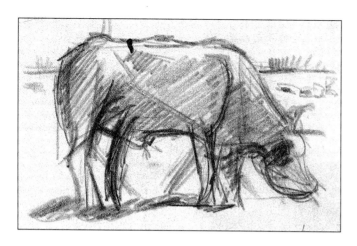

1.23 Theo van Doesburg, Study 1 for *Composition (The Cow)*, 1916. Pencil on paper, 4⅝ × 6¼ in (11.7 × 15.9 cm). Museum of Modern Art, New York. Purchase.

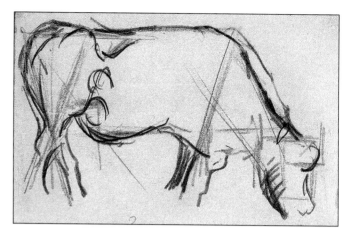

1.24 Theo van Doesburg, Study 2 for *Composition (The Cow)*, 1917. Pencil on paper, 4⅝ × 6¼ in (11.7 × 15.9 cm). Museum of Modern Art, New York. Purchase.

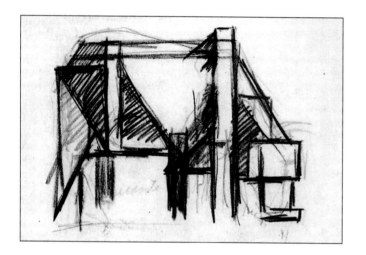

1.25 Theo van Doesburg, Study 3 for *Composition (The Cow)*, 1917. Pencil on paper, 4⅝ × 6¼ in (11.7 × 15.9 cm). Museum of Modern Art, New York. Gift of Nelly van Doesburg.

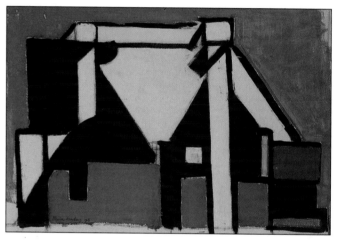

1.26 Theo van Doesburg, Study for *Composition (The Cow)*, (c. 1917; dated 1916). Tempera, oil, and charcoal on paper, 15⅝ × 22¾ in (39.7 × 57.8 cm). Museum of Modern Art, New York. Purchase.

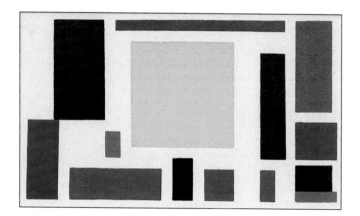

1.27 Theo van Doesburg, Study for *Composition (The Cow)*, c. 1917. Oil on canvas, 14¾ × 25 in (37.5 × 63.5 cm). Museum of Modern Art, New York. Purchase. All images © 1999 MOMA.

The transition from naturalism to geometric abstraction is encapsulated in a series by the early twentieth-century Dutch artist Theo van Doesburg (figs. 1.23–**1.27**). He gradually changed his drawing of a cow from 1.23, which could be called naturalistic, figurative, or representational, to image 1.27, which is an abstract arrangement of flat squares and rectangles. In 1.23 and 1.24, the cow's form is recognizable as that of a cow—it is composed of curved outlines and a shaded surface that creates a three-dimensional illusion. In image 1.25, the cow form is still recognizable, especially as it follows 1.23 and 1.24. It is now devoid of curves, but still shaded—it has become a series of volumetric (solid, geometric) shapes. Even in image 1.26, the general form of the cow is recognizable in terms of squares, rectangles, and triangles, but there is no longer any shading. As a result, each distinct color area is flat. In image 1.27, however, the shapes can no longer be related to the original natural form. It is thus a pure abstraction, and is also nonfigurative and nonrepresentational.

2

The Art of Prehistory

Who are we? Where do we come from? Where are we going? These are three of the most universal questions. They are about time—past, present, and future—as well as about the nature of the human condition. The more we know about our past, the better we understand our present. We will begin by going back in time to early periods of the human race in western Europe, to the study of prehistory. Prehistory refers to the time before people developed writing systems and, therefore, before the existence of written documents. In one sense, the term prehistory is a misnomer because objects and images are actually historical records of a sort. The challenge lies in discovering how to read such nonverbal information.

The Stone Age in Western Europe

To organize the vast span of prehistory, scholars currently divide the Stone Age in western Europe into three large time periods. The dates of these periods fluctuate as new research reshapes our understanding of prehistoric societies, revealing great complexity at very early times. Paleolithic (from the Greek *paleos*, meaning "old," and *lithos*, meaning "stone") is the earliest of the three periods. It is subdivided into three shorter periods: Lower (beginning c. 1,500,000 years ago), Middle (beginning c. 100,000/200,000 years ago), and Upper (beginning c. 45,000/50,000 years ago). The Mesolithic ("middle stone") period extends from around 8000–6000 B.C. in southeastern Europe, and c. 8000–4000 throughout the rest of Europe. The Neolithic ("new stone") period dates from c. 6000/4000–2000 B.C., and continues for another thousand years in northwestern Europe.

The designation of these early periods as Stone Age derives from people's dependence on tools and weapons made of stone. As metalworking technology developed in different regions at different times, metal would eventually supersede stone for many purposes. Then as now, technological change and social change went hand-in-hand, bringing the Stone Age to a gradual close.

Upper Paleolithic

(c. 50,000/45,000–c. 8000 B.C.)

By the beginning of the Upper Paleolithic era in Europe, our own subspecies, *Homo sapiens sapiens* (literally "wise wise man"), had supplanted early *Homo sapiens* people, who had developed complex cultures. We can gain some understanding of what Paleolithic society may have been like by interpreting the physical record left by these early humans. But because ideas cannot be fossilized, there is much that will never be known.

Very little is known about Paleolithic religion, for example, but inferences have been drawn from certain ritual burial practices. Red ocher—possibly symbolizing blood—was sprinkled on corpses, and various objects of personal adornment (such as necklaces) were buried with them. Bodies were arranged in the fetal position, often oriented toward the east and the rising sun, which must have seemed reborn with every new day. Such practices have been interpreted as a sign of belief in life after death and offer some insight into the way Paleolithic people answered the third question posed at the start of this chapter: Where are we going?

Paleolithic people were nomadic hunters and gatherers, who moved from place to place in search of food. They lived communally, building shelters at cave entrances and under rocky overhangs. Their tents were made of animal skins and their huts of mud, plant fibers, stone, and bone. Fire had already been used for some 600,000 years, and there is evidence of hearths in Paleolithic homes.

Although the invention of writing was still far off, people made symbolic marks on hard surfaces, such as bone and stone, possibly to keep track of time. The sophistication of Upper Paleolithic art suggests that language—the ability to communicate with words and tell stories—had also been developed, which in itself requires a sense of sequence and time. The high quality of painting and sculpture, tools and weapons, seems to indicate specialized groups of workers.

The earliest surviving works of Western art correspond roughly to the final stages of the Ice Age in Europe and date back to about 30,000 B.C. Before that time, objects were made primarily for utilitarian purposes, although many have esthetic qualities. It is important to remember, however, that our modern, Western concept of "art" would almost certainly have been alien to prehistoric people. For them, as for many later cultures, an object's esthetic value was inseparable from its function.

Upper Paleolithic Sculpture (c. 25,000 B.C.)

Upper Paleolithic artists produced a wide range of small sculptures made of ivory, bone, clay, and stone. These depict humans, animals, and combinations of the two. Many show a high level of technical skill, with finely carved lines representing natural surface details. Artists created other portable objects such as spear throwers (sticks against which spear shafts were fitted to increase the range and impact of the spear), musical instruments, and objects of personal adornment (such as beads and pendants). The esthetic quality of some of these works suggests a long prior artistic tradition.

Perhaps the most famous Paleolithic sculpture is the small limestone statue of a woman, the so-called *Venus of Willendorf* (fig. **2.1**), variously dated from 25,000 to 21,000 B.C. Although this figure can be held in the palm of one's hand, it is a monumental object with a sense of organic form. The term monumental can mean literally "very big" or, as is the case here, "having the quality of

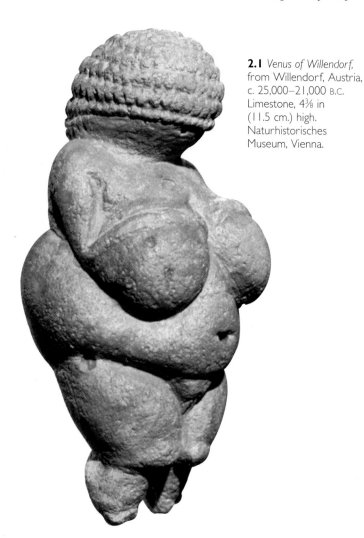

2.1 *Venus of Willendorf,* from Willendorf, Austria, c. 25,000–21,000 B.C. Limestone, 4⅜ in (11.5 cm.) high. Naturhistorisches Museum, Vienna.

Carving

Carving is a subtractive technique in which a sculptor uses a sharp instrument such as a knife, gouge, or chisel to remove material from a hard substance such as bone, wood, or stone. After an image is shaped, it can be sanded, filed, or polished. The *Venus of Willendorf* was not polished, although some Paleolithic sculptures were. It is made of limestone, which does not polish as well as other types of stone.

appearing very big." In fact, the *Venus of Willendorf* is only 4⅜ inches (11.5 cm) high. It is evidence of a well-developed esthetic sensibility and was carved by an experienced artist (see Box). The rhythmic arrangement of bulbous oval shapes emphasizes the head, breasts, torso, and thighs. The scale of these parts of the body in relation to the whole is quite large, while the facial features, neck, and lower legs are virtually eliminated. The arms, resting on the breasts, are so undeveloped as to be hardly noticeable. The *Venus of Willendorf* is a strikingly expressive figure. But what, we might ask, did she mean to the artist who carved her? And what was her function in her cultural context? Unfortunately, we can only speculate. The artist has emphasized those parts of the body related to reproduction and nursing. Furthermore, comparison of the front with the side and back shows that, although it is a **sculpture in the round** (see Box), more attention has been lavished on the front. This suggests that the figure was intended to be viewed from the front. Since frontality is characteristic of much religious art in later cultures, the combination of frontality and symbolic exaggeration here has led some scholars to conclude that the *Venus of Willendorf* represented a fertility goddess.

She is one of a number of prehistoric female figurines which scholars have nicknamed *Venus* (after the much later Roman goddess of love and beauty), although there is no evidence as to who, if anyone, the figurines were meant to represent. They all exaggerate the breasts and hips, suggesting a cultural preoccupation with fertility, on which the survival of the species depended. Unlike many Upper Paleolithic art forms, these female figurines are found throughout Europe, and are thought to be roughly contemporaneous (c. 25,000–21,000 B.C.). Some, like those in figures 2.1 and 2.2, are relatively naturalistic; others are **abstract**. Their interpretation as fertility goddesses is one possibility among several. Another theory suggests that these figures were used for some kind of ritual exchange between groups of people during periods of environmental instability, when such interaction would have been necessary for collective survival.

Most prehistoric sculptures are in the round, but Paleolithic artists also made **relief** sculpture (see Box). A good example of relief is the so-called *Venus of Laussel* (fig. **2.2**), which has traces of the red ocher **pigment** (see Box) also present on the *Venus of Willendorf*. Although there is

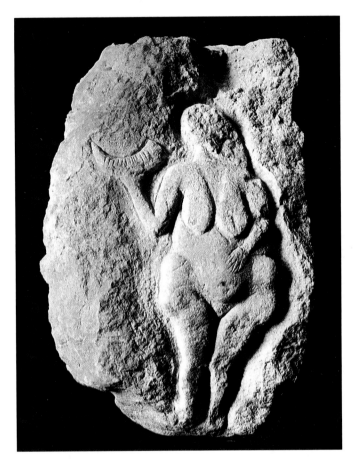

2.2 *Venus of Laussel*, from Laussel, Dordogne, France, c. 25,000–23,000 B.C. Limestone, 17⅜ in (44 cm) high. Fouilles Lalanne, Musée d'Aquitaine, Bordeaux, France.

Categories of Sculpture

Sculpture in the round and in **relief** are the two most basic categories of sculpture. Sculpture in the round refers to any sculpture that is completely detached from its original material, so that it can be seen from all sides, such as the *Venus of Willendorf*. The *Venus of Laussel* remains partly attached to its original material, in this case limestone, so that it is shown in relief, i.e. there is at least one angle from which the image cannot be seen. Sculpture in relief is more pictorial than sculpture in the round because some of the original material remains and forms a background **plane**.

There are different degrees of relief. In **high relief**, the image stands out relatively far from the background plane. In **low relief**, also called bas-relief (*bas* means "low" in French), the surface of the image is closer to the background plane. When light strikes a relief image from an angle, it casts a stronger shadow on high relief than on low relief and thus defines the image more sharply. Reliefs can also be sunken, in which case the image or its outline is slightly recessed into the surface plane, as in much ancient Egyptian carving (Chapter 4).

Pigment

Pigment (from the Latin *pingere*, meaning "to paint") is the basis of color, which is the most eye-catching aspect of most paintings. Pigments are colored powders made from organic substances, such as plant and animal matter, or inorganic substances, such as minerals and semiprecious stones. Cave artists either applied powdered mineral colors directly to damp walls, or mixed their pigments with a liquid, the **medium** or **binder**, to adhere them to dry walls.

Technically, the medium is a liquid in which pigments are suspended (but not dissolved). The term "**vehicle**" is often used interchangeably with "medium." If the liquid binds the pigment particles together, it is referred to as the binder or binding medium. Binders help paint adhere to surfaces, increasing the durability of images. Cave painters used animal fats and vegetable juices, water, or blood as their binding media.

Pigment is applied to the surface of a painting, called its **support**. Supports vary widely in Western art—paper, canvas, pottery, even faces and the surface of one's body. For the cave artist, the walls of the cave were the supports.

no archaeological evidence, the red color might have represented the blood of childbirth, an association reinforced by the form itself. The pelvis and breasts are exaggerated, although the arms are slightly more prominent than those of the *Venus of Willendorf*. In her right hand, the *Venus of Laussel* holds an animal horn.

In addition to female figurines, Upper Paleolithic artists produced many portable representations of animals. Most often found are horses, bison, and oxen; less frequently found are deer, mammoths, antelope, boar, rhinoceri, foxes, wolves, bears, and an occasional fish or bird. A bison carved from reindeer horn (fig. **2.3**) illustrates the

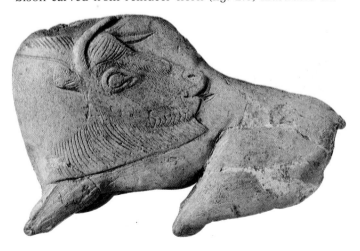

2.3 Bison with turned head, from La Madeleine, Tarn, France, c. 11,000–9000 B.C. Reindeer horn, 4⅛ in (10.5 cm) long. Musée des Antiquités Nationales, Saint Germain-en-Laye.

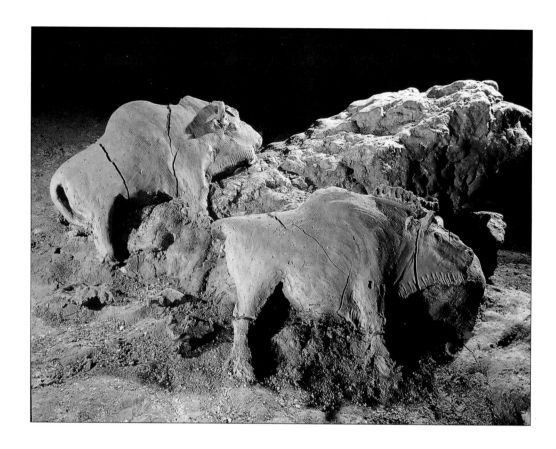

2.4 Bison, Tuc d'Audoubert, 13,000–8000 B.C. Unbaked clay, each one approx. 2 ft (61 cm) long. Ariège, Dordogne, France.

naturalism of Paleolithic animal art. The finely **incised** (cut) lines of the mane and the sharp turn of the head reveal a keen observation of detail, as well as the capacity to render the illusion that the animal is turning in space.

Two sculptures of bison were found more than 700 yards (640 m) inside a cave at Tuc d'Audoubert in Ariège, in the Dordogne region of France (fig. **2.4**). The animals are naturalistically modeled (see Box) in high relief from the clay floor of the cave. Their manes and facial features, on the other hand, are incised, probably with a sharp flint blade. The Tuc d'Audoubert bison seem to emerge from the ground as if rising out of the cave's mud floor. This transition between natural and created form is characteristic of much Stone Age art.

Modeling

Modeling, unlike carving, is an additive process and its materials (such as clay) are pliable rather than hard. The primary tools are the artist's hands, especially the thumbs, although various other tools can be used. Until the material dries and hardens, the work can still be reshaped.

Clay that has been heated (**fired**) in a **kiln** (a special oven) is more durable and waterproof. A Paleolithic kiln for firing clay statues of women and animals has been found in eastern Europe, and a variety of finely crafted, decorated clay vessels was made in western Europe during the Neolithic period.

Upper Paleolithic Painting in Spain and France (c. 30,000–c. 10,000 B.C.)

Most surviving European Paleolithic cave paintings are located in over two hundred caves in the cliffs of northern Spain, especially the Pyrenees Mountains, and the Périgord and Dordogne regions in France. The concentration of cave art in this part of Europe has puzzled scholars. Many now think that the treeless plains, uncovered as the glaciers retreated northward, would have supported unusually large herds of animals, which in turn would have supported whatever human populations existed in the area. The well-preserved state of these cave paintings when they were first discovered was due mainly to the fact that most of the caves are limestone and had been sealed up for thousands of years. After exposure to the modern atmosphere and visitor traffic, the paintings began to deteriorate so rapidly that some caves have been closed to the public.

Like the Tuc d'Audoubert bison, the paintings that have survived are primarily found deep within caves, in interiors which are difficult to reach and uninhabitable. They seem to have served as sanctuaries where fertility, initiation, and hunting rituals were performed and seasonal changes recorded. The predominance of animal representations is in part a reflection of the importance of hunting. But the animals most often depicted do not coincide with those that were hunted most, suggesting that these images had other meanings.

At Altamira, in Santander, Spain, a remarkable group of cave paintings was discovered in 1879 (figs. **2.5** and **2.6**).

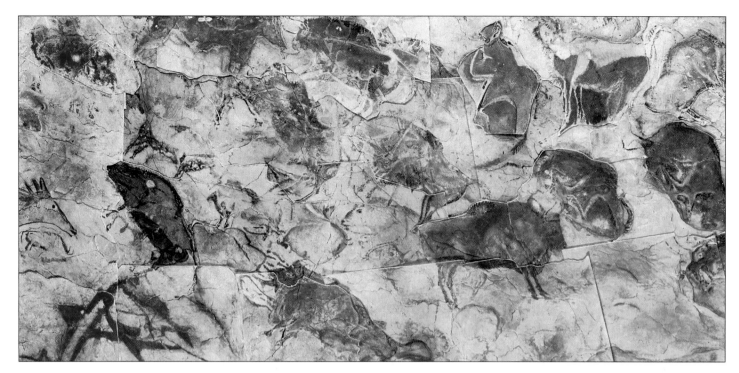

2.5 (above) Ceiling view, Altamira cave, Spain, c. 12,000 B.C. The outlines, limbs, and manes are of black manganese. The interiors are mainly of red ocher with some shading.

2.6 (below) Standing bison, Altamira cave, Spain, c. 12,000 B.C. 6 × 5 ft (1.8 × 1.5 m). The shaded application of ocher creates the impression of a three-dimensional mass. The black outline and details are of manganese.

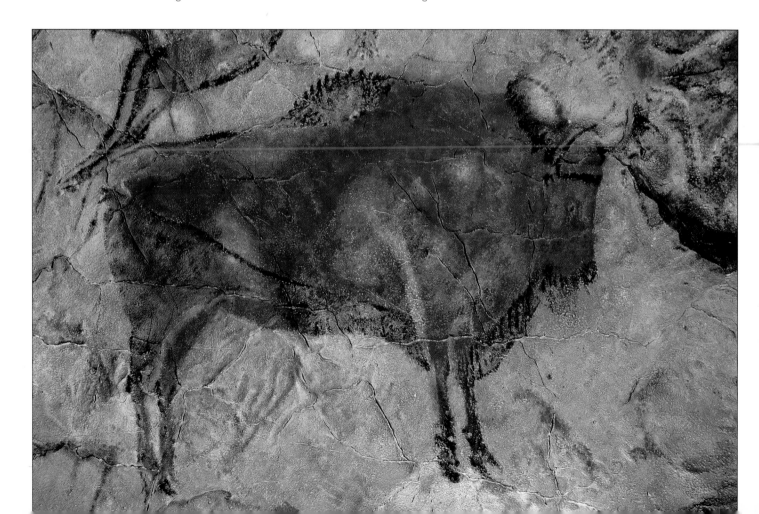

Here the natural bulges in the rock suggest the contours of various animals—mainly bison, but also boar, horses, deer, and a wolf. Artists perceived the outline in nature, and then enhanced the forms with reds, yellows, and browns, and shaded them in black. In addition to paint, carving was used to shape the figures. We can see from the view of the Altamira ceiling in figure 2.5 that the animals are rendered in various poses: standing, kneeling, and curled up.

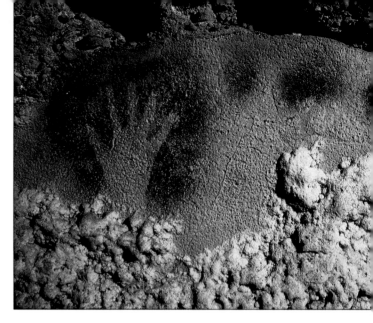

2.7 Handprints from Pech-Merle, Dordogne, France, c. 16,000 B.C. The cave at Pech-Merle is an underground complex, which seems to have been in use periodically for about five thousand years. In addition to handprints, the cave paintings include animals and geometric signs.

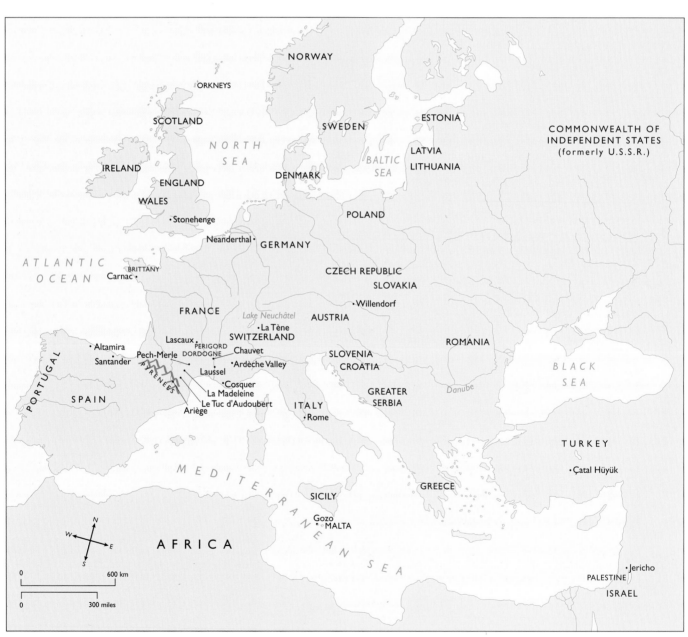

2.8 Map of prehistoric Europe.

The standing bison (fig. 2.6) illustrates the monumentality of Stone Age animal representations. The artist has emphasized the bison's thick neck and shoulder muscles, where its main physical strength resides, in contrast to its small head and thin legs.

Small handprints are also common in Paleolithic cave art (fig. **2.7**). In general, they seem to predate the relatively naturalistic paintings of animals. The hands were placed against a wall with the fingers spread out. Pigment was then applied around them, leaving the shape of the hand visible. Sometimes, the hand itself was covered with pigment and pressed onto the wall. Handprints were also made by pressing against a damp clay wall to leave an impression. The example in figure 2.7 is a small hand of the first type and it is juxtaposed with three black dots.

The significance of these hands has proved to be elusive. According to one scholar, André Leroi-Gourhan (see Box), the hand is a female sign and the dots a male one. Another scholar, Henri Breuil, believed such handprints may have been made during initiation ceremonies. Many of the hands appear to be missing one or more fingers, a fact that has elicited several interpretations, from ritual amputation to frostbite. Another hypothesis is that they represent a code of hand signals used by hunters to communicate silently while stalking their prey (similar signals are still used today in certain hunting societies).

Dating and Meaning of the Cave Paintings: Changing Interpretations

Dating

The French abbot Henri Breuil was the dominant figure in studies of western European cave painting from the early twentieth century until his death in 1961. He dated cave paintings according to a system of development in which "primitive" (in the sense of "schematic" or "abstract") images preceded naturalistic ones. In particular, he noted that some animals are rendered with profile heads and frontal horns, which he called "twisted perspective."

In the 1980s the French scholar André Leroi-Gourhan developed a system dividing cave painting into four styles that also progressed from "primitive" to complex and naturalistic. Today, however, scholars reject the notion of both an identifiable origin of cave painting and of its stylistic progression. They read artistic development more dynamically, as undergoing various stylistic shifts influenced by changes in technology and other cultural factors. Current scholarship also emphasizes the diversity of Upper Paleolithic art from place to place. The "animal art" of cave paintings in southern France and northern Spain exemplifies one such regional style.

Meaning

In the nineteenth century, reflecting the popular view of "Art for Art's Sake," works of art were thought to have been created for purely esthetic purposes. Cave paintings were believed to have been made by male artists in their leisure time. In his personal mythic account of the first artist, Whistler described him as a man who declined to hunt or fight. Instead, he "stayed by the tents with the women, and traced strange devices with a burnt stick upon a gourd ... this devisor of the beautiful—who perceived in Nature ... certain curvings, as faces are seen in the fire—this dreamer apart, was the first artist."[1]

At the turn of the century, the French archaeologist Salomon Reinach read art mainly in social terms. In his view, cave painting was the act of creating an image in order to influence reality, especially to produce magic that would ensure a successful hunt. In the 1920s, Breuil elaborated the notion of cave paintings as attempts at magical control of reality. He also believed that the caves themselves were used as religious sanctuaries, in which worship and initiation rites took place.

Leroi-Gourhan's interpretations were based on anthropological structuralism, which sought to identify universal structures in thought, social organization, and cultural expressions such as myth and religion. He disagreed with the hunting-magic theories and devised instead a system of reading certain signs as binary oppositions of male and female forces. For example, he interpreted triangles, ovals, and rectangles as female, and barbed shapes, dots, and short marks as signifying the phallus (see fig. 2.12). Subsequent interpretations have identified multiple sign systems, each of which had its own symbols, meanings, and functions.

The most recent views locate the significance of cave painting in an environmental context. Thus the depictions of animals reveal changes in season (for instance, a bison's heavy winter coat) and climate (such as the presence of particular species). The concentration of cave art in southwest France and northern Spain is now thought to indicate a corresponding increase in the population of those areas. As a result, rituals and ceremonies involving art became necessary, possibly to reinforce political power.

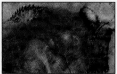

Standing bison, Altamira
(**2.6**)

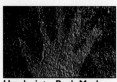

Handprints, Pech-Merle
(**2.7**)

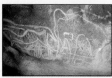

Mammoths and Horses, Chauvet cave (2.16)

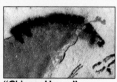

"Chinese Horse," Lascaux (2.11)

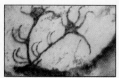

Reindeer, Lascaux
(**2.12**)

Cave art has often been interpreted as evidence of an intimate relationship between image-making and religious practice. Figure **2.9** from the cave of Trois-Frères in Ariège shows a hybrid creature—part human, part animal—in the midst of superimposed animals. Human figures are rare in Upper Paleolithic cave art, and their interpretation is debated. This particular painting seems to represent either a ritual or a supernatural event. In contrast to the animals, who are nearly always in profile, this creature turns and stares out of the rock. His pricked-up ears and alert expression suggest that he is aware of an alien presence, perhaps the viewers themselves. The figure can be read as a man dressed as a stag. His pose and costume suggest that he may be a shaman (see Box) engaged in a ceremonial identification with the animal. Alternatively, the figure can be interpreted as an animal-god.

Shamanism

Shamanism exists today in certain small-scale societies throughout the world, and seems to have been a feature of some prehistoric cultures. Shamans, from the Tunguso-Manchurian word *saman* (meaning "to know"), function as intermediaries between the human and the spirit worlds. They communicate with spirits by entering a trance—induced by rhythmic movement or sound, hallucinogenic drugs, fasting, and so forth—during which one or more spirits "possess" them. Shamans are revered healers and problem-solvers in their communities, and are feared for the harm they could do if angered. They foretell the future, cure the sick, and assist in such rites of passage as birth and death. Shamans are highly individualistic, often living on the fringes of society, and do not participate in organized religion. They generally wear ritual costumes made of animal skins and horns or antlers (see fig. 2.9), and carry ritual objects such as rattles. Dancing and chanting typically accompany shamanic ceremonies.

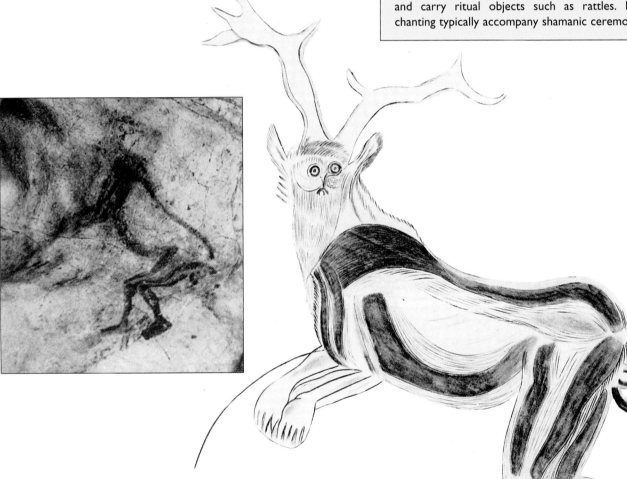

2.9a, b Shaman, Trois-Frères cave, Ariège, Dordogne, France, 13,000–11,000 B.C. 24 in (60 cm) high. Original cave painting and drawing by Henri Breuil. Breuil described the process of making his drawing from the original surface of the cave wall: "How the artist who drew it could have worked four meters (13 ft) above the floor was a problem which I had to solve myself and without a ladder … there is a small, projecting rock where one's right foot can rest; then, taking a firm hold … and making a complete half turn, it is possible to sit quite comfortably on the uneven surface.… It is difficult to hold at the same time a lamp, one's paper and pencil and a drawing board for the retouching of a tracing, taking care at the same time not to slide downwards."[2]

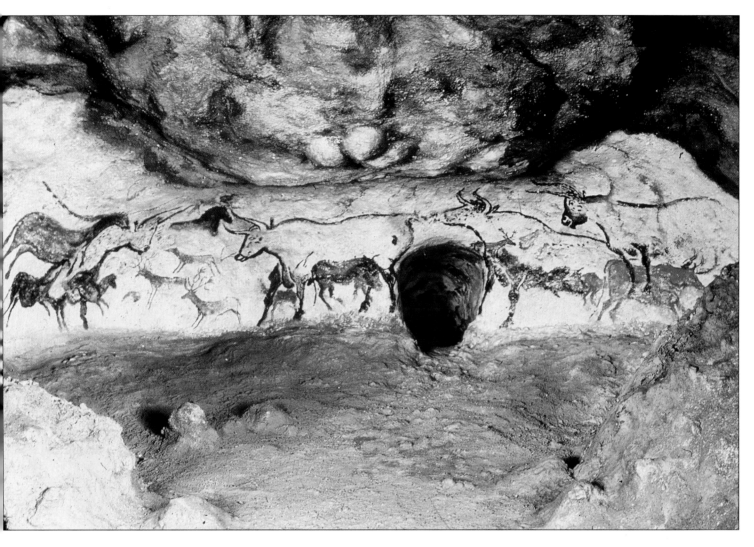

The Lascaux Paintings The most famous examples of cave art are the wall paintings at Lascaux, in the Dordogne (figs. **2.10**, **2.11**, **2.12**, and **2.13**). Located deep within the recesses of the caves, they represent a wide range of animal species and a few human stick figures painted with earth-colored pigments—brown, black, yellow, and red. These were ground from minerals such as ocher, hematite, and manganese and applied to the natural white limestone surfaces of the walls. The Lascaux artists created their figures by first drawing an outline and then filling it in with pigment. The pigment itself was stored in hollow bones plugged at one end, which may also have been used to blow the pigment onto the walls. Some of these bone tubes, still bearing traces of pigment, have been found in the caves. These finds, and their interpretation, exemplify the way in which deductions about the use of objects in a prehistoric society are made. Perhaps if the bones containing pigment had been found out of context, i.e. far from the paintings, different conclusions about their use might have been drawn.

The Lascaux animals are among the best examples of the Paleolithic artists' ability to create the illusion of motion and capture the essence of certain species by

2.10 Hall of Running Bulls, Lascaux, Dordogne, France, c. 15,000–13,000 B.C. Paint on limestone rock, individual bulls 13–16 ft (3.96–4.88 m) long. Note that the white bulls are superimposed over other animals. Cave artists did not always cover up previous representations before adding new ones.

slightly exaggerating characteristic features. The diagonal planes of the long white bulls on either side of the opening of the wall in figure 2.10 create the impression that the one on the left is walking downhill, while the one on the right is going upward. Since many Lascaux animals are superimposed, they have been read as examples of image-magic. According to this theory, the act of making the image was an end in itself, possibly a symbolic capture of the animal by fixing its likeness on the cave wall.

One example of Lascaux's art that has given rise to different interpretations is the so-called "Chinese Horse" (fig. 2.11), whose sagging body suggests pregnancy and the imminent delivery of a foal. The two diagonal forms in this detail, one almost parallel to the horse's neck and the other overlapping its lower outline, have been variously identified as plants or as arrows. Because of their similarity to extant (preserved) specimens, they may be harpoons.

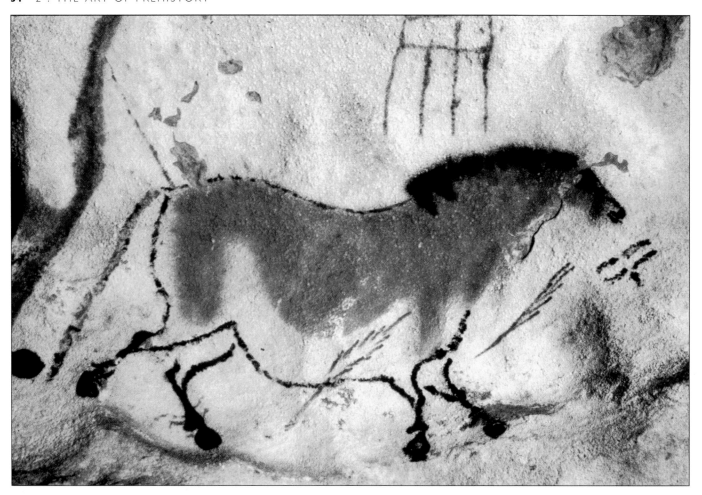

2.11 "Chinese Horse," Lascaux, Dordogne, France, c. 15,000–13,000 B.C. Paint on limestone rock, horse 5 ft 6 in (1.42 m.) long. The animal acquired its nickname because it resembles Chinese ceramic horses of the Han Dynasty.

Leroi-Gourhan argues that they are phallic symbols, and therefore male signs, while he reads the rectangle above the horse as female. The animal's pregnant appearance would be consistent with the paired male-female imagery of Leroi-Gourhan's structuralist approach to prehistoric European art. In any event, the elusive character of such images reveals the ability of Paleolithic artists to produce complex symbolic imagery, whereas our interpretations of the artist's intentions remain hypothetical.

Recent Discoveries: Cosquer and Chauvet Two Upper Paleolithic caves were discovered in the 1980s and 1990s. In 1985, the deep-sea diver Henri Cosquer found a passage 121 feet (36.88 m) below sea level near Marseilles on the southern coast of France. The ascending passage led to a cave, now named after him, that had remained above sea level when the coastal water level rose, cutting it off from land. Six years later, Cosquer discovered a wealth of art—paintings and engravings—on the walls and ceilings of the cave. The images have been securely dated to two periods. The first group, dating to c. 25,000 B.C., consists of stenciled hands surrounded by red and black pigment, and of repeated indented lines called "finger tracings." The second group, from c. 16,000 B.C., consists of painted and engraved animals.

One of the most significant features of Cosquer cave art is the large number of sea animals represented there. These include seals, auks, a fish, and forms presently interpreted as jellyfish (fig. **2.14**). Another unique element is the precise dating. This is possible because samples of the charcoal used in the paintings, as well as pieces of charcoal recovered from the cave floor, have been subjected to radiocarbon testing (see p. 13).

In 1994, three speleologists (cave explorers) found the entrance to an underground cave complex in the Ardèche Valley, in southeast France. They came upon an interior chamber, now named for Jean-Marie Chauvet, a member of the team. The cave proved to be the largest so far known in this region, and contains over three hundred wall paintings, engravings, Paleolithic bear skeletons and a bear's skull set on a rock, evidence of fires, and footprints. Radiocarbon analysis indicates a very early date of around 30,000 B.C. for some of the paintings. They are thus considerably older than those at Altamira, Trois-Frères, and Lascaux. The paintings are generally outlined in red or black pigment. As at other Upper Paleolithic caves in southern France and northern Spain, they represent mainly animals along with some signs—especially red dots and handprints. These animal images are unusual, however, in that there are many rhinoceri and large felines.

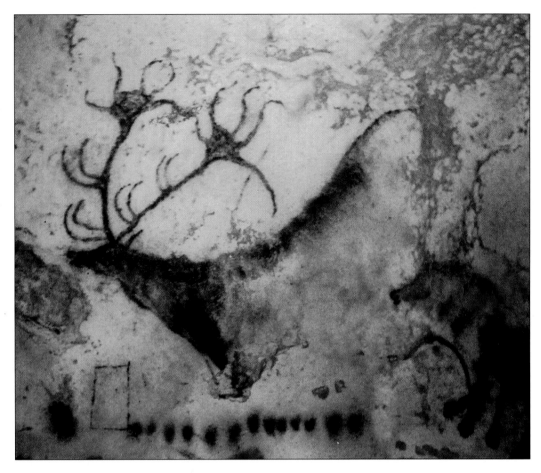

2.12 Reindeer, Lascaux, Dordogne, France, c. 15,000–13,000 B.C. Paint on limestone rock. Stags are less common than horses in Paleolithic art. Like the horse, however, this figure has a pronounced dorsal curve that enhances the impression of downhill movement.

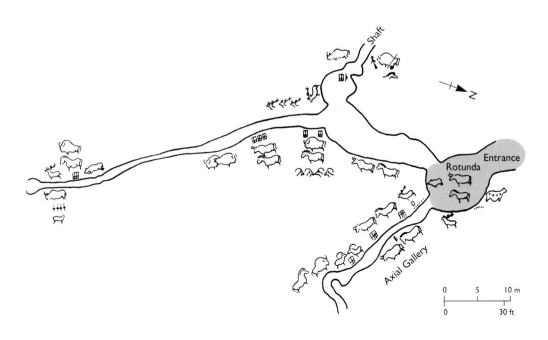

2.13 Diagram of Lascaux cave system (based on a diagram by the Service de l'Architecture, Paris).

2.14 Jellyfish, Cosquer cave, near Marseilles, France, c. 25,000 B.C. Painting on a black stalagmite.

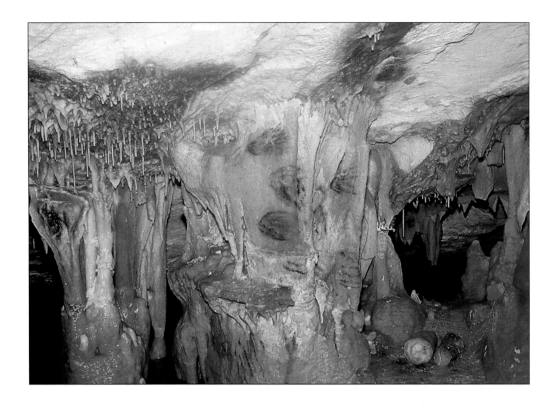

Only four of the Chauvet cave images may be reproduced at this time (three are shown here) because the rest are in litigation over picture rights—one of the many examples of ways in which politics and money interfere with scientific research and artistic expression.

The spotted figures identified as a panther and a hyena (fig. **2.15**) are, according to the explorers, unprecedented in cave art of the Ardèche region. They are outlined in red ocher, which is characteristic of the animals close to the cave entrance. The curved edges and the rock itself impart a sense of natural bulk similar to that found elsewhere in Paleolithic animal art. Also conveyed is the hyena's characteristic aggression: its head, accentuated by the spots, juts forward on a downward diagonal that visually overwhelms the smaller animal below.

Altogether, thirty-four images of mammoths were found at Chauvet, of which twenty-one are engraved into the rock and thirteen are painted. The two superimposed engraved examples in figure **2.16** are depicted as if following an engraved horse, whose mane is indicated by a thick line. This one was placed over a series of parallel incised lines identified as claw marks by explorers. The overlapping images are unexplained, but may have been made at different times and ritually repeated. As at Lascaux, we see *through* the animals in a way that is not naturalistic, and it is not clear whether the significance of the superimposition is formal or iconographic.

The so-called "Lion Panel," partly shown in figure **2.17**, represents various species of animals that run across

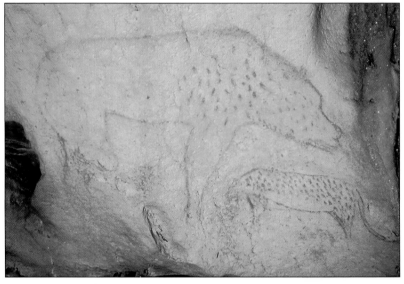

2.15 Hyena and Panther, Chauvet cave, Ardèche Valley, France, c. 25,000–17,000 B.C. Red ocher on limestone wall. Courtesy of J. Clottes, the Regional Office of Cultural Affairs, Rhône-Alpes, and the Ministry of Culture and Communication (Direction du Patrimoine, sous Direction de l'Archéologie).

a niche in the wall. Visible here are three large lions and numerous smaller, but more densely painted, rhinoceri. Some, like the Lascaux animals, are shaded. One faces a group that seems to be moving towards it. It is not clear whether this is a coherent scene or a ritual repetition. Some are superimposed—those at the top—while the others are spread across the surface of the wall. Under the

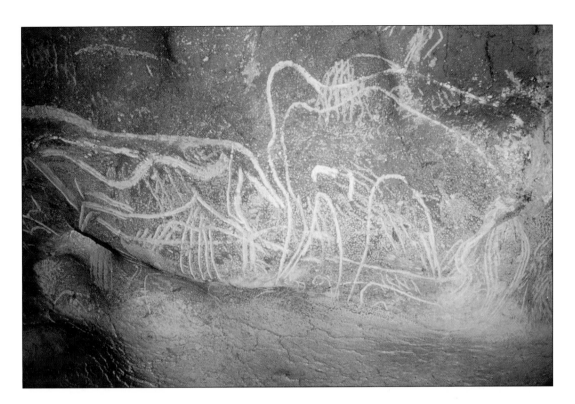

2.16 Mammoths and Horses, Chauvet cave, Ardèche Valley, France, c. 25,000–17,000 B.C. Engraving on limestone wall. Courtesy of J. Clottes, the Regional Office of Cultural Affairs, Rhône-Alpes, and the Ministry of Culture and Communication (Direction du Patrimoine, sous Direction de l'Archéologie).

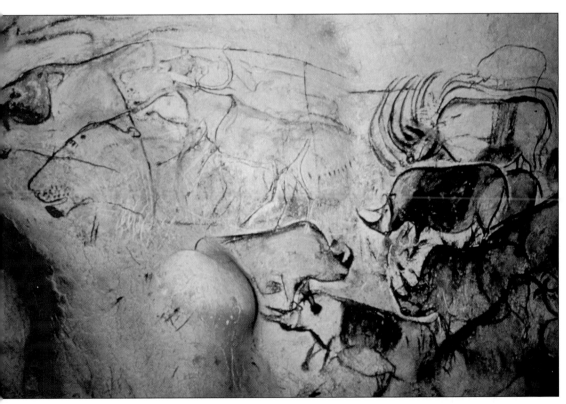

2.17 Left section of the "Lion Panel," Chauvet cave, Ardèche Valley, France, c. 25,000–17,000 B.C. Black pigment on limestone wall. Courtesy of J. Clottes, the Regional Office of Cultural Affairs, Rhône-Alpes, and the Ministry of Culture and Communication (Direction du Patrimoine, sous Direction de l'Archéologie).

painting of the lions, traces of red pigment can be seen, as well as the outline of a deer. Like the other animals rendered in black, these are deep within the interior of the cave, suggesting that the red paintings precede the black ones chronologically.

Since the Cosquer and Chauvet caves are recent discoveries, explorers and archaeologists are in the early stages of studying them. Like all finds of this kind, they expand the understanding of previously known sites even as they raise new questions.

Rock Paintings of Australia

(c. 75,000/50,000 B.C.–the present)

Rock paintings, carvings, and other art objects have continued to be produced since the Stone Age by certain cultures around the world. A few of these societies that have persisted into our own era appear to have something in common with those of Paleolithic western Europe. There is uncertainty in dating works created by such cultures and in pinning down the antiquity of their mythological traditions. Nevertheless, these "modern Stone Age" societies may provide valuable clues to the way art functioned in prehistoric Europe. Such comparisons must, of course, be made with caution, but they can suggest alternative ways of thinking about ancient art.

Australian Rock Art

In the outback of Australia, hunting and gathering societies, called Aboriginal, have had an unusually long history. Revolutionary archaeological finds in 1996 in a remote part of northwestern Australia at the site of Jinmium challenged basic assumptions about when and where humans evolved (fig. **2.18**). Stone tools and other objects from this site suggest that Australia was inhabited as long ago as 174,000 B.C. Carved rocks discovered there may be roughly 75,000 years old. Recent evidence—a red ocher "crayon"—indicates that people may have been

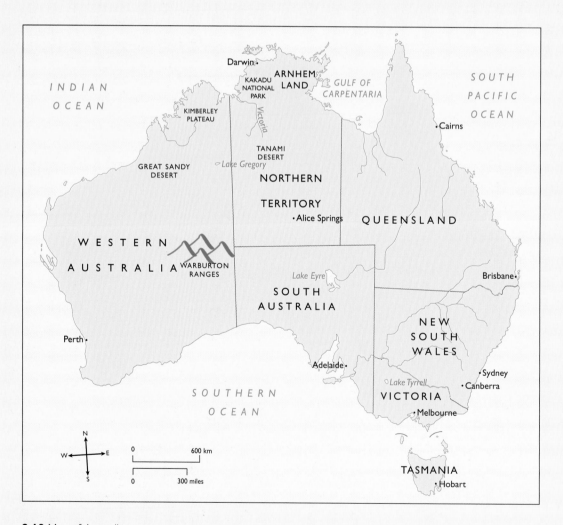

2.18 Map of Australia.

making rock paintings for the past 75,000 years. If accepted, these dates are far older than scholars had believed possible. Australia is an island that had been relatively isolated from the rest of the world until the eighteenth and nineteenth centuries. Nevertheless, there are remarkable visual similarities between European Paleolithic and Aboriginal rock paintings, including handprints, naturalistic animals, and hunting scenes.

Aside from these works, our knowledge of ancient Aboriginal mythology, ritual, tradition, and social customs comes from contemporary Aborigines. Their society is divided into clans that "own" certain myths and sacred images. Myth and imagery thus assume a concrete value and are considered to be cultural possessions. They have a totemic, or ancestral, significance, and it is thus possible that many of the animals represented in Australian rock art are, in fact, totems of particular clans.

The ancestral character of Australian Aboriginal art and religion is related to what has been translated into Western languages as the "Dreaming." This phenomenon is not a dream, but rather a mythological plane of existence. For Aborigines, the "Dreamtime" is the order of the universe and encompasses cosmological time from its beginning to an indefinite future. Included in Dreamtime are the ancestors who created and ordered both the world and the human societies that populate it. Dreamtime is accessible through the performance of certain rituals—such as creating rock paintings—accompanied by singing and chanting. In the Aboriginal Dreaming, therefore, is contained a wealth of cultural mythology, much of which is revealed in the visual arts.

The Wandjinas, or Cloud Spirits, for example, appear in numerous rock pictures, usually painted in black, red, and yellow on a white ground (fig. **2.19**). These creatures combine human with cloud forms and are ancestral creators from the Dreamtime. According to Aboriginal myth, Wandjinas made the earth, the sea, and the human race. They are depicted frontally with large heads, massive upper bodies, and lower bodies that taper toward the feet. Around their heads are feathers and lightning. Their faces typically lack mouths, although the eyes and nose are present. If Wandjinas are offended, they unleash lightning and cause rains and flooding, but they can also bring fertility. Paintings of them are believed to have special powers and therefore are approached with caution.

The oldest identifiable style of Aboriginal rock painting, referred to as the Mimi style, is found in Arnhem Land in northern Australia (fig. **2.20**). Mimi, in Aboriginal

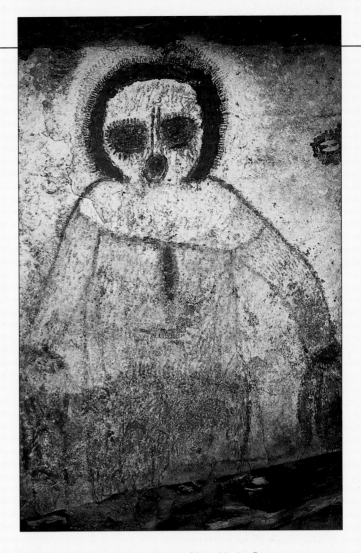

2.19 Wandjina, Rowalumbin, Barker River, Napier Range, Kimberly, Australia. These rock paintings were discovered in 1837 by an expedition led by George Grey. He described his first view of the Wandjinas as follows: "They appeared to stand out from the rock; and I was certainly rather surprised at the moment that I first saw this gigantic head and upper part of a body bending over and staring down at me."[3]

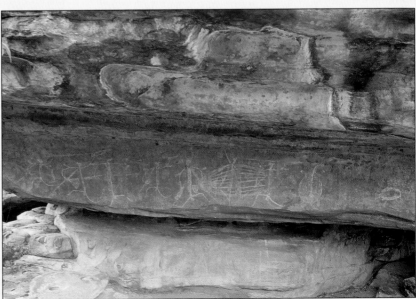

2.20 Mimi hunters, Kakadu National Park, Arnhem Land, Northern Territory, Australia. Rock painting. In the Mimi style, as here, figures are painted in red ocher. These hunters carry spears and boomerangs.

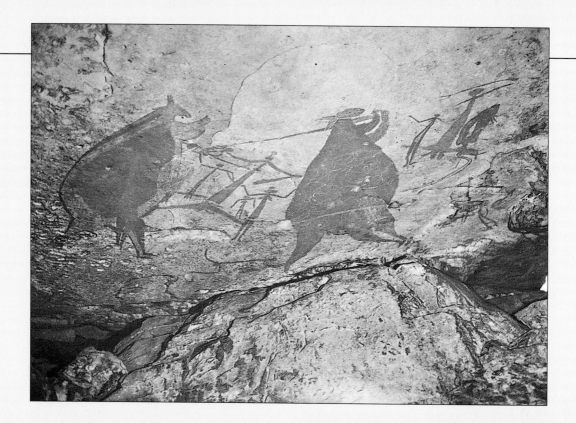

2.21 Men and women hunting kangaroos, Unbalanya Hill, Arnhem Land, Northern Territory, Australia. Rock painting.

myth, are elongated spirits living in rocks and caves. They are taller than humans, and are so light that they can be blown away and destroyed by the wind. If a Mimi entices a man to its cave and tricks him into eating its food or sleeping with a Mimi woman, then the human turns into a Mimi and cannot return to his human condition. Mimi are often represented hunting, as they are in figure 2.20, and are believed to have taught hunting to the Aborigines.

The kangaroo, which is indigenous only to Australia and adjacent islands, is a frequent subject of Aboriginal rock art. Kangaroos have been hunted for thousands of years, probably as a source of food. Those represented in figure **2.21** are trying to escape from a group of hunters, who are both male and female. That the kangaroos are hopping is clear from their poses—the one in the center has just landed and tilts slightly back on its feet. The kangaroo on the left leans forward as if to regain its balance. In paintings such as this, Aboriginal artists used two relatively different styles, a naturalistic one for animals and a schematic one for humans. This distinction is also characteristic of western European Upper Paleolithic cave paintings.

The kangaroo in figure **2.22** is a good example of the **polychrome** "X-ray" style. It is rendered in brown and white as if displaying the inner organic structure of bone and muscle. Because of its flattened pose, it is stylized rather than naturalistic. The fish-shaped head reflects the appearance of aquatic animals in Aboriginal rock iconography that took place following a rise in the sea level around 8000 B.C. The skeletal figure on the right is the fearsome Lightning Man, who is surrounded by an electrical circuit.

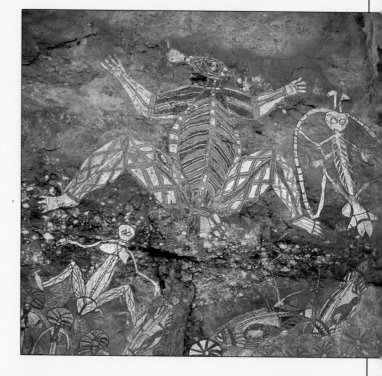

2.22 Kangaroo with Lightning Man, Nourlangie Rock, Kakadu National Park, Arnhem Land, Northern Territory, Australia. Rock painting. In Dreamtime, the Lightning Man, called Namarragon or Namarrkon, lived in the sky and carried a lightning spear. He tied stone clubs to his knees and elbows so that he would always be prepared to hurl thunder and lightning. For most of the year he lived at the far ends of the sky, absorbing the light of the Sun Woman. When the wet season came, he descended to the earth's atmosphere in order to keep an eye on the human race. When displeased, he hurled spears of lightning across the sky and onto the earth. Some 30 miles (48 km) east of Oenpelli, there is a taboo Dreaming site where Namarrkon is said to have settled. This site is avoided by Aborigines who fear his wrath.

Mesolithic (c. 8000–c. 6000/4000 B.C.)

The Mesolithic era in western Europe was a period of transition more noteworthy for its important cultural and environmental changes than for its artistic legacy. It followed the end of the Ice Age and the rapid development of a more temperate climate about 11,000 B.C. With the retreat of the glaciers, forests expanded. Animals that had been hunted in the Paleolithic era died out or migrated, and people began to congregate around bodies of water, where fishing became a major source of food. By the end of the Mesolithic period many nomadic hunter-gatherer societies had become increasingly settled, differentiated, predominantly agricultural communities.

Neolithic (c. 6000/4000–c. 2000 B.C.)

In western Europe the revolutionary shift from hunting and gathering to farming seems to have occurred at the dawn of the Neolithic period. This more settled existence contributed to the development of a new art form: monumental stone architecture. On a more modest scale, domestic architecture took on new forms, as did other arts such as sculpture, pottery, and jewelry.

The two most impressive types of monumental Neolithic architecture in western Europe are the limestone tombs and temples discovered on Malta, an island between Italy and North Africa, and a type of structure known as a **megalith** found in parts of France, Spain, Italy, and northern Europe (especially Great Britain). Megaliths (from the Greek *megas*, meaning "big") are huge stones, and such structures were built without the use of mortar.

Malta

The megaliths on Malta and the adjoining island of Gozo are now dated before 3000 B.C. Maltese temples are freestanding structures, the products of a civilization that lasted some eight hundred years and then disappeared following an invasion. The biggest temple, Ggantija (meaning "Tower of the Giants"), discovered on Gozo, is located on a hill and faces downward. Its **façade** (front) was originally nearly 50 feet (15.24 m) high, and its exterior was constructed of rough, uncut native limestone slabs, which were rolled to the site on limestone balls. The diagram in figure **2.23** shows that the exterior wall surrounded two

temples. The one to the south, at the left, is earlier, and its sanctuary, which is trilobed (i.e. having three rounded projections), is larger than the oval space preceding it. In the northern temple, at the right, the sizes are reversed—the sanctuary is small compared with the oval in front of it.

Attention was focused on the elaborate interior sanctuaries, which were reached through a series of decreasing and expanding spaces. The narrower spaces contained a **parapet** (a wall around a terrace or balcony), while one curve of the oval forecourt of the southern temple is lined with platforms that resemble altars. There is also evidence that the stone oval at the entrance to this temple was a hearth used in ceremonies and rituals.

Seventeen temples have been excavated so far on Malta. These, like Ggantija, show evidence of libations (poured offerings), divination (forecasting the future), collective human burial, and the presence of an important priesthood. Animal sacrifices—especially of rams and pigs—were performed in the Maltese temples, but there is no indication of human sacrifice. Artistic activity in this religious context includes paintings and sculptures on the walls of the innermost sacred chambers, as well as many female figures.

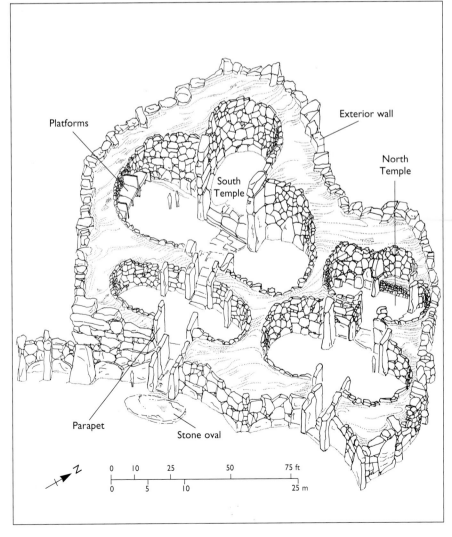

2.23 Reconstruction drawing of the temple at Ggantija, Gozo, Malta.

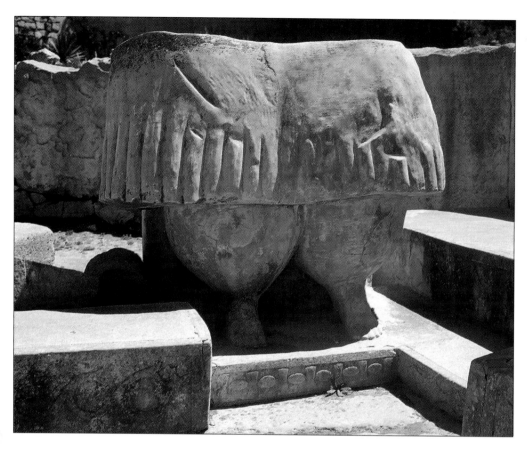

2.24 *Mother Goddess*, Tarxien, Malta, before 2500 B.C. Stone fragment.

The most dramatic surviving statue from the Maltese temples is a fragment of a huge figure, possibly a mother goddess (fig. **2.24**). Her large, bulbous legs, covered to just below the knees by a pleated skirt, leave no doubt that in her original state she was an imposing and literally gigantic figure. This colossal statue and the abundance of smaller obese female figures suggest the presence of a fertility cult. A number of them were ritually covered around the legs with red ocher, suggesting the blood of childbirth, while the rounded plans (see fig. 2.23) of the megalithic tombs and temples on Malta have been interpreted as symbolizing wombs.

The connection between an earth goddess and human burial is most direct at the Maltese site of Hal Saflieni, where a **necropolis**—or city of the dead—has yielded the remains of over seven thousand human bodies in addition to statues of females. The combination of womb-like architectural space with the sculptures of obese women on Malta points to the importance of a chthonian, or underground, goddess. At Ggantija, holes apparently provided worshipers with access to the underworld through ritual libations poured into them. Images of the sick or crippled, and sculptures of reclining females, suggest that the temple was endowed with curative powers. These seem to have been thought most effective if the invalid lay on the sanctuary floor.

Northern Europe

The Neolithic megaliths in Ireland, Britain, France, Spain, and Italy are of a different character from those discovered on Malta. Three distinctive types of stone structure regularly occur: the **menhir**, **dolmen**, and **cromlech**—these terms are Celtic in origin (see Box). They are not only visually impressive and mysterious reminders of the ancient past, but are also imbued with fascinating symbolic associations. For megalithic builders, stone as a material was an integral part of cults honoring dead ancestors. Whereas most Neolithic dwellings in western Europe were made of impermanent material such as wood, the tombs—or "houses of the dead"—were of stone so that they would outlast mortal time. Even today we associate these qualities of durability and stability with stone. For example, we speak of things being "written in stone" when we mean that they are unchanging and enduring, and to "stonewall" means to block a decision for as long as possible. One who is "stoned" is unable to move because of excessive consumption of alcohol or other drugs.

Menhirs Menhirs (from two Celtic words: *men*, meaning "stone," and *hir*, meaning "long") are unhewn or slightly shaped single stones (**monoliths**), usually standing upright in the ground. They were erected individually, in clusters, or in rows as at Carnac (fig. **2.25**) in Brittany, probably an important Neolithic religious center in what is now northern France. Menhirs might have symbolized the phallic power of the male fertilizing Mother Earth.

The Celts

Celtic terms are used for Neolithic megaliths in western Europe because a large number of them are located in regions later inhabited by Celtic peoples.

The Celts were first identified in the basin of the upper Danube River and southern Germany in the second millennium B.C. Although of mixed origins, they spoke related Indo-European languages. From the early ninth century B.C., the Celts began to migrate throughout western Europe, occupying France, Spain, Portugal, northern Italy (they sacked Rome in 390 B.C.), the British Isles, and Greece. Gaelic-speaking Celts settled in Ireland, Scotland, England, and Wales, and Celtic dialects are still spoken in Great Britain, Ireland, and northern France.

The rigidly organized social structure of the Celts was ruled by a chief. They worshiped many gods and believed in the immortality of the soul. Celtic priests, called Druids, supervised education, religion, and the administration of justice. The rich Celtic oral tradition forms the basis of much European folklore.

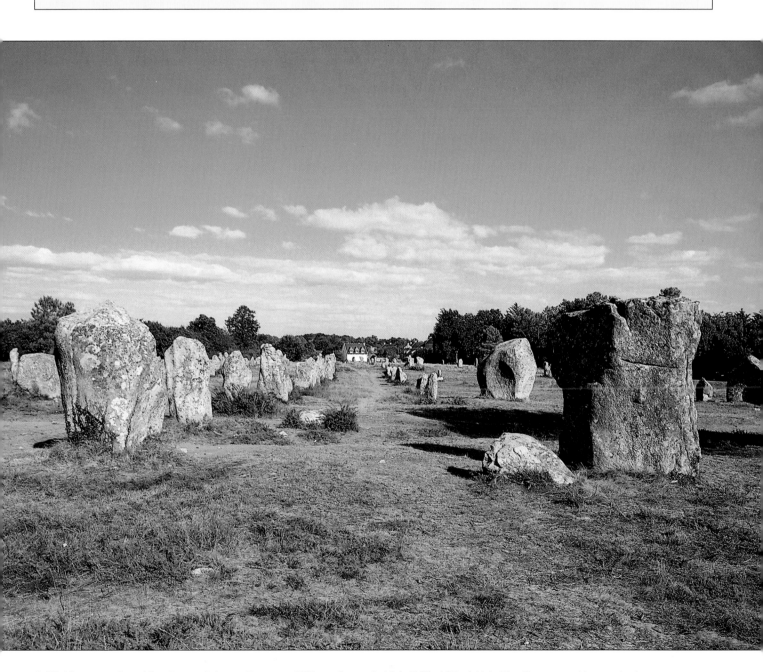

2.25 Alignment of menhirs, Carnac, Brittany, France, c. 4000 B.C. Stone, 6–15 ft (1.83–4.57 m) high. The Carnac menhirs, numbering almost three thousand, are arranged in parallel rows nearly 13,000 ft (4000 m) long. A small village has grown up around the menhirs.

Dolmens Dolmens (from the Celtic *dol*, meaning "table") are chambers or enclosures consisting of two or more vertical stones supporting a large single stone, much as legs support a table (fig. **2.26**). The earliest dolmens were built as tombs, each enclosing a body. Later additions turned them into passageways. Some interior dolmen walls were decorated with carvings and others were painted. Occasionally a pillar stood in the center of a burial chamber. Dolmens, like menhirs, were imbued by Neolithic people with symbolic associations. In contrast to the impermanence of houses built for the living (usually made of mud, plant fibers, and wood), stone burial monuments functioned as links between present and future time.

Cromlechs Cromlechs (from the Celtic *crom*, meaning "circle," and *lech*, meaning "place") are megalithic structures in which groups of menhirs are arranged to form circles or semicircles. By far the greatest number of Neolithic stone circles is found in Britain. Cromlechs must have played a major role in their cultures, since the effort required to build them was extraordinary. Although the function and symbolism of their circular forms have not been determined, cromlechs clearly marked sacred spaces.

The most famous Neolithic cromlech in western Europe is Stonehenge (fig. **2.27**), which was built in several stages from roughly 2800 to 1500 B.C. Rising dramatically from Salisbury Plain in southern England, Stonehenge has fascinated its visitors for centuries. The plan in figure **2.28** indicates all stages of construction (Neolithic and later), with the dark sections showing the megalithic circles as they stand today. Many of the original stones have now fallen. The aerial view in figure 2.27 shows the present disposition of the remaining stones and the modern pathway traversed by tourists.

This circular area of land on a gradually sloping ridge was a sacred site before 3000 B.C. Originally, barrows (burial mounds) containing individual graves were surrounded by a ditch roughly 350 feet (107 m) in diameter. A mile-long "avenue" was hollowed out of the earth and ran in an east-west direction. Fifty-six pits (known as Aubrey Holes after their seventeenth-century discoverer) were added inside the circular ditch, and filled with rubble or cremated human bones. Around the same period the Heel Stone, a block of sarsen (a local sandstone) 16 feet (4.88 m) high, was set in place outside the ditch in the entrance causeway to the northeast. The first stone circle, consisting of smaller stones called bluestones, imported from Wales (over 100 miles, or 160 km, away), was constructed around 2500 B.C.

Over the next four hundred years, a new group of people settled in western Europe and was assimilated into the native population. The origin of these Beaker People, so-called after their beaker-shaped pottery, is still a matter of debate. They brought with them a knowledge of metalworking, new building techniques, and pottery. Partly as a consequence of new technology, the Stone Age gave way to the Bronze Age. Nevertheless, before the total disappearance of the Stone Age in western Europe, its most famous architectural monument was completed, apparently by the Beaker People themselves. In the final stages of construction at Stonehenge, huge sarsen blocks were brought to the site from Marlborough Downs, a distance of some 20 miles (32 km). From these larger monoliths, the outer circle and inner U-shape were constructed.

The cromlech at Stonehenge is a series of concentric circles and horseshoe- or U-shaped curves (see figs. 2.27 and 2.28). The outer circle is a **post-and-lintel construction** (fig. **2.29**; see Box). Each post is a sarsen block 13 feet

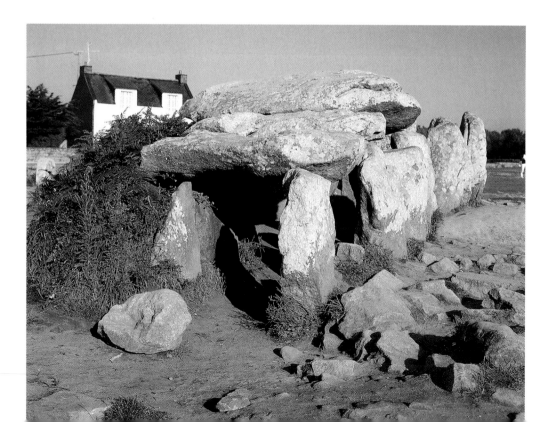

2.26 Dolmen, Crucuno, north of Carnac, Brittany, France, c. 4000 B.C.

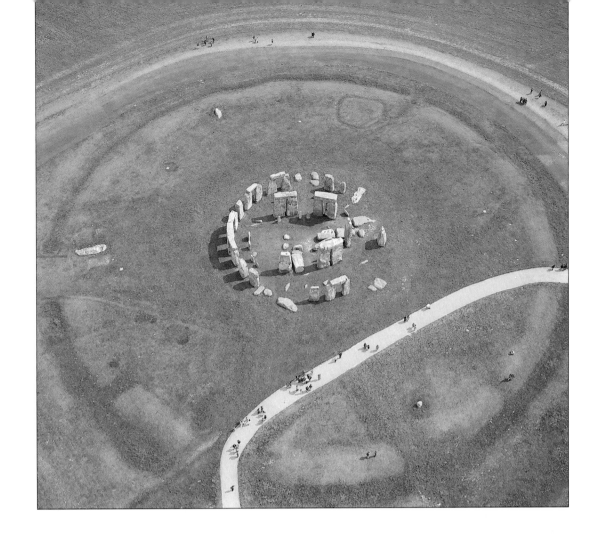

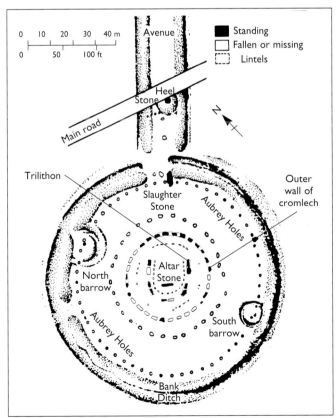

2.28 Plan of Stonehenge.

2.27 Stonehenge, Salisbury Plain, England, c. 2800–1500 B.C. Diameter of circle 97 ft (29.57 m), height approx. 13 ft 6 in (4 m). Interpretations of this remarkable monument have ranged from the possible—a kind of giant sundial used to predict seasonal change and astronomical phenomena—to the purely fanciful—a Druid ritual site, or a form of architectural magic conjured by Merlin, King Arthur's magician.

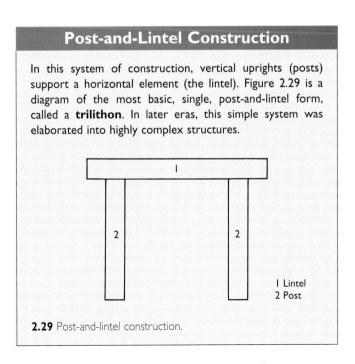

Post-and-Lintel Construction

In this system of construction, vertical uprights (posts) support a horizontal element (the lintel). Figure 2.29 is a diagram of the most basic, single, post-and-lintel form, called a **trilithon**. In later eras, this simple system was elaborated into highly complex structures.

1 Lintel
2 Post

2.29 Post-and-lintel construction.

(3.96 m) high, and is rougher on the outside than on the inside, bulging at its center and then gradually tapering at the top. Projecting above each post was a **tenon** which fitted into a hole carved out of the lintel (fig. **2.30**). For the outer wall, the lintels were slightly curved to create a circle when attached end-to-end.

From the inside ring (fig. **2.31**) one can see part of the outer ring, and several individual posts and lintels. A second, inner circle consists entirely of single upright bluestones. Inside those are five very large **trilithons** (a pair of sarsen posts supporting a single lintel) arranged in a U-shape (fig. **2.32**). An even smaller U-shape of blue-stones parallels the arrangement of the five posts and lin-tels. We do not know how bluestones weighing up to 40 tons (40,640 kg) and sarsens weighing up to 50 tons (50,800 kg) were transported, or how the lintels were raised above the posts, but such engineering feats required large-scale social organization and an enormous commitment of resources over a long period of time.

Within the U of bluestones, one stone lies horizontally on the ground. This is referred to as the "altar stone," although there is no evidence that it was ever used as an altar. While continuing archaeological activity steadily increases our knowledge of Stonehenge, we still cannot identify its function. Clearly the presence of circular stone rings throughout western Europe points to a common

1 Lintel
2 Upright
3 Mortice
4 Raised to fit hollow
  in top of upright
5 Tenon
6 Dished slightly

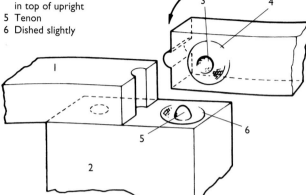

2.30 Lintel and tenon.

purpose. Some scholars think that rites, processions, and sacred dances were held in and around the megalithic structures, celebrating the resurgence of life in spring and summer. These practices correlate with what we know of early agricultural societies, for which the timing of seasonal change was of crucial importance.

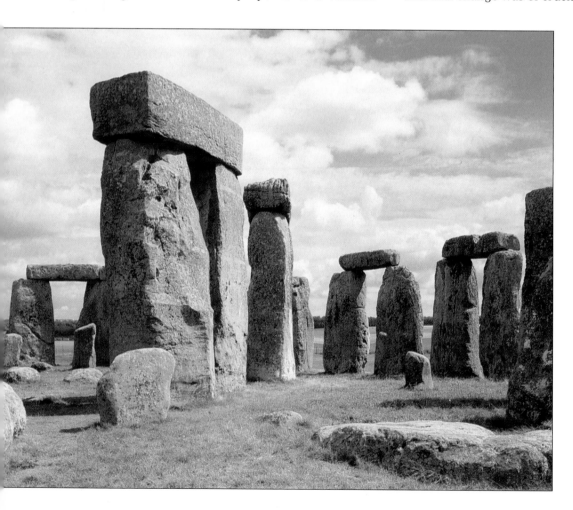

2.31 The inside ring of Stonehenge.

Also consistent with agricultural preoccupations are interpretations of Stonehenge and other megalithic structures as astronomical observatories, used to predict lunar eclipses and to keep track of time. At Stonehenge, for example, the absence of a roof reinforces the relationship of the structure with the sky and celestial phenomena. Carnac (see fig. 2.25) has been described as an observatory in which each menhir functions as a point on a landscape graph. Elsewhere, direct evidence of astronomical markings on carved stones has been found. The circular monuments in particular are aligned according to the positions of the sun and moon at critical times of year. Earlier cromlechs were oriented toward sunrise at the winter solstice, and later ones at the summer solstice. At Stonehenge, the avenue is aligned with the rising summer sun. An observer standing in the middle of the circle about 1800 B.C. would have seen the sun rise over the Heel Stone on June 21st, the summer solstice. Other stones are aligned with the northernmost and southernmost points of moonrise.

The greatest megalithic monument of the Neolithic era in western Europe was also among the last. Around 2000 B.C., as the use of metal increased, the construction of large stone monuments declined.

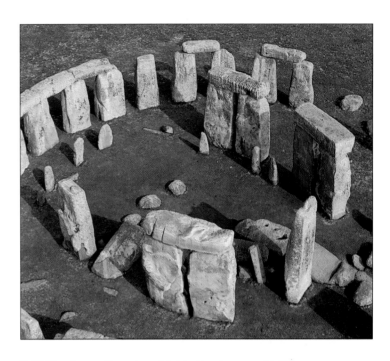

2.32 Stonehenge, its posts and lintels, bluestones, and trilithons.

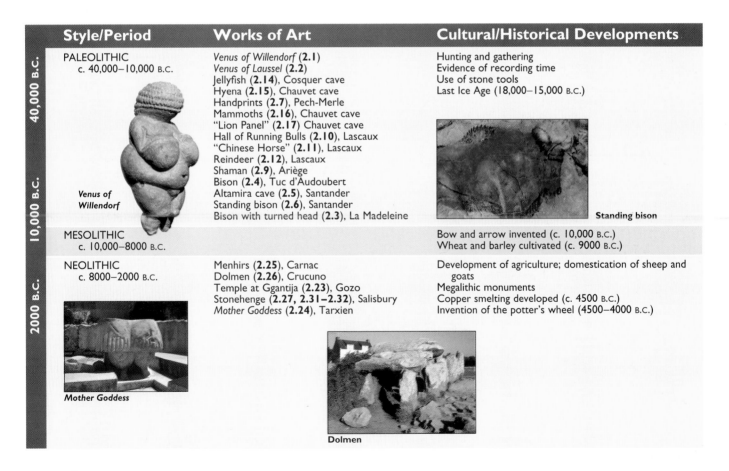

Style/Period	Works of Art	Cultural/Historical Developments
PALEOLITHIC c. 40,000–10,000 B.C.	*Venus of Willendorf* (**2.1**) *Venus of Laussel* (**2.2**) Jellyfish (**2.14**), Cosquer cave Hyena (**2.15**), Chauvet cave Handprints (**2.7**), Pech-Merle Mammoths (**2.16**), Chauvet cave "Lion Panel" (**2.17**) Chauvet cave Hall of Running Bulls (**2.10**), Lascaux "Chinese Horse" (**2.11**), Lascaux Reindeer (**2.12**), Lascaux Shaman (**2.9**), Ariège Bison (**2.4**), Tuc d'Audoubert Altamira cave (**2.5**), Santander Standing bison (**2.6**), Santander Bison with turned head (**2.3**), La Madeleine	Hunting and gathering Evidence of recording time Use of stone tools Last Ice Age (18,000–15,000 B.C.) Standing bison
MESOLITHIC c. 10,000–8000 B.C.		Bow and arrow invented (c. 10,000 B.C.) Wheat and barley cultivated (c. 9000 B.C.)
NEOLITHIC c. 8000–2000 B.C.	Menhirs (**2.25**), Carnac Dolmen (**2.26**), Crucuno Temple at Ggantija (**2.23**), Gozo Stonehenge (**2.27, 2.31–2.32**), Salisbury *Mother Goddess* (**2.24**), Tarxien	Development of agriculture; domestication of sheep and goats Megalithic monuments Copper smelting developed (c. 4500 B.C.) Invention of the potter's wheel (4500–4000 B.C.)

3

The Ancient Near East

It was in the ancient Near East that people first invented writing, one of the most significant developments in human history. Writing enabled communities to keep records and create a permanent body of literature. The Near East produced the first known epic poetry, written history, religious texts, and economic records. These provide insights into the origins of human thought and civilization. They also shed light on the artistic products of ancient Near Eastern civilization in a way that is not possible for preliterate times. Before exploring the invention of writing and its relation to art history, however, we shall consider the rise of Neolithic cultures in this part of the world (see Box).

The Neolithic Era

Neolithic cultures developed some four thousand years earlier in the Near East than in Europe. As was the case with Neolithic cultures in western Europe, those in the Near East emerged during the transition from a relatively nomadic hunting-and-gathering way of life to a more settled one centered around agriculture and animal herding. Droughts and floods made growing crops and establishing permanent communities difficult in certain areas. In response, people learned how to manage water supplies by building large-scale irrigation systems. The social structures that made this possible—organized labor and stabilized political power—contributed to the rise of increasingly complex, urban cultures.

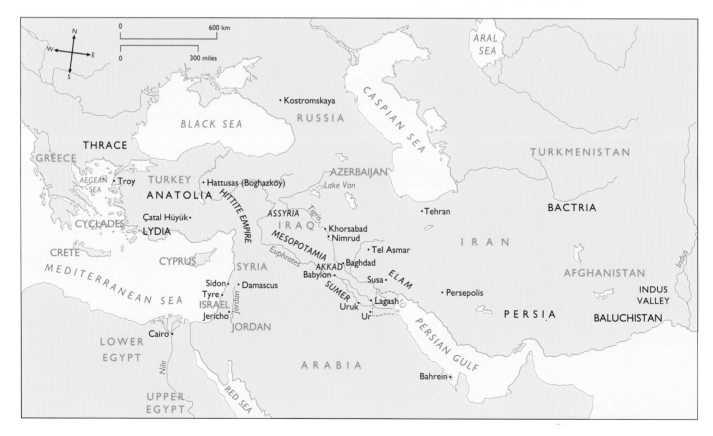

3.1 Map of the ancient Near East and the Middle East.

Chronology of the Ancient Near East and Principal Sites

NEOLITHIC ERA c. 9000–4500/4000 B.C.	Jericho (in modern Israel) Çatal Hüyük (in modern Turkey)
MESOPOTAMIA Uruk period c. 4500–3100 B.C.	Modern Iraq Uruk
Sumer Early Dynastic period c. 2800–2300 B.C.	Sumer Tell Asmar, Ur
Neo-Sumerian period c. 2150–1800 B.C.	Lagash
Akkad c. 2340–2180 B.C.	Akkad
Babylon Old Babylonian period c. 1830–1550 B.C.	Babylon
Neo-Babylonian period c. 612–539 B.C.	
Assyrian Empire c. 1100–612 B.C.	Assur
ANATOLIA Hittite Empire c. 1450–1200 B.C.	Modern Turkey Hattusas (modern Boghazköy)
ANCIENT IRAN c. 5000–331 B.C.	Modern Iran
Achaemenid Persia 559–331 B.C.	Persepolis (near modern Shiraz)
THE SCYTHIANS 8th–4th centuries B.C.	Modern Russia and Ukraine

Agricultural rituals celebrated fertility and the vegetation cycles of birth–death–rebirth. Perhaps the most constant artistic and religious presence in the Neolithic religions of the Near East was a female deity and her male counterpart. Neolithic architecture reflects increasingly elaborate concepts of sacred space in which religious buildings symbolize the cosmic world of the gods. Archaeologists have also excavated mud-brick fortification walls and found evidence of town planning. On a smaller scale, surviving examples of Neolithic pottery indicate that this art form had artistic as well as utilitarian importance.

Jericho

The Neolithic settlement of Jericho, located in the West Bank region of modern Israel, is one of the world's oldest fortified sites. It was originally built c. 8000–7000 B.C., when it was surrounded by a ditch and walls, 5 to 12 feet (1.52 to 3.65 m) thick, from which rose a tower some 30

feet (over 9 m) high. The biblical account of Joshua's attack on Jericho (Joshua 6) refers to a much later settlement at the site. His success lives on today in the refrain of the spiritual: "Joshua fought the battle of Jericho, and the walls came tumbling down."

Jericho's walls protected a city of rectangular houses and public buildings made of mud-brick and erected on stone foundations. Mud-brick was the mainstay of ancient Near Eastern architecture, used for ordinary buildings as well as for public architecture. Manufactured from an inexpensive, readily available material, it was easy to work with and suited to the climate. The walls of Jericho's mud-brick houses were plastered and painted.

In addition to providing shelter for the living, dwellings in Jericho housed the dead. Corpses buried under the floors indicate a concern with ancestors, a conclusion reinforced by one of the most intriguing archaeological finds, the so-called "Jericho Skulls" (fig. **3.2**). These uncanny skull "portraits" are almost literal renderings of the transition between life and death. The dead person's detached skull presumably served as a kind of **armature** on which to rebuild the face and thus preserve the memory of the deceased.

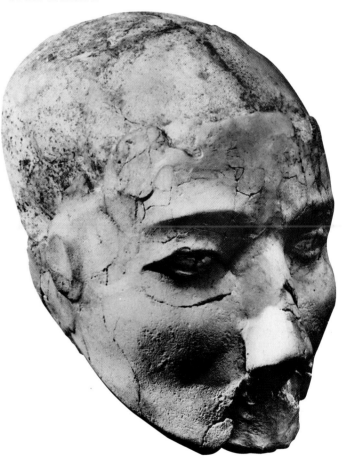

3.2 Neolithic plastered skull, from Jericho, c. 7000 B.C. Lifesize. Archaeological Museum, Amman, Jordan. Skulls such as this reflect an attempt to reconstitute the image of the dead person by modeling the features in plaster. The hair was painted and cowrie shells were embedded into the eye sockets.

Çatal Hüyük

Similar burials in houses occur at the site of Çatal Hüyük in Anatolia (modern Turkey). Dating from c. 6500–5500 B.C., it is the largest Neolithic site so far discovered in the ancient Near East.

In the ruins of Çatal Hüyük archaeologists found evidence of one of the most developed Neolithic cultures, in which agriculture and trade were well established and stoneware and ceramics were made. The layout of the town suggests that it was planned without streets. Instead, one-story mud-brick houses were connected to each other by their rooftops, and scholars assume that ladders provided access from ground level; it is possible, although not certain, that this was for defense. Windows were small, and a ventilation shaft allowed smoke from ovens and hearths to escape. The interiors of the houses were furnished with built-in benches made of clay, probably used for seats and beds. Skeletons were buried under floors and benches. Some of the skeletons were coated with red ocher, while the necks and heads of others were decorated with blue and green pigments. Deposits of jewelry and weapons accompanied the remains, suggesting that they were thought necessary in an afterlife.

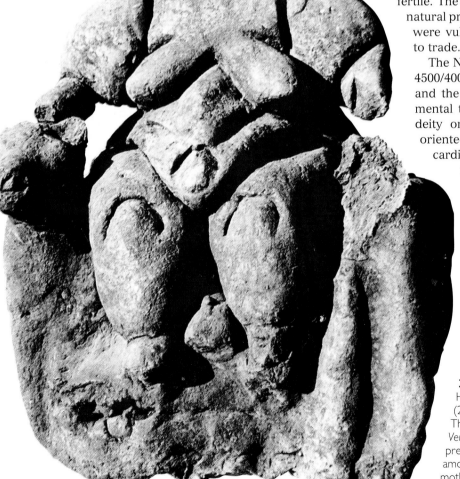

Little is known of the religious beliefs at Çatal Hüyük since it was a preliterate culture. However, archaeologists have identified chambers that may have functioned as shrines. Their elaborate decorations include representations of gods and goddesses (fig. **3.3**); male and female deities appear in human form, standing or seated with their sacred animals. Figure **3.4** is a painted plaster relief of two leopards. They are paired symmetrically and are thus more emblematic than the naturalistic Paleolithic cave paintings illustrated in Chapter 2.

In addition to representations of deities and their sacred animals, the Çatal Hüyük shrines contained murals painted on a white plaster background with natural pigments bound with fats. They illustrate hunting scenes, rituals, human hands, geometric patterns, and a variety of unidentified symbols.

Mesopotamia

Mesopotamia (in modern Iraq) was the center of ancient Near Eastern civilization. Its name is derived from the Greek *mesos* (middle) and *potamos* (river). Mesopotamia is literally the "land between the rivers"—the Tigris and the Euphrates. The Mesopotamian climate was harsh, and its inhabitants learned irrigation to make the land fertile. The southern terrain was open and without natural protection; as a result, Mesopotamian cities were vulnerable to invasion, but also accessible to trade.

The Neolithic period in Mesopotamia ended c. 4500/4000 B.C. It was followed by urbanization and the construction of the first known monumental temples, dedicated to each city's patron deity or deities. Mesopotamian temples were oriented with their corners toward the four cardinal points of the compass, suggesting religious beliefs relating sacred architecture to earth and sky (see Box).

3.3 Anatolian goddess giving birth, from Çatal Hüyük, Turkey, c. 6500–5700 B.C. Baked clay, 8 in (20.3 cm) high. Archaeological Museum, Ankara. The monumental forms are reminiscent of the *Venus of Willendorf* (see fig. 2.1) and other prehistoric fertility figures. There is controversy among scholars over whether such figures were mother goddesses.

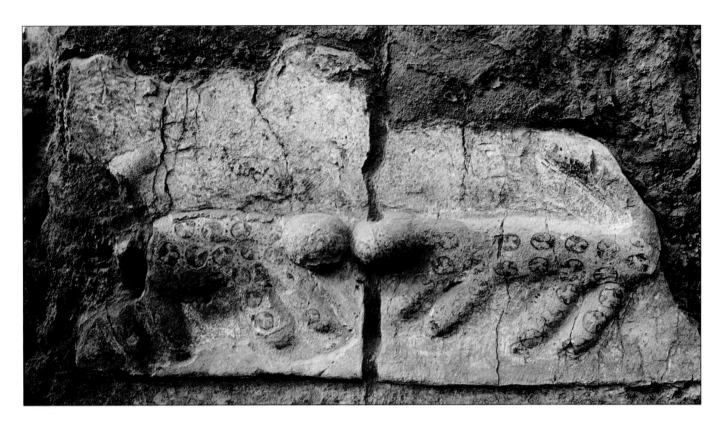

3.4 Two leopards, Shrine VIa, Çatal Hüyük, Turkey, c. 6000 B.C. Painted plaster relief, 27 × 65 in (68.5 × 165 cm).

Mesopotamian Religion

Mesopotamian religion was polytheistic (from the Greek *poly*, meaning "many" and *theos*, meaning "god"), that is, people believed in many gods. They were represented anthropomorphically (human in form and character), but were superhuman in power, and immortal. The main gods were:

Enlil	god of the air: a productive, beneficent creator who ensures good harvests
Anu	supreme god of the heavens
Enki (Akkadian Ea)	god of water, arts and crafts, and wisdom
Ninhursag	the Great Mother and Lady of the Mountain, goddess of the earth and Anu's consort
Utu (Akkadian Shamash)	sun god, judge, and protector—see figure 3.22
Nanna (Akkadian Sin)	goddess of the moon
Inanna (Akkadian Ishtar)	goddess of fertility, love, and war
Nergal and Ereshkigal	queen and king of the underworld, who rule from a lapis lazuli palace with seven gates.

Our knowledge of Mesopotamian religious practices comes from cuneiform texts of several types: prayers, rituals, legends, and myths. The mythological texts are primarily literary in nature, and some show remarkable parallels to the Old Testament.

The Sumerians conceived of the universe as created by a primal sea. By "universe" they meant a flat earth, the vault of heaven, and the atmosphere in between. Sun, moon, planets, and stars existed within this atmosphere. The human race was created out of clay for the sole purpose of serving the gods. When people died, their spirits were ferried across a river into a gloomy existence below the earth—hence the numerous inscriptions on tablets, in temples, and on sculptures asking the gods for long life.

Ceremonies were performed in Mesopotamian temples before a god's image, which was conceived of as literally inhabited by the god. Such images led a royal life, being fed, clothed, and housed (along with their entire families) in the temple.

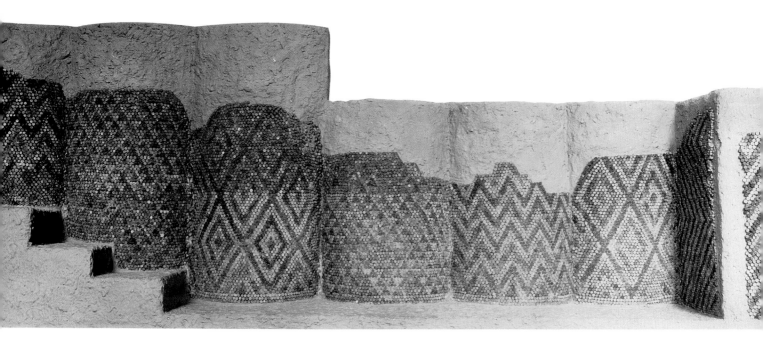

3.5 Cone mosaics, from Uruk. Staatliche Museen, Berlin.

Some temples were decorated with so-called **cone mosaics** (fig. **3.5**). Thousands of long, thin cones made of baked clay were embedded in mud walls and columns, leaving only the circular ends of the cones visible. They were dipped in black, red, or tan pigments and arranged in geometric patterns. Since they also reinforced the walls, the cones served a structural as well as an esthetic purpose.

Technological advances in early Mesopotamia included the potter's wheel and metalworking. Metallurgy brought about substantial changes in spheres of activity ranging from warfare to art. Metal weapons were superior to stone, and objects such as drinking vessels and ornaments could now be fashioned from new materials.

The Uruk Period (c. 4500–3100 B.C.)

The city of Uruk (known as Erech in the Bible and Warka in present-day Iraq) has given its name to a period sometimes known as Protoliterate, because the earliest known writing developed. This coincides with the rise of city-states (powerful, independent cities that rule their allied territories) within the Uruk period some time around 3500 to 3000 B.C.

It is possible that the New Year festival in honor of the goddess Inanna (see Box) is the subject of an impressive alabaster vase (fig. **3.6**) found at Uruk. It is 3 feet (91.4 cm) in height, and is decorated with four horizontal bands (or **registers**) of low relief. In the top register a goddess, possibly Inanna herself, receives a figure with a basket of fruit. In the next register nude men walk from right to left, also bearing offerings. In the third register rams alternate with ewes and march around the vase in the opposite direction.

Inanna

Evidence of the Mesopotamian goddess of fertility, love, and war is found in precincts dedicated to her as early as the fourth millennium B.C. Inanna to the Sumerians and Ishtar to the Akkadians, she was the wife of the shepherd-god Dumuzi, referred to in the Bible as Tammuz. Their courtship and sacred marriage, his death and return, and her descent into the underworld are sung in several Mesopotamian hymns.

Inanna had multiple aspects to which these hymns were addressed. She was the "holy priestess of heaven," "thundering storm," "lady of evening and of morning," and "joy of Sumer." She was also fearsome, and had to be propitiated with offerings like the alabaster vase in figure 3.6, which may depict Inanna herself. One of the hymns to Inanna has been translated as follows:

> In the pure places of the steppe,
> On the high roofs of the dwellings,
> On the platforms of the city,
> They make offerings to her:
> Piles of incense like sweet-smelling cedar,
> Fine sheep, fat sheep, long-haired sheep,
> Butter, cheese, dates, fruits of all kinds.[1]

In the course of the third millennium B.C., Inanna became the central deity in the most important rite of Sumer's New Year festival. In the *hieros gamos*, or sacred marriage, the Sumerian king (who stood for Dumuzi) and a priestess (standing for Inanna) were married in a ceremonial re-enactment of the divine union. The purpose of the rite was to ensure agricultural fertility for the coming year.

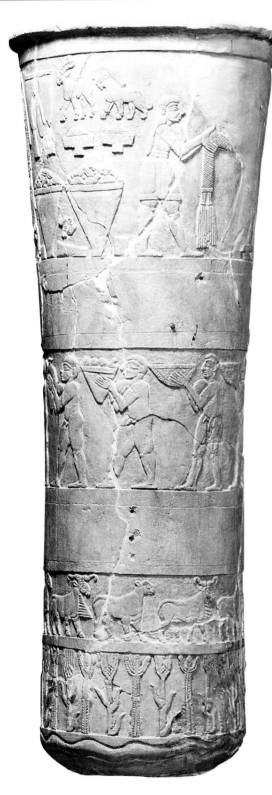

Barley stalks alternate with date palms at the bottom. The abundance of vegetal iconography on this vase suggests its association with agricultural festivals of renewal and rebirth.

Several **conventions** evident here remain characteristic of ancient Near Eastern art. Though the figures are stocky and modeled three-dimensionally, they occupy a flat space, which is partly defined by their poses. Legs and heads are in profile, the torsos turn slightly, and the eyes are frontal, creating a composite or synthesized view of the human form. There is no indication of space extending back behind the figures, who walk as if on a thin ledge. In the top register, figures and objects seem suspended in mid-air.

Despite the flat space of the Uruk vase and of much relief and pictorial art in ancient Mesopotamia, the white marble head of a female (fig. **3.7**), also from Uruk, demonstrates the artist's command of three-dimensional form. The eyebrows meet over the nose (a stylistic convention of Mesopotamian statues), and the face is organically modeled. The cheeks bulge slightly, creating the natural line from the nose to the corners of the mouth, and the lower lip curves outward from an indentation above the chin. Asymmetrical cheeks and the slight rise of the right side of the upper lip create the impression of an individual personality. The figure's eyebrows would originally have been **inlaid** (set into the surface), and other additions, such as hair and eyes, have probably disappeared.

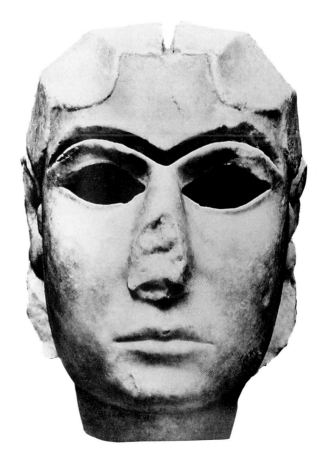

3.6 (above) Sculpted vase, from Uruk, c. 3500–3000 B.C. Alabaster, 3 ft (91.4 cm) high. Iraq Museum, Baghdad. The abundance of vegetation in the iconography of this vase reinforces its relationship to festivals of seasonal renewal and rebirth. The association of these rites with Inanna, the goddess of love and fertility, is almost certainly derived from the role of the Neolithic mother goddess.

3.7 (right) Female head, from Uruk, c. 3500–3000 B.C. White marble, 8 in (20.3 cm) high. Iraq Museum, Baghdad.

Ziggurats

The ziggurat, derived from an Assyrian word meaning "raised up" or "high," is a uniquely Mesopotamian architectural form. Mesopotamians believed that each city was under the protection of a god or gods to whom the city's inhabitants owed service, and they built imitation mountains, or ziggurats, as platforms for those gods. Mountains were believed to embody some of the immanent powers of nature: they were sources of the life-giving water that flowed into the plains and made agriculture possible. The Mesopotamian goddess Ninhursag, a source of nourishment, was also the Lady of the Mountain. As a symbolic mountain, therefore, the ziggurat satisfied one of the basic requirements of sacred architecture, namely the creation of a transitional space between people and their gods.

Ziggurats are examples of **load-bearing construction**, a system of building that began in the Neolithic period. Their massive walls had small openings, or none at all. They were usually solid, stepped structures, tapering toward the top, with wide bases supporting the entire weight of the ziggurat.

At Uruk the earliest surviving ziggurat (fig. **3.8**) dates from between 3500 and 3000 B.C. It was a solid clay structure reinforced with brick and asphalt. White pottery jars were embedded into the walls, their rims creating a surface pattern of white circles framing the dark round spaces of their interiors. Ziggurats remained characteristic structures throughout Mesopotamian history and became increasingly elaborate as belief systems and technology evolved.

The ziggurat at Uruk supported a shrine, the "White Temple," which was accessible by a stairway. Like the ziggurat, the temple was oriented toward the four cardinal points, an arrangement that became standard. Figure **3.9** shows the plan of the rectangular White Temple, which is believed to have been dedicated to Anu, the sky god. It was divided into several rooms off a main corridor, which contained the altar. The temple probably housed a statue of the god, although no such statue has been found.

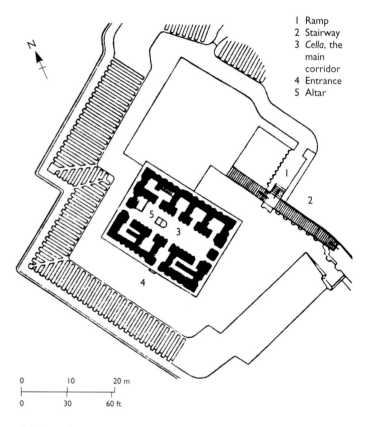

1 Ramp
2 Stairway
3 *Cella*, the main corridor
4 Entrance
5 Altar

3.9 Plan of the White Temple.

3.8 The White Temple on its ziggurat, Uruk, c. 3500–3000 B.C. Stone and polished brick, temple approx. 80 × 60 ft (24.38 × 18.29 m); ziggurat c. 140 × 150 ft (42.7 × 45.7 m) at its base and 30 ft (9.1 m) high. It was called the "White Temple" because of the white paint on its outer walls.

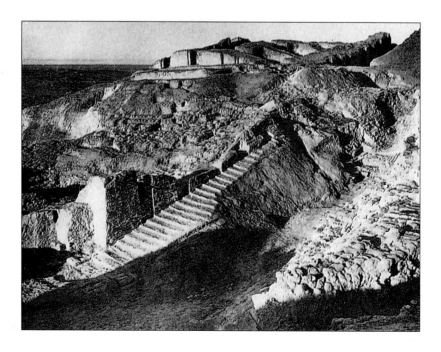

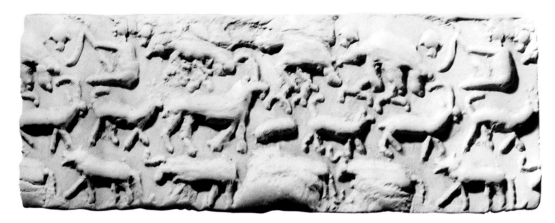

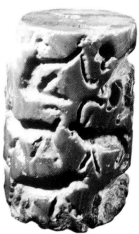

3.10 Cylinder impression and seal from Uruk, c. 3500–3000 B.C. Iraq Museum, Baghdad.

Cylinder Seals

The earliest examples of **cylinder seals,** which are classed as **glyptic art** (from the Greek word *glyptos,* meaning "carved"), were produced during the Uruk period. The seal in figure **3.10** is a small stone cylinder into which an image of a herd of animals has been carved. In a process known as intaglio printing, the seal's hard, incised surface would have been pressed against a soft surface, leaving a raised impression of the animals in reverse. When a cylinder seal was rolled across a clay tablet or the closure on a container, it created a repetitive band of images. Seal impressions were used originally to designate ownership, to keep inventories and accounts, and later to legalize documents. They offer a rich view of Mesopotamian iconography and of the development of pictorial style over a three-thousand-year period.

From Pictures to Words

The use of seal impressions to designate ownership contributed to the development of writing. In the course of the Uruk period, around 3500 to 3000 B.C., abstract wedge-shaped characters begin to appear on clay and stone tablets. The earliest written language known comes from Sumer, in southern Mesopotamia, and persisted as the language of the priestly and intellectual classes throughout Mesopotamian history. Its script is called **cuneiform** from the Latin word *cuneus,* meaning "wedge" (fig. **3.11**). After c. 2300 B.C. a Semitic language, Akkadian, belonging to a people who may have come from the west, became more prevalent than Sumerian. The Sumerian and Akkadian cultures coexisted for many centuries and their languages roughly correspond to the two main geographical divisions of Mesopotamia, Sumer and Akkad. Both lie between the Tigris and Euphrates Rivers, Sumer in the south and Akkad in the north.

Some time after the invention of writing, a Mesopotamian literature developed. The written word, which originated in response to a practical need for daily record-keeping, became a tool of creative expression. Much epic poetry of Mesopotamia deals with the origins of gods and humans, the history of kingship, the founding of cities and the development of civilization (see Box). These themes are also familiar in later literature. A Sumerian flood myth in which the human race is nearly destroyed, for example, describes an event much like Noah's flood (Genesis 6–8). According to Sumerian tradition, the flood occurred shortly before the invention of writing and therefore separated preliterate Mesopotamia from its literate, historical era.

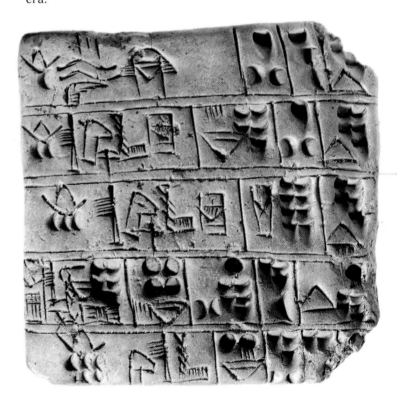

3.11 Clay tablet with cuneiform text, probably from Jemdet Nasr, Iraq, c. 3000 B.C. 3¼ × 3¼ in (8 × 8 cm). British Museum, London. This tablet is covered with cuneiform inscriptions, which were made by pressing a wedge-shaped stylus (writing implement) into the surface. In addition to the written word, Sumerians used a numerical system with a base of sixty, as well as a decimal system.

Gilgamesh

The *Epic of Gilgamesh* is the oldest surviving epic poem and is preserved on cuneiform tablets from the second millennium B.C. It recounts Gilgamesh's search for immortality as he undertakes perilous journeys through forests and the underworld, encounters gods, and struggles with moral conflict. The opening lines introduce Gilgamesh as the hero who saw and revealed the mysteries of life:

> The one who saw the abyss ...
> ... he who knew everything, Gilgamesh,
> who saw things secret, opened the place hidden,
> and carried back word of the time before the Flood.[2]

Gilgamesh finally attains immortality as the builder of Uruk's walls. He establishes urban civilization and lays the foundations of historical progress. The poem also refers to his having also "cut his works into a stone tablet." Just as the megalithic builders of Neolithic Europe revered stone as a permanent material, so Gilgamesh founded a city of stone walls and ensured that the record of his achievements was written in stone. This is consistent with the historical fact that the earliest writing was actually inscribed on stone or clay tablets. The works of Gilgamesh were thus literally as well as figuratively "carved in stone."

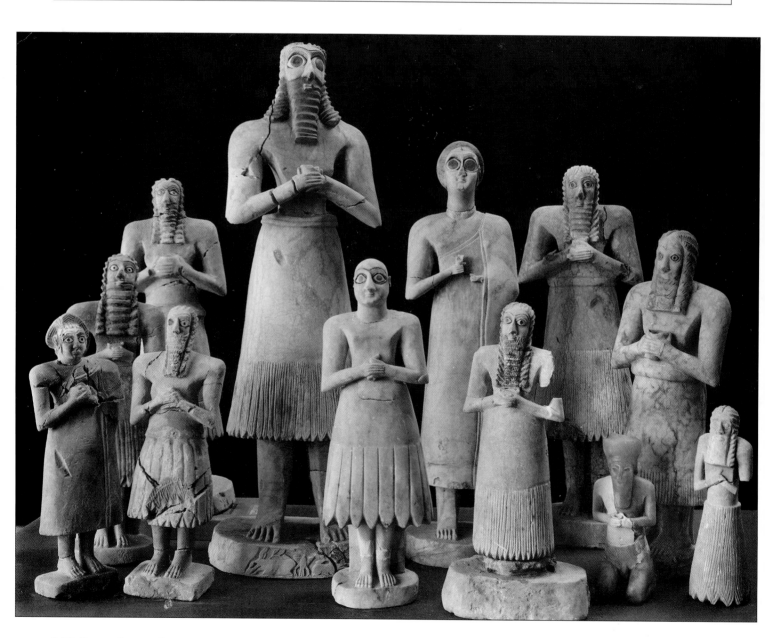

3.12 Group of statues from the Abu Temple at Tell Asmar, c. 2700–2500 B.C. Limestone, alabaster, and gypsum, tallest figure approx. 30 in (76.3 cm) high. Iraq Museum, Baghdad, and Oriental Institute, University of Chicago.

Sumer: Early Dynastic Period

(c. 2800–2300 B.C.)

The gradual transition to full literacy occurred during the growth of approximately a dozen powerful city-states ruled by dynasties, or royal families. Lists of these ancient Sumerian rulers have survived. Other documents provide the picture of a society in which people played increasingly specialized roles (such as canal-builders, artisans, merchants, and bureaucrats) under the administration of a class of priests. The priests' power derived from their role as intermediaries between the inhabitants of the cities and their gods.

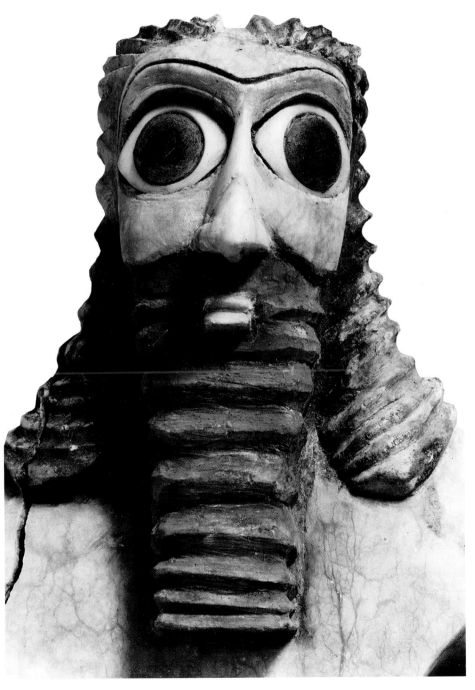

Tell Asmar

Many small cult figures were produced during the Early Dynastic period, such as those from Tell Asmar (figs. **3.12** and **3.13**), a Sumerian site about 50 miles (80 km) northeast of modern Baghdad, in Iraq. It is not known whether these figures were originally a unified group, but most hold a cup, and some hold a flower or branch. Male and female are distinguished by costume. Men tend to wear less above the waist than women (in this case, the bare-chested men wear skirts, while the women wear robes that cover one shoulder). The figures are made of pale stone, their hair, beards, and other features emphasized with black pitch. The eyes are shells and the pupils are inlaid with black limestone. The largest male statue has no attributes of divinity and is thought to represent an important or wealthy person dedicating himself to the god Abu. All the statues probably represent worshipers of varying status whose sizes were determined by the amount of money their donors paid for them. As such, these figures are rendered with so-called **hierarchical proportions**, a convention equating size with status.

The statues are cylindrical and many stand on curved bases, reflecting the Mesopotamian preference for rounded sculptural shapes. Also characteristic, as in the Uruk head (see fig. 3.7), is the combination of stylization—visible here in the horizontal ridges of the males' hair and beards—with suggestions of organic form in the cheeks and chin. The frontal poses and vertical planes of these figures endow them with an air of imposing solemnity. Their frontality is further emphasized by the prominence of large, wide-open eyes, staring straight ahead. The importance accorded the eye in these figures indicates that they are in the presence of divinity.

Ur

At the Sumerian site of Ur, the English archaeologist Sir Leonard Woolley (1880–1960) discovered evidence of the richness of Early Dynastic culture. The most impressive finds came from the "royal" cemetery, so-called because of the abundance of gold in the tombs. Burial pits at Ur were filled with chariots, harps, sculptures, headdresses, jewelry, and the bodies of people who may have been ritually

3.13 Head of a large male figure dedicated to the god Abu (detail of fig. 3.12).

killed in order to provide companions for the royal family in the afterlife.

The elegant lyre soundbox (fig. **3.14**) from Ur indicates not only the presence of music and musical instruments, but also the superb craftsmanship of early Sumerian artists. The significance of the gold bearded bull's head and the inlay decoration at the front of the box (fig. **3.15**) is uncertain, but it is likely that they served a ritual purpose and had mythological meaning. Certainly the motif of the bull's head is known from as early as around 6000 B.C., when it was one of the manifestations of the male god at Çatal Hüyük. At Ur the head was combined with a stylized human beard of **lapis lazuli**, illustrating the ancient Near Eastern taste for combinations of species.

Akkad (c. 2340–2180 B.C.)

The Akkadians were a Semitic-speaking Mesopotamian people who lived to the north of Sumer. We know little about them before their territorial expansion in the twenty-fourth century B.C. From their capital at Akkad (near modern Baghdad), the Akkadians dominated one city-state after another until they ruled Mesopotamia. They assimilated much of Sumerian culture, but there were some important changes. City-states were now subordinate to a larger political entity, an empire, and Akkadian became the dominant language. Some Akkadian gods were merged with those of Sumer, while Akkadian rulers elevated themselves to godlike status.

The founder of the Akkadian dynasty, Sargon I, reigned for over half a century, from c. 2332 to 2279 B.C. (see Box), gaining control of most of Mesopotamia and the lands beyond the Tigris and Euphrates Rivers. A near-lifesized bronze head (fig. **3.16**) may be his portrait. Its high level of artistry and technical skill indicates that metal sculpture on a monumental scale was not new, but earlier examples have not survived. It was made by the *cire-perdue*, or lost-wax, method discussed in Chapter 6 (see p. 154). Throughout history metal objects were often melted down for re-use, making large-scale metal sculptures from antiquity rare today. This head, found on a trash heap, is all that remains of a full-length statue.

Sargon of Akkad

With Sargon, we encounter another "first" in Western history—namely, the legendary birth story of one who is destined for greatness. These tales typically link humble origins to later fame. Sargon's story is inscribed on a tablet, and recounts his lowly illegitimate birth. His mother sends him down a river in a basket (which resonates with the biblical account of Moses in the bulrushes). A man named Akki, who is drawing water, finds Sargon and raises him as his own son. Later Sargon rules in the city of Agade, or Akkad, whose inhabitants are called Akkadians.

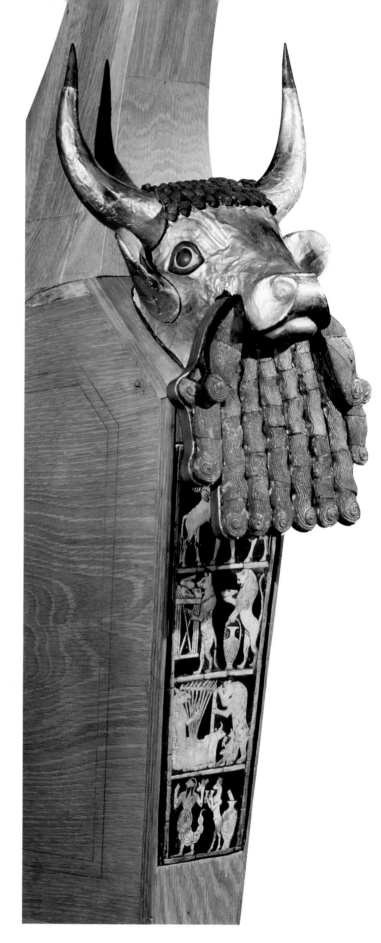

3.14 Lyre soundbox, from the tomb of Queen Puabi, Ur, c. 2685 B.C. Wood with inlaid gold, lapis lazuli, and shell, approx. 13 in (33 cm) high. University Museum, University of Pennsylvania, Philadelphia.

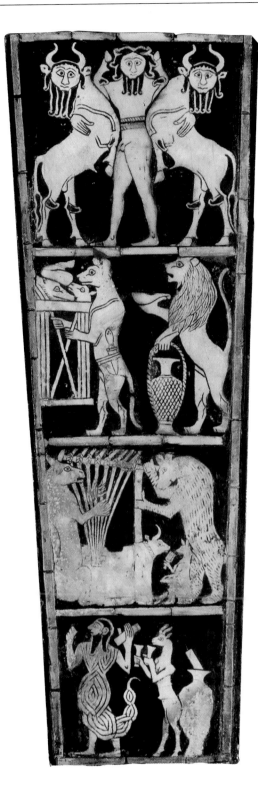

3.15 Inlay from front of soundbox (detail of fig. 3.14).

3.14 and **3.15** The scorpion-man, who appears in the bottom scene on the front of the box, may be one of the fearsome guardians of the sun described in the *Epic of Gilgamesh*. In addition to hybrid forms combining animals with other animals and animals with humans, ancient Near Eastern art is populated by animals—such as the goat holding a cup and walking upright—who act like humans. These figures could represent either mythological creatures or people dressed as animals.

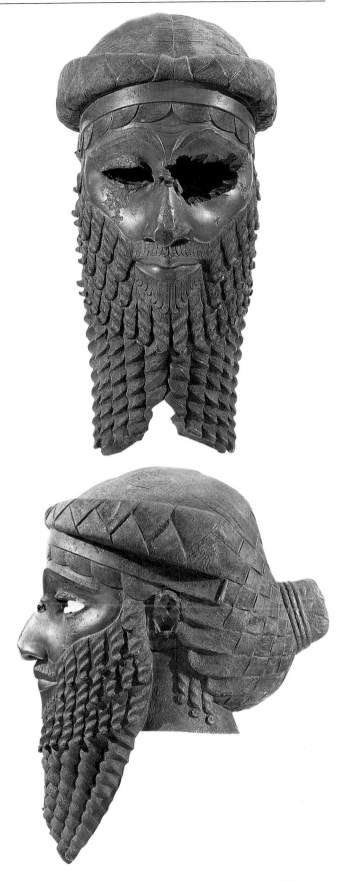

3.16a, b Head of an Akkadian ruler (Sargon I?), from Kuyunjik, Iraq, c. 2250 B.C. Bronze, 12 in (30 cm) high. Museum of Antiquities, Baghdad.

The power of this work resides in the self-confident, facial features emerging from the framework of stylized hair. The eye sockets would originally have been inlaid with precious stones, which have since been gouged out—perhaps for their intrinsic value, or perhaps to destroy the power of the image. At the back of the head, the hair is bound in a bun and is elaborately designed in a regular arrangement of surface patterns. Large curved eyebrows

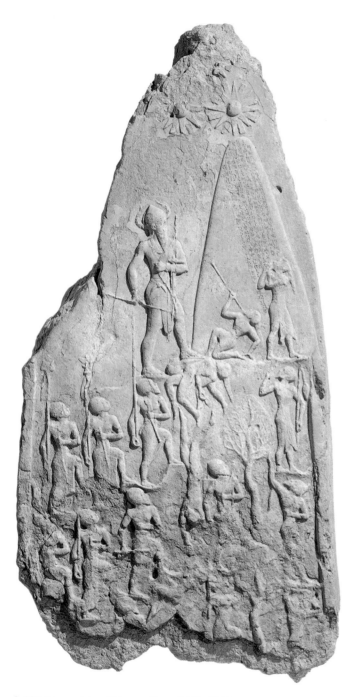

3.17 Victory stele of Naram-Sin, c. 2300–2200 B.C. Pink sandstone, 6 ft 6 in (1.98 m) high. Louvre, Paris. This stele suffered an ironic twist of fate when it was taken as booty by invaders from the southeast. What had been created to mark an Akkadian victory was looted to mark their defeat.

meet on the bridge of an assertive nose. A striking V-shape frames the lower face in the form of a beard made of spiraling curls. In this head, the energy and rhythm of the stylizations combine with an organic facial structure to produce an air of regal determination.

Sargon I's grandson, Naram-Sin, recorded his victory over a mountain people, the Lullubians, in a commemorative **stele** (fig. **3.17**)—an upright stone marker. This form of record-keeping used inscriptions and/or relief images to commemorate important events. When the *Epic of Gilgamesh* says that the hero "cut his works into a stone tablet" (see Box), the author was probably referring to a stele. Today when we speak of "making one's mark," we mean essentially the same thing as the Mesopotamians when they made marks in stone "markers" that were intended to last.

The stele of Naram-Sin is a good example of so-called *Machtkunst* (German for "power art"), for it proclaims the military, political, and religious authority of Naram-Sin. He is identified as a god by the horned cap of divinity, and dominates the scene by his large size and central position above the other figures. His long, prominent beard is a conventional sign of virility, and therefore of his potency as both man and ruler. Around his neck he wears a necklace with a protective bead. Also exerting a protective force are the stars shining prominently over Naram-Sin. Together with the landscape details, they reflect the Akkadian taste for depicting nature.

Two defeated enemies are before the ruler, one praying for mercy and the other trying to pull a spear from his neck. Naram-Sin and his victorious followers march unhindered up the mountain while the defeated soldiers fall. This opposition exemplifies the convention in which going up denotes success and downward movement denotes failure or death. In a related convention Naram-Sin steps on a defeated foe, indicating triumph. Furthermore, the nudity of Naram-Sin's victims indicates that they are dead.

To the degree that Naram-Sin's own body is exposed, the artist was displaying an image of physical perfection that was a sign of his inherent "goodness," or "rightness," as a ruler. He is intentionally portrayed with his right side most visible to the viewer, in keeping with a Mesopotamian belief that a ruler's right side—including his right arm and right ear—had to be both intact and well formed for his state to prosper.

Neo-Sumerian Culture

(c. 2150–1800 B.C.)

After flourishing for about a century, the Akkadian dynasty was defeated by the Guti, mountain people from the northeast who ruled Mesopotamia for roughly sixty years. Only one city-state, Lagash, managed to hold out, and it prospered. When the Sumerians overthrew the Guti, there was a revival of Sumerian culture in the newly united southern city-states, a period referred to as Neo-Sumerian.

Lagash

Gudea, the ruler of Lagash during the period of Guti dominance, initiated an extensive construction program which included several temples. His building activity was made possible by his ability to maintain peace in his own territory, despite continual political upheavals surrounding Lagash. Gudea embodied the transition between gods and humans. Just as the ziggurats linked earth with the heavens, so Mesopotamian rulers were viewed as the gods' chosen intermediaries on earth. Such ideas form the basis for the continuing belief in the divine right of kings.

Gudea's image is familiar from a series of similar statues made of diorite, a hard black stone, which had to be imported. He either stands or sits, usually with hands folded in an attitude of prayer (figs. **3.18** and **3.19**). Whether standing or seated, Gudea wears a robe over his

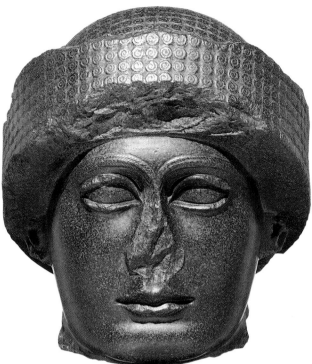

3.18 (above) Head of Gudea, from Lagash, c. 2150 B.C. Diorite, 9 in (22.9 cm) high. Museum of Fine Arts, Boston. Francis Bartlett Donation of 1912.

3.19a (left) Gudea with temple plan, from Lagash, Iraq, c. 2150 B.C. Diorite, 29 in (73.7 cm) high. Louvre, Paris.

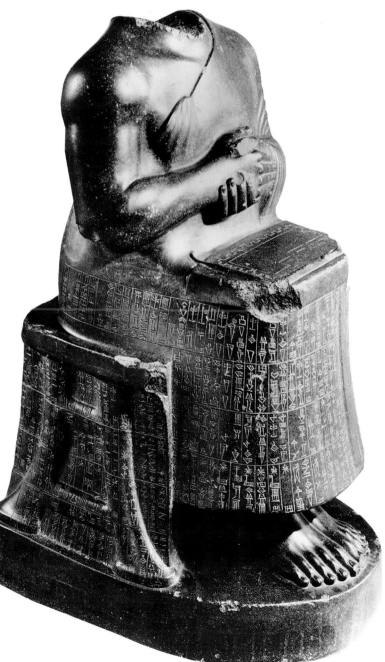

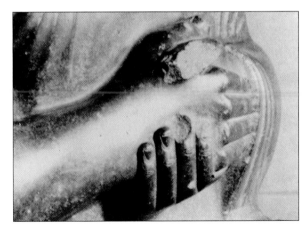

3.19b Gudea (detail of fig. 3.19a).

3.18 and **3.19a, b** Gudea's affinity with the Sumerian gods is revealed in his account of a dream in which a god instructed him to restore a temple. In the dream, Gudea saw the radiant, joyful image of the god Ningirsu wearing a crown and flanked by lions. He was accompanied by a black storm bird, while a storm raged beneath him. Ningirsu told Gudea to build his house; but Gudea did not understand until a second god, Nindub, appeared with the plan of a temple on a lapis lazuli tablet.

left shoulder leaving his right shoulder bare; the bottom of the robe flares out slightly into a bell curve. He is either bald or wears a round cap (fig. 3.18), which is decorated with rows of small circles formed by incised spiral lines.

The Gudea in figure 3.19 is compact; there is no space between the arms and the body, and the neck is short and thick. This contraction of space contributes to Gudea's monumentality, as does his controlled and dignified pose. The typical Mesopotamian combination of organic form with surface stylization can be seen in the juxtaposition of the incised eyebrows (fig. 3.18) with the more naturalistically modeled nose, cheeks, and chin.

The temple plan resting on the lap of the seated Gudea identifies his role as an architectural patron. His gesture of prayer establishes his relation with the gods and their divine patronage as revealed in his dream. In the ancient world, dreams were thought of as external phenomena, usually messages through which gods communicated with mortals, especially kings. As such, dreams, like temples, could establish a link between people and their gods. And it was precisely in those terms that Gudea described his completed temple. He said that it rose up from the earth and reached toward heaven, that its radiance illuminated his country. The metaphor in which the temple is a source of light relates the structure to the radiant Ningirsu who appears in the dream. The dream itself is a source of intellectual light, or enlightenment, originating with the gods and transmitted to their earthly representative in the person of Gudea. In all of these images, the temple, like dream and dreamer, functions as a symbolic bridge between heaven and earth.

The Stele of Ur-Nammu

The Neo-Sumerian period reached a peak under the first king of its last important dynasty, the Third Dynasty of Ur. It was Ur-Nammu who supervised the construction of the great ziggurat at Ur, which is reconstructed in figure **3.20**. Compared with the ziggurat in Uruk (see fig. 3.8), this later one at Ur was more complex. Three stages were constructed around a mud-brick core and culminated in a shrine, accessible by a short stairway on the northeast side. The mud-brick was faced with baked brick which was embedded in mortar made of bitumen (a type of asphalt). Leading to a vertical gate, which provided the only point of entry to the upper levels, were three long stairways, each composed of a hundred steps. The ziggurat walls curve gradually outward while sloping toward the center of the structure, which functioned esthetically to reduce the rigidity of straight walls. The ancient Near Eastern preference for rounded sculptural shapes thus carried over into architectural design.

The process of the construction of the ziggurat at Ur was recorded in the stele of Ur-Nammu (fig. **3.21**). Like the Akkadian king Naram-Sin before him (see fig. 3.17), Ur-Nammu recorded important events in his reign by commissioning commemorative stelai. Although most of Ur-Nammu's stele has been destroyed, fragments of it sur-

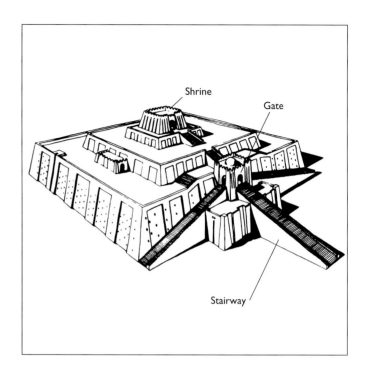

3.20 Reconstruction drawing of the ziggurat at Ur.

vive. In figure 3.21, three of the fragments have been superimposed over a reconstruction that has since been discredited by scholars. The surviving fragments, however, make it possible to draw certain preliminary conclusions about the original, as scholars continue to work on a more secure reconstruction.

The stele was carved in relief, with the space at the top denoting the heavens. Below and slightly to the left is the remnant of a seated deity. At the far left, a sky-borne goddess holds a vase of flowing water, an iconographic element referring to the life-giving aspect of water in the dry climate of Mesopotamia.

The second register shows Ur-Nammu before a more complete god at the right. The god holds a ring and staff, **attributes** (identifying features) that stand for kingship and justice. They are also a measuring rod and a line which were used in the construction of the ziggurats. The implication of this iconography is the relationship between the god's rule and that of the king. It is presumably at this point in the narrative that Ur-Nammu receives the god's order to build his house, the same order that Gudea received in his dream.

Most of the third register is lost. The old reconstruction depicts Ur-Nammu laden with building tools. He is assisted by a priest, who walks behind him. The remainder of the representation is indecipherable except for a diagonal ladder indicating a lost scene of building activity in the fourth register. The reverse of the stele, which is not illustrated, was probably decorated with similar scenes at the top and dedication ceremonies below.

A cuneiform tablet records Ur-Nammu's contribution to the building process. It states that the god Marduk ordered

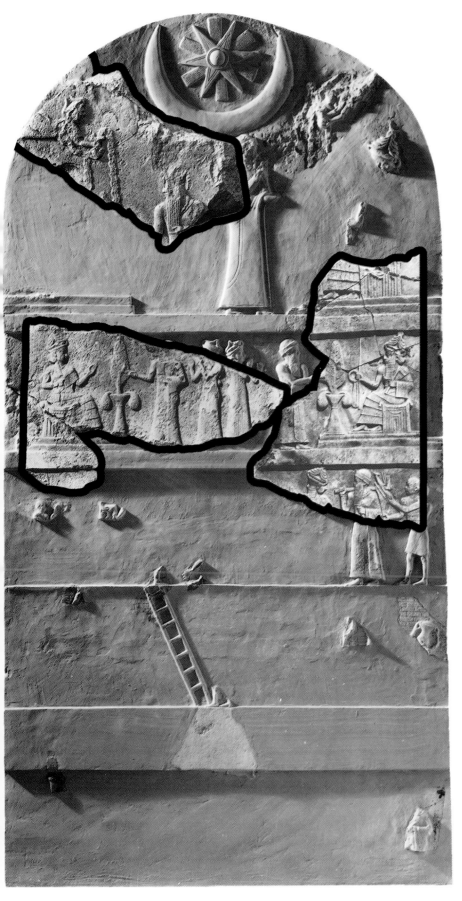

him to build the ziggurat with a secure foundation and stages that reach to the heavens: "I caused baked bricks to be made," the ruler continues; "…I caused streams of bitumen to be brought by the Canal Arahtu…. I took a reed and myself measured the dimensions…. For my Lord Marduk I bowed my neck, I took off my robe, the sign of my royal blood, and on my head I bore bricks and earth."[3]

In contrast to Naram-Sin's victory stele, with its relatively free arrangement of figures in a landscape setting, the composition of this stele reflects the Sumerians' hierarchical view of their universe: gods above, and kings, priests, and ordinary mortals following in descending order. Both the figures and the space they inhabit are larger at the top. The gods, reflecting their importance, are depicted as larger than mortals. The narrative sequence starts at the top, so that the idea of top and beginning are visually related. This connection persists in the terminology of the theatre and concert hall, in which "take it from the top" means to rehearse a scene or a musical movement from the beginning.

Ur-Nammu's ziggurat was eventually expanded into a sacred architectural complex containing several temples, workshops, factories, and a commercial center with law courts. Records of these structures were kept on clay and stone tablets.

Babylon (c. 1900–539 B.C.)

When the last Neo-Sumerian king was overthrown by foreign invaders, Mesopotamia reverted to rule by independent city-states. Over the next few centuries continuing warfare, as well as invasions from all directions, led to the frequent rise and fall of different cultural groups. Mesopotamia was next united under the Amorites, a Semitic-speaking people from Arabia, who established their capital at Babylon.

3.21 Stele of Ur-Nammu (three original fragments superimposed on a now-rejected reconstruction). Height 10 ft (3 m), width 5 ft (1.5 m).

Old Babylonian Period (c. 1830–1550 B.C.)

The most famous king of the Amorite dynasty was Hammurabi (flourished c. 1792–1750 B.C.). Hammurabi is best known for his Law Code (see Box), which he inscribed on a black basalt stele (fig. **3.22**). This text was based on local Sumerian legal traditions and remains an important historical document, articulating the relationship of law to society. Its cultural importance is reflected in its value as booty: Hammurabi's stele, as well as Naram-Sin's, was carried off to Susa (a rival city-state east of the Tigris River) by invading Elamite armies.

Babylon was sacked by Hittites from Anatolia (see below) c. 1600 B.C., ending the Old Babylonian period. For the next half millennium Mesopotamia was under the control of a weak foreign dynasty, the Kassites, one of many groups penetrating the region from Central Asia. This was a time of great political and cultural turmoil. Despite the disruption in patterns of trade, however, influences from farther west—what are now Syria, Egypt (see Chapter 4), and the Aegean world (see Chapter 5)—did reach Mesopotamia through immigrants from these lands. Meanwhile, Babylon remained a renowned cultural center.

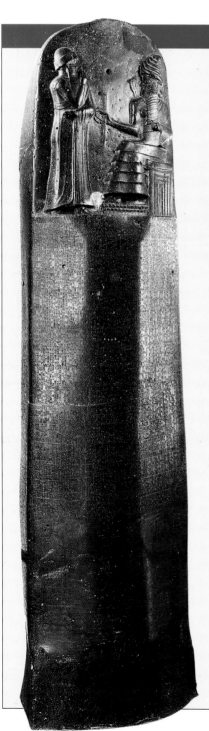

The Law Code of Hammurabi

The text of Hammurabi's Law Code, comprising 300 statutes, is written in Akkadian in 51 cuneiform columns. It provides a unique glimpse into the social and legal structure of ancient Mesopotamia. Though the stated purpose of Hammurabi's laws was to protect the weak from the strong, they also maintained traditional class distinctions: the lower classes were more severely punished for crimes committed against the upper classes than vice versa. There was no intent to create social equality in the protection of the weak, or in the expressed concern for orphans and widows, but rather to maintain the continuity and stability of society.

Three types of punishment stand out in the Law Code of Hammurabi. The Talion Law—the equivalent of the biblical "eye for an eye"—operated in the provision calling for the death of a builder whose house collapsed and killed the owner. In some cases, the punishment fit the crime; for example, if a surgical patient died, the doctor's hand was cut off. Perhaps the most illogical punishment was the ordeal, in which the guilt or innocence of an alleged adulteress depended on whether she sank or floated when thrown into water.

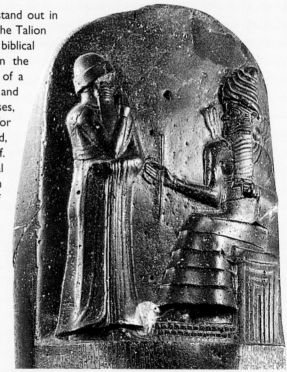

3.22b (right) Stele (detail of fig. 3.22a).

3.22a Stele inscribed with the Law Code of Hammurabi, c. 1792–1750 B.C. Basalt, height of stele approx. 7 ft (2.13 m), height of relief 28 in (71.1 cm). Louvre, Paris. Hammurabi stands before the Akkadian sun god, Shamash, who is enthroned on a symbolic mountain. Shamash wears the horned cap of divinity and an ankle-length robe. He holds the ring and rod of divine power and justice, and rays emanate from his shoulders. Here the conventional pose of the god in relief sculpture serves a double purpose: the torso's frontality communicates with the observer, while the profile head and legs turn to Hammurabi. Hammurabi receives Shamash's blessing on the Law Code, which is inscribed on the remainder of the stele. The god's power over Hammurabi is evident in his greater size; were Shamash to stand, he would tower over the mortal ruler.

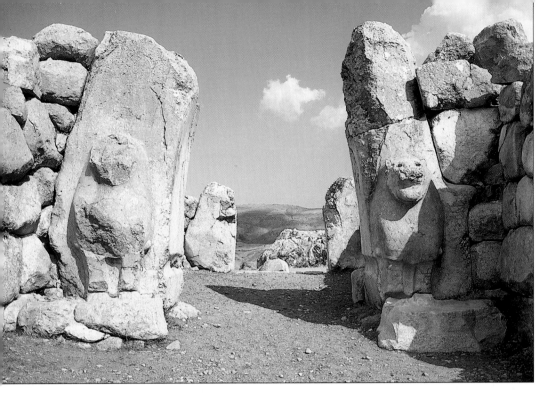

3.23 Lion Gate (Royal Gate), Hattusas, Boghazköy (in Turkey), c. 1400 B.C. Stone, lions approx. 7 ft (2.13 m) high. The lions face the visitor approaching the citadel. The direct confrontation, combined with the open, roaring mouths, served as a warning and symbolically protected the inhabitants against the forces of evil.

3.24 Hittite war god, from the King's Gate at Hattusas, Boghazköy, Turkey, c. 1400 B.C. 6 ft 6¾ in (2 m) high.

Anatolia: The Hittites

(c. 1450–1200 B.C.)

The Hittites were an Anatolian people whose capital city, Hattusas, was located in modern Boghazköy, in central Turkey. Like the Mesopotamians, they kept records in cuneiform on clay tablets, which were stored on shelves, systematically catalogued and labeled as in a modern library. These archives, comprising thousands of tablets, are the first known records in an Indo-European language. Because their written records have survived, the cultural and artistic achievements of the Hittites are fairly well documented.

The Hittites cremated their dead and buried the ashes and bones in urns, so that they left little tomb art. There is, however, much evidence of monumental palaces, temples, cities, and massive fortified walls decorated with reliefs. The predominance of fortifications and the location of palaces and **citadels** (urban fortresses) attest to the need for protection from invading armies as well as to the military power of the Hittites themselves.

The western entrance to the citadel at Hattusas (fig. **3.23**) is a good example of the monumental fortified Cyclopaean walls constructed by the Hittites. The guardian lions are a traditional motif in ancient art because of the belief that lions never sleep. Here they project forward from the stone wall as if emerging from natural into manmade form. Their heads and chests are in high relief, while some details, such as the mane, fur, and eyes, are incised. At 7 feet (2.13 m) tall, they would have towered over anyone approaching the gate.

The most distinctive Hittite sculptures are, like the guardian lions, in relief, usually carved on the lower levels of city walls. Figure **3.24** is an over-lifesized representation of a powerful Hittite war god. He is armed, helmeted, and wears a short tunic. Conforming to ancient Near Eastern

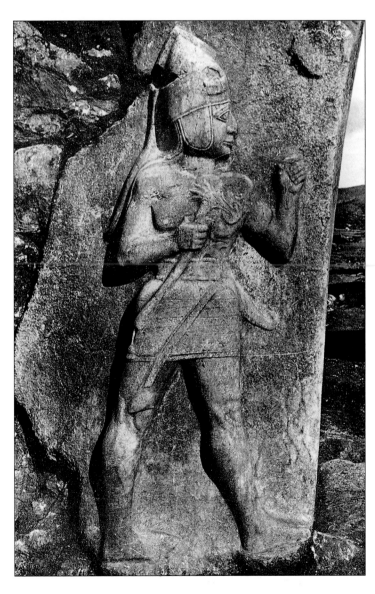

convention, his head and legs are depicted in profile with his torso in front view. And, as in the art of Mesopotamia, the sculptor has achieved a remarkable synthesis of stylization (the eye and knee caps) with organic form. Like the stele of Naram-Sin, this relief projects an image of divine authority.

Assyria (c. 1100–612 B.C.)

A northern Assyrian city-state emerged as the next unifying force in Mesopotamia. Located along the Tigris in modern Syria, its capital city was named for Ashur, the chief Assyrian deity, equivalent in authority to the Babylonian Marduk (whom he closely resembled) and the Sumerian Enlil. Excavations carried out in Ashur in the early twentieth century uncovered a culture extending back to 3000 B.C. At the end of Hammurabi's reign c. 1750 B.C., Ashur had become a prominent fortified city. By 1300 B.C. Ashur's rulers were in communication with the leaders of Egypt, indicating that they had achieved international status. Assyria borrowed much from Babylon, which remained culturally prominent during its political decline, as well as from foreign cultures to the west.

The Assyrian state is particularly well documented, both through its texts and the remains of architectural and sculptural projects undertaken to reflect the might and glory of its kings (see Box). The region in and around Assyria had a great deal more stone available than the rest of Mesopotamia. As a result, the Assyrians' determination to memorialize their accomplishments in stone could be satisfied without importing raw materials.

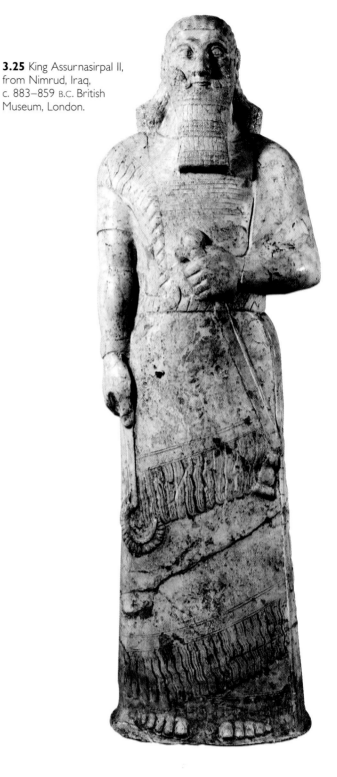

3.25 King Assurnasirpal II, from Nimrud, Iraq, c. 883–859 B.C. British Museum, London.

Assyrian Kings

Under Assurnasirpal II (reigned 883–859 B.C.), Assyria became a formidable military force. His records are filled with boastful claims detailing his cruelty. He says that he dyed the mountains red, like wool cloth, with the blood of his slaughtered enemies. From the heads of his decapitated enemies he erected a pillar, and he covered the city walls with their skins.

The first imperial king, Tiglath-Pileser I (reigned c. 1114–1076 B.C.), recorded his intent to conquer the world and claimed that the god Ashur had commanded him to do so.

The last powerful king of Assyria, Assurbanipal (reigned 668–633 B.C.), combined cruelty with culture. He established a great library, consisting of thousands of tablets recording the scientific, historical, literary, religious, and commercial pursuits of his time. Also included in his collection were the Mesopotamian creation and flood epics, which were deciphered in the late nineteenth century. Today, most of Assurbanipal's library is in the British Museum in London.

Assyrian military strength grew rapidly under Assurnasirpal II. The only known sculpture in the round representing him (fig. **3.25**) depicts an imposing figure in a rigid, frontal pose. He wears an ankle-length robe, his arms are close to his body, and his stylized hair and beard fill the space around his neck. He holds the scepter of kingship in his right hand and a mace in his left. Inscribed across his chest are his name, titles, and conquests. In contrast to Gudea, whose inscriptions recorded his architectural patronage, Assurnasirpal II's statue proclaims his god-given power.

The king's might is also the theme of alabaster reliefs that lined the walls of his palace in present-day Nimrud. Figure **3.26** shows him standing at the back of a horse-drawn chariot, his bow and arrow aimed at a rearing lion. The king's dominance over lions, a favorite subject in Assyrian art, is a metaphor for the subjugation of his enemies. The dynamic energy of the scene is reinforced by opposing diagonal planes and the accentuation of muscular tension. Overlapping of the horses creates an illusion of three-dimensional space.

The battle relief in figure **3.27** represents a city at war, with Assyrian invaders shooting arrows and attacking the defenders' walls with a battering ram. At the center of the relief, two wounded enemy soldiers have toppled from the ramparts and plunge to their deaths. Here, too, opposing diagonals convey energetic movement. The upper figures are cut off by the **crenellated** fortifications and the bowmen at the right overlap each other, enhancing pictorial depth. The wealth of such details in the Assyrian

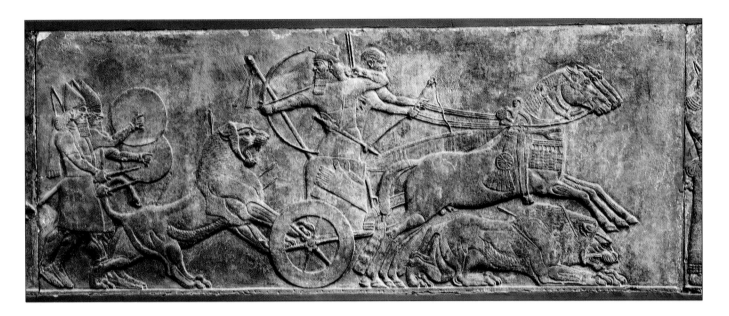

3.26 King Assurnasirpal II hunting lions, from Nimrud, Iraq, c. 883–859 B.C. Alabaster relief, 3 ft 3 in × 8 ft 4 in (99 cm × 2.54 m). British Museum, London.

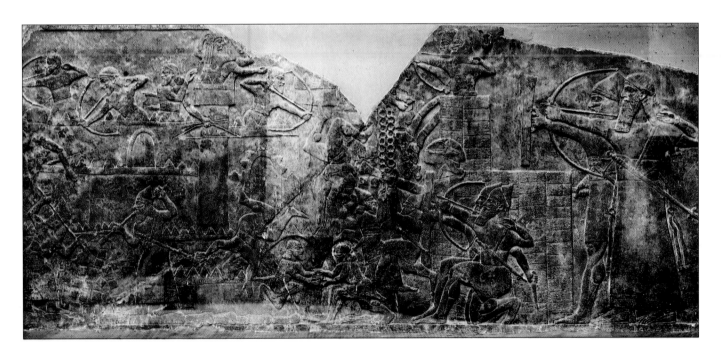

3.27 City attacked with a battering ram, relief, palace of King Assurnasirpal II, from Nimrud. Approx. 39 in (99 cm) high. British Museum, London.

reliefs, and in Assyrian art generally, makes them particularly valuable as cultural records.

Over the course of the empire's history, the Assyrian capital shifted several times. The palace that king Sargon II (reigned 721–705 B.C.) built at Dur Sharrukin (present-day Khorsabad, in the far north) is the most fully excavated large-scale example, revealing the complexity of Assyrian royal architecture. The plan of the city (fig. **3.28**) shows the fortified walls, the two gates leading into the city, and the location of the palace within the citadel. The latter was a defensive structure, designed as a last bastion protecting the king from enemies.

Figure **3.29** is the plan of the palace itself, a mud-brick structure on a **plinth**, or platform, whose rectangular rooms lay at right angles to each other. Number 5 on the plan (the concentric squares at the left) is Sargon's ziggurat. This was built in several levels, which were formed from a ramp in the shape of a squared-off spiral that decreased in size as it approached the top. This meant that priests and other high-status worshipers moved continuously around the structure as they ascended it.

Access to the palace required entering the huge gate of the citadel and traversing the open square. A ramp was provided so that chariots could be driven across the square to the palace gate. The approach to the throne room itself was through a carefully controlled program of architectural and sculptural propaganda, designed to intimidate visitors. They would have entered the palace complex through one of the entrances at the lower end of a courtyard (4 on the plan). From the courtyard, they proceeded to the ambassadors' courtyard (3), whose monumental reliefs, like those carved in the reign of Assurnasirpal II, reminded viewers of the king's military

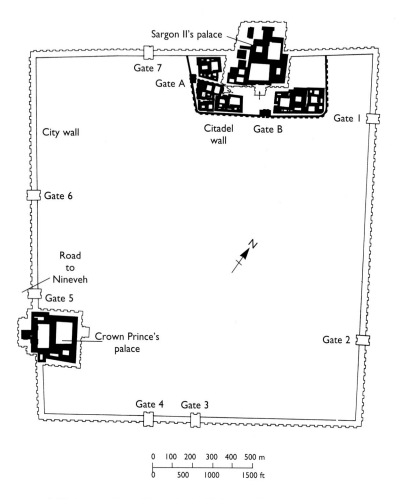

3.28 (above) Plan of Khorsabad with Sargon II's palace.

3.29 (right) Plan of Sargon II's palace. Sargon's pride in his palace and his wish to be remembered for it is revealed in his so-called Great Inscription: "Palace of Sargon, the great king, the powerful king, king of legions, king of Assyria, viceroy of the gods at Babylon, king of the Sumers and of the Akkads, favorite of the great gods. The gods Assur, Nebo [god of knowledge, literature, and agriculture], and Marduk have conferred on me the royalty of the nations, and they have propagated the memory of my fortunate name to the ends of the earth."[4] The throne room (2) was decorated with murals, and the walls of the ambassadors' courtyard (3) were highlighted with reliefs. The ziggurat (5) differed from others in Mesopotamia in having elaborate surface movement created by repeated recesses in the walls and crenellations at the top.

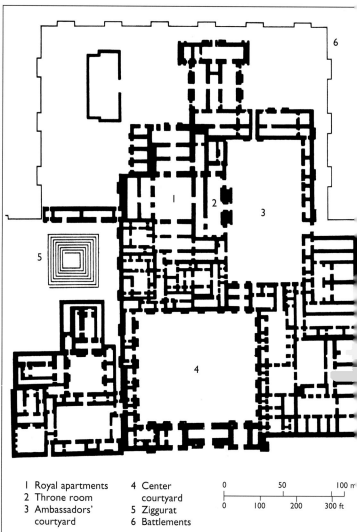

1 Royal apartments	4 Center
2 Throne room	courtyard
3 Ambassadors'	5 Ziggurat
courtyard	6 Battlements

achievements on the one hand and his relationship with the gods on the other. In order to reach the throne room (2), visitors had to pass through an entrance guarded by monumental limestone figures called **Lamassu** (fig. **3.30**).

Twice as tall as the Hittite lions guarding the gateway at Hattusas (see fig. 3.23), the Lamassu were divine genii combining animal and human features, in this case the body and legs of a bull with a human head. The hair, beard, and eyebrows are stylized. The figure wears the cylindrical, three-horned crown of divinity. As is typical of ancient Near Eastern art, this figure combines naturalism—the suggestion of bone and muscle under the skin—with surface stylization—the zones of patterned texture scattered across the body. Rising from above the forelegs in a sweeping curve are wings which fill the limestone blocks from which the Lamassu is carved.

The wings draw the eye of the viewer to the side of the Lamassu, a transition unified by the "re-use" of the forelegs in the side view, which essentially creates a "fifth leg." This striking visual device enhances the architectural function of an entrance, which is to mark a point of access: the Lamassu appears to confront approaching visitors and simultaneously seems to stride past them. By narrowing the space through which visitors must pass, the figure builds up tension as one approaches the king. Sargon's palace was thus an elaborate structural and pictorial expression of the notion that power resides in an interior space, access to which becomes a rite of passage. Once visitors entered the throne room, they were confronted with brightly painted walls and a throne backed up against a wall. Inscribed on the base of the throne were warnings against rebellion and revolution.

With the rise of Assyrian palace architecture, the importance of the ziggurat declined. Originally, Mesopotamian palaces had been adjuncts to the ziggurat and places from which a ruler ran the administration of a city-state. Under the militaristic Assyrians, the relationship between religious and administrative centers changed. The power of the Assyrian king was now reflected in immense fortifications and reliefs showing his victories and his cruelty, and the ziggurat became an accessory to the palace.

Throughout its history the Assyrian empire faced constant pressure from both within and without, and its militaristic art reflects the chronic warfare necessary to maintain control of its territory. Within a century after Sargon II's reign, the Assyrian empire collapsed. Its capital at Nineveh fell in 612 B.C. to an alliance of Medes (from what is today Iran) and Scythians (from modern Russia and the Ukraine). Babylonian clay tablets record the events surrounding the end of Assyrian power and the rise of a Neo-Babylonian empire.

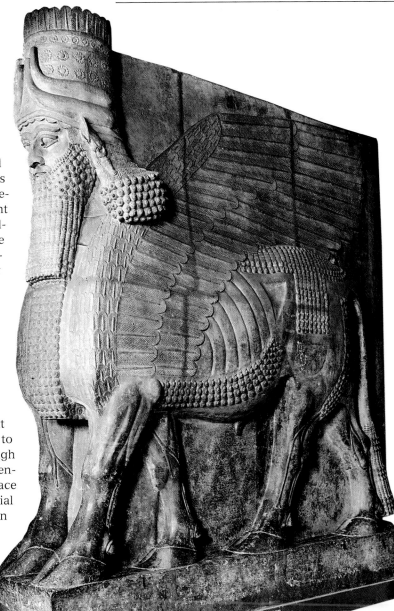

3.30 Lamassu, from the gateway, Sargon II's palace at Dur Sharrukin (now Khorsabad, Iraq), c. 720 B.C. Limestone, 14 ft (4.26 m) high. Louvre, Paris. The ancient visitor to the palace would experience the Lamassu first as standing and then as walking. The Lamassu stands as the observer faces him and walks as he passes by, all the while seeming to keep an eye out for the king's protection.

The Neo-Babylonian Empire

(612–539 B.C.)

Babylon had been ruled by Assyria for about two and a half centuries, during which time it exerted considerable cultural influence over its masters. When the new southern dynasty reversed the balance of power, the greatest of the Neo-Babylonian kings, Nebuchadnezzar (reigned 604–562 B.C.), restored some of Babylon's former splendor.

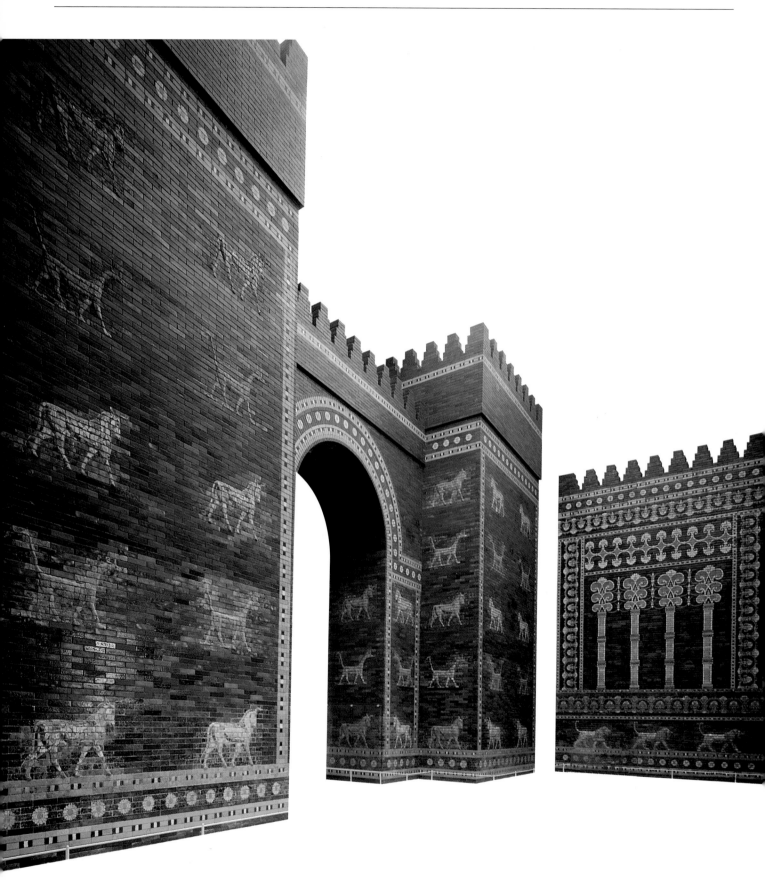

3.31 Ishtar Gate (reconstructed), from Babylon, c. 575 B.C. Glazed brick. Staatliche Museen, Berlin. The gate is restored and preserved indoors. The idea of a monumental gateway with a round arch as a kind of processional marker persists—for example, in the triumphal arches of imperial Rome (Chapter 8) and the 19th-century Arc de Triomphe in Paris.

Round Arches

An arch may be thought of as a curved lintel connecting two vertical supports, or posts. The round arch, as used in the Ishtar Gate, is semicircular and stronger than a horizontal lintel. This is because a round arch carries the thrust of the weight onto the two vertical supports rather than having all the stress rest on the horizontal. The Greeks, Etruscans, and Romans developed rounded arches for many other purposes besides gateways (see Chapters 7 and 8). Later still, in medieval Europe, round arches were revived in Romanesque churches and cathedrals (see Chapter 11).

Among the many architectural monuments Nebuchadnezzar commissioned for his capital city was a ziggurat dedicated to the god Marduk, which is thought to have been the Tower of Babel referred to in the Bible (see p. 8). Another was the Ishtar Gate (fig. **3.31**), one of eight gateways with round **arches** (see Box) that spanned a processional route through the city. The gate was named in honor of the Akkadian goddess of love, fertility, and war. It was **faced** (covered on the surface) with **glazed** bricks (see Box). Set off against a deep blue background are rows of bulls and dragons (sacred to Marduk), molded in relief. They, too, proceed in horizontal planes either toward or away from the arched opening. Geometric designs in white and gold frame the animal imagery and outline the gate's architectural forms.

In 539 B.C. Babylon came under the rule of yet another conqueror, Cyrus the Great of Persia (modern Iran), and became part of the Achaemenid empire.

Glazing

Glazing is a technique for adding a durable, water-resistant finish to clay objects. Glazes can be clear, white, or colored and are typically made from ground mineral pigments mixed with water. The minerals become vitreous (glass-like) and fuse with the clay bodies of the objects when fired at high temperatures in kilns.

Iran (c. 5000–331 B.C.)

To the east of Mesopotamia lay ancient Iran, whose name derives from the Indo-European Aryans, a people who may have entered the Near East in Neolithic times from the steppes of present-day Russia.

By the fifth millennium B.C. a distinctive pottery style had emerged in ancient Iran. A large painted pottery beaker from Susa, the capital of Elam in the southwest, exemplifies the artistic sophistication of the early Iranians (fig. **3.32**). It combines elegant form with a preference for animal subjects, which are characteristic of Iranian art. The central image is a stylized ibex, or wild goat, whose body is composed of two curved triangles; its head and tail are smaller triangles, with individual hairs on the beard and tail rendered as relatively parallel lines. The two large curved horns are particularly striking. They occupy two thirds of the framed space and encircle a stylized plant form.

The ibex stands still and upright in contrast to the dogs, whose outstretched forelegs suggest that they are racing around the upper part of the beaker. A sense of slower movement is created by the repeated long-necked birds who seem to be parading along the top row in the opposite direction. By using the largest visible surface of the beaker for the standing ibexes (there is a second one on the other side), and the top two registers for the repeated animals, the artist creates a unity between the painted images and the three-dimensional form of the object.

An unusual sculpture dating from c. 3000 B.C. merges leonine with human—apparently female—form (fig. **3.33**; see Box). Its polished surface and compact tension contribute to its curious combination of elegance and monumentality. It stands upright, and the twist of the upper torso is so pronounced that it is positioned at a right angle to the lower part of the body. The head is turned sharply to face in the same direction as the lower body. A sense of powerful force is achieved despite the small size—3½ inches (8.9 cm) high. Because this figure is unique in ancient art, and because its original context is unknown, its significance has so far eluded researchers.

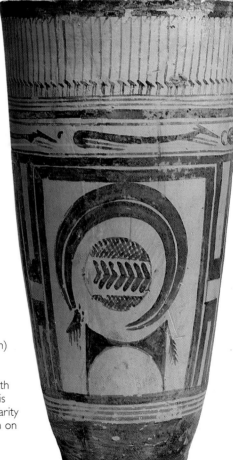

3.32 Beaker, from Susa, capital of Elam (now in Iran), c. 5000–4000 B.C. Painted pottery, 11¼ in (28.6 cm) high. Louvre, Paris. The images painted on the beaker are consistent with the fact that the viewer is more aware of its circularity at the rim and base than on the broader surface in between.

Destroying the Archaeological Record

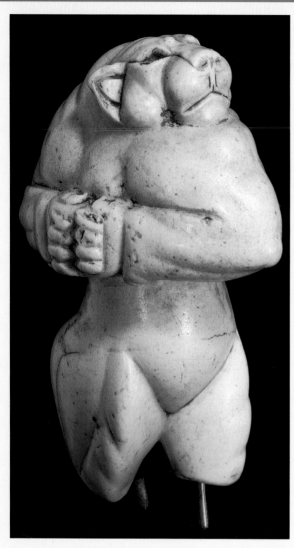

Objects such as the leonine sculpture in figure 3.33 create significant problems for archaeologists and raise questions about the plunder of archaeological sites. This particular work, like many others from ancient civilizations around the world, is certainly authentic (i.e. not a modern forgery), but has no **provenience**. That is, it appeared on the art market without any record of its place of origin. Presumably because it was one of the thousands of objects plundered for profit, the circumstances of its removal from the ground are unknown. It can be identified as Elamite on the basis of stylistic and iconographic analysis, through comparison with related works excavated in known circumstances, but it cannot be assigned a specific context. We do not know, for example, what city it is from, or whether it might have been found in a house, a palace, or a temple; its purpose is also unknown. Once the archaeological record of such an object is destroyed, a piece of history is lost forever. As a work of art, from a purely esthetic point of view, the figure is immensely satisfying. As a visual document and expression of a time and place, it remains a mystery.

3.33 Lion monster, c. 3500–3000 B.C. Crystalline limestone, 3½ in (8.9 cm) high. From the Collection of Robin B. Martin, on loan to the Brooklyn Museum, New York.

The Scythians (8th–4th century B.C.)

The influence of early Iranian art persists in the much later animal art of the Scythians, a migratory people from southern Russia. Because they were nomadic, the Scythians' art was portable. It is characterized by vivid forms and a high degree of technical skill. A stag from the seventh century B.C. (fig. 3.34) is typical of Scythian gold objects. The artist has captured a naturalistic likeness of the animal, while at the same time forming its antlers into an abstract series of curves and turning its legs into birds. Such visual metaphors, in which the forms of one animal are transformed into those of another, are characteristic of Scythian animal art. They also enhance the illusion of motion; although it is clear from the folded, bird-shaped legs that the stag is not moving, there is a sense of movement in the curvilinear patterning.

3.34 Stag, from Kostromskaya, Russia, 7th century B.C. Chased gold, 12½ in (31.7 cm) long. State Hermitage Museum, St. Petersburg. As with the Paleolithic cave paintings and carvings of western Europe (see Chapter 2), this Scythian work is the product of artists familiar with the animals around them.

Achaemenid Persia (539–331 B.C.)

The Persians, Indo-European-speaking people affiliated with the Medes, settled southeast of Susa in a region of Iran now known as Fars. The Assyrian empire was brought down by a coalition of Medes, Scythians, and Babylonians in 612 B.C., creating a power vacuum. King Cyrus II (reigned 559–530 B.C.), called Cyrus the Great, founded the Persian Achaemenid dynasty, which was to become the largest empire in the world. He first conquered the Medes, followed by Lydia (in Anatolia) and, in 539 B.C., Babylon (in Mesopotamia). Cyrus's son seized Egypt, and under later rulers the Achaemenids' vast territory stretched as far as the Aegean islands. The Assyrians—who had preceded the Persians as empire-builders in the ancient Near East—influenced the Persians in several ways, most notably in their manner of celebrating kingship.

The Persians followed the religious teachings of Zoroaster (c. 628–551 B.C.), who taught that the world's two central forces were light and dark: Ahuramazda was light and Ahriman, similar to the Christian concept of evil, was dark. There were no Achaemenid temples, since religious rituals were held outdoors, where fires burned on altars. The most elaborate Achaemenid architectural works were therefore palaces, of which the best example is at Persepolis (literally, "city of the Persians"). It was begun c. 520 B.C. by Darius I (reigned 521–486 B.C.), and work continued over many years under his successors, especially Xerxes and Artaxerxes I (fig. **3.35**). The palace at Persepolis was built on a stone platform 40 feet (12.2 m) high, and consisted of multi-columned buildings. Access to the platform was along a double stairway leading to the main gate, which was known as "All Lands."

The most important structure was the Apadana, or Audience Hall (fig. **3.36**), where the king received foreign delegations. This and the throne room were huge squares that gave onto open verandas. They contained tall columns constructed of a wooden core covered with painted plaster.

Reliefs lining the walls and stairways were originally painted, and emphasized the king's grandeur. In contrast to the aggressive military scenes on Assyrian reliefs, Persian reliefs depict solemn tribute-bearers calmly presenting offerings to the king. This distinction is consistent with the political styles of the two civilizations: unlike the cruel repression that characterized the Assyrian empire, the Persian empire was generally administered in an orderly and peaceful way. The wall in figure **3.37** is covered with the king's royal guards. The broad, slightly curved folds of their drapery contribute to the sense of slow, ceremonial movement. Their stylizations, particularly the curls of hair and beards, are typically Achaemenid. The vast numbers of these figures, like the repeated columns of the Apadana and the columned halls of Persepolis (see Box), are intended to focus attention on the centrality and greatness of the king.

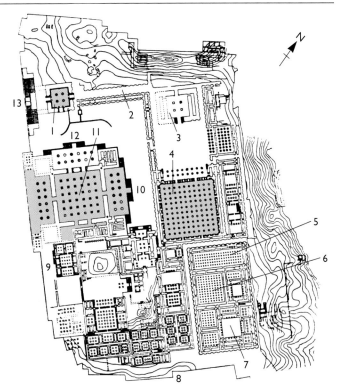

1 Gate House of Xerxes
  (Gate of All Lands)
2 Procession way
3 Unfinished Gate house
4 Hall of 100 columns
  (Throne Hall)
5 Hall of 100 columns
  (part of Treasury)
6 Hall of 99 columns
  (part of Treasury)
7 Storerooms
8 South terrace façade
  overlooking plain
9 Palace of Darius
  (Banquet hall)
10 East Apadana stairs
11 Apadana
12 North Apadana stairs
13 Stairs to Treasury

3.35 Plan of Persepolis.

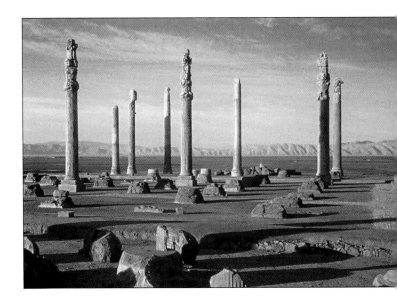

3.36 Apadana (Audience Hall) of Darius, Persepolis (in modern Iran), c. 500 B.C., approx. 250 ft² (23.2 m²). The Apadana was decorated with a hundred columns 40 feet (12.2 m) high. Originally painted, the shafts show influences from other cultures, including Egypt (Chapter 4) and Greece (Chapter 6), but the bull capitals were unique to Persia.

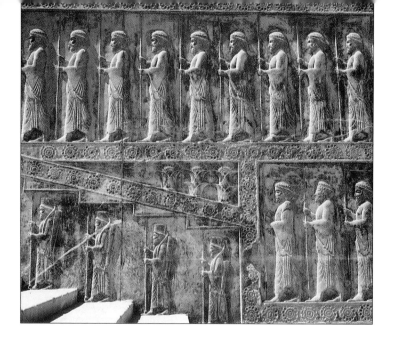

3.37 Royal guards, relief on the stairway to the Audience Hall of Darius, Persepolis.

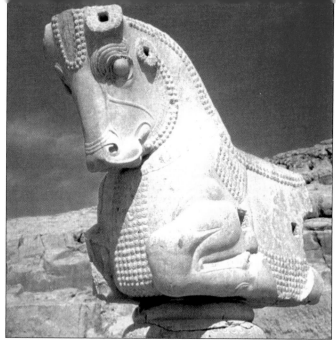

3.38 Bull capital, Persepolis, c. 500 B.C.

Paired bulls facing in opposite directions (fig. **3.38**) were set on top of the capitals at Persepolis. The bulls themselves form the **impost block**, whose function was to carry the wooden ceiling beams on a "saddle" created by joining the bulls' foreparts. With his legs tucked under him, the bull illustrated here conveys a sense of vitality despite its stylized details. The representation of bulls at the palace associates the king with the power and fertility that this animal traditionally embodies. Bull capitals at Persepolis are also an architectural metaphor for the position of the king as "head" of state.

Some of the iconography at Persepolis was assimilated from different Near East cultures. For example, motifs included crenellated walls like those of Sargon's palace at Khorsabad, Assyrian-derived guardians of the gateways, and Egyptian and Greek architectural elements. The Achaemenid capital city was described in an inscription of Darius, referring to his palace in Susa: "This is the palace I erected.... Its ornament was brought from afar."[5] According to Darius, Babylonians dug the earth, packed the rubble, and molded the brick. Cedar timber came from Lebanon, and was transported by Assyrians to Babylon. Gold came from Sardis and Bactria, silver and copper from Egypt, and ivory from Ethiopia. The stonecutters were Ionians and Sardians.

Achaemenid artists were also expert in metalwork. The gold lion drinking vessel, for example (fig. **3.39**), is clearly an object fit for a king. Not only the intrinsic value of its material but the complexity of its design and structure suggest that it comes from a royal workshop. It is formed from several pieces of gold, but their sophisticated fusion makes it difficult to locate the joints. Thin gold threads were used—altogether over 144 feet (44 m) of them—for the cup itself. Like the bull on the Persepolis capital, the gold lion tucks its legs under its body and seems to clench its paws, which conveys a sense of compressed space and muscular tension. Its combination of stylized elements—such as the horseshoe-shaped leg muscle, the bulges on either side of the nose, the wing feathers and body hair—

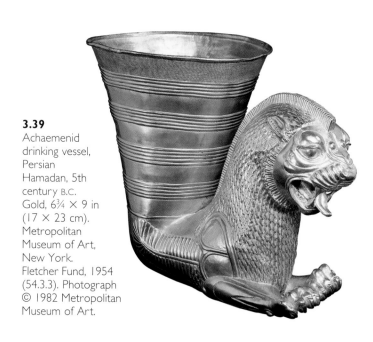

3.39 Achaemenid drinking vessel, Persian Hamadan, 5th century B.C. Gold, 6¾ × 9 in (17 × 23 cm). Metropolitan Museum of Art, New York. Fletcher Fund, 1954 (54.3.3). Photograph © 1982 Metropolitan Museum of Art.

Columns

A **column**, like a **pillar**, is a tall, slender upright. Columns can be freestanding and sculptural, but they are usually architectural supports—the "posts" of the post-and-lintel system of elevation. At Persepolis, columns consist of three main parts, a lower **base**, a vertical **shaft**, and a **capital** on top, on which the horizontal lintel rests. The term capital comes from the Latin word *caput*, meaning "head," and refers to its position at the top of the column.

with convincing organic form is typical of much ancient Near Eastern art. So is the metamorphosing of the work from one form (the lion) into another (the drinking vessel). But the specific nature of the stylizations and the merging of elegance with monumental power are characteristic of the Achaemenid esthetic.

Persian domination of the Near East came to an end nearly 200 years after Darius I began the palace at Persepolis. In 331 B.C. Alexander the Great, King of Macedonia (the northern part of modern Greece), conquered the Achaemenids and went on to create an even larger empire.

	Style/Period	Works of Art	Cultural/Historical Developments
9000 B.C.	NEOLITHIC c. 9000–4500/4000 B.C.	Plastered skull (**3.2**), Jericho Anatolian goddess (**3.3**), Çatal Hüyük Two leopards (**3.4**), Çatal Hüyük	Development of agriculture; domestication of sheep and goats (c. 6000 B.C.) Earliest cities in Mesopotamia (5000–4000 B.C.) Great Pyramids built at Giza, Egypt (2500 B.C.) Copper smelting developed (c. 4500 B.C.)
5000 B.C.	ANCIENT IRANIAN c. 5000–3000 B.C.	Beaker (**3.32**), Susa Lion monster (**3.33**), Iran	
4000 B.C.	URUK c. 4500–3100 B.C.	Cone mosaics (**3.5**), Uruk Sculpted vase (**3.6**), Uruk Female head (**3.7**), Uruk White Temple, ziggurat (**3.8**), Uruk Cylinder seal impression (**3.10**), Uruk Clay tablet, cuneiform text (**3.11**), Iraq	First bronze casting (c. 4000 B.C.) Sumerians settle at site of Babylon (4000–3000 B.C.) Height of Sumerian civilization (3500–3000 B.C.) Development of cuneiform script in Sumer (3500–3000 B.C.) Invention of the potter's wheel (c. 3100 B.C.)
3000 B.C.	SUMERIAN Early Dynastic c. 2800–2300 B.C. Neo-Sumerian c. 2150–1800 B.C.	Group of statues (**3.12**), Tell Asmar Lyre soundbox (**3.14**), Ur Head of Gudea (**3.18**), Iraq Gudea with temple plan (**3.19**), Iraq Ziggurat (**3.20**), Ur Stele of Ur-Nammu (**3.21**)	Gilgamesh, legendary King of Uruk (2750 B.C.) First known epic poem, *The Epic of Gilgamesh*, recorded on cuneiform tablets (2000–1000 B.C.)
2000 B.C.	AKKADIAN c. 2340–2180 B.C.	Head of Akkadian ruler (**3.16**) Victory stele of Naram-Sin (**3.17**)	
	OLD BABYLONIAN c. 1830–1550 B.C.	Stele, Law Code of Hammurabi (**3.22**)	
	HITTITE c. 1450–1200 B.C.	Lion Gate (**3.23**), Boghazköy Hittite war god (**3.24**), Hattusas	Troy destroyed by Mycenaeans (c. 1180 B.C) Beginning of Judaism (1200 B.C.)
1000 B.C.	ASSYRIAN c. 1100–612 B.C.	Assurnasirpal II (**3.25**), Nimrud Assurnasirpal II and Lions (**3.26**), Nimrud City attacked with a battering ram (**3.27**) Sargon II's palace (**3.28**), Khorsabad Lamassu (**3.30**), Khorsabad	Israelite kingdom founded; reign of David and his son Solomon (r. 961–922) (1000 B.C.) Phoenicians develop alphabetic script (c. 1100 B.C.)
	SCYTHIAN c. 800–550 B.C.	Stag (**3.34**), Kostromskaya	
500 B.C.	NEO-BABYLONIAN 612–539 B.C.	Ishtar Gate (**3.31**), Babylon	Neo-Babylonian Empire reaches zenith under Nebuchadnezzar (r. 605–562) (600–550 B.C.); conquest of Egypt (605) and Jerusalem (586) Birth of Buddha (c. 563 B.C.) Birth of Confucius (c. 550 B.C.)
300 B.C.	ACHAEMENID 539–331 B.C.	Apadana of Darius (**3.36**), Persepolis Royal guards (**3.37**), Persepolis Bull capital (**3.38**), Persepolis Achaemenid drinking vessel (**3.39**)	Birth of Herodotos, "Father of History" (485 B.C.)

Plastered skull

Tell Asmar head

Sargon I (?)

Hittite war god

Assurnasirpal II

4
Ancient Egypt

The Gift of the Nile

Located in northeast Africa (fig. **4.1**), Egypt was the home of one of the most powerful and longest lasting civilizations in the ancient world. In the Neolithic period, before about 7000 B.C., farming communities had settled along the banks of the Nile. They used stone tools, and made ivory and bone objects and handbuilt pottery. Until its unification around 3000 B.C., ancient Egypt had been divided into Upper Egypt in the south and Lower Egypt in the north. Egypt was defined by its most important geographical feature, the Nile, the world's longest river. Because annual floods kept the land fertile, Egypt was called "the gift of the Nile." The Nile flows northward for some 4160 miles (6695 km) from its source in Central Africa (modern Burundi) through Egypt. At Memphis, near Cairo, the Nile divides and spreads into its delta, a wide alluvial triangle of about 14,500 square miles (23,335 sq km), now lush and fertile but in antiquity a region of marsh and scrub. From the delta the river empties into the Mediterranean Sea.

The search for the source of the Nile became an obsession with nineteenth-century explorers. In fact, however, the Nile is actually a combination of two rivers. Rainfall in the highlands of East Equatorial Africa drains into a series of lakes, especially Lake Victoria, to form the headwaters of the White Nile. After flowing north through a large area of swamp, the river reaches Khartoum, where it joins its twin, the Blue Nile, rising in the Ethiopian mountains. North of Khartoum, the Nile enters what was ancient Nubia, where vegetation and marshland give way to desert on either side. At six points the river passes over outcrops of rock, known as the Cataracts (actually, very large waterfalls—from the Greek *katarrhaktes*, meaning "down-swooping"). At the northernmost of these, the First Cataract, the Nile enters Lower Egypt at Aswan.

Rainfall in Central Africa and melting snows from the Ethiopian highlands caused the Nile to flood each year, reaching its highest point in Egypt by the end of August. The average flood level measured nearly 25 feet (8 m), high enough to flood the whole valley up to the edge of the desert but not so high as to overwhelm villages and dykes. When the waters receded, the soaked earth was covered with a fresh deposit of rich, dark silt. This led the

Egyptians to call their land Kemet ("The Black") as opposed to the desert, Deshret ("The Red"). By autumn, the land was once again ready for planting, its fertility renewed.

This pattern was generally predictable from year to year, as were the sunny, cloudless skies. Occasionally, however, the Nile failed to rise to the expected levels and the resulting food shortages reminded the Egyptians of their dependence on the annual flood. This concern is reflected in a hymn to the Nile god Hapy (see Box), as well as in the Bible (Genesis 41), in which Joseph interprets

---

Hymn to Hapy

Hapy was the personification of the Nile, and was regularly honored with festivals and hymns. This one, from which only excerpts are given here, was written during the Middle Kingdom:

Hail to you, Hapy,
Spring from earth,
Come to nourish Egypt! ...

Who floods the fields that Re has made,
To nourish all who thirst;
Lets drink the waterless desert,
His dew descending from the sky ...

When he is sluggish, noses clog,
Everyone is poor;
As the sacred loaves are pared,
A million perish among men.
When he plunders, the whole land rages, ...

Food provider, bounty maker,
Who creates all that is good!
Lord of awe, sweetly fragrant,
Gracious when he comes ...

Conqueror of the Two Lands,
He fills the stores,
Makes bulge the barns,
Gives bounty to the poor.[1]

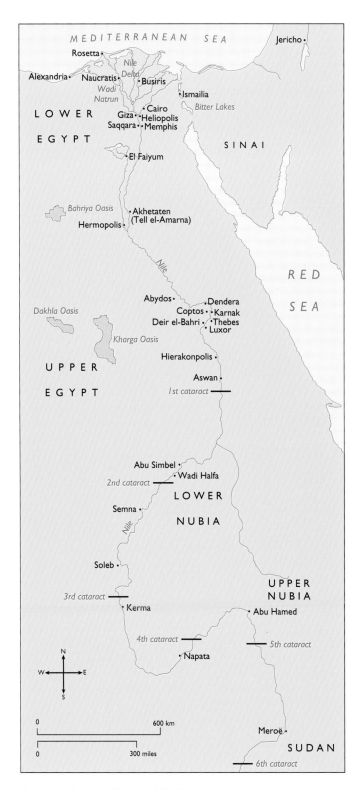

4.1 Map of ancient Egypt and Nubia.

Egyptians a sense of order and inevitability. Every natural phenomenon, especially the daily return of the sun and the annual flood of the Nile, seemed a continual rebirth and this theme was central to the development of Egyptian religion.

Religion

The Egyptians, like their Near Eastern neighbors, were polytheists. Gods were manifest in every aspect of nature, as well as in the Nile. They influenced human lives and ordered the universe, and they could appear in human or animal form, or as various human and animal combinations.

Archaeological evidence suggests that prehistoric Egyptian religion consisted of local gods or cults that were confined to a particular district, or *nome*. After the unification of Upper and Lower Egypt c. 3000 B.C., the importance of these local deities increased or diminished with the military or political fortunes of their districts. For example, the sky god Horus, usually represented as a falcon, was originally a local god who later achieved national status.

Egyptian gods had spheres of influence that could intersect or overlap, producing numerous compound deities. Single gods could also have multiple aspects: for example, Horus-the-child, representing the potential power of a child, and Horus-in-the-horizon, denoting the power of daybreak or sunset.

The result of this belief system was a pantheon (meaning "all the gods of a people," from the Greek *pan*, meaning "all," and *theoi*, or "gods") of enormous complexity (see Box). Over time the number was increased by the introduction of foreign gods into Egypt. Like most polytheists, the Egyptians did not find the religious ideas of other cultures incompatible with their own, and they incorporated new deities either singly or in combination. This process of fusion is known as syncretism. One such syncretistic immigrant assimilated into the Egyptian pantheon was the Syrian goddess Astarte, related to the Babylonian Ishtar (see Chapter 3).

The Pharaohs

From approximately 3000 B.C., Egypt was ruled by pharaohs, or kings, whose control of the land and its people was virtually absolute. Egyptian monumental art on a vast scale begins with pharaonic rule, originating when King Menes united Upper and Lower Egypt. Much of our knowledge of Egyptian chronology comes from ancient king lists, the most comprehensive of which was compiled in the fourth century B.C. by a priest, Manetho. His list begins with the legendary reign of the gods, followed by that of the human kings from Menes to Alexander the Great. He divided Egyptian history into thirty dynasties, or royal families (a thirty-first was added later).

Pharaoh's dream of seven fat and seven lean cattle as meaning seven years of plenty and seven of famine. The predictability of life—the rising and setting of the sun, the monthly waxing and waning of the moon, the annual flood, sowing and harvesting—induced in the ancient

Egyptian Gods

A few of the principal gods of ancient Egypt in their most typical guises are listed here:[2]

Amon the great god of Thebes; identified with Ra as Amon-Ra; sacred animals, the ram and goose

Anubis the jackal god, patron of embalmers; god of the necropolis, who ritually "opens the mouth" of the dead

Aten god of the sun disk; worshiped as the great creator god by Akhenaten

Bes helper of women in childbirth, protector against snakes and other dangers; depicted as a dwarf with features of a lion

Hapy god of the Nile in flood; depicted as a man with pendulous breasts, a clump of papyrus (or a lotus) on his head and bearing tables laden with offerings

Hathor goddess with many functions and attributes; often depicted as a cow, or woman with a cow's head or horned headdress; mother, wife, and daughter of Ra; protector of the royal palace; domestic fertility goddess; identified by the Greeks with Aphrodite (see p. 140)

Horus the falcon god, originally the sky god; identified with the king during his lifetime; the son of Osiris and Isis and avenger of the former

Imhotep chief minister of Zoser and architect of the step pyramid; deified and worshiped in the Late Period as god of learning and medicine

Isis the divine mother, wife of Osiris and mother of Horus; one of four protector goddesses, guarding coffins and **canopic** jars

Maat goddess of truth, right, and orderly conduct; depicted as a woman with an ostrich feather on her head

Mut wife of Amon; originally a vulture goddess, later depicted as a woman

Osiris god of the underworld, identified as the dead king; depicted as a mummified king

Ptah creator god of Memphis, patron god of craftsmen; depicted as a mummy-shaped man

Ra (Re) the sun god of Heliopolis, supreme judge; often linked with other gods, whose cults aspire to universality (e.g. Amon-Ra); depicted as falcon-headed

Serapis introduced into Egypt in the Ptolemaic period; with characteristics of Egyptian (Osiris) and Greek (Zeus) gods

Seth god of storms and violence; brother and murderer of Osiris, rival of Horus; depicted as pig, ass, hippopotamus, or other animals

---

One problem with Manetho's list has been to identify the sequence of the names. Since Egypt had no absolute system of dating (such as B.C./A.D.), each pharaoh treated the first year of his reign as year one. However, with the help of other king lists, inscriptions naming more than one king, references to astronomical observations which can be precisely dated, and correlations with evidence from outside Egypt, nineteenth- and twentieth-century scholars have compiled a relative chronology (see Box). Nevertheless, even this changes as new archaeological discoveries are made.

Modern scholars have divided Egyptian history into Predynastic and Early Dynastic periods, followed by the Old, Middle, and New Kingdoms, and the Late Dynastic period. These were punctuated by so-called "intermediate periods" of anarchy or central political decline, as well as by periods of foreign domination. For thousands of years following Menes's unification, Egypt had many periods of durable power, when artists worked for the state and its rulers within the confines of a political and religious hierarchy.

Between the Middle and New Kingdoms of Ancient Egypt there was a period of more than one hundred years during which a group of Semitic rulers, based in the northeastern Delta, controlled Lower Egypt. Known as the Hyksos, from the Egyptian *heqau-khasut* (meaning "princes of foreign countries"), these rulers are credited with having introduced the horse-drawn chariot to Egypt. During the New Kingdom, some important changes occurred. For example, the first queen to have assumed pharaonic status and to have presided over an artistic revival, Hatshepsut (see p. 97), co-ruled Egypt with Thutmose III from c. 1479 to 1458 B.C., and later the pharaoh Akhenaten (ruled c. 1349–1336 B.C.) made important changes in the hierarchy of gods.

From the end of the New Kingdom, Egypt's pre-eminent position as a powerful monarchy was weakened by infiltration from other states. During the Late Dynastic Period, Egypt twice fell under Persian rule—from 525 to 404 B.C. and again in 343 B.C. In 332 B.C. the Persians were defeated by Alexander the Great, who annexed all Persian territory, including Egypt, to his empire. After his death in 323 B.C., control of Egypt passed to the Macedonian general Ptolemy, whose successors ruled until the Roman conquest in 30 B.C. His descendants established the capital of Egypt at Alexandria, on the Mediterranean coast just west of the Delta, and infused Egypt with ideas from the Greek-speaking world.

The Egyptian Concept of Kingship

For the ancient Egyptians, kingship was a divine state. As in Mesopotamia (Chapter 3), kings mediated between their people and the gods. In Egypt, however, the kings were themselves considered gods. They ruled according to the principle of *maat*, divinely established order (personified by Maat, the goddess of truth and orderly conduct; cf. Box on p. 78). From the Third Dynasty, the compound god Amon-Ra, in the guise of the reigning pharaoh, was believed to impregnate the queen with a son who would be heir to the throne. This divine conception by Amon-Ra was part of each pharaoh's official personality and iconography. A queen could be either the king's mother or his principal wife. Marriages occasionally took place between a pharaoh and his sister, half-sister, or daughter, when this was politically useful. The ambiguous position of the queen by comparison with that of the pharaoh reflects her complementary role. Certain exceptions notwithstanding, Egyptian kingship was not for women. The queen was the king's means of renewal by providing him with male heirs to the throne or with daughters for creating alliances through advantageous marriages.

Chronology of Egyptian Kings		
(all dates before 664 B.C. are approximate)		
Predynastic Period		3300–2960 B.C.
Early Dynastic Period	Dynasties 1–2	2960–2649 B.C.
Old Kingdom	Dynasties 3–6	2649–2150 B.C.
First Intermediate Period	Dynasties 7–11	2143–1991 B.C.
Middle Kingdom	Dynasties 12–14	1991–1700 B.C.
Second Intermediate Period	Dynasties 15–17 (including the Hyksos Period)	1640–1550 B.C.
New Kingdom	Dynasties 18–20	1550–1070 B.C.
Third Intermediate Period	Dynasties 21–25	1070–660 B.C.
Late Dynastic Period	Dynasties 26–30	688–343 B.C.
	Persian Kings	343–332 B.C.
Ptolemaic Period	Macedonian Kings	332–30 B.C.

In entering into incestuous marriages, the king, like the gods, was distinct from the general population of Egypt. Although there are many uncertainties about daily life in ancient Egypt, texts indicate that monogamous marriage was considered a positive and natural state and that the Egyptian commoner tended to have one wife at a time. Infidelity, especially if committed by the wife, was grounds for divorce, as were impotence, infertility, dislike of a wife, or a wish to marry another woman. A primary purpose of marriage was the production of children, and household deities of fertility—including Hathor and Bes—were worshiped in the home. In Egypt, as in the Near East, homosexuality was viewed as counterproductive to the ideal of fertility. Widows and orphans were disadvantaged members of society, although adoption was an established institution.

Despite the gaps in our knowledge, it seems clear that Egyptian kingship derived its divinity from the association of pharaohs with gods. The royal family modeled its behavior on that of the gods, separating itself from those it ruled. Egyptian kings did not maintain power by setting an example to the public at large, but rather by their distinction from it. In the transfer of kingship from father to son, or some substitute for a son, Egypt created another avenue of identification with the gods.

The Palette of Narmer

The links between divine and earthly power noted in earlier civilizations reappear in an important Egyptian ritual object, the Palette of Narmer (figs. **4.2** and **4.3**); it dates from the beginning of pharaonic rule and, like the Akkadian stele of Naram-Sin (see fig. 3.17), is an excellent example of *Machtkunst*. On both sides, the palette is decorated in low relief. The large scene in figure 4.2 is depicted according to certain conventions that lasted for over two thousand years in Egypt. For example, King Narmer (thought to be Menes, the first pharaoh) is the biggest figure—his size and central position denote his importance. His composite pose, in which head and legs are rendered in profile view with eye and upper torso in frontal view, is an Egyptian convention. This is a conceptual, rather than a naturalistic, approach to the human figure, for the body parts are arranged as they are understood, and not as they are seen in nature. The entire body is flat, as is the kilt, with certain details such as the knee caps rendered as stylizations, rather than as underlying organic structure.

Narmer wears the tall, white conical crown of Upper Egypt (the *hedjet*) and threatens a kneeling enemy with a mace. He holds him by the hair, an act that symbolizes conquest and domination. Two more enemies, either fleeing or already dead, occupy the lowest register of the palette. Behind Narmer on a suspended horizontal strip is a servant whose small size, like the enemies' low positions, identifies him as less important than the king. In Egypt, as in Mesopotamia, therefore, artists used a system of

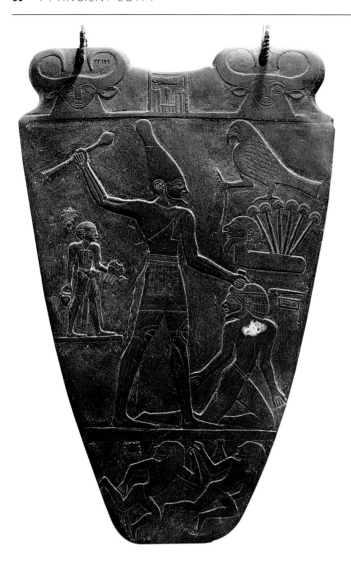

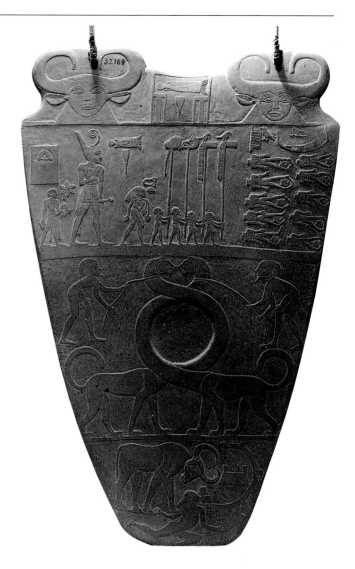

4.2 Palette of Narmer, from Hierakonpolis, c. 3000 B.C. Slate, 25 in (63.5 cm) high. Egyptian Museum, Cairo. This is called the Upper Egypt side because Narmer wears the white crown.

4.3 Palette of Narmer (reverse side of fig. 4.2). This is called the Lower Egypt side because the pharaoh wears the red crown.

hierarchical proportions. The servant holds Narmer's sandals indicating that the king is on holy ground (just as Muslims remove their shoes before entering a mosque). In front of Narmer, at the level of his head, is Horus, the falcon god of sky and kingship, who holds a captive human-headed creature at the end of a rope. From the back of this figure rise six **papyrus** plants, which represent Lower Egypt. The image of Horus dominating symbols of Lower Egypt parallels Narmer, crowned as the king of Upper Egypt and subduing an enemy.

At the top center of each side of the palette is a rectangle known as a *serekh* (see Box). A *serekh* contained a king's name in hieroglyphs (pictures symbolizing words that were the earliest Egyptian writing system; see Box). On either side of the *serekh*, frontal heads of the cow goddess Hathor indicate that she guards the king's palace.

The other side of the palette (fig. 4.3) comprises three registers below the Hathor heads and the pharaoh's name. At the top, Narmer wears the red crown of Lower Egypt

(the *deshret*). His sandal-bearer is behind him and he is preceded by standard-bearers. At the far right, ten decapitated enemies lie with their heads between their feet. These figures are meant to be read from above, as a row of bodies lying side by side. Such shifting viewpoints are characteristic of Egyptian pictorial style.

Two felines, roped by bearded men, occupy the central register. Their elongated necks frame an indented circle similar to those that held liquid for mixing eye makeup on smaller palettes. This one, however, was found as a dedication in a temple, and is larger than those used in everyday life. Although derived from such palettes, the Palette of Narmer was most likely a ceremonial, rather than a practical, object. It is not certain what the felines, called *serpopards*, signify, but their intertwined necks could refer to Narmer's unification of Egypt (signified by his two crowns). In the lowest register, a bull—probably a manifestation of Narmer himself—subdues another fallen enemy before architectural symbols.

Royal Names: *Serekhs* and Cartouches

During the First, Second, and Third Dynasties, the chief name, or "Horus name," of the reigning pharaoh was written in the top half of a rectangular frame known as a *serekh*, a flattened representation of his palace. This was symbolic of the king as the god Horus, himself depicted as a falcon surmounting the *serekh*.

During the third millennium B.C. it became customary for kings to take five titled names. The Horus name was followed by "He of the Two Ladies," signifying that the king was under the protection of two goddesses, the Wadjet of Lower Egypt and the Nekhbet of Upper Egypt. The third name was "Horus of Gold," a reference to the sunlit sky. In the Fourth Dynasty a fourth name was added, "King of Upper and Lower Egypt," known as the *prenomen* or throne name; it was enclosed in a cartouche, a rectangle with a semicircle at either end, signifying the passage of the sun around the universe and the pharaoh's dominion over it. Completing the series of five titles was a second cartouche, containing the *nomen* or birth name, "Son of Ra" (the sun god).

Figure **4.4** is a diagram of the *serekh* from the Palette of Narmer, and figure **4.5** shows Amenhotep IV's cartouches.

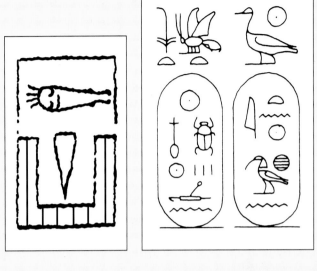

4.4 *Serekh* from the Palette of Narmer.

4.5 Cartouches of Amenhotep IV.

Every image on the palette conveys Narmer's might and importance. He is protected by the gods. He is taller, more central, and more powerful than any other figure. He destroys his enemies and their cities. The iconographic message of this work is a political one. Like much of the Egyptian art which survived the next two thousand years, the Palette of Narmer is a statement of power, for it celebrates the king's divine right to rule and illustrates his ability to do so.

The Egyptian View of Death and the Afterlife

For the ancient Egyptians, death was not the end of life but the transition to a similar existence on another plane. To ensure a fortuitous afterlife, the deceased had to be physically preserved along with earthly possessions and other reminders of daily activities. This was first achieved by simple burial in the dry desert sands. Later, coffins insulated the body and artificial means of preservation were used (see Box, p. 83). But, in case the body of the deceased did not last, an image could serve as a substitute. The dead person's *ka*, or soul, was believed able to enter the surrogate before journeying to the next world.

The *ka* was only one aspect of the Egyptian triple concept of the spirit. In its aspect as a "double," the *ka* was viewed as the life force that continued after death and permitted the deceased to eat and drink offerings provided by relatives and priests. The *akh* was more detached from the body than the *ka* and resided in the heavens as the spiritual transformation of the dead person. The third aspect of the spirit, the *ba*, was literally in touch with the deceased, and its mobility in and out of the body was reflected in its depiction in art as a bird with a human head.

Procedures such as mummification highlight the ancient Egyptian preoccupation with a continued material existence in the afterlife. Enormous resources were devoted to providing for the dead, both on an individual level and, in the case of the royal family and its court, on a grand scale involving the whole society. Much of the art and writings that have survived is funerary, preserved in the dry desert climate for thousands of years (see Box, p. 84).

The Old Kingdom (c. 2649–2150 B.C.)

Menes's unification of Egypt was followed by long periods of relatively stable, highly centralized government during which artists worked for the state and its rulers within the confines of a political and religious hierarchy. Egyptian artists worked, as did their contemporaries in Mesopotamia, for individual patrons as well as for the state. Since the ruling classes controlled the wealth in these hierarchical societies, their art is both more impressive and often better preserved than that of less wealthy patrons. We see this clearly in funerary art. Those in power could afford durable materials such as stone for their memorials, as well as precious materials such as gold and gems, and could finance elaborate burial sites designed to endure for eternity.

Writing and History

By around 3100 B.C. the Egyptians were using a form of picture-writing known as hieroglyphic (from the Greek *hieros*, or "sacred," and *glypho*, "I carve"). Examples of hieroglyphs can be seen in figure 4.22, where they denote the names and titles of Prince Rahotep and his wife Nofret. This method of writing was slow, so for everyday purposes the Egyptians developed a faster system, an abridged form of hieroglyphic called hieratic.

In the seventh century B.C. a simpler form of writing known as demotic (because it was used by the ordinary people, *demos* in Greek) became standard for all but religious texts. These three systems—hieroglyphic, hieratic, and demotic—remained in use until the Christian era when they were replaced by Coptic, which was composed of Greek letters and supplemented by seven demotic signs. From the fifth century A.D. to 1822, reading ancient Egyptian scripts was a lost art.

In 1799, soldiers of Napoleon's French Expeditionary Force, working on fortifications at the village of Rashid (called Rosetta by Europeans) in the Western Delta, discovered a slab of black basalt—the Rosetta Stone (fig. **4.6**)—built into an old wall. The importance of the Rosetta Stone lay in its three separate inscriptions, each a version of the same text in a different script and two languages—hieroglyphics, demotic, and Greek. The Greek version was soon translated and found to be a decree passed by a council of Egyptian priests in honor of the first anniversary of the coronation of the pharaoh Ptolemy V Epiphanes (205–180 B.C.).

Primary credit for the decipherment of the Rosetta Stone goes to Jean-François Champollion (1790–1832), a young French scholar who realized that hieroglyphs could be divided into two categories: ideograms, which recorded an idea pictorially, and phonograms, which denoted sounds representing one or more consonants (the Egyptian script had no vowels), independent of their meaning. Some hieroglyphs could be either ideograms or phonograms, depending on their context. Ideograms were also used as determinatives, which helped to indicate the meaning of a word spelled phonetically (e.g. a hieroglyph of walking legs to indicate motion, or of a hawk, the fastest bird, to represent swift things in general or anything for which speed is an attribute).

Once the Egyptian text on the Rosetta Stone was deciphered, the meanings of thousands of preserved Egyptian texts became available for study. Reading the king lists was the starting point for establishing a chronology of ancient Egypt, and other texts have clarified ancient Egyptian art and its cultural context.

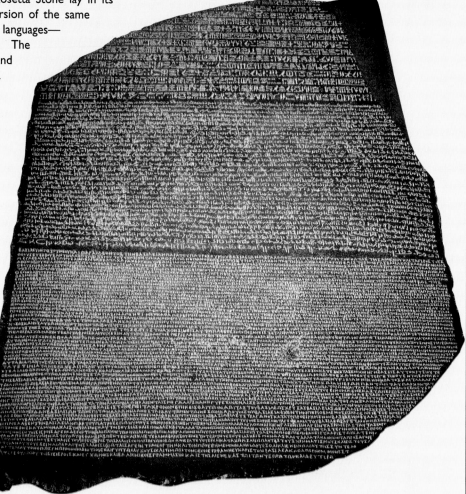

4.6 Rosetta Stone, 196 B.C. Basalt, 3 ft 9 in (1.14 m) high. British Museum, London. The stone was probably about 5–6 feet (1.52–1.82 m) high originally, with a rounded top (now missing) that contained the winged disk of Horus of Edfu depicted over the figure of Ptolemy V standing in the presence of various gods. A similar scene on a stele of 182 B.C., with the text of the same decree, enabled scholars to fill in the missing portions around the edge of the stone.

Mummification

By c. 3000 B.C., the Egyptians had invented a seventy-two-day process of embalming corpses. According to Herodotos (*History,* II, 85–90), writing in the fifth century B.C., the first step was the removal of the internal organs, except for the heart, which was believed to be the seat of understanding and was therefore left intact. The body was then packed in dry natron (a natural compound of sodium carbonate and sodium bicarbonate found in Egypt), which dehydrated the cadaver and dissolved its body fats. Then the corpse was washed, treated with oils and ointments, and bandaged with as many as twenty layers of linen in a way that conformed to its original shape. The substances applied to its skin caused the body to turn black; later travelers took this to mean that the body had been preserved with pitch, for which the Arabic term is *mumiya*—hence the English terms "mummy" and "mummification." Ornaments placed on the body or inside the wrappings included amulets (charms against evil or injury), scarabs (a representation of a scarab beetle used as a protective device and symbol of the soul; fig. **4.7**), *wedjats* (Eyes of Horus; fig. **4.8**) and *djeds* (pillars symbolizing stability).

No less important than preservation of the body was preservation of the organs which had been removed. These were embalmed and placed in four so-called canopic jars (fig. **4.9**), but the brain was discarded as useless. Each jar held a particular organ and was under the protection of one of Horus's four sons. Each son had a characteristic head (man, ape, jackal, and falcon). Until c. 1300 B.C. the jars had human-headed stoppers, but later they were carved in the form of the head of the relevant protective deity. Even in the Late

Period, when the organs were usually wrapped and replaced in the body cavity, a substitute set of canopic jars was left at the burial site.

Before c. 2000 B.C. a mask made of linen stiffened with plaster (a material known as **cartonnage**) was molded to the contours of the face, creating an effect reminiscent of the skulls from Neolithic Jericho (see fig. 3.2). After that time, a separate mask often covered the face, and these came to be made from valuable materials, including, for those who could afford it, gold.

A single mummy might have been nested inside several coffins. Eventually, the mummy's shape—bandaged and masked—became the model for the coffin itself. Coffins were made of wood or plaster-reinforced linen and placed inside stone sarcophagi.

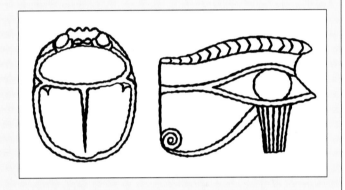

4.7 A scarab.　　　　**4.8** A *wedjat* (the eye of Horus).

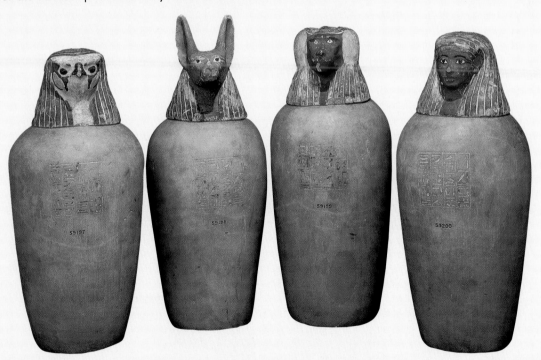

4.9 Canopic jars of Neshkons. British Museum, London.

Funerary Texts

Funerary texts written on tomb walls, coffins, and papyrus reveal the Egyptian use of words as magic to protect the deceased. These texts contain spells designed to preserve the dead person's name and pleas for his well-being in the afterlife. They recount his virtues, attest to his good character, and invoke the protection of his body from harmful creatures such as snakes and scorpions. Over seven hundred different formulae have been identified, but no single tomb contains a complete set of the texts. At first, Pyramid Texts were confined to the pyramids of the Pharaohs, but around the twentieth century B.C. they begin to appear on non-royal coffins, which may be evidence of a relaxation of royal prerogatives.

The Pyramid Text quoted below, known as *Utterance 407*, is from the east wall of the antechamber of the pyramid of Teti (Sixth Dynasty) at Saqqara. It describes the king joining the sun god Re after death, and refers to the Opening of the Mouth ritual (see p. 100), followed by the assertion that he will become a judge in the afterlife:

> Teti has purified himself:
> May he take his pure seat in the sky!
> Teti endures:
> May his beautiful seats endure!
> Teti will take his pure seat in the bow of Re's bark:
> The sailors who row Re, they shall row Teti!
> The sailors who convey Re about lightland,
> They shall convey Teti about lightland!
> Teti's mouth has been parted,
> Teti's nose has been opened,
> Teti's ears are unstopped.
> Teti will decide matters,
> Will judge between two,
> Teti will command one greater than he!
> Re will purify Teti,
> Re will guard Teti from all evil![3]

During the Middle Kingdom, the wooden coffins of commoners were inscribed with Coffin Texts, which included myths and funerary incantations. Also from this period are the earliest known maps—called the *Book of Two Ways*—designed to help the dead find their way in the perilous transition from life to afterlife, the journey through the underworld. They were also guided by the *Book of the Dead*, the modern name for the compilations of religious and magical texts found in numerous burials, which the ancient Egyptians called the *Chapter of Coming-forth by Day*. The title refers to the ability of the deceased to leave their tombs. Although no complete copy of this book exists, numerous extracts have survived.

From Hatshepsut's reign on, the *Book of the Dead* was written on papyrus. More expensive texts were illustrated with colored chapter headings. The example in figure **4.10** has a blank space for the name of the deceased, to be filled in after purchase, implying that it was not a custom-made commission. It depicts the *Judgment Hall of Osiris*, in which the entire life of the deceased is judged by a tribunal of forty-two assessor deities (shown in two rows above the weighing scene). Anubis (the jackal-headed god) and Horus (the falcon-headed god) operate the scale. The heart of the deceased, contained in a small canopic jar on the left scale, is weighed against Maat, the goddess of truth and right. Thoth (the ibis-headed scribe of the gods) holds a palette and reed for recording the results. The deceased stands at the far right, raising his arms in triumph. The larger figure to the left is Osiris himself, presiding over the tribunal. In front of Osiris is a table laden with food and other offerings. The monster Amemet, part lion and part hippopotamus, sits on the second table, waiting to devour the hearts of those found wanting.

4.10 Scene from a *Book of the Dead*, 4th century B.C. or later. Papyrus, 10.2 in (26 cm) high. British Museum, London.

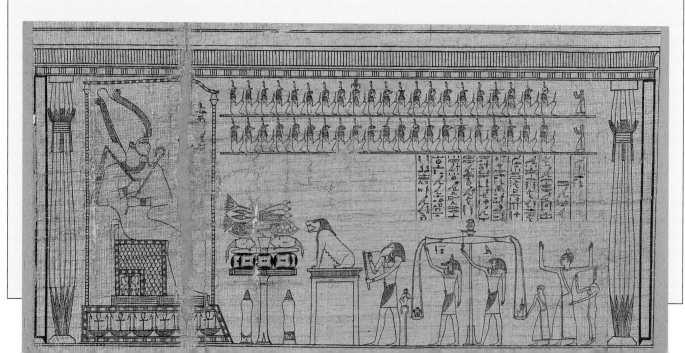

Pyramids

The most monumental expression of the Egyptian pharaoh's power was the pyramid, his burial place and zone of passage into the afterlife. Pyramids were preceded by smaller structures called **mastabas**, from the Arabic word for "bench" (fig. **4.11**). These were originally made of mud-brick, and later were faced with cut stones. A mastaba is a single-story trapezoidal structure containing a vertical shaft leading to an underground burial chamber where the dead body lay in a **sarcophagus** (from the Greek *sarcos*, meaning "flesh," and *phagein*, "to eat"). Another room (the *serdab*), located at ground level, contained the *ka* statue of the deceased. Adjoining this was an additional room for receiving mourners with offerings. Eventually, the number of underground chambers was increased in some mastabas to accommodate burials of entire families.

Around 2600 B.C., King Zoser's architect Imhotep constructed a colossal structure within a sacred architectural precinct at Saqqara, on the west bank of the Nile about 30 miles (48 km) south of Cairo. To the basic mastaba Imhotep added five more mastaba forms of decreasing size, one on top of the other, resulting in a "step pyramid" (fig. **4.12**). Inside, a vertical shaft some 90 feet (27.4 m) long led to the burial chamber. The exterior was faced with limestone, most of which has now disappeared. The purpose of Zoser's building complex was to function as a vast architectural "stage set"—some of the buildings were only façades backed with rubble—to serve him in the afterlife.

Later on, the site was maintained as a cult center for both Zoser and Imhotep. In contrast to Mesopotamia, where it is the name of the royal patron that has lasted, at Saqqara it was the architect who received credit for the conception and execution of the building.

The next major development in pyramid design was the purely geometric pyramid, an evolution of Imhotep's stepped pyramid. Four triangular sides slant inwards from a square base so that the apexes of each triangle meet over the center of the square. Originally, the sides were smooth

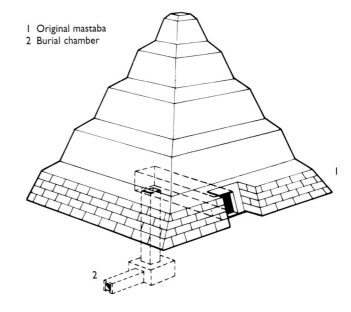

1 Original mastaba
2 Burial chamber

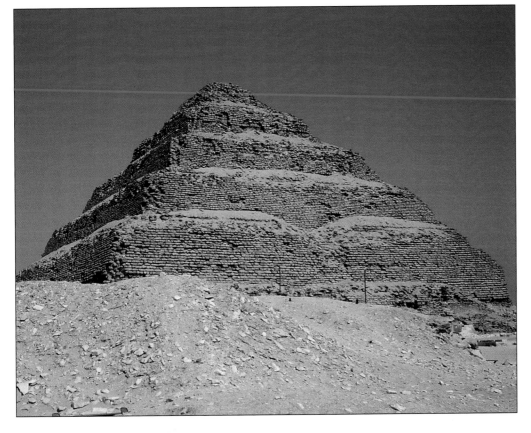

4.11 The step pyramid with a mastaba base.

4.12 Step pyramid, funerary complex of King Zoser, Saqqara, Egypt, c. 2750 B.C. Limestone, 200 ft (61 m) high. Its architect, Imhotep, was a priest at Heliopolis and is reputed to have been the first Egyptian to build monumental stone structures. His name is inscribed inside the pyramid, where he is designated "First after the King of Upper and Lower Egypt." He became a legendary figure in ancient Egypt, revered for his wisdom as a magician, astronomer, and healer, and was worshiped as a god.

and faced with polished limestone. A capstone, probably gilded, reflected the sun and signified the pharaoh's divine solar identification. Surveying techniques made it possible to orient the four corners of the plan precisely to the cardinal points of the compass. The purpose of this was to align the pyramids with significant positions of the sun.

Of the eighty-odd pyramids known to exist, the three outstanding examples were built by, and for, three Old Kingdom pharaohs of the Fourth Dynasty: the pyramid of Khufu (the largest, known as the Great Pyramid); the pyramid of his son Khafre, 22 feet (6.6 m) shorter and 15 percent smaller in volume; and the pyramid of Khafre's son Menkaure, only 10 percent of the size of Khufu's (fig. **4.13**). All three are near Cairo at Giza, on the west bank of the Nile, facing the direction of sunset (symbolizing death), as was customary for Old Kingdom burial sites. Across the river to the northeast was Heliopolis (from the Greek *helios*, meaning "sun," and *polis*, or "city"), the center of the cult associated with the sun god Ra.

Although the Giza monuments have been surrounded by desert since antiquity, recent archaeological excavations suggest that the site was once a river harbor. Each of

4.13 Pyramids at Giza, Egypt, c. 2500–2475 B.C. Limestone: pyramid of Khufu approx. 480 ft (146 m) high; base of each side 755 ft (230 m) long. The Giza pyramids were built for three Old Kingdom pharaohs of the 4th Dynasty, Khufu (c. 2500 B.C.), Khafre (c. 2490 B.C.), and Menkaure (c. 2475 B.C.). Khufu's pyramid—the largest of the three—was over twice as high as Zoser's step pyramid at Saqqara.

the pyramids was connected by a causeway (or elevated road) to its own valley temple at the edge of the original flood plain of the Nile. Upon the death of the king, his body was transported across the Nile by boat to the valley temple. It was then carried along the causeway to its own funerary temple, where it was presented with offerings of food and drink, and the Opening of the Mouth ceremony was performed (see p. 100).

The pyramid was intended primarily as a resting place for the king's body, and burial chambers were constructed either in the rock under the pyramid or in the pyramid itself. In Khufu's case (fig. **4.14**), the burial chamber is in the middle of the pyramid, slightly less than halfway between the ground and the top. It is reached by a sloping passageway which runs into the Grand Gallery, an enormous foyer 153 feet long and 28 feet high (46.5 × 8.5 m) with a **corbelled** roof. The King's Chamber measures 34 by 17 feet (10.33 × 5.16 m), and its roof is composed of nine slabs of granite weighing 400 tons. The granite sarcophagus containing the body of Khufu was so large that it could not have been moved through the passages of the pyramid. Instead, it was placed in the chamber and the pyramid was built around it.

In addition to the king's chamber, there were smaller chambers, possibly for the body of the queen, the organs of the deceased, and worldly goods for the journey to the afterlife. The chambers were connected by a maze of passages, including dead-end passages designed to foil grave robbers. In this latter objective the builders failed; during

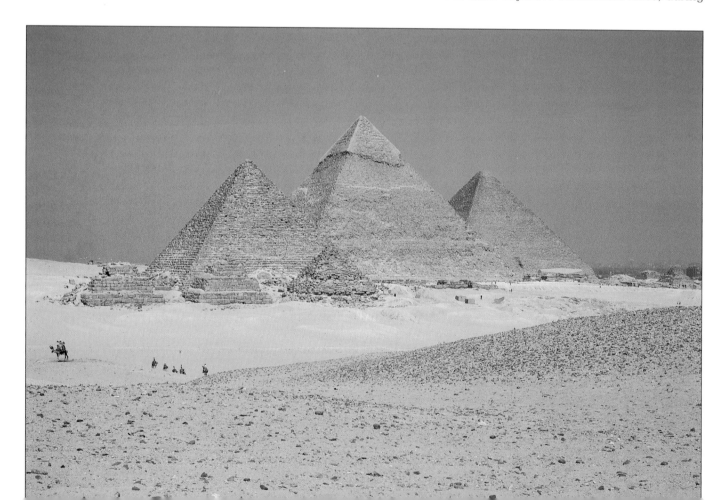

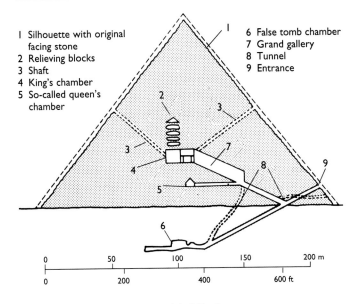

1 Silhouette with original
   facing stone
2 Relieving blocks
3 Shaft
4 King's chamber
5 So-called queen's
   chamber

6 False tomb chamber
7 Grand gallery
8 Tunnel
9 Entrance

4.14 Cross-section of the pyramid of Khufu.

the Middle Kingdom a succession of thieves penetrated the pyramids at Giza and plundered them.

Construction of the pyramids was a considerable feat of engineering and organization (see Box). The fifth-century-B.C. Greek historian Herodotos (c. 484–430 B.C.), who traveled to Egypt and questioned the priests at Heliopolis, reported that the laborers "worked in gangs of a hundred thousand men, each gang for three months"[4] (*History,* II, 124). Modern scholars have theorized that frequently two or three pyramids were under construction during the reign of the same pharaoh, more than one for himself plus one for his dead predecessor, and that, during the Fourth Dynasty at least, pyramid construction was a more or less continuous process. Some of the workers were probably seasonal—for example, peasants during the flooding of the Nile—but there would also have been a core of full-time, highly skilled masons and other craftsmen. Housing for 4000 workers has been excavated near the pyramid of Khafre.

Construction of the Pyramids

The pyramid of Khufu, the largest of the Giza pyramids, contains an estimated 2,300,000 blocks of stone weighing a total of 6,500,000 tons. Its square base has sides of 755 feet (230 m), and occupies more than 13 acres (the equivalent of ten New York City blocks). The original height (before deterioration) was 480 feet (146 m), equivalent to a forty-story modern building.

The Giza pyramids consisted of three main types of stone: a core of local limestone; blocks of the same stone more precisely cut; and blocks of white limestone, used for facing, which were quarried further up the Nile and carried to the site by boat. The quarrying of the stones must have been done with copper tools or by inserting wooden wedges into the limestone and then wetting them so that they expanded and cracked the stone along horizontal and vertical planes (fig. **4.15**). Granite, which was used in the king's burial chamber and for the capstone, could not be cut by these methods. It was probably heated by fires laid along straight lines and then suddenly cooled with water to produce cracks.

To transport blocks to the site, Egyptians used sledges pulled by hand over sand wetted to make it less resistant.

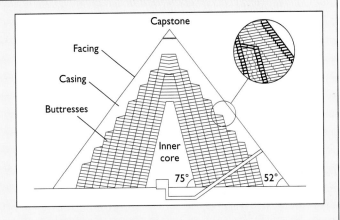

4.16 Cross-section of a pyramid.

The magnitude of this task can be judged from the weight of the stones: although their average weight was 2½ tons, the granite slabs weighed up to 50 tons each.

Construction methods changed over time, but the Giza pyramids appear to have been built according to a standard system (fig. **4.16**). The inner core was buttressed by a series of masonry walls built at an angle of 75 degrees and decreasing in height toward the outside of the pyramid. Both the casing stones and the facing stones, instead of being perfectly horizontal, were inclined slightly inward to reduce the risk of falling masonry. It is believed that, as a pyramid grew in height, a single access ramp was built around it, and the blocks were hauled up by manpower (as illustrated in reliefs on nearby temple walls). Once the capstone was in place, the facing stones (their outer surface cut at an angle of 52 degrees) were set, starting at the top and working downward, and the access ramp was dismantled.

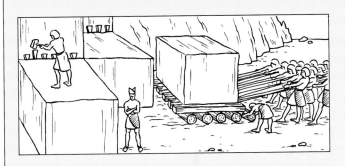

4.15 Stone quarries.

4.17 Plan of the Giza funerary complex.

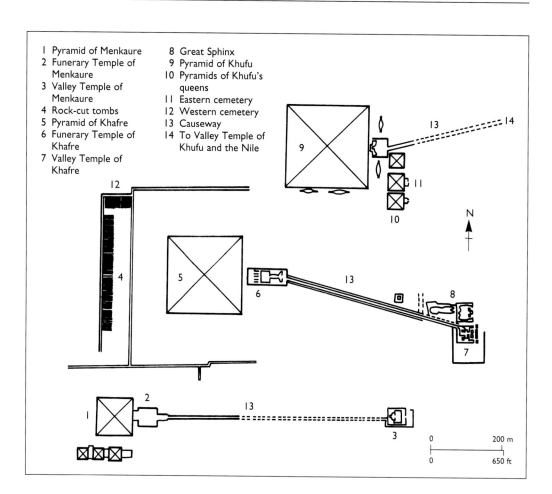

1	Pyramid of Menkaure	8	Great Sphinx
2	Funerary Temple of Menkaure	9	Pyramid of Khufu
3	Valley Temple of Menkaure	10	Pyramids of Khufu's queens
4	Rock-cut tombs	11	Eastern cemetery
5	Pyramid of Khafre	12	Western cemetery
6	Funerary Temple of Khafre	13	Causeway
7	Valley Temple of Khafre	14	To Valley Temple of Khufu and the Nile

4.18 Colossal statue of Khafre, known as the Great Sphinx, Giza, c. 2500 B.C. Sandstone, 66 ft (20.12 m) high, 240 ft (73.15 m) long. In Egypt, as elsewhere in the Near East, lions guarded entrances, especially to temples and palaces. Lions were particularly appropriate as guardians because they were thought to be watchful and to sleep with their eyes open. They were also associated with the sun as the eye of heaven.

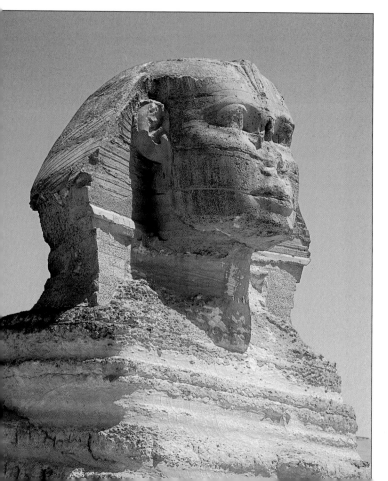

The pyramids at Giza were part of a vast funerary complex (fig. **4.17**) that included temples, chapels for offerings and ceremonies, mastabas for noble families, and causeways linking the structures. From the pyramid of Khafre, a processional road led to his valley temple guarded by the Great **Sphinx** (fig. **4.18**), a colossal human-headed creature with a lion's body carved out of the rock. The location of the sphinx suggests that it represented Khafre himself. It also faces the rising sun, which reinforces its association with the pharaoh. Surrounding the sphinx's head is the trapezoidal pharaonic headcloth (the *Nemes* headdress) that fills up the naturally open space above the shoulders and enhances the sculpture's monumentality.

Sculpture

Nearly all the Egyptian sculpture that has been preserved was originally created for tombs or temples. Egyptian artists followed certain conventions both for sculptures in the round and in relief. The more important the personage represented, the more rigorously the conventions were observed.

An over-lifesized diorite statue of Khafre (fig. **4.20**) illustrates the conventional representation of a seated pharaoh. Khafre sits in an erect, regal posture, both hands on his lap, his right fist clenched and his left hand lying flat above his knee. The sculptor began with a rectangular

The Egyptian Canon of Proportion

Canons of proportion are commonly accepted guidelines for depicting the ideal human figure by specifying the relationships of the parts of the body to one another and to the whole. They vary from culture to culture and have evolved over time. The canons followed by Egyptian artists changed only slightly from the Old to the New Kingdom, a reflection of the unusual stability of ancient Egypt. The illustration here is based on the Old Kingdom canon as it was used at Saqqara during the reign of Zoser (fig. **4.19**).

The surface for the relief or painting is divided into a grid of squares, each equivalent to the width of the figure's fist. The distance from the hairline to the ground is eighteen fists, from the base of the nose to the shoulder one fist, and from the fingers of a clenched fist to the elbow 4½ fists. The length of a foot (heel to toe) is 3½ fists.

Note the characteristic way of depicting the human body: the shoulders and the one visible eye are frontal; the head, arms, and legs are shown in profile, while the waist is nearly in profile but is turned sufficiently to show the navel. One purpose of this system was to arrive at a conventional, instantly recognizable image. The persistence of such canons contributed to the continuity of Egyptian style over a two-thousand-year period.

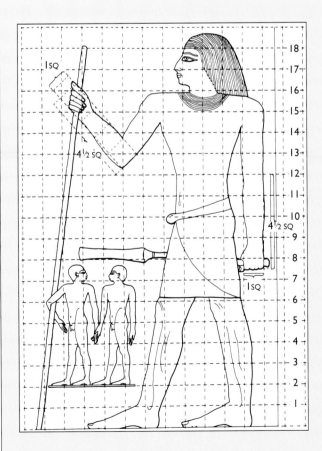

4.19 Egyptian canon of proportion.

block of stone to which the planes of the figure still conform. Khafre's throne and its base comprise a stepped arrangement with two verticals (corresponding to the king's torso, upper arms, and calves) meeting three horizontals (his forearms, thighs, and feet) at right angles. Spaces between body and throne are eliminated because the original diorite remains, serving to unify the king and his throne. The symbolic identification of king and throne is thus formally enhanced by the sculptors of this period.

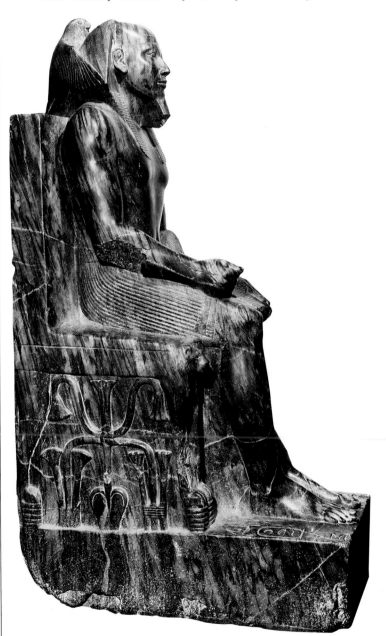

4.20 Seated statue of Khafre, from Giza, c. 2500 B.C. Diorite, 5 ft 6 in (1.68 m) high. Egyptian Museum, Cairo. The standing lions carved on Khafre's throne are the king's guardians, and images of regal power in their own right. Horus, who protects the back of Khafre's head, was the son of Isis, a mother goddess called the "Pharaoh's throne." Both gods reinforce Khafre's divine right of kingship. The association of a ruler and his throne is reflected in modern usage when we refer to the "seat of power."

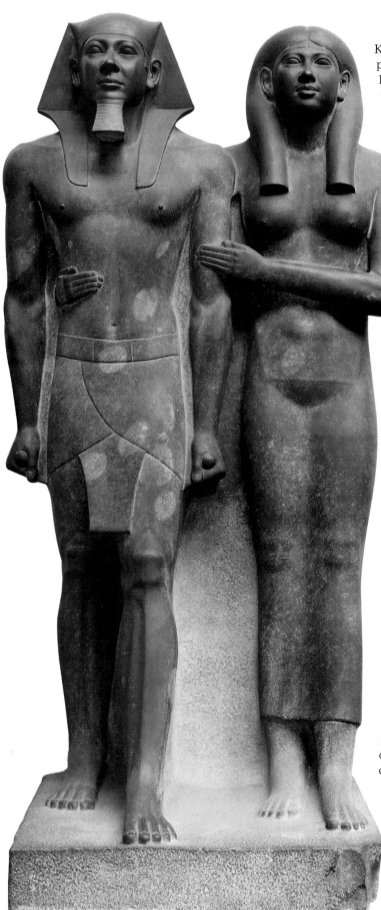

A good example of standing figures from the Old Kingdom is the statue of Khafre's son Menkaure (whose pyramid at Giza is illustrated in figure 4.13) and Queen Khamerernebty (fig. **4.21**). The artist began with an upright rectangular block, which remains visible in the base, between the figures, and at the back. Menkaure is portrayed frontally and stands as if at attention, arms at his sides and fists clenched. His left leg extends forward in an assertive stance signifying his power. The trapezoidal *Nemes* headdress closes up the space around the head as in the sphinx at Giza. Both the knee cap and the ceremonial beard are rectangular, echoing the form of the original block.

A comparison of the representations of Menkaure and Khamerernebty illustrates certain conventional differences between males and females in Egyptian art. Within the rigorously social hierarchy of ancient Egypt, a queen was below a king in rank, a position indicated not only by her slightly smaller size but by her stance. Her left foot does not extend as far forward as her husband's, nor are her arms as rigidly positioned as his. In addition, her arms are bent, the right one reaching around the king's waist and the left one bent at the elbow and holding the king's left arm. The openness of her hands lacks the tension of the king's clenched fists. Her drapery, in contrast to Menkaure's, outlines the form of her body and, like her wig, is more curvilinear. The less imposing, more naturalistic, and less formal portrayal of the queen in comparison with the king is a function of her lower rank.

The statues of Khafre and of Menkaure and Khamerernebty were originally found in their valley temples, and were part of a series of similar figures. Their function was to embody the *ka* of the royal personages they depicted and to receive food and drink brought by worshipers. Priests were believed to have the magic power to transform the images into real people who could eat the offerings.

The sculptures of Prince Rahotep and his wife Nofret (fig. **4.22**) also exhibit distinctions between representations of male and female. Princess Nofret is fully clothed and her right hand lies flat, protruding from her garment. Her husband wears only a lower garment and both fists are clenched. Since the soft limestone from which these figures are carved is porous, their original paint has been preserved. This fortunate circumstance reveals the elaborate jewelry worn by aristocratic Egyptian women and the stylized eye outlines also current in Mesopotamian art. The difference in Rahotep's brown skin tone and Nofret's, which is yellow ocher, is a convention of Egyptian painting and painted sculpture.

4.21 Menkaure and Queen Khamerernebty, from Giza, 2548–2530 B.C. Slate, 4 ft 6½ in (1.39 m) high. Courtesy, Museum of Fine Arts, Boston.

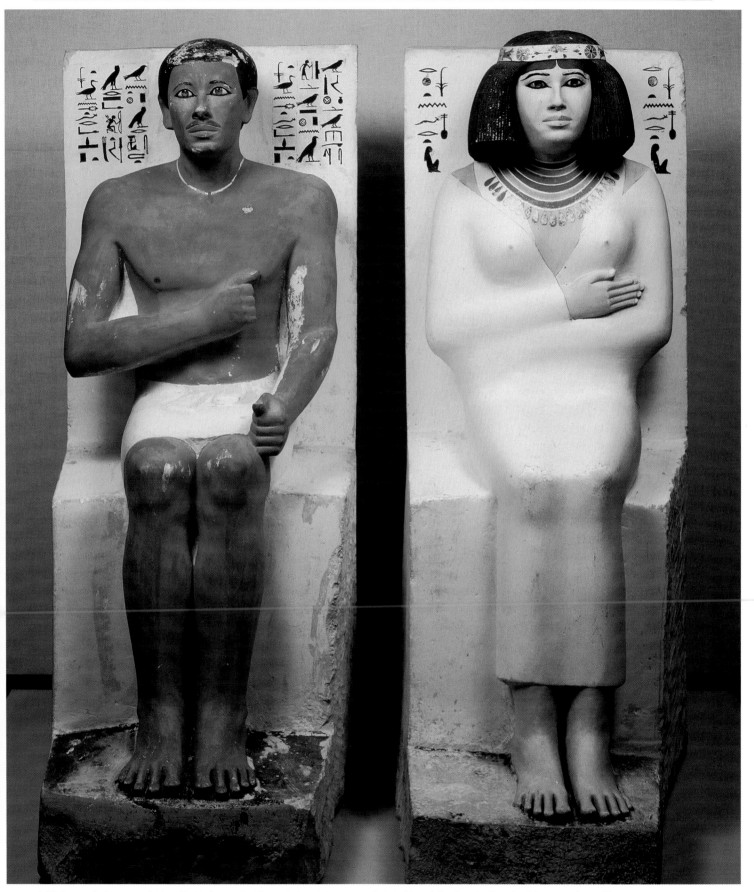

4.22 Prince Rahotep and his wife Nofret, c. 2610 B.C. Painted limestone, 3 ft 11¼ in (1.2 m) high. Egyptian Museum, Cairo. The eyes are inlaid with rock crystal; facial features and Nofret's headband and necklace are painted.

Papyrus Manuscripts

The Egyptians wrote on stone, bronze, dressed leather, **vellum**, wooden boards coated with **gesso**, and *ostraka* (pieces of broken pottery). Their most important writing surface, however, was made from the papyrus plant, which grew in the marshes along the Nile. (Today papyrus does not grow north of Khartoum.)

Papyrus stems were cut into lengths of about 12 inches (30 cm). The rind was peeled off and the pith cut lengthwise into thin slices. One layer of slices was laid side by side with a second layer on top of it at right angles. The two layers were bonded together by pressing, with no adhesive other than the natural starch of the papyrus. Once dry, the resulting smooth and light-colored surface was polished with a wood or stone tool.

The maximum size of papyrus sheets was about 19 inches in height and 17 inches in width (48 × 43 cm). They could be joined together at the edges (with the fibers running in the same direction) and then rolled up for future use, keeping the horizontal fibers on the inside. Some papyri as long as 130 feet (40 m) have survived. Scribes used the side with the horizontal fibers first, holding the papyrus in their left hand and unrolling it as they went. They wrote in either vertical columns or horizontal rows. For shorter texts sheets were cut into halves or quarters. These papyrus documents are manuscripts, i.e. written by hand (from the Latin *scriptum* and *manus*).

Pigments for writing texts were solid tablets made of carbon (black) or of ground ocher (red) mixed with gum. They were dissolved as the scribe wet his brushes and rubbed them over the tablet's surface—much as watercolor paint is used today. Brushes were made from the trimmed stems of other marsh plants. Bristles to hold a supply of wet pigment were made by chewing one end of their stems to separate the fibers. During the Late Period, pens were also used; these were made from reeds cut to a point and split in two at the tip.

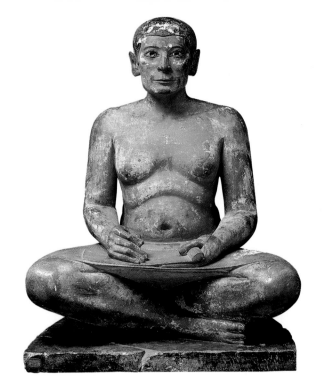

4.23 Seated scribe, from Saqqara, c. 2400 B.C. Limestone, 21 in (53.3 cm) high. Louvre, Paris. The scribe retains his original paint, which makes his eyes seem lifelike. In ancient Egypt scribes were among the most educated people, having to study law, mathematics, and religion, as well as reading and writing.

The Middle Kingdom (c. 1991–1700 B.C.)

Monumental architecture continued in the Middle Kingdom, though much of it was destroyed by New Kingdom pharaohs for use in their own colossal building projects. Besides pharaohs' pyramids, a new form of tomb was introduced. This was rock-cut architecture, in which the sides of cliffs were excavated to create artificial cave-chambers. Rock-cut tombs became popular with aristocrats and high-level bureaucrats in the Eleventh and Twelfth Dynasties, and then, in the New Kingdom, with the rulers themselves.

Middle Kingdom sculpture is often somewhat more naturalistic, and royal figures less imposing than in the Old Kingdom. Forms tend to be more rounded and faces show occasional hints of an expression. Although the graceful seated statue of Lady Senuwy (figs. **4.24** and **4.25**) retains the closed space between arms and body, and lower legs and seat, associated with statues of Old Kingdom pharaohs, there is a narrow space behind the figure that emphasizes the gradual curve of the wig and back. Compared with the statue of Nofret (fig. 4.22), Lady Senuwy is slim and her features more delicate. Hers is one of the finest and most elegant large-scale statues from the Middle Kingdom.

The political turbulence and invasions of the First Intermediate Period that preceded the Middle Kingdom disrupted confidence in the pharaoh's absolute divine power. Although pharaonic rule quickly reasserted itself, certain works of art reflect a new national mood. This can be seen by comparing two well-preserved wooden statuettes of Sesostris I (figs. **4.26** and **4.27**) with the

Compared with the sculptures of Khafre and Rahotep, the seated scribe (fig. **4.23**) is less monumental, though no less impressive. He sits cross-legged, in the pose that is conventional for scribes. A papyrus scroll (see Box) extends across his lap, and his right hand is poised to write. In contrast to statues of pharaohs and nobles, the lower rank of the scribe allows the sculptor to reflect his relatively individual character. Furthermore the sculptor has cut away the limestone between the arms and body as well as around the head and neck, thereby reducing the monumentality of this statue as compared with that of Khafre. The depiction of the scribe is also more personalized than that of either Khafre or Rahotep—he has a roll of fat around his torso, a pot belly, and sagging breasts. This particular scribe must have been of high status, because he had his own tomb.

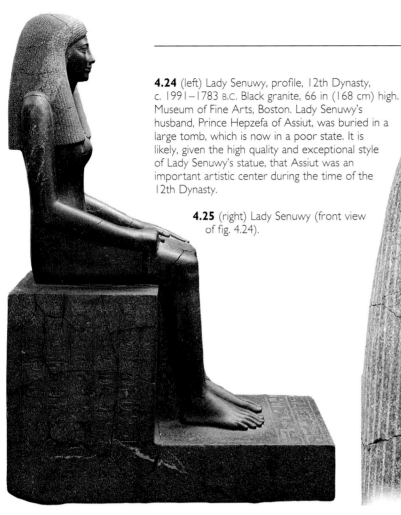

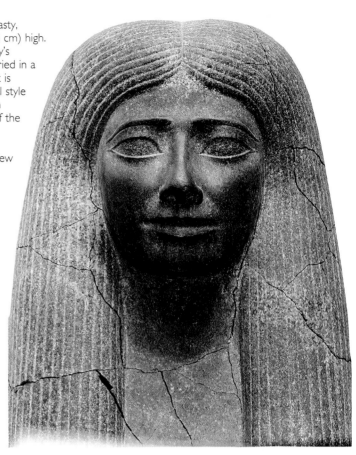

4.24 (left) Lady Senuwy, profile, 12th Dynasty, c. 1991–1783 B.C. Black granite, 66 in (168 cm) high. Museum of Fine Arts, Boston. Lady Senuwy's husband, Prince Hepzefa of Assiut, was buried in a large tomb, which is now in a poor state. It is likely, given the high quality and exceptional style of Lady Senuwy's statue, that Assiut was an important artistic center during the time of the 12th Dynasty.

4.25 (right) Lady Senuwy (front view of fig. 4.24).

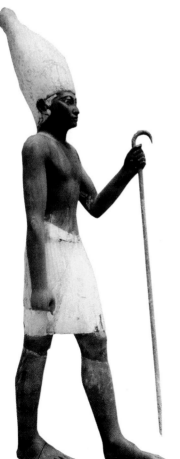

4.26 Sesostris I, from Lisht, 12th Dynasty. Wood. Egyptian Museum, Cairo.

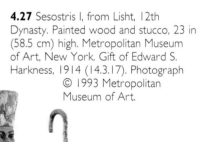

4.27 Sesostris I, from Lisht, 12th Dynasty. Painted wood and stucco, 23 in (58.5 cm) high. Metropolitan Museum of Art, New York. Gift of Edward S. Harkness, 1914 (14.3.17). Photograph © 1993 Metropolitan Museum of Art.

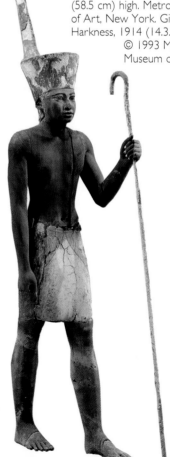

fragmentary portrait of Sesostris III (fig. **4.28**). The figure of Sesostris I on the left wears the conical white crown of Upper Egypt (the *hedjet*) and the other figure, the red crown of Lower Egypt (the *deshret*). Because these are made of wood, they are entirely carved in the round. Nevertheless, they are slimmer and less imposing than the Old Kingdom images of Khafre (see fig. 4.20) and Menkaure (see fig. 4.21).

The portrait of Sesostris III is one of the best examples of the new approach to royal representation in the Middle Kingdom. Sesostris III referred to himself as the shepherd of his people, and his portrait seems to show concern. There are bags under his eyes, and his cheeks are fleshy. Lines of worry crease the surface of his face, and his forehead forms into a slight frown. This is no longer solely an image of divine, royal power.

Instead, by departing from earlier conventions of royal representation, a specific personality emerges.

The coffin in figure **4.29** illustrates some of the textural qualities of Middle Kingdom painting. The detailed, occasionally illusionistic patterns were drawn by an artist with a fine linear sensibility. Slight shading creates a tactile quality enhanced by the grain of the cedar surface. The eyes are those of Horus, and are framed above the painted "false door" of the coffin over which they watch. The "door" itself allowed the *ka* to leave and re-enter the coffin at will.

4.28 (left) Sesostris III, c. 1850 B.C. Quartzite, 6½ in (16.5 cm) high. Metropolitan Museum of Art, New York. Gift of Edward S. Harkness, 1926.

4.29 (below) Painted coffin of Djehuty-nekht, from Bersheh, 12th Dynasty, c. 1991–1783 B.C. Cedar. Museum of Fine Arts, Boston.

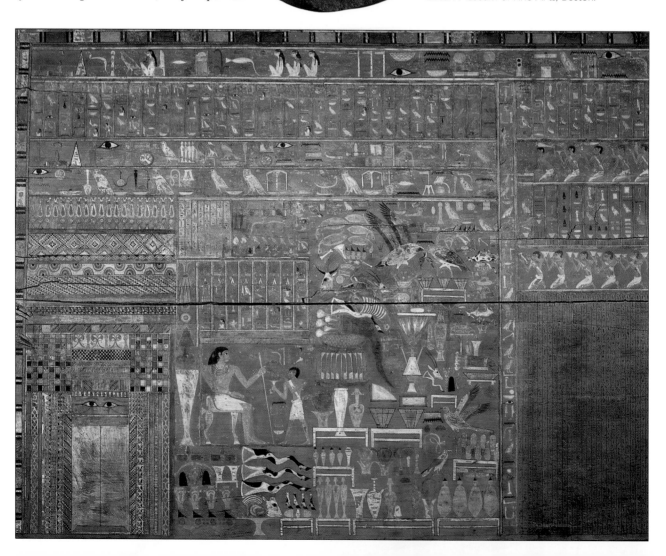

The New Kingdom

(c. 1550–1070 B.C.)

After the instability of the Second Intermediate Period, during which the so-called Hyksos invasion occurred, Egypt once again recovered its political equilibrium. The pharaohs of the New Kingdom re-established control of the entire country and reasserted their power.

Temples

As durable and impressive as the tombs, Egyptian temples provided another way of establishing the worshiper's relationship with the gods. The first known Egyptian temples in the Neolithic period were in the form of huts preceded by a forecourt. From the time of Menes at the beginning of the dynastic period, a courtyard, hallway, and inner sanctuary were added. The columned hallway, called a

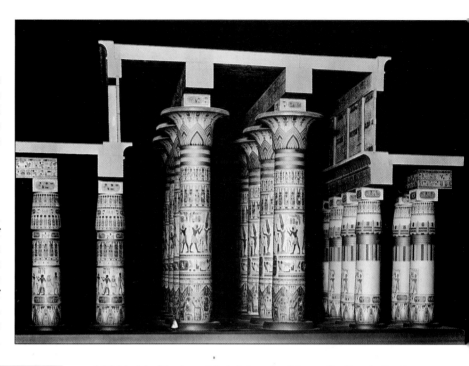

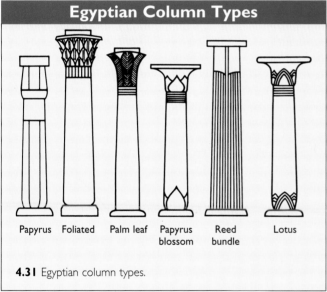

Egyptian Column Types

Papyrus | Foliated | Palm leaf | Papyrus blossom | Reed bundle | Lotus

4.31 Egyptian column types.

4.30 Model of the hypostyle hall, temple of Amon-Ra, Karnak, Egypt, c. 1290 B.C. Metropolitan Museum of Art, New York. Bequest of Levi Hale Willard, 1890. The central hypostyle columns have capitals that seem to grow upward and curve outward from the shaft like the lotus blossom. The shafts were covered with painted low-relief scenes and hieroglyphs. Their enormous scale is hard to imagine from a photograph, but the base of each column would reach to the waist of an adult of average height. The side columns are papyrus.

hypostyle (from the Greek *hupo*, meaning "under," and *stulos*, "pillar"), is shown in its fully developed New Kingdom form in figure **4.30**. It was constructed in the post-and-lintel system of elevation and had two rows of tall central columns flanked by rows of shorter columns on either side (see Box).

The standard Egyptian temple, called a **pylon** temple after the two massive sloping towers (pylons) flanking the entrance, was designed symmetrically along a single axis. The plan in figure **4.32** is typical, showing the spaces through which worshipers moved from the bright out-

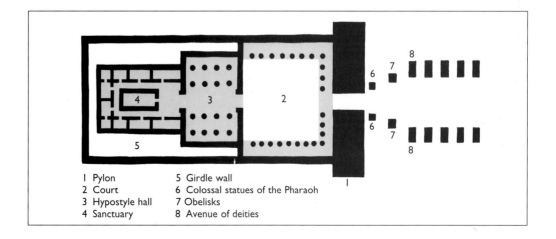

1 Pylon	5 Girdle wall
2 Court	6 Colossal statues of the Pharaoh
3 Hypostyle hall	7 Obelisks
4 Sanctuary	8 Avenue of deities

4.32 Plan of a typical pylon temple.

doors to the dark inner sanctuary. When they arrived at the entrance, they confronted two rows of gods in animal form facing each other. At the end of the row were two **obelisks** (tall, tapering, four-sided pillars ending in a pointed tip called a **pyramidion**) and two colossal statues of pharaohs (fig. **4.33**).

From the courtyard, the worshiper entered the hypostyle hall, its massive columns casting shadows and creating an awe-inspiring atmosphere. The upper, or **clerestory**, windows let in small amounts of light that enhanced the effect of the shadows. Most people never entered the temples, but watched from the outside the pro-

cessions for which the temples were planned. The elite were allowed to enter the courtyards, while the priests carried the images of the gods in and out of the innermost sanctuaries in boat-shaped shrines called barks. The transitional quality of this architecture is carefully designed to evoke the feeling of a mysterious enclosure, a space implicitly inhabited by pharaohs and gods.

The New Kingdom temple of Amon-Mut-Khonsu at Luxor is dedicated to a triad of gods. This triad was worshiped at the New Kingdom capital city of Thebes and its importance steadily increased. The plan of the temple (fig. **4.34**) shows that the hut and courtyard of the Neolithic era had developed by this date into a much more elaborate structure. At the far end is the sanctuary—the "holy of holies"—a small central room with four columns shown at the far left of the plan. Many pharaohs contributed to the construction of this temple, each adding to its complexity. Later, Alexander the Great and the Romans made further additions.

Ancient Egyptian temples were considered microcosms of the universe, and as such they contained both earthly and celestial symbolism. Column designs were derived from the vegetation of Egypt and represented the earth. In the temple of Amon-Mut-Khonsu (fig. **4.35**), for example, the original ceiling was painted blue and decorated with birds and stars denoting its symbolic role as the heavenly realm.

It is clear from Egyptian temple architecture, as well as from the pyramids, that colossal size was important to the builders of ancient Egypt. The scale of these structures emphasized the enormous power of the gods and the pharaoh, and made ordinary worshipers feel insignificant by comparison. Similarly, the vast numbers of colossal columns were intended to create an overwhelming effect. There were many large statues of the pharaoh lining the temple courtyards, as there were rows of deities preceding the entrances. This insistence on repetition was designed to impress the worshipers with the king's power.

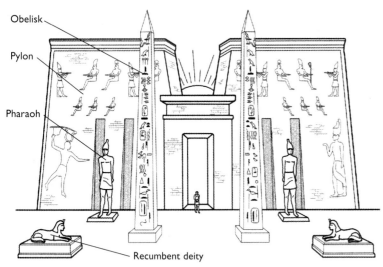

Obelisk
Pylon
Pharaoh
Recumbent deity

4.33 (above) Diagram of a pylon façade. The obelisks were derived from the sacred *benben*-stone worshiped as a manifestation of Amon at Heliopolis. At dawn, the rays of the rising sun caught the *benben*-stone before anything else, and the stone was thus believed to be the god's dwelling place. The obelisks flanking the pylon entrance were arranged in relation to positions of the sun and moon and, like the pyramids, were probably capped with gold.

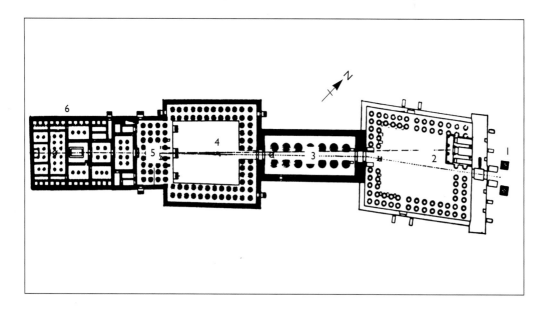

4.34 Plan of the temple of Amon-Mut-Khonsu, Luxor, Egypt, begun c. 1390 B.C. Reading the plan from right to left, number 1 refers to the pylons, flanking the entrance. From the entrance, one proceeded through three open-air colonnaded courtyards (2, 3, 4). Then the worshiper was plunged into the darkened and mysterious realm of the hypostyle hall (5), beyond which lay the sanctuary complex (6).

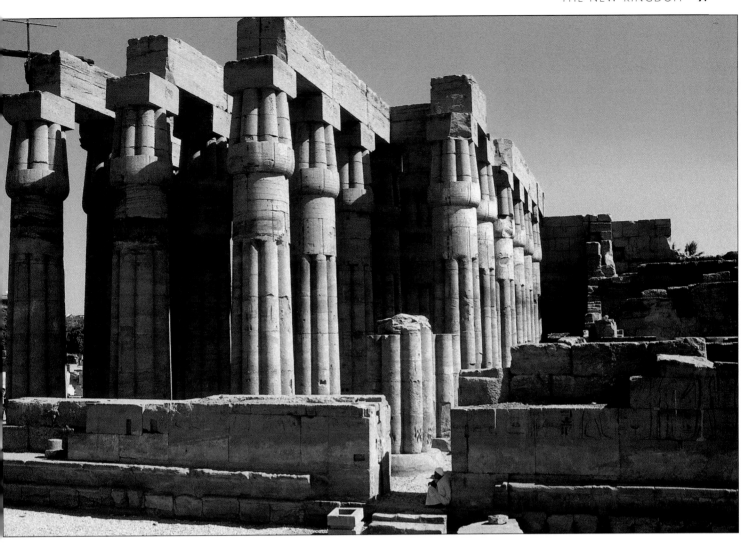

4.35 View of the hypostyle from the courtyard, temple of Amon-Mut-Khonsu, Luxor, begun c. 1390 B.C. Columns 30 ft (9 m) high. Here the capitals are constructed in the form of bundles of papyrus reeds.

Hatshepsut's Mortuary Temple and Sculpture Thutmose I (reigned c. 1504–1492 B.C.) was the first Egyptian pharaoh buried in a rock-cut tomb carved out of a cliff face in the Valley of the Kings, which is across the Nile from Luxor and Karnak.

The Eighteenth Dynasty is also notable for its female pharaoh, Hatshepsut (reigned c. 1479–1458 B.C). She was the wife and half-sister of Thutmose I's son, Thutmose II. When Thutmose II died, *his* son by a minor queen, Thutmose III, was under age. Around 1479 B.C. Hatshepsut became regent for her stepson/nephew, but exerted her right to succeed her father and was crowned King of Egypt in 1473 B.C. Although female rulers of Egypt were not unprecedented, Hatshepsut's assumption of specifically male aspects of her office—such as the title of king—was a departure from tradition. Despite her successor's attempts to obliterate her monuments, many of them survive to document her productive reign.

It is not known why Hatshepsut became king, nor why Thutmose III tolerated it. Hatshepsut's strong character and political acumen must have contributed to her suc-

cess. She claimed that her father had chosen her as king and she used the institution of co-regency to maintain her power without having to eliminate her rival. Above all, she selected her officials wisely, particularly Senenmut, who was her daughter's guardian, as well as her First Minister and Chief Architect.

Hatshepsut, like other pharaohs, assumed royal titles and iconography and had her own divine conception depicted in her temple reliefs. In keeping with the conventional scene, the compound god Amon-Ra was shown handing the *ankh* symbol (♀)hieroglyph for "life," to her mother Queen Ahmose. In this imagery, Hatshepsut proclaimed her divine right to rule Egypt as a king. She also referred to herself in texts as the female Horus, evoking the traditional parallel between a pharaoh and Horus. (Horus was the falcon-headed son of the underworld god Osiris, born after the murdered Osiris was brought back to life. Horus claimed kingship as the son of the dead Osiris. Likewise, when the Egyptian throne was handed down from father to son, it was seen as a symbolic transfer from Osiris to Horus.)

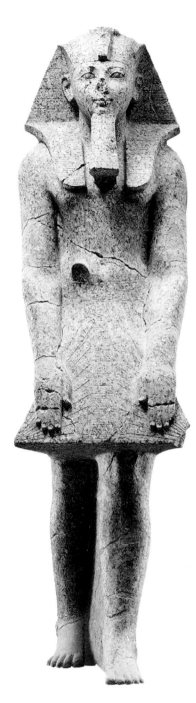

4.36 Granite statue of Hatshepsut as pharaoh, 18th Dynasty, c. 1473–1458 B.C. Granite, 7 ft 11 in (2.41 m) high. Metropolitan Museum of Art, New York. Hatshepsut was the second known queen who ruled Egypt as pharaoh. The earlier queen, Sobekneferu, ruled in the 12th Dynasty, but, unlike Hatshepsut, did not preside over an artistic revival.

4.37 Funerary temple of Queen Hatshepsut, Deir el-Bahri, Egypt, c. 1480 B.C. Sandstone and rock. Construction of this temple began in the reign of Thutmose I and continued during the reign of his daughter Hatshepsut. Most of the projecting colonnades have been restored after vandalism during the reign of Thutmose III. They adorn the three large terraces, which are connected to each other by ramps. The inner sanctuary is located inside the cliff.

Despite such acknowledgments of her gender, Hatshepsut chose to be represented as a man in many of her statues. The example in figure **4.36** depicts her in the traditional assertive pose of standing pharaohs, wearing a ceremonial headdress and beard. Instead of the clenched fists of Old Kingdom pharaohs such as Menkaure (see fig. **4.21**), Hatshepsut extends her arms forward and lays her hands flat on her trapezoidal garment.

The main architectural innovation of Hatshepsut's reign was the terraced mortuary temple at Deir el-Bahri (fig. **4.37**). The primary function of the Egyptian mortuary temple, which was usually constructed from a pylon plan, was twofold: first, to worship the king's patron deity during his lifetime, and, second, to worship the king himself after his death. The function of the Deir el-Bahri complex as a mortuary temple for both Hatshepsut and her father reinforced her image as his successor. At the same time, the major deities Amon, Hathor, and Anubis were worshiped in shrines within the temple complex. On the exterior, terraces with rectangular supports and polygonal columns blended impressively with the vast rocky site.

Hatshepsut's architect Senenmut was the main artistic force behind the temple and its decoration. His special status is reflected in the fact that his tomb, which was never completed, was begun inside the royal religious complex, and its unfinished ceiling was decorated with texts usually reserved for a pharaoh's burial. Senenmut's contribution to the artistic renewal under Hatshepsut is evident in a series of characteristic self-portraits. These show him kneeling in prayer to Amon and were located in the temple behind doors to the chapels and niches for stat-

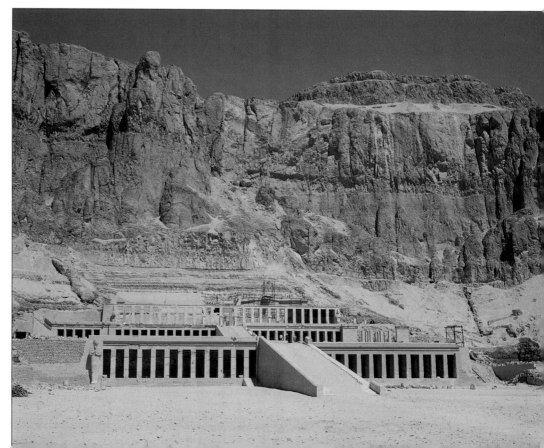

ues. When the doors were opened during religious rites, the figures of Senenmut became visible.

In the black granite statue in figure **4.38**, Senenmut holds his ward, the young princess Nefrura, daughter of Hatshepsut. The figures are frontal and, despite their rather iconic, even rigid poses, there is a suggestion of protectiveness in Senenmut's large hands enveloping his ward. Above all, however, this iconography, like Senenmut's self-portrait temple carvings, project an image of his power by depicting his close relationship with the pharaoh.

At the end of Hatshepsut's reign, Thutmose III, then in his late twenties, finally assumed sole power (c. 1458 B.C.). He demolished the images and cartouches of Hatshepsut and emphasized his own role as the successor of his father, Hatshepsut's brother/spouse Thutmose II. Whereas Hatshepsut's reign had been notable for diplomatic missions, Thutmose III became a great conqueror, gaining control of Nubia and invading the Near East. Reflecting his interest in foreign alliances were his marriages to three women with Syrian names.

Painting

Like sculpture and architecture, what survives of ancient Egyptian painting was used primarily in the service of the rulers and gods. Walls of Egyptian New Kingdom tombs and temples were covered with reliefs and paintings. Both provided the *ka* with familiar scenes from the earthly existence of the deceased. They also offer the modern viewer a wealth of information about life in ancient Egypt.

Fresco Most Egyptian wall paintings were **frescoes**, painted using the *fresco secco*, or dry fresco, technique. Pigments were mixed with water and applied to a dry plaster wall. As a result, the paintings were less durable than those made using the later *buon fresco*, or true fresco, technique (see p. 117). In *buon fresco*, pigments are applied to wet plaster with which they bond as it dries, preventing the flaking to which *fresco secco* is prone. Egyptians also used water-based paint on papyrus and on sculptures such as the scribe in figure 4.23.

A New Kingdom *fresco secco* from the tomb of Nebamun (fig. **4.39**) shows him enjoying a favorite sport, bird-hunting. He is accompanied by his wife and daughter

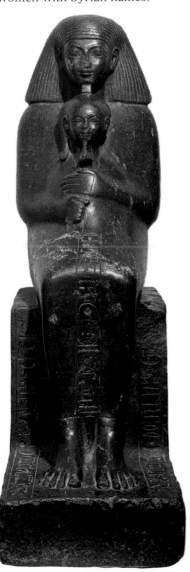

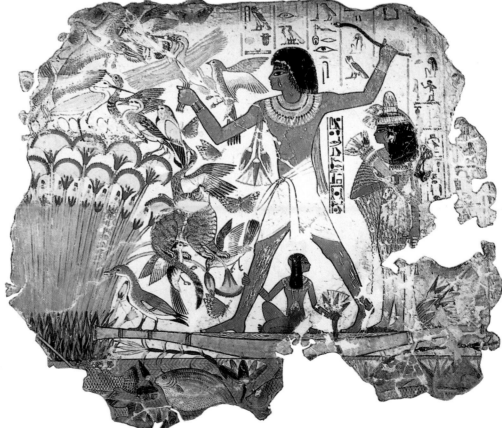

4.38 (left) Statue of Senenmut and Nefrura, 18th Dynasty, c. 1500–1480 B.C. Black granite, 24 in (60 cm) high. British Museum, London. The number of statues of Senenmut is exceptional for an official who was not a member of the royal family. The fate of Nefrura at the end of Hatshepsut's reign is not known.

4.39 (above) Nebamun hunting birds, from the tomb of Nebamun, Thebes, Egypt, c. 1400 B.C. Fragment of a *fresco secco*. British Museum, London.

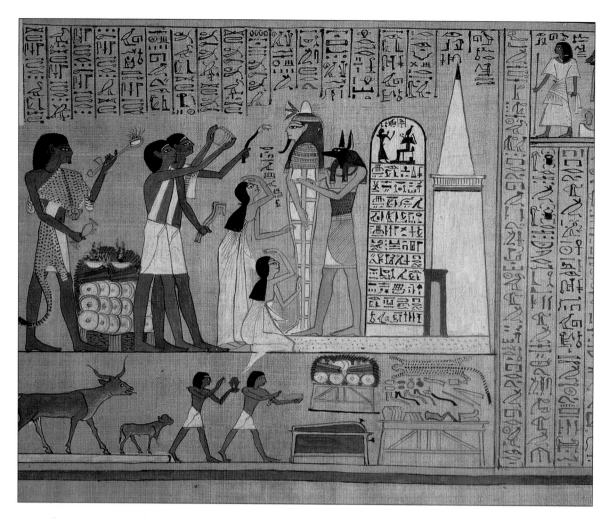

and surrounded by animals and landscape. Following the conventional Egyptian pose, his head and legs are in profile, and his torso and eye are frontal. He also wears a trapezoidal kilt. Nebamun's wife and daughter are small and curvilinear by comparison, continuing the Old Kingdom tradition of increasing naturalism for decreasing rank. Paintings of this period, however, were slightly more naturalistic than during the Old Kingdom. Note that Nebamun's wife is rendered with brown skin rather than with the conventional lighter skin of Egyptian women in art, as seen in the statues of Rahotep and Nofret (see fig. 4.22). The birds turn more freely in space than the human figures, and on the fish there is evidence of shading, which conveys a sense of volume.

Papyrus A New Kingdom painting on papyrus from the *Book of the Dead* (fig. **4.40**) illustrates the Opening of the Mouth ceremony, which ritually "opened the mouth" of the dead body and restored its ability to breathe, feel, hear, see, and speak. In this scene, described in the rows of hieroglyphics at the top, the ritual is performed on the Nineteenth Dynasty mummy of the scribe Hunefer. Reading the image from left to right, we see a priest in a leopard skin, an altar, and two priests in white garments with upraised ritual objects—a hook, a bull's leg, and a

4.40 Opening of the Mouth Ceremony, from the *Book of the Dead* of Hunefer, New Kingdom, 19th Dynasty, c. 1307–1196 B.C. Pigment on papyrus. British Museum, London.

knife. Two mourning women are directly in front of the upright mummy. Behind the mummy is Anubis, the jackal-headed mortuary god. The two forms behind him are a stele, covered with hieroglyphs and surmounted by a representation of Hunefer appearing before a god, and a stylized tomb façade with a pyramid on top. Note the similarity between the iconography of the power-revealing scene at the top of the stele and that on the Law Code of Hammurabi (see fig. 3.22). Both are images of *Machtkunst*, and signify communication between the god and a mortal. In both, the seated god combines a frontal and profile pose, while the smaller mortal—as if commanding less space—is more nearly in profile.

In spite of the remarkable social, political, and artistic continuity of ancient Egypt, it is clear from the fresco fragment in figure 4.39 and from Hunefer's papyrus that certain changes had occurred in the two thousand years between the beginning of the Old Kingdom and the New Kingdom. The most important cultural change, however, took place from around 1349 B.C., when a revolutionary pharaoh, Amenhotep IV, came to power.

The Amarna Period (c. 1349–1336 B.C.)

Generations of scholars have tried to answer the questions surrounding King Amenhotep IV, who challenged the entrenched religious cults and threatened the very existence of the established priesthood that had held power in Egypt for centuries. By the Fifth Dynasty, the sun god Ra had superseded Horus as the supreme deity. Ra's cult was introduced north of Cairo at Heliopolis, the city of the sunrise. By the Twelfth Dynasty, Amon had superseded Ra in this position, and then in the Eighteenth Dynasty, Amenhotep IV adopted a new, and unpopular, religious system that was relatively monotheistic.

His primary god was Aten, the sun disk, and Amenhotep accordingly changed his name to Akhenaten (meaning "servant of the Aten"). He effaced the names and images of the other gods. Presumably to escape the influence of the priests, he moved the capital down the Nile (i.e. north) from the major cult center of Thebes to Akhetaten (now known as Tell el-Amarna, from which the term for this period is derived). Akhenaten chose the site and name for his new capital because the sun rising over the horizon at that point resembled the hieroglyph for sunrise.

Nothing is known of the origin of his ideas, which greatly influenced artistic style during his reign. Statues of Akhenaten (fig. **4.41**) and his family differ dramatically from those of traditional pharaohs. He looks as if he had unusual, if not deformed, physical features. Here Akhenaten holds the crook and flail, which are attributes of Osiris and of Egyptian royalty. He wears the combined *hedjet* and *deshret* crowns of Upper and Lower Egypt. Carved into the surface of his body—by his right shoulder and at his waist—are his cartouches (see fig. 4.5).

Despite the traditional attributes of pharaonic power and the iconography of royalty, however, Akhenaten broke with artistic convention. Rather than always being represented as an assertive and dominating king identified with the gods, Akhenaten often shows himself as a priest of Aten. In the statue illustrated in figure 4.41, however, he is shown as a pharaoh, despite being elongated, thin, potbellied, and curvilinear. Although some scholars believe that Akhenaten suffered from acromegaly—a condition caused by an overactive pituitary gland, resulting in enlarged hands, feet, and face—others think these proportions reflect changes consistent with his religious and social innovations. More recent scholarship argues that the Amarna style reflects an exaggeration of Akhenaten's actual appearance. The entire royal family, and eventually others as well, were similarly represented.

The best-known sculpture from Akhenaten's reign is a painted limestone bust of his wife, Nefertiti (fig. **4.42**). The well-preserved paint adds to its naturalistic impression. This is enhanced by the organically modeled features, the sense that taut muscles lie beneath the surface of the neck, and the open space created by the long, elegant curves at the sides of the neck. Instead of wearing the queen's traditional headdress, Nefertiti has her hair pulled up into a tall crown, creating an elegant upward motion.

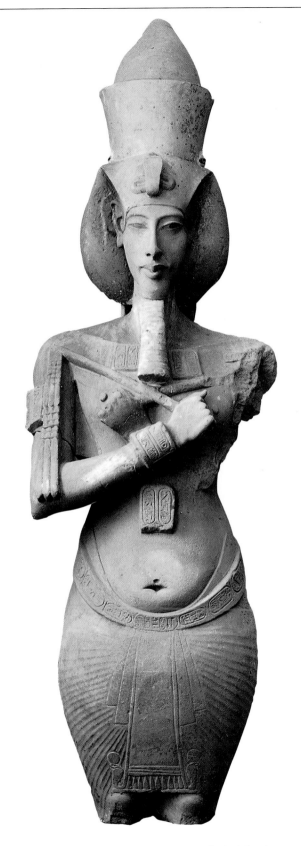

4.41 Akhenaten, from Karnak, Egypt, Amarna Period. Sandstone, approx. 13 ft (3.96 m) high. Egyptian Museum, Cairo. Akhenaten was the son of Amenhotep III and his principal wife Tiy. Amenhotep III ruled Egypt for thirty-eight years. During Tiy's lifetime, he married a Mittani (from Mesopotamia), two Babylonian princesses, and then made his own daughter his principal wife.

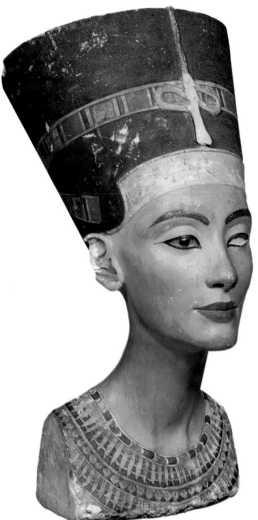

A small relief in which Akhenaten and Nefertiti play with their children illustrates some of the stylistic and iconographic changes under Akhenaten (fig. **4.43**). The king and queen are seated, and rendered with a naturalism unprecedented for Egyptian royal figures. Their fluid, curved outlines—repeated in their drapery patterns—add a new sense of individual motion within three-dimensional space, which is enhanced by the flowing bands of material behind their heads.

Although the children are represented with the unnatural proportions of miniature adults, their behavior and relative freedom of movement endow them with convincingly childlike character. The child on Nefertiti's lap points eagerly toward her father, while the other one, perched on her shoulder, seems to be pulling on her mother's earring. Akhenaten holds a third child, whom he kisses. The intimacy of a scene such as this reflects the new humanity characteristic of the Amarna style.

Hieroglyphs are carved at the top of the scene; several cartouches are visible on the right. In the middle of the hieroglyphs is the sun disk Aten, with rays of light that end in hands—some holding the *ankh* hieroglyph—which seem to reach out to the royal family. Unlike earlier representations of gods in Egyptian art, Aten was embodied in the pure shape of the circle rather than in human or animal form.

Akhenaten's new cult posed a danger to the established priesthood and its traditions. At the close of his eighteen-

4.42 Bust of Nefertiti, Amarna Period. Painted limestone, approx. 19 in (48 cm) high. Ägyptisches Museum, Staatliche Museen, Berlin. Nefertiti was Akhenaten's principal wife, even though he also had Mittani and Babylonian wives, presumably for diplomatic reasons. Nefertiti was given artistic prominence and was important in Akhenaten's sun cult. The blue crown in this sculpture is unique to her.

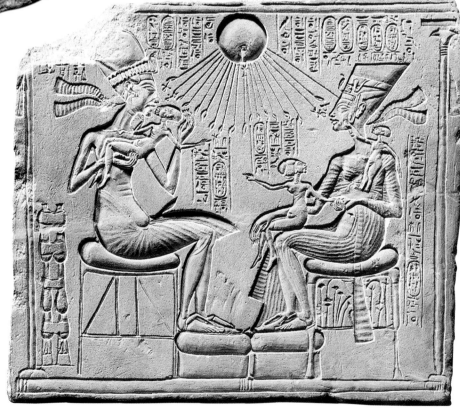

4.43 Akhenaten and Nefertiti and their children, Amarna Period. Limestone relief, 13 × 15 in (33 × 38 cm). Staatliche Museen, Berlin.

year reign, despite certain innovations, Egypt reverted to its previous beliefs, reinstated the priestly hierarchy, and revived traditional artistic style. Akhenaten's tomb has been identified, but his mummy has never been located. Subsequent Egyptian rulers did their best to eradicate any trace of his religion and its expression in art.

Tutankhamon's Tomb

After Akhenaten's death, the pharaoh Tutankhamon (reigned c. 1336–1327 B.C.) returned to the worship of Amon, as his name indicates. He died at eighteen and his only claim to historical significance is the fact that his tomb, with its four burial chambers, was discovered intact. In 1922 an English Egyptologist, Howard Carter, was excavating in the Valley of the Kings, to the west of the Nile and the New Kingdom temples of Karnak and Luxor. To the delight of his patron Lord Carnarvon, Carter found one tomb whose burial chamber and treasury room had not yet been plundered. It yielded some five thousand works of art and other objects, including the mummified body of the king himself.

Tutankhamon's mummy wore a solid gold portrait mask (fig. **4.44**). It was inlaid with blue glass in imitation of lapis lazuli, a blue stone considered valuable by the Egyptians because it had to be imported from Afghanistan or Iran. Three coffins, one inside the other, protected the mummy. All three had the form of the king as Osiris. The two outer coffins were made of gilded wood; the innermost coffin was solid gold and weighed 243 pounds (110 kg). The mummy and its three coffins rested inside a large rectangular stone sarcophagus. The coffinette in figure **4.45** is one of four that contained the pharaoh's organs. These small coffins were housed in a wooden shrine that was placed in another room of the tomb. The shape of the canopic coffins conforms to that of the large coffins and they also show Tutankhamon as Osiris. Each was made of beaten gold, decorated with inlaid colored glass and semi-precious stones.

A comparison of Tutankhamon's effigy with the images produced under Akhenaten shows that the rigid, frontal pose has returned. The natural spaces are closed—for example, around the head and neck by the *Nemes* headdress and around the body by virtue of the crossed arms and tight drapery—thus restoring the conventional iconography of kingship. Like Akhenaten, Tutankhamon holds the crook and

flail. Protecting his head are two goddesses, Wadjet the cobra and Nekhbet the vulture. The wings wrapped around Tutankhamon's upper body belong to the deities on his forehead, and their claws hold signs indicating the unity of Upper and Lower Egypt. In this iconography, Tutankhamon, like Narmer nearly two thousand years earlier, is represented as being under divine protection and as the ruler over a vast domain. The hieroglyphs in the vertical band running from his hands to his feet include an **apotropaic** frontal eye (designed to avert evil) and his cartouche.

Over forty years after Carter's discovery, the contents of Tutankhamon's tomb became one of the world's most popular and widely-traveled museum exhibitions, appearing in Paris, London, Russia, and the United States. But Lord Carnarvon did not live to see it. Just five months after Tutankhamon's tomb was opened, Carter's patron died of an infection, which the popular press attributed to the mummy's curse.

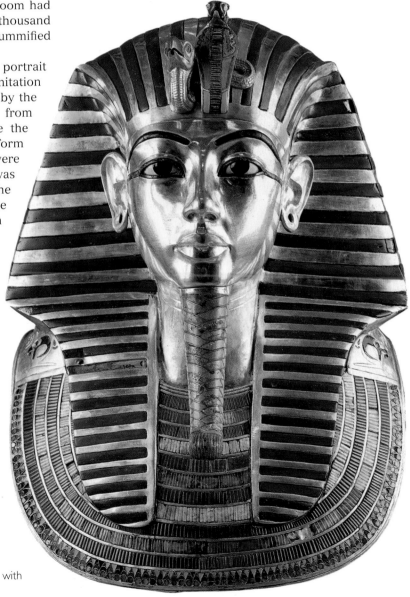

4.44 Mask of Tutankhamon, c. 1333–1323 B.C. Gold inlaid with enamel and semiprecious stones. Egyptian Museum, Cairo.

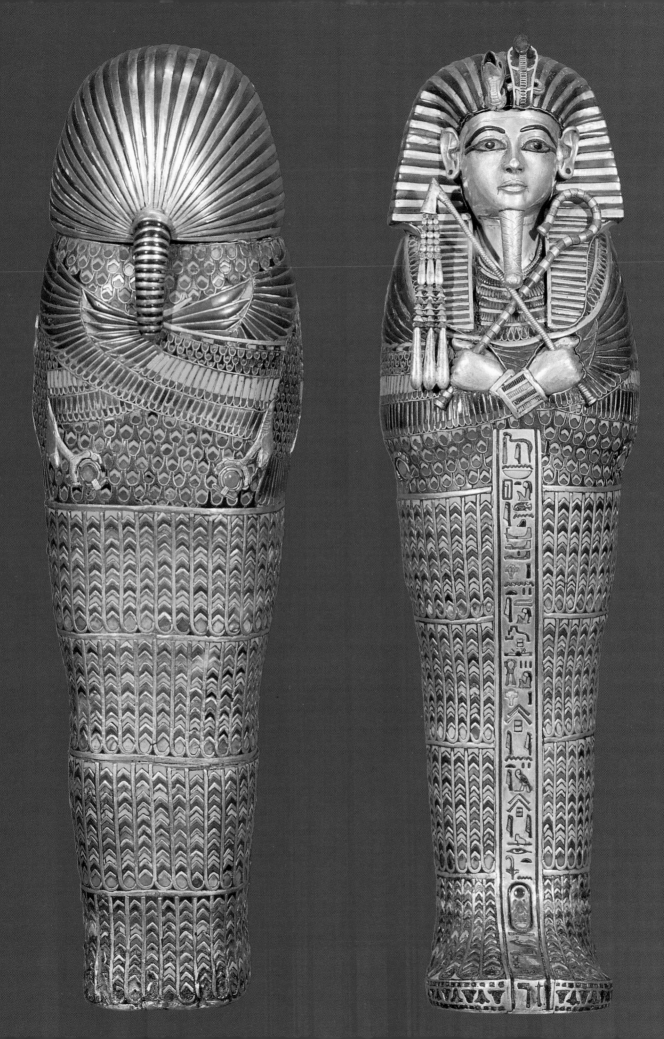

Egypt and Nubia

Throughout the history of ancient Egypt, in written texts and in works of art, there are continual references to other lands both in the Near East and on the African continent. The land called Punt by the Egyptians, for example, is believed to have been located to the southeast along the Red Sea. It was a source of exotic spices and incense, and appears as the destination of an Egyptian expedition on reliefs from Hatshepsut's Deir el-Bahri temple. According to those reliefs, Punt was rich in palm trees and giraffes, and was ruled by an obese woman (fig. **4.46**). To date, however, little is known of Punt and its relation to Egyptian trade. It remains for archaeologists to explore further this part of the ancient world.

Early Kush

Much more information is available about the land south of the Nile's First Cataract (now southernmost Egypt and the Sudan), which was called Nubia by the Romans. To the Egyptians, this area was variously the Land of the Bow (after the Nubians' standard weapon), the Land of the South, and Kush. As in Egypt, the Nile's floods were crucial to the development of Nubian culture, which was enhanced by the wealth of its natural resources—gold, copper, and semiprecious gems—and its location along a major African trade route. As a result of these advantages, Nubia had links to sub-Saharan Africa, to Egypt, and to the Mediterranean world.

In Neolithic Nubia, agriculture had developed and cattle was domesticated. Artisans began making distinctive pottery that was technically and artistically accomplished. The finest Nubian work is the "eggshell" pottery, so-called for the thinness of its walls. The two examples in figure **4.47** are decorated with fingerprints (on the right) and designs derived from basket weaving (on the left). In the former, the artist simultaneously creates a design and makes a personal signature, or "mark." In the latter, the artist incorporates the material "history" of the craft itself into the surface pattern.

During the Old Kingdom, Egypt frequently raided Nubia, usually for natural resources and probably also to capture slaves. By the Middle Kingdom, however, Egypt had definite plans to subjugate Lower (northern) Nubia, and Twelfth Dynasty pharaohs invaded the region with a view to mining copper and gold and taking control of the valuable trade route. Their successes were reinforced by the construction of massive fortresses and a highly organized communication system.

The Kerma Culture

In the seventeenth and sixteenth centuries B.C., the so-called Kerma culture flourished just south of the Nile's Third Cataract in Upper (southern) Nubia. The influence of

4.45 (opposite) Canopic coffinette (coffin of Tutankhamon), c. 1333–23 B.C. Gold inlaid with enamel and semiprecious stones, 15¾ in (39 cm) high. Egyptian Museum, Cairo.

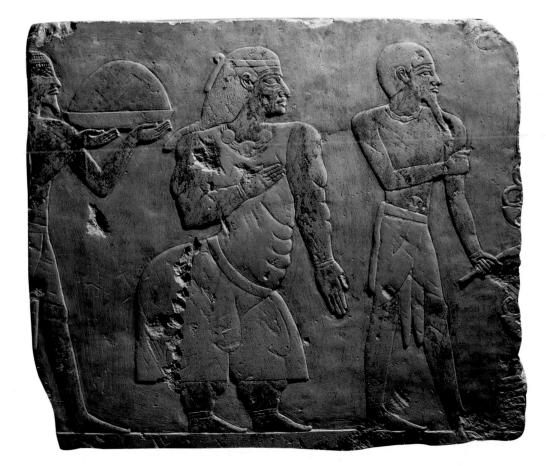

4.46 (right) King and Queen of Punt, from Hatshepsut's funerary temple, Deir el-Bahri, c. 1480 B.C. Painted relief. Egyptian Museum, Cairo.

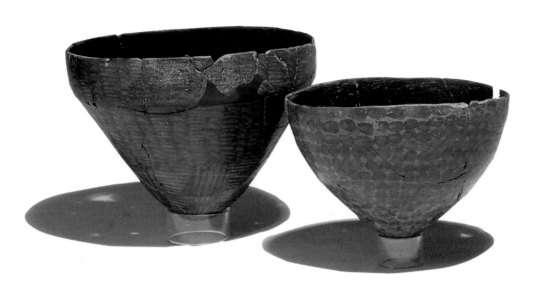

4.47 Nubian "eggshell" vessels, c. 3100–2890 B.C. Ceramic. Left: 6⅛ in (15.4 cm) high. Right: 4⅝ in (12.2 cm) high. British Museum, London.

Egypt, which had occupied Kerma since c. 2500 B.C., is reflected in the form of the Western Deffufa, a large structure of mud-brick (fig. **4.48**). The vertical mass at the right was connected to the larger rectangular mass on the left, and the interior contained a central passage with steps leading to a flat roof. Although the Deffufa's function is not known for certain, the similarity of its form to Egyptian temples with pylon entrances reinforces the view that it was a religious building and that the passage served as an inner sanctuary. The Deffufa is a complex site containing over fifty levels of stratification. Surrounding the monumental Deffufa in the period c. 1700–1650 B.C. were other structures, including shops, houses, and possibly a royal audience hall, as well as streets.

Since the Kushite language was not written down until much later, archaeologists must rely on physical evidence for clues to the religious beliefs of Nubia. Graves, which were hollow pits surmounted by a tumulus, or mound of earth, were filled with the belongings of the deceased. During the height of the Kerma culture, dead Kushite rulers were clothed in leather and placed on beds inside chambers under the tumuli, revealing the early association of death with sleep.

The abundance of jewelry, weapons, food, and sacrificial sheep in the graves suggests that Nubia, like Egypt, had a concrete view of the afterlife. One large grave contained skeletons of hundreds of victims who had been ritually killed and buried in a "sacrificial corridor," possibly to honor or accompany a deceased ruler. In this custom, the Nubians differed from the Egyptians, who, to the best of our knowledge, did not practice human sacrifice at the pharaoh's funeral.

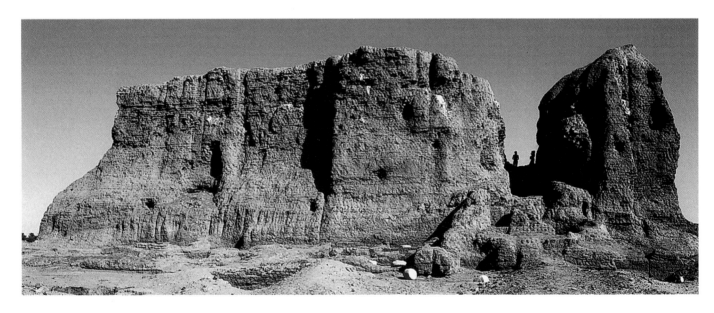

4.48 Western Deffufa, Kerma, 17th–16th century B.C.

Reconquest

When the Egyptian delta was conquered by the Hyksos c. 1600 B.C., the Kushites seized the opportunity to expand their own power. They moved north to Aswan by the First Cataract, took control of the trade route, and enjoyed considerable cultural expansion. Once the Hyksos were expelled, however, the Egyptians recolonized Nubia. The Egyptian viceroy who ran the administration of Nubia carried the titles "King's Son of Kush," and "Overseer of the Southern Lands." Egypt once again profited from the Nubian gold mines and imported Nubian captives for labor or slave markets, and even to work as policemen.

A Nineteenth Dynasty fresco fragment from Thebes depicts Nubians with gifts for the Egyptian pharaoh (fig. **4.49**). The man at the left carrying interlocked gold rings is followed by another with ebony logs and giraffe tails. A monkey perches on the third figure, who holds a leopard skin and carries a basket of fruit. Behind him, the arms of a fourth man leading a monkey on a leash are visible.

A painted relief from the Theban tomb of Huy, Nubia's viceroy under Tutankhamon, shows Heqanufer, the local prince of Mi'am, bowing to the pharaoh (fig. **4.50**). A princess follows in an ox-drawn chariot. Works such as these illustrate the natural resources of Nubia—especially gold—that the Egyptians wanted, as well as the degree to which Nubians adopted Egyptian culture.

In the course of the New Kingdom's Eighteenth and Nineteenth Dynasties, the Egyptians built their most imposing temples in Nubia. Figure **4.51** shows the façade of Ramses II's rock-cut temple at Abu Simbel, one of a

4.49 Nubians bringing offerings to Egypt, Thebes, 19th Dynasty, c. 1400 B.C. Fresco. British Museum, London.

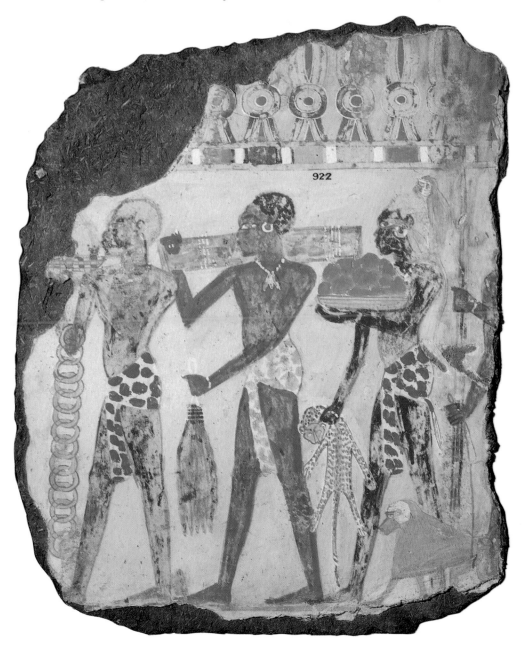

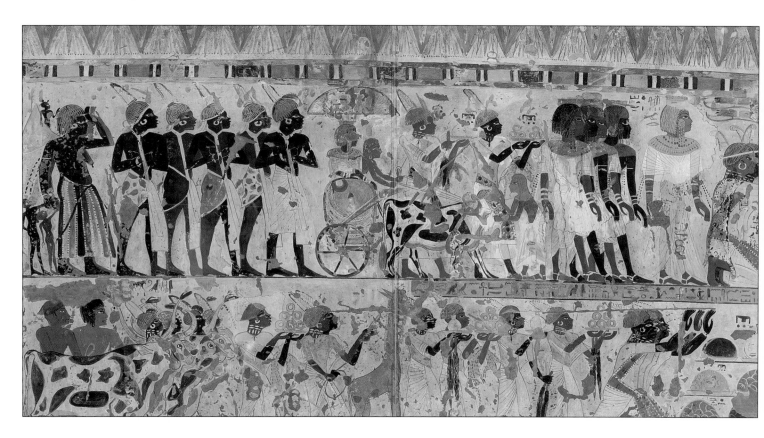

4.50 Presentation of Nubian tribute to Tutankhamon (restored), tomb chapel of Huy, Thebes, 18th Dynasty, c. 1360 B.C. Wall painting, 6 × 17¼ ft (1.82 × 5.24 m). Metropolitan Museum of Art, New York. Egyptian Exhibition of Metropolitan Museum of Art. Rogers Fund, 1930 (30.4.21).

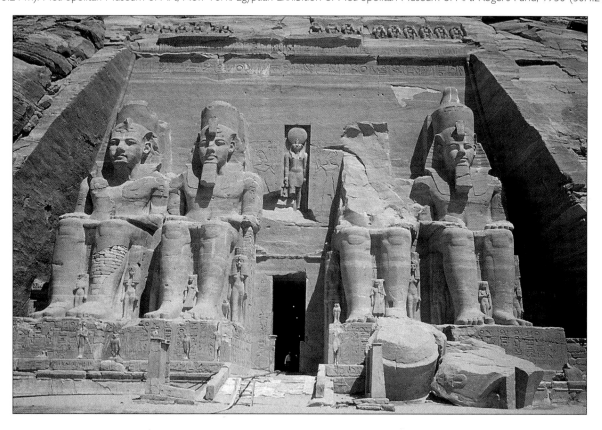

4.51 Temple of Ramses II, Abu Simbel, Nubia, 1237 B.C.

series of six colossal structures south of Aswan. Four huge seated statues of Ramses II represent him in a traditional royal pose. The trapezoidal shapes of the ceremonial beards and headdresses are formal echoes of the space framing them. Ramses' purpose in having works such as this constructed in Nubia was to proclaim to the Nubians his identification with the gods Amon and Ra, as well as to emphasize Egyptian domination over Nubia. A smaller temple nearby, dedicated to his wife, Queen Nefertari, conveyed her identification with the goddess Hathor (Ra's wife). Pharaoh and queen together, therefore, presided over Nubia, asserting their divinity in vast monuments of stone (see Box).

During the last hundred years of the New Kingdom (c. 1170–1070 B.C.), both Egypt and Nubia declined. The Egyptian colonial administration collapsed along with its building programs. And Nubia, with a decreasing population, entered three hundred years of obscurity.

The "50" Sons of Ramses II: A Recent Archaeological Find

In 1995, an excavation led by the American archaeologist Kent Weeks revealed the largest New Kingdom tomb so far known in Egypt's Valley of the Kings. Although robbed in antiquity, the tomb is a rich find, still in the early stages of excavation. It contains at least sixty-seven chambers, and inscriptions indicate that fifty or more of Ramses II's sons were buried there (very few human remains have been recovered to date). It was formerly assumed that each male member of the royal family had a separate tomb; this new evidence, therefore, raises questions about family relationships at the highest level of Egyptian society, as well as about communal burial practices in ancient Egypt.

The Napatan Period

Beginning in the eighth century B.C., Nubia (still called Kush by the Egyptians) re-emerged into what would be an era of artistic development and political influence. Scholars divide this phase of Nubian history into two distinct stages. In the earlier stage, called Napatan after a religious center, Nubians invaded Egypt and established Kushite control of their former colonizers. Four Kushite kings of Egypt in the Twenty-fifth Dynasty conquered the country, revived artistic production, and continued the Egyptian cult of Amon.

The small granite sphinx of Taharqo reflects the appropriation of Egyptian pharaonic iconography by these foreign kings, and their use of Egyptian artistic conventions (fig. 4.52). Although endowed with Nubian facial features, Taharqo's sphinx wears the pharaonic headcloth, and is protected by Wadjet the cobra and Nekhbet the vulture

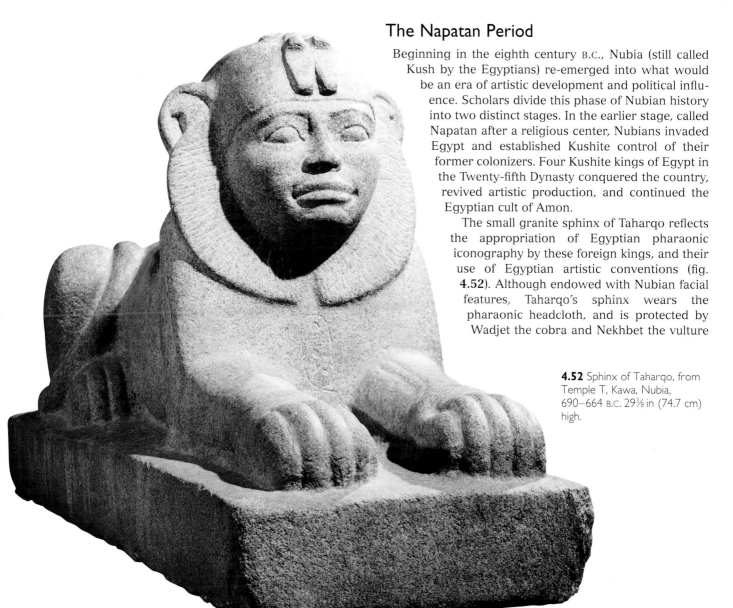

4.52 Sphinx of Taharqo, from Temple T, Kawa, Nubia, 690–664 B.C. 29⅜ in (74.7 cm) high.

on his forehead. There is also a cartouche in sunken relief on the figure's chest.

The Kushite royal residence was at Memphis, a Nile city south of Cairo. But a virgin princess, designated as "God's Wife of Amon," was chosen to control the religious center in Thebes. She, in turn, chose her own successor, thus ensuring that the royal family maintained religious control. Figure **4.53** shows a statuette of Amenirdis I, a Kushite princess of the late eighth century B.C., who held this high priestly office. The statue's frontal pose, blocklike form, and stylized headcloth reflect the assimilation of Egyptian conventions by the Nubians. A striking Nubian feature of her costume is the pair of feathers above her head, which are Nubian signs of royalty that occur also in Heqanufer's relief.

Meroë

In the seventh century B.C., the Assyrians (see Chapter 3) invaded Egypt and ousted the Kushite kings. By the third century B.C., a new stage of Nubian cultural development can be identified. The economic and artistic high point of this period is referred to as Meroitic, after the site of Meroë, south of Napata. Royal Kushite burials shifted from Napata to Meroë itself when Meroitic culture began to absorb a combination of influences from sub-Saharan Africa on the one hand and from Greece (Chapter 6) and Rome (Chapter 8) on the other. Meroë's location in relation to important trade routes between Africa, the Red Sea, and the Mediterranean contributed to its significance. It imported bronze, glass, and silver, and exported ebony, ivory, and gold. Meroë also provided the Roman emperors with elephants. Under the Greek Ptolemies (305–30 B.C.), who ruled Egypt after Alexander the Great wrested it from the Persians, the Kushites continued to trade with Egypt.

Archaeological exploration of Meroë is still incomplete, but the significance of the area in antiquity is clear from classical accounts. In about 430 B.C., Herodotos (*History*, II, 29) described the arduous journey by ship, followed by forty days on foot and another ship journey, from Aswan to Meroë. He reported that two important Greek gods, Zeus and Dionysos (see Chapter 6), had pen-

4.53 Statuette of Amenirdis I, Kush, Nubia, late 8th century B.C. 11 in (28.3 cm) high. British Museum, London.

etrated Meroë and were worshiped there. At the same time, however, it is clear from inscriptions that Egyptian gods such as Amon and Isis were the objects of popular cults. There were also indigenous Nubian gods. In religious beliefs therefore—as in politics, economics, and the arts—Meroë was a melting pot, which contributed to, and was also a result of, its strategic international position.

Meroitic inscriptions dating from the second century B.C. have been discovered, but they are imperfectly understood. Since no related languages have survived, scholars once again must rely on physical evidence. The most impressive buildings from Meroë are the pyramids whose ruins are illustrated in figure **4.54**. They are derived from Egyptian pyramids, but rise more steeply than those at Giza, and have flat, rather than pointed, caps. Scholars believe that these flat tops may each have supported a sun disk, indicating worship of a sun god. Burial chambers were underground, and the deceased, as in Egypt, were mummified. The outer stone blocks, and the structures themselves, are smaller than Old Kingdom Egyptian royal pyramids. They are closer in form to New Kingdom examples built for private individuals, even though those at Meroë were royal tombs.

In 1820–21, a French traveler, F. Cailliaud, accompanied the Egyptian army into the Sudan and made drawings of the pyramids at Meroë. The example in figure **4.55** belonged to Queen Amanishakheto (first century B.C.) and was in a relatively good state of preservation. According to Cailliaud's drawing, the entrance, inspired by Egyptian temple pylons, was decorated with reliefs of the ruler's triumph over Meroë's enemies. Excavations of the interior of the pyramid were carried out some thirteen years later by the Italian physician Giuseppe Ferlini. His account of the excavation reflects the careless and unscientific procedures current in nineteenth-century archaeology, including the destruction of some objects and the removal of others from the site.

Among the goldwork from Amanishakheto's tomb were nine so-called shield rings, of which figure **4.56** is a typical example. The god Amon is depicted in the guise of a naturalistic ram's head under a sun disk. Behind the disk stands a chapel façade with smaller circles flanked by *uraei*. Blue glass is fused into the circle, which is soldered onto its gold background. The red glass on top of the sun disk was glued into the gold circle. It is not certain what purpose was served by the shield rings, but it is possible that they were pendants similar to the decorative pieces worn by Nubian women of today on their foreheads.

The excavation of Amanishakheto's tomb confirms Meroë's artistic independence from Egypt as well as its absorption of both Egyptian and Greek forms. Stonecutters from Greece may have worked at Meroë. Amanishakheto's

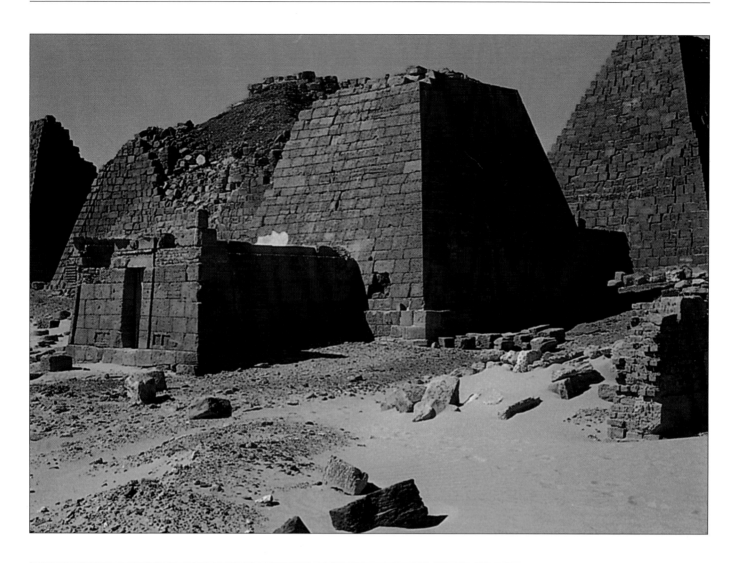

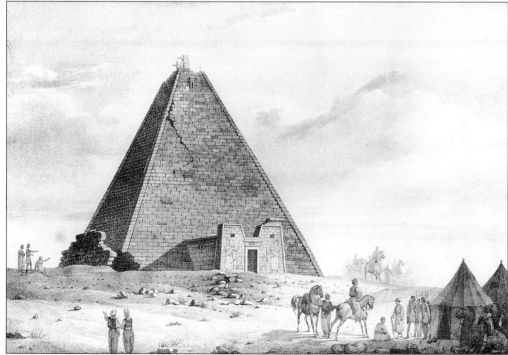

4.54 (above) Ruins of the Meroë pyramids, Nubia, 3rd–1st century B.C.

4.55 Tomb of Amanishakheto, Meroë, Nubia, late 1st century B.C. Drawing from F. Cailliaud, *Voyage à Méroé*, Paris, 1823–27, plate XLI.

tomb has also contributed to our knowledge of local society, the position of women, and the organization of the royal family in this part of sub-Saharan Africa. The king's mother, who was given the title Kandake, was below the king in the royal hierarchy, but in certain cases, such as Amanishakheto's, the Kandake herself ruled. This is reflected in a New Testament text referring to a eunuch "under Candace [Kandake], queen of the Ethiopians" (Acts 8:27).

After the first century A.D., Nubian civilization fell into a gradual decline. The Ethiopian kingdom of Axum rivaled Meroë for trade routes, particularly with Rome. Meroë was occupied by nomads during the fourth century, which marked the end of the region's thriving culture. From the sixth to the twelfth centuries, Christianity (Chapter 9) made inroads into Nubia, and trade with Mediterranean cultures, especially Egypt, was revived. For the next four hundred years, Nubia was infiltrated by various groups. In the fourteenth century, it became predominantly Islamic (Chapter 10).

Egypt itself underwent a series of conquests, first by the Assyrians (c. 673–657 B.C), followed by the Persians in 525 B.C., and by Alexander the Great in 332 B.C. In 58 B.C. the Romans invaded Egypt and annexed it in 30 B.C. Since the early seventh century Egypt has been part of the Islamic world.

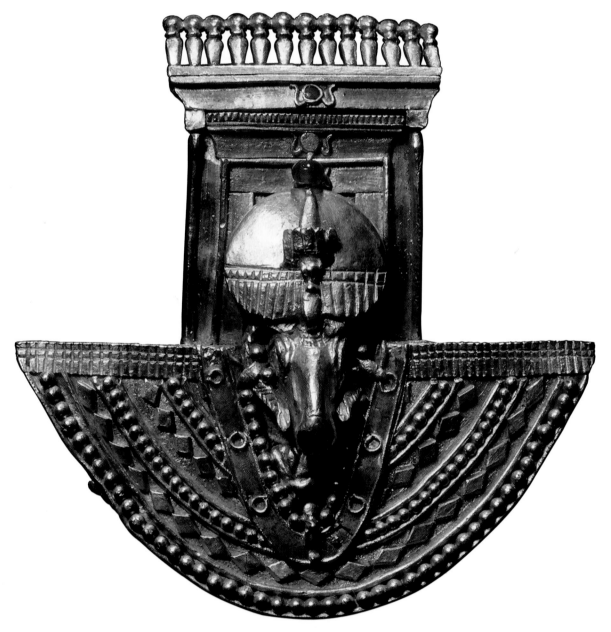

4.56 Shield ring with Amon as a ram, Meroë, Nubia, c. 200 B.C. Gold, fused glass, and carnelian, 2½ in (5.6 cm) high. Staatliche Sammlung Ägyptischer Kunst, Munich.

Style/Period	Works of Art	Cultural/Historical Developments
PREDYNASTIC c. 3300–2960 B.C.	Palette of Narmer (**4.2, 4.3**), Hierakonpolis	Egypt unified under a single pharaoh (3000 B.C.) Hieroglyphic writing appears (c. 3000 B.C.) Papyrus scrolls exported (3000 B.C.)
OLD KINGDOM c. 2649–2150 B.C.	Step pyramid (**4.12**), Saqqara Rahotep and Nofret (**4.22**) Great Pyramids (**4.13**), Giza The Great Sphinx (**4.18**), Giza Seated statue of Khafre (**4.20**), Giza Menkaure and Khamerernebty (**4.21**), Giza Seated scribe (**4.23**), Saqqara	Copper widely used in Egypt (2700 B.C.) Egyptian conquest of Nubia (2600 B.C.) Potter's wheel in common use in Mesopotamia (c. 2500 B.C.) Egyptians discover use of papyrus (2500–2000 B.C.)
MIDDLE KINGDOM c. 1991–1700 B.C.	Painted coffin of Djehuty-nekht (**4.29**) Lady Senuwy (**4.24, 4.25**) Sesostris I (**4.26, 4.27**) Sesostris III (**4.28**)	*Gilgamesh* epic written in Sumer (c. 2000 B.C.) Earliest Minoan palace built at Knossos, Crete (c. 2000 B.C.) Nile floods used for irrigation purposes (2000–1500 B.C.) The Hyksos establish themselves in Egypt (c. 1750–1550 B.C.) Horse-drawn chariot introduced to Egypt (c. 1750–1550 B.C.)
NEW KINGDOM c. 1550–1070 B.C. The Armana Period c. 1349–1336 B.C. Egypt and Nubia	Funerary temple of Queen Hatshepsut (**4.37**) Hatshepsut as pharaoh (**4.36**) Senenmut and Nefrura (**4.38**) Nebamun hunting birds (**4.39**) Temple of Amon-Mut-Khonsu (**4.35**), Luxor Statue of Akhenaten (**4.41**), Karnak Akhenaten and Nefertiti and their children (**4.43**) Bust of Nefertiti (**4.42**) Mask of Tutankhamon (**4.44**) Small coffin of Tutankhamon (**4.45**) Opening of the Mouth Ceremony (**4.40**) Temple of Amon-Ra (**4.30**), Karnak Western Deffufa (**4.48**), Kerma Statuette of Amenirdis I (**4.53**), Kush Nubian "eggshell" vessels (**4.47**) Nubians bringing offerings to Egypt (**4.49**), Thebes King and Queen of Punt (**4.46**), Deir el-Bahri Painted relief (**4.50**), Huy, Thebes Temple of Ramses II (**4.51**), Abu Simbel Sphinx of Taharqo (**4.52**), Kawa Meroë pyramids (**4.54**), Nubia Tomb of Amanishakheto (**4.55**), Meroë "Shield ring" with Amon as ram (**4.56**), Meroë	Citadel at Mycenae (Greece) constructed (c. 1600–1500 B.C.) The Hyksos expelled from Egypt (1550 B.C.) Dominance of Mycenaean Greeks in eastern Mediterranean (1400–1200 B.C.) Destruction of palaces at Crete (c. 1400 B.C.) Akhenaten's religious reforms (1375–1350 B.C.) Death of Tutankhamon (c. 1340 B.C.) Exodus of the Hebrews, led by Moses, from Egypt to Canaan (mid 13th c. B.C.) Egypt invaded by the "sea peoples" (c. 1230 B.C.) Beginning of Judaism (c. 1200 B.C.) Iron in common use (c. 1200 B.C.) Dorians invade Greece from the north (c. 1100 B.C.) Egypt loses control of Nubia (c. 1100 B.C.) Phoenicians develop alphabetic script (1100 B.C.)

Palette of Narmer

Seated scribe

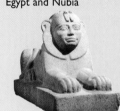

Nefertiti bust

Sphinx of Taharqo

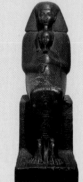

Senenmut and Nefrura

5

The Aegean

From about 3000 to 1200 B.C., three distinct cultures—Cycladic, Minoan, and Mycenaean—flourished on the islands in the Aegean Sea and on parts of mainland Greece (fig. **5.1**). These cultures chronologically overlapped the Old, Middle, and New Kingdoms of ancient Egypt (see Chapter 4), and there is evidence of contact between them. Before the late nineteenth century, however, Aegean culture was remembered only in myths and legends—most of the works of art discussed in this chapter were discovered around 1850. As a result, much less is known of the Aegean cultures than of those in Egypt and the ancient Near East.

Cycladic Civilization (c. 3000–1200 B.C.)

The Cyclades, so-named because they form a circle (from the Greek *kuklos*), are a group of islands in the southern part of the Aegean Sea. Typical of many island populations, the inhabitants of the Cyclades were accomplished sailors, fishermen, and traders. They also hunted and farmed, the latter requiring permanent village settlements. Cycladic culture is essentially prehistoric because of the absence of a writing system. Scholars therefore rely on physical evidence and written accounts dating from the later, historical period of Greece (beginning around 900 B.C.). In the fifth century B.C., for example, the Greek historian Herodotos described the inhabitants of the Cyclades as notorious pirates. But the earliest surviving artistic evidence of Cycladic culture dates from the Bronze Age, when people learned to make bronze from copper and tin. Many works of art, including pottery, metalwork, and marble sculpture from Cycladic graves have a provenience despite extensive plundering.

The most impressive examples of Cycladic art date from the early Bronze Age and are made of marble. They range in height from nearly 5 feet (1.5 m) (figs. **5.2** and **5.3**) to only a few inches (fig. **5.4**). Today they are called idols (from Greek *eidolon*, meaning "image") because they are thought to have been objects of worship. Most were found lying down in graves.

Figures of females are much more numerous than those of males. Their purpose is unknown, but it is assumed that they were carried in religious processions, for they are unable to stand on their own. The large female in figure 5.2 has long, thin proportions, with the breasts and pubic triangle accentuated. The view from the side (fig. 5.3) shows that the idol forms a narrow vertical, extending at the back from the top of the head to the hips. Legs and feet fall into three slight zigzag planes, and the angle of the feet makes it impossible for them to support the statue.

Seen from the front, the figure is composed mainly of geometric sections. Note that the head is a slightly curving rectangle—its only articulated feature is the long, pyramidal nose. The neck is cylindrical, and the torso is divided into two squares by the horizontals of the lower arms. The right angles of the elbows create a three-sided frame around the upper torso, which the breasts seem to transform into a second face. Although the overriding impression of its shapes is geometric, certain features,

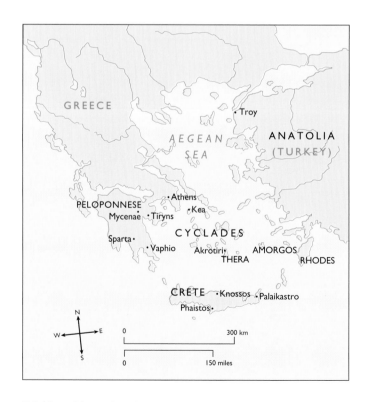

5.1 Map of the ancient Aegean.

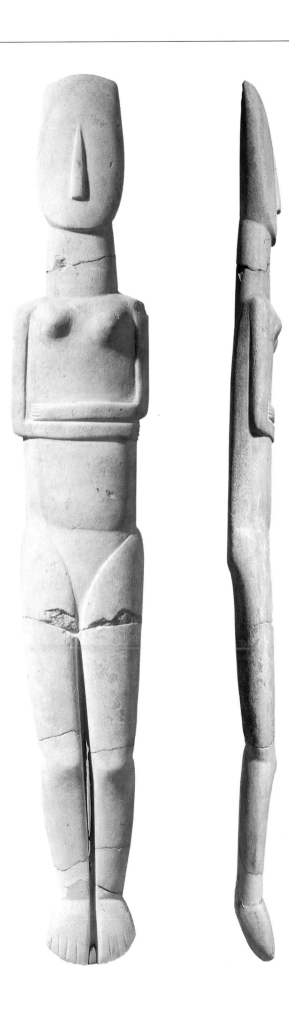

such as the breasts and knees, have a very convincing organic quality. They seem to protrude naturally from beneath the exterior surface of the body. Despite formal differences between the Cycladic idols representing women and earlier prehistoric sculptures such as the *Venus of Willendorf* (see fig. 2.1) and the so-called *Mother Goddess* of Malta (see fig. 2.24), all are images of divine, female power.

The male Cycladic idols are composed mainly of cylindrical shapes and are often depicted playing musical instruments. The man in figure 5.4 plays a double pipe, and tilts his head so far back that it is nearly at a right angle to his neck. The area of greatest formal movement in this sculpture is where the diagonals of the arms and pipe meet the tilting head and long neck. Arms, legs, and torso are shorter and sturdier than those of the female. The relative solidity of this statue is reinforced by the horizontal plane of the feet and their little **pedestal**, which provide actual support.

Minoan Civilization (c. 3000–1500 B.C.)

The modern Greek island of Crete, to the south of the Cyclades and northwest of the Nile delta, was the home of another important Bronze Age culture. It was destroyed twice, once in 1700 B.C. by an earthquake and again, two or three centuries later, by an invasion from the Greek mainland. The culture that flourished on Crete was all but forgotten until the early twentieth century, when the British archaeologist Sir Arthur Evans (1851–1941) decided to search for it. Inspired by his knowledge of later Greek myths about the pre-Greek Aegean, Evans initiated excavations that would establish a historical basis for the myths.

In Greek mythology (see Box, p. 140), Crete was the home of the tyrant King Minos, son of Zeus and the mortal woman Europa. Minos broke an oath to Poseidon, who had guaranteed his kingship. In revenge, the sea god caused Minos' wife to fall in love with a bull. The offspring of their unnatural union was the Minotaur, a monstrous creature, part man and part bull, who lived at the center of a labyrinthine maze in the Palace of Minos at Knossos. Every year the Minotaur killed seven girls and seven boys sent as annual tribute from Athens on the Greek mainland to Minos. Eventually, the Athenian hero Theseus killed the Minotaur and was rescued by Minos' daughter Ariadne from the labyrinth. They set sail from Crete and landed on the island of Naxos, where Theseus deserted Ariadne. The Greek wine god Dionysos found Ariadne and married her. Theseus, meanwhile, had sailed home to Athens, but he forgot the prearranged signal to his father, King Aegeus, indicating that he was returning safely. Believing his son dead, Aegeus threw himself into the sea and drowned. The Aegean Sea is named after the unfortunate king.

5.2 Female Cycladic idol, from Amorgos, 2700–2300 B.C. Marble, 4 ft 10½ in (1.49 m) high. National Archaeological Museum, Athens.

5.3 Female Cycladic idol (side view of fig. 5.2).

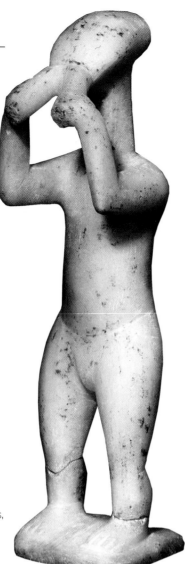

5.4 Male Cycladic flute player, from Keros. Marble, c. 2500–2200 B.C. National Archaeological Museum, Athens.

5.5 Plan of the Palace of Minos, Knossos, Crete, 1600–1400 B.C. Area approx. 4 acres (1.6 hectares).

The Palace at Knossos

Sir Arthur Evans called the culture he discovered Minoan, after the legendary King Minos. "Minos" may be either a generic term for a ruler, like the designations "king" and "pharaoh," or the name of a particular ruler. The major Minoan site was Knossos, which had been inhabited since early Neolithic times. Its palace (fig. **5.5**) was the traditional residence of Minos, and the largest of several known palaces on Crete.

In Greek mythology the palace was called a "labyrinth," which Evans believed originally meant "house of the double axe." The latter was a cult object in the Minoan era, and is represented in paintings and reliefs throughout the palace at Knossos. Double axes may have been used to sacrifice bulls, which were sacred animals in ancient Crete. The later Greek meaning of "labyrinth," a complex, maze-like structure, may have been applied to the palace because of the asymmetrical, meandering arrangement of rooms, corridors, and staircases (see plan in figure 5.5). Greek coins of Knossos which were minted in the historical period generally contained maze patterns.

The palace itself (fig. **5.6**) was not fortified, for the fact that Crete is an island was its primary protection against invasion. Like other Aegean and Near Eastern palaces, Knossos was more than a royal residence; it also served as a commercial and religious center. Industry, trade, and justice were administered from the palace, which had a well-organized system for receiving and distributing local agricultural products and imported luxury goods. Much of this wealth was stored in large **terracotta** (literally "cooked earth") jars (see below).

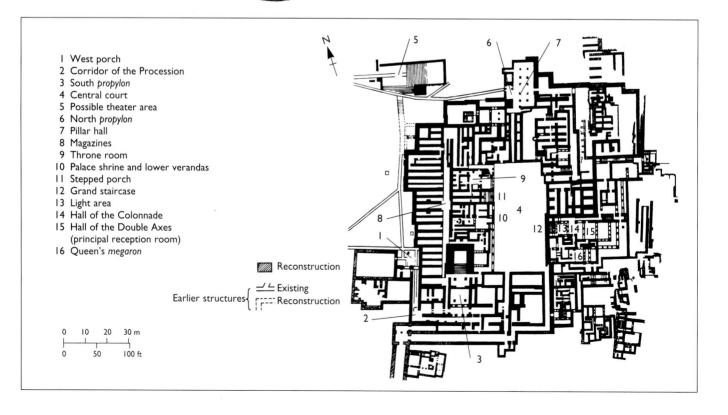

1 West porch
2 Corridor of the Procession
3 South *propylon*
4 Central court
5 Possible theater area
6 North *propylon*
7 Pillar hall
8 Magazines
9 Throne room
10 Palace shrine and lower verandas
11 Stepped porch
12 Grand staircase
13 Light area
14 Hall of the Colonnade
15 Hall of the Double Axes
  (principal reception room)
16 Queen's *megaron*

Reconstruction

Earlier structures { Existing
Reconstruction

0 10 20 30 m
0   50   100 ft

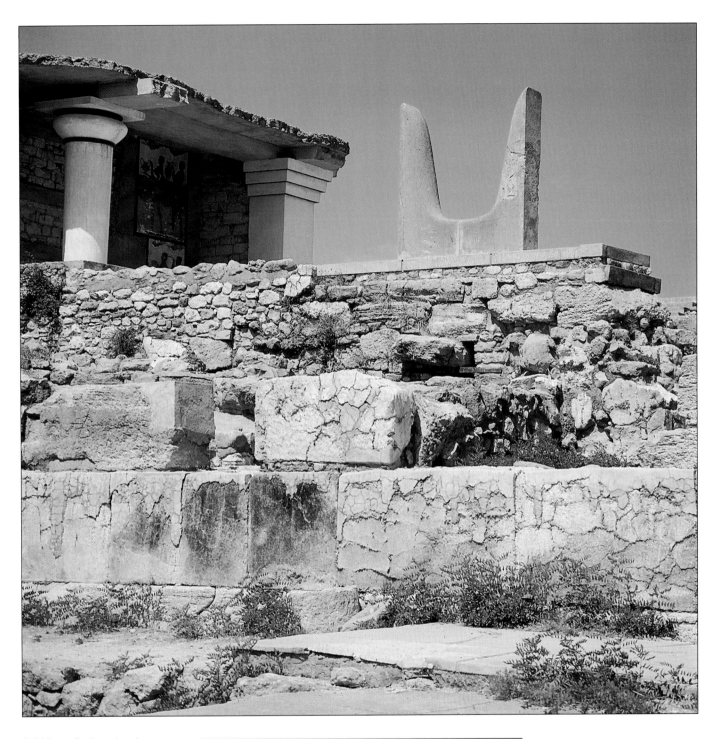

5.6 View of palace showing wooden columns and limestone bulls' horns near the south entrance, Palace of Minos, Knossos.

Minoan Fresco

Whereas Egyptian wall paintings were *fresco secco*, Minoan wall paintings were *buon* (true) *fresco*—pigments were mixed with water and applied to damp lime (calcium-based) plaster. As the plaster dried, the coloring was absorbed into the fabric of the wall, making *buon fresco* more durable than *fresco secco*. Minoan artists used *fresco secco* for additional details painted over the true fresco, which had to be applied quickly before the plaster dried.

The palace at Knossos used post-and-lintel construction with low ceilings, stone masonry walls, and short, wooden columns that taper downward toward the base. Because their **capitals** appear inflated, or puffed up (fig. **5.7**), they are called pillow capitals. Those shown here have been reconstructed on the basis of fragments of fresco painting (see Box) that originally decorated the interior palace walls. These three painted columns come from the western portico (porch) at the north entrance to the palace.

The painted plaster relief behind the columns is based on the original fragments shown in figure **5.8** depicting a charging bull. It recalls the myth of the Minotaur. The bull's ancient significance as a sacred, royal symbol recurs at Knossos—note the horns perched on the edge of the wall in figure 5.6.

The so-called *Toreador Fresco* (fig. **5.9**) is perhaps the best-known wall painting from Knossos. It represents a charging bull, two girls, and one boy. The girl at the left grasps the bull's horns, the boy somersaults over his back, and the girl at the right stands ready to catch him. Given

the sacred character of the bull in the Minoan era and the myth of the Minotaur, it is believed that this fresco depicts a ritual sport, possibly involving the sacrifice of the bull, of the athletes, or both. As in Egyptian paintings, females are depicted with lighter skin color than males, and in each case a profile head is combined with a frontal eye. In other ways, however, the Minoan paintings differ from those of Egypt—for example, in the predominance of curvilinear form and the dynamic movements of figures in space. Although in the *Toreador Fresco* three different human figures are represented, their poses correspond to a sequence of movement that could be made by a single figure. Such depictions of time and sequencing are more characteristic of Minoan than of Egyptian iconography. Bordering the fresco are rows of patterned designs simulating different colored marble.

5.7 Partly restored west portico of the north entrance passage with a reconstructed relief fresco of a charging bull. Palace of Minos, Knossos.

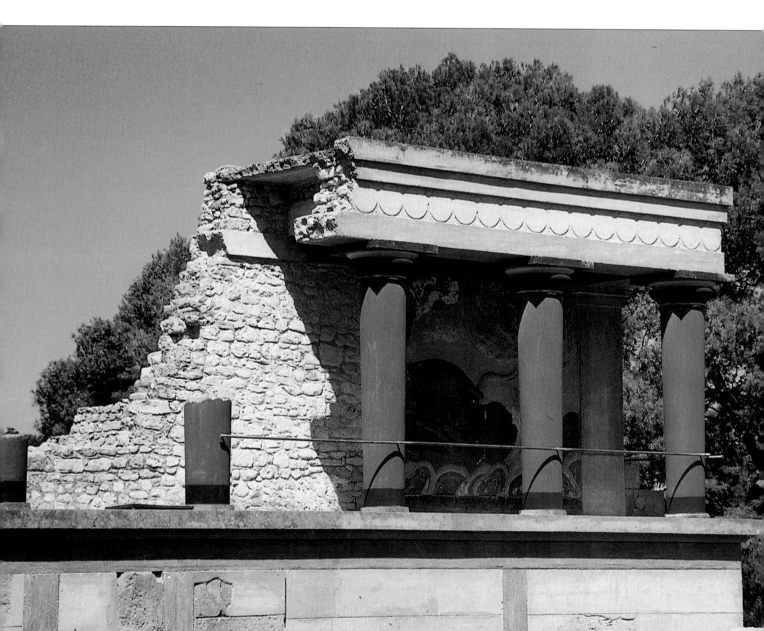

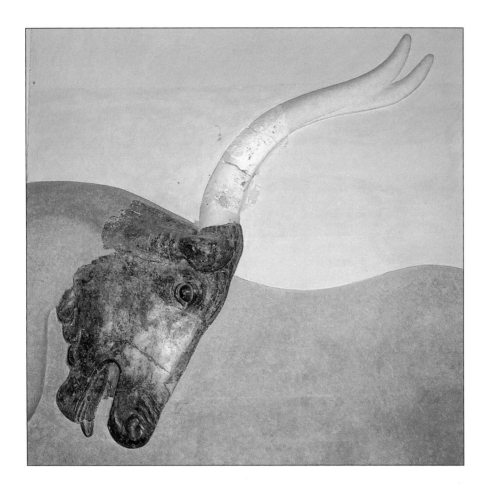

5.8 Original bull's head, as reconstructed in figure 5.7. Relief fresco. Archaeological Museum, Herakleion, Crete. Note the paler quality of the color of the original before reconstruction.

5.9 *Toreador Fresco*, from Knossos, c. 1500 B.C. Reconstructed fresco, 32 in (81.3 cm) high (including border). Archaeological Museum, Herakleion, Crete. This wall painting was discovered in a fragmentary condition and has been pieced back together. The darker areas belong to the original mural while the lighter sections are modern restorations.

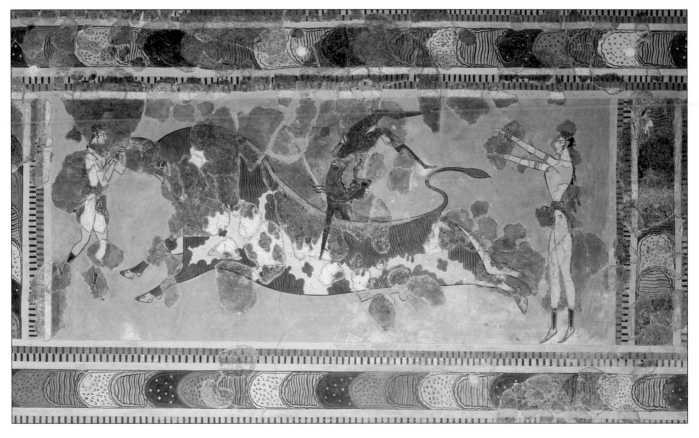

One of the most imposing, albeit heavily restored, Knossos frescoes decorated the so-called "throne room" (fig. **5.10**). The throne—actually a stone chair—is made of gypsum; its seat is indented and tilted back for increased comfort. Scholars generally believe that a woman, probably a priestess, sat here as part of a religious ritual, for symbolic griffins such as those in the fresco behind the throne always flank a female in Aegean art. These griffins, a mixture of eagle and lion, are set in a landscape of undulating terrain and tall flowers.

Though posed symmetrically and stylized, the griffins are rendered with curved outlines and rudimentary shading that creates a sense of three-dimensional contour. By placing some of the plants behind the animals, the artist has enhanced the illusion of depth. The expansive, generalized quality of this particular landscape, which differs from the more constrained and detailed Egyptian landscapes, is characteristic of Aegean painting.

Minoan Religion

Little is known of Minoan religious beliefs. We have only archaeological evidence to shed light on Minoan religion because scholars have been unable to decipher the Minoan language (see Box). Shrines were located on mountaintops or inside the palaces, which played an

Minoan Scripts

In the Aegean two kinds of script, Linear A and Linear B, are preserved on clay tablets. Linear A, the written Minoan script and language, developed about 2000 B.C. and remains undeciphered, while Linear B had come into use by about 1400 B.C. or later. The scripts were similar, but Linear B was used to write early Greek after the Mycenaean domination of Crete. As it was used mainly for inventory lists and palace records, Linear B provides evidence of Mycenaean administration, but reveals little about the culture.

important role in religious ceremonies. Images of what seem to be priests and priestesses, of bulls, double axes, trees, columns, and elevated poles occur in scenes of religious ceremonies. Trees, pillars, and poles were venerated in rites celebrating the coming of spring, apparently a practice dating back to the Bronze Age.

Another recurring motif in Minoan art is a female—a goddess or priestess—holding snakes. The precise significance of the small statue of the so-called *Snake Goddess* (fig. **5.11**) is not known. However, the motif of a male or female deity dominating animals, referred to as the

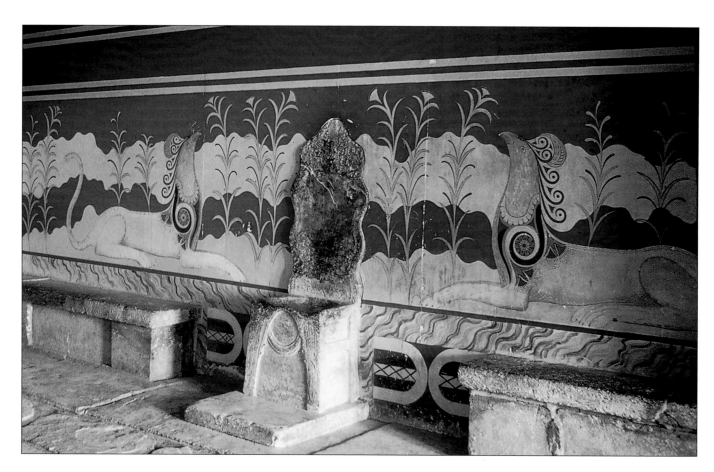

5.10 View of the "throne room," Knossos, with a heavily restored fresco depicting griffins.

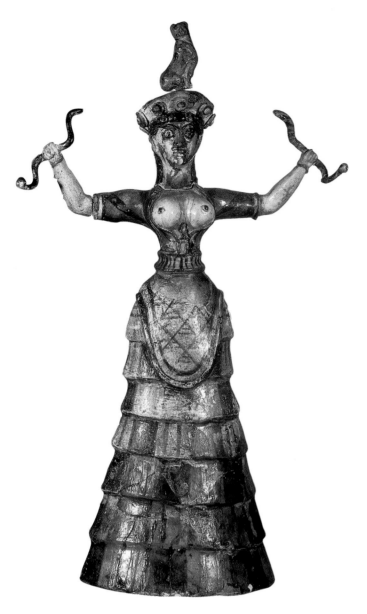

5.11 *Snake Goddess*, from Knossos, c. 1600 B.C. Faïence, 13½ in (34.3 cm) high. Archaeological Museum, Herakleion, Crete. This frontal figure has a thin, round waist and wears a conical flounced skirt. Her breasts are exposed, and a cat perches on top of her headdress. Faïence is a technique for glazing earthenware and other ceramic vessels by using a glass paste which, after firing, produces bright colors and a lustrous sheen.

"Master" or "Mistress of the Beasts," occurs earlier in the ancient Near East and later in Greek art. As creatures of the earth, snakes were associated with fertility and agriculture, and did not have the evil connotations with which they later became endowed in the West.

Pottery The storage jar, or *pithos*, in figure **5.12** is from the west wing of the palace at Knossos. Its lively surface decoration consists of thin bands of incised circles and wider strips of circles and diagonals—the so-called rope pattern—in relatively high relief. The energetic quality of the geometric designs on the *pithos* also characterizes Minoan vessels with painted decoration. For example, the spouted jar from the older palace at Knossos illustrates the earlier type of Kamares ware, dating to c. 1800 B.C. (fig.

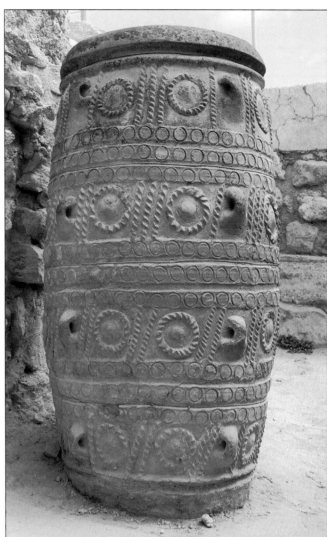

5.12 *Pithos*, west porch, Knossos. Terracotta.

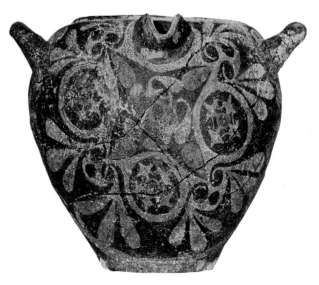

5.13 A spouted jar, c. 1800 B.C. Kamares ware. Archaeological Museum, Herakleion, Crete.

5.13). (The term "Kamares" is from the Kamares Cave, in the mountains above Phaistos, where examples of this type of pottery were first discovered.) Compared with Egyptian imagery, the Kamares example is freer and more curvilinear. The abstract pattern formed by white on the characteristic blue-black ground of Kamares ware suggests floral design, with its undulating motion and whirling, circular arrangement of shapes. A few details are enhanced by the orange, which adds to the vibrant quality of the jar's design. (Note that blue and orange are opposites on the color wheel, figure 1.18, and therefore their juxtaposition is particularly striking.) Kamares ware is an art of shape and color, in which patterns are integrated in a balanced, organic manner with the shape of the vessel.

The Octopus Vase (fig. **5.14**) from Palaikastro, like both the *pithos* and the Kamares jar, is enlivened by vigorous surface design related to natural forms. Although the image of an octopus and other forms of sea life are discernible on the vase, the artist's obvious delight in the swirling patterns of the arms and their little round suction cups retains an abstract character. These, in turn, are repeated formally in the large oval eyes of the octopus, which echo the holes made by the handles and seem to stare directly at the viewer. The iconography of this object also reflects the fact that the Minoans, like the inhabitants of the Cyclades, were seafarers.

Discoveries at Thera

In the 1960s the island now known as Santorini in the southern Cyclades yielded exciting new archaeological material. Called Thera by the ancient Greeks, Santorini is a volcanic island, parts of which are covered with thick layers of ash and pumice. The Greek archaeologist Spyridon Marinatos began to excavate near the modern town of Akrotiri, on the south coast of the island facing Crete.

His excavations confirmed that an enormous volcanic eruption had buried a flourishing culture with a well-developed Aegean artistic tradition. The date of this disaster has been placed as late as 1500 B.C., or as early as around 1628 B.C.—in either case it occurred during the heyday of Minoan civilization. Since no human remains have been found in the ashes, the inhabitants were evidently able to evacuate the island before the volcano erupted.

The geographical location of Thera, north of Crete, places it squarely within the trading and seafaring routes between the Aegean, Egypt, Syria, and Palestine. To date, archaeologists have uncovered large portions of an ancient and affluent town. The paved, winding streets and houses of stone and mud-brick indicate a high standard of living. Homes had basements for storage, workroom

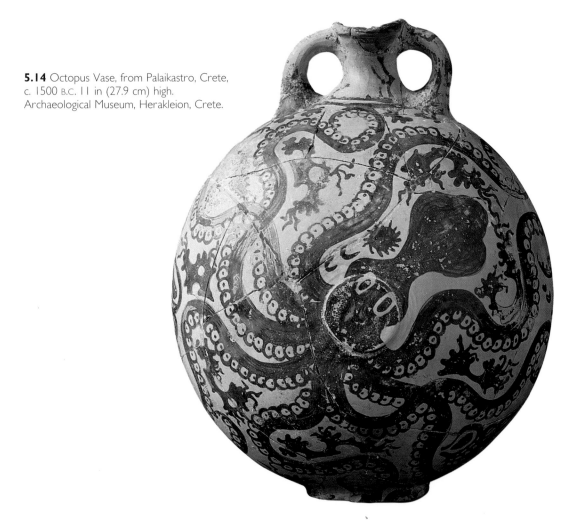

5.14 Octopus Vase, from Palaikastro, Crete, c. 1500 B.C. 11 in (27.9 cm) high. Archaeological Museum, Herakleion, Crete.

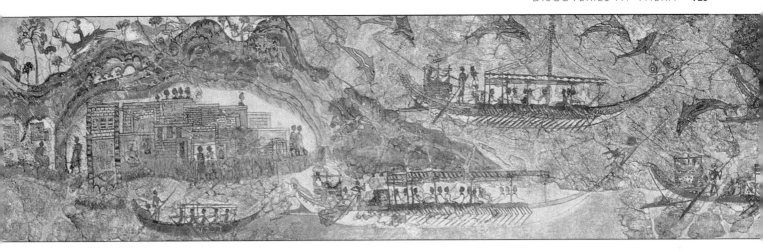

5.15 *Ship Fresco* (left section), from Akrotiri, Thera, c. 1650–1500 B.C. 15¾ in (40 cm) high. National Archaeological Museum, Athens.

space, and upper-story living quarters. Mills attached to houses reflect an active farming as well as seafaring economy. Walls, as in Crete, were reinforced with timber and straw for flexibility in the event of earthquakes. Interior baths and toilets were connected by clay pipes to an extensive drainage and sewage system under the streets. Such elaborate attention to comfortable living conditions is not found again in the West until the beginning of the Roman Empire over a thousand years later (see Chapter 8).

The Frescoes

Equally remarkable was the attention paid to art in Theran culture. The walls of public buildings as well as private houses were decorated with frescoes, which constitute an important new group of paintings. They represent a wide range of subjects: landscapes, animals, people engaging in sports and rituals, boats, and battles. When first discovered, most of the frescoes were covered with volcanic ash which had to be carefully removed by brush. The paintings had fallen from the walls and were restored piece by piece to their original locations.

Theran pictures are characteristically framed at the top with painted borders, often created by abstract geometric patterns. The most significant painting discovered on Thera is the large *Ship Fresco*, the left section of which is reproduced in figure **5.15**. It was painted in a long horizontal strip, or **frieze**, that extended over windows and doorways (fig. **5.16**). The scene includes harbors, boats, cities and villages, human figures, landscape, sea life and

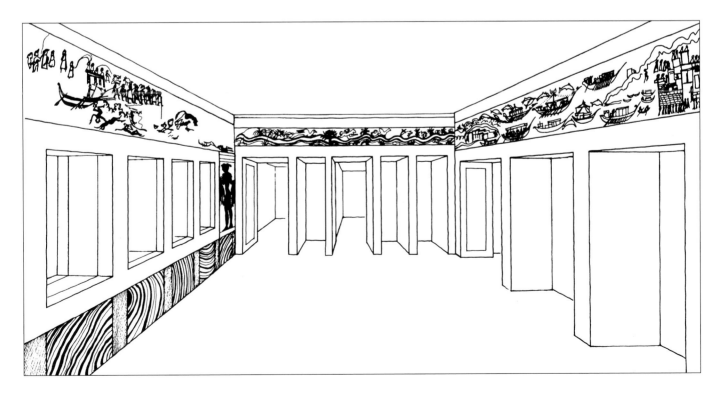

5.16 Diagram showing the original arrangement of the *Ship Fresco* at Akrotiri, *in situ*.

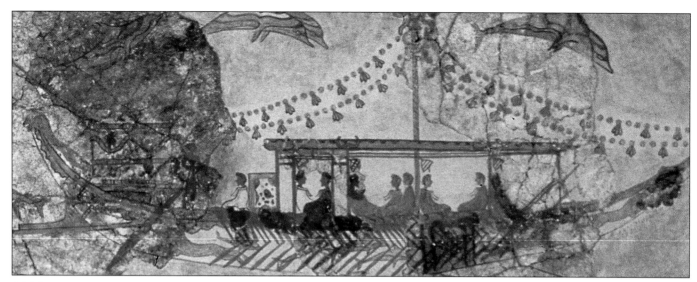

5.17 *Ship Fresco* (detail of boats in fig. 5.15).

land animals, all of which provide information about the culture of ancient Thera. Some of the houses, for example, have several stories, the boats are propelled by paddles and sails, and the style of dress is distinctively Theran.

Various interpretations of the *Ship Fresco* have been proposed, from the straightforward return of a fleet to the depiction of a ceremonial rite. Although there is some overlapping to show depth, the landscape is rendered with no sense of spatial diminution and appears to "frame" the city. Distance is indicated by proximity to the top of the fresco—boats below, buildings on land, hills, trees, and animals at the horizon. The detail in figure **5.17** suggests that the event depicted here is celebratory. Garlands swing from the mast and alert passengers sit upright. The leaping dolphins above, like the stags in figure **5.18**, seem to reflect the general aura of excitement that pervades the scene.

The fresco of *Boxing Children* (fig. **5.19**) offers a larger-scale depiction of human figures than does the *Ship Fresco*. As is true of painted figures from Egypt and Crete, these stand on a thin strip rather than in a naturalistic space. They also retain the convention of a frontal eye in a profile face. Like Minoan figures, and in contrast to Egyptian ones, the curved outlines and shifting planes of movement create a sense of vigorous, sprightly energy. The significance of these boxers remains controversial, but it is likely that they are engaged in a coming-of-age ritual. The boy on the left wears jewelry and is receiving a blow from the boy on the right. His lighter face and upwardly turned eye show that he has been hit by his opponent and is in pain. This indicates either that he is the initiate, or that of the two he is being emphasized.

In contrast to the boxers, the so-called *Crocus-Gatherer* (fig. **5.20**) is light-skinned, following the convention of Minoan and Egyptian representations of females. She holds a basket in her left hand and reaches for a flower with her right. Although her body is frontal—she is in a squatting position—she turns her head to speak to her

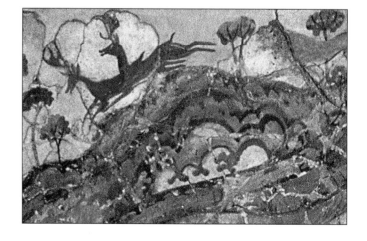

5.18 *Ship Fresco* (detail of stags in fig. 5.15). This fragment depicting the two stags pursued by a mountain lion shows the cracks where the fresco has been pieced together. Thousands of such fragments have been dusted, saturated with acetone to remove moisture, sent to a conservation laboratory, photographed, glued to matching fragments, and then reassembled on the wall in an aluminum frame.

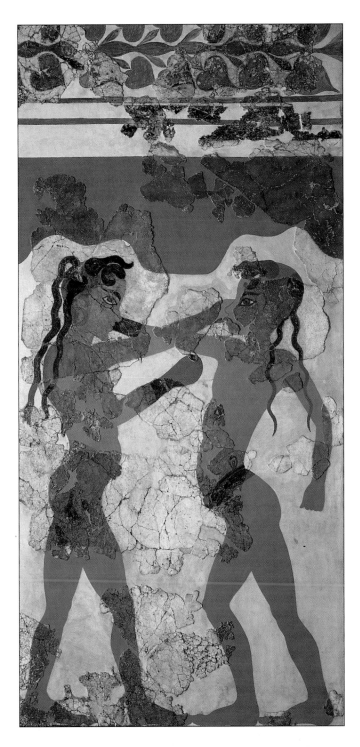

5.19 *Boxing Children*, from Akrotiri, Thera, c. 1650–1500 B.C. Fresco, 9 ft × 3 ft 1 in (2.74 × 0.94 m) high. National Archaeological Museum, Athens.

a specific individual. Again more like Minoan than Egyptian painting, she is set in a spacious landscape amid mountains and rocks. The iconography of this fresco is based on religious ritual. Crocuses are the source of saffron, which was considered valuable for medicinal as well as for ritual purposes. The girl depicted here is one of four collecting saffron for presentation to a nature goddess; elsewhere in the sequence, a monkey presents the saffron to an enthroned goddess.

When hitherto unknown cultures such as that on Thera are uncovered for the first time, modern views of history are necessarily modified. The precise role of Thera in the Minoan era still remains to be determined. Some people believe it is the source of the story of the lost Atlantis, described by Plato in his *Timaeus* and *Kritias*; others strongly disagree. In any case, such archaeological finds reveal the dynamic nature of history and human culture, the similarities as well as differences linking us to the past, and the continuing relevance of past to present.

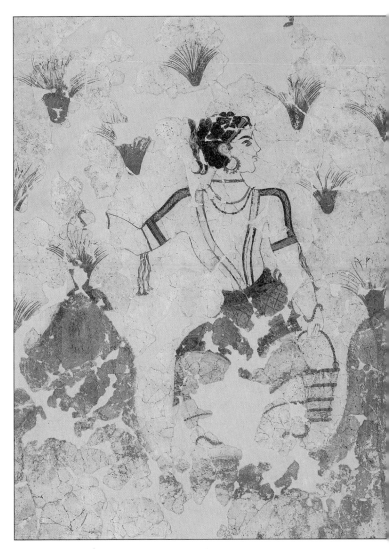

5.20 *Crocus-Gatherer*, from Thera, before 1500 B.C. Fresco, approx. 35 × 32 in (89 × 81 cm). National Archaeological Museum, Athens.

companion. Her curly black hair, whose ringlets echo the lines of her ear, is held in place by a blue headband. She wears a large earring and three necklaces, a short-sleeved dress and an overskirt. The stylized outline of her eye is reminiscent of ancient Near Eastern eye outlines (see fig. 3.7), although her physiognomy creates the impression of

Mycenaean Civilization

(c. 1600–1200 B.C.)

In the late 1860s, Heinrich Schliemann, a successful young German businessman, became an archaeologist. Like Evans, Schliemann was convinced that certain Greek myths were based on historical events. He focused his search on the legends of the Trojan War and its heroes described by Homer (see Box). In 1870, Schliemann first excavated the site of Troy on the west coast of Turkey. Years later he excavated Mycenae, the legendary city of Agamemnon, in the northeast of the Peloponnese, on the Greek mainland. The subsequent excavations of other similar Greek sites have revealed that a Mycenaean culture flourished between 1600 and 1200 B.C. After the eruption of Thera, the Aegean was dominated by the Mycenaeans, who began by conquering Crete and ruling the island from Knossos.

Also called Late Helladic after "Hellas," the historical Greek name for Greece ("Greece" was the name used by the Romans), Mycenaean culture takes its name from its first excavated and foremost site of Mycenae. Here, as elsewhere, the citadel was built on a hilltop and fortified with massive stone walls (fig. **5.21**). The palace, or **megaron** (literally "large room" in Greek), was rectangular. One entered the *megaron* through a front porch supported by two columns and continued through an antechamber into the throne room, in which four columns surrounded a circular hearth (fig. **5.22**). The king's throne was centered, facing the hearth. This arrangement had pre-Mycenaean antecedents on the Greek mainland, and would be elaborated in later Greek temple architecture.

Like the Minoans, the Mycenaeans apparently had no temples separate from their palaces. Shrines have been found within the palaces, which were lavishly decorated and furnished with precious objects and painted pottery. Figure **5.23** is a reconstruction of the *megaron* at Mycenae. The walls, floors, and perhaps the interior columns were covered with paintings.

5.21 View of the citadel, Mycenae.

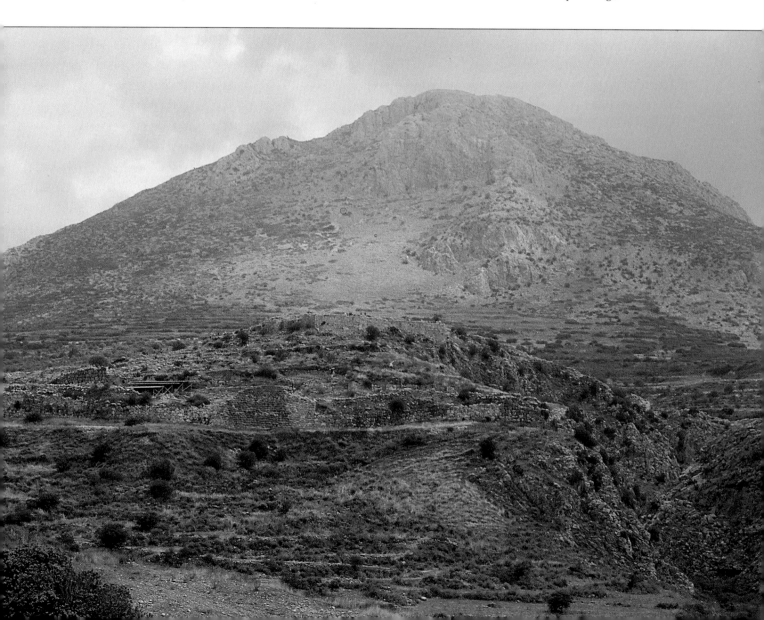

The Legend of Agamemnon

Mycenae was the legendary home of King Agamemnon, who led the Greek army against King Priam of Troy in the Trojan War. Agamemnon's brother, King Menelaus of Sparta, had married Helen, known to history as the beautiful and notorious Helen of Troy. Priam's son Paris abducted Helen, and Agamemnon was pledged to avenge the offense against his family. But as soon as the Greek fleet was ready to sail, the winds refused to blow, because Agamemnon had killed a stag sacred to the moon goddess Artemis. As recompense for the stag, and in return for allowing the winds to blow, Artemis exacted the sacrifice of Agamemnon's daughter Iphigenia.

Ten years later the war ended and Agamemnon returned to Mycenae, bringing with him the Trojan seeress Kassandra. He was murdered by his wife Klytemnestra, who had not forgiven him for Iphigenia's death, and her lover Aegisthos. Agamemnon's children, Orestes and Elektra, killed Klytemnestra and Aegisthos to avenge their father's death.

These tales were well known to the historical Greeks: the Trojan War from *The Iliad*, written in the eighth century B.C. and attributed to Homer; and the tragedy of Agamemnon's family from plays of Aeschylos and Euripides (fifth century B.C.). Like the myths of Theseus and the Minotaur, however, the account of Agamemnon's family was considered to belong to the realms of imagination and legend until the archaeological discoveries of Schliemann at the end of the nineteenth century.

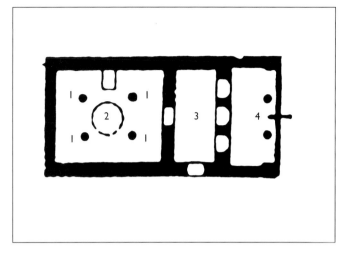

5.22 Plan of the Mycenaean *megaron*. Within a rectangular structure, the throne room had four columns (1) enclosing a circular hearth (2) in the center. Access to the throne room was through an antechamber (3) and a front porch (4) with two columns.

5.23 Reconstruction drawing of the Mycenaean *megaron* showing the front porch with two columns and the interior hearth enclosed by four columns.

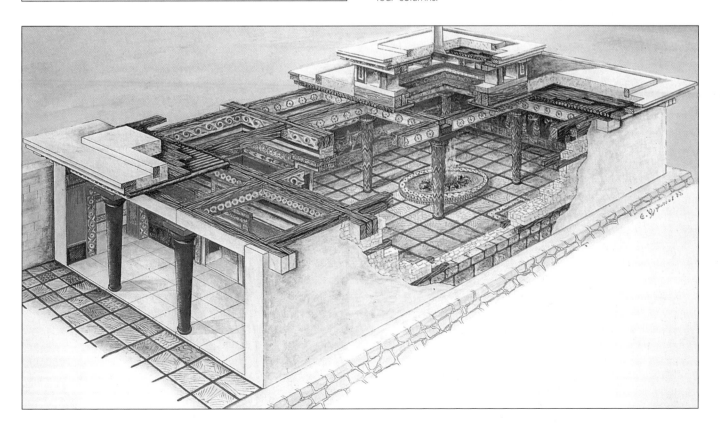

The best-preserved fresco from Mycenae shows similarities with Minoan fresco style. The so-called Mycenaean "Goddess" (fig. **5.24**) was discovered in the cult center of the citadel. Her face is rendered in profile with a frontal eye, but her naturalism is enhanced by the curvilinear form of her body. She smiles slightly, and seems to contemplate the necklace held in her right hand. The thin black lines framing her torso, outlining her eye, and defining her eyebrow recall those of the Theran *Crocus-Gatherer* (see fig. 5.20). Her elaborate jewelry and coiffure indicate that she was a personage of high status or possibly a goddess.

Unlike the nobility, most of the citizens lived in small stone and mud-brick houses below the citadel. In times of siege, they sought refuge within its walls. The defensive fortifications of the Mycenaean cities reflect a society more involved in war than were the Minoans, and thus more concerned with protection from invaders. These considerations led to building the thick, monumental walls that surround most Mycenaean citadels. They were constructed of large, rough-cut, irregular blocks of stone such as those visible in figure 5.25. Because of the enormous weight of such stones, the later Greeks called the walls Cyclopaean (see Box).

The Lion Gate crowned the entrance to the citadel of Mycenae (fig. **5.25**). Its opening is framed by a post-and-lintel structure, and the triangular section over the lintel consists of a relieving triangle (see p. 132). This was formed by **corbelling**, or arranging layers, called courses, of stones so that each level projects beyond the lower one.

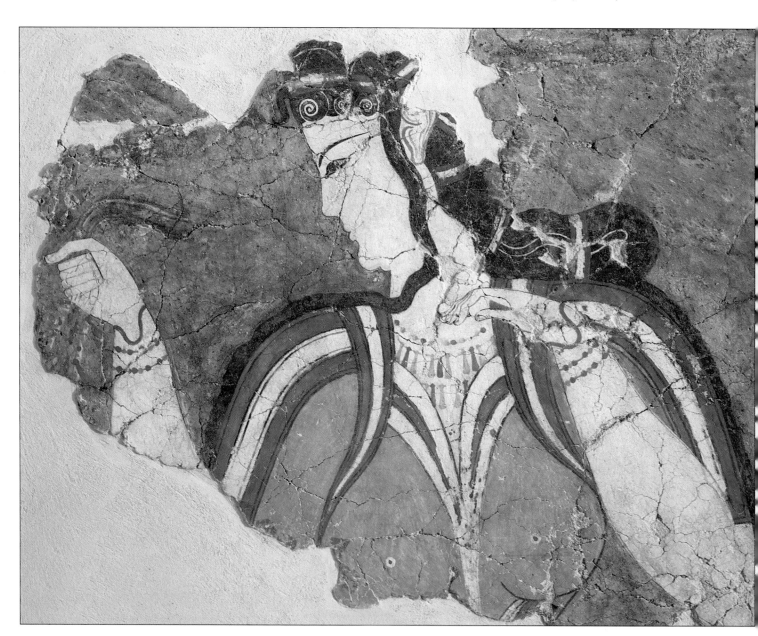

5.24 "Goddess," from the citadel of Mycenae. Fresco, approx. 1200 B.C. National Archaeological Museum, Athens.

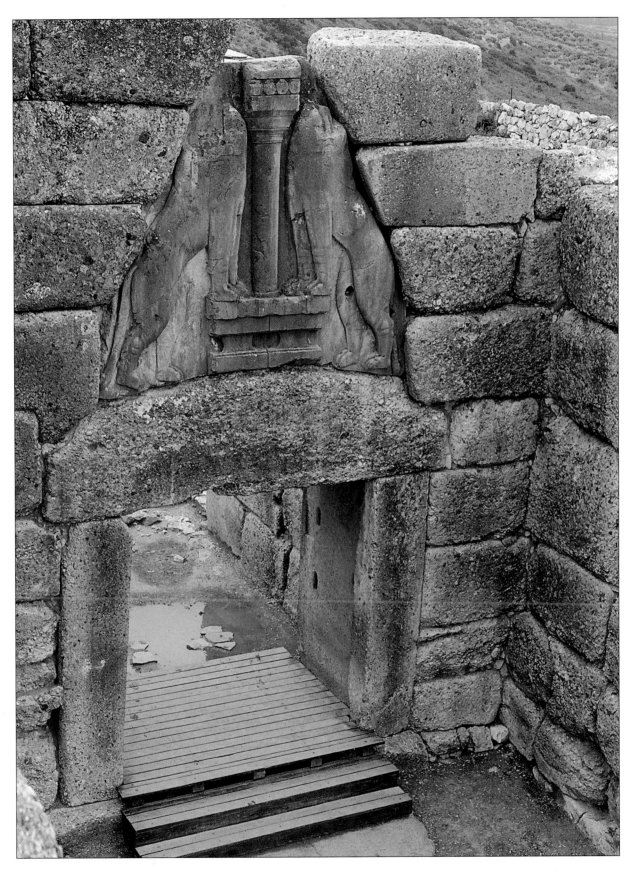

5.25 Lion Gate, Mycenae, 1500–1300 B.C. Limestone, approx. 9 ft 6 in (2.9 m) high. The presence of a Minoan column at Mycenae is an example of the kind of evidence used by archaeologists to demonstrate the influence of Minoan art.

When the stones meet at the top they create an arch. Filling in the triangle is a relief of two lions placing their paws on a concave Minoan altar. They flank a Minoan-style column, which is a symbol of the Nature Goddess. The relief is thus an image showing the lions obedient to the goddess as "Mistress of the Beasts," and the power immanent in her symbol. The heads of the lions are missing. Originally they were carved separately to project frontally and fulfill their traditional role as guardians of an entrance.

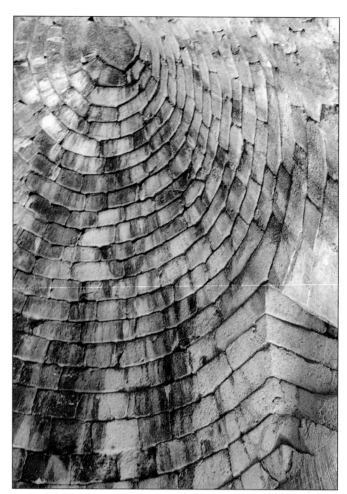

5.27 Vault, interior of the Treasury of Atreus, Mycenae, c. 1300 B.C. Stone, height approx. 43 ft (13 m), diameter 47 ft 6 in (14.48 m).

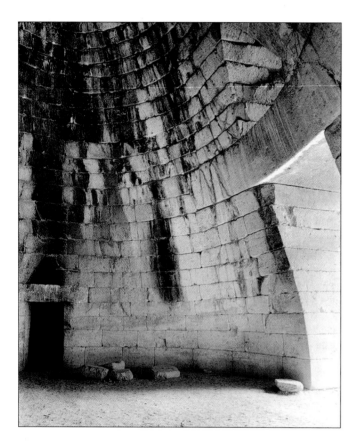

5.26 Interior of a *tholos* tomb, showing the entrance lintel and a door to the side chamber, Treasury of Atreus, Mycenae, c. 1300 B.C. Diameter of interior 43 ft (13 m), height 40 ft (12 m); doorway 17 ft 8 in × 8 ft 10 in (5.4 × 2.7 m).

Cyclopaean Masonry

Cyclopaean masonry is named for a mythological race of Giants, or Cyclopes, who were believed strong enough to lift the blocks of stone found at Mycenaean sites. The Cyclopes are described by Homer in *The Odyssey* as having a single round eye in the center of their foreheads (the name derives from the Greek *kuklos*, meaning "circle," and *ops*, meaning "eye"). In Book 9 of *The Odyssey*, Odysseus escapes from the Cyclops Polyphemos by putting out his single eye with a stake and tying himself and his men to the undersides of a flock of sheep.

The most dramatic surviving structure at Mycenae exemplifies the culmination of Mycenaean royal tomb architecture in the thirteenth century B.C. This tomb, or ***tholos*** (Greek for "round building"), has been called both the Treasury of Atreus and the tomb of Agamemnon, who was Atreus' son (figs. **5.26** and **5.27**). It is not known who was buried there, but because of its enormous size, it was doubtless intended for royalty.

Figure 5.27 shows a section of the ceiling with corbeled courses in a circular arrangement of rectangular stones corresponding to the curved sides. The courses diminish in diameter as they approach the top of the chamber, which is crowned by a round capstone. Most likely the construction of such large tombs had been influenced by the design of smaller *tholoi* used earlier for communal burials on Crete. There is also some connection between the *tholoi* and earlier Mycenaean shaft graves, which were set within circular walls. One such grave circle inside the citadel itself can be seen in the aerial view in figure 5.28. The reconstruction of these ruins (fig. **5.29**) shows the massive, Cyclopaean walls and the disposition of the graves within them. Toward the top of the picture, the inside of the Lion Gate is visible, with the back of the slab containing the relief illustrated in figure 5.25.

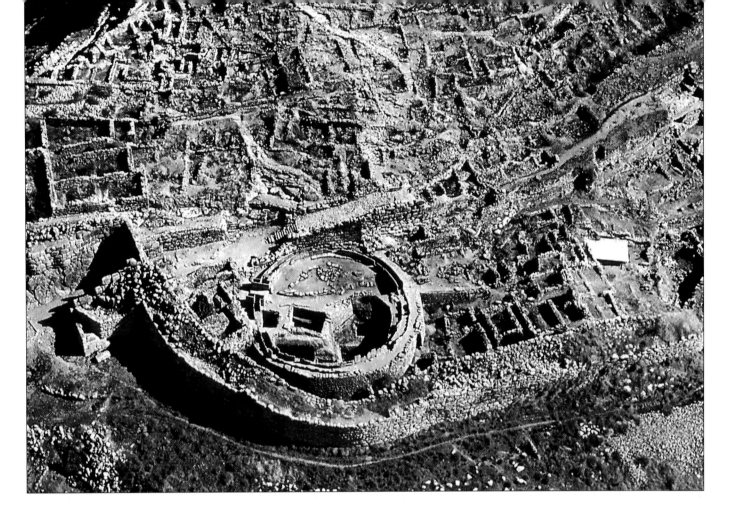

5.28 Aerial view of Grave Circle A and its surroundings, Mycenae.

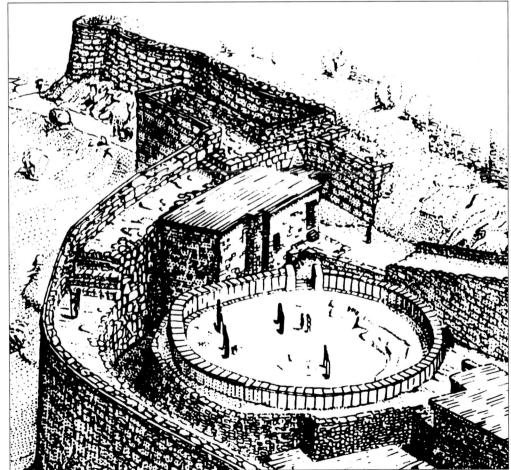

5.29 Reconstruction drawing of Grave Circle A, Mycenae, as it was in the late 13th century B.C.

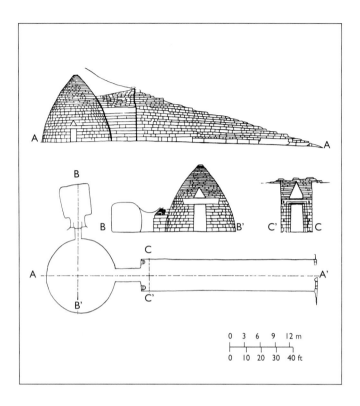

5.30 (above) Plan and sections of a *tholos*.

The *tholos* was entered through a *dromos*, or roadway, 118 feet (36 m) long, whose walls were faced with rectangular stone blocks (fig. **5.30**). Above the rectangular entrance to the *tholos* was an enormous lintel weighing over 100 tons. It separates the doorway from a triangle that relieves the weight borne by the lintel. Figure **5.31** shows the entrance and *dromos* of another important royal tomb, identified by local villagers as the tomb of Klytemnestra. Like the triangle above the Lion Gate, this one was originally filled in with carved stone blocks.

Once the dead body had been placed inside the *tholos*, the door was closed and the entrance walled up with stones until such time as it had to be reopened for later burials. All that would have been visible from the exterior was the mound of earth covering the tomb and the *dromos*. Unfortunately, both of the royal tombs discussed above were plundered before their modern excavation. However, excavations of unplundered graves, especially the earlier shaft graves at Mycenae, have yielded remarkable objects.

5.31 Façade and *dromos* of the tomb of Klytemnestra, Mycenae, c. 1300–1200 B.C. Façade 34½ ft (10.5 m) high; doorway 17¾ ft (5.4 m) high, 8¼ ft (2.48 m) wide. Originally the door was framed by half-columns made of gypsum.

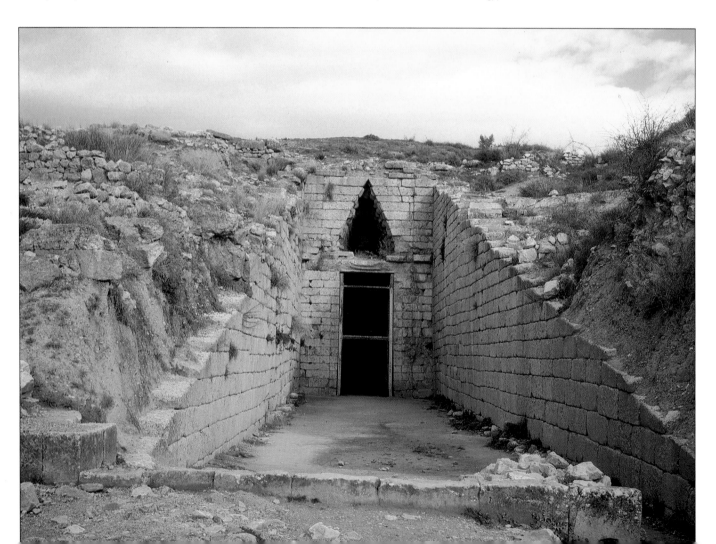

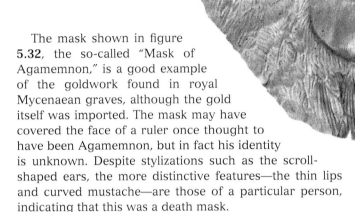

5.32 "Mask of Agamemnon," from Mycenae, c. 1500 B.C. Beaten gold, approx. 12 in (30.5 cm) high. National Archaeological Museum, Athens. Although little is known of Mycenaean religion, it is thought that such death masks were intended to guarantee a dead person's identity in the afterlife.

The mask shown in figure **5.32**, the so-called "Mask of Agamemnon," is a good example of the goldwork found in royal Mycenaean graves, although the gold itself was imported. The mask may have covered the face of a ruler once thought to have been Agamemnon, but in fact his identity is unknown. Despite stylizations such as the scroll-shaped ears, the more distinctive features—the thin lips and curved mustache—are those of a particular person, indicating that this was a death mask.

Two gold cups from a *tholos* tomb at the site of Vaphio, in the region around Sparta (fig. **5.33**), were also buried with a king. There is some controversy over the origin of the two cups, but the one on the left seems to be the work of a Minoan artist, while the one on the right is Mycenaean. The scene on the left cup shows a man tying up a bull, possibly for the ritual Minoan bull sport. Landscape forms—trees and earth—are depicted with considerable naturalism. Also reflecting a concern for naturalism is the sense of time, noted above in the *Toreador Fresco* (see fig. 5.9): here the bull first sniffs the ground and then is enticed by a cow. The man's thin waist and flowing curvilinear outlines further recall the human figures in Minoan painting.

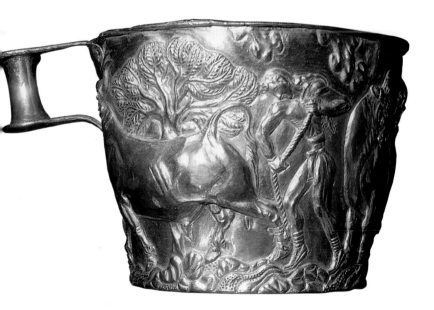
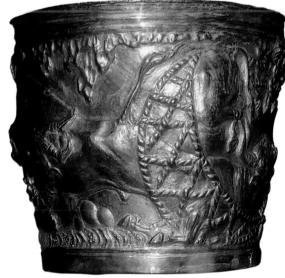

5.33 Minoan and Mycenaean cups from Vaphio, near Sparta, c. 1500 B.C. Gold, 3½ in (8.9 cm) high. National Archaeological Museum, Athens.

The cup on the right is Mycenaean in execution, but its iconography is Minoan. It is cruder than the Minoan cup, and stresses the violence of the struggling bull caught in a net rather than landscape forms. The style of the Mycenaean cup is more powerful than the Minoan one, and its forms are generally more abstract. The relief on both cups was made by the *repoussé* technique (from the French *pousser*, meaning "to push"), in which an artist hammers out the scenes from the inside of the cup. Final details were added on the outside. On the Vaphio cups a smooth lining of gold was attached on the inside.

The rediscovery of the Minoan-Mycenaean civilizations in the late nineteenth and early twentieth centuries, and the more recent finds at Thera, have restored some miss-ing links of Western history. Minoan and Mycenaean cultures came to light as a result of the conviction of a few scholars—notably Sir Arthur Evans, Heinrich Schliemann, and Spyridon Marinatos—that certain old legends and myths had a basis in fact. There remains much to be learned, and archaeologists continue to probe the earth for clues to the past. Although the fall of Mycenae was followed by several hundred years of a so-called "Dark Age," about which we have archaeological but no literary information, the Aegean cultures provide a transition from Egypt and the ancient Near East to the later art and culture of historical Greece, which is the subject of the next chapter.

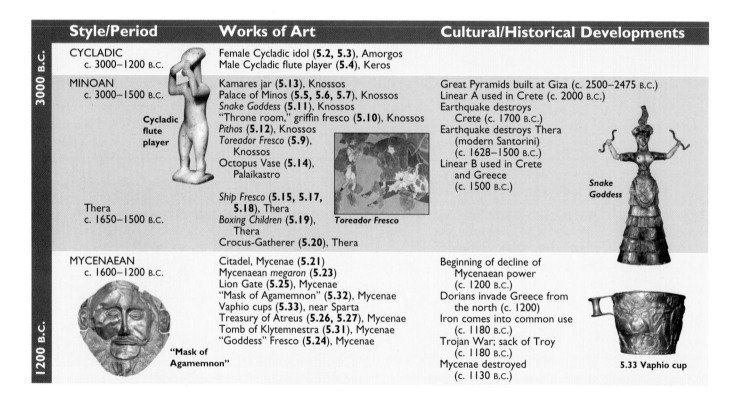

	Style/Period	Works of Art	Cultural/Historical Developments
3000 B.C.	CYCLADIC c. 3000–1200 B.C.	Female Cycladic idol (5.2, 5.3), Amorgos Male Cycladic flute player (5.4), Keros	
	MINOAN c. 3000–1500 B.C.	Kamares jar (5.13), Knossos Palace of Minos (5.5, 5.6, 5.7), Knossos *Snake Goddess* (5.11), Knossos "Throne room," griffin fresco (5.10), Knossos *Pithos* (5.12), Knossos *Toreador Fresco* (5.9), Knossos Octopus Vase (5.14), Palaikastro	Great Pyramids built at Giza (c. 2500–2475 B.C.) Linear A used in Crete (c. 2000 B.C.) Earthquake destroys Crete (c. 1700 B.C.) Earthquake destroys Thera (modern Santorini) (c. 1628–1500 B.C.) Linear B used in Crete and Greece (c. 1500 B.C.)
	Thera c. 1650–1500 B.C.	*Ship Fresco* (5.15, 5.17, 5.18), Thera *Boxing Children* (5.19), Thera Crocus-Gatherer (5.20), Thera	
1200 B.C.	MYCENAEAN c. 1600–1200 B.C.	Citadel, Mycenae (5.21) Mycenaean *megaron* (5.23) Lion Gate (5.25), Mycenae "Mask of Agamemnon" (5.32), Mycenae Vaphio cups (5.33), near Sparta Treasury of Atreus (5.26, 5.27), Mycenae Tomb of Klytemnestra (5.31), Mycenae "Goddess" Fresco (5.24), Mycenae	Beginning of decline of Mycenaean power (c. 1200 B.C.) Dorians invade Greece from the north (c. 1200) Iron comes into common use (c. 1180 B.C.) Trojan War; sack of Troy (c. 1180 B.C.) Mycenae destroyed (c. 1130 B.C.)

Cycladic flute player

Toreador Fresco

Snake Goddess

"Mask of Agamemnon"

5.33 Vaphio cup

6

The Art of Ancient Greece

The time referred to as the historical Greek period emerged some four hundred years after the decline of the Minoan-Mycenaean cultures around 1200 B.C. (fig. **6.1**). Because the art of writing had been lost, little is known of Greek history from 1200 to 800 B.C. Beginning around 800 B.C., however, Greek culture is relatively well documented, including the achievements of its artists, writers, philosophers, and scientists. These made a signifi-

cant and long-lasting impact on Western civilization. (The period covered in this chapter continues through the first century B.C.) Writing was revived, and the Greek language could be read and understood. It has persisted relatively unchanged to the present day. The Greek alphabet was an adaptation of Phoenician, a script written for a Near Eastern Semitic language. The English word "alphabet," in fact, combines the first two letters of the Greek alphabet—

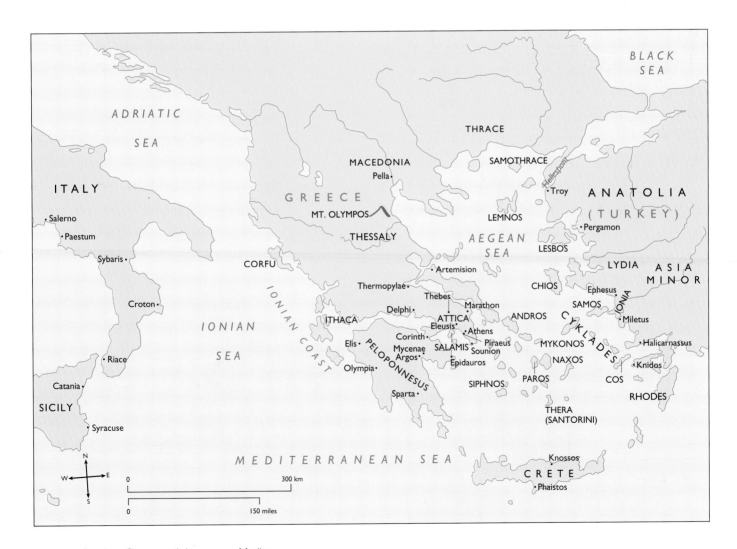

6.1 Map of ancient Greece and the eastern Mediterranean.

alpha and *beta*, equivalent to the Semitic *aleph* and *beth*, and to the modern English "A" and "B."

The exact origins of the Hellenes, as the Greeks called themselves, are unknown. By c. 800 B.C., two related Greek peoples had settled in Greece—the Dorians inhabited the mainland, and the Ionians occupied the easternmost strip of the mainland (including Athens), the Aegean islands, and the west coast of Anatolia (modern Turkey). Later, the Greeks established colonies in southern Italy, Sicily, France, and Spain. As such colonizing activity suggests, the Greeks were accomplished sailors and their economy depended to some degree on maritime trade. They were also successful in cultivating their rocky terrain and in manufacturing pottery and metal objects.

Cultural Identity

Greece was not unified by a strong sense of its identity as a nation until the invasions of 490 and 480 B.C. by the Persians, who were longstanding enemies of the Greeks. But after defeating the Persians, the Greeks thought of

Delphi

The Greek site of Delphi on the northern slopes of Mount Parnassos in Phokis was one of the most spectacular settings in the ancient world—and it remains so today. In the Mycenaean era (c. 1600 B.C.), Delphi had been a sanctuary dedicated to the Titan earth goddess Gaia. By the eighth century B.C., it had become the sanctuary of Apollo, whose temple lies at the beginning of the Sacred Way (figs. **6.2** and **6.3**). According to Greek myth, when Apollo left Delos, he went to Delphi and killed the Python, a dragon who guarded the oracle and stood for the mysterious power of the underworld. In this transfer of Delphi from Gaia and the Python to Apollo, the Greeks saw a development from the forces of darkness to the rationality of light, from the primitive to the intellectual, and from a matriarchal past to patriarchy.

Delphi was also the site of the Pythian Games. At first these contests were held every eight years and were reserved for music and poetry—in honor of Apollo. From 582 B.C., the Games were expanded to include sports, as at Olympia, and took place every four years. The victors were rewarded with a wreath from Apollo's sacred laurel tree, and with a portrait statue erected in the sanctuary.

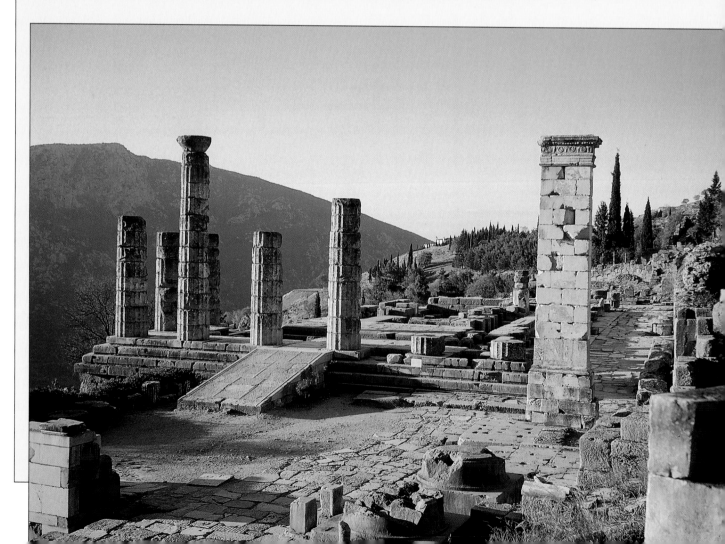

themselves as the most civilized culture in the world, a view reflected in their sense of being a single people, superior to all others. The modern meaning of the word "barbarian" is "uncivilized" or "primitive," but for the ancient Greeks any foreigner was a barbarian (*barbaros*). Greeks considered anyone who spoke a foreign language—unintelligible words sounding like "bar-bar"—to be less civilized than they.

Greece was not only the most civilized country in its own estimation, it was also the most central. The site of the sacred oracle at Delphi (see Box), where futures were fore-told, omens read, and dreams interpreted, was called the *omphalos*, or navel, of the world. The oracle, actually a priest or priestess believed to be divinely inspired, advised on political matters as well as on private ones. As a result, the Delphic oracle drew emissaries from all over the Mediterranean world and became an established center of international influence. Inscribed in stone at Delphi was the prescription "Know thyself," which expressed a new emphasis on individual psychology and insight.

There was also a new perception of history. Rather than marking the passing of time in terms of kings and

6.2 (opposite) Temple of Apollo at Delphi. East view.

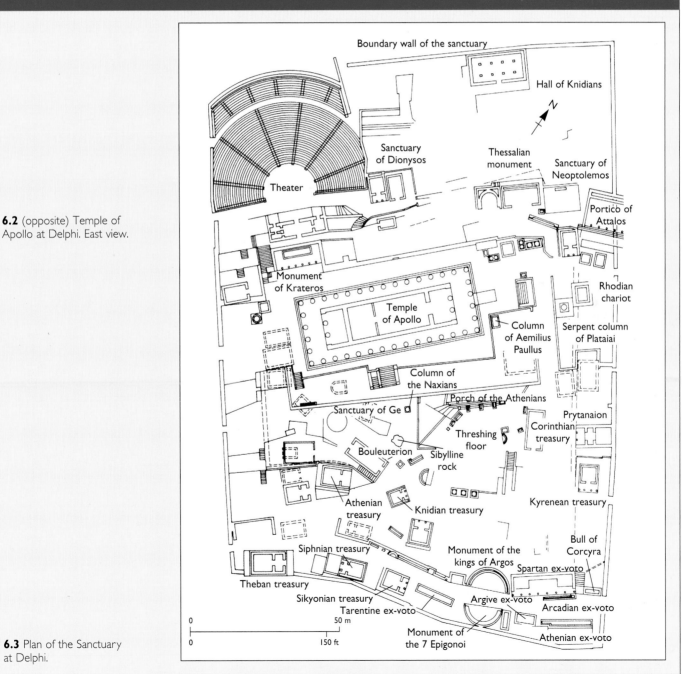

6.3 Plan of the Sanctuary at Delphi.

dynasties as the Egyptians and the Mesopotamians had, the Greeks reckoned time in Olympiads—four-year periods beginning with the first Olympic Games, held in 776 B.C. The Games (called Panhellenic, meaning "all the Greeks") were restricted to Greek-speaking competitors, and reinforced the Greek sense of cultural unity. The Olympic Games were so important that all wars on Greek territory were halted so that athletes could travel safely to Olympia to participate. In this way the destructive forces of battle were transformed into the more peaceful pursuit of athletic competition.

Government and Philosophy

The Athenians abhorred the rule of autocratic kings and pharaohs that characterized many of the other Mediterranean cultures. When the Greek rebels Harmodios and Aristogeiton killed the son of the tyrant Peisistrates in the sixth century B.C., Athens honored them as champions of liberty. The Athenian citizens commissioned portrait statues of the heroes—this was one of the highest honors in ancient Greece because it preserved an individual's fame for posterity. The Persians symbolically challenged Athenian liberty by plundering the statues of Harmodios and Aristogeiton, which were not replaced until 477/6 B.C., after their defeat.

The Greek aversion to tyranny led to the establishment of independent city-states. Each city-state, or *polis*, required some degree of citizen participation in its government. Even though the Greeks, like most ancient Mediterranean cultures, kept slaves and did not allow women to engage in politics (see Box), the *polis* was an important foundation of modern democracy. The ideas embodied in the Athenian democracy of the second half of the fifth century B.C. inspired Thomas Jefferson when he wrote the Declaration of Independence and framed the American Constitution in the late eighteenth century. The very word "democracy" is derived from the Greek *demos* (people) and *kratos* (power).

Women in Ancient Greece

In the period of Greek history depicted by Homer, aristocratic women led lives of relative independence, as did the women of Sparta from the sixth century B.C. onward. In Athens and other parts of Greece during the Classical period (fifth century B.C.), however, women lived under severe constraints. They ventured outside the house mainly for religious processions and festivals restricted to women, and could not vote or hold public office. In the words of Aristotle: "The deliberative faculty is not present at all in the slave, in the female it is inoperative, in the child undeveloped."

In the private sphere, women occupied segregated quarters of the house. Greek marriages were monogamous. As in all ancient cultures, marriage was an economic transaction arranged by the parents of the couple, generally within a circle of relatives so as to preserve property within the family. The woman was usually much younger than the man and they often had no previous acquaintance. If an unmarried woman had no brothers, she was obliged upon the death of her father to marry his closest relative in order to carry on the family.

Once married, a woman became her husband's responsibility. She had no independent status and her life was devoted to childbearing and looking after the family and household. Perikles is quoted by the Greek historian Thucydides (c. 460–400 B.C.) as having said that a woman should "be spoken of as little as possible among men, whether for good or ill." Women could own nothing apart from personal possessions, and could not be party to any transaction worth more than a nominal amount. A man could divorce his wife by declaration before witnesses; a wife could do so only by taking her husband to court and proving serious offenses.

Athenian men were required by law to marry daughters of Athenian citizens. As a result, some men developed relationships outside marriage with *hetairai*, or companions who often were courtesans. *Hetairai* generally came from Ionia and were more intellectual and better educated than Athenian women. The best-known *hetaira* of the fifth century B.C. is the Milesian Aspasia, who was the companion of Perikles. He eventually divorced his wife to marry her.

Ideas about female emancipation begin to appear in literature from the end of the fifth century B.C., and some of the most memorable characters in Greek plays are females, although they were acted by male youths. From the fourth century onward—and increasingly so in the Hellenistic period (third to first century B.C.)—education was accessible to some women and there are reports of women studying philosophy, painting, and writing poetry.

The Roman historian Pliny the Elder mentions by name one Iaia of Kyzikos, who lived in the early first century B.C. Her "hand," he wrote, "was quicker than that of any other painter, and her artistry was of such high quality that she commanded much higher prices than the most celebrated painters of the same period."

Sappho, the most famous poetess in antiquity, lived at the turn of the seventh century B.C. and was much admired by Plato and other writers. Little is known of her life, except that she was born on the island of Lesbos (from which comes the word "lesbian"). Her poems, inspired by Aphrodite, tell of her love for girls and were accompanied by the music of the lyre. Today her work survives only in fragments, but she is known to have written nine books of odes, elegies (poems that mourn the dead), and *epithalamia* (lyric odes to a bride and bridegroom). She composed in various meters—the Sapphic meter is believed to have been her invention.

Plato on Artists

Great philosopher though he was, Plato did not have much use for artists. In Book X of *The Republic*, he proposes banishing them from his ideal state. For Plato, art had no reality except as technique (*techne*) and as imitation (*mimesis*) of nature. But nature itself, he argued, is *only* a mere shadow of the essential truth, which he called the "Good and Beautiful" (*kalos k'agathos*), and it is the philosopher, rather than the poet or artist, who is capable of interpreting it.

The original creator, according to Plato, is God, who creates in relation to the philosophical essence. Craftsmen and artisans are below God, for they make useful objects that, like nature, only reflect the essential. The painter, who makes an image of the object, is lower still, and therefore even farther from the truth.

Poets do not fare much better than artists in Plato's ideal state, for, in his view, they appeal to passion rather than to truth. Although Plato loved Homer, he recommended banishing his works along with those of the artists, and admitting only hymns to God and poetry praising famous men.

Greek philosophers discussed the nature of government at length. Foremost among them is Plato (c. 428–348 B.C.). His writings include *The Republic* and *The Laws*, which examine his ideal state and the laws required for its proper functioning. Plato's spokesman and teacher, Socrates (see Box and fig. **6.4**), had developed a new method of teaching known as Socratic dialogue—a process of question and answer through which the truth of an argument is elicited from the student. Demanding close observation of nature and human character, the Socratic method reflects the Greek interest in the centrality of man in relation to the natural world, which is consistent with the Greek artists'

pursuit of naturalism and the study of anatomy.

Aristotle, Plato's most distinguished student and tutor of Alexander the Great, stands out among the ancient Greek philosophers for the diversity of his interests. In addition to natural sciences such as botany, physics, and physiology, Aristotle wrote on philosophy, metaphysics, ethics, politics, logic, rhetoric, and poetry. His *Poetics* established the basis for subsequent discussions of tragedy, comedy, and epic poetry in Western literary criticism. Aristotle did not discuss the visual arts as specifically as Plato had, but his views on esthetics have had a substantial influence on Western philosophy.

Socrates: "Know Thyself"

Socrates (470–399 B.C.) left no writings. He was the philosophical spokesman and central figure of Plato's *Dialogues*, who advocated self-knowledge in the search for truth. Ultimately a martyr to his intellectual integrity, Socrates chose death rather than exile from the Athens he loved. He explains the philosophical rationale for his choice in Plato's *Apology*.

Figure 6.4 reflects the appearance of Socrates as described by the Athenian general Alkibiades in Plato's *Symposium*. Alkibiades compares Socrates to two unattractive satyrs (mythological creatures who are part human and part goat), Silenos and Marsyas (the latter found the flute which Athena had discarded and challenged Apollo to a musical contest). Silenos was associated with the drunken orgies of Dionysos, and Alkibiades notes that small statues of Silenos found in Athenian shops open up to reveal the image of a god. Similarly, he says, Socrates' words open up into images of Truth and Beauty: "They are ridiculous when you first hear them; ... he clothes himself in language that is like the skin of the wanton Satyr." The ignorant laugh, but whoever looks below the surface sees the divine beauty in his words. According to Alkibiades, these words have even more charm than the music of Marsyas, for Socrates charms and stirs the souls of his listeners. "I saw in him," Alkibiades says, "divine and golden images of such fascinating beauty that I was ready to do in a moment whatever Socrates commanded."

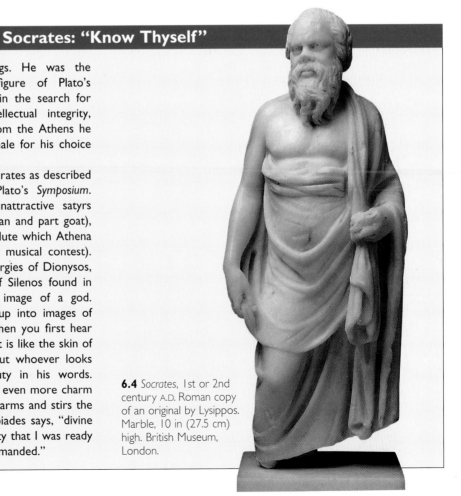

6.4 *Socrates*, 1st or 2nd century A.D. Roman copy of an original by Lysippos. Marble, 10 in (27.5 cm) high. British Museum, London.

Philosophy and science, as well as philosophy and esthetics, were very much interrelated in ancient Greece. In the seventh century B.C., for example, Thales of Miletos had founded the first Greek school of philosophy, and argued that the origin of all matter was water. In the sixth century B.C., the Pythagorean philosophers of Samos recognized that the earth was a sphere. It was here that the Pythagorean theorem was formulated: "A² + B² = C²" (the square of the hypotenuse of a right-angled triangle is equal to the sum of the squares of the other two sides). Similar mathematical relationships determined the proportions of Classical Greek temples (see p. 168). In the fourth century B.C., Euclid developed number theory and plane geometry.

Greek Gods and Roman Counterparts

Greek God	Function/Subject	Attribute	Roman Counterpart
Zeus (husband and brother of **Hera**)	King of the gods, sky	Thunderbolt, eagle	**Jupiter**
Hera (wife and sister of **Zeus**)	Queen of the gods, women, marriage, maternity	Veil, cuckoo, pomegranate, peacock	**Juno**
Athena (daughter of **Zeus**)	War in its strategic aspects, wisdom, weaving, protector of Athens	Armor, shield, Gorgoneion, Nike	**Minerva**
Ares (son of **Zeus** and **Hera**)	War, carnage, strife, blind courage	Armor	**Mars**
Aphrodite	Love, beauty	**Eros** (her son)	**Venus**
Apollo (son of **Zeus** and **Leto**)	Solar light, reason, prophecy, medicine, music	Lyre, bow, quiver	**Phoebus**
Helios (later identified with **Apollo**)	Sun		**Phoebus**
Artemis (daughter of **Zeus** and **Leto**)	Lunar light, hunting, childbirth	Bow and arrow, dogs	**Diana**
Selene (later identified with **Artemis**)	Moon	Crescent moon	
Hermes (son of **Zeus** and **Maia**)	Male messenger of the gods, trickster and thief; good luck, wealth, travel, dreams, eloquence	Winged sandals, winged cap, *caduceus* (winged staff entwined with two serpents)	**Mercury**
Hades (brother of **Zeus**, husband of **Persephone**)	Ruler of the underworld	**Cerberus** (a triple-headed dog)	**Pluto**
Dionysos (son of **Zeus** and **Semele**)	Wine, theater grapes, panther skin	*Thyrsos* (staff), wine cup	**Bacchus**
Hephaestos (son of **Hera**)	Fire, the art of the blacksmith, crafts	Hammer, tongs, lameness	**Vulcan**
Hestia (sister of **Zeus**)	Hearth, domestic fire, the family	Hearth	**Vesta**
Demeter (sister of **Zeus**)	Agriculture, grain	Ears of wheat, torch	**Ceres**
Poseidon (brother of **Zeus**)	Sea	Trident, horse	**Neptune**
Herakles (son of **Zeus** and a mortal woman, the only hero admitted by the gods to Mount Olympos and granted immortality)	Strength	Lion skin, club, bow and quiver	**Hercules**
Eros (son of **Aphrodite**)	Love	Bow and arrow, wings	**Amor/Cupid**
Iris	Female messenger of the gods (especially of **Hera**), rainbow	Wings	
Hebe (daughter of **Zeus** and **Hera**)	Cup-bearer of the gods, youth	Cup	
Nike	Victory	Wings	
Persephone (daughter of **Zeus** and **Demeter**, wife of **Hades**)	The underworld	Scepter, pomegranate	

Literature and Drama

The literary legacy of Greece is one of the most remarkable bequeathed to Western civilization. *The Iliad*, attributed to Homer, is the account of the Trojan War and its heroes, and *The Odyssey* the story of Odysseus' ten-year journey home to Ithaca after the war. These epic poems were originally recited, and then were written down some time between the eighth and sixth centuries B.C. They are noteworthy for their literary style and new emphasis on the power and psychology of human heroes. The same is true of the tragedies of Aeschylos, Sophokles, and Euripides, and the comedies of Aristophanes, all of which laid the foundation of Western theater. Aeschylos' trilogy *The Oresteia*, written during the fifth century B.C., dramatized the tragedy of Agamemnon's family after his return to Mycenae from the Trojan War (see p. 127). And it was Sophokles who gave the world the Oedipos plays, from which Freud recognized that poets had understood human psychology long before the development of psychoanalysis. The events and characters of Greek literature were often illustrated by the artists, whose interest in psychology paralleled that of the writers and philosophers.

"Man is the Measure of All Things"

The ancient Greek contributions to Western civilization are inextricably linked to this saying, which set Greece apart from other ancient Mediterranean cultures. In Greek religion, gods were not only anthropomorphic (human in form), but had human-like personalities and conflicts (see Box). They participated in human events, such as the Trojan War, and tried to influence their outcome. The gods are referred to as the Olympians, because they resided on Mount Olympos after having overthrown their primitive, cannibalistic forerunners, the so-called Titans.

The Greeks also differed from other Mediterranean cultures, especially Egypt, in their views of death and in their rituals for the dead. For example, they believed that certain rituals were necessary for the "shade" of the deceased to pass into the shadowy underworld of Hades. Without proper burial rituals, a spirit might be condemned to wander restlessly forever. Rather than engage in elaborate efforts to preserve the physical body from decay (as in Egypt), the

Greeks erected grave-markers, which were memorials to the deceased rather than offerings to the gods.

Like science, philosophy, and literature, the surviving works of art from ancient Greece emphasize the individual above all. In contrast to the continuity of Egyptian art, Greek art evolved rapidly from stylization towards naturalism. The treatment of nature and humanity's place in it—ideal as well as actual—differentiated the Greek use of canons (see p. 89) from the Egyptian. In Greek art, measurements were in relation to human scale and organic form.

The Greek attitude to artists indicated a new interest in the relationship of creators to their work. As far as one can tell, the Greeks were the first Western people to sign their works (for example, fig. 6.9). They were also the first to mention female as well as male artists, indicating that—despite the restricted role of women in Greek society—a few exceptional women achieved professional success. The Greeks gave their artists a new status consistent with their cultural view that man, rather than gods, is the "measure of all things."

Painting and Pottery

The earliest Greek style, called Geometric (c. 1000–700 B.C.), is known only from pottery and small-scale sculpture. The Orientalizing style (c. 700–640 B.C.) shows influences from Eastern art and, around the same time, monumental sculptures began to develop. The broad stylistic categories of Greek art following Orientalizing are Archaic, Classical, and Hellenistic.

Geometric Style
(c. 1000–700 B.C.)

Since most of the monumental mural paintings of ancient Greece have been lost, the development of pictorial style is best known through images on pottery. The earliest recognizable style in Greek art after the destruction of the Mycenaean cultures c. 1200 B.C. is **Geometric**. The lively, rectilinear **meander patterns** circling the body of the amphora (or two-handled storage jar) in figure **6.5** are typical of developed Geometric pottery design. Each pattern is framed by circular horizontal

6.5 Geometric amphora, 8th century B.C. Terracotta, 5 ft 1 in (1.55 m) high. National Archaeological Museum, Athens.

borders that emphasize the shape of the pot, and two rows of stylized animals seem to proceed slowly around the neck. Because the original function of the amphora was to serve as a grave-marker, its main scene is a *prothesis*, or lying-in-state of the dead. The deceased lies on a horizontal bier, held up and flanked by rows of figures who create a sense of motion through ritual gestures of mourning. Their torsos are composed of flat black triangles, and their heads are rounded. Typical of Geometric vase painting are the flat, two-dimensional renderings, and the lively, stylized forms painted in a dark glaze (actually a **slip**, or refined clay) over a light surface.

Orientalizing Style (c. 700–640 B.C.)

In the eighth century B.C., influences from the Near East and Egypt enter Greek art in a recognizable way. The

Greek assimilation of Eastern iconography reflects contact and trade, as well as an interest in the artistic possibilities of certain motifs and forms.

In the Orientalizing amphora shown in figure **6.6**, dated c. 675–650 B.C., the shapes have become larger and more curvilinear than those of the Geometric style, and the geometric patterns are now relegated to borders of the mythological representations. The scene on the neck (fig. **6.7**) illustrates Odysseus and his men driving a stake into the eye of the Cyclops Polyphemos, who had eaten some of his men. The poses of Odysseus and his companion show similarities with earlier Aegean painting, particularly the nearly frontal shoulder, profile legs and head, and frontal eye. As in Minoan and Theran nudes (see the *Boxing Children* in figure 5.19), there is a hint of a turn at the waist to account for the spatial discrepancy between torso and legs.

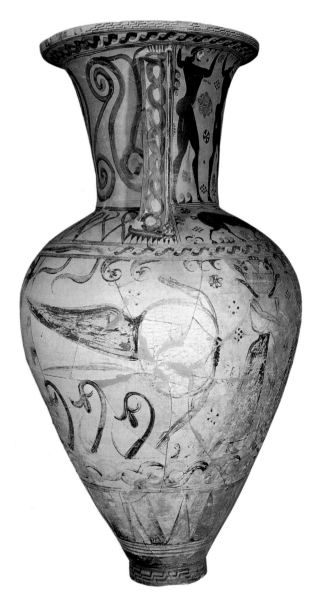
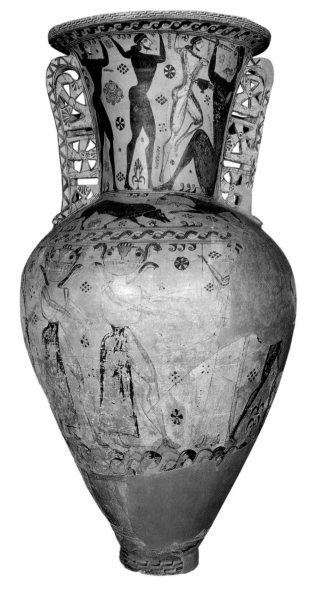

6.6a, b Polyphemos Painter, Amphora, 675–650 B.C. Terracotta, 4 ft 8 in (1.42 m) high. Eleusis Museum, Eleusis.

6.7 Polyphemos Painter, Amphora neck showing the blinding of Polyphemos (detail of fig. 6.6). In Book IX of *The Odyssey*, the one-eyed Titan, the Cyclops Polyphemos, imprisons the Greek Odysseus and his men in his cave on the island of Sicily. After Polyphemos devours six of the men, Odysseus gives him wine and blinds him with a large stake. The cunning Odysseus has previously told the Cyclops that his name is Nobody, so that when Polyphemos calls for help he can only report that Nobody is harming him. The next day, Odysseus and his men tie themselves to the underbellies of Polyphemos' sheep. When in the morning Polyphemos sends his sheep out of the cave to graze, he feels their backs to make sure that the Greeks are not using his sheep to escape. But he does not feel their undersides, and so Odysseus and the rest of his men go free.

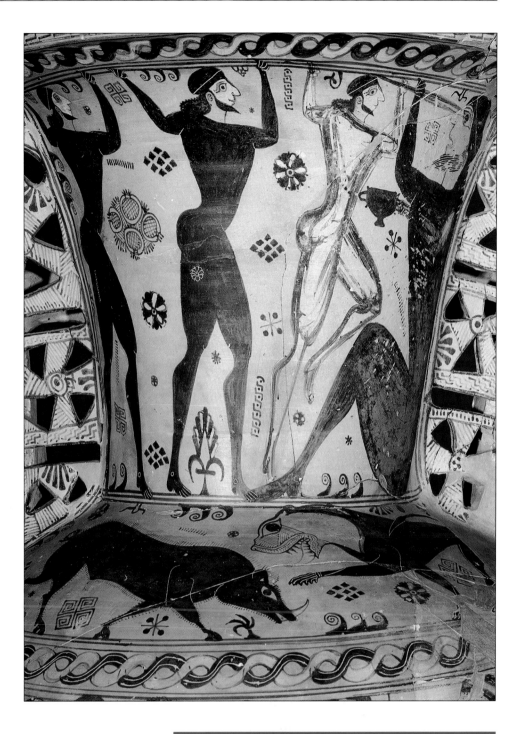

On the body of the vase, the artist has represented the beheading of Medusa by the hero Perseus (see Box). Medusa's two immortal Gorgon sisters, shown in figure 6.6b are running from her decapitated body lying horizontally in figure 6.6a. The Gorgon heads resemble those on bronze cauldrons that were imported into Greece from the Near East, and the protruding snakes suggest the cauldron **protomes**, or tops of animals. Both events depicted on this amphora represent Greek heroes—Odysseus and Perseus—as destroying the primitive forces of terror (Medusa) and cannibalism (Polyphemos).

Medusa

Medusa, the only mortal of the three Gorgon sisters, turned to stone any man who looked at her. She had snaky hair, glaring eyes, fanged teeth, and emitted a loud roar. Following the wise advice of Athena to look at her only in the reflection of his shield, Perseus decapitated Medusa. He took her head to Athena, who adopted it as her shield device. The Medusa head, or *gorgoneion*, subsequently became a popular armor decoration in the West, symbolically petrifying—i.e. killing—one's enemies.

Greek Vase Media and Shapes

Greek vases were made of terracotta. On **black-figure** pieces, the artist painted the figures in black silhouette with a slip made of clay and water. Details were added with a sharp tool by incising lines through the painted surface and exposing the orange clay below. The vase was then fired (baked in a kiln) in three stages. The final result was an oxidization process that turned the surface of the vase reddish-orange and the painted areas black.

For **red-figure** vases, the process was reversed. Figures were left in red against a painted black background, and details were painted in black.

On **white-ground** vases, a wash of white clay formed the background. Figures were then applied in black, and additional colors were sometimes added after the firing.

As early as the Archaic period, certain shapes of vase became associated with specific uses (fig. **6.8**).

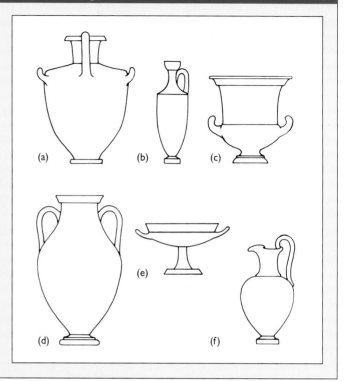

6.8 Greek vase shapes include (a) the **hydria**, a water jar with three handles; (b) the **lekythos**, a flask for storing and pouring oil; (c) the **krater**, a bowl for mixing wine and water (the Greeks drank their wine diluted); (d) the **amphora**, a vessel for storing honey, olive oil, water, or wine; (e) the **kylix**, a drinking cup; and (f) the **oenochoe**, a jug for pouring wine.

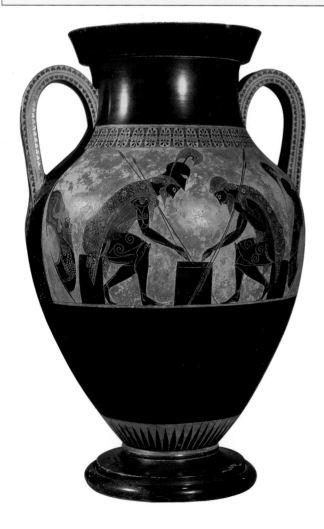

6.9 (left) Exekias, Amphora showing *Achilles and Ajax Playing a Board Game*, 540–530 B.C. Terracotta, whole vessel 24 in (61 cm) high. Musei Vaticani, Rome. This amphora was signed by Exekias as both potter and painter. He integrates form with characterization to convey the impression that Achilles, the younger warrior on the left, will win the game. On the right, Ajax leans farther forward than his opponent so that the level of his head is slightly lower, and he has removed his helmet. Achilles' helmet and tall crest indicate his dominance.

Archaic Style (c. 640–490 B.C.)

The painting technique used during the Archaic period (from the Greek *archaios*, meaning "old") is known as **black-figure** (c. 600–480 B.C.) (see Box). The amphora with a scene of *Achilles and Ajax Playing a Board Game* is an excellent example; patterning still functions as a border device (fig. **6.9**). And, as in Orientalizing, the central image is a narrative scene. Exekias, the most insightful and dramatic black-figure artist known to us, was a panel painter as well as a vase painter. In this scene, he transforms the personal rivalry between the two Greek heroes of the Trojan War into a board game. He emphasizes the intense concentration of Homer's protagonists by the combined diagonals of their spears and their gaze, all of which focus our attention on the game-board. Ajax and Achilles are identified by inscriptions. They wear elaborately patterned cloaks, arm and thigh armor enlivened with elegant spiral designs, and greaves (shin protectors). The stylized frontal eye persists from Mesopotamian, Egyptian, and Aegean art, but here the postures are rendered more three-dimensionally.

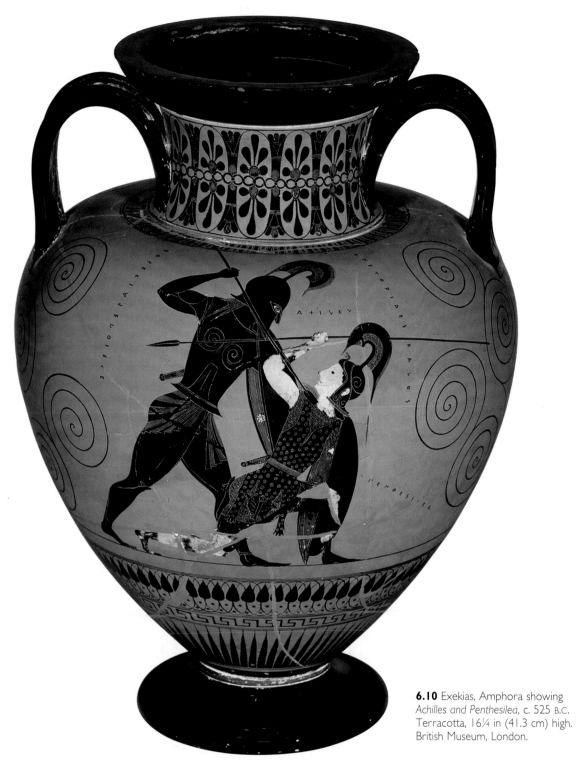

6.10 Exekias, Amphora showing *Achilles and Penthesilea*, c. 525 B.C. Terracotta, 16¼ in (41.3 cm) high. British Museum, London.

In another vase painting, Exekias uses the power of the gaze and the device of diagonal spears to enhance the tragic love between Achilles and the Amazon queen, Penthesilea (figs. **6.10** and **6.11**). The Greek hero leans forward, his entire body a forceful, towering diagonal, and drives his spear into the neck of his opponent. Identified with the luxurious East by her leopard skin, Penthesilea is on her knees in defeat. Both figures, as in the previous example, are partly three-dimensional, but their heads are in strict profile. With blood gushing from her neck, Penthesilea turns back to confront the gaze of her attacker. She sees that Achilles has, at the point of her death, fallen in love with her. Compared with the scene in figure 6.9, the confrontation here is intensified by the "locked in" gaze of the two combatants and is unrelieved by the intervening board-game. Exekias' ability to capture such dramatic moments is consistent with contemporary developments in Greek theater, and foreshadows Classical tragedy.

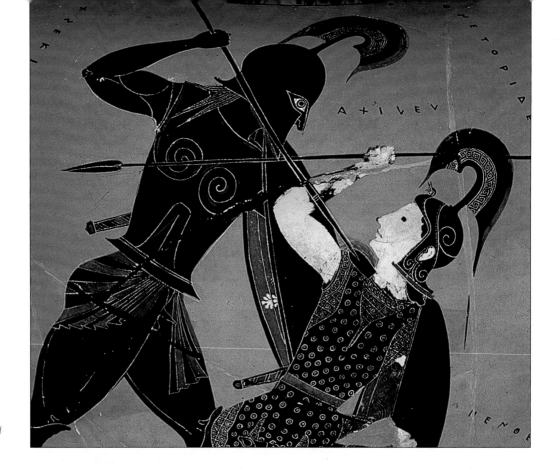

6.11 (right) Exekias, *Achilles and Penthesilea* (detail of fig. 6.10).

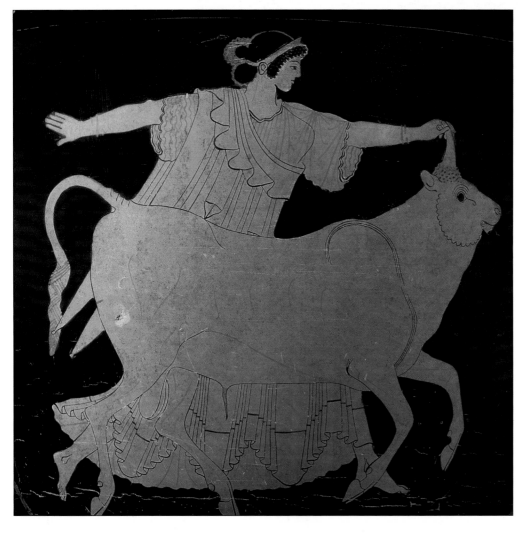

6.12 (left) Berlin Painter, Bell krater showing the *Abduction of Europa*, c. 490 B.C. Terracotta, whole vessel 13 in (33 cm) high. Museo Archeologico, Tarquinia. In this scene Zeus takes the form of a bull and abducts the mortal Europa. The Greeks would have recognized the irony of the unsuspecting Europa being fascinated by Zeus' horn and rushing to her fate.

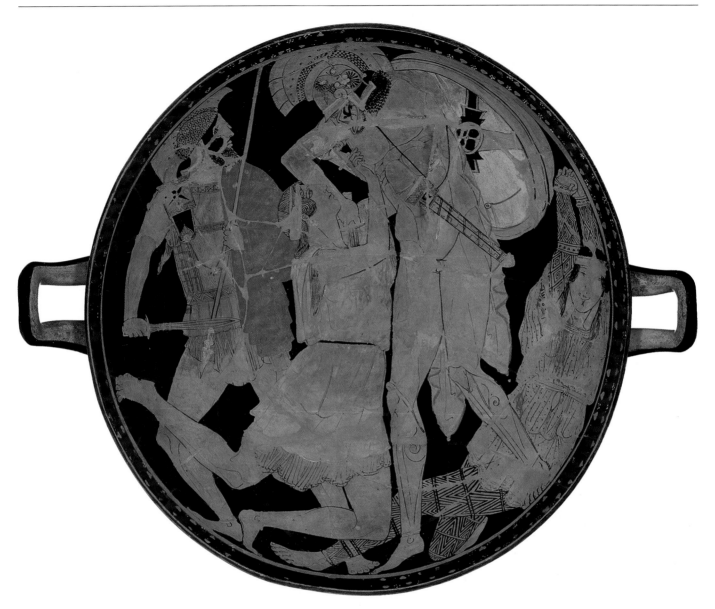

Late Archaic to Classical Style (c. 530–400 B.C.)

The **red-figure** painting technique was introduced in the late Archaic period and continued to be used until around 400 B.C. It permitted freer painting and the representation of more natural form than had been possible in black-figure. Furthermore, the red color now used for skin tones was closer to the actual skin color of the Greeks than black had been.

The scene on a bell krater of about 490 B.C. by an artist known as the Berlin Painter (fig. **6.12**) illustrates the transition from black-figure to red-figure painting. The decorative surface patterns have decreased and more attention is given to organic form and movement. Black lines indicating the folds of Europa's dress appear three-dimensional in form and suggest the motion of her body—especially the large step that she takes with her heels lifted off the ground.

By some thirty-five years later, red-figure painting had become less stylized, and human figures were represented with greater naturalism. This development can be seen in

6.13 Penthesilea Painter, Cup interior showing *Achilles and Penthesilea*, c. 455 B.C. Terracotta, diameter 17 in (43 cm). Antike Sammlungen, Munich.

another painting of Achilles and Penthesilea by the so-called Penthesilea Painter (fig. **6.13**). The large figures that seem about to burst the rim of the cup suggest that the scene was based on a larger mural painting. At the right, a dead Amazon curves in line with the frame, while a vigorous Greek readies his dagger and spear at the left. In the center Achilles and Penthesilea enact their tragic fate. Compared with the black-figure version by Exekias, this is more crowded, the figures are closer together, and there is more overlapping. We see Achilles plunging his sword straight down into the Amazon, as she clasps his breast. Although this artist maintains the profile confrontation and the riveted gaze of Exekias' painting, he achieves dramatic power by the sheer physical force of the figures, especially the Greeks.

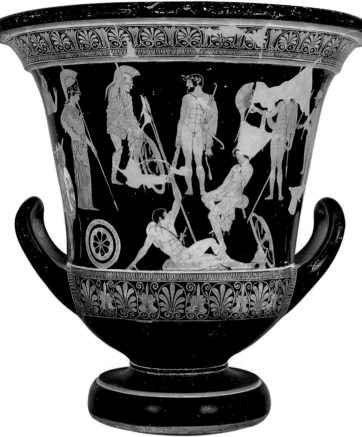

6.14 Niobid Painter, Kalyx krater, side showing unidentified scene, c. 455–450 B.C. 21¼ in (54 cm) high. Louvre, Paris.

Encaustic: Luminous Painting

From the second half of the fifth century B.C. Greek artists colored their sculptures with **encaustic**—one of the oldest and most luminous painting media. It is made by mixing dry powder pigments with molten beeswax. Colors are applied with a brush or a spatula and then fused in with heat—hence the term "encaustic," which means "burnt in." Greek artists liked to refer to their "waxes" just as modern artists refer to their "oils."

Because of its luminosity, encaustic can create a particularly naturalistic impression. The poet Anacreon (c. 570–478 B.C.) was reportedly so amazed by an encaustic likeness that he exclaimed, "Quickly, O wax, you will speak!" Unfortunately, Greek encaustic paintings are now known only from descriptions.

In addition to increased organic form, the Greek painters of the mid-fifth century B.C. began to set figures in nature and to depict elements of landscape. The kalyx krater by an artist known as the Niobid Painter has an unidentified scene on one side (fig. **6.14**); the other, depicting the *Death of the Children of Niobe* (the Niobids) (fig. **6.15**), has a rudimentary tree and sloping terrain. Niobe

was a mortal woman who boasted that she was greater than Leto because she had fourteen children. Apollo (the son of Zeus and Leto) and his twin sister Artemis, who were expert archers, killed all of Niobe's children. Figure 6.15 shows Artemis removing an arrow from her quiver, while Apollo takes aim at his next victim. The gods' power is emphasized by the fact that they tower over the mortals, two of whom lie dead, draped over the rocky landscape in the foreground.

Classical to Late Classical Style
(c. 420–4th century B.C.)

During the late fifth century B.C., a technique of painting known as white-ground became popular on *lekythoi*, which were used as grave dedications. The example in figure **6.16**, of c. 410 B.C., shows a warrior sitting by a grave. He is rendered as if in a three-dimensional space—his body moves naturally, bending slightly at the waist, and his head inclines as if in meditation or mourning. The drapery falls over his legs as it would in reality, and his left leg and shield are **foreshortened**.

The Greek interest in naturalism led to a delight in illusionism and *trompe-l'oeil* (see p. 6). Zeuxis, for example, as mentioned in Chapter 1, was reputed to have painted

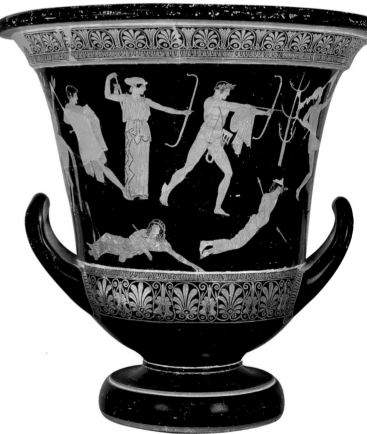

6.15 Niobid Painter, Kalyx krater, side showing the *Death of the Children of Niobe*, c. 455–450 B.C. 21¼ in (54 cm) high. Louvre, Paris.

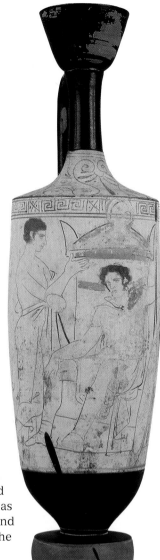

6.16 Reed Painter, *Warrior by a Grave* (detail of white-ground *lekythos*), c. 410 B.C. Terracotta, 18⅞ in (48 cm) high. National Archaeological Museum, Athens. The use of foreshortening, which depicts the round shield as an oval because it is partly turned, indicates the Greek artist's interest in rendering forms as they appear in natural, three-dimensional space.

grapes that fooled birds into believing they were real. By the late fifth century, Zeuxis was painting from live models and therefore directly from nature. One anecdote relates that he died laughing while staring at his painting of an old woman and that he painted Helen of Troy (see p. 127) as a *hetaira*, or courtesan, and charged admission when the picture was exhibited.

During the fourth century B.C, Apelles of Kos (see Chapter 1) reputedly painted such realistic horses that live horses neighed when they saw them. He became Alexander the Great's court painter (see below); one of his portraits depicted Alexander with a thunderbolt so realistically that the fingers seemed to stand out from the picture plane. Apelles also painted Alexander's mistress, Pancaspe, and fell in love with her. As a measure of his esteem for Apelles, Alexander gave Pancaspe to him.

Apelles, like Zeuxis, had a sense of humor. He liked to hide when his works were exhibited in order to hear viewers' comments. On one occasion, when a shoemaker observed that the artist had made a mistake in his rendition of a sandal strap, Apelles corrected it. Later the same shoemaker criticized a leg, and Apelles objected to his pre-

sumption. He told him not to rise above the sandal, which was his only area of expertise. This became the origin of the expression: "Let a shoemaker stick to his last."

Mosaic

The best preserved examples of large-scale Greek pictorial style are mosaics from the Hellenistic period (c. 323–31 B.C.), although many earlier mosaics have been found. The pebble mosaic in figure **6.17** represents a stag hunt. Diagonal planes, curved, shifting outlines, and sharp contrast between the white figures and dark gray background give the composition a sense of animation, which is reinforced by the elaborate floral border. Note also the suggestion of muscle tension rendered by shading, and the flowing cloaks of the hunters. The opposing diagonals of the figures enhance the impression of struggle between hunters and stag and between stag and dog. Because the artist conveys a sense of three-dimensional space, the two hunters and their dog appear to surround their prey.

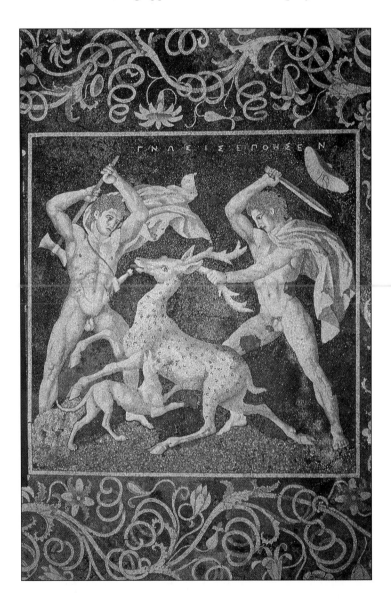

6.17 *Stag Hunt*, from Pella, c. 300 B.C. Pebble mosaic, 10 ft 4 in × 10 ft 4 in (3.15 × 3.15 m). Archaeological Museum, Pella. In floor mosaics, the image is created by embedding colored pebbles into a surface and defining the outlines with metal strips inlaid to keep the stones in place. The use of pebbles tends to dull the colors. Despite the limitations of the medium, an illusion of organic figures moving freely in three-dimensional space is achieved here.

Sculpture

Orientalizing Style: The Lions of Delos
(7th century B.C.)

The row of impressive white marble lions (fig. **6.18**) on the island of Delos continues the traditional guardian function of such animals. Located in the middle of the Cyclades, Delos is a small island that was an important trading center inhabited from the third millennium B.C. Delos had been revered as Apollo's sanctuary, because it was the god's birthplace. According to the myth, Zeus seduced Leto, a daughter of the Titans. His jealous wife Hera pursued the pregnant Leto until she found refuge on a barren rock in the sea. There she gave birth to the twin gods Apollo and Artemis, and thereafter Delos was a fertile island.

Because of its importance as a religious site, Delos was subjected to a long-lasting struggle for control. In the late seventh century B.C., it was under the rule of the neighboring island of Naxos. The Naxians erected the marble lions on the road leading north from the temple of Leto, and today five of them survive. They sit on their haunches, looking alert and ready to spring. The sense of contained energy combined with monumental form and stylization—most evident in the rib-cage—is characteristic of the early Greek styles. At the same time, the simplicity of the lions and their gleaming marble surfaces recall the Cycladic idols that had been produced in the Bronze Age.

The ancient belief that lions sleep with their eyes open accounts for the guardian function of the Delos lions, as it had in Egypt, the Aegean, and the Near East. Their focus on the temple of Apollo's mother is consistent with the tra-

6.18 Terrace of the Lions, Delos, 7th century B.C. Marble, over-lifesize.

ditional association of lions with the sun, which continues to the present day in the zodiac: Leo (the lion) is the house of the sun.

Archaic Style (c. 640–490 B.C.)

Monumental sculpture of human figures began in Greece during the Archaic period. It is not known why the Greeks began making such works when they did, but it is clear that the early Archaic artists were influenced by Egyptian technique and convention.

In creating lifesize human figures, the Greeks learned from the Egyptians how to carve blocks of stone, but adapted the technique to suit their own tastes. The *New York Kouros* (fig. **6.19**) was made around 600 B.C. by an artist known as the Dipylon Master. A comparison of this figure with the statue of Menkaure (fig. 4.21) highlights the similarities and differences between Egyptian and Archaic Greek lifesize statues of standing males. The *Kouros* maintains the standard Egyptian frontal pose. His left leg extends forward, with no bend at knee, hips, or waist, and his arms are at his sides, fists clenched and elbows turned back. Nevertheless, the Dipylon Master has made changes to emphasize human anatomy. The *Kouros* is cut away from the original rectangular block of marble, leaving open spaces between arms and body and between the legs. This openness and the smaller shoulders decrease the tension and monumentality of the *New York Kouros* when compared with Menkaure.

Both figures are rendered with characteristic stylizations. In contrast to the rectangularity of Egyptian convention, various features of the *Kouros* are curved—the round knee caps topped by two arcs and the lower outline of the rib-cage. The hair is composed of little circles arranged in parallel rows, ending in a bottom row of small cones. It falls over the back of the shoulders, but does not fill up as much space as Menkaure's wig.

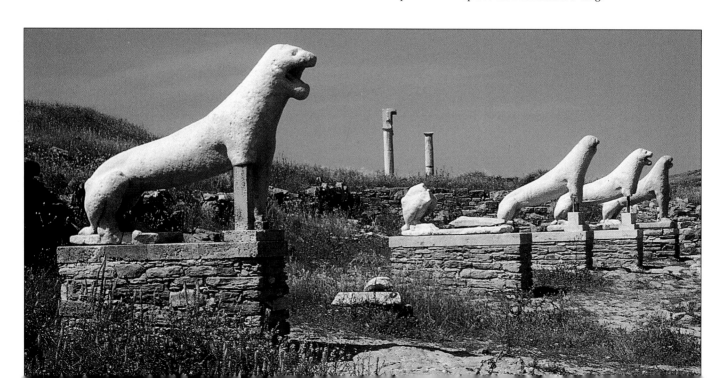

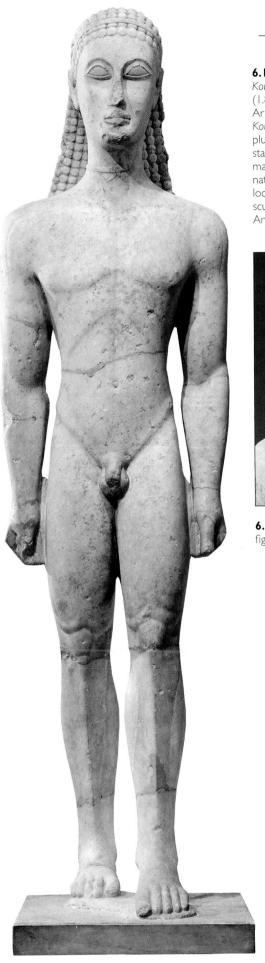

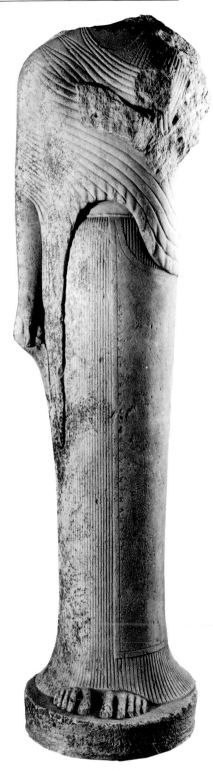

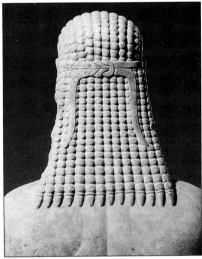

6.19a (left) Dipylon Master, *New York Kouros*, from Attica, c. 600 B.C. Marble, 6 ft (1.84 m) high. Metropolitan Museum of Art, New York. Fletcher Fund, 1932. *Kouros*, the Greek for "boy" (*kouroi* in the plural), is used to denote a type of standing male figure, typically carved from marble and usually commemorative in nature. This *kouros* is named for its present location. It is the earliest known lifesize sculpture of a standing male from the Archaic period.

6.19b (above) *New York Kouros* (detail of fig. 6.19a).

6.20 (right) The Cheramyes Master, *Hera of Samos*, from Samos, c. 560 B.C. Marble, 6 ft 3½ in (1.9 m) high. Louvre, Paris.

The most obvious difference between the statues of Menkaure and the *New York Kouros* is the nudity of the latter. The Greek convention of nudity for male statues from the Archaic period signals the interest in human form, whereas Archaic statues of females were clothed for reasons of propriety.

In the *Hera of Samos* (fig. **6.20**), as in the Delos lions, we find the characteristic Archaic combination of tension and geometric form. A votive figure, dedicated to Hera by a

6.21a (far right) *Peplos Kore*, c. 530 B.C. Parian marble, from Paros, 3 ft 11⅔ in (1.21 m) high. Acropolis Museum, Athens. The *Peplos Kore* still retains traces of paint on her dress and in her eyes, reminding us that Greek artists originally used color to enliven the appearance of their white marble figures.

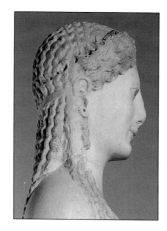

6.21b *Peplos Kore* (detail of fig. 6.21a).

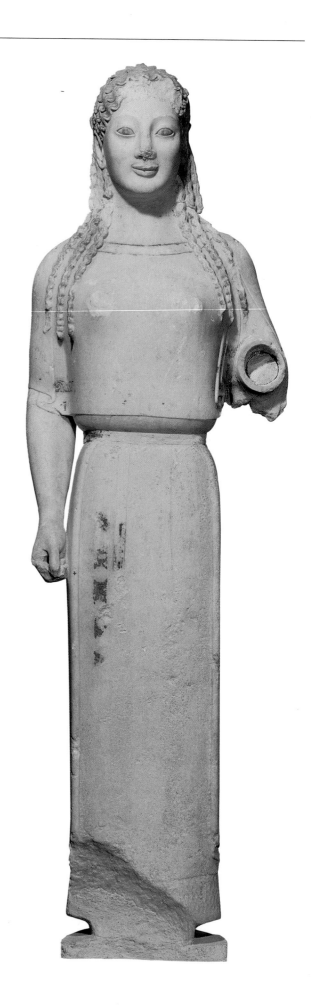

man whose name is engraved on the skirt, it originally stood outside the temple of Hera on the island of Samos. The statue occupies a vertical plane, and the cylinder of her *chiton* (linen dress) is smooth except for finely incised folds. The upper part seems more three-dimensional, revealing the shape of the arms and breasts beneath. The elegance of this figure and the unified flow of curves at the bottom of the *chiton* create an unusual synthesis of grace and monumentality.

Archaic sculptures of standing women are referred to as *korai* (singular *kore*, Greek for "girl"). The *Peplos Kore* (fig. **6.21**) is named for her *peplos* (a woolen dress, pinned at the shoulders). Her pose is slightly less rigid than that of the earlier *New York Kouros*, as she bends her left arm forward. Compared with the *Hera*, the drapery of the *Peplos Kore* reveals the contours of the body. Further distinguishing the *Peplos Kore* from earlier Archaic figures is the so-called "Archaic smile," which accentuates the fact of being alive. The artist has handled the smile organically by curving the lips upwards and raising the cheekbones in response.

Early Classical Style (c. 490–450 B.C.)

From 499 to 494 B.C., Athens gave aid to the Ionian cities in their unsuccessful revolt against Persia. This provoked Darius the Great, King of Persia, to invade mainland Greece in 490 B.C., only to be defeated by the Athenians at the Battle of Marathon. Another invasion in 480 B.C. by Darius' son Xerxes was finally turned back in 479 B.C; this marked the end of Persian efforts to conquer Greece. A change in artistic style seems to have coincided with the Persians' final departure from Greek soil. The Early Classical style, sometimes called Severe (because the smile has disappeared and the forms are simpler) or Transitional (because it bridges the gap between Archaic and Classical), produced radical changes in the approach to the human figure.

The best example of the new developments can be seen in the marble *Kritios Boy,* attributed to the sculptor Kritios (fig. **6.22**). It is not known if the sculpture was made before or after the Persian War, but it reflects a moment of self-awareness in Greek history that is marked by the change from Archaic to Early Classical. Stylization has decreased, remaining primarily in the smooth, wavy hair and the circle of curls around the head. The flesh now seems to cover an organic structure of bone and muscle. The Archaic smile has disappeared and the face, like the body,

has become idealized and neutral in expression. But perhaps the most important developments are that the head is turned slightly, and the right leg, which is forward, bends at the knee, so the left leg appears to hold the body's weight. The torso shifts so that the right hip and shoulder are lowered, a pose referred to as **contrapposto** (from the Latin *positus,* meaning "positioned," and *contra,* meaning "against"). Its use here makes the *Kritios Boy* seem relaxed, and the frontality and rigid stance of the Archaic *New York Kouros* have been modified.

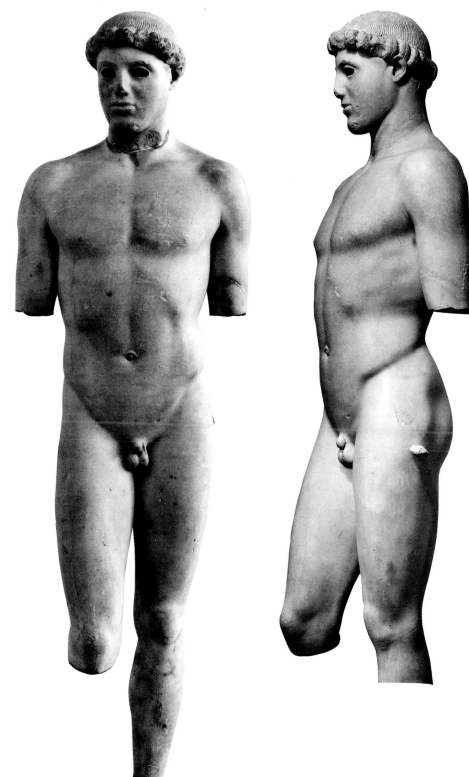

6.22a, b Attributed to Kritios, *Kritios Boy,* from the Acropolis, Athens, c. 480 B.C. Parian marble, 33 ⅞ in (86 cm) high. Acropolis Museum, Athens.

Another Early Classical development, which originated in the Archaic period, was the widespread use of bronze as a medium for large-scale sculpture cast by the "lost-wax" process (see Box). For smaller objects, however, bronze casting had been used since the Aegean period. Of the few Greek over-lifesize bronzes that have survived, the bronze statue representing either Zeus hurling his thunderbolt or Poseidon his trident (fig. **6.23**) is one of the most impressive. By virtue of his pose, the god seems to command space. He focuses his aim, tenses his body, and positions himself as if ready to shift his weight, perfectly balanced between the ball of his right foot and his left heel. His slightly bent knees create the impression that he will spring at any

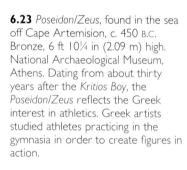

6.23 *Poseidon/Zeus*, found in the sea off Cape Artemision, c. 450 B.C. Bronze, 6 ft 10¼ in (2.09 m) high. National Archaeological Museum, Athens. Dating from about thirty years after the *Kritios Boy*, the *Poseidon/Zeus* reflects the Greek interest in athletics. Greek artists studied athletes practicing in the gymnasia in order to create figures in action.

The Lost-Wax Process

In casting bronze by the **lost-wax** method (also known by the French term *cire-perdue*), the artist begins by molding a soft, pliable material such as clay or plaster into the desired shape and covering it with wax. A second coat of soft material is superimposed on the wax and attached with pins or other supports. The wax is then melted and allowed to flow away, leaving a hollow space between the two layers of soft material. The artist pours molten bronze into the mold, the bronze hardens as it cools, and the mold is removed. The bronze is now in the shape originally formed by the "lost" wax. It is ready for tooling, polishing, and for the addition of features such as glass or stone eyes and ivory teeth to heighten the organic appearance of the figure.

moment. The intensity of his concentration and the force of an imminent thrust extend the viewer's experience of the sculpture to the weapon's destination.

The Early Classical *Diskobolos* (*Discus Thrower*) is known only from Roman copies in marble (fig. **6.24**). The bronze original was cast by Myron between c. 460 and 450 B.C. at the end of the period. Even in the copy, however, it is clear that the *contrapposto* is considerably more pronounced than that of the earlier *Kritios Boy*. A formal analysis of the statue shows that its design is based on the intersection at the neck of two arcs. One arc can be traced from the head, through the curve of the back to the left heel, and another from one hand to the other. The overriding movement of the *Diskobolos* is circular—the torso twists forward and brings the shoulders into line with the right thigh. As a circle, the plane creates a unity of form with the domed head, the round discus and base, and finally with the pose. For, in fact, Myron did not so much create a pose as freeze in time the circular motion of a pivoting athlete.

In 1972, a pair of original Greek bronzes known as the *Warriors from Riace* was discovered in the sea off the southern coast of Italy near Riace. The figure illustrated here (fig. **6.25**) is in a remarkably good state of preservation after extensive restoration work. Inlaid eyes (made of bone and glass-paste), copper eyelashes, lips, and nipples, and silver teeth create a vivid, lifelike impression compared with statues that have lost such details. Most scholars assign a date of about 450 B.C. to the work, placing it at the end of Early Classical and the beginning of Classical. The dome-shaped head and flat, curvilinear stylizations of the hair are familiar Early Classical elements, while the self-confident, dynamic pose and organic form are consistent with Classical.

Classical Style (c. 450–400 B.C.)

The fifty-year span of Greek history from c. 450 to 400 B.C. is referred to as the Classical, or High Classical, period. It corresponds to the aftermath of the Persian Wars, when Greek art evolved from the lavish designs of the Orientalizing and Archaic styles. The association of the Near Eastern cultures with luxury and opulence led the Greeks to reject the earlier, more decorative styles in favor of a new simplicity.

The modern term "classical," which has multiple meanings—including "traditional," "lasting," and "of high quality"—referred originally to the Greek accomplishments of the second half of the fifth century B.C. Works of art produced in this period not only reflect the

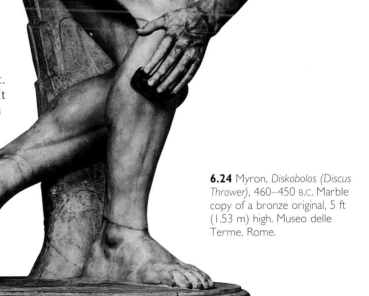

6.24 Myron, *Diskobolos (Discus Thrower)*, 460–450 B.C. Marble copy of a bronze original, 5 ft (1.53 m) high. Museo delle Terme, Rome.

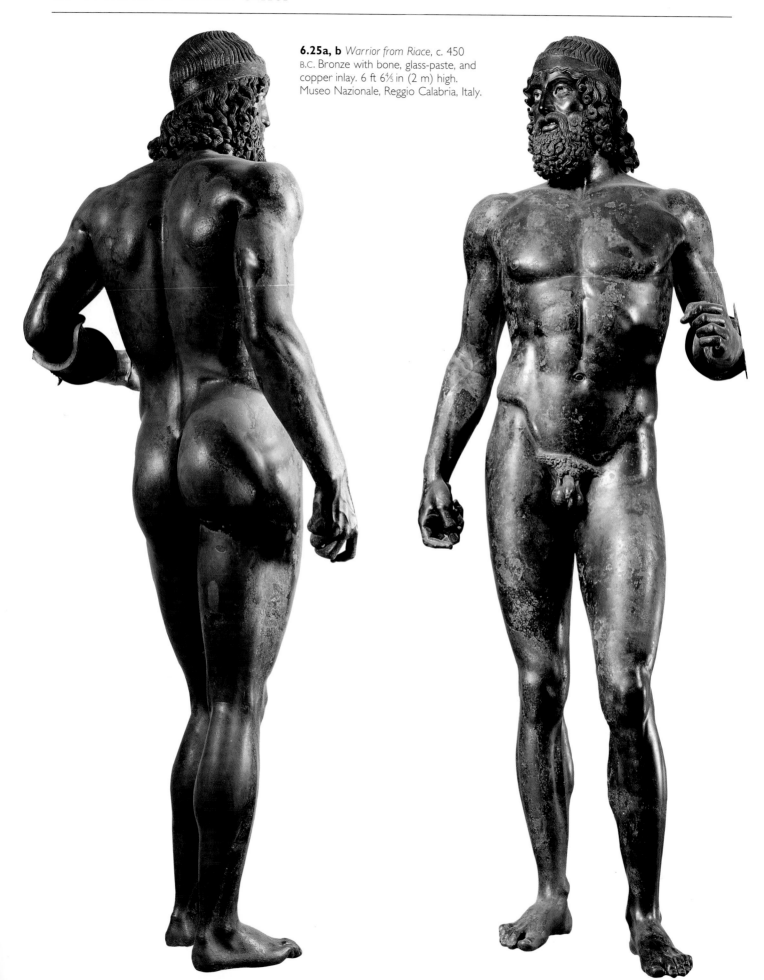

6.25a, b *Warrior from Riace*, c. 450 B.C. Bronze with bone, glass-paste, and copper inlay. 6 ft 6⅘ in (2 m) high. Museo Nazionale, Reggio Calabria, Italy.

cultural and intellectual achievements of Greece itself; they have also had a far-reaching influence on subsequent Western art and culture. It is virtually impossible to understand any aspect of Western development fully without some familiarity with the achievements of Classical Greece.

Polykleitos of Argos

Polykleitos of Argos was esteemed by his contemporaries, and his work is still thought of as the embodiment of Classical style. He is known to have created a canon, which is no longer extant. Most of his sculpture was cast in bronze and is known today only through later Roman copies in marble. Ancient records document the fact that the *Doryphoros* (*Spear Bearer*) was originally bronze (fig. **6.26**). The figure held a spear in his left hand and stands like the *Kritios Boy*, although with a slight increase in *contrapposto* and in the inclination of the head. The gradual S-motion of the body is more pronounced and there is a greater sense of conviction in the body's underlying organic structure—notably the bulging knee caps, the ribcage, and veins in the arms. The head is dome-shaped, as in the *Kritios Boy*, the *Warrior from Riace*, and the *Diskobolos*, but the circle of curls has been eliminated and the short, wavy hair lies flat on the surface of the head and face.

A marble replica of a bronze sometimes attributed to Polykleitos is the *Wounded Amazon* of c. 430 B.C., which also embodies Classical style (fig. **6.27**). Compared with the Archaic *Peplos Kore* of a century earlier (fig. 6.21), the figure is relaxed; her body turns somewhat languidly, and she inclines her head and twists at the waist. The Archaic stylizations have disappeared, as has the smile. The hair is parted in the middle and seems to grow from the scalp. Whereas Archaic drapery has a columnar, architectural quality, Classical drapery follows the form and movement of the body.

Classical artists idealized the human form. Figures are usually young, with no trace of physical defect. They are nicely proportioned and symmetrical in form (not necessarily in pose), but lack personality and facial expression. These qualities are evident in the *Amazon*, who turns toward a wound in her right side without indicating any pain or discomfort. The Classical preference for idealization thus overrides narrative content. Such conventions of Classical taste are evident not only in sculpture but reflect those of Greek theater of the fifth century B.C. No violence or impropriety was performed on stage: when the plot involved such events, they were narrated by a messenger.

6.26 Polykleitos, *Doryphoros* (*Spear Bearer*), c. 440 B.C. Marble copy of bronze original, 6 ft 11½ in (2.12 m) high. Museo Nazionale Archeologico, Naples. Typical of Roman copies is the "tree trunk" supporting the back of the right leg, and the block of marble connecting the hip with the right wrist. Since bronze is a stronger medium than marble, it can stand on its own more readily and needs no such additional supports.

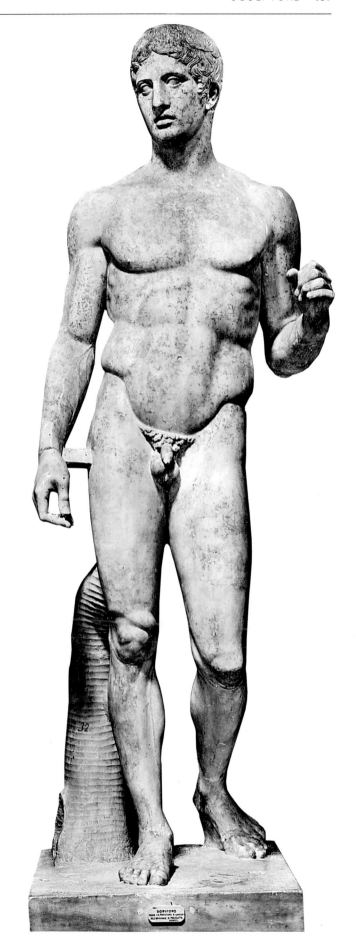

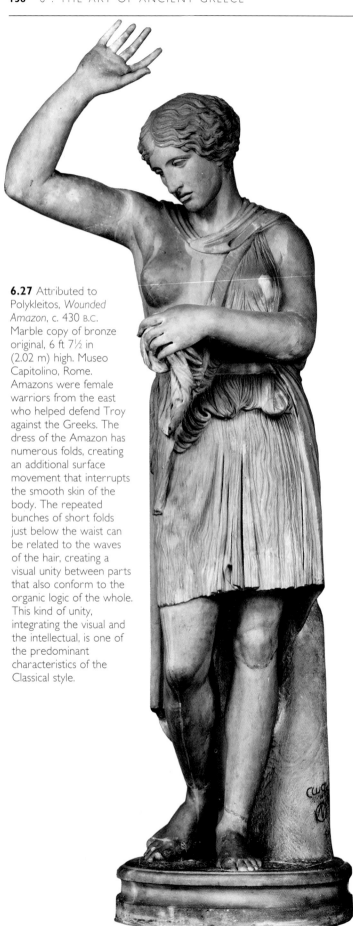

6.27 Attributed to Polykleitos, *Wounded Amazon*, c. 430 B.C. Marble copy of bronze original, 6 ft 7½ in (2.02 m) high. Museo Capitolino, Rome. Amazons were female warriors from the east who helped defend Troy against the Greeks. The dress of the Amazon has numerous folds, creating an additional surface movement that interrupts the smooth skin of the body. The repeated bunches of short folds just below the waist can be related to the waves of the hair, creating a visual unity between parts that also conform to the organic logic of the whole. This kind of unity, integrating the visual and the intellectual, is one of the predominant characteristics of the Classical style.

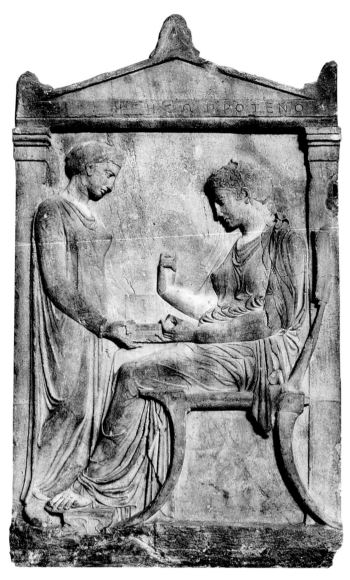

6.28 Stele of Hegeso, c. 410–400 B.C. Marble, 5 ft 9 in (150 cm) high. National Archaeological Museum, Athens.

Grave Stelai

A similar combination of organic form and idealization also characterizes Classical grave stelai. In the Archaic period, these markers took the form of vertical stone slabs, usually with an image of the deceased and members of his or her family carved in relief on the shaft and surmounted by a **finial**, or decorative element. By the second half of the fifth century B.C., the typical grave stele had become squarer, and the figures were carved in the Classical style. In the Stele of Hegeso (fig. **6.28**), the deceased gazes at a necklace which she has removed from the box held by her servant. The draperies reveal naturalistic forms and poses, while also creating their own graceful rhythms. Both Hegeso and her servant gaze downward, somewhat languidly, and convey an air of melancholy that is characteristic of such memorials.

The Development of Greek Architecture and Architectural Sculpture

The Greeks, like all ancient peoples, thought of temples as houses for the gods. In Greece, form was determined by function and the temple plan was derived from the *megaron* plan found in Mycenaean palaces (see p. 126). At its most basic, the *megaron* consisted of a rectangular room with a front porch, or **portico**, having two columns. The god's cult statue was housed in the main room, or hallway (the **naos**), and looked toward the east to an outdoor altar where sacrifices were performed. The main rituals inside the temple involved the care of the statue itself, usually ceremonial dressing and cleaning. Temple interiors also became sanctuaries for fugitives.

Archaic Style (c. 640–490 B.C.)

In the course of the sixth century B.C., during the Archaic period, the basic temple form was developed further, often into two rooms with interior columns, front and back porches, and an outer colonnade on all sides. This latter feature was, in part, influenced by the monumental temples of Egypt which had huge stone columns, capitals, and bases. In Greece, the proportions changed and the size diminished in accordance with human scale and the maxim that "man is the measure of all things." As in Egypt, the system of elevation was post and lintel, but in Greece the columns were placed on the outside and formed a wall of columns separate from the *naos*; such temples are referred to as **peripteral**. The façades were elaborated by the Greeks into the so-called **Orders** of architecture (see Box).

Figure **6.29** is the plan of Apollo's temple on the mainland at Corinth. Constructed around 550 B.C., it is early Doric, and some of the massive, fluted columns are still standing (fig. **6.30**). Their shafts rise directly from the top step and have no base. The capitals, which are reminiscent of the Minoan pillow capitals, support the remnants of a horizontal architrave. We can see from the plan that the temple had a second room (or *opisthodomos*) behind the *naos* that housed the cult statue of Apollo.

1 *Naos* (Inner sanctuary)
2 Hallway separated from the *naos* by a solid wall
3 Base of cult statue
4 Solid wall
5 Column of peristyle
6 *Pronaos* (Front porch)
7 *Opisthodomos* (Back porch)
8 Steps

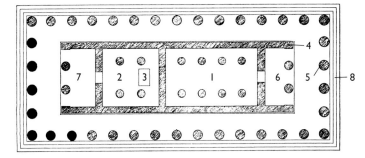

6.29 Plan of the temple of Apollo at Corinth.

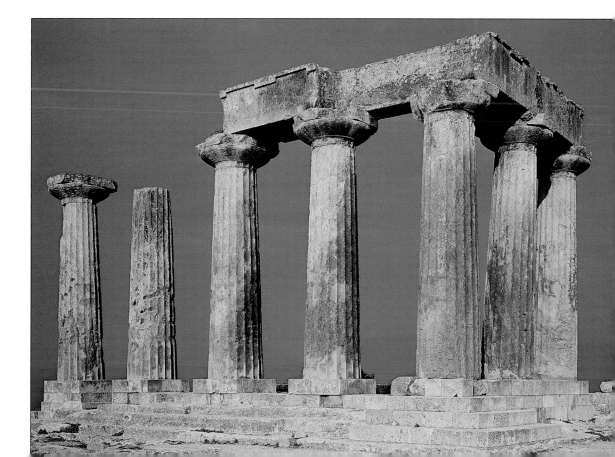

6.30 View of the temple of Apollo at Corinth, c. 550 B.C. Limestone, originally faced with stucco.

The Orders of Greek Architecture

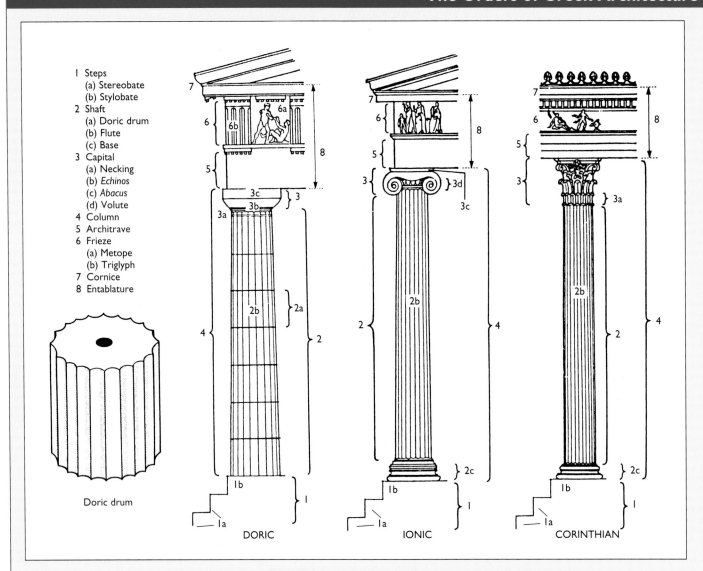

1 Steps
  (a) Stereobate
  (b) Stylobate
2 Shaft
  (a) Doric drum
  (b) Flute
  (c) Base
3 Capital
  (a) Necking
  (b) *Echinos*
  (c) *Abacus*
  (d) Volute
4 Column
5 Architrave
6 Frieze
  (a) Metope
  (b) Triglyph
7 Cornice
8 Entablature

Doric drum

DORIC   IONIC   CORINTHIAN

The Doric and Ionic Orders of Greek architecture (fig. **6.31**) had been established by about 600 B.C. and were an elaboration of the post-and-lintel system of elevation (see p. 45). Ancient Greek buildings, like their sculptures, were more human in scale and proportion than those in Egypt. And unlike the animal-based forms of ancient Iran, the Greek Orders were composed of geometric sections, each with its own individual meaning and logic. Each part was related to the others and to the whole structure in a harmonious, unified way.

The oldest Order, the Doric, is named for the Dorians, who lived on the mainland. Ionic—after Ionia, which includes the Ionian islands and the coast of Anatolia—is an Eastern Order. Its greater elegance results from taller, thinner, curvilinear elements and surface decoration. The Corinthian capital is most easily distinguished by its **acanthus** leaf design.

6.31 Doric, Ionic, and Corinthian Orders.

Doric Order

The Doric Order begins with a base of three steps. Its shaft rises directly from the top step (the **stylobate**), generally to a height about five and a half times its diameter at the foot. The **shaft** is composed of individual sections—**drums**—cut horizontally and held together in the middle by a metal dowel (peg) encased in lead. Shallow, concave grooves known as **flutes** are carved out of the exterior of the shaft. Doric shafts do not stand in an exact vertical plane, but taper slightly from about a quarter of the way up. The resulting bulge, or **entasis** (Greek for "stretching"), indicates that the Classical Greeks thought of their architecture as having an inner organic structure, with a capacity for muscular tension.

At the top of the shaft, three elements make up the Doric capital, which forms both the head of the column and the transition to the horizontal lintel. The **necking** is a snug band at the top of the shaft. Above it is the *echinos* (Greek for "hedgehog" or "sea urchin")—a flat, curved element, like a plate, with rounded sides. The *echinos* forms a transition between the curved shaft and the flat, square *abacus* (Greek for "tablet") above. The *abacus* in turn creates a transition to the **architrave**—literally, a "high beam."

The architrave is the first element of the **entablature** (note the "tabl" related to "table"), which forms the lintel of this complex post-and-lintel system. The **frieze**, above the architrave, is divided into alternating sections—square **metopes** and sets of three vertical grooves, or **triglyphs** (Greek *tri*, meaning "three," and *glyphos*, meaning "carving"). Finally, projecting over the frieze is the top element of the entablature—the thin, horizontal **cornice**. In Classical architecture, a triangular element known as a **pediment** rested on the cornice, crowning the front and back of the building.

The harmonious relationship between the parts of the Doric Order is achieved by formal repetitions and logical transitions. The steps, sides of the *abacus*, architrave, metopes, frieze, and cornice are rectangles lying in a horizontal plane. The columns, spaces between columns, flutes, and triglyphs are all vertical. The outline of the three steps, the *echinos*, and each individual drum is a trapezoid (a quadrilateral with two parallel sides).

Groups of three predominate: three steps; a capital consisting of necking, *echinos*, and *abacus*; triglyphs; and the entablature, which is made up of architrave, frieze, and cornice. The sudden shift from the horizontal steps to the vertical shaft is followed by a gradual transition via the capital to the entablature. The pediment may be read as a logical, triangular crown completing the trapezoid formed by the outline of the steps.

Ionic Order

The more graceful Ionic Order has a round base with an alternating convex and concave profile. The shaft is taller in relation to its diameter (height is about nine times the diameter at the foot). The fluting is narrower and deeper. Elegant **volutes**, or **scroll** shapes, replace the Doric *echinos* at each corner, and virtually eclipse the thin *abacus*. In the Ionic frieze, the absence of triglyphs and metopes permits a continuous narrative extending its entire length.

Corinthian Order

There is no evidence of the existence of the Corinthian Order earlier than the latter part of the fifth century B.C. The origin of the term Corinthian is obscure, but it suggests that the acanthus-leaf capital was first designed by the metalworkers of Corinth and later transferred to marble. Unlike Doric and Ionic columns, Corinthian columns were used mainly in interiors by the Greeks—they were associated with luxury, and therefore with "feminine" character.

In many cases, the *opisthodomos* was reserved for the safe-keeping of valuables dedicated to the god and eventually became an official treasury. Sometimes treasuries were separate buildings, consisting of a rectangular room with a front porch that housed costly objects dedicated by individual cities at the large sanctuaries. An Archaic treasury of this kind in the Ionic Order can be seen in the reconstructed Siphnian Treasury (fig. **6.32**) from the sanctuary at Delphi.

The small Treasury, 12 feet (3.66 m) in height, was built by the inhabitants of the Ionian island of Siphnos. The reconstruction in figure 6.32 shows a well-proportioned structure decorated with relief sculpture on the continuous Ionic frieze and sculpture on the triangular pediment. This is part relief, but the upper section is cut away at the back. The two **caryatids**, the statues of women functioning as columns, are early examples of their type; the earliest are also found at Delphi, in the Knidian Treasury. The winged sphinxes at the apex of the pediment were ultimately derived from Near Eastern prototypes. At the corners are winged females representing Nike, the Greek goddess of victory. Their lively grace, enhanced by the curves of their wings, adds a decorative element to the relatively ornate Ionic building. The **egg and dart** and **leaf and dart** patterns bordering various elements of the façade increase

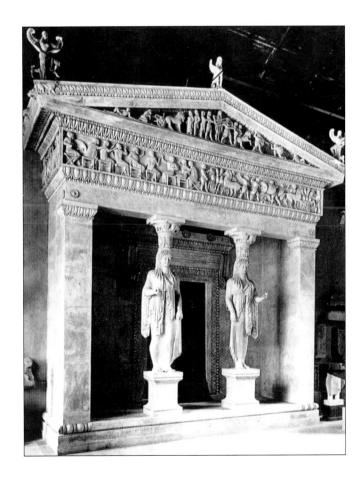

6.32 Former reconstruction of the façade of the Siphnian Treasury in the sanctuary of Apollo at Delphi, 530–525 B.C. Delphi Museum.

the richness of the design by comparison with the heavy structural appearance of Apollo's Doric temple at Corinth.

The subject of the pediment, a scene from the Trojan War, lends itself to action. The seated deities on the frieze (fig. **6.33**), representing Aphrodite, Artemis, and Apollo, are arguing about the outcome of the war with an intensity conveyed through animated gestures and stylized surface patterns. The two goddesses lean forward, while Apollo turns back toward them. His turn is unusual in Archaic art for it reflects an attempt to suggest three-dimensional spatial movement. He is shown in back view from the waist up, while his head and legs are in profile. The drapery curves indicate a new awareness of the naturalistic twist required by such a pose, and hint at the shoulderblade under the flesh.

6.33 Seated gods from the Ionic frieze of the Siphnian Treasury. Parian marble, height of frieze 24¾–26⅞ in (63–68.3 cm).

Early Classical

The temple of Zeus at Olympia, in the Peloponnese, shows the development of Doric architecture in the transitional Early Classical period. It was finished around 456 B.C., but the cult statue, which was one of the Seven Wonders of the ancient world, was not completed and installed until about twenty years later. Although it has long since been destroyed, the statue has been reconstructed from its image on coins (fig. **6.34**); the diagram shows a section (fig. **6.35**) as viewed from the east façade (fig. **6.36**). The proportions of the plan (fig. **6.37**), as compared with those of Apollo's temple at Corinth (see fig. 6.30), have decreased in length by the space of two columns. The building had a long, single *naos* with two rows of seven interior columns and an outer colonnade in a ratio of six columns to thirteen—at Corinth the ratio was six columns to fifteen.

The Olympia **metopes** depicted the twelve Labors of Herakles, six on the west and six on the east (figs. **6.38**, **6.39**, and **6.40**). As a site sacred to Zeus and a center of politics and athletics, the sanctuary at Olympia had special

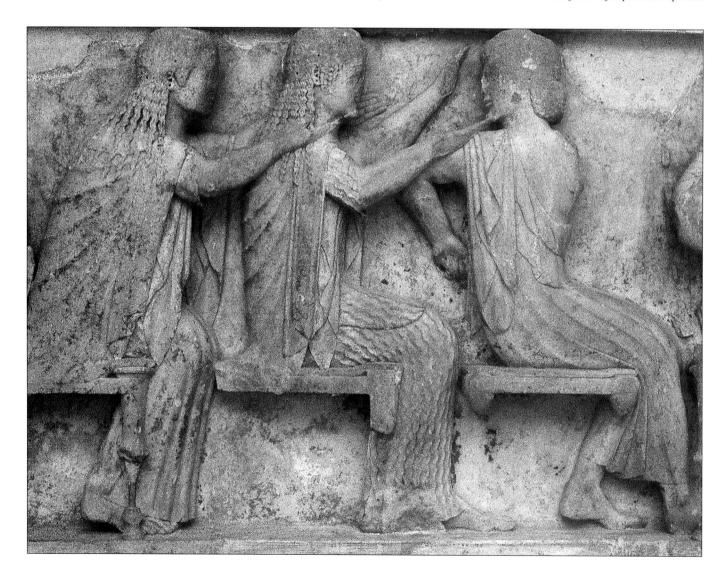

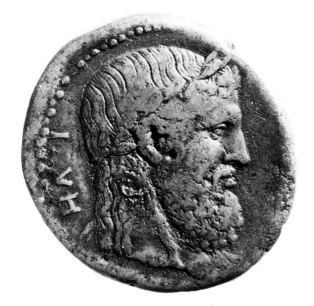

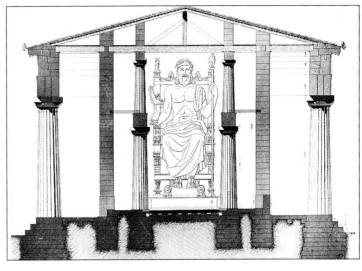

6.35 Sectional drawing of the temple of Zeus at Olympia, 465–457 B.C., showing the cult statue seen from the façade. The cult statue was the work of Phidias and was made later. It was a colossal statue, originally around 40 ft (12.2 m) high, and made of chryselephantine (from the Greek *chrusos*, meaning "gold," and *elephantos*, meaning "ivory"), attached to a wooden frame.

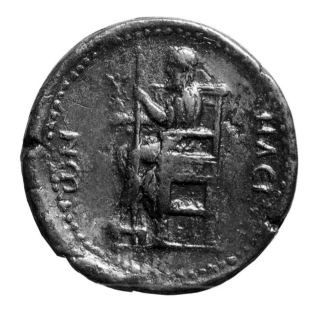

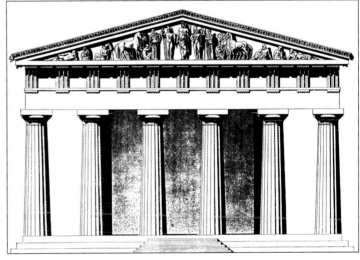

6.34a, b After Phidias, *Head of Zeus* and *Enthroned Zeus*, 2nd century B.C. Obverse and reverse of a coin minted by Hadrian to celebrate the 228th Olympiad in A.D. 133. Staatliche Museen, Berlin and Archaeological Museum, Florence.

6.36 Reconstructed east façade of the temple of Zeus at Olympia.

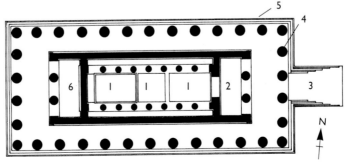

1	*Naos*	4	Peristyle column
2	*Pronaos*	5	Steps
3	Ramp	6	*Opisthodomos*

0   5   10   15   20 m

0 10 20   40   60   80 100 ft

6.37 Plan of the temple of Zeus at Olympia.

The Labors of Herakles

By the Archaic period, Olympia, which had long been a sacred sanctuary, was a cult center in honor of Zeus. Zeus' son Herakles established the borders of the Olympian precinct and was the legendary founder of the Olympic Games. The combination of brain and brawn that made Herakles a model for Greek athletes is illustrated by the twelve Labors he performed for Eurystheus, King of Tiryns (a Mycenaean site), at the command of the Delphic oracle. Because of his Labors and other exploits Herakles was granted immortality.

6.38 *Herakles and Atlas, the Golden Apples of the Hesperides*: Metope from the east side of the temple of Zeus at Olympia. Marble, 5 ft 3 in (1.6 m) high.

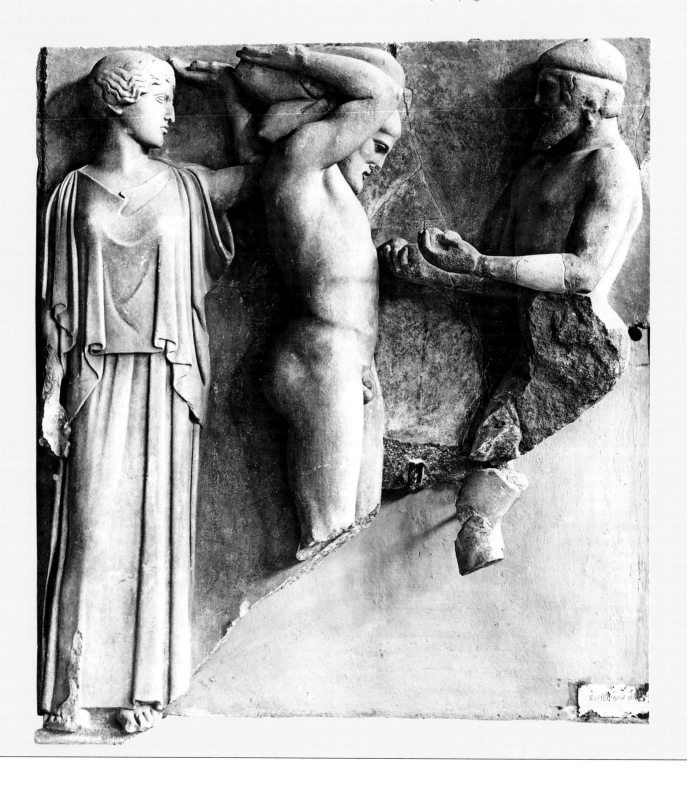

As represented on the metopes of the temple of Zeus in Olympia, Herakles is endowed with intelligence and a canny problem-solving ability as well as with strength. In several instances he is assisted by Athena, who typically offers wise advice, and by Hermes, usually in his aspect as a trickster. Herakles performs six Labors on the Greek mainland (depicted on the west metopes at Olympia) and six in foreign lands (on the east metopes). They are as follows:

1. Herakles kills the Nemean Lion. The lion's skin becomes one of his attributes.

2. The Lernean Hydra was a poisonous water-snake with seven heads that regenerated whenever one was cut off. Herakles cut off the heads and burned the stumps to prevent the heads from growing back.

3. Herakles kills the dangerous birds in the marshes of Stymphalos (depicted here bringing them back to Athena).

4. Herakles ropes and captures the huge Cretan Bull.

5. Herakles tames Artemis' sacred Keryneian Hind.

6. Herakles kills Hippolyte, the Amazon queen, and steals her magic girdle.

7. Herakles captures the Erymanthian Boar alive by chasing it into a snowfield and catching it in a net. He brings it to the king who hides in a storage jar.

8. Herakles tames the Mares of Diomedes, King of Thrace, by feeding them the flesh of their own master.

9. Herakles travels to an island at the extreme west of Oceanos (the river believed to encircle the earth). There he kills the triple-bodied monster, Geryon, as well as the guardian dog and giant, and brings back Geryon's herd of oxen.

10. Herakles had to obtain the golden apples from the Tree of Life in the North African Garden of the Hesperides. He offers to relieve Atlas from the burden of carrying the world on his shoulders if Atlas will obtain the apples for him. In the metope illustrated here (fig. 6.38), Herakles supports the world, his head bowed by its weight, while Atlas holds the apples. Having accomplished his mission, Atlas is reluctant to resume his burden, but Athena (on the left) persuades him to do so.

11. Herakles drags into daylight the three-headed dog Kerberos, guardian of Hades. In this task, Herakles is assisted by Hermes, who leads souls to the underworld.

12. The Augean Stables in Elis housed huge herds of cattle, whose dung had not been cleared for thirty years. Herakles wagered the king that he could clean the stables in a single day. He made two holes in the stable walls, through which he diverted the River Alpheios, thereby accomplishing his task.

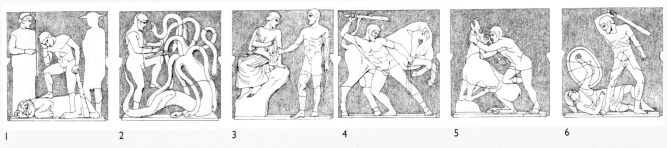

6.39 Olympia, diagram of the west end of the *naos* from the temple of Zeus, showing the Labors of Herakles: 1. Herakles kills the Nemean Lion 2. Herakles battles the Lernean Hydra 3. Herakles brings the Stymphalian Birds to Athena 4. Herakles captures the Cretan Bull 5. Herakles tames the Keryneian Hind 6. Herakles kills the Amazon queen Hippolyte.

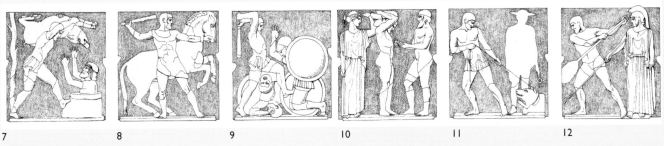

6.40 Olympia, diagram of the east end of the *naos* from the temple of Zeus, showing the Labors of Herakles: 7. Herakles with the Erymanthian Boar 8. Herakles with one of the Mares of Diomedes 9. Herakles kills Geryon 10. Herakles and the Golden Apples of the Hesperides 11. Herakles and Kerberos 12. Herakles cleans the Augean Stables.

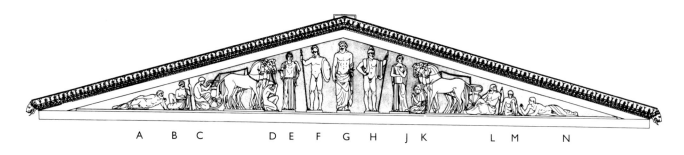

6.41 Reconstruction drawing (after Studniczka) of the east pediment of the temple of Zeus at Olympia: a. unidentified reclining figure   b. seer   c. Myrtilos with Oinomaos' chariot   d. youth   e. Sterope   f. Oinomaos   g. Zeus   h. Pelops   j. Hippodameia   k. girl in front of Pelops' chariot   l. seer   m. squatting youth   n. unidentified reclining figure.

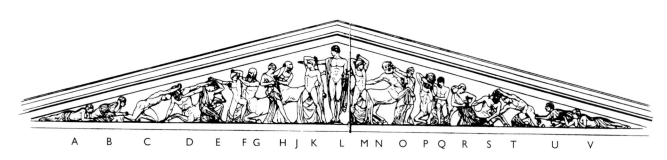

6.42 Reconstruction drawing (after Treu) of the west pediment of the temple of Zeus at Olympia: a, b. two Lapith women   c, d, e. Lapith rescues a Lapith woman from attack by a Centaur   f, g. Centaur assaults a Lapith boy   h, j, k. Perithöos protects his bride from a Centaur   l. Apollo   m, n, o. Theseus battles with a Centaur for a Lapith woman   p, q. Centaur sinks his teeth into a Lapith boy's arm   r, s, t. Lapith protects a Lapith woman from attack by a Centaur   u, v. Lapith women watching the battle.

significance for the Greeks. This is reflected in the iconography of the temple's sculptural program. On the pediments, two separate myths were represented in sets of freestanding sculptures, which alluded to recent historical events. For years, two neighboring Greek cities, Elis and Pisa, had been vying for control of Olympia. Finally, around 470 B.C., Pisa was destroyed by the Eleans. As a result of its victory, Elis increased its wealth and used the money to build a temple dedicated to Zeus. The temple's sculptural program was designed in such a way that ancient myths could be read in relation to contemporary events.

The subject of the east pediment (fig. **6.41**) is the chariot race between Oinomaos, the old mythical king of Pisa, and Pelops, a young man from Lydia, in Anatolia, who hoped to win the hand of the king's daughter. Because Oinomaos had been warned by an oracle that his son-in-law would kill him, he challenged his daughter's suitors to a race. Each previous unsuccessful suitor had been put to death, but Pelops had the linchpin removed from the wheel of Oinomaos' chariot, which overturned and killed him, thus fulfilling the prophecy. At the center of the pediment, Zeus stands with Oinomaos and Pelops, who has won the race. The two quadrigas (chariots drawn by four horses) on either side refer to the life-and-death race, and

at each corner are unidentified reclining figures. To the Eleans who built the temple, the story of Oinomaos and Pelops mirrored their own victory over the Pisans.

The west pediment (fig. **6.42**) represents the mythical battle between the Lapiths (a Greek tribe) and the Centaurs, who were part human and part horse. According to this myth, the Lapiths invited the Centaurs to a wedding, at which the latter became drunk and tried to rape the Lapith boys and girls. Apollo's imposing presence at the center of this scene refers to his personification of intellect and reason (fig. **6.43**). He symbolically holds back the forces of disorder and irrationality as he directs the action with his gesture. Apollo's power and rectitude are implicit in his "straight," vertical pose, using only his outstretched *right* arm and divine gaze to control the Centaurs. The pediment clearly reflects the alliance of the Elean victors with Apollo's superior reason, while their defeated enemies are allied with the primitive Centaurs.

The geometric clarity of Apollo's commanding pose and gesture is contrasted with the energetic zigzags of the Centaur, and its contorted facial expression. Apollo is idealized through his youthful form and calm demeanor, while the Centaur's features suggest old age, with straining muscles and bulging veins. But some stylization—the patternistic treatment of the god's hair, ending in carefully

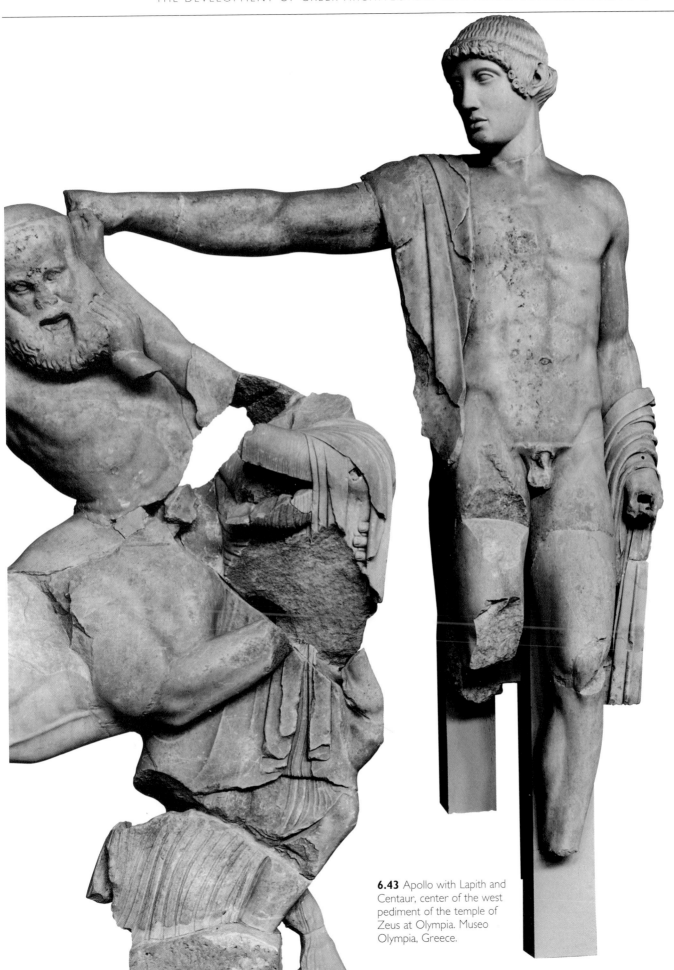

6.43 Apollo with Lapith and Centaur, center of the west pediment of the temple of Zeus at Olympia. Museo Olympia, Greece.

arranged curls—persists (fig. **6.44**). Nevertheless, compared with the Archaic sculptures on the Siphnian Treasury, the Apollo, like the *Kritios Boy* and the *Diskobolos*, conveys a convincing sense of organic form.

Classical Style (c. 450–400 B.C.)

Athens, the capital of modern Greece, is located on the Saronic Gulf, just inland from the port of Piraeus. In the second half of the fifth century B.C., Athens was the site of the full flowering of the Classical style in the arts. This section considers that culmination as it was embodied in the buildings on the Acropolis (figs. **6.45** and **6.46**), particularly the Parthenon. The Acropolis (from the Greek *akros*, meaning "high," or "upper," and *polis*, meaning "city") is an elevated rock supporting several temples, precincts, and other buildings. During the Mycenaean period, it had been a fortified citadel, and its steep walls made the Acropolis difficult for invaders to scale.

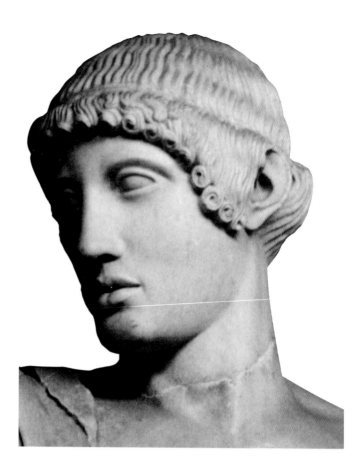

6.44 (right) Apollo (detail of fig. 6.43).

6.45 (below) View of the Acropolis, Athens.

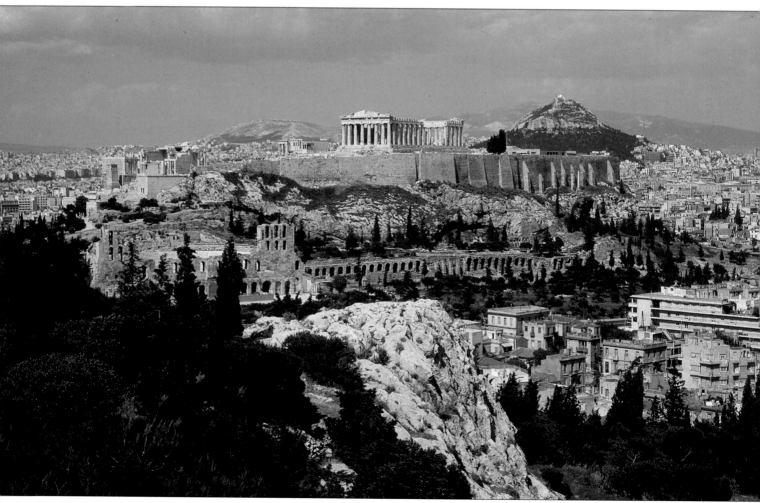

6.46 Plan of the Acropolis. This plan includes only the four Classical buildings that were rebuilt after the destruction of the Acropolis at the end of the Persian Wars (c. 480 B.C.). Like most Greek temples, they were made of marble, which was available in large quantities from quarries on the mainland and on the islands.

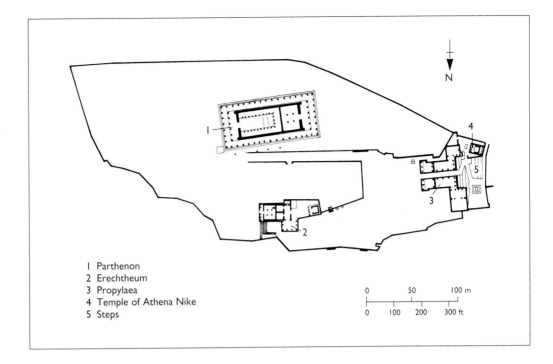

N

1 Parthenon
2 Erechtheum
3 Propylaea
4 Temple of Athena Nike
5 Steps

0   50   100 m
0   100   200   300 ft

The Classical period in Athens is also called the Age of Perikles, after the Greek general and statesman (c. 500–429 B.C.) who initiated the architectural projects for the Acropolis. He planned a vast rebuilding campaign to celebrate Athenian art and civilization after the devastation of the Persian Wars. The Propylaea (or entranceway) and the Parthenon (448–432 B.C.) were completed during his lifetime, but work on the Nike Temple (427–424 B.C.) and the Erechtheum (421–405 B.C.) was not begun until after his death.

Financing for Perikles' building program had come from the Delian League. Because of Athens' sea power, it was able to force the rest of Greece to buy its protection against the Persian invaders. The treasury which housed the funds was located in Apollo's sanctuary on the island of Delos, but was transferred to Athens in 454 B.C.

Athenian political rhetoric, which claimed to protect other Greek cities in the League, informs the iconography of the buildings on the Acropolis. It was also Perikles' justification for spending the war chest on art and architecture in Athens. The controversy that arose over this issue is described in Plutarch's *Life of Perikles*: Perikles' political enemies in the Athenian assembly accused him of disgracing their city by taking the League's money. "Surely," they argued, "Hellas is insulted with a dire insult and manifestly subjected to tyranny when she sees that with her own enforced contributions for the war [against the Persians], we are gilding and bedizening our city, which, for all the world like a wanton woman, adds to her wardrobe precious stones and costly statues and temples worth their millions."[1]

Perikles replied that, as long as Athens waged war for her allies "and kept off the Barbarians," she alone deserved the money. "Not a horse, not a hoplite [a heavily-armed Greek foot-soldier], but money simply" was, according to Perikles, the only contribution of the other Greek cities. And furthermore, once Athens had sufficiently equipped itself for war, it was only natural that she "should apply her abundance to such works as, by their completion, will bring her everlasting glory." This, he added, would also provide employment for many workers.

The Parthenon (448–432 B.C.)

The Parthenon was designed by the architects Iktinos and Kallikrates (see Box). Phidias, a leading Athenian artist of his generation and a friend of Perikles, supervised the sculptural decorations. Completed in 432 B.C. as a temple to Athena, the patron goddess of Athens, the Parthenon celebrates Athena in her aspect as a virgin goddess. *Parthenos*, Greek for "virgin" (and the root of the word *parthenogenesis*, meaning "virgin birth"), was one of Athena's epithets.

The Parthenon (figs. **6.47**, **6.48**, and **6.49**) stands within a continuum of Doric temples. We have seen two earlier examples, at Corinth and at Olympia, but no previous Greek temple expresses Classical balance, proportion, and unity to the same extent as the Parthenon. Its exceptional esthetic impact is enhanced by its so-called refinements, which are slight architectural adjustments to improve the visual impression of the building. For example, lines that look like horizontals actually curve upward toward the middle, thereby correcting the tendency of the human eye to perceive a long horizontal as curving downward in the middle. Other refinements involve the columns, all of which tilt slightly inwards; those toward the corners of the building are placed closer together, creating a sense of stability and the illusion of a frame at each end.

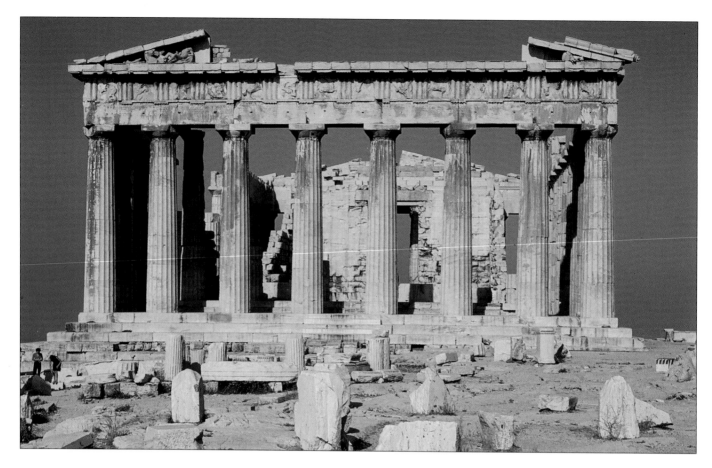

6.47 East end of the Parthenon, Athens, 447–438 B.C. Pentelic marble, 111 × 237 ft (33.8 × 72.2 m). Once through the Propylaea at the western edge of the Acropolis, the visitor emerges facing east. Ahead and a little to the right are the remains of the western wall of the Parthenon. Its damaged state reflects centuries of neglect and misuse. In the 5th century A.D. the Parthenon became a Christian church, and in the 15th century the Turks conquered Athens and converted the temple into a mosque. They stored gunpowder in the building! When it was shelled by artillery in 1687, most of the interior and many sculptures were destroyed. Centuries of vandalism and looting, plus modern air pollution, have further contributed to the deterioration of the Parthenon.

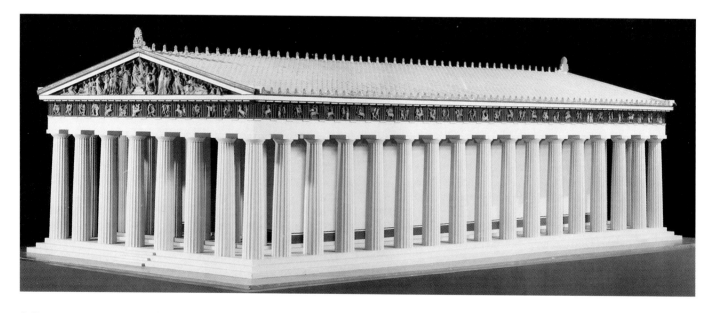

6.48 Reconstruction of the Parthenon, Athens. Metropolitan Museum of Art, New York. Purchase, Bequest of Levi Hale Willard, 1890. This view is from the northeast corner—the eastern perimeter and the long north side are visible.

Plan of the Parthenon

The Parthenon is constructed as a rectangle, which is divided into two smaller rectangular rooms. A front and back porch and a **peristyle (colonnade)**, supported by the three steps of the Doric Order, complete the structure. The temple was made entirely of marble, which was cut and fitted without the use of mortar.

The three lines on the perimeter of the plan represent the steps. The black circles indicate columns—those comprising the peristyle number eight on the short sides (east and west) and seventeen on the long sides (north and south), counting the corner columns twice. Each corner column serves a short and a long side, making a smooth visual transition between them.

The inside wall of the Parthenon, supported by two steps, consists of six columns on a front and back porch, leading to a solid wall with a doorway to an inner room. The solid walls

are indicated by thick black lines.

The western entrance leads to the smaller room, which served as a treasury. The eastern entrance leads to the *naos*, or inner sanctuary. It was originally dominated by a monumental gold and ivory statue of Athena—its base is indicated on the plan by the rectangle inside the *naos*. An inner rectangle of Doric columns repeats the shape of the room and surrounds the statue on three sides.

Although constructed primarily in the Doric Order, the Parthenon had two features that were Ionic. Firstly, there were four Ionic columns inside the treasury. And secondly, a continuous Ionic frieze ran around the top of the outside of the inside wall, which cannot be seen on the plan. The inclusion of Ionic elements in the Parthenon expresses the Athenian interest in harmonizing the architectural and sculptural achievements of both eastern and western Greece.

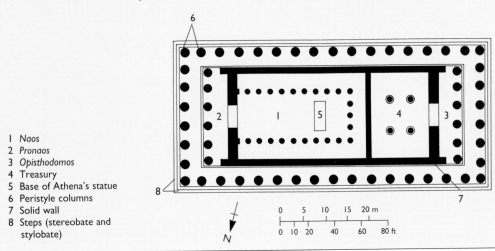

1 Naos
2 Pronaos
3 Opisthodomos
4 Treasury
5 Base of Athena's statue
6 Peristyle columns
7 Solid wall
8 Steps (stereobate and stylobate)

N

0   5   10   15   20 m
0 10 20   40   60 80 ft

6.49 Plan of the Parthenon, Athens.

The Parthenon sculptures, located in four sections of the building, were integrated harmoniously with the architecture. Their narrative content proclaimed the greatness of Classical Athens.

The Parthenon Pediments A drawing of 1674 by the Frenchman Jacques Carrey illustrates the condition of the pediments at that time (fig. **6.50**). Carrey's rendering of the sculpture on the east pediment reveals a relatively good state of preservation, although the central figures had by then disappeared. The three goddesses on the left half of the east pediment (fig. **6.51**)—possibly Iris or Hebe, and Demeter and Persephone, reading from the viewer's right to left—are posed so that they fit logically into the triangular space. Their repeated diagonal planes relate to the two diagonals of the pediment, while the graceful curves of their garments harmonize with the architectural curves of the Doric order below. The reclining male nude to the left could be either Herakles or Dionysos. His limbs, like those of the goddesses, form a series of zigzag planes. His torso forms a gentle curve, repeated in the domed head and

organic musculature. Despite the naturalism of the pose and organic form, however, this figure is idealized like those of Polykleitos—there is no facial expression or individual personality.

Mirroring the two seated females and the male on the left of the pediment is the group of three goddesses on the right (fig. **6.52**). Their identity has been disputed by scholars because they have no attributes. Though posed slightly differently from their counterparts on the left, the groups otherwise match each other closely. The reclining goddess relates to Dionysos/Herakles, and the two seated figures balance those of Demeter and Persephone in their poses and in the curvilinear garments outlining their bodies.

The most striking correspondence between the two sides of the east pediment occurs at the angles. On the far left are the marble remnants of Helios' horses, pulling the chariot of the sun. They rise, beginning their daily journey across the sky. On the far right, a single horse's head descends, echoing the triangular corner of the pediment (fig. **6.52**). This horse, from the chariot of the moon

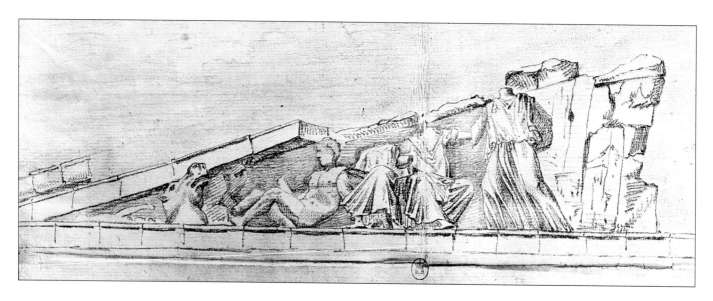

6.50a, b (above and opposite) *The East Pediment of the Parthenon in 1674*, from a drawing by Jacques Carrey. Sculptures finished by 432 B.C. Bibliothèque Nationale, Paris. Greek temple sculptures and their background areas were originally painted. The sculptures in the broken center section of this pediment used to represent Athena's birth on Mount Olympos: Zeus is in the middle and a Nike is crowning Athena with a laurel wreath. According to the myth, Hephaestos struck Zeus on the head with an axe, and Athena emerged fully grown and armed. As the goddess of wisdom, as well as of war and weaving, she was born like an idea from the head of the supreme god.

goddess Selene, shows Phidias' understanding of anatomy which he transformed into the Classical esthetic. He creates the illusion of a triangular cheek-plate with one curved side, blood vessels, and muscles pushing against the inside of the skin. The right eye seems to bulge from its socket, and the ear and mane to emerge convincingly from beneath the surface. The open mouth forms another triangular space, echoing the head, cheek-plate, and the pediment itself.

The Doric Metopes The Parthenon metopes illustrate four mythological battles. The best preserved were originally on the south frieze and represent the battle between

Lapiths and Centaurs—also the subject of the west pediment at Olympia. The violent energy of the battle (fig. **6.53**) contrasts dramatically with the relaxing gods on the east pediment. The strong diagonals of the Lapith, the repeated curved folds of his cloak, and the backward thrust of the Centaur's *contrapposto* enliven the metope.

The other three metope battles depicted Greeks against Amazons on the west, the Trojan War on the north, and Olympians overthrowing Titans on the east. Each set of metopes expressed an aspect of the Greek sense of superiority. The Lapiths and Centaurs symbolized the universal human conflict between animal instinct or lust—exemplified by the drunken Centaurs—and rational self-control—

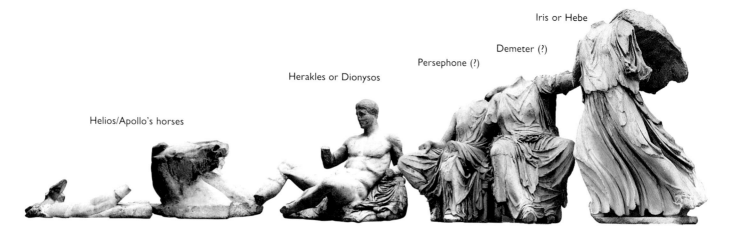

6.51 Sculptures from the left-hand side of the east pediment of the Parthenon, finished by 438 B.C. Pentelic marble, left figure 5 ft 8 in (1.73 m) high. British Museum, London. The pediments are almost 100 feet (30.5 m) wide at the base and 11 feet (3.35 m) high at the central peak. The depth of the pediment bases is, however, only 36 inches (91.4 cm), thus restricting the space available for the sculptures. Since the sides of the pediments slope toward the corner angles, Phidias had to solve the problem of fitting the sculptures into a diminishing triangular space.

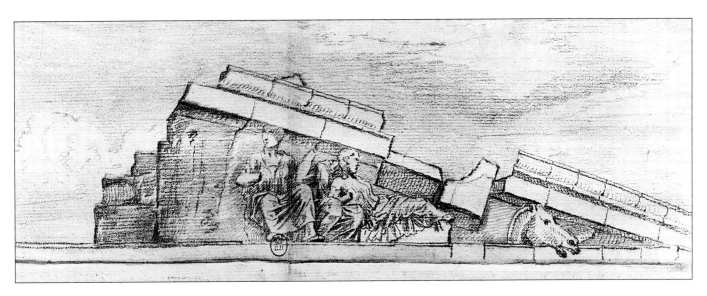

embodied by the Lapiths. The Greek victory over the Amazons symbolized the triumph of Greek warriors over the monstrous female warriors from the east. In the Trojan War, West again triumphed over East, and in the clash between Titans and Olympians, the more human Greek gods wrested control of the universe from their primitive, cannibalistic predecessors. As at Olympia, the sculptural program of the Parthenon represented mythological battles as a way of alluding to recent, and historical, victories. The political subtext of the battles on the Parthenon metopes is thus the Athenian triumph over the Persians.

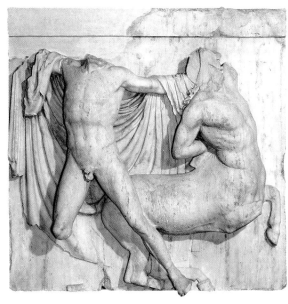

6.53 (right) *Lapith and Centaur*, from South Metope XXVII of the Parthenon. Pentelic marble, 4 ft 5 in (1.35 m) high. British Museum, London. Each metope is approximately 4 feet square (1.22 m²) and contains high relief sculpture. There were fourteen metopes on the short east and west sides, and thirty-two on the long north and south sides. Most are scenes of single combat.

Group of three unidentified goddesses

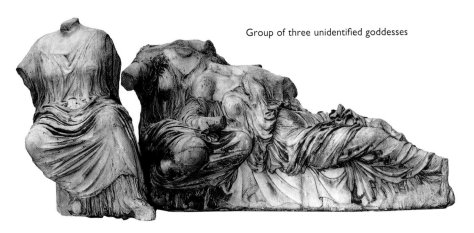

Horse of Selene

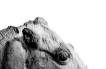
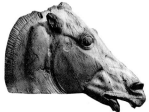

6.52 Sculptures from the right-hand side of the east pediment of the Parthenon. Pentelic marble, left figure 4 ft 5 in (1.35 m) high. British Museum, London. At the left corner of the whole pediment Helios' horses mark the rising of the sun, because Athena was born in the east at dawn. The horse of the moon descends at the right corner. The location of the scene on this pediment also corresponds to the sunrise in the East. Thus, in this arrangement, the artist has formally integrated sculpture and architecture with iconography, time, and place.

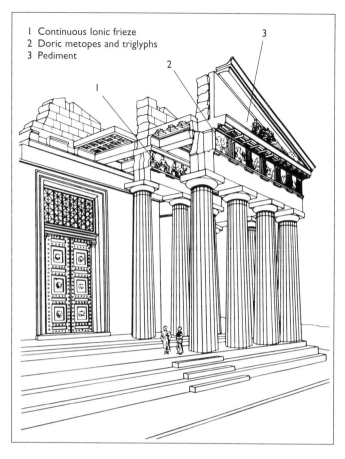

1 Continuous Ionic frieze
2 Doric metopes and triglyphs
3 Pediment

6.54 Cutaway perspective drawing of the Parthenon showing the Doric and Ionic friezes, and a pediment (after G. Niemann).

6.55 The Parthenon, looking up through the outer Doric peristyle at the Ionic frieze.

The Ionic Frieze Over the outside of the inner (*naos*) wall of the Parthenon (figs. **6.54** and **6.55**), an Ionic frieze 525 feet (160 m) long illustrated the Great Panathenaic procession (fig. **6.56**). This was held every four years, and the entire city participated in presenting a sacred *peplos* to Athena. The continuous nature of the Ionic frieze, uninterrupted by triglyphs, is consistent with its content. Thus the shape of the frieze corresponds with the form of a procession. In order to maintain the horizontal plane of the figures, Phidias adopted a sculptural convention of **isocephaly** (from the Greek *isos*, meaning "equal" or "level," and *kephale*, meaning "head"). When a work is isocephalic, all the heads are set at approximately the same level.

The Naos The *naos* contained the cult statue of Athena. In the reconstruction in figure **6.57**, she is armed and represented in her aspect as the goddess of war. She stands and confronts her viewers directly, wearing Medusa's head on her leather aegis and holding a statue of Nike (goddess of victory) in her right hand and a shield in her left. Both shield and pedestal were decorated with reliefs by Phidias. The colossal scale of this statue was unprecedented, and embodied Athena's importance as the patron goddess of Athens. (Phidias' statue of Zeus at Olympia was later, even though the temple itself predated the Parthenon.) Athena's central position in the Parthenon pediments and the offering of the *peplos* in the Ionic frieze signified her wisdom and power as well as the Athenians' devotion to her. The sectional drawing in figure **6.58** shows her position in the temple as seen from the entrance. Compared with the section of Zeus' temple at Olympia, the Parthenon is wider, which gives it a lighter, less box-like quality, reflecting the pleasing proportions of the Classical style in architecture.

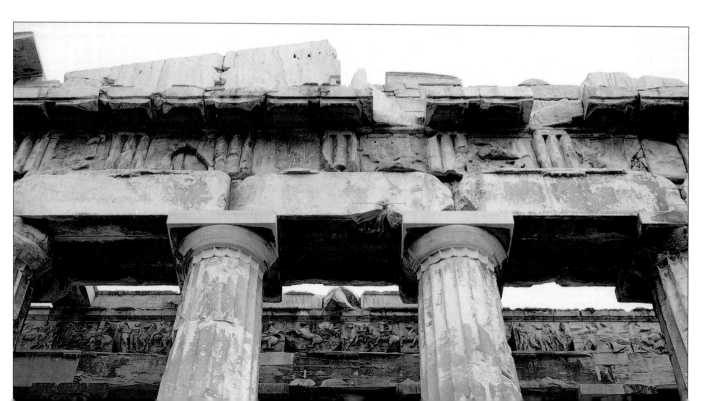

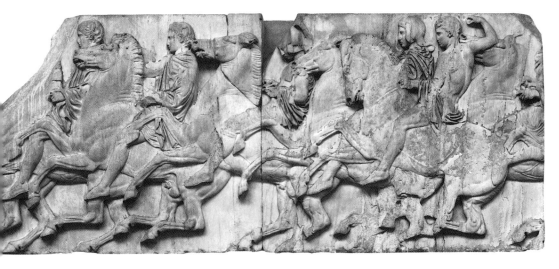

6.56 Equestrian group from the north frieze of the Parthenon, c. 442–439 B.C. Pentelic marble, 3 ft 5¾ in (1.06 m) high. British Museum, London. This illustrates Phidias' technique of making the horses small in relation to the riders. He carved the horses' legs in higher relief than their bodies and heads. The effect is to cast heavier shadows on the lower part of the frieze which, together with the multiple zigzags, increases the illusion of movement.

6.57 (left) Neda Leipen and Sylvia Hahn, reconstruction of Phidias' *Athena*, from the *naos* of the Parthenon. Original dedicated 438 B.C. Wood covered with gold and ivory plating, model approx. 4 ft (1.22 m) high. Royal Ontario Museum, Toronto. Like many cult statues, that of Athena was over-lifesize, standing 40 feet (12 m) high on a pedestal. Phidias constructed the statue around a wooden frame, covering the skin area with ivory, and the armor and drapery with gold. The original statue has long since disappeared and has been reconstructed from descriptions, small copies, and images on coins.

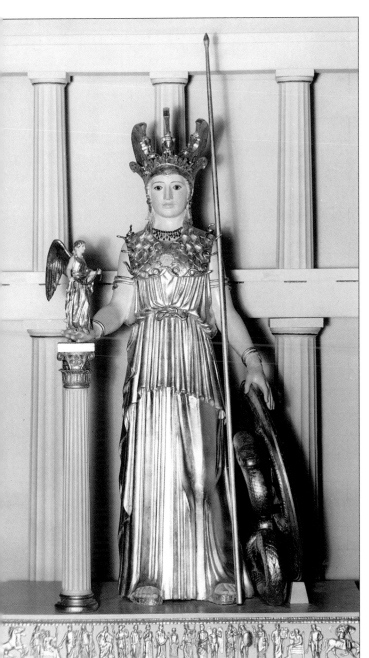

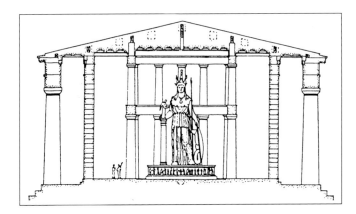

6.58 Sectional drawing showing the cult statue of Athena from the entrance of the Parthenon.

The Temple of Athena Nike Athena was honored as the goddess of victory in the small marble Ionic temple of Athena Nike, which crowns the southern edge of the Acropolis (fig. **6.59**). It has a square *naos*, and a front porch, with four Ionic columns and four steps at the front and back. This repetition reflects the Classical insistence on unifying the parts with the whole. The small size and graceful Ionic Order of the Nike temple contrast with the heavier proportions of the Doric columns in the Parthenon.

The Nike temple, like the Parthenon, celebrated a military victory, but it is not known which one. The issue is complicated by the fact that it was designed before the Parthenon, but finished later. The original gold statues of Nike were housed in the temple, but have since disappeared. The best surviving sculpture from the Nike temple

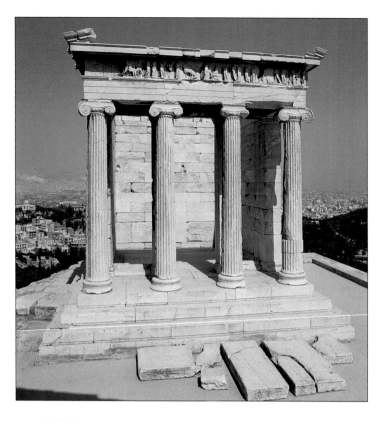

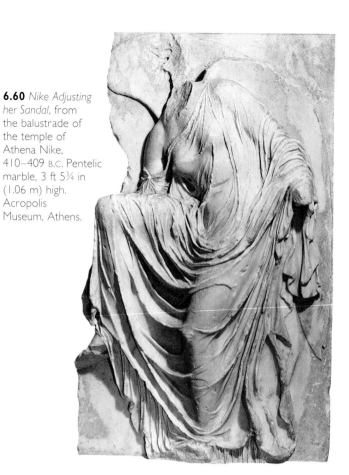

6.60 *Nike Adjusting her Sandal,* from the balustrade of the temple of Athena Nike, 410–409 B.C. Pentelic marble, 3 ft 5¾ in (1.06 m) high. Acropolis Museum, Athens.

6.59 (above) Temple of Athena Nike from the east, Acropolis, Athens, 427–424 B.C. Pentelic marble.

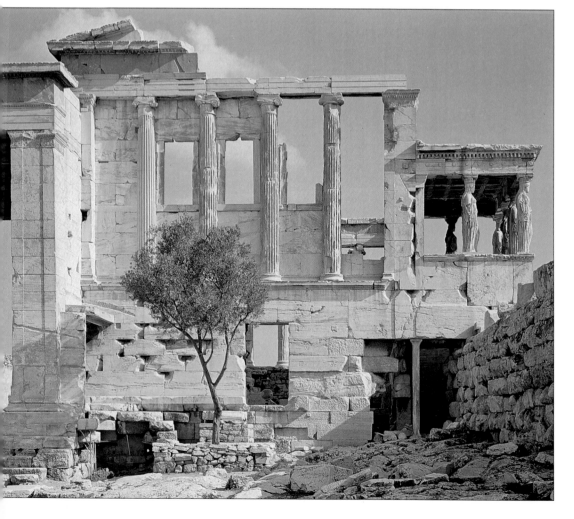

6.61 The Erechtheum, west side, Acropolis, Athens, 421–405 B.C. Porch figures approx. 8 ft (2.44 m) high. This temple was named for Erechtheus, a legendary king of Athens who was worshiped with Athena and various other gods and ancestors. As a result of the large number of dedicatees, the building itself is unusually complex for a Classical Greek temple.

is the relief of *Nike Adjusting her Sandal* (fig. **6.60**), originally located on a **balustrade** of the parapet. This figure combines a graceful, curved torso with diagonal planes in her legs. The sheer, almost transparent drapery (called "wet drapery" because it appears to cling to the body) falls in a pattern of elegant, repeated folds. Behind Nike are what remains of her open wings. Their smooth surfaces contrast with the folds of the drapery, and, at the same time, echo and frame the torso's curve.

The Erechtheum The Erechtheum (fig. **6.61**) is on the northern side of the Acropolis, opposite the Parthenon. It replaced an old temple to Athena that housed a wooden, Archaic statue of the goddess. The temple was destroyed by the Persians, but the Athenians decided to display the ruins to remind citizens of the sacrilegious act of sacking the Acropolis. A more complex Ionic building than the Nike temple, the Erechtheum is built on an uneven site. The eastern room was dedicated to Athena Polias, or Athena in her aspect as patron of the city.

The small southern porch (fig. **6.62**) is distinctive for its six caryatids, a convention already in place in the Siphnian Treasury (see fig. 6.33). But these now stand in a relaxed *contrapposto* pose; the drapery defines the body in an ideal form characteristic of the Classical style. As an ensemble, a perfect symmetry is maintained so that each set of three, right and left, is a mirror image of the other. The two corner caryatids, like the corner columns of the Parthenon, are perceived as being aligned with the front figures when viewed from the front, and with the side figures when viewed from the sides, thus creating a smooth visual transition between front and side.

In the metaphorical transformation of columns into human form, several features are necessarily adapted. For example, the vertical drapery folds covering the support leg recall the flutes of columns. In the capital over the caryatid's head, the volute is omitted, but the *echinos* has been retained in the molded headdress which creates a transition from the head to the *abacus*. At the same time, the headdress is an abstract geometric form, related to organic human form only by its proximity to the head. Whereas the Doric *echinos* effects a transition from vertical to horizontal and from curved elements to straight, the headdress satisfies the additional transition from human and organic to geometric and abstract. These caryatids thus illustrate the harmonious metaphorical relationship between ideal and organic, human and abstract, that characterizes Classical style.

6.62 The caryatid porch of the Erechtheum, south side.

Late Classical Style (4th century B.C.)

By the end of the fifth century B.C., Athens had lost her political supremacy. Other Greek city-states, especially Sparta, began to exert political and military power over Greece. In the fourth century B.C., Philip II of Macedon, in northeastern Greece, conquered the Greek mainland and his son Alexander the Great extended his empire. Nevertheless, the intellectual leaders of that period, notably Plato and Aristotle, continued to flourish in Athens.

The outdoor theater came into its own as an architectural form after the fifth century B.C. (see Box). The best example is the theater at Epidauros (figs. **6.63** and **6.64**). It

Greek Theater

Greek theater originally grew out of rituals performed in honor of the wine god, Dionysos. The early theaters were hollow spaces in the hills, and in the fifth century B.C. these were developed to incorporate wooden benches arranged around an opening in a rock. Thus virtually embedded in nature, these theaters integrated drama with landscape. It was in such theaters—one was located below the Acropolis in Athens—that the great dramas by Aeschylos, Sophokles, and Euripides were performed. Greek theater began with a chorus of actors who sang and danced, and gradually individual roles performed by separate players emerged.

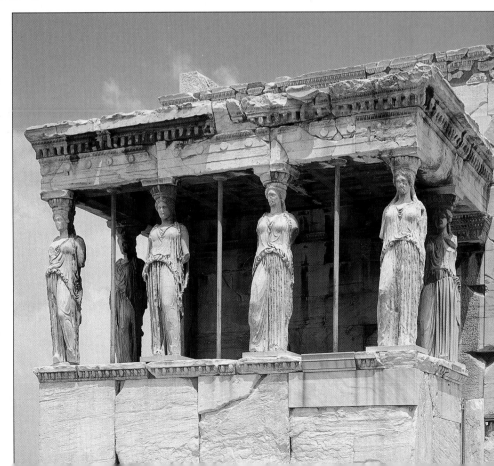

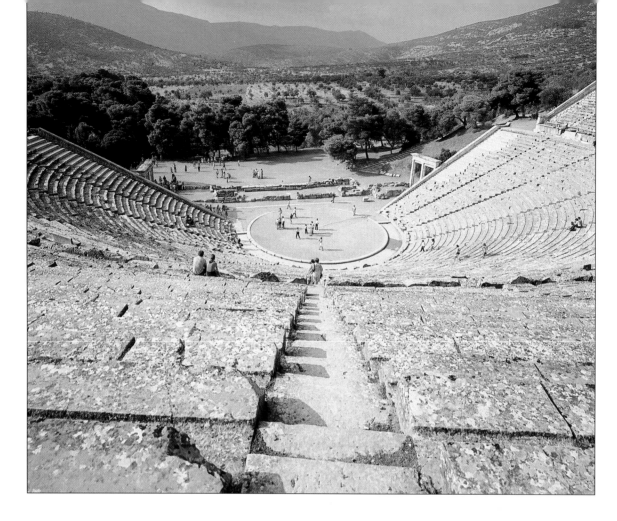

6.63 Theater at Epidauros, c. 350 B.C. Stone, diameter 373 ft (114 m). Curved rows of stone seats formed an inverted conical space in these impressive structures. Behind the *orchestra* was the rectangular stone backdrop, or *skene* (from which the modern English word "scene" is derived), and actors entered from the sides.

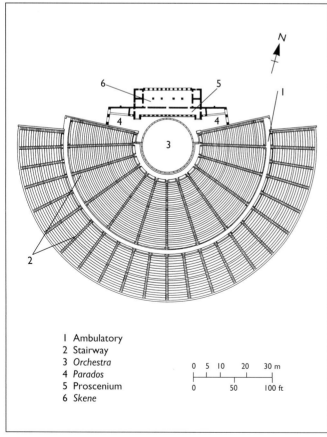

1 Ambulatory
2 Stairway
3 *Orchestra*
4 *Parados*
5 Proscenium
6 *Skene*

0 5 10   20   30 m
0   50   100 ft

6.64 Plan of the theater at Epidauros.

had a slightly more than semicircular seating area, with radiating stairways and a walkway a little more than halfway up—not unlike a modern sports arena. The auditorium was built around the *orchestra* (literally a place for dancing), a round space for the chorus where the action of the play unfolded. This was about 80 feet (24.5 m) in diameter and contained an altar dedicated to Dionysos.

Sculpture

The leading Athenian sculptor of the Late Classical style was Praxiteles. A gentle S-shape, sometimes called the "Praxitelean curve," outlines the stance of Praxiteles' most famous statue, the *Aphrodite of Knidos* (fig. **6.65**), which is known only from Roman copies. The east Greek city of Kos originally commissioned the *Aphrodite*, but rejected the finished work because of the nudity, and it was then accepted by the Anatolian city of Knidos. It represents the goddess standing next to a water jar (*hydria*) after her bath. She picks up drapery with her left hand and, while the gesture of her right hand implies modesty, at the same time it calls attention to her nudity. Compared with Classical sculptures, the *Aphrodite* has slightly fleshier proportions and a heavier, fuller face.

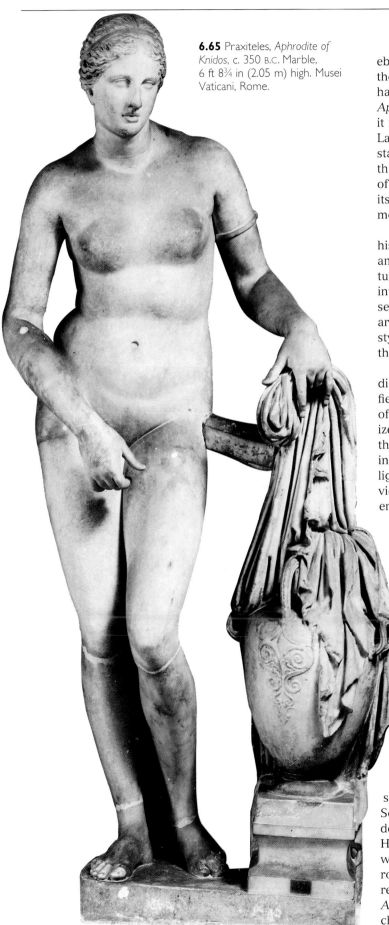

6.65 Praxiteles, *Aphrodite of Knidos*, c. 350 B.C. Marble, 6 ft 8¾ in (2.05 m) high. Musei Vaticani, Rome.

More than any earlier Greek sculptor, Praxiteles celebrated the female nude. In fact, it was with this work that the female entered the canon of beauty in Greek art, which had been previously restricted to the male nude. The *Aphrodite* was celebrated by the Knidians, who exhibited it in such a way that viewers could completely encircle it. Later anecdotes emphasize the erotic qualities of the statue. Others emphasize its realism, relating, for example, that the goddess emerged from the waves off the coast of Anatolia to see her likeness. So astonished was she by its accuracy that she cried out "Where did Praxiteles see me naked?".

Lysippos of Sikyon (near Corinth), who was famous for his portrayals of athletes and portraits of great men, was among the important Greek sculptors of the fourth century B.C. whose work survives mainly in Roman copies. He introduced a new, more naturalistic approach to representing the human figure. In so doing, he became the key artist in the transition from Late Classical to Hellenistic style. His genius brought him to the attention of Alexander the Great, who made him his court sculptor.

The Roman historian Pliny the Elder (see p. 213) distinguished between the canon of Polykleitos, exemplified by the *Doryphoros* (see fig. 6.26), and the newer style of Lysippos. Whereas Polykleitos' figures were idealized youths, according to Pliny, Lysippos preferred thinner bodies, smaller heads, more detailed hair, and an increase in surface movement. The result was a taller, lighter appearance and a livelier stance. This, in Pliny's view, changed external form in the direction of greater emotional accuracy. It also took into account the position of the viewer in relation to the sculpture by opening up the space around its central axis. One effect of Lysippos' canon can be seen in the *Apoxyomenos* (literally, in Greek, "one scraping himself")—originally a bronze and now known only in Roman marble copies (fig. **6.67**). It represents a victorious athlete scraping the oil off his arm with a strigil.

The two views illustrated in figure 6.67 show the turn in the athlete's body compared with the relaxed *Doryphoros*, who stands within a single vertical axis. Here there is more movement away from the center, because of the wider opening between the legs and the outstretched arms. The athlete seems to swivel, which draws observers into his space, and engages them with his action.

Lysippos' sculpture of Socrates (see p. 139)—the example shown here is a statuette (see fig. 6.4)—corresponds to Plato's description of his teacher's character. Socrates is represented as if walking slowly and thinking deeply, his wrinkled brow conveying a pensive mood. He is known to have been considered ugly and faun-like, with a snub nose, flowing mustache and beard, small rounded shoulders, and a pot belly, yet it is an affectionate rendition. When this sculpture is juxtaposed with the *Apoxyomenos*, some idea of Lysippos' range of types and character becomes clear.

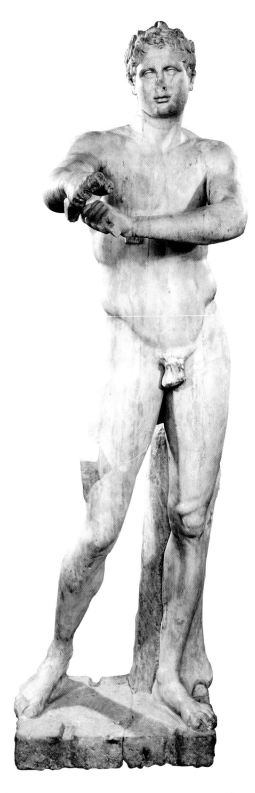

The "Hermes of Praxiteles"

Sometimes the stylistic categories of canonical Western art history are thrown into doubt when new discoveries are made. The so-called *Hermes of Praxiteles* is a case in point. For generations, art historians have identified this sculpture (fig. **6.66**) as a fourth-century-B.C. work by Praxiteles (c. 370–330 B.C.). It has the slightly fleshy proportions of the Late Classical style, and the *contrapposto* creates the S-shaped curve associated with him. The planar movement seems to fit comfortably between that of the Classical and Hellenistic styles. But when the sandals were studied in relation to the known shoe styles of ancient Greece, it was discovered that these did not belong to the fourth century. As a result, scholars have concluded that the work must belong to a later period. It is now generally thought to be Roman.

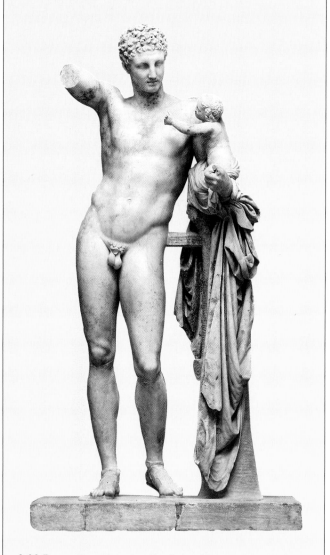

6.66 Formerly attributed to Praxiteles, *Hermes and the Infant Dionysos,* c. 340 B.C. Marble, with vestiges of red paint on lips and hair, 7 ft 1 in (2.16 m) high. Archaeological Museum, Olympia.

6.67a, b (above and opposite) Lysippos, *Apoxyomenos* (*Athlete with a Strigil*). Marble, Roman copy of a bronze original of c. 320 B.C. 6 ft 9 in (2.05 m) high. Musei Vaticani, Rome. According to Pliny, this sculpture was particularly admired by the Roman emperor Tiberius, who had it moved from the public baths to his bedroom, but returned it because the Roman citizens protested their loss.

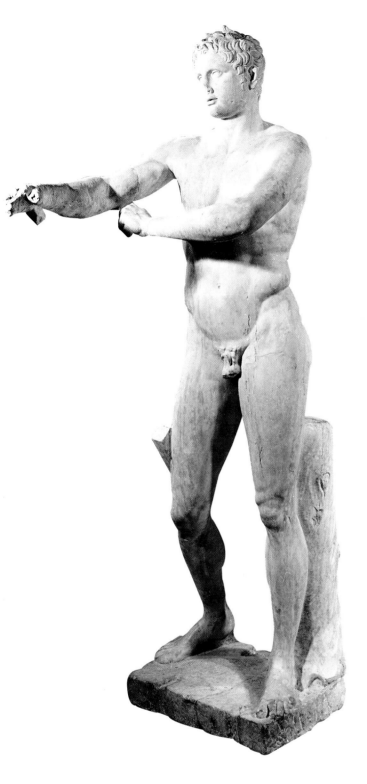

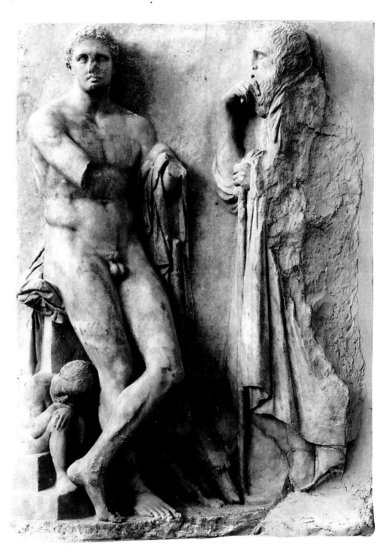

6.68 Attic grave stele, from near Athens, c. 350–330 B.C. Marble, 5 ft 6 in (1.7 m) high. National Archaeological Museum, Athens.

pathos that become typical of Greek art in subsequent centuries.

The Late Classical style formed a transition between the idealized sculptures of the second half of the fifth century B.C. and the Hellenistic style. In Hellenistic art, idealism gives way to increasing melodrama and new types of representation are developed.

Fourth-Century Grave Stelai

A similar taste for individual characterization can be seen in the grave stelai of the Late Classical period (fig. **6.68**). Compared with the Stele of Hegeso (see fig. 6.28), the relief here is more deeply carved, so that the deceased youth almost looks like a freestanding figure leaning against a marble wall. He has died in the prime of life, a loss accentuated by the sculptor through the youth's heroic form and the representation of the aged, grieving father at the right. The weeping boy seated on the steps at the left and the dog sniffing the ground add touches of

Hellenistic Period (323–31 B.C.)

The Hellenistic period extended from the death of Alexander the Great (323 B.C.) to the beginning of the Roman Empire under Augustus, who assumed power in 31 B.C. and became emperor four years later (see Chapter 8). The term "Hellenistic" refers to the spread of Greek culture beyond Greece—especially to the East—as a result of Alexander's conquests.

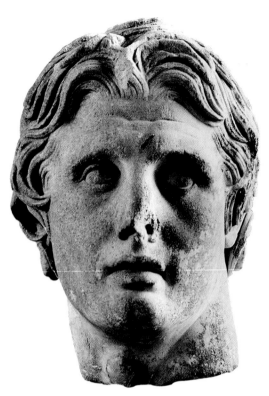

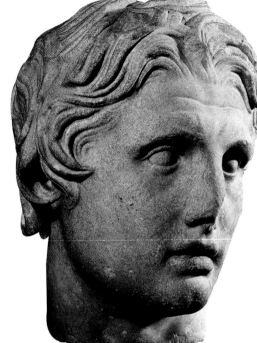

6.69a Head of Alexander, from Pergamon, c. 200 B.C. Marble, 1 ft 4 in (0.41 m) high. Archaeological Museum, Istanbul.

6.69b Alexander (side view of fig. 6.69a).

When Philip II, King of Macedon, died in 336 B.C., his monarchy had already begun to dominate Greece. Within eleven years, his son Alexander had subjugated the rest of Greece and conquered Egypt, Phoenicia, Syria, and Persia (the latter in revenge for Xerxes' invasion of Greece). In 325 B.C. he pushed the limits of his kingdom to the Punjab, but rebellious troops forced his return westward. Wherever Alexander went, the process of Hellenization followed until it encompassed virtually the entire Middle East. Even though Greek culture was dominant at this period, however, it was exposed to diverse languages and customs and was therefore enriched by cross-fertilization.

Alexander died at the age of thirty-three. No single successor emerged after his death and his kingdom was broken up into independent monarchies. During the second century B.C., European tribes invaded Greece from the north, and the Romans (see Chapter 8) began to exert their influence in Europe and the Mediterranean.

Hellenistic Sculpture

Hellenistic style continues the developments introduced by Lysippos and further expands the diversity of sculpture formally and iconographically, as well as psychologically. There is an increase in portrait types, children and old people are represented, theatricality and melodrama express extremes of emotion, and the inner character of figures is conveyed through an emphasis on formal realism.

6.70 Polyeuktos, *Demosthenes*, c. 280 B.C. Marble copy of a Roman original, 6 ft 6 in (2.02 m) high. Ny Carlsberg Glyptotek, Copenhagen. This statue was one of several of Athenian heroes opposed to the Macedonian rule of Athens that was set up in the *agora*, or marketplace, of the city. Demosthenes was forced by the Macedonians to flee Athens. When he reached the island of Poros, he drank poison rather than submit to the enemy. An inscription on the base of the sculpture reads: "If your strength had equalled your resolution, Demosthenes, the Macedonian Ares [i.e. Alexander the Great] would never have ruled the Greeks."[2]

Lysippos had established the official royal image of Alexander, but none of those portraits survives. Nevertheless, the type he created is known through descriptions and posthumous portraits of Alexander by later artists. One such example from the site of Pergamon in western Turkey shows Alexander's slightly tilted head, as if he is gazing toward the heavens, with dreamy eyes, parted lips, fleshy facial texture, and a furrowed brow (fig. **6.69**). The wavy hair, brushed upwards at the center of his forehead, became characteristic of Alexander's portraits, and the general type was used in the Hellenistic period as a standard for all royal portraiture.

The full-length portrait of the orator Demosthenes by Polyeuktos, also a Roman copy, is an example of Hellenistic interest in character (fig. **6.70**). Demosthenes' life was beset by difficulties, including financial hardship and a speech impediment. He was a serious stutterer as a young man, but he trained himself to become the greatest public speaker in Athens. His political enemies succeeded in having him exiled from Athens on a trumped-up charge of corruption. In Polyeuktos' rendition, Demosthenes is an elderly, haggard man, with long, thin arms. His dejection shows on his face and an inner tension is conveyed by the agitation of his hands. The difficulties of his life are an integral part of the statue, which endows the portrait with a new, biographical accuracy.

The *Winged Nike*, also known as the *Winged Victory*, from Samothrace (fig. **6.71**) and the *Old Market Woman* (fig. **6.72**) are further sculptural examples of the contrast between the vigor of youth and the weight of old age. The Nike is represented as if alighting on the prow of a ship to commemorate a naval victory. The wind whips her draperies with a sense of movement more activated than in Classical sculpture, and her wings are outspread in triumph. The forward diagonal of her torso seems forced against the elements, and the position of her wings suggests that they have not yet settled. Adding to the sense of movement are the drapery masses sweeping across the front of the body, which are contrasted with the seemingly transparent drapery at the torso. The more deeply cut folds also increase the areas of shadow in the skirt swirling around her legs, making it appear darker as well as heavier than the drapery covering the torso. From the side, the diagonal planes of the body and the outspread wings come into view.

6.71 *Winged Nike (Winged Victory)*, from Samothrace, c. 190 B.C. Marble, approx. 8 ft (2.44 m) high. Louvre, Paris. The shifting spatial thrusts of the Nike are characteristic of the new Hellenistic command of form and motion in space.

By contrast, the draperies of the *Old Market Woman* seem heavy; her garment hangs in drooping folds as she bends forward, bearing the weight of her basket. For the first time in Greek art, artists began to depict the qualities of old age that are apparent here—a bent and bony frame, wrinkled skin, sunken cheeks, and sagging breasts. Both figures engage the viewers in ways that are consistent with the character they convey.

Hellenistic sculpture of children also shows a variety of types, which reflects the new approach to realism. The *Boy Wrestling with a Goose*, for example, is a study in contained energy locked in conflict (fig. **6.73**). He is depicted as a naturalistic toddler, with baby fat and childlike proportions. His stance is slightly precarious, as he leans back, pulling at the the goose's neck. The repeated diagonal planes and open spaces draw viewers into the work

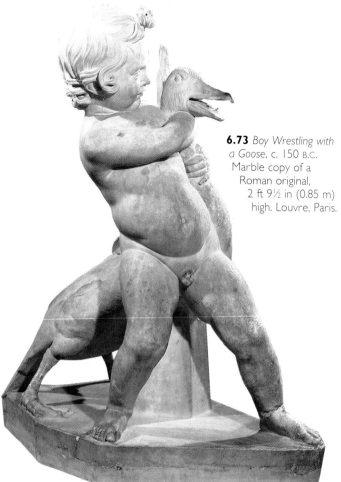

6.73 *Boy Wrestling with a Goose*, c. 150 B.C. Marble copy of a Roman original, 2 ft 9½ in (0.85 m) high. Louvre, Paris.

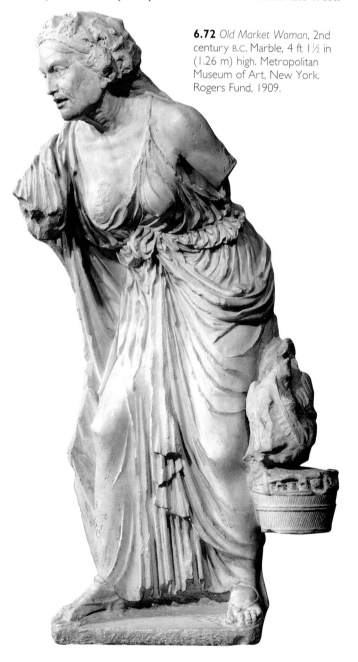

6.72 *Old Market Woman*, 2nd century B.C. Marble, 4 ft 1½ in (1.26 m) high. Metropolitan Museum of Art, New York. Rogers Fund, 1909.

and lead them to the formal climax of the struggle—the juxtaposition of the boy's head with that of the goose. By contrast, the bronze sculpture of the *Sleeping Eros* depicts relaxation (fig. **6.74**). The god's weight lies heavily on the slanted surface of his support, and his arm hangs limply in response to the force of gravity. Although Eros twists at his waist and the diagonals open up spaces, all the tension of the wrestling boy is gone.

The bronze *Boxer* from around the turn of the first century B.C. reveals the ravaging effects of this violent and brutal sport (fig. **6.75**). His face, turned awkwardly over his right shoulder, is covered with scars. He wears the leather knuckle-straps worn by Greek boxers which inflicted serious injury on one's opponents. He himself has a broken nose and teeth, as well as ears that have suffered from years of beating. His arms are still muscular, but his ribs are beginning to protrude from his chest, indicating the sagging flesh of age. Neither the function nor context of this figure is known, but it shows a man who has weathered a lifetime of fighting in a realistic, rather than an idealized, way.

The Hellenistic interest in melodramatic pathos is again evident in the sculptural group of *Laocoön and his Two Sons* (fig. **6.76**), a Roman adaptation of a Hellenistic work. It depicts an incident from the end of the Trojan War, in which Laocoön and his sons are devoured by a pair of serpents (see Box). The choice of such a moment lends itself to the Hellenistic taste for violent movement. The zigzags and strenuous exertions of the human figures are bound by the snakes winding around them.

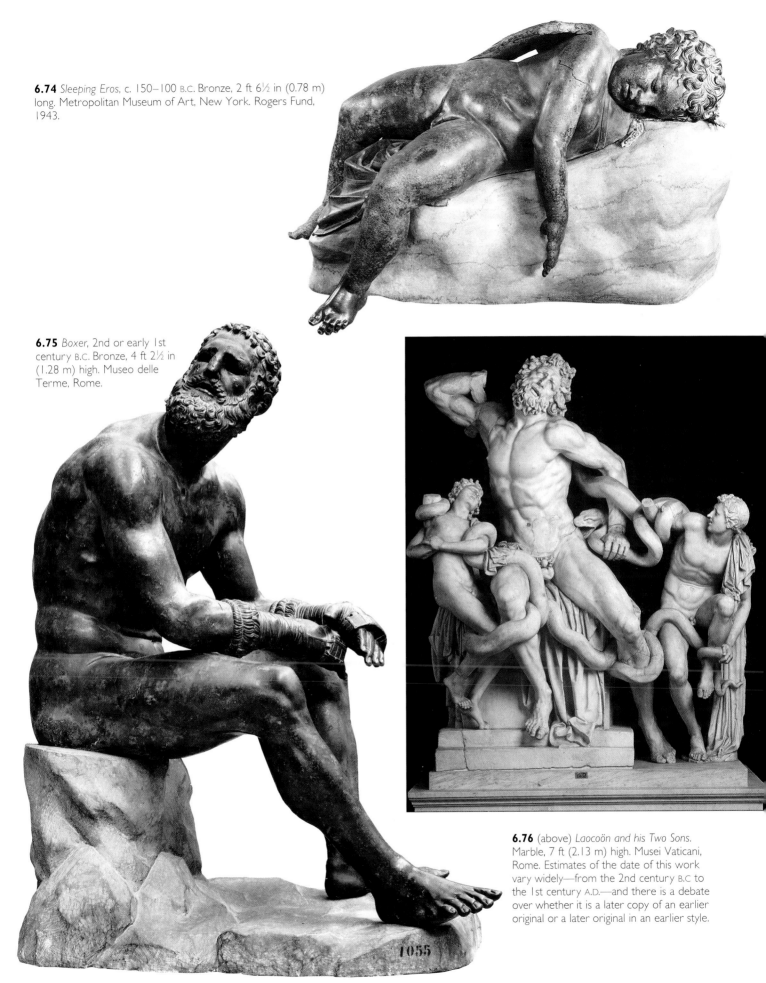

6.74 *Sleeping Eros*, c. 150–100 B.C. Bronze, 2 ft 6½ in (0.78 m) long. Metropolitan Museum of Art, New York. Rogers Fund, 1943.

6.75 *Boxer*, 2nd or early 1st century B.C. Bronze, 4 ft 2½ in (1.28 m) high. Museo delle Terme, Rome.

6.76 (above) *Laocoön and his Two Sons*. Marble, 7 ft (2.13 m) high. Musei Vaticani, Rome. Estimates of the date of this work vary widely—from the 2nd century B.C to the 1st century A.D.—and there is a debate over whether it is a later copy of an earlier original or a later original in an earlier style.

The Trojan Horse

According to a lost Homeric epic, the Greeks constructed a colossal wooden horse and filled it with armed soldiers. They tricked the Trojans into believing it was an offering to Athena that they should take inside their city walls. Laocoön, a Trojan seer, warned the Trojans that he did not trust the Greeks, "even bearing gifts." Thereupon, Athena sent two serpents to kill the seer and his children. The Trojans took this as a sign that Laocoön was not to be believed, and accordingly opened their gates and pulled in the horse. The Greek soldiers emerged, let in the rest of the Greek army, and sacked Troy. References to the story are also found in *The Odyssey* (IV. 271; VIII. 492; XI. 523).

In the *Laocoön*, Classical restraint and the symmetry of the Parthenon sculptures have been abandoned. There is extra weight to the left as Laocoön's powerful frame pulls away from the serpent biting his right hip. A counterbalancing diagonal is produced by the sharp turn of his head, and is repeated by the leg, torso, and head of the boy on the right. In contrast to the Classical *Wounded Amazon* of Polykleitos (fig. 6.27), Laocoön and his children express pain through facial contortion (fig. **6.77**) and physical struggle—bulging muscles, veins, flesh pulled taut against the rib-cage.

In the Great Altar of Zeus erected at Pergamon (fig. **6.78**), the Hellenistic taste for emotion, energetic movement, and exaggerated musculature is translated into relief sculpture. The two friezes on the altar celebrated the city and its superiority over the Gauls, who were a constant threat to the Pergamenes. Inside the structure, a small frieze depicted the legendary founding of Pergamon.

Outside, the traditional depiction of the gods fighting the Titans was transformed. In a detail illustrating Athena's destruction of Alkyoneus (fig. **6.79**), a son of the Titan earth goddess Gaia (Apollo's predecessor at Delphi) (see p. 136), the energy inherent in the juxtaposed diagonal planes seems barely contained. This mythical battle between pre-Greek Titans and Greek Olympians recurs in Hellenistic art partly as a result of renewed political threats to Greek supremacy. But unlike the Classical version on the Parthenon metopes, that at Pergamon is full of melodrama, frenzy, and pathos. King Attalus I defeated the powerful Gauls, who invaded Pergamon in 238 B.C. This victory made Pergamon a major political force. Later, under the rule of Eumenes II (197–c. 160 B.C.), the monumental altar dedicated to Zeus was built to proclaim the victory of Greek civilization over the barbarians. Greece tried to reassert its superiority, as Athens had done in building the Parthenon following the Persian Wars. But Hellenistic art, especially in its late phase, reflects the uncertainty and turmoil of the period. By the end of the first century B.C., the Romans were in complete control of the Mediterranean world and, with the ascendancy of Augustus in 31 B.C., the scene was set for the beginning of the Roman Empire.

Compared with the art of the other Mediterranean cultures we have surveyed, Greek art stands out for its prime concern with the expression of what is human. This is equally reflected in the science, philosophy, government, literature, theater, and religion of ancient Greece. As far as one can tell from surviving texts, the Greeks were the first in the West to write historically about art and artists. Of the Greek styles covered in this chapter, it is the Classical style that has had the most lasting impact on Western art and thought. The very notion of "Classical" has set a standard to which Western artists have responded in various ways. Subsequent styles, as well as individual artists, can be seen as both continuing the Classical tradition and rebelling against it. In either case, indifference to the Classical achievements was—and remains—virtually impossible.

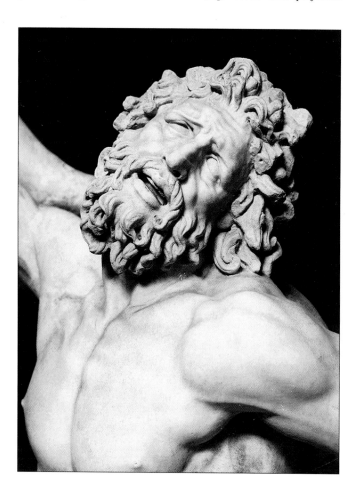

6.77 Head of Laocoön (detail of fig. 6.76).

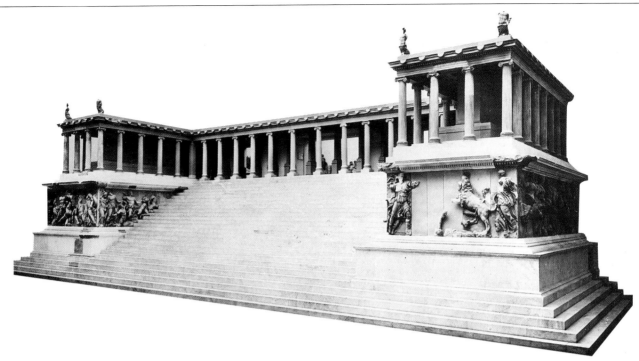

6.78 Altar of Zeus, west front, reconstructed and restored, from Pergamon, c. 175 B.C. Marble, great frieze on the exterior base of the colonnade over 36 feet (11 m) long, Pergamonmuseum, Berlin. The altar originally stood within the elaborate enclosure, in the open air, reminding the viewer of Zeus' role as supreme ruler of the sky.

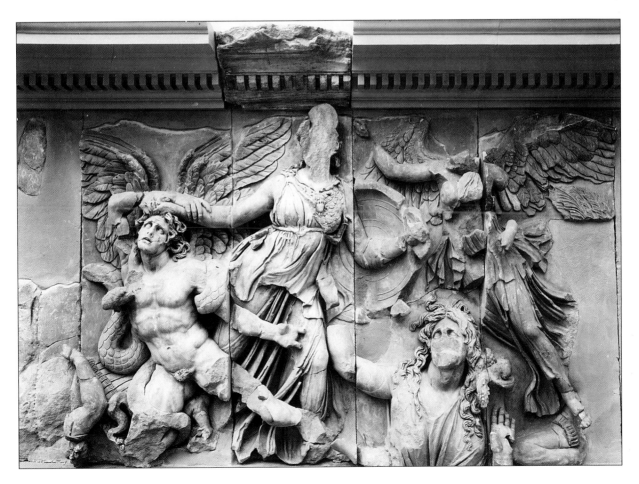

6.79 *Athena Battling with Alkyoneus*, from the great frieze of the Pergamon Altar, east section, c. 180 B.C. Marble, 7 ft 6 in (2.29 m) high. Antikensammlung, Staatliche Museen, Berlin.

Style/Period	Works of Art	Cultural/Historical Developments
GEOMETRIC c. 1000–700 B.C.	Geometric amphora (**6.5**)	Development of heroic legend in Greece: Homer's poems (*Iliad* and *Odyssey*) put into present form (8th c. B.C.) Etruscans settle central Italy (c. 900–700 B.C.) Adoption of Phoenician alphabet by Greeks (c. 800 B.C.) Traditional date for beginning of Olympic Games (776 B.C.) First Greek colony on Italian mainland (Cumae) (760 B.C.)
ORIENTALIZING c. 700–640 B.C.	Athenian amphora (**6.6, 6.7, 6.9, 6.10**) Terrace of Lions, Delos (**6.18**) **Geometric amphora**	Circumnavigation of Africa by Phoenicians (c. 700–600 B.C.) Coins used as units of currency imported from Asia Minor into Greece (c. 650 B.C.)
ARCHAIC c. 640–490 B.C. **Achilles and Ajax**	Dipylon Master, *New York Kouros* (**6.19**), Attica Cheramyes Master, *Hera of Samos* (**6.20**), Samos Temple of Apollo (**6.30**), Corinth Exekias, *Achilles and Ajax Playing a Board Game* (**6.9**) Siphnian Treasury (**6.32, 6.33**), Delphi Temple of Apollo (**6.2**), Delphi *Peplos Kore* (**6.21**) Exekias, *Achilles and Penthesilea* (**6.10**)	Solon's reforms in Athens (593 B.C.) Thales of Miletus, beginning of natural philosophy (585 B.C.) Pythagoras, Greek mathematician and philosopher (581–497 B.C.) Pisistratos tyrant of Athens (560 B.C.) Cyrus of Persia gains control of Media (550 B.C.) Persians conquer Asia Minor (546 B.C.) Roman Republic established (510 B.C.) First democratic government established in Greece (510–508 B.C.) Persian Wars (499–449 B.C.); Ionian cities revolt from Persia with aid of Athens (499); Athenians defeat Persians at Battle of Marathon (490) Use of lost-wax process begins in Greece (6th century)
EARLY CLASSICAL c. 490–450 B.C.	Berlin Painter, *Abduction of Europa* (**6.12**) Kritios, *Kritios Boy* (**6.22**) Myron, *Diskobolos* (**6.24**) Temple of Zeus (**6.38, 6.43, 6.44**), Olympia Penthesilea Painter, *Achilles and Penthesilea* (**6.13**) Niobid Painter, Kalyx krater (**6.14, 6.15**) *Poseidon/Zeus* (**6.23**) *Warrior from Riace* (**6.25**), Reggio Calabria	Herodotos, the "Father of History" (485–424 B.C.) Aeschylos, *Oresteia* (458 B.C.) Beginning of Perikles' dominance (458 B.C.) Age of Greek drama: Aeschylos (523–456), Sophokles (496–424), Euripides (c. 480–406), Aristophanes (c. 450–c. 385)
CLASSICAL c. 450–400 B.C. **Diskobolos**	Reed Painter, *Warrior by a Grave* (**6.16**) The Parthenon (**6.47, 6.50–6.57**), Athens Polykleitos, *Doryphoros* (**6.26**) Polykleitos, *Wounded Amazon* (**6.27**) Temple of Athena Nike (**6.59, 6.60**) The Erechtheum (**6.61, 6.62**), Acropolis, Athens Stele of Hegeso (**6.28**)	Hippokrates, Greek physician, the "Father of Medicine" (c. 460–c. 377 B.C.) Demokritos, Greek philosopher and scientist who developed an atomic theory of the universe (c. 460–c. 370 B.C.) Age of Classical Greek philosophy: Socrates (470–399), Plato (c. 427–c. 347), Aristotle (384–322) Beginning of the Parthenon (447 B.C.)
LATE CLASSICAL c. 400–300 B.C.	Theater (**6.63**), Epidauros Praxiteles, *Aphrodite of Knidos* (**6.65**) Attic grave stele (**6.68**)	The Peloponnesian War; Athens defeated by Sparta; Spartan hegemony in Greece (404–371) Trial and execution of Socrates (399 B.C.) Plato, *The Republic* (c. 380–360 B.C.) Alexander the Great conquers Egypt, Palestine, Phoenicia, and Persia (333–331 B.C.)
HELLENISTIC 323–31 B.C. **Laocoön and his Two Sons**	Lysippos, *Apoxyomenos* (**6.67**) Lysippos, *Socrates* (**6.4**) *Stag Hunt* (**6.17**), Pella Polyeuktos, *Demosthenes* (**6.70**) Head of Alexander (**6.69**), Pergamon *Winged Nike* (**6.71**), Samothrace *Old Market Woman* (**6.72**) *Boy Wrestling with a Goose* (**6.73**) *Sleeping Eros* (**6.74**) Bronze Boxer (**6.75**) *Laocoön and his Two Sons* (**6.76, 6.77**) Altar of Zeus (**6.78, 6.79**), Pergamon	Death of Alexander (323 B.C.) Euclid, *Elements of Geometry* (323 B.C.) The Colossus of Rhodes (290 B.C.) Archimedes, Greek mathematician (287–212 B.C.) Heyday of Alexandria (Egypt) as the center of the new Hellenistic culture (275–215 B.C.) **Sleeping Eros**

Time markers (left axis): 1000 B.C., 700 B.C., 500 B.C., 450 B.C., 300 B.C.

7

The Art
of the Etruscans

Etruscan civilization, which flourished between c. 1000 and 100 B.C., was contemporary with the Greek culture discussed in the previous chapter. The Iron Age predecessors of the Etruscans, known as Villanovans, after a site near modern Bologna in northern Italy, had elaborate burials that included objects of iron, bronze, and ivory. The Etruscans are important in Western history both in terms of their own art and culture and because of the significant links they provided between ancient Greece and Rome. Their homeland, Etruria (modern Tuscany), occupied the west-central part of the Italian peninsula. It was bordered on the south by the River Tiber, which runs through Rome, and on the north by the Arno (fig. **7.1**).

The Greeks called the Etruscans Tyrrhenians, after whom the sea was named, and the Romans called them Tusci or Etrusci. Like the Greeks, the Etruscans never formed a single nation, but coexisted as separate city-states with their own rulers. Unlike the Romans, they never established an empire.

Although the ancient Greek historian Herodotos thought that the Etruscans had come from Lydia, in modern Turkey, scholars today believe that they were indigenous to, or at least developed their civilization in, Italy. They lived as a distinct group of people whose culture contributed to, and benefited from, the larger Mediterranean world. From the seventh to the fifth centuries B.C.—the period of their greatest power—the Etruscans controlled the western Mediterranean with their fleet, and were an important trading nation. They rivaled the Greeks and the Phoenicians and established commercial trade routes throughout the Aegean, the Near East, and North Africa. At the same time, the Etruscans were largely responsible for extending Greek influence to northern Italy and Spain.

The Greeks and Romans considered the Etruscans to be a decadent, bloodthirsty people with a predilection for piracy, superstition, and magic. Archaeological evidence indicates that on occasion they practiced human sacrifice. But this reputation was only partly justified and, since the mid-nineteenth century, with the development of new archaeological techniques, the study of the Etruscans has become more scholarly.

The Etruscan language resembles none other that is presently known and its origin is uncertain. The alphabet was taken from the Greeks in the seventh century B.C. In contrast to Greek script, but similar to Phoenician (from which the Etruscan alphabet, like the Greek, ultimately derives), Etruscan is written from right to left. All Etruscan literature—which, according to Roman sources, was rich and extensive—has disappeared. The writing that has survived is mostly in the form of epitaphs on graves or religious texts. Only a few Etruscan words, most of them names and inscriptions, have been deciphered.

7.1 Map of Etruscan and Roman Italy.

Etruscan Materials

Unlike Greek architecture, that of the Etruscans was constructed primarily of mud-brick. Columns were made of wood and decorative details of terracotta or **tufa**, a soft, porous, volcanic rock that was easy to work.

Statues were typically made of terracotta or bronze, and the Etruscans were justly renowned for them in Classical Athens. They were skilled in bronze casting and engraved mythological scenes on the backs of bronze mirrors. For jewelry, gold was the preferred material.

The earliest Etruscan paintings were on a tufa ground, and later ones were applied to clay plaster. Most surviving Etruscan examples are fresco, but some have been discovered in **tempera**, a combination of pigment with water and egg yolk. The egg yolk makes the mixture thicker than fresco, and thus tempera paintings can be richer in color. The term derives from the French word *temper*, meaning "to bring to a desired consistency." It is not known when tempera was first used, but it became progressively more popular in Italy during the fifteenth century A.D.

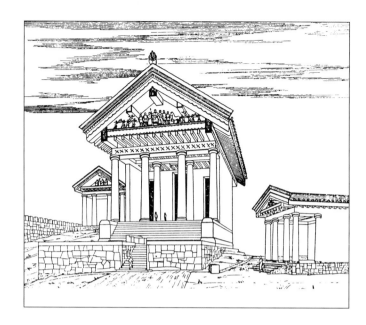

7.2 Reconstruction drawing of the three temples on the Arx of Cosa, c. 100 B.C.

Vitruvius on Architecture

Marcus Vitruvius Pollio, known as Vitruvius, was a Roman architect and engineer. During the Augustan period (30 B.C.–A.D. 14), Vitruvius wrote *De architectura*, a treatise on architecture in ten books, which was based on his own experience and on earlier works by Greek and Etruscan architects. It covered city planning and urban building, including the choice of site, materials, and construction types. Although the treatise has no particular literary merit, it is a good source of information on the architectural ideas and practices of antiquity.

Our major source of information about the Etruscans comes from the tombs and *necropoleis,* which the Romans left undisturbed and which are buried under modern Italian towns. Most of these were carved out of rocky ground, especially in the south, and their contents provide by far the richest examples of Etruscan art. Very few Etruscan buildings have survived, partly because of the nature of the materials used—wood, mud, and tufa (see Box). There are some remains of fortifications and urban organization, with streets arranged in a grid pattern.

Architecture

Greece was the inspiration for large-scale architecture in Etruria. The oldest known Etruscan temple, now in a fragmentary state, dates from the sixth century B.C.; earlier Etruscans had worshiped in open-air sanctuaries. The idea of erecting temples within such sanctuaries and sacred precincts came from Greece, and remains of temple foundations indicate that their plans were based on Greek prototypes. Late Archaic Etruscan temples, however, are distinct from the Greek in having gabled porches, but not pediments. Etruscan architects used **wattle and daub** construction for the superstructure by reinforcing branches (wattle) with clay and mud (daub). Stone was used only for the podium. Roofs were tiled and decorative sculpture was made of terracotta.

Three late Etruscan temples from the Hellenistic period have been reconstructed (fig. **7.2**) according to the ideal proportions described by the Roman architect and engineer Vitruvius (see Box). They show that, in addition to the plan, the Etruscans incorporated the Greek wooden roof and portico. In contrast to Greek temples, however, these are set on a high podium rather than on steps, and the side walls are solid. This arrangement emphasizes the entrance wall as being at the front of the temple, whereas the Greeks' use of colonnaded walls minimizes the distinction between front and sides. It also gives Etruscan temples a heavier, more massive quality than their Greek counterparts.

Pottery and Sculpture

Vines and olive trees, and the agricultural techniques associated with them, were as important in Etruria as in Greece. The Etruscans adopted—and adapted—such Greek social customs as the *symposium* or drinking party, and the practice of banqueting in a reclining position. For these functions they imported thousands of Greek vases. Etruscan tombs have yielded most of these imported

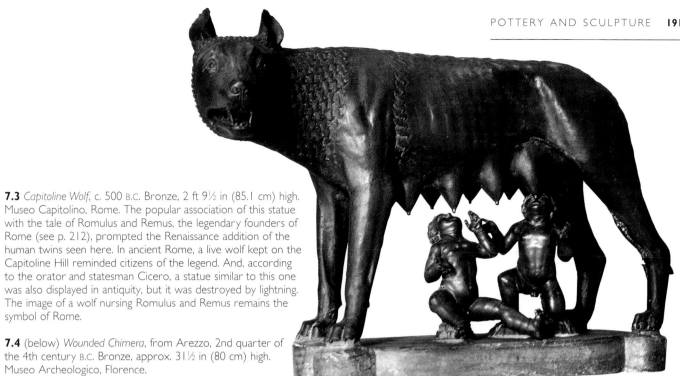

7.3 *Capitoline Wolf*, c. 500 B.C. Bronze, 2 ft 9½ in (85.1 cm) high. Museo Capitolino, Rome. The popular association of this statue with the tale of Romulus and Remus, the legendary founders of Rome (see p. 212), prompted the Renaissance addition of the human twins seen here. In ancient Rome, a live wolf kept on the Capitoline Hill reminded citizens of the legend. And, according to the orator and statesman Cicero, a statue similar to this one was also displayed in antiquity, but it was destroyed by lightning. The image of a wolf nursing Romulus and Remus remains the symbol of Rome.

7.4 (below) *Wounded Chimera*, from Arezzo, 2nd quarter of the 4th century B.C. Bronze, approx. 31½ in (80 cm) high. Museo Archeologico, Florence.

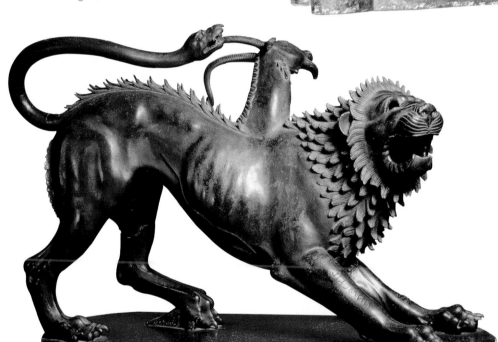

Greek black- and red-figure vases, which were important sources of Greek pictorial style in Italy. Scenes and characters from Greek mythology liberally populate Etruscan imagery. A particularly rich source for these images appears in engravings on the backs of bronze mirrors, which were an Etruscan specialty (cf. fig. **7.8**).

The few surviving examples of Etruscan sculpture indicate a thriving industry in bronze. As in Greece, Etruscan artists cast bronze by the lost-wax method. The statue of a nursing she-wolf of around 500 B.C., the so-called *Capitoline Wolf*, captures the aggressive anger of a

mother protecting her cubs (fig. **7.3**). She turns and becomes tense, as if suddenly startled, and bares her teeth at an unseen intruder. The stylized patterns of fur, especially around the neck, have clear affinities with Greek Archaic style.

The bronze *Wounded Chimera* from the fourth century B.C. depicts the mythological monster with a lion's body, a serpent's tail, and a goat's head—here emerging from the back (fig. **7.4**). The figure originally belonged to a group showing the Greek hero Bellerophon, who rode the winged horse Pegasus, killing the Chimera. Its pose

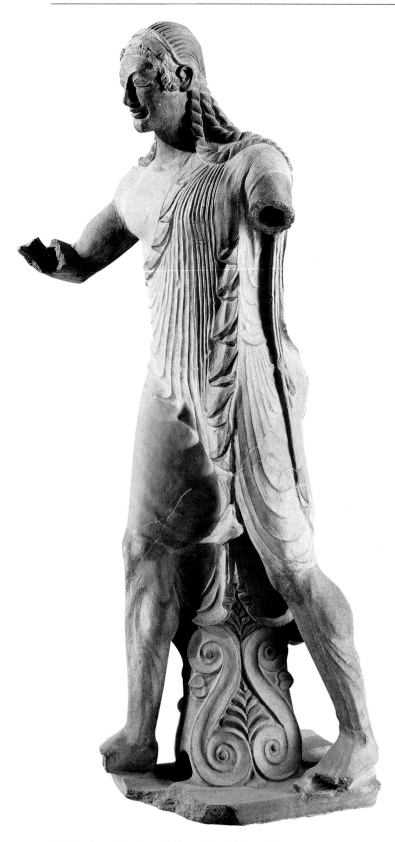

7.5 *Apollo of Veii*, from Veii, c. 515–490 B.C. Painted terracotta, approx. 5 ft 10 in (1.78 m) high. Museo Nazionale di Villa Giulia, Rome. Terracotta was a favorite Etruscan material for sculpture. It was modeled while still wet, and the smaller details were added with hand tools. In this statue, Apollo's energetic forward stride reflects the Etruscan interest in gesture, motion, and posture.

convincingly indicates a sense of withdrawal from danger, and it seems ready to spring toward an adversary. The hair along the spine literally stands on end; fear is also suggested through the open mouth, turned head, and raised eyebrows. The Archaic stylizations, especially the mane and whiskers, are similar to certain Achaemenid motifs (see p. 74), and thus reflect the influence of the Near East on Etruscan art.

To a considerable extent, the development of Etruscan art paralleled that of Greece, and the same terms are used to designate stylistic categories—Archaic, Classical, and Hellenistic—even though the Etruscan dates are only roughly contemporaneous with their Greek counterparts. The Archaic style, for example, continued in Etruria for a short time after it had been abandoned in Greece. This can be seen in the lifesize terracotta *Apollo of Veii* (fig. **7.5**), which originally decorated the roof of a temple. It corresponds to the Greek Late Archaic in style, but slightly overlaps Greek Early Classical in time.

The figure has some organic form (around the chest, for example), but the curvilinear stylizations and flat surface patterns of the drapery folds are more characteristic of Archaic. The same is true of the diagonal calf muscles fanning out from below the knees, with the lines on top of the feet suggesting that the toes continue to the ankles. The stylized hair, arranged in long locks, and the smile also belong to Greek Archaic convention. Despite the Greek influence on the *Apollo*, however, the sharp clarity of its forms and stylizations, as well as its determined stride, is characteristic of the forcefulness of early Etruscan art.

Closer to Greek Classical style is the bronze *Mars of Todi* (fig. **7.6**), dating from the early fourth century B.C. Named for the site of its discovery at Todi, north of Rome, it is the only nearly lifesize Etruscan bronze known from before the second century B.C. Although later than the Greek Classical period, the *Mars* has certain affinities with the *Spear Bearer* (see fig. 6.26), especially its *contrapposto* pose. The figure represents a warrior (hence the designation Mars, after the Roman god of war). He wears a leather cuirass (breastplate) and a tunic, and he holds a libation bowl in his right hand and the remnant of a lance, on which he probably leaned, in his left. The rendering of the anatomy is organic, but the pose seems self-consciously animated compared with the relaxed pose of the *Spear Bearer*, and the anatomy is not unified as it is in Greek Classical sculpture.

Women in Etruscan Art

The Etruscans differed significantly from the Greeks in their attitude to women. Judging from Etruscan art, Etruscan women participated more in public life with their husbands, and held higher positions than in ancient Greece—a state of affairs of which the patriarchal Greeks heartily disapproved. Wealthy Etruscan women were unusually fashion-conscious and wore elaborate jewelry commensurate with their rank.

The abundance of bronze mirrors that have been excavated from Etruria were used only by women (fig. **7.8**). They were typically decorated with mythological scenes, and their inscriptions indicate that the women to whom they belonged were literate. The greater emphasis on women in Etruscan society is consistent with the prominence in the arts of the mother goddess and other female deities well beyond the Bronze Age. Etruscan artists frequently depicted myths in which women dominate men by being older, more powerful, or higher in divine status. For example, the scene illustrated here shows the adult Herakles being breastfed by the goddess Uni, the Etruscan equivalent of Hera, in the presence of male and female divinities.

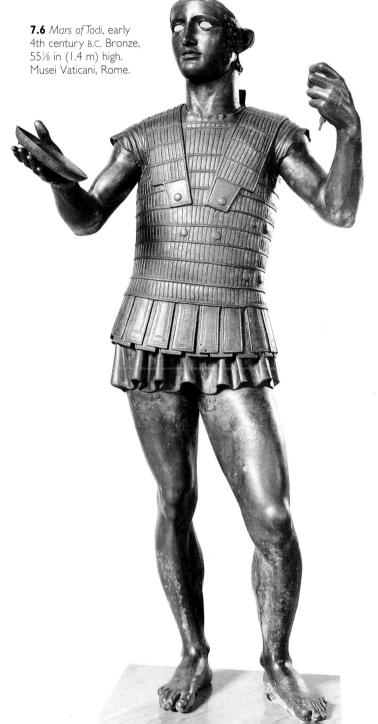

7.6 *Mars of Todi*, early 4th century B.C. Bronze, 55⅛ in (1.4 m) high. Musei Vaticani, Rome.

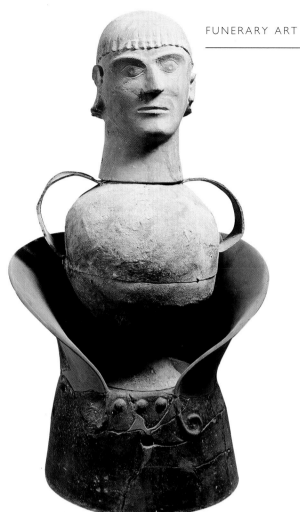

7.7 Cinerary urn, from Chiusi, 7th century B.C. Hammered bronze and terracotta, approx. 33 in (83.8 cm) high. Museo Etrusco, Chiusi. The metaphorical nature of this object, in which the body, base, and handles of the urn are equated with the corresponding human anatomy, implies a religious significance. The container of the ashes was probably intended to symbolize a reversal of the process of cremation, as if to keep the dead person alive through his or her image.

Funerary Art

The Etruscans clearly believed in an afterlife that was closer to the Egyptian concept than to the Greek, but it is not known what their view of the afterlife was. It seems to have been as materialistic as in ancient Egypt, since items used in real life such as women's mirrors, jewelry, men's weapons, and banquet ware accompanied the deceased.

Cinerary Containers

Before the seventh century B.C., many Etruscans cremated their dead. They buried the ashes in individual tombs or cinerary urns, which often had lids in the form of human heads. The vessels themselves sometimes had body markings. In figure **7.7** both the urn and the wide-backed chair on which it stands are made of bronze, but the head is terracotta. Its individualized features suggest that it was intended to convey at least a general likeness of the deceased.

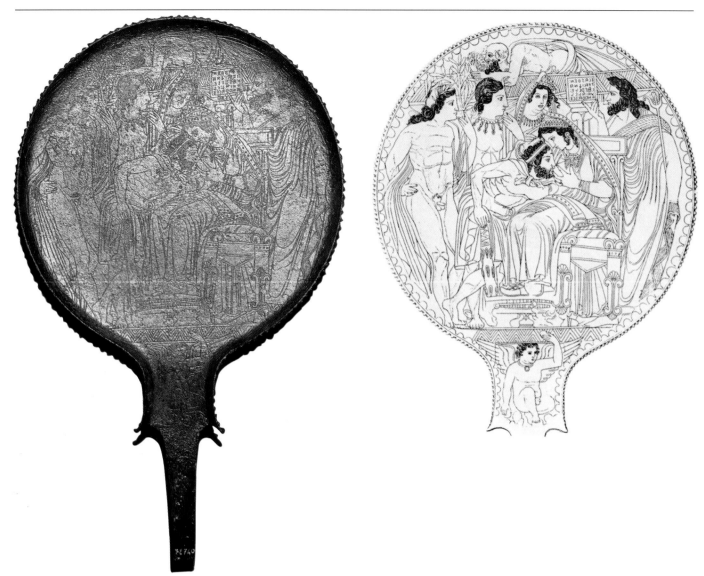

7.8a, b Scene from the back of a mirror, from Volterra, showing Uni (Hera) nursing Herakles in the presence of other gods. Bronze, engraved, c. 300 B.C. Museo Archeologico, Florence. The Greek version of the myth illustrated here is known only from literature and does not appear in Greek art. It recounts the story of Zeus deceiving Hera into nursing—as a sign of acceptance and adoption—his son Herakles (meaning "the glory of Hera") by the mortal woman Alkmene. But Hera pulled away, and the milk from her breast spurted into the heavens, creating the Milky Way. In the Etruscan version, which is also represented on two other mirrors, Uni (Hera) willingly nurses Herakles (Hercle in Etruscan). The fact that he is an adult reflects his acceptance into the pantheon of the gods and his attainment of immortality. Two gods, Aplu (the Etruscan Apollo) and Nethuns (the Etruscan Neptune), and two unidentified goddesses witness the initiation ritual. Behind Uni, another witness holds up a tablet with the inscription: "This shows how Hercle became Uni's son." The satyr at the top of the mirror drinks wine—the antithesis of milk in Etruscan religion.

An unusual limestone cinerary statue represents a particularly monumental female with a swaddled child lying across her lap (fig. **7.9**). The woman's facial expression, consistent with Greek Early Classical, reveals a hint of mourning as the corners of the mouth turn down slightly and the forehead is creased. She is frontal and conforms to the planes of her chair. On either side of the chair is a sphinx, here with a woman's head and a lion's body. The identity of these figures is unknown, although the woman is probably an enthroned goddess. In Egypt, the Near East, the Aegean, and elsewhere, leonine guardians are associated with royalty and divinity, but their significance in Etruscan art remains uncertain.

Many cinerary urns took the form of houses and provide us with a a glimpse of Etruscan domestic architecture. The Iron Age urn from the Villanovan civilization, for example, is in the form of a hut, the first known house type in central Italy (fig. **7.10**). It consists of a single room enclosed by a circular wall, and has a thatched roof supported by interior vertical posts. The example shown in figure **7.11** may have represented an upper-class house or palace, for it has an elegant, symmetrical façade with an arched doorway, and a second-story gallery. (The arch, which was invented in Mesopotamia and used in Greece, was assimilated by the Etruscans and later elaborated by the Romans.) At the corners of the urn, Corinthian

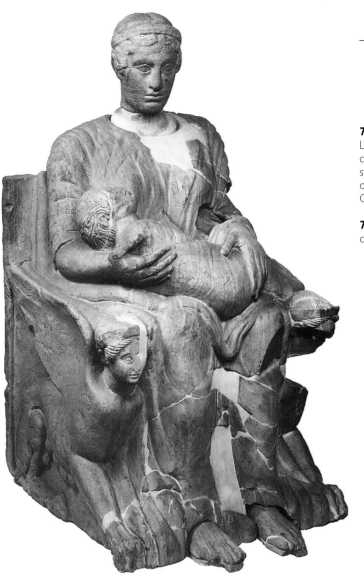

7.9 (left) *Mater Matuta*, from Chianciano, near Chiusi, 460–440 B.C. Limestone, lifesize. Museo Archeologico, Florence. This figure corresponds chronologically to the beginning of the Greek Classical style. Although the woman is organically sculpted and the drapery outlines her body, she nonetheless retains the stylized hair of the Early Classical period.

7.10 (below) Urn in the shape of a hut, from Tarquinia, 9th–8th century B.C. Museo Archeologico, Tarquinia.

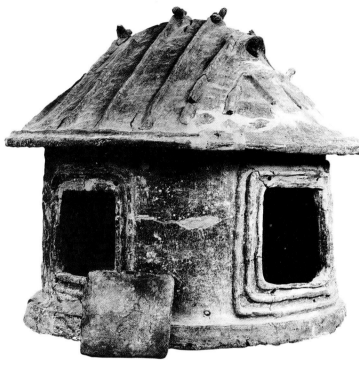

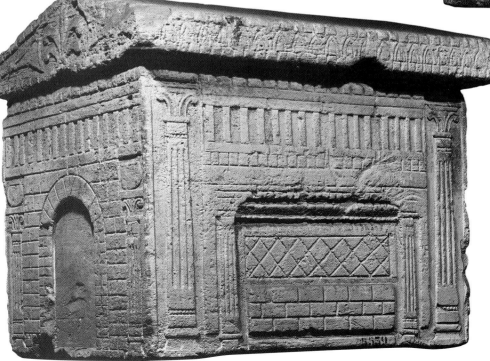

7.11 Cinerary urn in the form of a house, from Chiusi, c. 650–700 B.C. Museo Archeologico, Florence.

pilasters reinforce the structure. These are the flat, vertical elements that project from, and are engaged in, the wall. The lid of the urn corresponds to the roof, with a curved pediment over the entrance and a palmette relief in the center.

Architectural urns provide clues to the development of Etruscan sculptural and architectural styles. The human-headed urns reflect both a wish to preserve the likeness of the deceased and the importance of ancestors who were considered divine in the afterlife. Urns-as-houses express the metaphor in which the tomb or burial place is a "house for the dead." The little Etruscan architectural urns actually reverse the metaphor: instead of the house being the tomb, the tomb is the house.

Tombs

The attitudes to death suggested by objects such as the urns recur in the Etruscan custom of building larger-scale architectural tombs to "house" their families. Tombs were originally small and intended for individual burials, but beginning in the seventh century B.C. several rock-cut chambers were covered by larger earth mounds, or **tumuli**, and were grouped together to replicate cities. In fact, it is from the Etruscan *necropoleis* that scholars have been able to reconstruct entire city and town plans and to derive information about the urban architecture of Etruria.

The plan of the burial site known as the Tomb of the Shields and the Chairs at Cerveteri (fig. **7.12**) has a complex arrangement: the stepped passage (**1** on the plan) is flanked by similar tomb chambers (**2**), accessible through

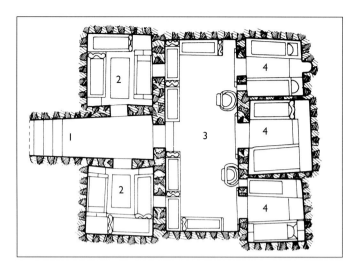

7.12 Plan of the Tomb of the Shields and the Chairs, Cerveteri, c. 700–650 B.C. Approx. 29 × 34 ft (9 × 10.5 m).

a door on each side of the entrance; at the far end is a set of three rooms (**4**); the central room (**3** on the plan and fig. **7.13**) has walls decorated with reliefs of round shields. There is a door at the right, with a lintel over the opening, and rectangular windows. Built-in furniture includes benches and a typically Etruscan curved-back chair with a footstool similar to that in the cinerary urn (see fig. 7.8). Funerary complexes such as this combined the universal need to provide burials with the particular Etruscan association of tombs with houses. They were intended to be dwelling places for the deceased.

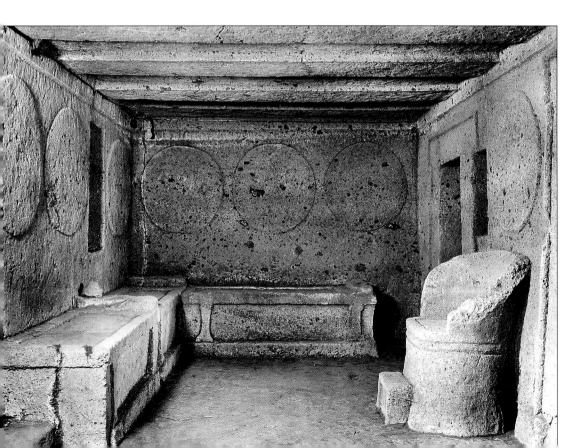

7.13 Interior of the central room in the Tomb of the Shields and the Chairs (number 3 on the plan above), Cerveteri, c. 600 B.C. Tufa, approx. 29 × 11½ ft (9 × 3.5 m).

Sarcophagi

Etruscan artists developed a new funerary iconography, which they translated into monumental sculpture in the sarcophagi of wealthy individuals. For example, a painted terracotta sarcophagus of around 520 B.C. from Cerveteri is in the form of a dining couch (fig. **7.14**). Like the urns, it was made to contain cremated remains rather than the bodies of the deceased. The figures represent a married couple—the family unit was an important element in Etruscan art and society. The wife and husband are given similar status, reflecting the position of women in ancient Etruria. They are rendered with Archaic features—long

7.14a, b Sarcophagus, from Cerveteri, c. 520 B.C. (front and back). Painted terracotta, 6 ft 7 in (2 m) long. Museo Nazionale di Villa Giulia, Rome.

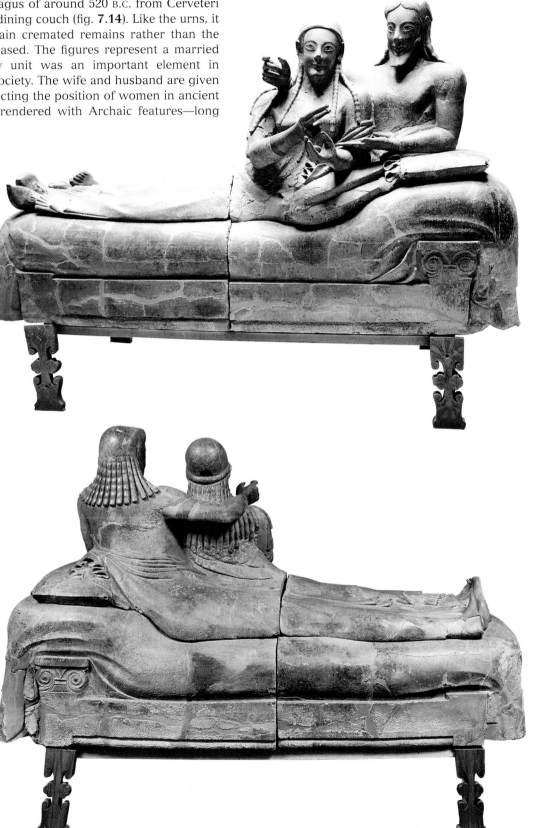

stylized hair, smiles with corresponding raised cheek-bones and upwardly slanting eyes, a circular cap for the woman and neatly parted hair for the man. The elegance of their curves and soft areas of their bodies, their finely pleated drapery, and almond-shaped eyes indicate influences from Greek Ionia. In contrast to Greek sculpture, however, these figures have no sense of skeletal structure and "stop" abruptly at the waist, indicating the Etruscan preference for stylistic effects over anatomical accuracy. The sharp bend at the waists and the animated gestures create the illusion of lively, sociable dinner companions, reclining in the style adopted for banqueting from the Greeks. The couple seems very much alive, as if to deny the fact of their deaths.

Another, later type of Etruscan sarcophagus represents individual figures or couples in bed on the lid. A sarcophagus lid from Vulci (fig. **7.15**) shows an embracing husband and wife. The folds of the sheet echo the curves of their arms, with shorter, more animated curves and diagonals over the zigzags of legs and feet.

Tomb Paintings

Etruscans used painted images as well as architecture and sculpture in the service of the dead. Hundreds of paintings have been discovered in the underground tombs of Tarquinia, a site northwest of Rome rich in archaeological finds. Tomb paintings were usually frescoes, although occasionally tempera was applied to dry plaster. Similar paintings probably adorned public and private buildings, although there are no surviving examples. Until the fourth century B.C., the most frequently represented subjects in Etruscan tomb paintings were funeral rites or optimistic scenes of aristocratic pleasures—banquets, sports, dances, and music-making.

A painting from the Tomb of the Augurs, in Tarquinia, dates from c. 540 B.C., and represents two mourners (fig. **7.16**). The figures stand on a horizontal ground line flanking the closed door leading to the Underworld, and there is little indication of depth. Plant stems rise directly from the ground line and are the same brownish color. Aside from the blue leaves, the colors of the costume match the solemn mood. The mourners wear a simple, light yellow inner garment that falls to about mid-calf, but their shorter outer garment is black, as are their boots. Their gestures are the traditional stylized gestures of mourning and have a theatrical quality. They direct our attention to the closed door that leads to the next life, an image that reaffirms the architectural metaphor equating house and tomb. The form of the door, with the horizontal lintel at the top extending beyond the sides, is similar to the actual door visible in the Tomb of the Shields and the Chairs (see fig. 7.12).

A fresco in the Tomb of the Leopards, at Tarquinia, shows men and women reclining on banqueting couches while servants wait on them (fig. **7.17**). The seated banqueters have the same bend at the waist and animated gestures as the couple on the Cerveteri sarcophagus (fig.

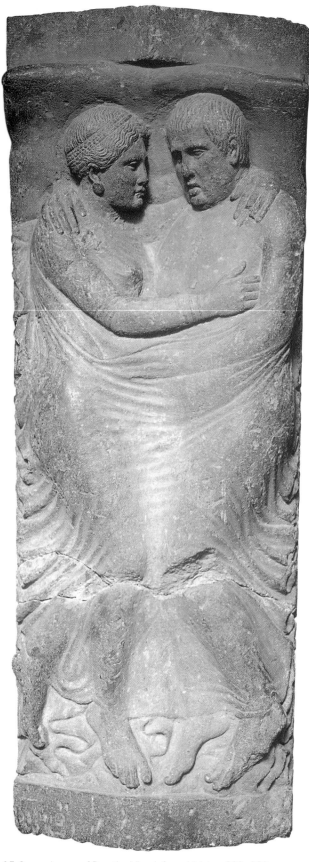

7.15 Sarcophagus of Ramtha Visnai, from Vulci, c. 300–280 B.C. Limestone, 7 ft 1¾ in × 2 ft 6¾ in (2.18 × 0.78 m). Courtesy Museum of Fine Arts, Boston. Gift of Mr. and Mrs. Cornelius C. Vermeule III. This restful scene expresses the ancient identification of sleep with death. The correlation is virtually universal—in Greek mythology, for example, Sleep and Death were twins—but in Etruscan tomb iconography the metaphor is rendered literally.

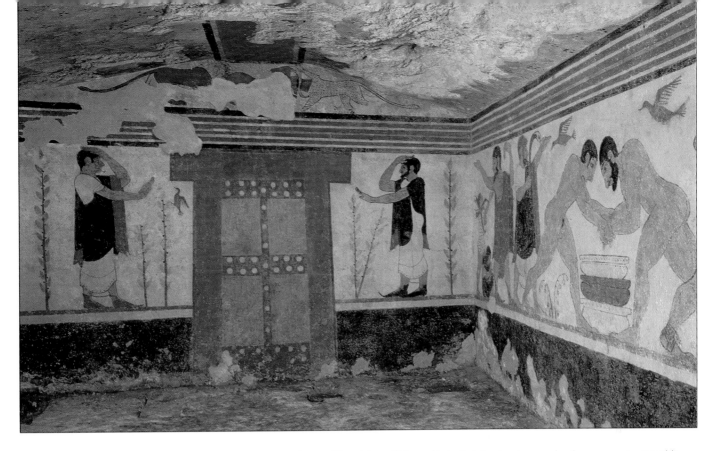

7.16 *Mourners at the Door of the Other World*, Tomb of the Augurs, Tarquinia, c. 510 B.C. Note that the boots worn by the mourners resemble those of the war god in the Hittite relief from Boghazköy (see fig. 3.24). Pointed boots are typically worn by mountain people and are another example of influence from the Greek Ionian cities and Asia Minor. The scene at the right shows two wrestlers.

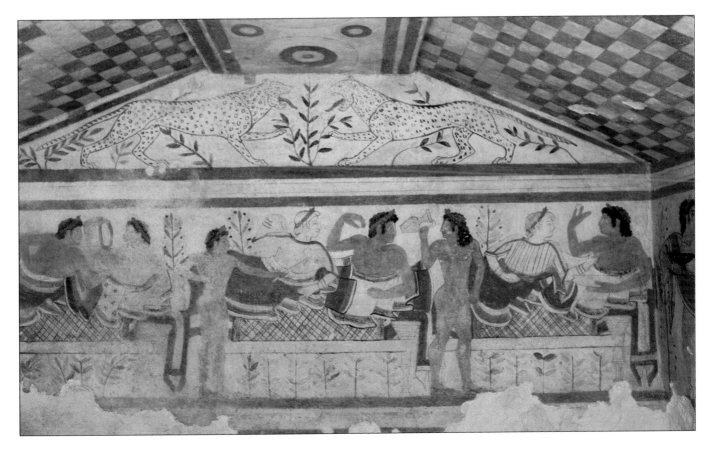

7.17 Tomb of the Leopards, Tarquinia, 480–470 B.C. Fresco. Here the influence of Egyptian and Aegean painting is quite evident. Women are lighter skinned than men, profile heads contain a frontal eye, and figures are outlined in black and dark brown.

7.14), but their heads are in profile. Colors are mainly terracotta tones of brown on an ocher background, with drapery patterns, wreaths, plants, and other details in blues, greens, and yellows. As in Egyptian, Minoan, and Greek painting, Etruscan women are rendered with lighter skin tones than men. Above the banqueting scene, two leopards flank a stylized plant and symbolically protect the tomb from evil influences. The wall to the right is decorated with musicians, and one man holds a wine cup.

Compared with paintings in Greece, Etruscan paintings disregard anatomical accuracy and naturalistic movement in space, and the overall impression is one of spontaneity. Even though figure 7.17 illustrates an interior scene, for example, the presence of trees indicates a willingness to merge what is naturally outside with what is architecturally inside.

Despite Greek influence, which was omnipresent in the Mediterranean, the Etruscans remained a culturally distinct group, retaining their own language, religion, and customs for nearly a millennium. Occupying a large section of Italy for much of the period of the Roman Republic, Etruscans were also independent of the Romans in language and religious beliefs. Yet they taught the Romans a great deal about engineering, building, drainage, irrigation, and the art of augury—how to read the will of the gods and foretell the future from the entrails of animals and the flight of birds. In matters of fashion and jewelry, the Etruscans were the envy of Greek and Roman women alike. Their technical skill and craftsmanship prompted advances in jewelry such as gold granulation, as well as in dentistry. Etruscans made bridges and dentures which enhanced physical well-being, as well as being cosmetically pleasing.

Etruscan kings ruled Rome until the establishment of the Roman Republic in 510 B.C. By the early third century B.C., Etruria had become part of Rome's political organization, and two centuries later it had succumbed to full Romanization.

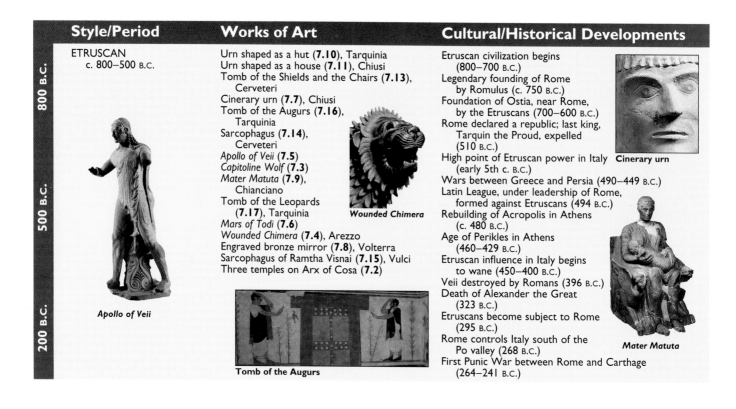

Style/Period	Works of Art	Cultural/Historical Developments
ETRUSCAN c. 800–500 B.C.	Urn shaped as a hut (**7.10**), Tarquinia Urn shaped as a house (**7.11**), Chiusi Tomb of the Shields and the Chairs (**7.13**), Cerveteri Cinerary urn (**7.7**), Chiusi Tomb of the Augurs (**7.16**), Tarquinia Sarcophagus (**7.14**), Cerveteri Apollo of Veii (**7.5**) Capitoline Wolf (**7.3**) Mater Matuta (**7.9**), Chianciano Tomb of the Leopards (**7.17**), Tarquinia Mars of Todi (**7.6**) Wounded Chimera (**7.4**), Arezzo Engraved bronze mirror (**7.8**), Volterra Sarcophagus of Ramtha Visnai (**7.15**), Vulci Three temples on Arx of Cosa (**7.2**)	Etruscan civilization begins (800–700 B.C.) Legendary founding of Rome by Romulus (c. 750 B.C.) Foundation of Ostia, near Rome, by the Etruscans (700–600 B.C.) Rome declared a republic; last king, Tarquin the Proud, expelled (510 B.C.) High point of Etruscan power in Italy (early 5th c. B.C.) Wars between Greece and Persia (490–449 B.C.) Latin League, under leadership of Rome, formed against Etruscans (494 B.C.) Rebuilding of Acropolis in Athens (c. 480 B.C.) Age of Perikles in Athens (460–429 B.C.) Etruscan influence in Italy begins to wane (450–400 B.C.) Veii destroyed by Romans (396 B.C.) Death of Alexander the Great (323 B.C.) Etruscans become subject to Rome (295 B.C.) Rome controls Italy south of the Po valley (268 B.C.) First Punic War between Rome and Carthage (264–241 B.C.)

800 B.C.   500 B.C.   200 B.C.

Apollo of Veii

Wounded Chimera

Cinerary urn

Mater Matuta

Tomb of the Augurs

China:
Neolithic to First Empire

(c. 5000–206 B.C.)

The Tomb of Emperor Qin: I

(late 3rd century B.C.)

It is not only in the West that people created tombs with a view to taking their lives with them into death. In 1974, a group of peasants in the Chinese province of Shaanxi discovered evidence of an ancient burial hidden in an enormous mound of earth (see fig. 1.2). Subsequent archaeological excavations revealed this to have been the burial of Shihuangdi, who became known as Emperor Qin (ruled 221–206 B.C.) after the states he ruled. He was the first emperor of a united China and it is from his name, Qin (pronounced *Ch'in*), that the name China is derived. A later historian described Shihuangdi's tomb chamber (which has not yet been opened) as

> filled with [models of (?)] palaces, towers, and [a] hundred officials, as well as precious utensils.... Artisans were ordered to install mechanically triggered crossbows set to shoot any intruder. With quicksilver the various waterways of the empire, the Yangtze and Yellow Rivers, and even the great ocean itself were created and made to flow and circulate mechanically. The heavenly constellations were depicted above and the geography of the earth was laid below. Lamps were fueled with whale oil so that they might burn forever without being extinguished.[1]

While not every detail of this account has been confirmed, it is certain that Shihuangdi unified China in the late third century B.C., installed himself as emperor, patronized monumental building campaigns and the arts with a view to solidifying his political position, and strengthened the country he ruled. Among his lasting accomplishments was the codification of the law, which he was famous for ruthlessly enforcing. He standardized weights, measures, and currency, established a written language, and adopted a canon for imperial art. His administrative system and division of China into provinces has lasted to the present day. He constructed a national network of roads, which facilitated the efficient mobilization and movement of troops. Emperor Qin also commissioned monumental palace architecture, and most of the Great Wall of China was built during his reign.

Precursors: Neolithic to the Bronze Age (c. 5000–221 B.C.)

Before the Qin Dynasty, China had a long cultural and artistic tradition. In contrast to the Mediterranean world, whose civilizations rose and fell (that of Egypt lasted the longest), China has maintained a cultural continuity from the Neolithic era to the present. Although the origins of Chinese culture are obscure, legends refer to an early Bronze Age Xia Dynasty and to stages in civilization brought about by heroes known as the Five Rulers.

There is evidence that between the fourth and third millennia B.C. pottery production was thriving. Crude Mesolithic pottery had been replaced by remarkably thin-walled, wheel-thrown wares: first, earthenware with black and red painted decoration, and then polished black vessels. By the third and second millennia B.C., jade was being imported from Siberia and carved into stylized animal figurines and other ceremonial objects.

Bronze was first used in the second millennium B.C. in the fertile valley of the Yellow River (fig. **7.A**), and its importance as both medium and symbol in ancient China cannot be overestimated (see Box and fig. **7.B**). As a material, bronze was of great value. It denoted power and was associated with the aristocracy who monopolized its manufacture, use, and distribution. Social rank was measured by the number and size of bronzes one owned. Bronze was also used for weapons, which led to new success in warfare, and productivity in general increased as a result of improved metal tools. Ritual objects—preferably

Major Periods of Early Chinese History		
BRONZE AGE		
Shang Dynasty	c. 1700–1050 B.C.	
Zhou Dynasty	c. 1050–221 B.C.	
IRON AGE		
Qin Dynasty	221–206 B.C.	

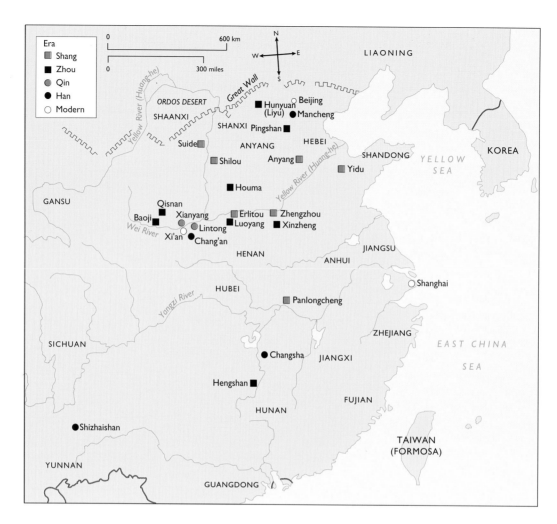

7.A Map of archaeological sites of China.

made of bronze—served the dead as well as the living, and bronze vessels containing offerings were dedicated to deceased ancestors. These were often used by shamans, who were members of the ruling aristocracy. They performed sacrifices to the spirits of ancestors or gods who, in turn, were believed to protect the living. In times of war, the ritual bronzes were melted down and made into weapons, to be recast into vessels when peace returned.

The two main Bronze Age dynasties were the Shang (c. 1700–1050 B.C.) and the Zhou (c. 1050–221 B.C.). Until its existence was documented by modern archaeology, the Shang Dynasty was believed by many scholars to have been a legend. But we now know that the Shang was a complex agricultural society with a class system, an administrative bureaucracy, and urban centers. City walls were made of earth, and there is evidence of some monumental architecture in the later Shang period. Of particular note are rectangular halls, over 90 feet (27.4 m) in length, with interior pillars arranged symmetrically. The Shang Dynasty also produced the earliest form of China's **calligraphic** writing system. This is known from inscriptions on so-called oracle bones used in divination rites in the mid-second millennium B.C (see Box).

The four-ram wine vessel (fig. **7.D**) is a good example of Shang Dynasty bronze casting in its homeland, the Anyang region of modern Hunan Province. Four rams, decorated in low relief with an abstract motif of crested birds, project from the body of the vessel, their legs forming its base. Above the rams, around the vessel's shoulder, are four horned dragons. The entire surface is enlivened by curvilinear patterns that create an unusual synthesis of naturalism and geometric abstraction. While the insistence on symmetry (fig. **7.E**) arrests formal movement, the surface patterns animate the object.

The Zhou originated in modern Shanxi. A predominantly warrior culture, they conquered the Shang and established a feudal state that lasted for a period of eight hundred years. Their chief god was conceived of as heaven (*tian*) and as the father of the Zhou king, reinforcing his imperial power. The late Zhou period produced the two great philosophies of China, Daoism and Confucianism (see Box). In the arts, the Zhou continued and elaborated Shang styles and techniques, especially in bronze. Whereas Shang forms can usually be identified, Zhou forms, though reminiscent of natural shapes, are elusive.

Bronze: The Piece-Mold Method

Bronze is essentially an alloy of copper and tin. Although the earliest manufactured metal objects were made exclusively of copper, it was soon discovered that adding tin increased its hardness, lowered its melting point, and made it easier to control.

In the Stone Age, most artifacts had been made from easily portable materials such as bone, clay, and stone. The introduction of bronze was a watershed in China, as in other civilizations, and precipitated a significant shift in the nature of its society. Sources of copper and tin had to be discovered, the ore mined, and the metal extracted. This was a huge undertaking as far as copper was concerned, since its ore yields only a tiny proportion of refined metal. Elaborate kilns and fires of great intensity were needed to melt the large batches of metal. Cooling the finished objects to avoid cracks and other defects required constant supervision. Such tasks could be accomplished only in a society that was settled (i.e. non-nomadic) and in which labor was specialized.

The Chinese produced bronze vessels in twenty-seven basic shapes by an indigenous technique derived from pottery-making. This differed from the lost-wax method (see p. 154) popular in Greece and elsewhere. First, a clay model of the vessel was made and then it was encased with an outer layer of damp clay. When the outer layer dried, it was cut off in sections and fired to form a mold. Meanwhile, a thin layer of the model was removed and became the core of the mold. The sections of the mold were reassembled around the core and held in place by bronze pegs (or **spacers**). Molten bronze was then poured into the space between the mold and the core through a pouring duct. The thickness of the final object was a function of the difference in size between core and mold. When the bronze had cooled, the mold and core were removed and the surface of the bronze was polished with abrasives.

Ancient Chinese bronzes remain unsurpassed in the technical virtuosity of their ornamentation. Decoration was an integral part of the casting process, created by designs on

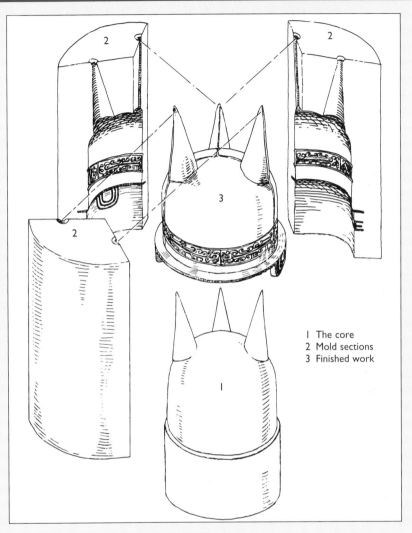

1 The core
2 Mold sections
3 Finished work

7.B Diagram showing the Chinese system of bronze casting.

the inner surface of the mold. Portions of especially complicated pieces were cast separately and fitted together. This piece-mold process made it possible to cast vessels of enormous size with elaborate surface ornamentation. It was not until the late Bronze Age that the Chinese began to cast bronze by the simpler lost-wax process, which permitted more flexibility of design but required more finishing after casting.

During the late Zhou Dynasty, China underwent several centuries of social upheaval. There is evidence of new influence from the animal art of the Scythian nomads (see p. 72), particularly in the **interlace** patterns and motifs characterized by metaphorical transitions from organic to geometric forms. This type of shifting imagery can be seen in a late Zhou **finial** (an ornament at the top of an object) rendered in the shape of a dragon (fig. **7.F**), a masterpiece of formal complexity as the dragon both bites, and is bitten by, a bird. Such iconographic representations of oral aggression and transformation are similarly expressed in certain objects of the European Middle Ages (see figs. 11.22 and 11.24).

Shihuangdi began his reign as the centuries of upheaval known as the Warring States period (475–221 B.C.) came to an end. His evident wish to perpetuate his life after death

Writing: Chinese Characters

The Chinese writing system uses characters that represent entire words instead of letters in an alphabet. These characters have been written and read—in columns, running from top to bottom and right to left—for at least 3000 years. Because of the sophistication of the earliest known characters, their prototypes may have originated as long ago as 4000 B.C., when they were applied to perishable materials such as textiles and leather. At Anyang, China's first city and capital of the Shang Dynasty (c. 1700–1050 B.C.), archaeologists found characters written on oracle bones used in divination. Archivists at the Shang court wrote with brush and ink on slices of bamboo or wood that were then bound into books.

Figure **7.C** shows the evolution of oracle script into seal script (still used for carved seals today) and finally into the same characters' standard modern forms. Many of the 4500 Shang characters known, of which one third have been identified, were **pictographs** (literally "written pictures"), or stylized renderings of specific objects: the sun is circular; the moon is a partial circle (showing its changing shape in contrast to that of the sun); rivers consist of wavy lines; and mountains have three peaks facing upwards. Other characters called **ideographs** (literally "written concepts") were more abstract, representing ideas through combinations of pictographs. The combination of sun and moon, for example, forms the idea of brightness.[2]

Chinese characters have become less pictorial over the centuries. Today about 90 percent of the 10,000 commonly used characters (out of a repertory of nearly 50,000) are composed of elements that convey meaning coupled with elements indicating pronunciation. Thus the combination of the character for "female person" with a character for the sound *ma* creates the notion of "mother." The five traditional styles in which the characters are written have all been in use for at least 2000 years and writing is considered the highest art form in China.

Evolution of Chinese Characters

PICTOGRAPHS

	Shang Dynasty (c. 1700–1050 B.C.) "oracle" script	Zhou Dynasty (c. 1050–221 B.C.) "seal" script	20th century
Sun			
Moon			
River			
Mountain			

IDEOGRAPHS

sun + moon = bright

MEANING AND SOUND GRAPHS

"female person" + (meaning)   *mă* (sound) = "mã" (mother)

7.C Chinese characters showing pictographs (oracle and seal script), ideographs, and meaning/sound graphs.

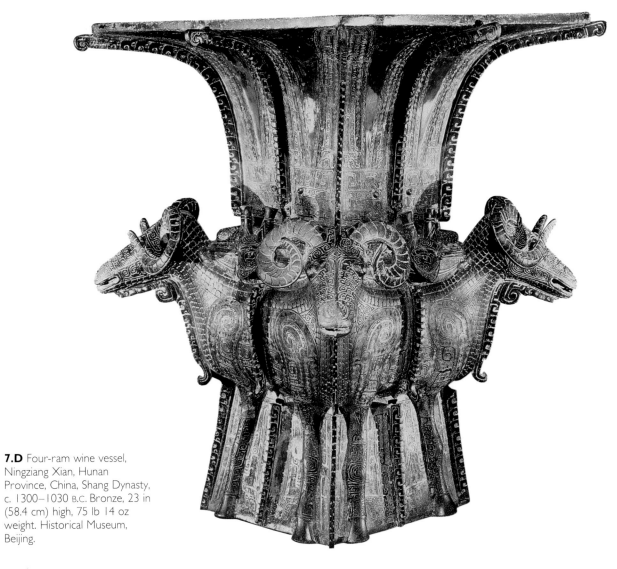

7.D Four-ram wine vessel, Ningziang Xian, Hunan Province, China, Shang Dynasty, c. 1300–1030 B.C. Bronze, 23 in (58.4 cm) high, 75 lb 14 oz weight. Historical Museum, Beijing.

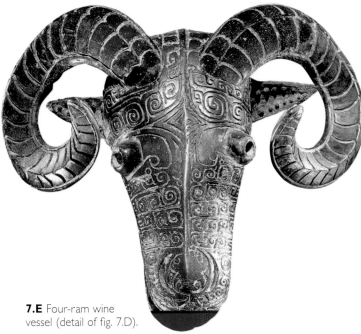

7.E Four-ram wine vessel (detail of fig. 7.D).

Chinese Philosophy

Daoism and Confucianism were the two great philosophies of ancient China. Daoism is based on the *Daode jing*, a text attributed to its legendary founder, Laozi, and thought to have been written in the fourth century B.C. It teaches individualism and transcendence through direct connection with the natural world. According to the *Daode jing*, "*Dao* [the Way] invariably does nothing and yet there is nothing that is not done."[3] Confucius (whose Chinese name is Kongzi, 551–479 B.C.), on the other hand, emphasized strict adherence to social conventions and rituals—based on those of the Shang and Zhou Dynasties—for the proper functioning of the state. Confucius' teachings were collected in the *Analects*, among whose maxims is: "Devote yourself earnestly to the duties due to men, and respect spiritual beings, but keep them at a distance. This may be called wisdom."[4] These two disparate philosophies have been reflected in Chinese art for the past two thousand years.

had a long tradition in China. Until the fourth century B.C., in the late Zhou Dynasty, rulers continued to be buried with their belongings and their animals. Slaves and servants, relatives and other members of the nobility were ritually killed in order to accompany the deceased. By the end of the Bronze Age in China, however, human sacrifice for burials had ceased. Wooden figures, or *mingi* (meaning "substitutes"), were used instead.

The Tomb of Emperor Qin: II

(late 3rd century B.C.)

Some seven hundred thousand people labored for fifteen years to build the Qin emperor's tomb complex. According to the historian's account cited above, Qin tried to take the entire universe with him—not just his friends, family, and possessions. In fact, he took approximately seven thousand lifesize painted terracotta warriors and horses, which were equipped with real chariots and bronze weapons. Their purpose was to provide Shihuangdi with a military bodyguard in the afterlife.

The hierarchy of military rank from infantryman to officer is represented in Emperor Qin's soldiers, deployed outside the burial chamber according to contemporary battle strategy. Although the figures conform to ideal types, they convey a sense of personality that is just short of portraiture. The hollow torsos are supported by sturdy cylindrical legs. Small details made separately were stuck to the surface while the clay was still wet. When the statues dried, they were fired, painted, and set on bases.

One of these, a terracotta kneeling archer (fig. **7.G**), shows the warrior holding his bow and wearing plated armor and a kilt. His raised cheekbones and eyebrows, along with the slight suggestion of a smile, give him an air of individuality despite his conventional pose. The detail of the back of his head (fig. **7.H**) shows incised lines, representing hair that has been tightly pulled into a topknot and strands of braids. Also visible are the modeling marks, made by the artist's thumbs, at the back of the neck and in the folds of the scarf. The officer (figs. **7.I** and **7.J**) stands upright, his hands forming a ritual gesture. He frowns slightly, as if weighing an important tactical decision, and his high rank is denoted by height and costume. In addition to an armored tunic, he wears a double robe with wide sleeves and an elaborate headdress tied under his

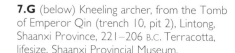

7.F Dragon finial, from Qin-Zun, China, late Zhou Dynasty. Bronze inlaid with gold and silver, 5 ft 5⁄16 in (1.64 m) high. Cleveland Museum of Art.

7.G (below) Kneeling archer, from the Tomb of Emperor Qin (trench 10, pit 2), Lintong, Shaanxi Province, 221–206 B.C. Terracotta, lifesize. Shaanxi Provincial Museum.

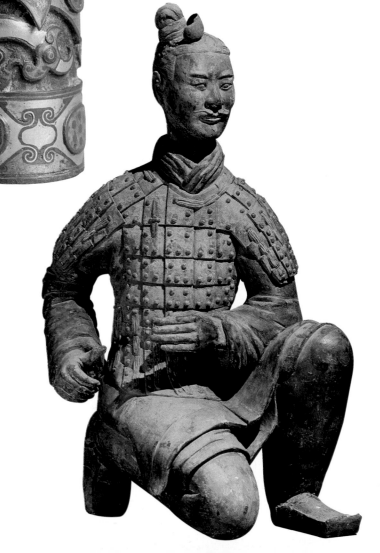

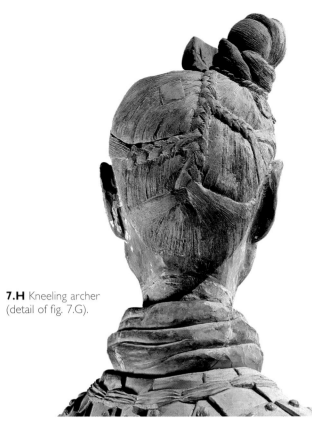

7.H Kneeling archer (detail of fig. 7.G).

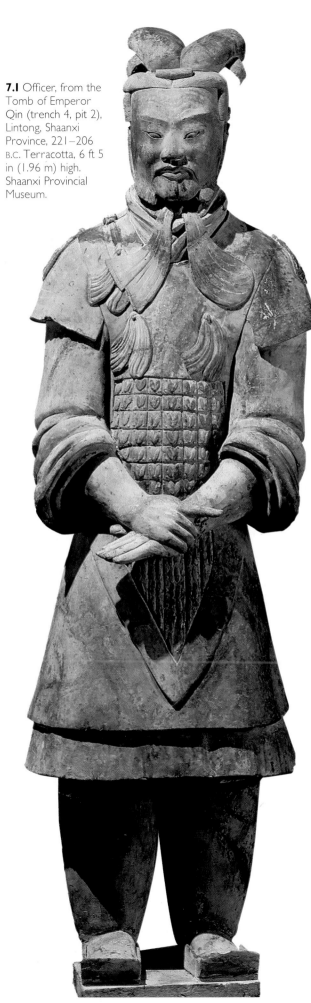

7.I Officer, from the Tomb of Emperor Qin (trench 4, pit 2), Lintong, Shaanxi Province, 221–206 B.C. Terracotta, 6 ft 5 in (1.96 m) high. Shaanxi Provincial Museum.

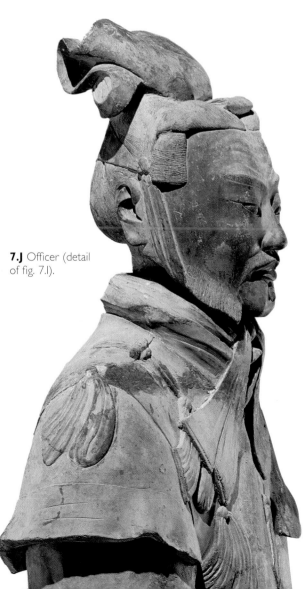

7.J Officer (detail of fig. 7.I).

chin. The cavalryman (fig. **7.K**) is shorter and more plainly attired. He wears the short robe and vest that made riding easier and replaced the long robe worn before 300 B.C. He stands at attention and holds the reins of his horse, whose saddle replicates the leather and bronze of a real saddle.

At the time of writing, Emperor Qin's burial chamber remains to be excavated, partly because it is thought to have been booby-trapped to protect against vandals. The burial chamber was located below streams and sealed off with bronze as another protective device. The emperor's 7000 bodyguards, like the army that defended his imperial power, served as guardians of his body in death.

7.K Cavalryman, from the Tomb of Emperor Qin (trench 12, pit 2), Lintong, Shaanxi Province, 221–206 B.C. Terracotta, man 5 ft 10 in (1.79 m) high, horse 5 ft 7 ½ in (1.69 m) high. Shaanxi Provincial Museum.

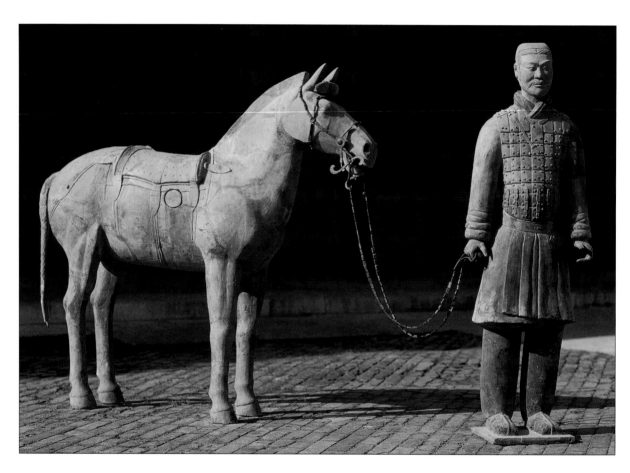

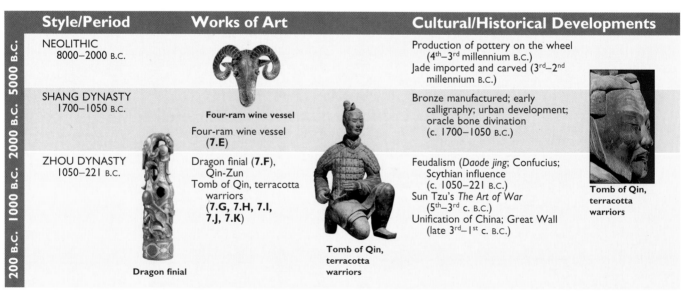

Style/Period	Works of Art	Cultural/Historical Developments	
NEOLITHIC 8000–2000 B.C.		Production of pottery on the wheel (4th–3rd millennium B.C.) Jade imported and carved (3rd–2nd millennium B.C.)	
SHANG DYNASTY 1700–1050 B.C.	**Four-ram wine vessel** Four-ram wine vessel (**7.E**)	Bronze manufactured; early calligraphy; urban development; oracle bone divination (c. 1700–1050 B.C.)	
ZHOU DYNASTY 1050–221 B.C.	Dragon finial (**7.F**), Qin-Zun Tomb of Qin, terracotta warriors (**7.G, 7.H, 7.I, 7.J, 7.K**)	Feudalism (*Daode jing*; Confucius; Scythian influence (c. 1050–221 B.C.) Sun Tzu's *The Art of War* (5th–3rd c. B.C.) Unification of China; Great Wall (late 3rd–1st c. B.C.)	**Tomb of Qin, terracotta warriors**

Dragon finial

Tomb of Qin, terracotta warriors

5000 B.C.   2000 B.C.   1000 B.C.   200 B.C.

8
Ancient Rome

The political supremacy of Athens lasted only about fifty years; Rome's endured for nearly five hundred. Greece had been unified culturally, but Rome was a melting pot of cultures and ideas. Despite Greece's belief in its own superiority over the rest of the world, it had never achieved long-term political unity. The political genius of Rome lay in its ability to encompass, govern, and assimilate cultures very different from its own. As time went on, Roman law made it increasingly easy for people from distant regions to attain citizenship, even if they had never been to Rome. Nevertheless, there was no doubt that the city itself was the center of a great empire. Rome's designation of itself as *caput mundi*, or "head of the world," signified its position as the hub of world power.

From the death of Alexander the Great in 323 B.C., Rome began its rise to power in the Mediterranean. By the first century A.D., the Roman Empire extended from Armenia and Mesopotamia in the east to the Iberian peninsula in the west, from Egypt in the south to the British Isles in the north (fig. **8.1**). Everywhere the Roman legions went, they took their culture with them, particularly their laws, their religion, and the Latin language. Only Greece and the Hellenized world kept Greek, rather than Latin, as the official language.

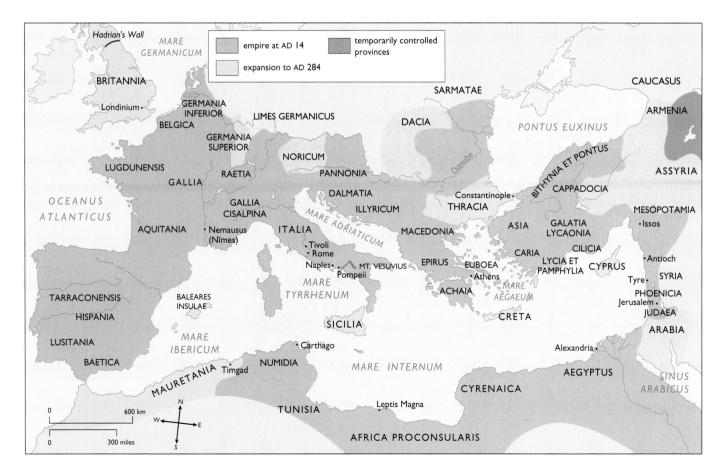

8.1 Map of the Roman Empire, A.D. 14–284.

Virgil's *Aeneid*

During the reign of Rome's first emperor, Augustus, Virgil wrote the *Aeneid*, a Latin epic to celebrate Aeneas as the legendary founder of Rome. Composed in twelve books, it opens with the fall of Troy. Aeneas is a Trojan hero who carries his aged father Anchises and the household gods (the Lares and Penates) as he leads his young son Ascanius from the burning city of Troy. Like Odysseus (see fig. 6.7 and pp. 246–248) and Gilgamesh (see p. 56) before him, Aeneas travels far and wide, even visiting the underworld. Virgil's frequent references to "pius Aeneas" evoke his hero's sense of duty and destiny. They also imply comparison with Augustus, and create an image of him as a predestined second founder of Rome, that is, as the ruler of a great empire under divine guidance. The connotations of this epic for the readers of first-century Augustan Rome were clearly that the founding of their city and Roman domination of the world had been the will of the gods.

In the *Aeneid*, Virgil defines the Roman view of its relationship to Greece and to Greek art by emphasizing that Rome's destiny was political rather than artistic:

> Others will cast more tenderly in bronze
> Their breathing figures, I can well believe,
> And bring more lifelike portraits out of marble;
> Argue more eloquently, use the pointer
> To trace the paths of heaven accurately
> And accurately foretell the rising stars.
> Roman, remember by your strength to rule
> Earth's peoples—for your arts are to be these:
> To pacify, to impose the rule of law,
> To spare the conquered, battle down the proud.[1]

Ovid

Another Roman poet who lived during the reign of Augustus was Publius Ovidius Naso (43 B.C.–A.D. 18), known as Ovid. His surviving poems include the *Amores* (which describe love in different moods) and the *Heroides* (love poems in the form of letters from legendary heroines to their husbands or lovers). Ovid's poetry is irreverent and witty. His longest work is the *Metamorphoses*, a hexameter poem in fifteen books. Its theme is the miraculous transformations of gods, and it contains a collection of Greek and Roman myths which have inspired countless works of art. In the Middle Ages, Ovid was applied to Christian themes and "moralized." During the Renaissance, especially in Italy, artists again used Ovid as an iconographic source for works depicting mythological subjects.

In A.D. 8, the Emperor Augustus banished Ovid to Tomi on the Black Sea, where he died ten years later. His crime is unknown, but it may have been the immoral theme of the *Ars Amatoria*, a treatise on the arts of seduction.

Roman citizenship was accessible to many more people than Athenian citizenship had been, and the position of women in Roman society was more dignified than in Athens. Instead of being confined to their quarters, they ate with their husbands and were free to go out. Some women were involved in law, literature, and politics.

Before the second century B.C., Roman marriage took the form of transfer of control of the woman from her father to her husband. To some degree, this required the bride's consent. If a woman lived with a man for a year without being absent for more than two nights, the couple was considered legally married. From the second century B.C. onward, the pace of emancipation accelerated. Married women could retain their legal identity, controlling their property, managing their affairs, and becoming independently wealthy. Divorce was more common, and during the Empire marriage was so unpopular that laws were passed to encourage it and to increase the birthrate.

There were also important differences between Greek and Roman approaches to history and politics, which, in some sense, parallel the differences in their views of art. The Greeks had written about their artists and given them a historical and biographical identity, and Greek art was a model throughout the Mediterranean world. In Rome, art had its local styles, but the Romans continued to be greatly influenced by Greek sculpture. They also identified their own gods with counterparts in the Greek pantheon and adopted Greek iconography. Roman artists copied Greek art, and Roman collectors imported Greek works by the thousand. Although Greek monumental paintings have not survived, it is known that they too influenced Roman painters, especially in the Hellenistic period.

While Greek art had tended toward idealization, Roman art was generally commemorative, narrative, and based on history rather than myth. As in the Hellenistic style, Roman portraitists sought to preserve the features of their subjects. They went even further in the pursuit of specific likenesses, making wax death masks modeled directly on the face of the deceased, and copying them in marble.

The purpose of Roman portraiture was genealogical. As a family record, it connected present with past, just as Aeneas connected Roman origins with the fall of Troy and, through his mother Venus, with the gods. Roman interest in preserving family lineage also extended to names. The typical Roman family was grouped into a clan, called a *gens*, by which individuals traced their descent. Portraits, whether sculptures or paintings, thus had a twofold function: they both preserved the person's image and contributed to the history of the family. Similarly, Roman reliefs usually depicted historical narrative, commemorating the actions of a particular individual rather than mythical events. Most commemorative reliefs adorned architectural works, and it was in architecture that the Romans were most innovative.

According to the official chronology, the city of Rome was founded in 753 B.C., but legend traces the origins of Rome and the Latin people to the Trojan hero Aeneas (see Box). Rome also had its local heroes, the twins Romulus

Chronology of Roman Periods and Corresponding Works of Art and Architecture

PERIOD AND RULERS	WORKS OF ART
Early Kings Rule by kings and a senate	
Late Kings Etruscan rulers. Ends 509 B.C.	
The Republic (509–27 B.C.) Rule by Senate and patrician citizens Punic Wars (264–146 B.C.)	*The Battle of Issos*, "Alexander Mosaic," House of the Faun, 2nd century B.C. **(8.55–8.57)** Temple of Portunus, late 2nd century B.C. **(8.26)** Temple of the Sibyl, early 1st century B.C. **(8.28)**
Transition to Empire Julius Caesar (46–44 B.C.)	Villa of the Mysteries, c. 65–50 B.C. **(8.59–8.62)** *Odyssey Landscapes* c. 50–40 B.C. **(8.63)** Bust of Julius Caesar, mid-1st century B.C. **(8.45)**
Octavian/Augustus (27 B.C.–A.D.14)	Roman forums, 1st century B.C.–2nd century A.D. **(8.12)** Pont du Gard, late 1st century B.C. **(8.25)** Ara Pacis,13–9 B.C. **(8.33–8.35)** *Augustus of Prima Porta*, early 1st century A.D. **(8.50)** House of the Silver Wedding, early 1st century A.D. **(8.4)** Patrician with Two Ancestor Busts, A.D. c. 13 **(8.47)**

Early Empire
Julio-Claudian Dynasty (14–68)
    Tiberius (14–37)
    Caligula (37–41)
    Claudius (41–54)
    Nero (54–68)
	Young Woman with a Stylus, 1st century A.D. **(8.64)**
	Still Life, A.D. c. 50 **(8.67)**
	
	Landscape with Boats, 1st century A.D. **(8.66)**
	Hercules Strangling the Serpents, A.D. 63–79 **(8.68–8.69)**
	Colosseum, A.D. 72–80 **(8.21–8.22)**

Flavian Dynasty (69–96)
    Vespasian (69–79)
    Titus (79–81)
    Domitian (81–96)
	Arch of Titus, A.D. 81 **(8.40–8.41)**
	Portrait of a young Flavian lady, A.D. c. 90 **(8.48)**
	Portrait of an older Flavian lady, A.D. c. 90 **(8.49)**

The so-called "Good Emperors" (96–180)
    Nerva (96–98)
    Trajan (98–117)
    Hadrian (117–138)
    Antoninus Pius (138–161)
    Marcus Aurelius (161–180)
	City of Timgad, early 2nd century **(8.7)**
	Basilica Ulpia, 98–117 **(8.13–8.14)**
	Prometheus Sarcophagus, c. 110 **(8.44)**
	Trajan's Column, 113 **(8.36–8.37)**
	Trajan's markets, early 2nd century **(8.15)**
	Bust of Trajan, early 2nd century **(8.46)**
	Insula, 2nd century **(8.5)**

A period of political stability and economic prosperity	Pantheon, c. 117–125 **(8.30)** Medallions from the Arch of Constantine, c. 117–138 **(8.43)** Hadrian's Villa and Canopus, 118–138 **(8.10)** Statue of Antinous, c. 131–138 **(8.51)** Equestrian statue of Marcus Aurelius, 164–166 **(8.52)** Artemidoros' mummy case, 100–200 **(8.70)**
Beginning of Decline Commodus (180–192) Political unrest and economic decline	

The Severan Dynasty (193–235)
    Septimius Severus (193–211)
    Caracalla (211–217)
    Severus Alexander (222–235)
	Baths of Caracalla, 211–217 **(8.20)**
	Circus at Leptis Magna, early 3rd century **(8.24)**
	Bust of Caracalla, early/mid-3rd century **(8.53)**

Anarchy (235–284)	
Period of Tetrarchs (284–306) Diocletian (284–305) institutes four co-rulers in an unsuccessful effort to restore stability to the Empire.	
Late Empire Constantine I (306–33)	Arch of Constantine, c. 313 **(8.42)** Monumental head of Constantine, 313 **(8.54)** Dacian silver vase, helmet, 4th century **(8.38–8.39)**

and Remus, who were said to have been descended from Aeneas. Tradition had it that Romulus and Remus were abandoned as infants and nursed by a wolf (see fig. 7.3). Romulus later killed Remus, built Rome on the Palatine Hill, and became its first king. He ruled Rome until the late eighth century B.C., and was followed by six kings, some of whom were Etruscans. In 510 B.C. the last king was overthrown and the Republic was established. For the next five centuries Rome was ruled by two consuls, a senate and an assembly. The consuls were elected every year and shared the military and judicial authority of the former kings. The senate was composed of former magistrates and an assembly of citizens.

The Republic lasted until 27 B.C., when Octavian (who later took the title "Augustus") became the first emperor. The term "Augustus" originally meant "revered" and had religious connotations, but it came to mean "he who is supreme." For the next three hundred years, Rome was ruled by a succession of emperors. In A.D. 330 Constantine

---

Roman Building Materials

Marble had been the favorite building material of the Greeks, but was less readily available, and therefore a luxury, to the Romans. They used it mainly as a final decorative facing, or outer layer, over a core of other material. Suetonius, the Roman lawyer and author of the *Lives of the Twelve Caesars* (A.D. c. 121), wrote that Augustus found Rome a city of brick and left it a city of marble. Today, much ancient Roman marble facing has disappeared because of subsequent looting, leaving visible the inside core of the structure (cf. the Colosseum, fig. 8.21).

The Romans also used **travertine**—a hard, durable limestone that mellows to a golden yellow—and the soft, easily carved tufa, which had been popular with the Etruscans (see p. 190). Above all, the Romans built with concrete, a suitable material for large-scale public structures. Their concrete was a rough mixture of mortar, gravel, rubble, and water. It was shaped by wooden frames, and often wedge-shaped stones, bricks, or tiles were inserted into it before it had hardened, for reinforcement and decoration. Alternatively, a facing of plaster, stucco, marble, or other stone was added.

The Goths

The Goths were a confederation of Germanic tribes who fought the Roman Empire from the third to the fifth centuries A.D. and were partly responsible for the destruction of the Western Roman Empire in the fifth century. They originated in Scandinavia in the first century B.C. By the third century A.D. they had settled near the Black Sea and raided the eastern Roman provinces, including Dacia (see fig. 8.1). In 253 and 267 they invaded Asia Minor and overran Greece in 268.

During the fourth century, the Goths split into two groups. One settled in the Danube region and became known as the Visigoths. For a while they coexisted peacefully with the Romans, lived in land ceded to them by the Roman emperor Theodosius (reigned 379–395), and fought in the Roman army. After the death of Theodosius, the Roman Empire was divided between his two sons. The Visigoths, under Alaric, invaded Italy and sacked Rome in 410. They then established themselves in southwestern Gaul (at Toulouse, in modern France) and controlled much of what is now the south of France and Spain. Around 507, the Visigoths lost most of Gaul to the Franks under Clovis, but retained their territory in Spain until the Moors (see Chapter 10) defeated them in 711.

The eastern Goths, who lived north of the Black Sea (in modern Ukraine), became the Ostrogoths. They were conquered around 370 by the Huns, nomadic invaders from western Asia. After the death in 453 of Attila, king of the Huns, the Ostrogoths regained their freedom. They moved into the Balkans and became Roman allies. But around 490 they invaded Italy and their leader, Theodoric the Great, was recognized as ruler of Italy from 493 to 526. In 553, the Ostrogothic kingdom in Italy was overcome by the forces of the Byzantine Empire under Justinian (see p. 284).

---

established an Eastern capital of the Roman Empire in Byzantium, which he renamed Constantinople (now Istanbul, in modern Turkey). After this period the Western Empire, which had kept Rome as its capital, declined. The Goths overran the Western Empire in 476, which is considered to be the date of the fall of Rome (see Box).

Architectural Types

During the Empire, the Romans carried out extensive building programs, partly to accommodate their expanding territory and its growing population, and partly to glorify the state and the emperor. In so doing, the Romans assimilated and developed building and engineering techniques from the Near East, Greece, and Etruria (see Box). They also recognized the potential of certain building materials, particularly concrete, which allowed them to construct the monumental public buildings that are such an important part of the Roman legacy.

Domestic Architecture

Roman interest in the material comforts of living conditions led to the development of sophisticated domestic architecture. Many examples have been preserved as a result of the eruption of Mount Vesuvius in A.D. 79. Volcanic ash covered Pompeii, near modern Naples, a port noted for agriculture and commerce; the nearby seaside resort of Herculaneum was buried in mud and lava, and was therefore more difficult to excavate than Pompeii. An

Arches, Domes, and Vaults

Just as the Romans recognized the potential of concrete, which had been invented in the ancient Near East, so too they greatly developed the arch and the **vault** (fig. **8.2**), which had previously been used in the ancient Near East and Etruria.

The round arch (see p. 71) may be thought of as a curved lintel used to span an opening. A true arch is constructed of tapered (wedge-shaped) bricks or stones, called **voussoirs**, with a **keystone** at the center. The point at which the arch begins to curve from its vertical support is called the **springing**, because it seems to spring away from it. The arch creates an outward pressure, or thrust, which must be countered by a supporting **buttress** of masonry.

The arch is the basis of the vault—an arched roof made by a continuous series of arches forming a passageway. A row of round arches produces a **barrel** or **tunnel vault**, so-called because it looks like the inside of half a barrel or the curved roof of a tunnel. It requires continuous buttressing and is a difficult structure in which to make openings for windows. Vaults formed by a right-angled intersection of two identical barrel vaults are called **groin** or **cross-vaults**.

Arches and vaults have to be supported during the process of construction. This is usually done by building over wooden frames known as **centerings**, which are removed when the keystone is in place and the mortar has set.

A **dome** is made by rotating a round arch through 180 degrees on its **axis**. In its most basic form, it is a hemisphere. As is true of arches and vaults, domes must be buttressed and, since their thrust is equally dispersed in all directions, the buttressing must be from all sides. They can be erected on circular or square bases. Ancient Roman domes, such as the one on the Pantheon (fig. 8.31), were generally set on round bases. Domes on square bases are discussed in Chapter 9.

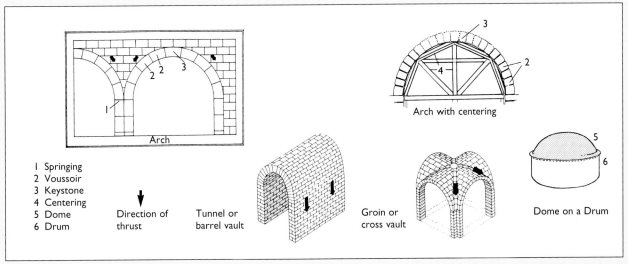

8.2 Arch, arch with centering, tunnel or barrel vault, groin or cross-vault, and a dome on a drum.

Pliny the Elder and Pliny the Younger

Gaius Plinius Secundus (A.D. 23/24–79), known as Pliny the Elder, was a Roman official who held military and civil positions in North Africa, Gaul (modern France), and Spain. He wrote on grammar, military history, and oratory; most of his writings are lost, but his greatest achievement survives, the encyclopedic *Naturalis historia* (*Natural History*). This consists of thirty-seven books, covering topics that range from the elements of the universe, through continental geography and ethnology (of Europe, Asia, and Africa), to human physiology, zoology, botany, and the medicinal properties of plants, and discusses metallurgy as it relates to the use of minerals for medical purposes and to the arts. Pliny's history of ancient art remains a fundamental source.

Pliny the Elder died in A.D. 79, during the eruption of Mount Vesuvius, an event described by his nephew, Pliny the Younger. The latter's voluminous correspondence includes a vivid account of his uncle's role as commander of the fleet at Misenum, north of Pompeii. When he noticed a column of smoke rising from the nearby mountains, the elder Pliny launched a small boat and went to investigate. He soon realized that he was witnessing an eruption and, under a hail of stones, dictated his observations to a secretary. The next day, he went to the seashore for a closer look, and was asphyxiated by the sulfurous fumes.

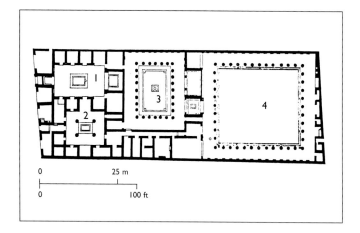

8.3 Plan of the House of the Faun, Pompeii, 2nd century B.C.:
1. *atrium* 2. *atrium tetrastylum* 3, 4. courtyards surrounded
by peristyles.

eyewitness to the eruption of Vesuvius, Pliny the Younger
(see Box on p. 213), described the disaster from a safe distance across the Bay of Naples, yet both Pompeii and
Herculaneum were forgotten until 1592, when a Roman
architect digging a canal discovered some ancient ruins.
Serious archaeological excavations of the buried cities did
not begin until the eighteenth century and they are still
continuing today.

Roman domestic (from the Latin *domus*, meaning
"house") architecture was derived from both Etruscan and
Greek antecedents, but developed characteristics of its
own. The main feature of the Roman *domus* was the *atrium*
(figs. **8.3** and **8.4**), a large hall entered through a corridor
from the street. The *atrium* roof usually sloped inward,
while a rectangular opening, the *compluvium*, allowed
rainwater to collect in an *impluvium* (a sunken basin in the
floor), from which it was channeled into a separate cistern.
The *compluvium* was also the primary source of light in
the *domus*. But, by the end of the first century B.C., the
peristyle, with its colonnade, had become the focal point of
the *domus* and the *atrium* was little more than a foyer, or
entrance hall. Additional rooms surrounded the peristyle,
and were used as slave quarters, wine cellars, and storage
space.

These houses had plain exteriors without windows.
Rooms fronting on the street functioned as shops, or
tabernae (from which we get the English word "tavern").
Behind the unassuming façades were interiors that were
often quite luxurious—decorated with floor and wall
mosaics, paintings, and sculptures. The typical professional or upper-class Roman house also had running
water and sewage pipes.

For the middle and lower classes, especially in cities, the
Romans built concrete apartment blocks or tenements,
called *insulae* (the Latin word for "islands")—as in figure
8.5. According to Roman building codes, the *insulae* could
be as high as five stories. On the ground floor, shops and
other commercial premises opened onto the street. The

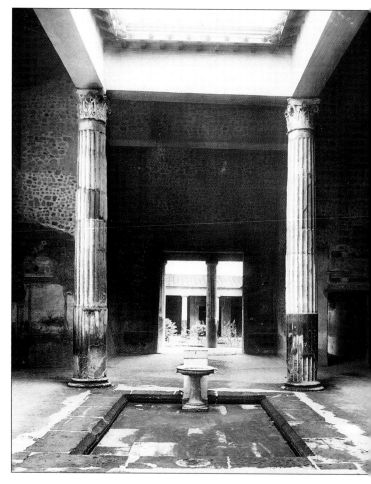

8.4 *Atrium* and peristyle, House of the Silver Wedding, Pompeii, early
1st century A.D. Standing with our backs to the entrance, we can see
the *compluvium* in the roof, which is supported by four Corinthian
columns. The *impluvium* is in the center of the floor. Visible on the
other side of the *atrium* is the *tablinium*, probably used for
entertaining and for storing family documents and images of
ancestors.

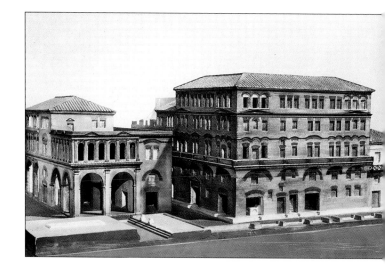

8.5 *Insula*, Ostia, reconstruction, 2nd century. Brick and concrete.

upper floors were occupied by families, who lived separately but shared certain facilities. As early as the first century A.D., most of Rome's urban population lived in such *insulae*. Their blocklike construction conformed to the typical town plan of the Empire. Such plans were organized like a military camp, or **castra**, in which a square was divided into quarters by two streets intersecting in the middle at right angles. The *cardo* ran from north to south and the *decumanus* from east to west. Each quarter was then subdivided into square or rectangular blocks of buildings, such as the domestic houses and the *insulae*.

Under the emperor Trajan (see below), a new city was founded in Timgad, in North Africa, which followed the plan of the *castra* (fig. **8.6**). Its purpose was to provide a retirement colony for Trajan's soldiers. The plan was basically square, with gates for access to the city along roadways. Its relatively good state of preservation is seen in the aerial view in figure **8.7**, which shows the ruins of the theater, the square forum next to it, and the large triple arch spanning the cobbled road.

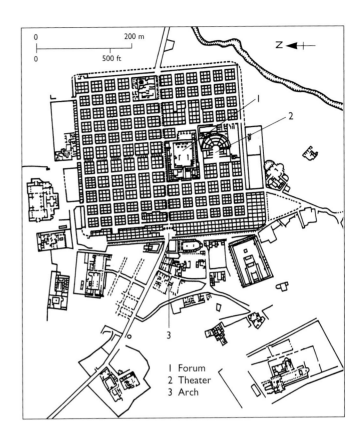

8.6 (right) Plan of Timgad, Algeria, early 2nd century.

8.7 View from the west of the ruins of Timgad, Algeria, early 2nd century.

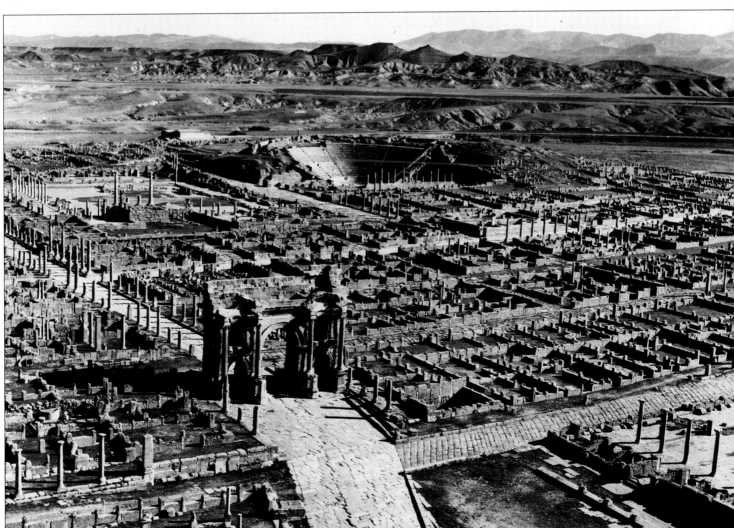

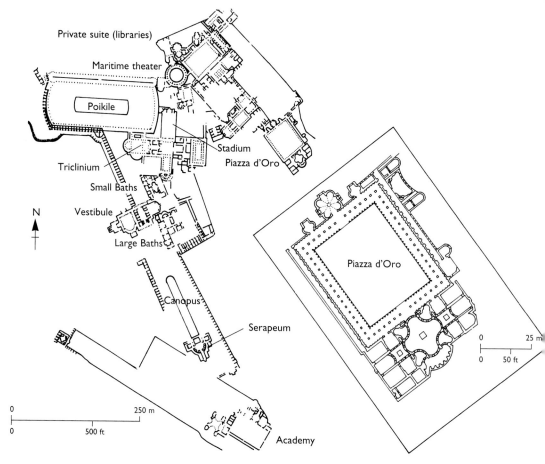

8.8 Plan of Hadrian's Villa, Tivoli, A.D. 118–138.

In addition to urban domestic architecture, the Romans invented the concept of the country **villa** as an escape from the city (see Box). Villas varied according to the tastes and means of their owners, and naturally the most elaborate belonged to the emperors. Hadrian's Villa (fig. **8.8**), built from A.D. 118 to 138 near Tivoli, 15 miles (24 km) outside modern Rome, consisted of so many buildings—including libraries containing works in Greek and Latin, baths (fig. **8.9**), courtyards, temples, plazas, and a theater—that it occupied more than half a square mile (1.3 square km).

When Hadrian traveled, he collected ideas for his villa and later had monuments reproduced on its grounds. When visiting Alexandria, for example, Hadrian admired the **Serapaeum**, a temple dedicated to Serapis—the Egyptian god who combined features of Osiris, Zeus, and Hades, and was worshiped as ruler of the universe. Hadrian constructed his own canal and temple and named them after the Egyptian structures. He used Ionic columns in the Serapaeum, and Corinthian columns at the far end of the Canopus (fig. **8.10**) to support a structure of round arches alternating with lintels. Sculptures occupy the arched spaces; some of these are copied from the caryatids on the Athenian Erechtheum porch (see fig. 6.62). The entrance to the Serapaeum, which also contained sculptures and fountains, is visible at the far end of the canal.

Nero's Golden House

The emperor Nero spent four years (A.D. 64–68) overseeing the construction of his villa. It was called the Domus Aurea, or Golden House, because of its extensive use of gold decoration, and was a monument to his grandiosity. At the sight of it Suetonius declared "All Rome is transformed into a villa!"

There was nothing ... in which [he] was more ruinously prodigal than in building ... Its vestibule ... had a triple portico a mile long. There was a pond, too, like a sea ... pastures and woods, with great numbers of wild and domestic animals. In the rest of the palace all parts were overlaid with gold and adorned with gems and mother-of-pearl. There were dining rooms with ... ceilings of ivory, whose panels could turn and shower down flowers and were fitted with pipes for sprinkling the guests with perfumes. The main banquet hall was circular and constantly revolved day and night, like the heavens. He had baths supplied with seawater and sulphur water. When the palace was finished in this manner and he dedicated it, he deigned to say nothing more in the way of approval than that he was at last beginning to be housed like a human being.[2]

The entrance hall was large enough to accommodate an enormous statue of Nero, 120 feet (36 m) high, which he had commissioned. Because of the resentment that such displays engendered in the citizens of Rome, Nero's successor, Vespasian, had the statue decapitated. He then transformed it into a sun god by substituting a new head, and called this revised statue the Colossus, the origin of the name for the Colosseum (see pp. 223–4).

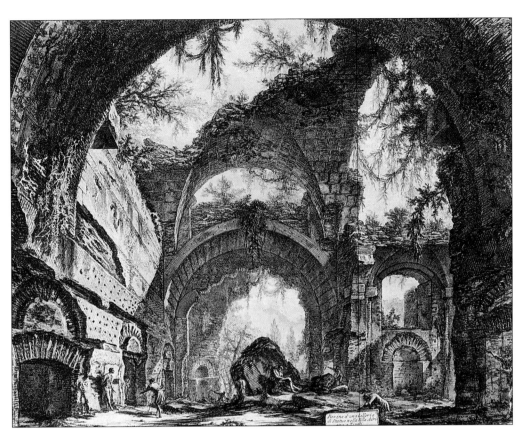

8.9 Piranesi, *The Great Baths, Hadrian's Villa, Tivoli*, from *Views of Rome*, 1770. Etching, 18 × 22 in (45.7 × 55.6 cm). Istituto Nazionale per la Grafica, Rome.

8.10 Canopus, Hadrian's Villa, Tivoli, A.D. c. 123–135.

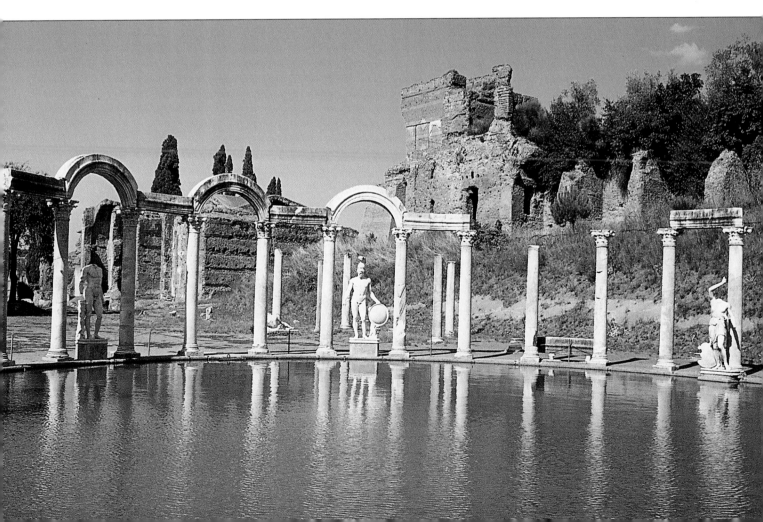

Public Buildings

As life in Rome and its provinces became increasingly complex, the need for public spaces and public buildings grew. Citizens gathered in open squares and civic and administrative functions were performed in public buildings. These activities led to the development of two characteristic architectural types, the forum and the basilica.

The Forum The forum (Latin pl. *fora*) was typically a square or rectangular open space, bounded on three sides by colonnades and on the fourth by a basilica (see below). Originally the forum was a market-place, its prototype being the smaller Greek *agora*. The Roman forum was a complex of buildings that "grew" out into the public space from an existing temple. This gave the forum a sense of order compared with the more random development of the *agora*. In Rome, the first known forum, the Forum Romanum, dates from the sixth century B.C. and it was this

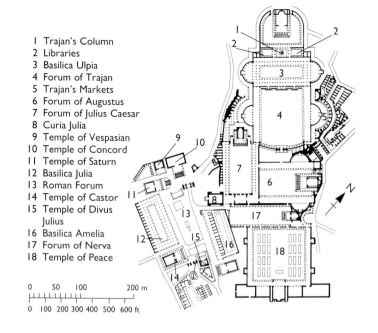

1 Trajan's Column
2 Libraries
3 Basilica Ulpia
4 Forum of Trajan
5 Trajan's Markets
6 Forum of Augustus
7 Forum of Julius Caesar
8 Curia Julia
9 Temple of Vespasian
10 Temple of Concord
11 Temple of Saturn
12 Basilica Julia
13 Roman Forum
14 Temple of Castor
15 Temple of Divus
   Julius
16 Basilica Amelia
17 Forum of Nerva
18 Temple of Peace

0   50   100   200 m

0 100 200 300 400 500 600 ft

8.11 Plan of the Roman and imperial forums, Rome. When Roman civic leaders wished to address the populace, they entered the forum. Today a forum means a place or opportunity for addressing groups of people—candidates for political office are said to have a forum for their views if they can arrange a time and place for the voters to hear them speak.

Julius Caesar

Gaius Julius Caesar (c. 100–44 B.C.) was the greatest general and political figure of his generation, and an author famed in his own day for his Classical Latin prose. His sole surviving writings are the *Commentaries*, a personal account of the Gallic and Civil wars. By the age of forty, Caesar shared the leadership of Rome with Pompey (his son-in-law) and Crassus, an arrangement known as the First Triumvirate (literally "Three Men"). He was consul in 59 B.C., and proconsul in Gaul (58–49 B.C.), where he waged a series of campaigns, going on to extend Roman rule north to Britain.

After the death of Crassus, Caesar vied with Pompey for political control. In 49 B.C., Caesar led an army across the Rubicon (the river north of Rimini on the east coast of Italy that marked the boundary of Roman citizenship), and expelled Pompey. The following year, he again defeated Pompey—at the Battle of Pharsalus—and drove him to Egypt, where he was murdered. While in Egypt, Caesar had a celebrated romance with its queen, Cleopatra, who bore him a son, Caesarion.

After successful campaigns in Asia Minor and in Spain against the sons of Pompey, Caesar returned to Rome. In 46 B.C., the senate appointed him temporary dictator in order to give him the power to control growing civil unrest. Caesar used his power to enact several radical measures, including expanding the franchise of the provinces, regulating taxation, and reforming the calendar. His contempt for republicanism and his aristocratic tendencies aroused suspicion, and people feared that he intended to remain dictator permanently. On March 15, 44 B.C., a group of conspirators led by Marcus Junius Brutus and Gaius Cassius stabbed him to death, an event memorialized in Shakespeare's admonition to "beware the Ides of March," the Ides being the Roman term for the fifteenth day of the month.

particular urban space that was conceived of as *caput mundi*. The Forum Romanum was regularly expanded during the Republic and the Empire. In the first century B.C., the Forum Julium became the prototype for all later imperial forums. Planned by Julius Caesar (see Box) and completed by Augustus, it must have presented a magnificent architectural spectacle (it is now in ruins). The plan in figure **8.11** indicates the variety of forms and the degree to which the Romans added to the basic rectangular conception of the forum, while the reconstruction in figure **8.12** illustrates the complexity of their layout.

8.12 Reconstruction of the forums, Rome, c. A.D. 46–117. Museo della Civiltà Romana, Rome.

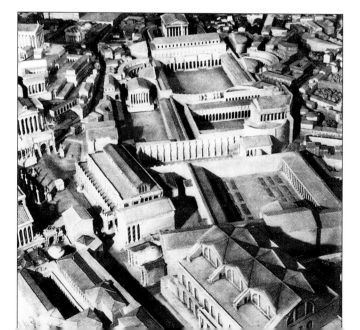

As a commercial center, the forum was a regular feature of most Roman town plans. Gradually, however, the shops were transferred elsewhere and the forum remained a focal point for civic and social activity. It was a more or less enclosed space, usually restricted to pedestrian traffic. Important temples and meeting places for the town council (or *curia*) and the popular assembly (*comitium*) were integrated into the forum.

The Basilica A basilica (from the Greek *basilikos*, meaning "royal") was a large roofed building, usually at one end of a forum. It was used for commercial transactions and also served as a municipal hall and law court. According to Vitruvius (see p. 190), basilicas should be located in the warmest site so that in winter businessmen can confer in comfort. Basilicas were typically divided into three **aisles**: a large central aisle was flanked by smaller ones on either side, separated from one another by one or two rows of columns. The extra height of the center aisle, or **nave**

(from the Latin *navis*, meaning "ship," and derived from the idea of an inverted boat), permitted the construction of a second-story wall above the colonnades separating the nave from the aisles. Clerestory windows were built into the additional wall space to admit light into the building.

As shown in figure **8.13**, Trajan's Forum adjoins the Basilica Ulpia (the name "Ulpia" comes from the *gens* to which Trajan belonged), which is basically rectangular in plan with an apse, or curved section, at each end. The apses contained statues of gods or emperors, provided space for legal proceedings, and often included a throne occupied by a statue of the emperor. The huge size of the basilica created a need for lighting, which the Romans solved by piercing the walls with clerestory windows above the colonnades on either side of the nave (fig. **8.14**). The colonnades themselves provided an articulated space for spectators, for people awaiting trial, and for those transacting business. Roofing was made of timber and covered with tiles, and the interior was adorned with marble and bronze.

1 Trajan's Column
2 Libraries
3 Apse
4 Central space (Nave)
5 Aisle
6 Forum of Trajan

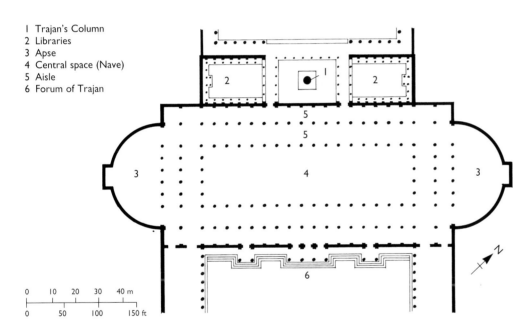

8.13 Apollodorus of Damascus, Plan of the Basilica Ulpia, Forum of Trajan, A.D. 98–117.

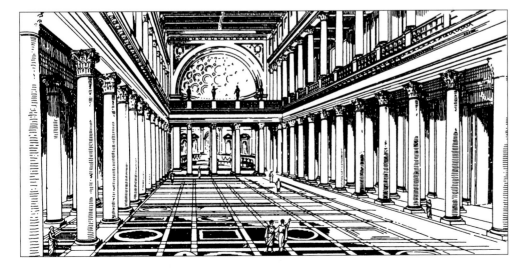

8.14 Reconstruction drawing of the interior of the Basilica Ulpia.

The Markets of Trajan Trajan intended the Basilica Ulpia to be the largest in Rome. The markets built during his reign were as noteworthy for their huge size as for their innovative engineering and architecture (fig. **8.15**). Their concrete core was faced with brick, with a few details in wood and stone. They were conceived as part of the total urban renovation that included Trajan's Forum (which was faced with marble); the isometric drawing of the surviving markets (fig. **8.16**) shows their relation to each other. Their original area is unknown, but they probably contained over two hundred rooms (evidence of 127 survives today). They rise from the Forum along the incline of the Quirinal Hill.

The view from the west in figure 8.15 gives some idea of the imposing quality and architectural variety of Trajan's markets. They are constructed as a series of tiered, apsidal spaces with barrel-vaulted ceilings. Groin vaults were used for the main hall. In the upper levels—shown in the analytical drawing (fig. **8.17**)—clerestory windows, as in the basilica, provided a source of interior lighting. The rooms housed offices and over one hundred and fifty shops linked by a complex system of stairways and arcades. Outlines, like those of the forums, were irregular and the whole lacked symmetry. Shifting axes, flowing masses and spaces, and patterns of light and shadow created a dynamic interplay of solid forms with voids. As a totality, the markets served a social and commercial function for large numbers of people. The architect exploited the formal appeal of the façade, while departing from traditional columns and colonnades.

Public Baths Another type of monumental construction popular in ancient Rome was the public bath. Besides being a place for bathing and swimming, the public bath was a museum filled with sculpture. It also provided facilities for playing ball, running, and wrestling. Romans attended the baths for health, hygiene, exercise, relaxation, and socializing. Amenities included a cold room (*frigidarium*), a warm room (*tepidarium*), a hot room (*caldarium*), steam rooms, changing rooms, libraries, and gardens.

Although every Roman city throughout the Empire had baths, Rome was particularly well supplied; a catalog of buildings of A.D. 354 lists 952 baths of various sizes. Particularly magnificent were the baths of the Emperor Caracalla, who ruled from A.D. 211 to 217 (see figs. **8.18** and **8.19**). The aerial view of the ruins of Caracalla's baths gives some idea of their size (fig. **8.20**).

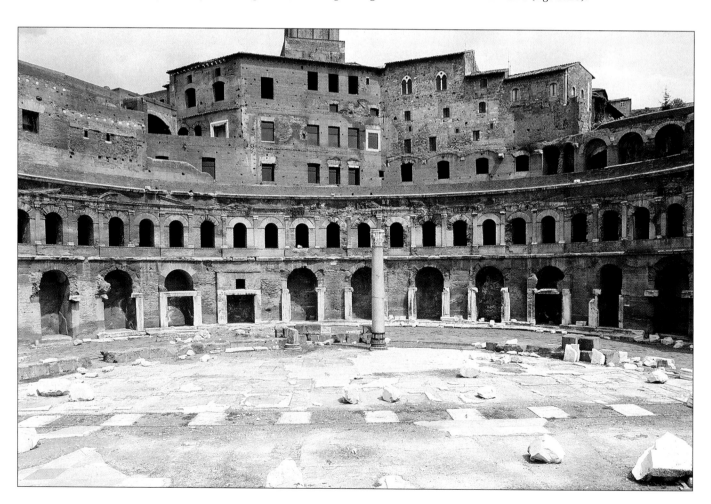

8.15 The remains of Trajan's markets as seen from the west.

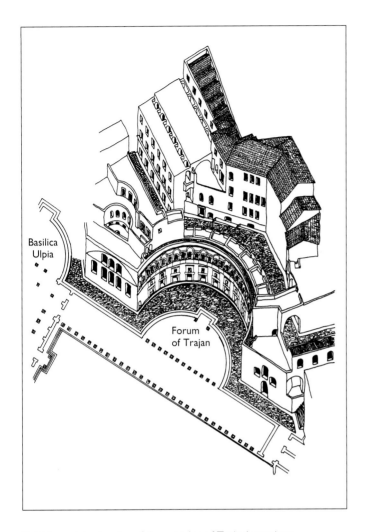

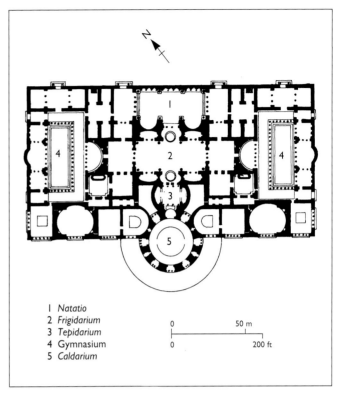

8.18 Plan of the Baths of Caracalla, Rome, A.D. 211–217. The total complex occupied approximately 35 acres (130,000 sq. m). It was constructed on two axes with the *frigidarium* at their intersection. As in the typical basilica construction, light entered the baths through clerestory windows and illuminated the myriad surface patterns created by marble, glass, painted decoration, and water.

1 *Natatio*
2 *Frigidarium*
3 *Tepidarium*
4 *Gymnasium*
5 *Caldarium*

0   50 m
0   200 ft

8.16 Isometric drawing of the remains of Trajan's markets.

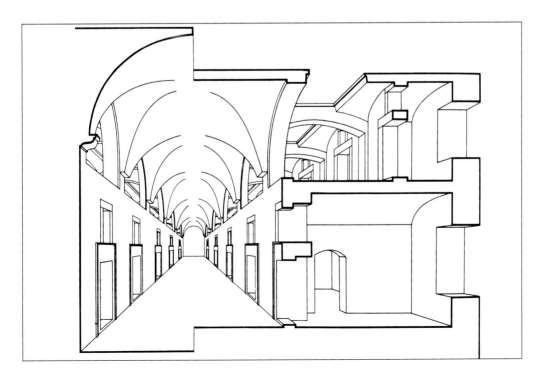

8.17 Analytical drawing of the *aula* (main hall) of Trajan's markets.

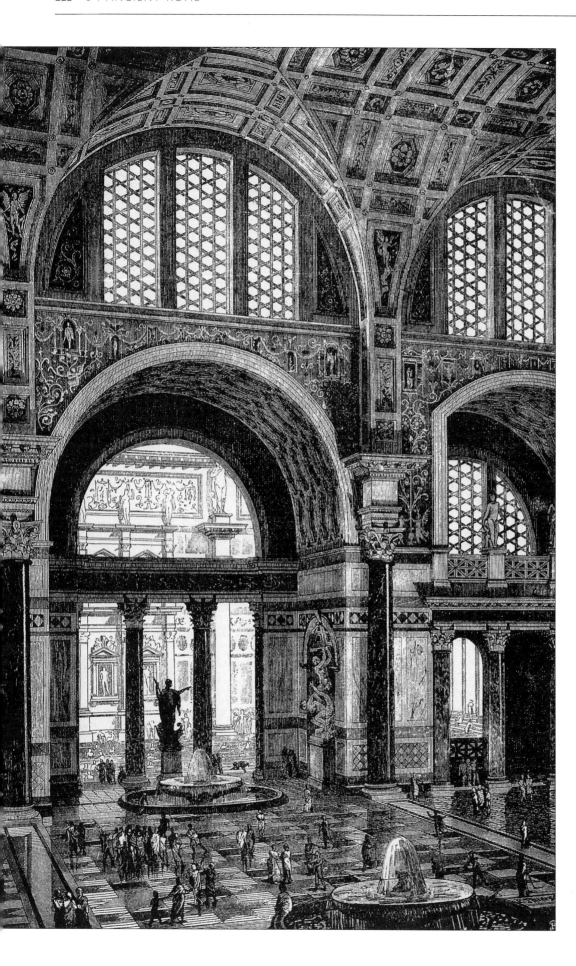

8.19 Restoration drawing of the Baths of Caracalla. The plan in figure 8.18 shows the enormous Corinthian columns that supported the groin vaults of the ceiling in this central hall.

The Colosseum Buildings such as the Colosseum (itself begun in A.D. 72 under Vespasian and inaugurated in A.D. 80 by his son Titus) were primarily for public spectacles (figs. **8.21**, **8.22**, and **8.23**). Their Greek antecedent was the outdoor theater (see fig. 6.63). Similar to a modern sports arena, the Colosseum in Rome is actually a massive **amphitheater** (from the Greek *amphi*, meaning "around" or "both," and *theatron*, meaning "theater").

The exterior of the Colosseum consists of **arcades** with three stories of round arches framed by entablatures and engaged columns. The ground floor columns are Tuscan (a later development of Doric), the second floor columns are Ionic, and those on the third floor are Corinthian. On the fourth floor are small windows and engaged, rectangular Corinthian pilasters. This system, in which the columns are arranged in order of visual as well as structural strength, with the "heaviest" Doric type at the bottom, was regularly followed in Roman architecture. The surface of the outer wall also becomes flatter as it rises, which carries the viewer's eye upward, while the repeated round arches of the circular arcades direct the eye around the building. The projecting cornice at the very top serves esthetically to crown the structure.

The Colosseum was built around a concrete core, with an extensive system of halls and stairways for easy access. Two types of vault were used in the corridor ceilings—the simpler barrel vault and the groin vault (also called a cross-vault). The upper wall was fitted with sockets, into which poles were inserted as supports for awnings; these were stretched by sailors across the open top of the arena to protect spectators from bad weather. The Colosseum was designed for gladiatorial contests and combats between men and animals, or between animals alone. Because it was located over a pond formerly on Nero's property, it was possible to construct a built-in drainage system for washing away the blood and gore of combat. The Colosseum remains a monument to one of the paradoxes of imperial Roman culture—catering to the popular taste for cruelty and violence, while at the same time showing a practical concern for creature comforts.

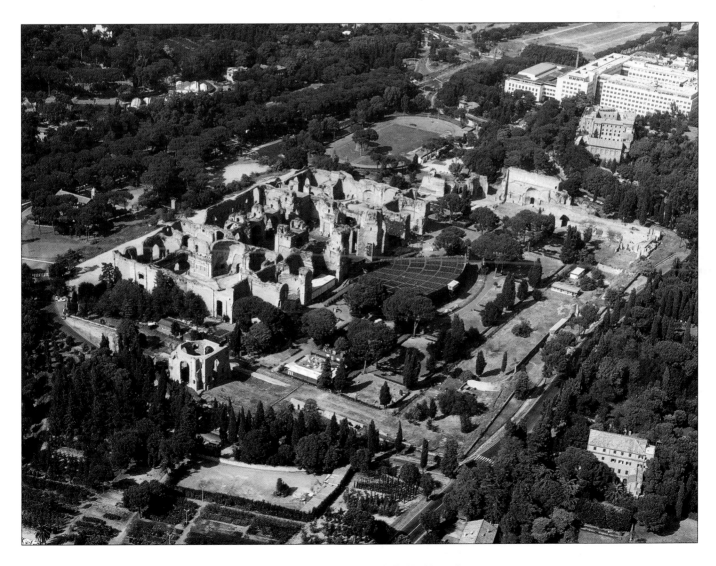

8.20 Aerial view of the ruins of the Baths of Caracalla, Rome, A.D. c. 211–217. Marble and concrete.

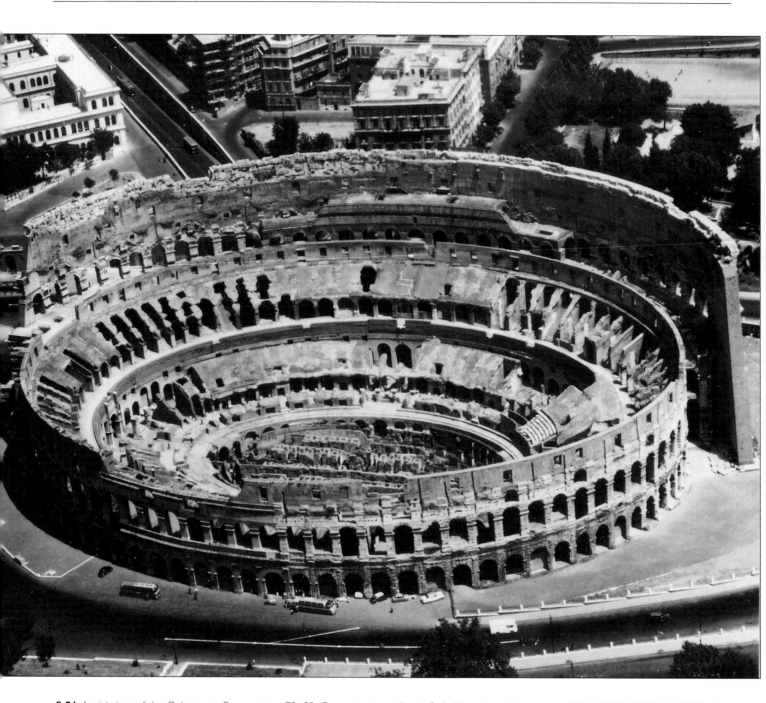

8.21 Aerial view of the Colosseum, Rome, A.D. c. 72–80. Concrete, travertine, tufa, brick, and marble, approx. 615 × 510 ft (187.5 × 155.5 m). Construction of the Colosseum started A.D. c. 72 under the emperor Vespasian, who had come to power in A.D. 69. It was inaugurated in A.D. 80, a year after his death. More than 50,000 spectators proceeded along corridors and stairways through numbered gates to their seats. The concrete foundations were 25 feet (7.6 m) deep. Travertine was used for the framework of the piers, and tufa and brick-faced concrete for the walls between the piers. Originally there was marble on the interior, but it has completely disappeared.

The Circus   A less bloodthirsty form of public entertainment in ancient Rome took place in the **circus**. Principally designed for chariot races, the circus could accommodate up to a dozen four-horse chariots. The resulting structures ranged in length from 1300 to 1970 feet (400 to 600 m). It has been estimated that the Circus Maximus, or Largest Circus, in Rome could hold more than 200,000 spectators. A more typical Roman circus (fig. **8.24**), dating to the early third century A.D., was located at Leptis Magna, in present-day Libya, at the southern extreme of the Roman Empire.

Circus races began from the starting gates, or *carceres* (from the Latin word for jail: cf. "incarcerate" in English), because the gates remained closed until the race started. The race itself consisted of seven circuits in a counter-clockwise direction. As the racers completed each lap, a marker indicated the number of remaining laps.

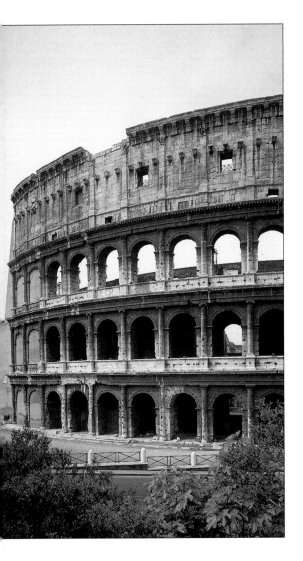

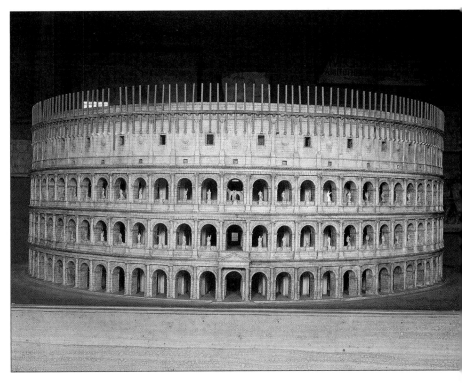

8.22 (left) Side view of the Colosseum.

8.23 (above) Reconstruction model of the Colosseum, Rome. Museo della Civiltà Romana, Rome.

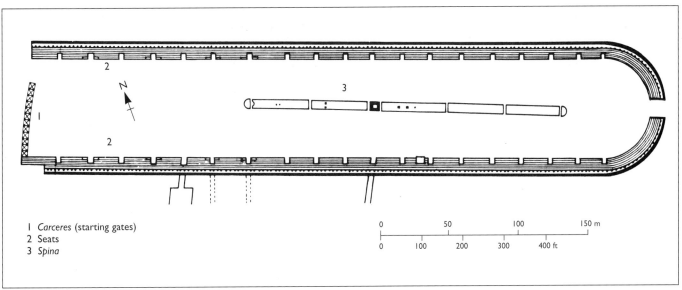

1 *Carceres* (starting gates)
2 Seats
3 *Spina*

8.24 Plan of the circus at Leptis Magna, Libya, early 3rd century. The two long sides and the semicircular eastern end had seats. A low dividing wall, or *spina* ("spine"), ran up the middle of the **arena** (the sandy running surface). It was decorated with statues, fountains, and other ornaments. Conical pillars marked the ends of the wall where the contestants had to turn.

The Greek forerunners of the circus were the hippo-drome for horse racing, and the stadium for footracing. Greek tastes, however, were less violent, and the need for public spectacles much more limited. The Roman populace craved entertainment, and the impetus for the huge imperial Roman building programs was as much to satisfy this craving as to express the power inherent in the emperor's ability to finance and execute them.

Aqueducts An example of the Roman ability to turn necessity into practicality was the development of the bridge and **aqueduct** (or conductor of water, from the Latin *ducere*, meaning "to lead," and *aqua*, meaning "water"). The most impressive example of a section of a Roman aqueduct is the Pont du Gard (fig. **8.25**), located in

modern Nîmes in the south of France. Between 20 and 16 B.C. Marcus Agrippa (son-in-law and adviser to Augustus) commissioned an aqueduct system to bring water to Nîmes from natural springs some 30 miles (48 km) away. Much of the aqueduct was built below ground or on a low wall, but when it had to cross the gorge of the Gardon, it was necessary to build a stone bridge to carry it.

The Pont du Gard was constructed in three tiers, each with narrow barrel vaults. Those on the first two tiers are the same size, while the third-story vaults, which carried the channel containing the water, were smaller. The vous-soirs (see p. 213) that make up the arches weigh up to 6 tons (6,096 kg) each. They were precisely cut to standard measurements, **dressed** (shaped and smoothed), and then fitted into place without mortar or clamps.

8.25 Pont du Gard, near Nîmes, France, late 1st century B.C. Stone, 854 ft (260 m) long, 162 ft (49 m) high. The aqueduct system maintains a constant decline of 1 in 3000, resulting in a total drop of only 54 feet (16.5 m) over its whole length of 30 miles (48 km).

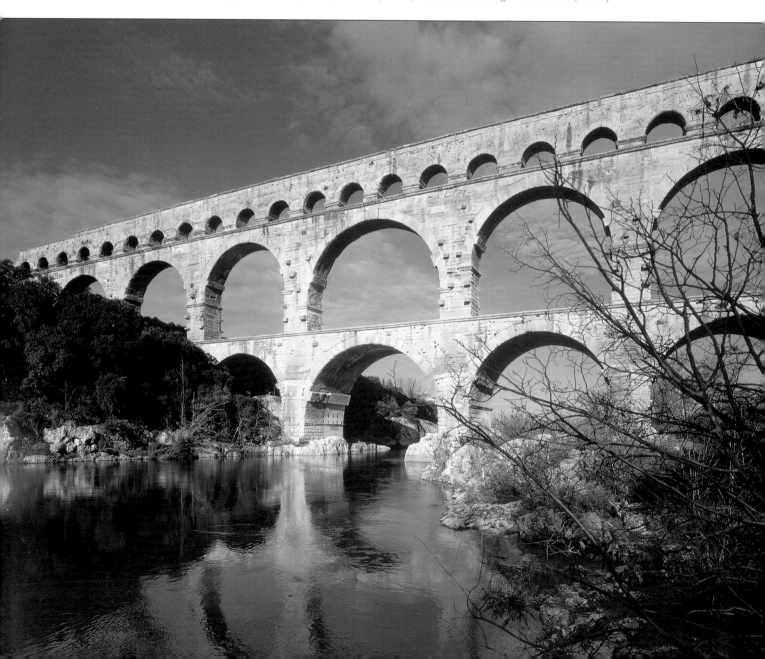

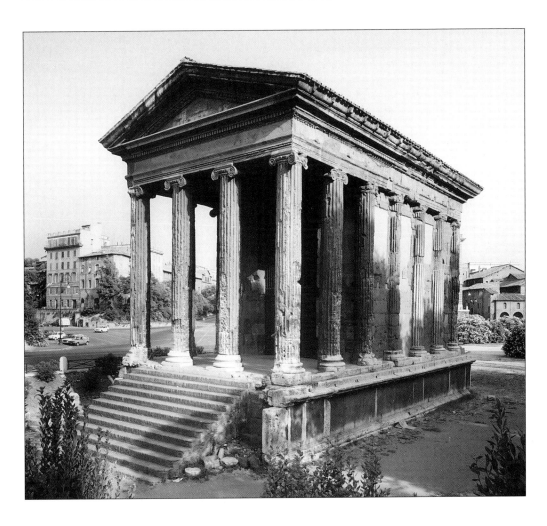

8.26 Temple of Portunus (formerly known as the Temple of Fortuna Virilis), Rome, late 2nd century B.C. Stone.

8.27 (below) Plan of the Temple of Portunus.

The vault system of construction was well suited to a massive engineering project such as the Pont du Gard bridge and aqueduct. With the tunnel vaults arranged in a continuous series side by side, the lateral thrust of each vault is counteracted by its neighbor, so that only the end vaults need buttressing. The placement of larger vaults below and smaller ones above serves both a structural purpose—support—and an esthetic one: the repeated arches not only carry water, but also formally carry one's gaze across the river.

Religious Architecture

Temples Roman temples were derived from both Greek and Etruscan precedents. From the Etruscan type came the podium (base) and the frontality of the temple (see p. 190). From Greece came the columns, the *cella* (equivalent to the Greek *naos*), the porch (*pronaos*), the Orders, and the pediment. Many Greek architects worked in Rome and its provinces following the Roman conquest of Greece in 146 B.C. Their activity led to an infusion of Greek elements and a gradual shift toward the use of marble.

The Temple of Portunus (figs. **8.26** and **8.27**), built in Rome in the late second century B.C., shows Greek influence in the entablature, which is supported on all four

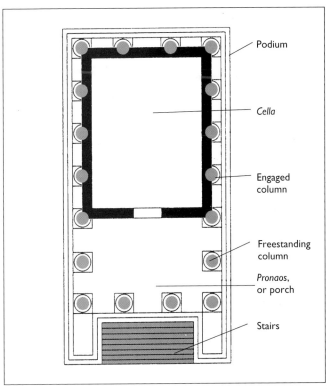

Podium

Cella

Engaged column

Freestanding column

Pronaos, or porch

Stairs

sides by slender Ionic columns. The corner columns, as in the Parthenon, serve both the long and the short sides simultaneously. Etruscan influence is apparent in the deeper porch, raised podium, and in the steps, which are restricted to the front porch and thus give the temple a well-defined frontal aspect. Later, during the Empire, the frontality of the temple, raised on its podium, seemed to preside over the ritual space before it, and was seen as a metaphor for the emperor's domination of the city and its inhabitants.

One aspect in which the Roman temple differs from the Greek is in the relation of the columns to the wall. Whereas Greek temples are typically **peripteral** (surrounded by a colonnade of freestanding columns), the columns of the Temple of Portunus are freestanding only on the porch. The other columns are engaged in the back and side walls of the *cella*, hence the term pseudo-peripteral. The Romans had thus moved beyond the Greek use of the column as the primary means of support and the colonnade as the organizing principle of architectural space. In the Temple of Portunus, the wall, made of rubble-faced concrete, is the supporting element, and the engaged columns, which originally were faced with travertine, have a purely decorative function.

Another Roman temple with both Greek and Etruscan elements, dating from the early first century B.C., is the circular Temple of the Sibyl at Tivoli (figs. **8.28** and **8.29**; see Box). It is reminiscent of earlier round temples from Greece, of the *tholos* design of Mycenaean and Etruscan tombs, and of the round Etruscan huts (see fig. 7.10).

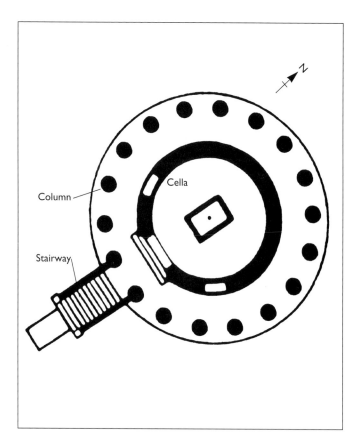

8.29 Plan of the Temple of the Sibyl.

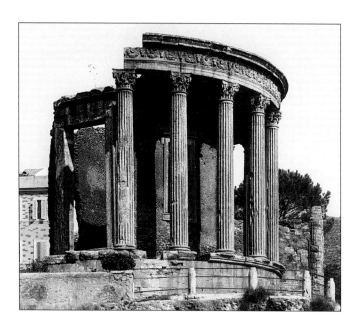

8.28 Temple of the Sibyl, Tivoli, early 1st century B.C. The foundations are of tufa, the temple itself of concrete faced with travertine ashlar. Also known as the Temple of Vesta (Goddess of the Hearth), the building is thought to be based on an earlier structure in Rome, where the sacred flame of the city was kept. In the eighteenth century, the column-capitals were copied for use on the façade of the Bank of England.

Sibyls

Sibyls were women in Greek and Roman antiquity who interpreted events and predicted the future. They were generally priestesses presiding at oracular sites such as Delphi (see p. 136), and were believed to be divinely inspired. In Christian art, for example on the Sistine Ceiling (see Vol. II), they are often represented as having foretold the coming of Christ.

Like the Temple of Portunus, the Temple of the Sibyl stands on a podium. Its eighteen fluted Corinthian columns support an entablature with a continuous frieze of oxen-heads alternating with garlands. The steps are located only in front of the entrance.

The Pantheon The Pantheon, the most monumental ancient Roman temple, was built during the reign of Hadrian (figs. **8.30**, **8.31**, and **8.32**). It consists of two main parts: a traditional rectangular portico supported by massive granite Corinthian columns; and a huge concrete **rotunda** (round structure), faced on the exterior with brick. Inscribed on the pediment of the portico is the name of Augustus' friend Marcus Agrippa, who had dedicated an earlier temple on the same site. The entire Pantheon

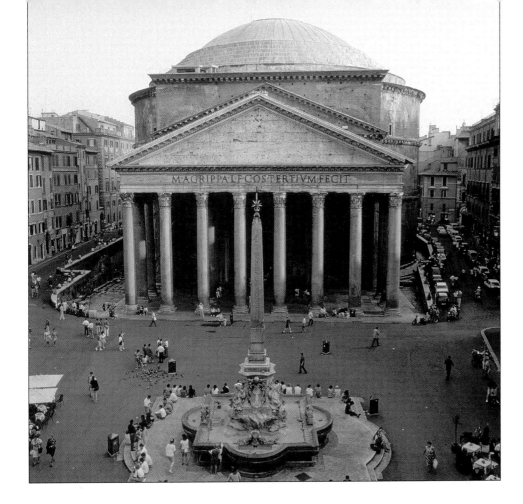

8.30 Exterior view of the Pantheon, Rome, A.D. 117–125. Marble, brick, and concrete. The Pantheon was built under Hadrian's rule and was dedicated in a literal sense to all *(pan)* the gods *(theoi)*—more specifically, to the five true planets then known (Jupiter, Mars, Mercury, Saturn, and Venus), and possibly also the sun and moon.

stands on a podium with steps leading to the portico entrance. The building was originally approached through a colonnaded forecourt, which has since been destroyed. The forecourt masked the striking absence of symmetry between the rectangular portico and the huge, cylindrical rotunda.

Once inside the rotunda, the visitor is confronted by a vast domed space illuminated only from the open **oculus** (Latin for "eye") in the center of the dome (fig. 8.32). The dome and the drum are in perfect proportion, the distance from the top of the dome to the floor being identical with the diameter of the drum. The marble floor consists of patterns of circles and squares, and the walls contain niches (each one for a different deity) with Corinthian columns supporting alternating triangular and rounded pediments. Between each niche is a recess with two huge columns flanked by two corner pilasters. A circular entablature forms the base of a short "second story." This, in turn, bears the whole weight of the dome, which is channeled down to the eight piers. The dome itself has five **coffered** bands (rows of recessed rectangles in the ceiling). These reduce the weight of the structure, and also create a decorative pattern on the interior of the dome.

Commemorative Architecture

An important category of Roman architecture was developed specifically to celebrate the actions of individuals, usually an emperor or a general. The historical and political nature of such commemorative works was related to the importance of portraiture.

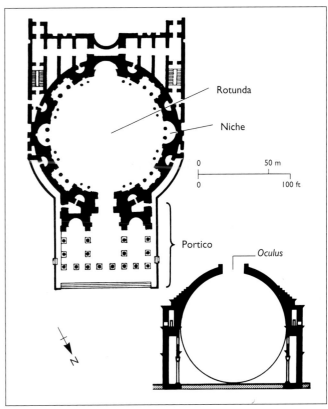

8.31 Plan and section of the Pantheon. The section shows the thickness of the dome tapering toward the top, from approximately 20 to 6 feet (6–1.8 m). Note the stepped buttresses on the lower half of the dome.

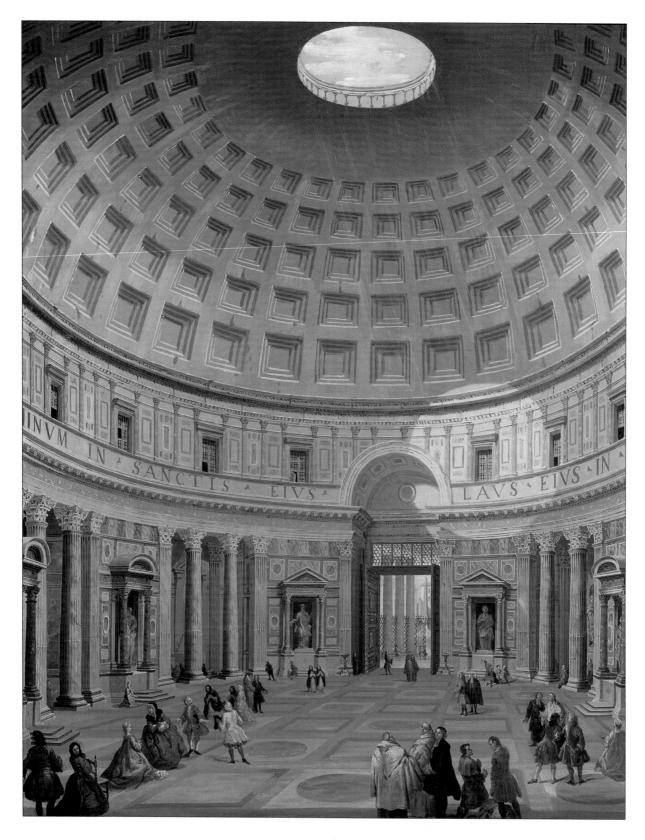

8.32 Giovanni Paolo Panini, *The Interior of the Pantheon*, c. 1740. Oil on canvas, 4 ft 2½ in × 3 ft 3 in (1.28 × 0.99 m). National Gallery of Art, Washington, DC. Samuel H. Kress Collection. The coffers were originally painted blue, and each had a gold rosette in the middle, enhancing the dome's role as a symbol of the sky, or the dome of heaven. The blue paint repeated the blue sky that was visible through the oculus. It in turn cast a circle of light inside the building, reminding ancient Roman visitors of the symbolic equation between the sun and the eye of Jupiter, the supreme celestial deity of Rome.

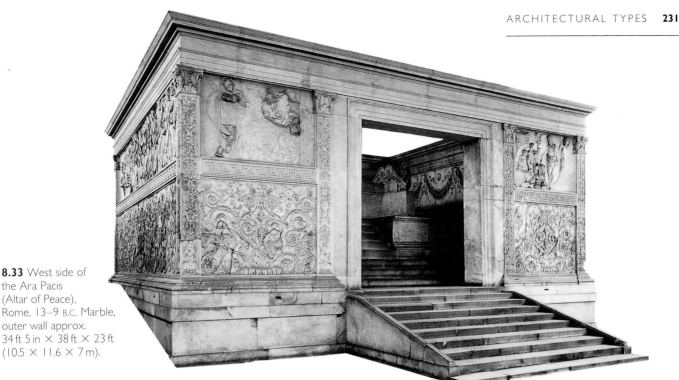

8.33 West side of the Ara Pacis (Altar of Peace), Rome, 13–9 B.C. Marble, outer wall approx. 34 ft 5 in × 38 ft × 23 ft (10.5 × 11.6 × 7 m).

The Ara Pacis (13–9 B.C.)   One of the greatest marble monuments of Augustus' reign was the Ara Pacis (Altar of Peace; fig. **8.33**), located on the Campus Martius (literally "the field dedicated to Mars," the god of war). Its purpose was to celebrate the *pax Augusta*, or "Peace of Augustus," after the emperor had made peace with the Gauls and returned to Rome. The altar (visible here through the opening) stood on a podium and was enclosed on the sides by a large rectangular marble frame. Visitors approached by a stairway located on the western side. Each year, magistrates, priests, and Vestal Virgins (virgins consecrated to the service of Vesta, goddess of the hearth) made sacrifices on it. They ascended the stairs, entered the sacred space, and performed the sacrifices while facing east, toward the sunrise.

The exterior of the marble frame is decorated with reliefs. Elegant vinescroll **traceries**, indicating peace and fertility under Augustus, are represented on the lower half of the frame, while the upper half illustrates the procession in honor of the founding of the altar. On the north side, senators and other officials, some with wives and children, are shown proceeding to the entrance. The south side represents members of the imperial family (fig. **8.34**). Not seen in this illustration, the figure of Augustus has his

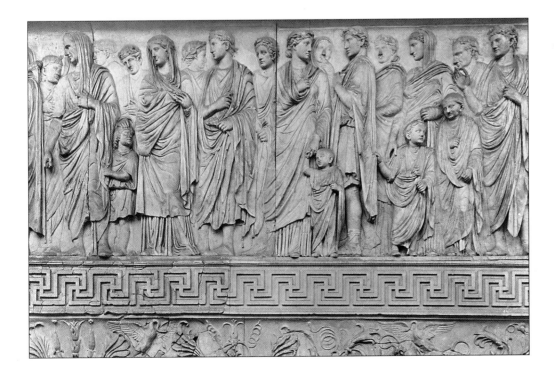

8.34 South side of the Ara Pacis, showing a detail of an imperial procession. Marble relief, approx. 5 ft 3 in (1.6 m) high.

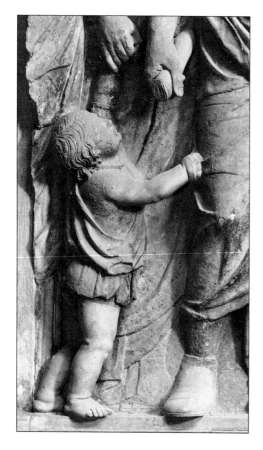

8.35 Ara Pacis, showing a detail of a child tugging at an adult's toga. Note the artist's careful observation of human nature in the child's chubby rolls around his ankles and dimpled elbows and knees. He is tired of walking and wants to be picked up and carried. Such accurate psychological characterization of specific age-related behavior is consistent with the Roman interest in portraiture.

head draped in the manner of the *Pontifex Maximus*, the title denoting his role as the state's religious leader. Visible at the left of the relief illustrated are his wife Livia and his son-in-law and adviser Agrippa. The presence of children (fig. **8.35**) is interpreted as referring to Augustus' policy of encouraging large families with tax relief.

There is good reason to believe that Roman artists used the Ionic frieze of the Parthenon as a source for the Ara Pacis. But the Greek temple commemorated the supremacy of Athens in a way that combined history (victory in the Persian Wars) with mythology (the Doric metopes and the pediments) and ritual (the Panathenaic procession). The Ara Pacis, in contrast, commemorates a specific historical event. Techniques of carving also differ, for the Ara Pacis is in higher relief than the Panathenaic procession, contributing to the characteristic Roman taste for spatial illusionism. Higher relief is reserved for the more prominent foreground figures, while lower relief is used for figures that appear to be in the background. The feet of the foreground figures, for example, project from the base of the relief. As in the Parthenon frieze, there is some variety of pose among the figures so that the potential monotony

of the procession is avoided. The Roman figures also have a greater range of facial expression and age—portraits of children as well as old people are represented.

Trajan's Column   Single, freestanding, colossal columns had been used as commemorative monuments from the Hellenistic period onward. The unique Roman contribution was the addition of a documentary, ribbon-like narrative frieze, best exemplified in Trajan's Column (fig. **8.36**), which was completed by A.D. 113. It was erected in honor

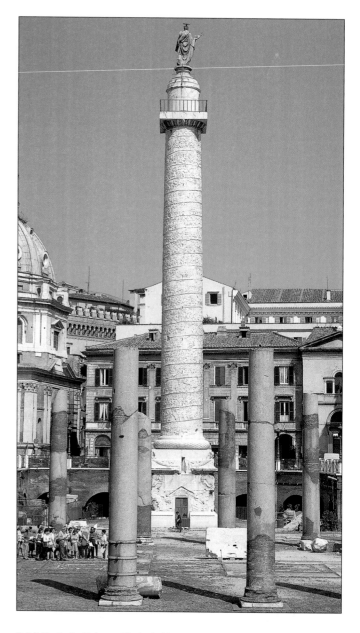

8.36 Trajan's Column, Trajan's Forum, Rome, dedicated A.D. 113. Marble, 125 ft (38 m) high, including base; frieze 625 ft (190 m) long. Although the upper scenes could not have been seen from the ground, they would have been visible from the balconies of nearby buildings. A gilded bronze statue of Trajan, since destroyed, originally stood at the top of the column. It has been replaced by a statue of St. Peter.

of his victories over the Dacians, the inhabitants of modern-day Romania (see Box). There were originally two libraries flanking the column, one for Greek texts and the other for Latin.

The column consists of marble drums cut horizontally and imperceptibly joined together. Supporting it is a podium decorated with sculptures illustrating the spoils of war and containing a repository for Trajan's ashes. Inside the column shaft, a spiral staircase was illuminated by openings cut into the marble. The exterior shaft is covered with a continuous low-relief spiral sculpture over 625 feet (190 m) long and containing some 2500 figures. In the first four bands of the spiral, at the beginning of the narrative (fig. **8.37**), the Roman army prepares its campaign. On the first level, a giant bearded river-god of the Danube appears under the arch of a cave. He watches as Trajan leads the Roman army out of a walled city. Boats and soldiers fill the river. The second level contains army camps, war councils, reconnaissance missions, and the capture of a spy. Background figures are raised above foreground figures, virtually eliminating any unfilled space. Zigzagging buildings faced with brickwork patterns and the diagonals of the boats add to the sense

of surface movement. The formal crowding conveys the bustling activity of armies preparing for war. In addition to its power as a commemorative statement, the frieze on Trajan's Column is one of the most informative historical records of life in the Roman army.

Trajan's Column and other monumental Roman columns are commemorative markers standing in a vertical plane. Their sculptural decorations narrate the emperor's achievements, while their height signifies his success.

The Triumphal Arch The triumphal arch was another Roman innovation that commemorated the military exploits of a victorious general or emperor. Rather than reaching upward, however, the arches marked a place of earthly passage by framing a space along a roadway. The act of passing through the arch symbolized an emperor's triumphant entry, or re-entry, into a city.

Since many Roman cities, including Rome itself, were walled, the Romans cut arches into the walls. These were often in sets of three, and served as entrances for the general populace. The earliest surviving examples of the triumphal arch, as distinct from entrances in a long city wall, precede the reign of Augustus by a century. They typically consisted of a rectangular block enclosing one or more round arches, and a short barrel vault like those on the Pont du Gard (fig. 8.25). Most had either one or three openings, with two being quite rare. Pilasters framed the openings and supported an entablature, which was surmounted by a rectangular section, or **attic**. This feature usually bore an inscription and supported sculptures of chariots drawn by horses or, occasionally, by elephants. Elephants, in ancient Rome, were imported from Africa and owned only by emperors. Because of their bulk, strength, and long lifespan, elephants were symbolic of the emperor's power and immortality.

One of the finest examples of an arch with a single opening is the Arch of Titus (fig. **8.40**), erected in A.D. 81 to commemorate Titus' capture of Jerusalem and suppression of a Jewish rebellion in A.D. 70–71. Its columns are of the Composite Order, a Roman Order combining elements of the Greek, in this case Ionic and Corinthian. On the curved triangular spaces between the arch and the frame, winged Victories hold laurel wreaths. Reliefs on either side of the **piers** (large rectangular supports) which form the passageway depict scenes of Titus' triumphs. In the center of the vault (not visible in fig. 8.40), Titus is carried up to heaven on the back of an eagle, representing his apotheosis.

In a relief on the inner wall (fig. **8.41**), Titus' soldiers carry off their booty from the Jewish Wars (see Box). As in the frieze of the Ara Pacis, the figures project illusionistically from the surface of the relief. Soldiers hold up the *menorah* (the sacred Jewish candelabrum with seven candlesticks), whose weight and prominence reflect its importance for the Jews and hence its role as a symbol of Roman victory. The base of the *menorah* is carved in perspective, as is the triumphal arch set at an oblique angle to the surface on the far right.

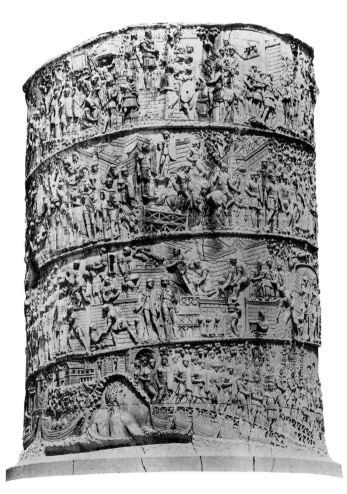

8.37 The four lowest bands of Trajan's Column (detail). Marble relief, each band 36 in (91.4 cm) high.

The Dacians

The Dacians, an Indo-European people related to the Thracians of northern Greece, occupied an area of modern Romania along the Danube. Because of their expertise in metallurgy, especially in working precious material such as gold and silver, they were a natural target for Roman conquest. In A.D. 101 the Romans under Trajan began campaigning against the Dacians and by 106 had occupied the whole country. The wealth of Dacian booty taken by Trajan paid for many Roman buildings and lavish gifts for his soldiers. It also helped to finance the soldiers' retirement colony at Timgad (see p. 215).

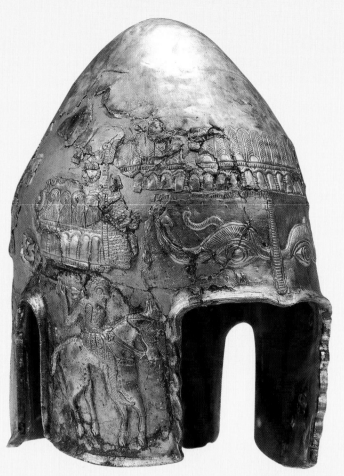

8.39 Dacian helmet, 4th century. Gilded silver, 3⅛ in (8 cm) high. National History Museum, Bucharest.

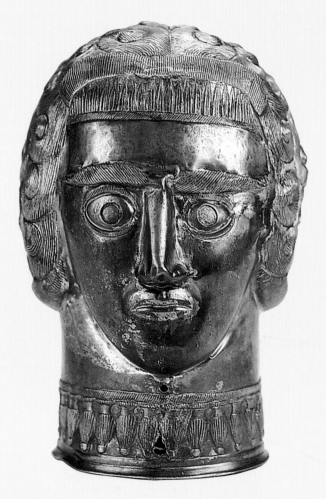

8.38 Dacian vase in the shape of a human head, 4th century. Silver, 6½ in (16.8 cm) high. National History Museum, Bucharest.

Two objects discovered in a Thracian tomb of the fourth century A.D., which was excavated in 1971, give some idea of Dacian wealth. The tomb itself was built around a wooden core, approached, as at Mycenae (see fig. 5.31), by a dromos. Two funerary rooms yielded precious objects and a chariot. The silver vase in figure **8.38** is in the form of a human head, with stylized plant forms across the forehead and a ring of vases on the neck. The inlaid pupils have disappeared. Characteristics of Greek sculpture and of ancient Near Eastern stylizations indicate the assimilation of features from different Mediterranean cultures. The helmet (fig. **8.39**), with a pair of apotropaic eyes on the front, provides further evidence of such assimilation, in this instance probably of Scythian influence. The eyes and ears give the helmet an anthro-pomorphic quality related to that of the vase. Certain details, notably the plant forms and the horned animals depicted in relief at the sides, combine stylization with naturalism in a manner reminiscent of Achaemenid art (see p. 73).

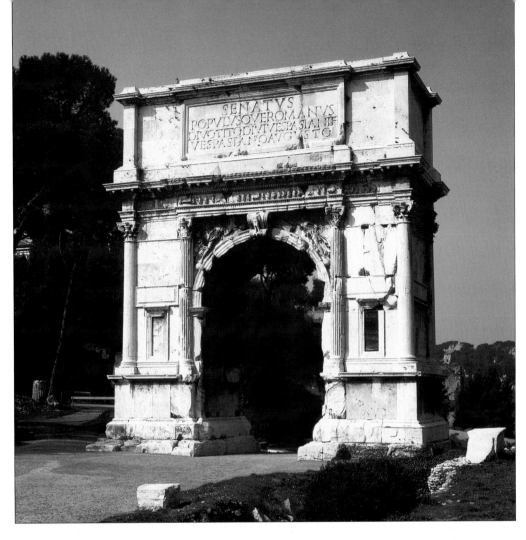

8.40 Arch of Titus, Rome, A.D. 81. Marble over concrete core, approx. 50 ft (15 m) high, approx. 40 ft (12 m) wide. The arch stands on the Via Sacra, or Sacred Way, in Rome. The Latin inscription on the attic proclaims that "the senate and people of Rome (SPQR) [dedicate the arch] to divine Titus, Vespasian Augustus, son of divine Vespasian."

8.41 (below) Relief from the Arch of Titus, detail showing *The Spoils of the Temple of Jerusalem Exhibited in Rome.* Marble, 6 ft 7 in (2 m) high.

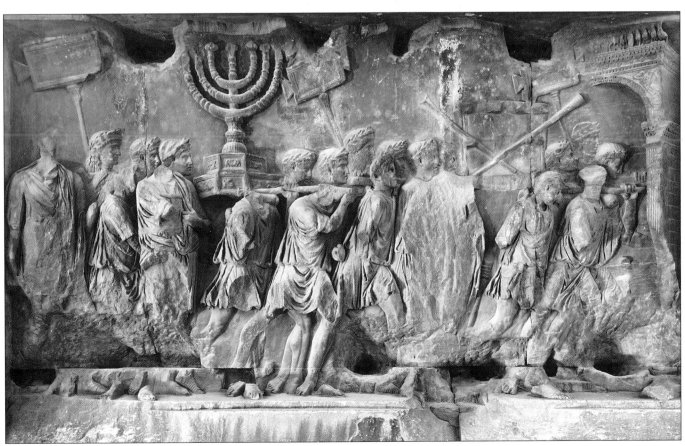

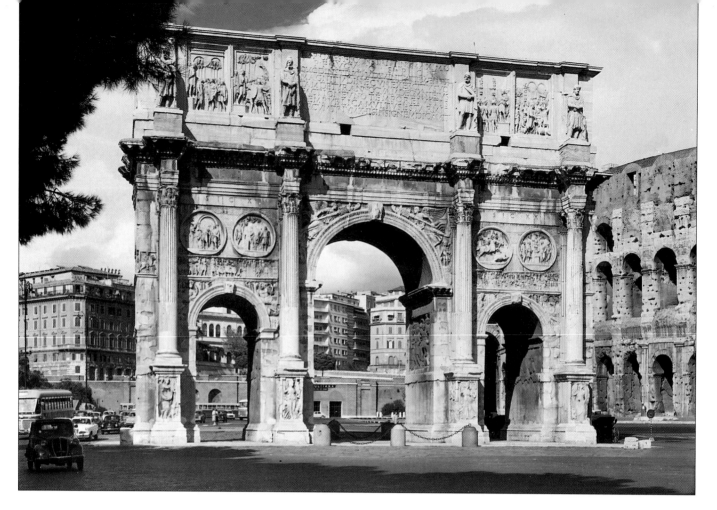

8.42 Arch of Constantine, Rome, A.D. c. 313. Marble, 70 ft (21.3 m) high, 85 ft 8 in (26.1 m) wide.

Over two hundred years after the dedication of the Arch of Titus, the emperor Constantine the Great (ruled A.D. 305–339) erected the largest triumphal arch in Rome, near the Colosseum (fig. **8.42**). It commemorated his assumption of sole imperial power in 312, after defeating his rival Maxentius at the Battle of the Milvian Bridge. This elaborate arch with three openings is decorated both with original reliefs and with those removed from earlier monuments in honor of other emperors (Trajan, Hadrian, and Marcus Aurelius; see below).

The juxtaposition of reliefs from different periods illustrates certain changes that took place in Roman sculpture in the course of the Empire. The medallions in figure **8.43** are *spolia*, which are pieces taken from older reliefs and reused in new ones. They date from the early decades of the second century A.D. and are thought to be Hadrianic. On the left, three riders in a landscape hunt a boar. On the right, three worshipers stand before an altar of Apollo.

The horizontal relief below the medallions dates from Constantine's reign. Constantine himself, now headless, sits in the middle, and makes a public speech. At either end are statues of Hadrian and Marcus Aurelius, both of whom were influenced by Greek taste. Lined up and listening to Constantine are figures accented by the arrangement of arches and columns. The style of the later reliefs is less naturalistic than that of the medallions: the proportions of the figures are stubbier, their heads are enlarged, their poses

Josephus and the Jewish Wars

Josephus (A.D. c. 37–100), a Jewish soldier and historian, wrote a history of the Jewish Wars which covers the capture of Jerusalem by Antiochus Epiphanes in 170 B.C. to Titus' seizure of Jerusalem in A.D. 70 (which he witnessed). Under the Flavian emperors (Vespasian, Titus, and Domitian, who together ruled from A.D. 69 to 97), Josephus was granted Roman citizenship, and he favored cooperation with the Romans. The history includes a description of the triumphal procession celebrating the victory of Vespasian (ruled A.D. 69–79) and his son Titus (ruled A.D. 79–81) after the sack of Jerusalem. His account reflects the Roman love of material splendor and its role in projecting an image of imperial power. He was struck by the abundance of gold and silver objects, which flowed "like a river," by the Babylonian tapestries, and jewels set in golden crowns. "The most interesting of all," he wrote:

> were the spoils seized from the temple of Jerusalem: a gold table weighing many talents, and a lampstand, also made of gold, which was made in a form different from that which we usually employ. For there was a central shaft fastened to the base; then spandrels extended from this in an arrangement which rather resembled the shape of a trident, and on the end of each of these spandrels a lamp was forged. There were seven of these, emphasizing the honor accorded to the number seven among the Jews.[3]

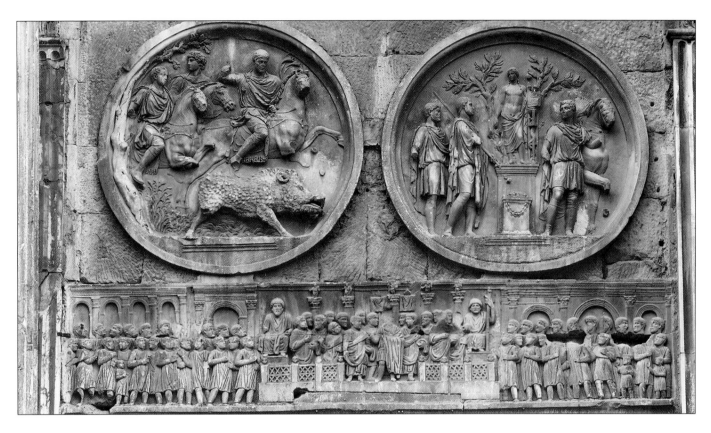

8.43 Medallions (Hadrianic, A.D. 117–138) and frieze (Constantinian, early 4th century) from the Arch of Constantine, Rome. Frieze approx. 3 ft 4 in (1.02 m) high.

are more repetitious, and their carving is flatter. Since we do not know why reliefs of two different periods appear on the same arch, it is difficult to explain their iconographic relationship, or even to confirm that there is one. What is clear, however, is the stylistic change. The reliefs belonging to Constantine's reign have lost the naturalism of the Ara Pacis and the Arch of Titus.

Sculptural Types

Sarcophagi

The Romans produced three basic types of funerary art. They used cinerary urns for cremation, possibly the result of Etruscan influence. Graves were marked in the Greek style by stelai or tombstones with inscriptions and/or reliefs. But the most typical item of funerary art for the Romans was the sarcophagus, which originated during the reign of Hadrian.

The Prometheus Sarcophagus (fig. **8.44**) is decorated with reliefs illustrating the Greek myth of Prometheus (see p. 8). He is

8.44 Prometheus Sarcophagus, A.D. c. 110. Marble. Museo Capitolino, Rome. The effigy of a sleeping child on the lid originally belonged to another sarcophagus. His head rests on a pillow and he holds poppies in his right hand. Poppies (well known for their narcotic quality) were an attribute of sleep in the ancient world, and in this context are a reminder of the traditional association of sleep and death.

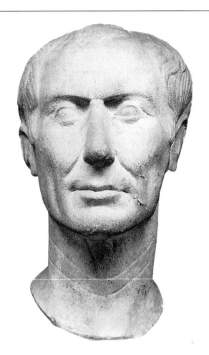

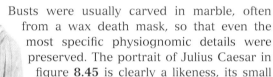

8.45 (left) Bust of Julius Caesar, from Tusculum, mid-1st century B.C. Marble, 13 in (33 cm) high; head 8⅔ in (22 cm) high. Museo di Antichità, Turin.

8.46 (right) Bust of Trajan, 1st half of 2nd century A.D. Marble, Musei Vaticani, Rome.

8.47 (below) Patrician with Two Ancestor Busts, A.D. c. 13. Marble, lifesize. Museo Capitolino, Rome.

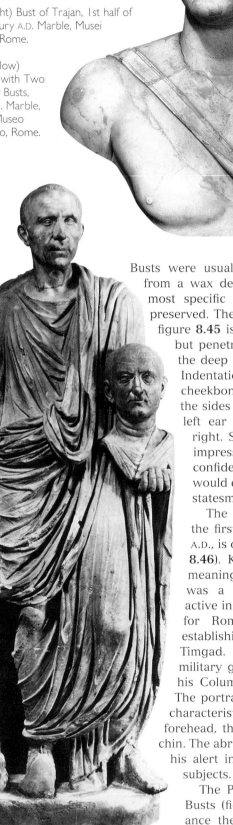

shown in the center as a bearded man making humans from clay, while Minerva gives each of his figures a soul in the form of a butterfly. On the right are personifications of night and the moon. A Cupid stands over a dead body and holds an upside-down torch; its extinguished flame is a symbol of death. Hercules (the Roman name for the Greek Herakles) leads Prometheus before Jupiter, while Atropos (the Fate of the forces of death) records the life of the deceased. On the left are Clotho and Lachesis (the Fates of the life forces) with the gods of earth, ocean, and wind. A personification of the sun appears above in a horsedrawn chariot. Although the crowded imagery on this sarcophagus deals with a range of different subjects, it is all related in one way or another to creation, life, and death.

Portraits

Just as tomb effigies are a metaphorical way of making the dead seem alive, so portraiture is often intended as a means of keeping the deceased alive in memory. When the subject of a Roman portrait was an emperor, the image was also a means of extending his authority throughout the empire.

One of the portrait types most characteristic of Rome was the head detached from the body, or **bust**. It had never been part of Greek tradition, but was common among the Etruscans.

Busts were usually carved in marble, often from a wax death mask, so that even the most specific physiognomic details were preserved. The portrait of Julius Caesar in figure **8.45** is clearly a likeness, its small but penetrating eyes contrasting with the deep spaces under the eyebrows. Indentations are carved out under the cheekbones and creases spread from the sides of the nose, and the figure's left ear is slightly higher than the right. Such facial details create the impression of a specific personality, confident and self-assured, as one would expect of a great general and statesman.

The bust of Trajan, dating from the first half of the second century A.D., is one of many that survive (fig. **8.46**). Known as *optimus princeps*, meaning "the best leader," Trajan was a popular emperor. He was active in improving the quality of life for Roman citizens—for example, establishing the retirement colony at Timgad. He was also considered a military genius, as commemorated in his Column (see figs. 8.36 and 8.37). The portrait bust of Trajan shows the characteristic smooth hair covering his forehead, the long nose, and prominent chin. The abrupt turn of his head suggests his alert interest in the welfare of his subjects.

The Patrician with Two Ancestor Busts (fig. **8.47**) reflects the importance the Romans accorded to pre-

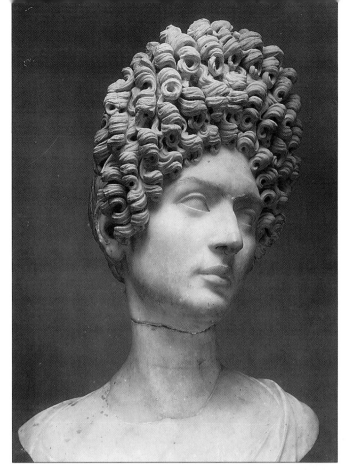

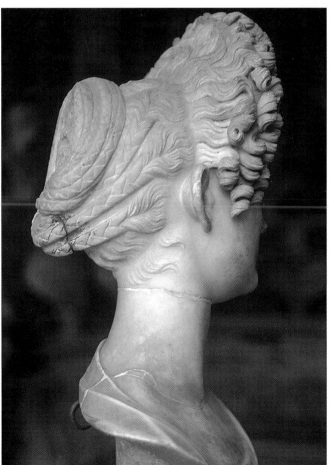

8.48a, b Portrait of a young Flavian lady (front and side), A.D. c. 90. Marble, 2 ft 1 in (63.5 cm) high. Museo Capitolino, Rome.

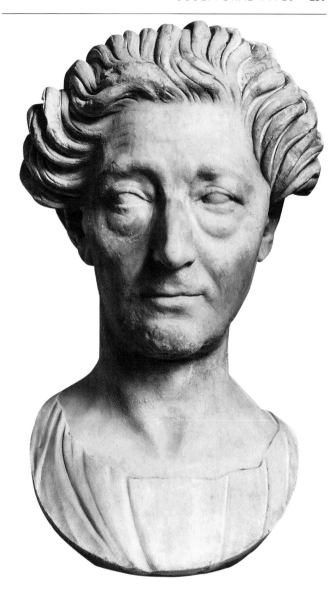

8.49 Portrait of an older Flavian lady, A.D. c. 90. Marble, 9½ in (24.1 cm) high. Museo Laterano, Rome.

serving family genealogy in stone. The two ancestors are elderly and appear serious, but the original head of the patrician has been lost and a substitute added. His toga (the round-edged outer garment worn in public by Roman citizens) draws our attention to the two heads by the arrangement of its folds. A series of short, horizontally curved folds directs us from the patrician's waist to the bust at the left. A contrasting group of longer folds curves up gradually from the hem to the bust at the right. The toga thus creates a formal unity between the patrician and his ancestors that condenses time by bridging the gap between the dead and the living.

Portraits of upper-class Roman women became popular in the first century A.D. Those illustrated here contrast the elaborate coiffure of a young Flavian lady (fig. **8.48**) with the more subdued hairstyle of an older woman (fig. **8.49**). The young woman wears the characteristic curls framing the face and rising upward in a top-heavy fashion.

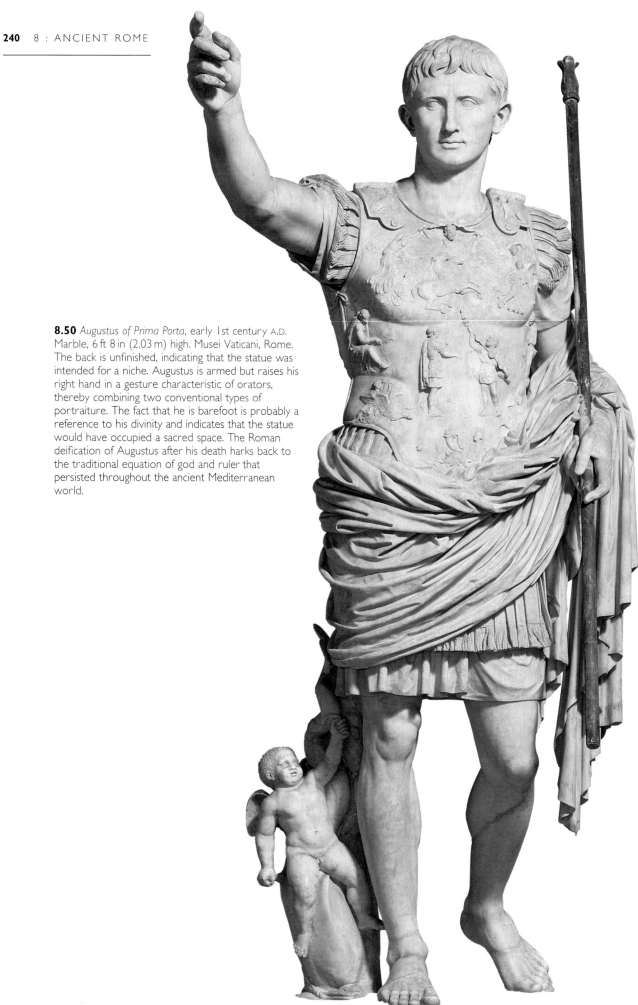

8.50 *Augustus of Prima Porta*, early 1st century A.D. Marble, 6 ft 8 in (2.03 m) high. Musei Vaticani, Rome. The back is unfinished, indicating that the statue was intended for a niche. Augustus is armed but raises his right hand in a gesture characteristic of orators, thereby combining two conventional types of portraiture. The fact that he is barefoot is probably a reference to his divinity and indicates that the statue would have occupied a sacred space. The Roman deification of Augustus after his death harks back to the traditional equation of god and ruler that persisted throughout the ancient Mediterranean world.

Deep carving creates strong oppositions of light and dark that add to the sense of mass supported by the delicate, smoothly carved surfaces of the face and neck. The older woman is carved with wrinkles, and bags under the eyes to show the results of ageing. Her hair also frames her face, but less elaborately so. It weighs down on her head, rather than rising up as that of the young woman does, and thus corresponds to the "weight" of her age. The older woman also seems to have grown wise and knowing.

One of the most important subjects of Roman sculpture in the round was naturally the emperor himself. In the *Augustus of Prima Porta* (fig. **8.50**) the emperor is portrayed as both orator and general. Even though the head is a likeness, it is idealized. Augustus was seventy-six when he died after a long reign, but this statue represents a self-confident, dominating, and above all youthful figure. A possible source for this idealization is the *Doryphoros* of Polykleitos (fig. 6.26). The similar stance suggests that the artist who made the *Augustus* was familiar with the Greek statue, probably from Roman copies, if not from the original.

The iconography of this statue again emphasizes the power of Rome embodied in Augustus as emperor. By his right leg, Cupid (Venus' son) rides a dolphin and serves as a reminder that Augustus traced his lineage to Aeneas (also a son of Venus), and was thus descended from the gods. Among the little reliefs carved on Augustus' armor is Mother Earth with a cornucopia, indicating the emperor's identification with the land as a source of plenty. The association of Augustus with the earth also has an implied reference to Roman territorial conquests. Another scene depicts a Parthian returning a military standard looted from the Romans. A canopy spread out by a sky god at the top of the breastplate alludes to the scene of surrender below.

The portrait statue of Antinous represents the Bithynian youth of great beauty who was the beloved of the emperor Hadrian (fig. **8.51**). The style of the work reflects Hadrian's attraction to Greek art and philosophy. Antinous drowned in the Nile in A.D. 130 and, after his death, Hadrian founded an Egyptian city (Antinoopolis) in his honor and dedicated many statues to him throughout the Roman Empire. Hadrian donated this particular statue to Apollo's sanctuary at Delphi (see p. 136). The relaxed pose, idealization, and naturalistic form of the *Antinous* recall the Classical style of the fifth century B.C. in Greece and it is likely that it was carved by a Greek artist. The nature of the head, with its luxurious curls and fleshy body, reflects Hellenistic influence.

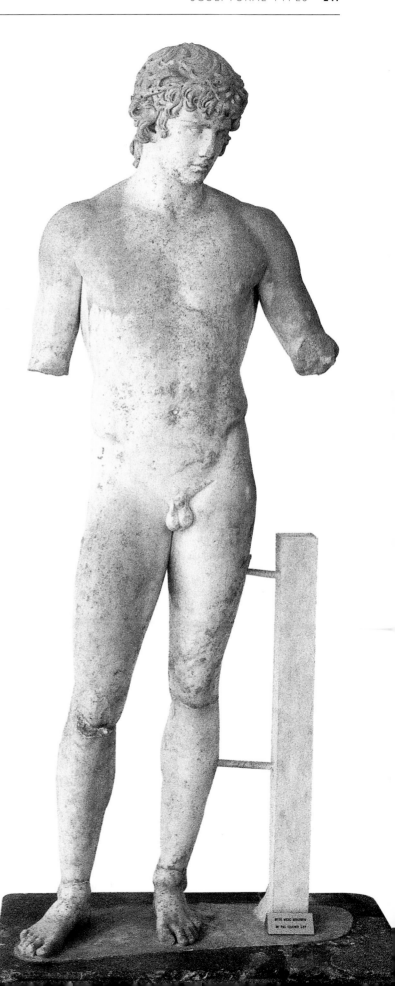

8.51 *Antinous*, c. A.D. 131–138. Marble, 70⅞ in (180 cm) high. Archaeological Museum, Delphi. When Antinous drowned in the Nile in 130, Hadrian was desolate. Priests tried to console him, saying that his beloved had become a star in the constellation of Aquila (the eagle). Since the eagle was the attribute of Jupiter, as well as the emblem of the Roman legions, it had special imperial symbolism.

A type of imperial portrait invented by the Romans is the equestrian monument. The only surviving example is an equestrian bronze statue of the emperor Marcus Aurelius (reigned A.D. 161–80) (fig. **8.52**; see Box). His beard reflects the Greek fashion set by Hadrian. Also suggesting Greek influence is the artist's representation of convincing organic form in both emperor and horse. Veins, muscles, and skin folds of the horse are visible as he raises his right foreleg, turns his head, and lifts his left hind leg so that only the toe of his hoof touches the ground. His apparent eagerness to set out is controlled and counteracted by the more sedate emperor, who originally held reins that have since disappeared.

Unlike the philosopher-emperor Marcus Aurelius, Caracalla (reigned A.D. 211–217) was a vicious tyrant. Despite his abilities as an administrator, he instituted a period of terror that continued for more than a hundred years. He began his rule with his brother Geta, but murdered him and massacred his followers. The force of his maniacal personality is captured in the marble portrait shown in figure **8.53**, especially in the flattened nose, furrowed brow, and downward turn of the mouth. A bestial, slightly subhuman quality is also suggested in the treatment of the facial hair, a strong contrast to Marcus Aurelius' stylish beard.

The emperor Constantine is depicted in a colossal marble head, over 8 feet (almost 3 m) high, which is detached from its body (fig. **8.54**). It is clearly a portrait, as evidenced by such features as the long nose, cleft chin, clean-shaven cheeks, and thick neck; yet the predominant impression left by this sculpture is derived from its monumental size, the staring geometric eyes, and stylized hair. The restrained Classical character of earlier imperial sculptures has disappeared, giving way to a new style, which expresses the emperor's power and makes him seem aloof from his subjects.

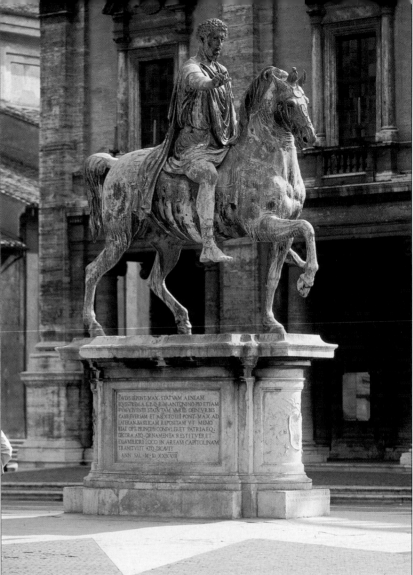

8.52 Equestrian statue of Marcus Aurelius (before restoration), A.D. 164–166. Bronze, 11 ft 6 in (3.5 m) high. Piazza del Campidoglio, Rome. In this statue the emperor is unarmed, and his right arm is extended in the conventional gesture of an orator. But domination and conquest are implied by equestrian iconography. Documents indicate that a conquered enemy originally cowered under the horse's raised foreleg. This harks back to Egyptian and Near Eastern motifs in which a small size and lowly position denote defeat.

Marcus Aurelius: Emperor and Philosopher

Marcus Aurelius (ruled A.D. 161–180) was a Stoic philosopher and author of the *Meditations*, which he wrote in Greek. He had been interested in the arts from his youth and had the greatest respect for artists. "In their devotion to their art," he wrote, "[they] wear themselves to the bone, and immersing themselves in their tasks, go without washing or eating."[4] Despite Marcus Aurelius' admiration for artists, however, he agreed with Plato (see p. 139) that art was mere imitation (*mimesis*) and therefore inferior to nature.

Mosaic and Mural Painting

Roman murals are among the most significant legacies of the eruption of Mount Vesuvius (see p. 212). Hundreds of wall paintings, as well as floor and wall mosaics, have been discovered among the ruins of Pompeii and Herculaneum. These provide the greatest evidence of Hellenistic painting, most of which no longer survives.

The "Alexander Mosaic"

The earliest known example of Greek historical art is a mosaic from Pompeii that includes portraits of Alexander the Great and the Persian king Darius III (fig. **8.55**). It is based on a Greek fresco of the fourth century B.C., showing Alexander defeating Darius at the Battle of Issos (333 B.C.). Notable for its three-dimensional illusionism, it uses

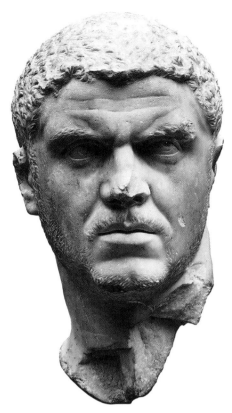

8.53 Bust of Caracalla, first half of the 3rd century. Marble, 1 ft 2¼ in (36.2 cm) high. Metropolitan Museum of Art, New York.

shading to convey a sense of mass and volume, with shadows cast on the horizontal ground, and foreshortening—as in the central horse, seen from the rear. Repeated diagonal spears, clashing metal, and the crowding of horses and men evoke the din of battle, while the sense of action is arrested through such details as the fallen horse and the soldier gazing in terror at the oncoming troops. The lone tree at the left echoes the movement of figures and weapons, and is also a reminder that the scene is taking place in a natural setting.

To the left of the tree, and accentuated by the diagonal sweep of its branch, is Alexander astride his famous horse, Bucephalos (fig. 8.56). Alexander's shoulders and torso are rendered frontally, while his head turns toward Darius. His wavy hair is similar to that of the royal portrait type established by Lysippos in the fourth century B.C. (see fig. 6.4). The strong diagonal of his glance, carried across the picture plane by the spear cutting across the tree, leads the viewer to the dying Persian between the two foreground horses (fig. 8.57), who turns toward his foreshortened shield to watch the reflection of his own death throes. This motif, which exemplifies Hellenistic realism, has been attributed to a new knowledge of optics derived from Euclid's treatise on the subject, written c. 300 B.C.

Mural Paintings

Roman mural paintings were executed in *buon fresco*: pigments mixed with a binder of limewater were applied to the walls before the plaster had dried. A small amount of wax was added to increase the surface shine when the dry painting was polished and buffed. As a result of the dura-

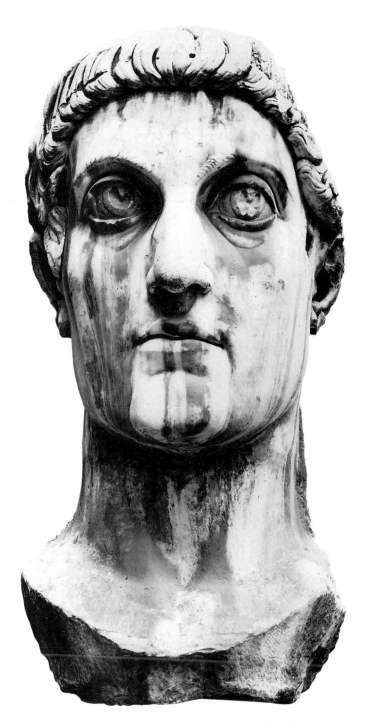

8.54 Monumental head of Constantine, from the Basilica of Constantine, Rome, A.D. 313. Marble, 8 ft 6 in (2.59 m) high. Palazzo dei Conservatori, Rome. The statue's original location on the throne in the apse of the basilica reflected the emperor's power over the Roman people.

bility of this technique, as well as the covering of volcanic ash, many murals from Pompeii and Herculaneum have survived in relatively good condition and they provide a remarkable panorama of Roman painting.

Scholars have divided Roman wall paintings into four styles, two dating to the period of the Republic, and two to the Empire. Artists of the First Style (c. 200–80 B.C.) used stucco for architectural features modeled in relief, which were painted to replicate different kinds of stone. Because of the taste for architectural illusionism,

8.55 The Battle of Issos, from the House of the Faun, Pompeii, 2nd century B.C., after an original Greek fresco of c. 300 B.C. Mosaic, 106¾ × 201½ in (271 × 512 cm). Museo Archeologico Nazionale, Naples. Also known as the "Alexander Mosaic," this work is made of **tesserae**, or little tiles, of color. They are arranged in gradual curves called *opus vermiculatum*, or "worm-work," because they seem to replicate the slow motion of a crawling worm. Monumental mosaics such as this one were found on the floors of houses of the wealthy.

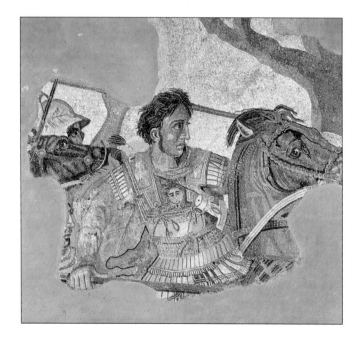

8.56 Detail of figure 8.55, showing Alexander and Bucephalos.

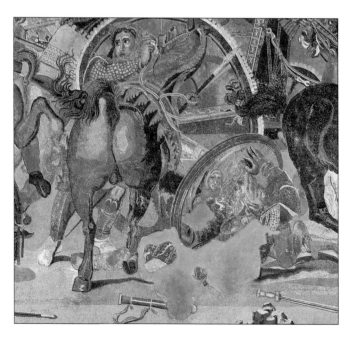

8.57 Detail of figure 8.55, showing a dying Persian.

this style is sometimes called the Masonry style. It arrived in Italy from various Hellenized cultures, although its origin is uncertain. There are examples of paintings in this style dating from as early as the fourth century B.C. in Greece, southern Russia, Asia Minor, Egypt, and North Africa. At Pompeii, artists assimilated some of its elements and produced their own version.

By the period of the Second Style (c. 80 B.C.– A.D.15), the latter part of which falls into the beginning of the Empire under Augustus, the wealthy classes—the nobility and the merchants—had become active patrons. As a result, artists flocked to Italy from other areas, especially Greece. The Second Style is generally characterized by the illusionistic extension, or "opening," of the actual wall surface into a deeper architectural or landscape setting.

The best examples of Second Style frescoes are found at a country villa near Pompeii known as the Villa of the Mysteries. The building itself (figs. **8.58** and **8.59**) is set on a platform, which elevates it from the surrounding landscape. From the interior, however, the landscape was visible through windows and openings in the colonnades, so that the view appeared to be framed, whether by the window or by the columns. This effect influenced the nature of the paintings, which occupy some twelve rooms, including the *atrium* and the peristyle (*peristilio*).

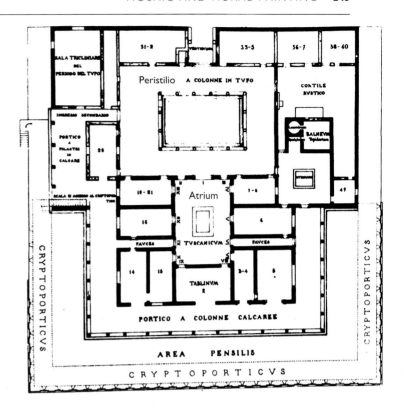

8.58 Plan of the Villa of the Mysteries, near Pompeii, c. 65–50 B.C.

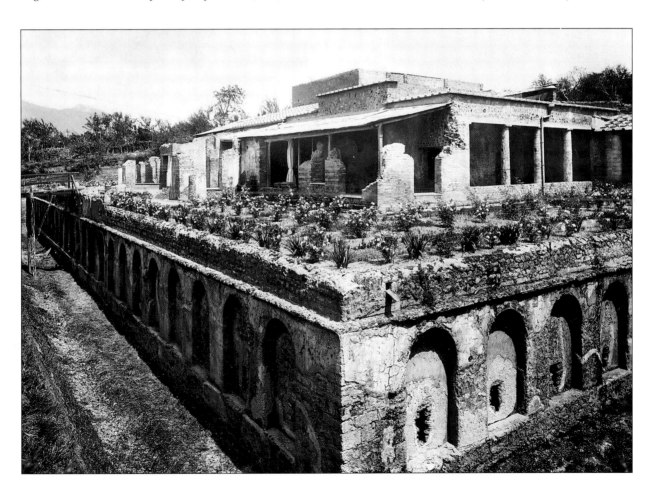

8.59 View of the Villa of the Mysteries, near Pompeii, c. 65–50 B.C.

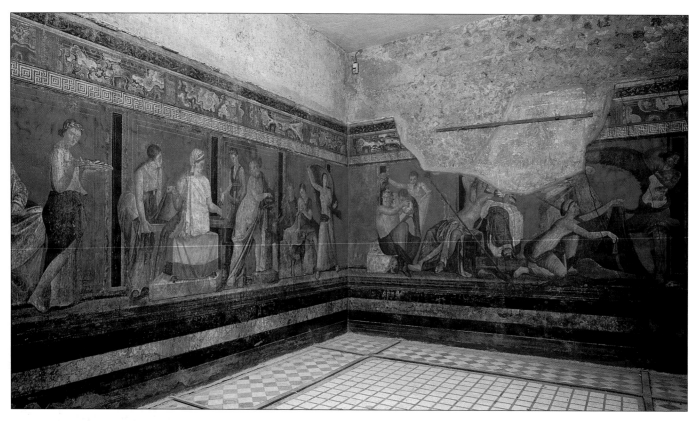

8.60 View of the frescoes at the Villa of the Mysteries, near Pompeii, c. 65–50 B.C.

In the southwest corner, painted pilasters separate each section, or *oecus*, of a long narrative illustrating what is thought to be a mystery rite in honor of Bacchus, the Roman god of wine (fig. **8.60**). Above the pilasters is a meander pattern surmounted by a painted frieze populated with Cupids. Nearly lifesize figures enact the ritual on a shallow, stage-like floor, which projects illusionistically beyond the surface of the wall. The vivid red background, known as Pompeiian red, contributes to the dynamic and dramatic quality of the scenes. The detail in figure **8.61** shows a girl kneeling at the lap of a seated woman while being beaten by the winged woman on the other side of the corner (fig. 8.60). The narrative thus continues around the walls of the room, uninterrupted by shifts in the actual architecture. To the right of the seated figure, a woman holds a *thyrsos*, the phallic staff used in Bacchic rites, usually with a pine cone or grape cluster at one end. In front of her is a twirling Maenad (a frenzied female follower of Bacchus), who plays the cymbals as she dances. The organic structure of her body and her pronounced *contrapposto* show the artist's command of three-dimensional space, which points to the influence of the Hellenistic style.

Although neither the exact meaning of these scenes nor their narrative order is agreed upon by scholars, it is clear that some kind of sacred event is taking place. Its mysterious character is enhanced by the inconsistent sources of light and absence of cast shadows, which is at odds with the naturalism of the figures and the perspectival space. The *Dancing Satyr* (fig. **8.62**) both reinforces and mocks the ritual eroticism that is a subtext of the larger narrative.

A different type of Second Style painting was discovered in a house on the Esquiline Hill in Rome. Known as the *Odyssey Landscapes*, they depict scenes from Books X through XII of *The Odyssey*. The *Odyssey Landscapes* transport the viewer from urban Rome to a distant mythological time and place. They depict large-scale landscapes, with small figures in pale colors framed by painted pilasters. Their perspective is more atmospheric than linear, so that the illusion of depth increases as the forms lose clarity.

Figure **8.63** illustrates a scene from Book X, in which Odysseus has landed on an island inhabited by cannibalistic, dark-skinned giants. They pull on trees, lift up boulders, and carry off Odysseus' sailors for their dinner. Odysseus describes the attack on his men by the Laestrygonians as follows:

> The mighty Laestrygonians came thronging from all sides, a host past counting, not like men but like the Giants. They hurled at us from the cliffs with rocks huge as a man could lift, and at once there rose throughout the ships a dreadful din, alike from men that were dying and from ships that were being crushed. And spearing them like fishes they bore them home, a loathly meal.[5]

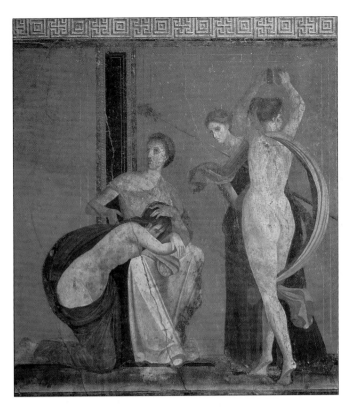

8.61 (above) Fresco from the Villa of the Mysteries, south wall, 5 ft 3 in (1.62 m) high.

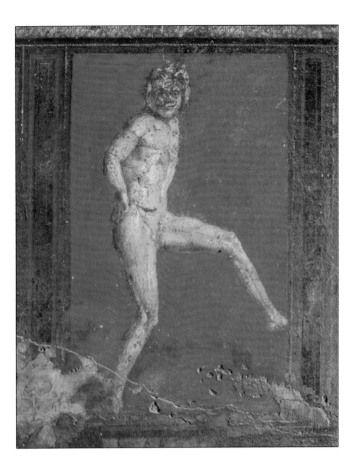

8.62 (above) *Dancing Satyr*, fresco from the Villa of the Mysteries.

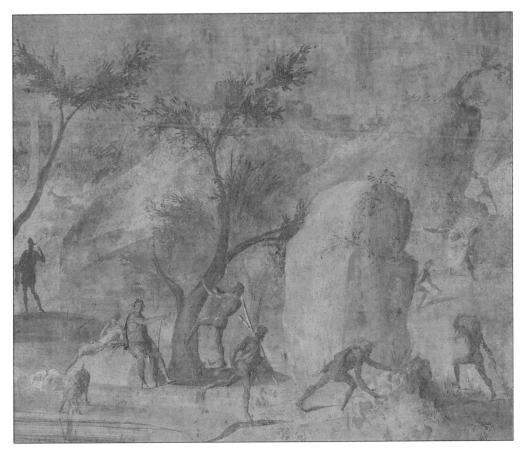

8.63 (left) *Odysseus Being Attacked by the Laestrygonians*, from the Esquiline Hill, Rome, c. 50–40 B.C. Fresco, 3 ft 10 in (1.16 m) high. Musei Vaticani, Rome.

The painted scene, as in Homer's description, is filled with action. It is characterized by vigorous curves and diagonals, which are relieved by the more relaxed figures at the left. The artist's attention to details of naturalism, such as the cast shadows, the reflection of the animal drinking from a pool of water, and the background haze, again indicates Hellenistic influence. But the prevalence of landscape with human figures, like the pilaster frames, was a Roman innovation.

Portraiture was common in Roman upper-middle-class houses, and relief sculptures with round frames (tondos) were used for portraits of ancestors. But painted tondo portraits such as the Third Style *Young Woman with a Stylus* (fig. **8.64**) were unusual. Shading enhances the cylindrical volume of the neck and the planes of the drapery folds. The dome-shaped head is ringed by curls, echoing the circular frame. Formal unity is thus maintained between figure and frame, and yet the artist creates the impression of an individual frozen in thought. The girl wears a hairnet of the type fashionable during the reigns of the Flavian emperors Nero and Vespasian, and the stylus and book suggest that she was literate. More typical of the Third Style is the fresco in figure **8.65**, which creates the illusion of a framed painting on a flat wall. It does not depict distant landscape or narrative. Instead the artist focuses on thin, delicate ornamentation and sets a miniature arrangement of trees, architecture, and human figures against a monochrome background.

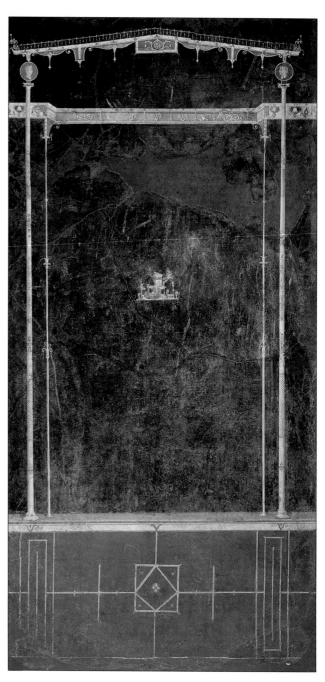

8.65 Columns and pediment with pavilion, villa at Boscotrecase, near Pompeii, late 1st century B.C. Fresco, 7 ft 11 in × 4 ft (3.65 × 1.21 m). Metropolitan Museum of Art, New York. Rogers Fund, 1920.

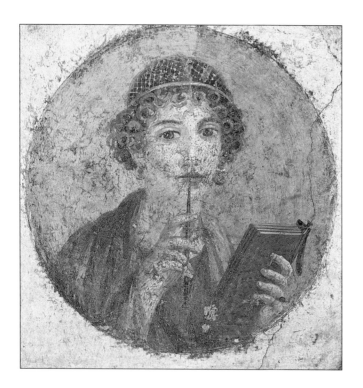

8.64 *Young Woman with a Stylus* (sometimes called Sappho), from Pompeii, 1st century A.D. Fresco, 11⅜ in (28.9 cm) diameter. Museo Nazionale Archeologico, Naples. The subject holds wax writing tablets in her left hand and a **stylus** in her right. Her contemplative expression suggests that she is pondering what to write next.

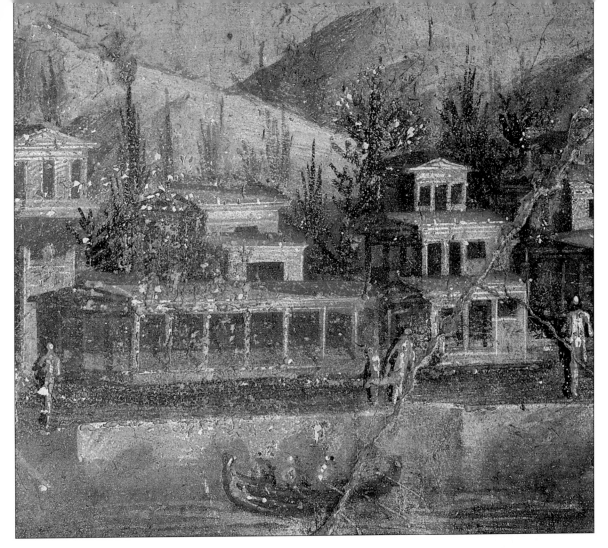

A new development in Third Style fresco painting was the villa landscape, in which the architecture is increasingly consistent. An example from Pompeii, the *Landscape with Boats* (fig. **8.66**), shows how nature and architecture have become of primary interest, with people given less prominence than in either the Roman Second Style or in Greek art. Here the buildings are set at oblique angles to the picture plane, which creates a convincing illusionistic recession in space. Behind the buildings are trees and mountains, the shaded surfaces of which enhance the sense of volume, while their placement toward the top of the wall makes them appear to be in the background. Human figures, notably those in the boat, occupy the foreground.

The still life in figure **8.67** of around A.D. 50 is an example of the early Fourth Style, which combines elements from all three earlier styles. Here objects are set on steps or shelves, whose spatial projection is indicated by abrupt shifts from light to dark. The spherical character of the peaches is indicated by their gradually shaded surfaces. Patches of white on the glass jar suggest light bouncing off a shiny, transparent surface. There is a further implication that the source of light is at the left, since the jar and peaches cast shadows to the right. The **highlights** of light, together with the shading, create an illusion of three-dimensionality on the flat surface of the wall. Such solid, volumetric effects are characteristic of the Fourth Style.

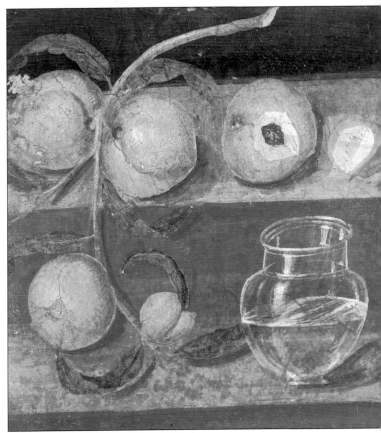

A more complex narrative mural painting, from the House of the Vettii in Pompeii, represents the Greek myth in which the infant Hercules strangles a pair of snakes (fig. 8.68). Hercules was the son of Jupiter and the mortal Alkmene. Juno was made jealous by her husband's infidelity, and tried to kill the infant by sending two snakes to his nursery. Her plot failed when Hercules killed the snakes instead.

In this painting, a toddler-age Hercules is the focus of attention. At the right, Alkmene's mortal husband Amphitryon (who believes himself to be Hercules' father) watches in amazement. Alkmene's reaction to her son, however, is more ambivalent. On the one hand, her pose takes her away from the event as she seems to be running out of the picture plane. On the other hand, she turns to stare at Hercules, her riveted gaze enhanced by her wide-eyed expression. Amphitryon and Hercules are depicted in *contrapposto*, but reversed in relation to each other. The play of shading across their torsos defines the natural structure of their bodies as well as their spatial positions. The figure at the left is rendered from the back, as if he, like the observer, has just happened on the scene.

The architectural elements within the picture add to the effect of depth. A slightly receding row of Ionic columns, like the oblique pavilions in figure 8.65, is an attempt at perspective. The floor of the room is rendered as a horizontal, enabling the viewer to determine the spatial locations of figures and objects. Amphitryon's footstool and the altar behind Hercules are placed so that each has a corner facing the picture plane. By darkening one side of the altar, the artist creates the illusion that both sides recede. The entire scene thus seems to occupy a convincing, if not mathematically precise, three-dimensional space.

Although the painting represents a Greek myth, certain iconographic details refer to the imperial concerns of Rome. Amphitryon is clearly a ruler, wearing a laurel wreath, enthroned, and holding a scepter. Perched on the altar is the eagle, which is at once a reference to Jupiter and to the Roman army. Likewise, the divine origins of Hercules recall the Roman legends tracing the origins of Rome to Aeneas and through him to the Greek gods. Hercules' formal similarity to the Hellenistic sculpture of *Laocoön* (see fig. 6.76) relates the image, like Aeneas himself, to the fall of Troy.

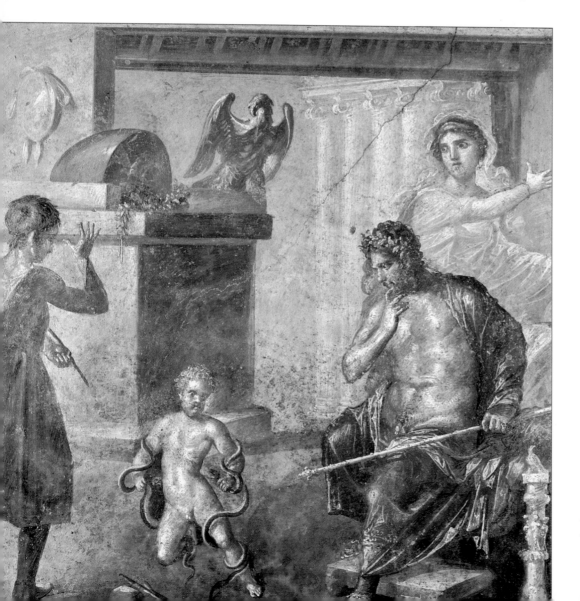

8.68 Hercules *Strangling the Serpents*, House of the Vettii, Pompeii, A.D. 63–79. Fresco.

Figure **8.69** shows the painting with another mythological scene at the right: this depicts Pentheus, the ruler of Thebes, being torn apart and killed by the Maenads, who had become enraged at his rejection of Bacchic rites. Here, Pentheus kneels in defeat, surrounded by the frenzied women about to tear him limb from limb. Both the mythological and architectural paintings in this room have the effect of windows cut into the wall, but they do not carry the entire wall into a fictive distance, as do those of the previous styles.

8.69 View of *Hercules Strangling the Serpents* in situ, House of the Vettii, Pompeii, A.D. 63–79.

Cross-Cultural Trends

Faiyum Painting

Roman and Greek pictorial art, sculpture, architecture, religion, and even certain ideas about politics and government had much in common with each other. But the Romans translated what they borrowed from Greece into their own idiom. Together, Greek and Roman culture have had an enormous impact on the foundation and development of Western civilization. But, since Greece was itself subject to Eastern and Egyptian influences, and Rome had a remarkable ability to assimilate foreign cultures, aspects of the entire Mediterranean world contributed to Western culture.

Cross-fertilization in the visual arts can be seen in a group of paintings produced in Egypt under the Roman Empire. These works differ considerably from Roman

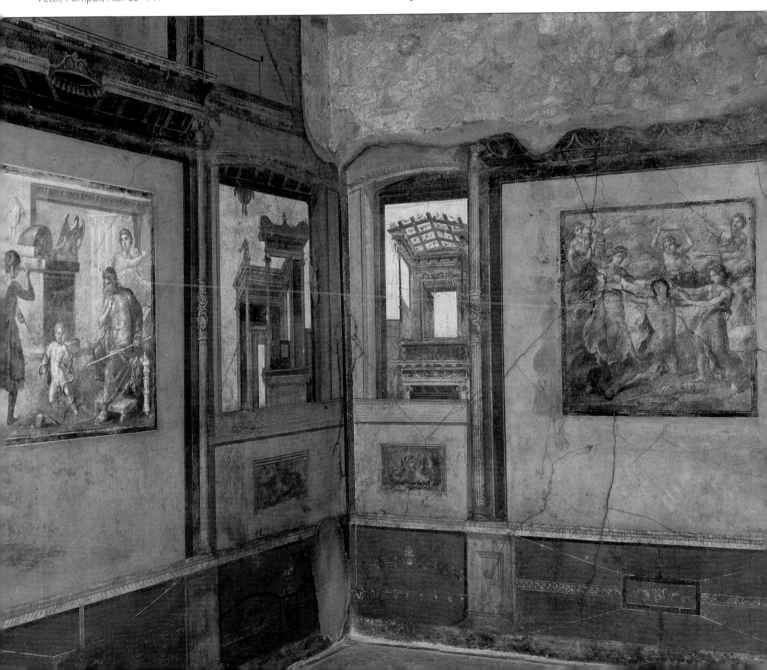

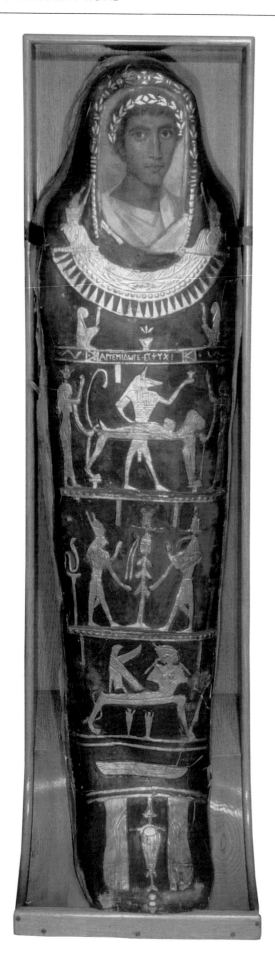

murals, and reflect a revival of vivid illusionism. They are believed to have been related to Hellenistic portraiture, of which no examples survive. Most come from the district of Faiyum, an area about 60 miles (97 km) south of Cairo in the Nile Valley. The earliest date to the first decades of the first century A.D., but the majority are from the second and third centuries.

Egypt had continued the practice of mummification (see p. 83), but the masks which had previously been placed over the mummy cases were replaced by portraits painted in encaustic on wood, and later by tempera on wood. Figure **8.70** shows the mummy case of Artemidoros, a citizen of Faiyum, with his portrait painted directly on the wooden surface. The white tunic over the shoulders is typical of Hellenistic style. The slightly three-quarter view of the face and thick black eyebrows, the highlight on the nose, and shaded modeling of the forms are characteristic of Faiyum portraits and contribute to their realistic effect.

Below the portrait are mythological scenes, including an image of Anubis, the jackal-headed mortuary god of the dead, in the top register. The stylization of the scenes, compared with the convincing likeness of the portrait, suggests that the ability to recognize the identity of the deceased continued to be a necessary feature of the Egyptian afterlife under Roman rule. In addition, the alert quality of the head, also found in banqueting figures on Etruscan sarcophagi, conveys a sense of immediacy that makes the dead person appear to be alive. Artemidoros, like the wax portrait described by the Greek poet Anacreon (see p. 148), indeed seems as if he is about to speak.

During the course of the Roman Empire, a new religion was born. Christianity was legally sanctioned by Constantine the Great in A.D. 313. According to Constantine's biographer Eusebius, Bishop of Caesarea, in Samaria (now Israel), and the first historian of the Christian Church, the emperor was himself baptized. For well over the next thousand years, Christianity was to dominate Western art and culture, and new conventions of style would develop to express its new message.

Rome and Carthage

The history of the Roman Empire includes extensive cross-cultural influences throughout the Mediterranean world and as far east as Pakistan and India. A significant thread of Roman history was intertwined with the North African city of Carthage. Located in Tunisia, Carthage was bordered by Libya on the east and Algeria on the west. It was valuable to Rome as a source of agricultural produce, marble, and shipbuilding.

8.70 Mummy case of Artemidoros, from Faiyum, A.D. 100–200. Stucco casing with portrait in encaustic on limewood with added gold leaf, 67.3 in (171 cm) high, 17.7 in (45 cm) wide, 14.4 in (36.5 cm) deep. British Museum, London.

The native inhabitants of Tunisia, the nomadic Libyans (known as Berbers), occupied the region from the ninth millennium B.C. In the ninth or eighth century B.C., the Semitic Phoenicians from Tyre, in modern Lebanon, founded Carthage and called it New City. To the Greeks it was Carchedon and to the Romans, Carthago. By the sixth century B.C., Carthage was the largest and most prosperous Mediterranean city, and an ally of the Etruscans. From the third to the second century B.C., Carthage was engaged in a series of wars with Rome, which are known as the Punic Wars (from *Poeni*, meaning "Phoenicians"— with its associated adjective *punicus*).

The Punic Wars left their mark on the history and literature of the Roman Empire, and two Carthaginian generals—Hamilcar Barca and his son Hannibal—have assumed legendary proportions. Hannibal performed one of the great feats of military history when he led his army and its elephants over the Alps in 218 B.C. (In the end, however, only one elephant survived.) Two years later Rome had amassed over 100,000 troops, and in 202 B.C. the Roman general Publius Cornelius Scipio defeated Hannibal. In the fourteenth century A.D., at the dawn of the Renaissance in Italy (see Chapter 14), the Italian poet Petrarch wrote his epic poem *Africa* (1338–41), celebrating the war between Scipio and Hannibal.

The Romans never forgot how close they had come to defeat, and Carthage played a significant role in the legend of the founding of Rome. In *The Aeneid*, Carthage is one of Aeneas' most memorable stops on his journey from Troy to Italy, for he meets the Carthaginian queen, Dido, who falls in love with him. According to tradition, Dido was originally the Princess Elissa of Tyre. She married her uncle, whom her brother the king killed for his money. Elissa fled to Cyprus and then to Tunisia, where she founded the city of Carthage. Early sources relate that the local ruler promised Elissa, now known as Dido, the amount of land which could be enclosed by the hide of an ox. Dido had the hide cut into thin strips and arranged them end to end, thereby enclosing a large area. When Aeneas finally leaves Carthage to follow his destiny to found Rome, Dido commits suicide and dies on a funeral pyre. She calls out for a hero to avenge her and her people—that avenger was Hannibal.

The Carthaginian relief in figure **8.71** shows Aeneas fleeing Troy with his father and son (see p. 210). Although the carving is rather clumsy, it reflects Roman influence.

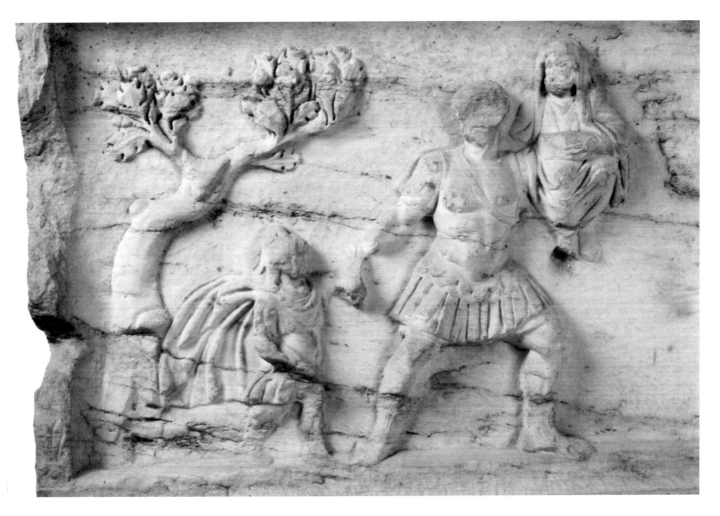

8.71 *Aeneas Fleeing Troy*, altar relief from Byrsa Hill, Carthage, Tunisia, early 1st century A.D. Bardo Museum, Tunisia.

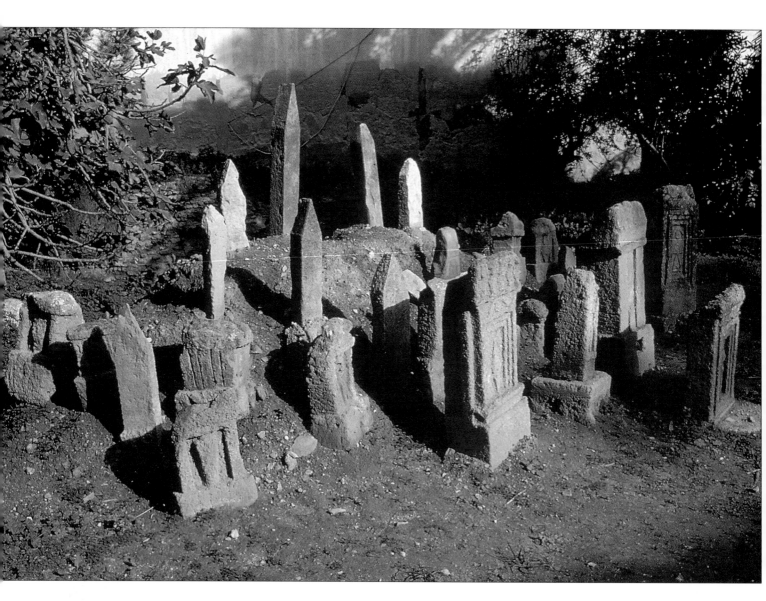

8.72 View of the Tophet, Carthage. The Bible (2 Kings 23:10) refers to the Tophet, a site in the Valley of Hinnon near Jerusalem, where the worshipers of Baal sacrificed their children. In the 7th century B.C., the king of Judah destroyed the Tophet and condemned the ritual of child sacrifice.

The site of Carthage has been known from antiquity, but it was not systematically excavated before the early 1970s, when developers began to threaten the ancient ruins. UNESCO agreed to assist in sponsoring international excavations led by French, British, German, and American archaeological teams. As a result, the historical and cultural past of Carthage has begun to emerge from the mists of legend and myth—much like the Minoan and Mycenaean civilizations.

Dido's role in the history of Carthage, her relationship with Aeneas, and its tragic aftermath are among the legends investigated by archaeologists. The original territory settled by Dido was thought to be on Byrsa Hill, which overlooks the harbor of Carthage. When the excavations

The Punic Gods

The Punic religion was an amalgam of several Mediterranean influences combined with indigenous elements. The rulers of the Punic pantheon were Baal Hammon, creator of the universe, and his female consort, Tanit. Baal was a form of the supreme sky god akin to the Phoenician El, the Egyptian Seth, and the Greek Chronos (called Saturn by the Romans). Baal controlled rain and thunder, and wielded a thunderbolt. As giver of rain, he fertilized the earth and embodied the forces of creativity. Tanit is not a Phoenician name, and may have been originally a Libyan fertility goddess. In ancient Carthage, she was queen of the dead, and a mother goddess associated with the Greek Hera and the Roman Juno.

Other important Punic gods were Eshmoun (from Phoenicia), who became equated with Asklepios (the Greek god of medicine), and Melqart, who was god of the city of Tyre and later associated with Hercules.

were under way, evidence of domestic buildings and a town defended by fortified walls was discovered.

Further excavations have revealed that Carthaginians practiced child sacrifice: there were mass killings in times of stress and sacrifices to appease the city gods, Baal Hammon and Tanit (see Box). Archaeologists estimate that from 400 to 200 B.C. over 20,000 children between infancy and the age of four were cremated and their ashes buried in the Tophet (fig. **8.72**). Burials were in urns marked by vertical stelai, which show the influence of Greek grave-markers (see p. 158). The contents of the urns, in contrast, show Egyptian influence—in amulets, images of the god Ptah (see p. 78), and of the apotropaic eye of Horus.

Figure **8.73** is a Neo-Punic stele with engraved signs and an inscription combining Greek and Phoenician letters. The goddess Tanit is shown in her standard iconography as a triangular body with upraised arms and elbows bent to form a right angle. The crescent moon is her emblem and the sun disk above it is Baal Hammon's. Tanit's sign appears also on thousands of "baby bottle" vessels from the Hellenistic period (fig. **8.74**). The body of the vessel is transformed into a face with two eyes and a nose that functions as a "nipple." Liquid was poured into the "bottle" through the spout at the top. Tanit's emblem beneath the spout is probably associated with her role as the mother goddess.

The art and architecture of Carthage reflect its cultural mix. Roman and Near Eastern ideas and motifs, together with native traditions, inform many Carthaginian works. The mausoleum at Dougga (fig. **8.75**), for example, is a tomb tower, apparently built by a Phoenician architect. His name—Ateban, son of Iepmatath—is inscribed on the monument in a script having both Libyan and Punic characteristics. The Order of the columns is Greek, and they rise, as in most Doric temples, from the top of three steps. The structure is crowned, on the other hand, by the pyramid form characteristic of Egypt. Showing Near Eastern, as well as Egyptian, influence are the guardian animals at the four corners and the apex of the pyramid. The synthetic nature of this mausoleum exemplifies the cross-cultural influences in the North Africa of antiquity.

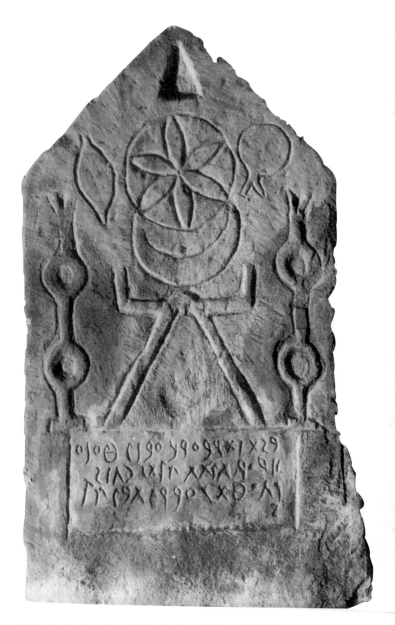

8.73 Neo-Punic stele with inscription and sign of Tanit, from Teboursouk, Tunisia, 1st century B.C.–1st century A.D.

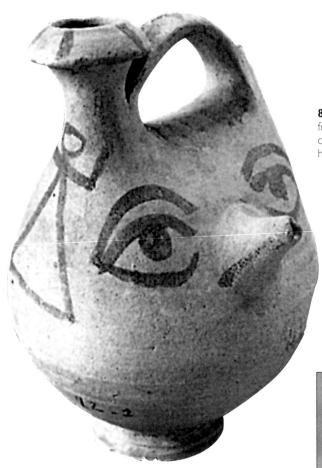

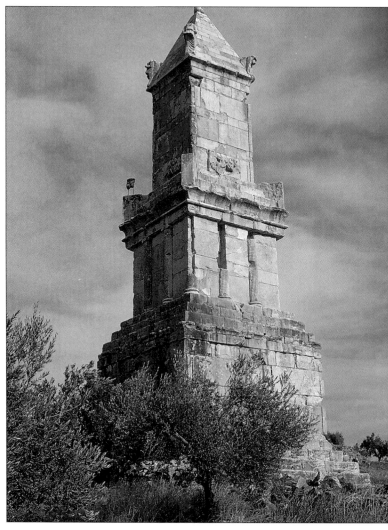

8.74 "Baby bottle" vessel from a Punic tomb, 4th-3rd century B.C. 4⅓ in (11 cm) high. Bardo Museum, Tunisia.

8.75 Mausoleum, Dougga, Tunisia, 2nd century B.C.

Style/Period	Works of Art	Cultural/Historical Developments

500 B.C.

REPUBLIC
509–27 B.C.

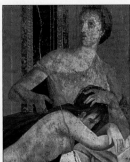

Villa of the Mysteries frescoes

"Baby-bottle" vessel (**8.74**)
Tophet (**8.72**), Carthage
Villa of the Mysteries (**8.59**), Pompeii
Mausoleum (**8.75**), Dougga, Tunisia
House of the Faun (**8.3**), Pompeii
Temple of Portunus (**8.26**), Rome
Temple of the Sibyl
  (**8.28**), Tivoli
Bust of Julius Caesar
  (**8.45**), Tusculum
Villa of the Mysteries
  frescoes (**8.59–8.62**),
  Pompeii
Odyssey Landscapes
  (**8.63**), Esquiline Hill
Villa at Boscotrecase
  (**8.65**), Pompeii
Landscape fresco
  (**8.66**), Pompeii

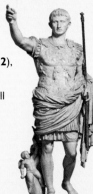

Augustus of Prima Porta

Age of Perikles in Athens (460–429 B.C.)
Etruscan influence in Italy begins to wane (450–400 B.C.)
First Punic War between Rome and Carthage
  (264–241 B.C.)
Carthaginians led by Hannibal invade Italy (218–211 B.C.)
Roman expansion: annexes Spain (201 B.C.), controls Asia
  Minor, Syria, Egypt, Greece (146 B.C.)
Sulla first dictator of Rome (82–79 B.C.)
Slave rebellion led by Spartacus (72–71 B.C.)
Julius Caesar conquers Gaul (58–50 B.C.)
Classical Age of Latin literature (Virgil, Horace, Livy,
  Ovid) (50–10 B.C.)
Julius Caesar becomes dictator (46 B.C.)
Flowering of Latin literature (Caesar, Catullus, Cicero,
  Lucretius)
Library of Alexandria destroyed by fire (47 B.C.)
Caesar reforms Roman calendar; introduction of solar
  year (46 B.C.)
Julius Caesar assassinated (44 B.C.)
Caesar's assassins defeated at Philippi by Octavian and
  Mark Antony (42 B.C.)
Antony marries Cleopatra (37 B.C.)
Julio-Claudian dynasty (31 B.C.–A.D. 68)
Augustus (Octavian) becomes emperor (27 B.C.)

0

EMPIRE
27 B.C.–A.D. 476

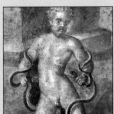

Infant Hercules

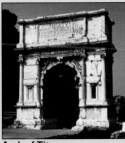

Arch of Titus

A.D. 500

Neo-Punic stele (**8.73**), Teboursouk
Ara Pacis (**8.33–8.35**), Rome
Roman and Imperial forums (**8.11–8.12**),
  Rome
Patrician with Two Ancestor Busts (**8.47**)
Augustus of Prima Porta (**8.50**)
Aeneas Fleeing Troy (**8.71**), Carthage
Young Woman with a Stylus (**8.64**), Pompeii
Still life fresco (**8.67**), Herculaneum
"Alexander Mosaic" (**8.55**), Pompeii
Hercules Strangling the Serpents (**8.68–8.69**),
  Pompeii
Colosseum (**8.21–8.22**), Rome
Arch of Titus (**8.40**), Rome
Portrait of a Flavian Lady
  (**8.48–8.49**)
Basilica Ulpia (**8.13–8.14**),
  Rome
Trajan's Column (**8.36**),
  Rome
Pantheon (**8.30**), Rome
Timgad (**8.7**), Algeria
Mummy case of
  Artemidoros (**8.70**),
  Faiyum
Hadrian's Villa (**8.10**),
  Tivoli
Statue of Antinous (**8.51**)
Bust of Trajan (**8.46**)
Statue of Marcus Aurelius
  (**8.52**)
Baths of Caracalla (**8.20**),
  Rome
Bust of Caracalla (**8.53**)
Head of Constantine (**8.54**), Rome
Arch of Constantine (**8.42**), Rome

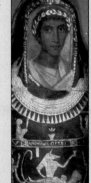

Artemidoros

Death of Virgil, Roman poet and author of *The Aeneid*
  (19 B.C.)
Judaea annexed by the Romans (6 A.D.)
Crucifixion of Christ at Jerusalem (c. 30 A.D.)
Roman conquest of Britain (43–85 A.D.)
St. Paul preaches Christianity in Asia Minor and Greece;
  sent to Rome for trial (c. 60 A.D.)
Great fire in Rome; Nero persecutes the Christians
  (65 A.D.)
Revolt of Jews; Romans sack Jerusalem (70 A.D.)
Flavian dynasty (Vespasian, Titus, Domitian) (69–96 A.D.)
The four Gospels written (75–100 A.D.)
Eruption of Vesuvius, destruction of Pompeii and
  Herculaneum (79 A.D.)
Death of Pliny the Elder (79 A.D.)
The "Five Good Emperors" (Nerva, Trajan, Hadrian,
  Antoninus Pius, Marcus Aurelius) (96–100 A.D.)
Roman Empire at its zenith (98–117 A.D.)
Trajan's conquest of Dacia (101–106 A.D.)
Trajan's conquest of Armenia and Mesopotamia
  (113–117 A.D.)
Dead Sea Scrolls written (c. 130–168 A.D.)
Jews expelled from Jerusalem; Jewish diaspora begins
  (132–135 A.D.)
Marcus Aurelius drives back invasions of Goths and Huns
  (c. 161–180 A.D.)
Bishop of Rome becomes Pope (c. 200 A.D.)
Codification of Jewish law in the Mishnah (c. 200 A.D.)
Imperial residence moved to Constantinople (c. 250 A.D.)
Edict of Milan; Christianity legalized (313 A.D.)
Sack of Rome by the Visigoths (410 A.D.)

Developments in South Asia

The Indus Valley Civilization

(to the 3rd Century A.D.)

In 326 B.C., Alexander the Great led his armies into the northwest corner of South Asia (fig. **8.A**)—parts of modern Afghanistan, Pakistan, and India—then a part of the Achaemenid Empire (see p. 73). In so doing, he was eroding the power of Greece's traditional enemies—the Persians. In the second century B.C. Indo-Greeks ruled to the south and, later, the Roman Empire established outposts in South Asia. Building upon a much older network of land and sea trade routes, the unprecedented territorial expansion of Greece and Rome created new contacts linking the Mediterranean and western Europe with parts of the East.

Transmitting cultural influence in the opposite direction—from East to West—were Buddhist missionaries sent to Greece and the Middle East in the third century B.C. by the Indian emperor Ashoka (ruled c. 273–232 B.C.). Merchant caravans traveled along the Silk Road, the 5000 miles (8052 km) of linked trade routes that stretched from China to Rome by the first century B.C. (fig. **8.B**). From China, they transported great quantities of finished goods such as silk, bronzes, ceramics, and lacquer wares. Wool and linen textiles, glassware, and valuable raw materials went eastwards from the Mediterranean world. As a result of such exchanges, certain styles and motifs infiltrated Eastern art from the West, while others flowed in the opposite direction.

The Indus Valley Civilization

(c. 2700–1750 B.C.)

The valley of the Indus River is located in modern Pakistan and northwest India, covering a vast area roughly equivalent to that of western Europe. Early in the third millennium B.C., its culture developed from a nomadic to a settled, urban civilization. Compared with the Mesopotamian and Egyptian civilizations, which were also centered around rivers, the Indus Valley culture adapted to a wider variety of natural environments. The first of hundreds of Indus Valley sites to be excavated (in the 1920s) were Mohenjo-daro and Harappa, which appear to have been artistic centers. The high point of Mohenjo-daro culture came in the second half of the third millennium B.C., during which time its population peaked at around fifty thousand. In addition to monumental stone architecture, archaeologists found evidence of houses, mostly two stories high, made of mud-brick and of more durable baked brick. The excavations also uncovered sewage systems, bronze and copper tools, large painted vases made on a potter's wheel and fired, and sculptures of terracotta, bronze, and stone. At Mohenjo-daro, as at most other large Indus Valley sites, streets in an eastern

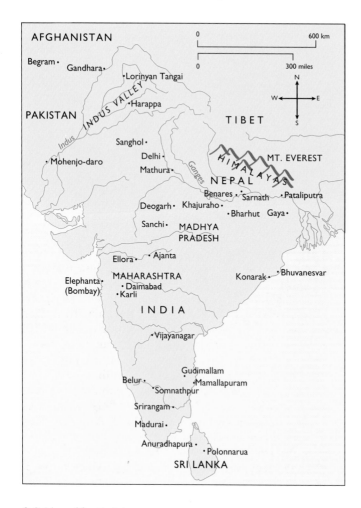

8.A Map of South Asia.

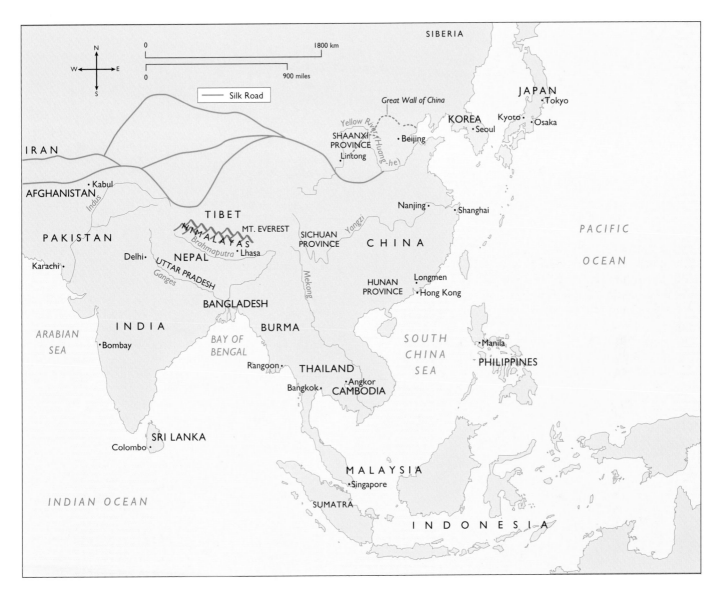

8.B Map of the Buddhist world.

residential section were laid out according to a grid. The ruins of a citadel in the west suggest that there was a need for defensive architecture. It is curious that so far there is no evidence of religious or royal architecture, whether temples, tombs, or palaces. The existence of writing, like urbanization, distinguishes Indus Valley society from other cultures of the region.

Glyptic art, which was popular in Sumer and Akkad (see pp. 57–58), is found in the Indus Valley civilization and to some scholars suggests contact with Mesopotamia. But Near Eastern seals are cylinders rolled across a soft surface, while those in the Indus Valley are square, and held by a knob at the back. They were stamped face down to make an impression. Whereas Mesopotamian seals were indented so that the images they made were raised, the Indus Valley seals were carved in relief so that their stamped images were indented. The

example in figure **8.Ca**—one of some two thousand seals depicting a range of subjects—represents a humped bull, or zebu, standing in a square space with an inscription incorporated into the overall design. The animal's stylized beard and thin, curved horns have a linear quality, while a sense of natural bulk is conveyed through the zebu's body, especially its hindquarters. Such rendering of organic form has remained typical of South Asian art.

Also characteristic is the iconography of the bull, which is often presented—as in Mesopotamia—in connection with human figures. Unique to South Asia, however, is the male figure seated in what seems to be a meditative yoga pose. He is sometimes horned and ithyphallic (having an erect and prominent phallus), which is probably symbolic of his power and fertility (fig. **8.Cb**) Scholars speculate that he may have been a precursor of the Hindu god Shiva (see p. 439).

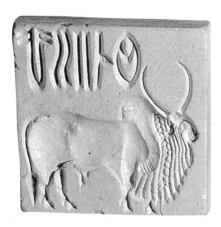

8.Ca Square stamp seal showing a zebu, from Mohenjo-daro, Indus Valley, c. 2300–1750 B.C. White steatite, 1½ in (3.81 cm) high. National Museum, New Delhi.

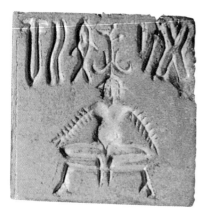

8.Cb Square stamp seal showing a yogi, Indus Valley civilization, c. 2500–1500 B.C. White steatite, approx. 1¼ in × 1¼ in (3.2 × 3.2 cm).

No monumental paintings are known from the Indus Valley civilization. Most of the few examples of Indus Valley sculpture from Mohenjo-daro and Harappa reflect the same full-bodied style that characterizes the bull seal, but there are rare examples of more stylized images. A work such as the *Bearded Man* (fig. **8.D**) from Mohenjo-daro is reminiscent of Mesopotamian art and seems to combine Sumerian qualities with indigenous South Asian forms. Like the humped bull in figure 8.C, it is a synthesis of compact monumentality, stylization (the beard, hair, ears, and trilobed drapery pattern), and organic quality in the structure of the face (especially the lips and nose). The figure's heavy-lidded, inward gaze, however, contrasts sharply with the wide-eyed stare of Mesopotamian statues such as those from Tell Asmar (see figs. 3.12, 3.13).

Entirely different in their esthetic effect, and more purely organic, are the nude sculptures (figs. **8.E** and **8.F**), which have more in common with later South Asian art. The *Dancing Girl* (fig. 8.E) from Mohenjo-daro is nude except for a necklace and arm bands that may have had a ritual purpose. Despite her thin proportions, she conveys an organic quality that derives both from the forms themselves (the indication of bone under the left shoulder, for example) and from the convincingly relaxed pose.

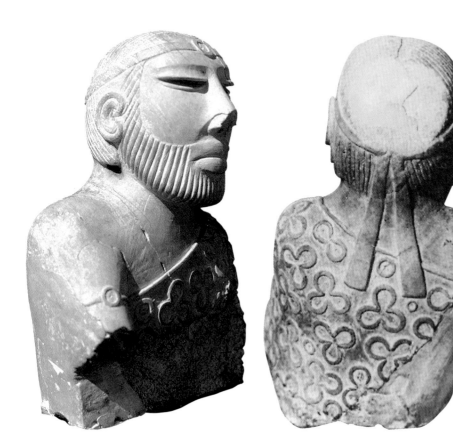
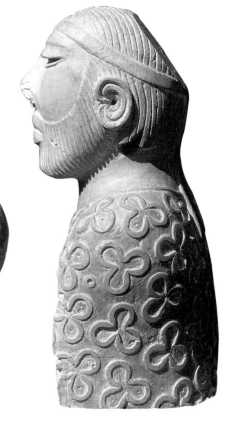

8.Da, b, c *Bearded Man*, from Mohenjo-daro, Indus Valley, c. 2000 B.C. Limestone, 7 in (17.78 cm) high. National Museum, New Delhi.

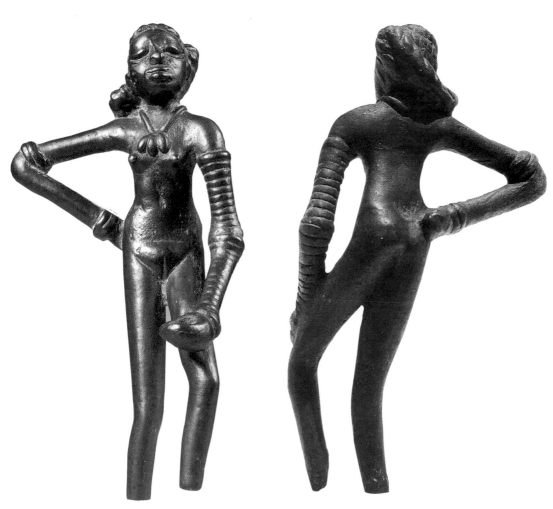

8.Ea, b *Dancing Girl*, from Mohenjo-daro, Indus Valley Civilization, c. 2300–1750 B.C. Bronze, 4¼ in (10.79 cm) high. National Museum, New Delhi.

The *Nude Male Torso* (fig. 8.F) differs from the *Dancing Girl* in its more massive proportions and compactness. Its quality of **prana** (the sense that the image itself is filled with living breath) typifies South Asian sculpture. Although it is less than 4 inches (10 cm) high, the *Torso,* like the *Venus of Willendorf* (see fig. 2.1), has the impact of a much larger work. The original meaning and function of this figure is not known, nor is the purpose of the small circles in the shoulders to which arms may have been attached.

The Indus Valley civilization declined around the middle of the eighteenth century B.C., perhaps owing to a combination of floods, invasions, and political overextension.

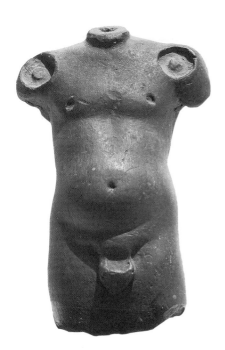
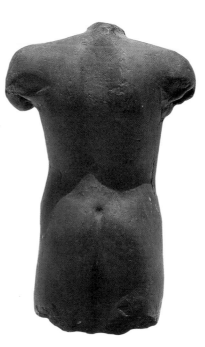
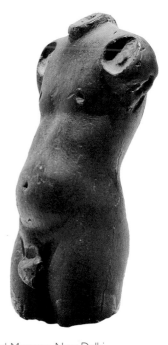

8.Fa, b, c *Nude Male Torso*, from Harappa, Indus Valley, c. 2000 B.C. Red sandstone, 3¾ in (9.52 cm) high. National Museum, New Delhi.

The Vedic Period (c. 1759–322 B.C.)

Around 1750 B.C. waves of semi-nomadic Indo-European (Aryan) peoples invaded the Indus Valley and the surrounding regions from the northwest. There is no archaeological record of Aryan cities, burials, or works of art. Most of what we know about the invaders, who spoke an early version of Sanskrit, comes from their sacred literature, the *Vedas* (see Box). One of the later Vedic texts, the *Upanishads*, describes the Aryan social hierarchy that became the Hindu caste system (see Box). Descriptions in the *Vedas* of Aryan conquests are consistent with the archaeological evidence of fortified cities (citadels) found in the Indus Valley. Likewise, Vedic references to phallic worship by the local population appear to be confirmed by certain images from Harappa and Mohenjo-daro.

The founder of Buddhism (see Box), Shakyamuni Buddha, was born Prince Siddhartha Gautama in the mid-sixth century B.C. Buddha's teachings were a reaction against the traditional Vedic religious hierarchy controlled by Brahmin priests. Two main Buddhist traditions emerged, both stressing the virtues of compassion and selflessness. One emphasizes the importance of breaking

The Early *Vedas*

The *Vedas* (from the Sanskrit verb meaning "to know") are collections of Aryan religious literature. For thousands of years the *Vedas* were transmitted orally from one generation of Brahmin priests to the next, syllable by syllable. The earliest, which date to the beginning of the second millennium B.C., invoke the Vedic gods in thousands of hymns chanted at sacrificial rituals. A second set codifies ritual practice and serves as handbooks for priests. Vedic priests sacrificed to the gods at fire altars. The fire itself embodied the god Agni (cf. "to ignite"), whose smoke carried offerings upward to the other deities. Agni was born when two sticks of wood were rubbed together, and he was therefore a natural product of the very material he consumed. Indra, the warrior god, personified thunder. Varuna was the guardian of cosmic order, and Rudra (the Howler) destroyed the unrighteous. Uma was the goddess of dawn, and Surya was the sun who crossed the sky in a chariot (as in Greek mythology). Soma, a polymorphous deity associated with an intoxicating elixir, was born like Aphrodite from the foam of the sea, and Yama was the god of death.

Buddha and Buddhism

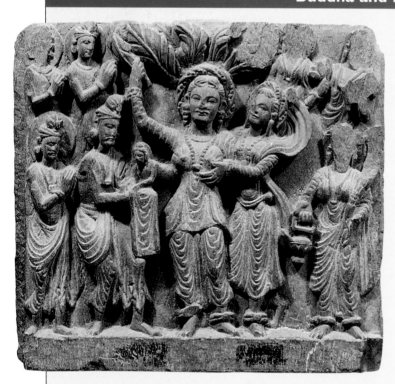

8.G *Birth of the Buddha*, from Gandhara, India, 2nd–3rd century. Relief, grey schist, 15 in (38 cm) high, 16½ in (42 cm) wide. Ashmolean Museum, Oxford. Queen Maya stands under a *sal* tree in the Lumbini Grove and holds one of its branches. She is surrounded by human and divine attendants. To her right, the Vedic god Brahma receives the infant Siddhartha as he emerges from her side.

Prince Siddhartha Gautama is believed to have been born around 563 B.C. in what is now Nepal. According to legend, his mother, Queen Maya, gave birth to him through her side, while reaching up to touch a *sal* tree in the Lumbini Grove (figs. **8.G–8.H**). Siddhartha's father, the head of the Shakya clan, was told in prophecies that his son was destined either to rule the world or become a great spiritual leader. In accordance with his own preference, Siddhartha's father raised his son in the sequestered atmosphere of the court. But at the age of twenty-nine, Siddhartha ventured outside the palace walls and encountered the suffering of humanity—disease, old age, and death. Disturbed by what he saw, he renounced materialism, left his wife and family, and rode out to save the world.

At first, Siddhartha became an ascetic and a beggar, devoting himself to meditation. He practiced extreme austerities while continuing his quest for knowledge. But after six years, starving and no closer to his goal, he ended his fast and adopted a moderate Middle Way. Then, in 537 B.C., while meditating under a *pipal* tree, Siddhartha resisted the seductive temptations of the demon Mara, and achieved enlightenment. Henceforth this tree was known as the sacred *bodhi* ("enlightenment") tree, and its site as *bodhgaya* (literally, a "place of enlightenment"). Siddhartha, having become a buddha ("one who has awakened"), was now known as Shakyamuni ("the sage of the Shakya clan"). He preached his First Sermon in the Deer Park at Sarnath, which set in motion the Wheel (*Chakra*) of the Law (*Dharma*) and founded Buddhism. He spent the remainder of his life traveling and preaching his new philosophy. In 483 B.C., the last great miracle of Shakyamuni Buddha's life, the *Mahaparinirvana*, occurred: when he died, at the age of eighty, the cosmos caused his cremated remains to shine like pearls.

The *Upanishads*

The *Upanishads*, composed c. 800–600 B.C., are literally "knowledge derived from sitting at the feet of the teacher." These are the final set of Vedic texts. Instead of emphasizing priesthood and ritual, as the second set does, the *Upanishads* are philosophical and speculative. They illuminate the inner meaning of the earliest *Vedas* and explore the nature of knowledge and truth.

Individuals undergo numerous births in the cycle of different lives *(samsara)*. In what form one is reborn depends on his or her *karma*—accumulated "credit" or "debt" created by a person's good or bad actions. Karmic status reflects one's position in the social hierarchy, known as the caste system. There were four castes: at the top were Brahmin priests, followed by warriors, farmers, and artisans. Lower yet were those without a caste—the "outcasts." Acceptance of one's proper place within this system leads, through a series of progressively better lives, to liberation *(moksha)* from the cycle of rebirth. *Nirvana* is the union of the liberated individual soul with Brahmin, the cosmic soul.

In social terms, Buddhism can be seen as an attempt to reform the rigidity of the caste system. Shakyamuni Buddha taught the Four Noble Truths as the basis of *Dharma*, according to which life is suffering (1), caused by desire (2). But one can overcome desire by conquering ignorance (3), and pursue an upright life by following the Eightfold Path (4):

1. Right understanding	5. Right calling
2. Right goals	6. Right effort
3. Right speech	7. Right alertness
4. Right behavior	8. Right thinking

In order to escape suffering, Shakyamuni Buddha advocated the extinction of all desire and all sense of self through meditation and spiritual exercises, which his disciples codified. Shakyamuni established the world's first monastic communities (the *Sangha*) and, after his death, Buddhist monasteries proliferated. Missionary monks spread Buddhist doctrine throughout the world.

Mirroring the multiplicity of Vedic deities, many buddhas emerged around the figure of Shakyamuni. Complementing these were wise and compassionate supernatural beings called bodhisattvas (from the Sanskrit for "enlightenment" and "existence"). Bodhisattvas delay their own buddhahood in order to help others attain enlightenment. In art they are identified by their princely attire, and they often flank a buddha. In later periods, the importance of Shakyamuni Buddha was overshadowed by cults of various buddhas and bodhisattvas, especially in the Himalayas and the Far East.

the cycle of reincarnation and achieving *nirvana*, and the other, the attainment of enlightenment for everyone. The latter accepts several buddhas in addition to Shakyamuni, as well as **bodhisattvas** (see Box). The first tradition promoted an ascetic, meditative path to spiritual growth, whereas the other taught that prayer and faith could also be routes to salvation. Despite its virtual disappearance from India by the tenth century, Buddhism eventually spread throughout Asia. The first of the Buddhist traditions was adopted primarily in Sri Lanka and Southeast Asia, and the second in China, Japan, and Korea.

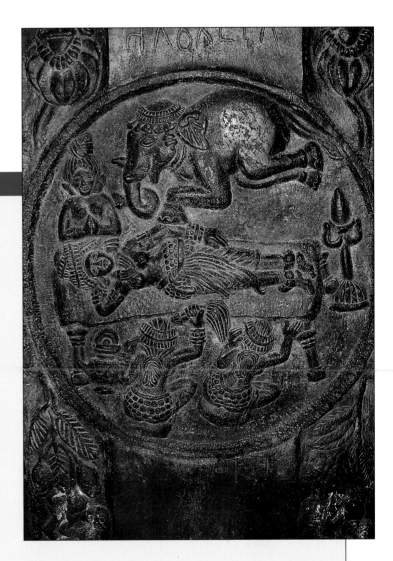

8.H *Dream of Queen Maya*, from Madhya Pradesh, India, Shunga period, 2nd century B.C. 19 in (48.3 cm) high. Relief from a *vedikā* of the Bharhut stupa, Indian Museum, Calcutta. Queen Maya's dream of a white elephant was interpreted as precognition of her pregnancy with Prince Siddhartha. The perspective of this scene defies our experience of natural reality, giving it a shifting quality. We see Maya from above, while the elephant floating over her is depicted in profile and the attendants at the side of her bed are in back view.

Buddhist Architecture and Sculpture

The Maurya Period (c. 321–185 B.C.)

Some eight hundred years after the Aryan invasion, urban culture began to reappear in northern India. The first ruler to unify a large territory after this revival was Chandragupta Maurya, who founded the Maurya

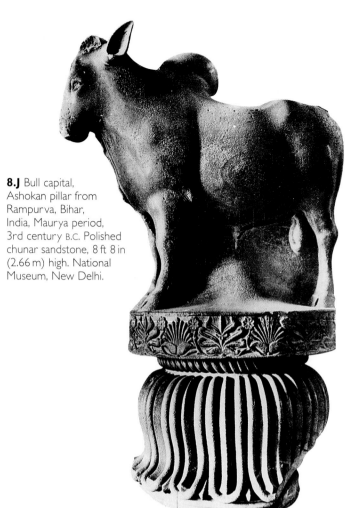

8.J Bull capital, Ashokan pillar from Rampurva, Bihar, India, Maurya period, 3rd century B.C. Polished chunar sandstone, 8 ft 8 in (2.66 m) high. National Museum, New Delhi.

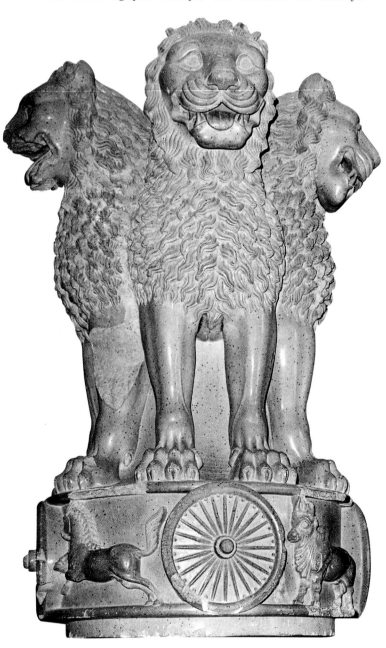

8.I Lion capital, Ashoka pillar, from Sarnath, Uttar Pradesh, India, Maurya period, mid-3rd century B.C. Polished chunar sandstone, 7 ft (2.13 m) high. Museum of Archaeology, Sarnath. According to tradition, the Buddha set in motion the Wheel of Law (*Dharmachakra*) in his first sermon expounding the Four Noble Truths in the Deer Park at Sarnath.

Dynasty in 321 B.C. From this point on, historical records increase. Chandragupta's grandson, Emperor Ashoka (ruled c. 273–232 B.C.), was one of South Asia's greatest kings, uniting almost all of the Indian subcontinent and parts of Central Asia. A dozen years into his reign, at the peak of his military success, he renounced warfare and embraced the nonviolent message of Buddhism, which he promoted throughout his empire and beyond.

Ashoka erected a number of monumental monolithic stone pillars, 50 feet (15.2 m) high. They are thought to have been derived from a Vedic royal tradition of free-standing wooden poles crowned by copper animals, perhaps associated with early tree worship. Like the *bodhi* tree, under which Shakyamuni attained enlightenment, such pillars probably represent the axis of the world. This axis was believed to link heaven and earth, separating as well as connecting them. On these pillars, as on rocks and stone tablets, Ashoka inscribed edicts on Buddhist themes that reflected his political, social, and moral philosophy. Although there is no evidence of a connection between these pillars and later Roman single monumental columns (see p. 232), they clearly served a similar political purpose. Whereas Trajan's Column (cf. fig. 8.36) depicted his military campaigns and stood as a metaphor for both his earthly victories and his future apotheosis, Ashoka's pillars were legislative documents in stone. They, too, by virtue of their height, can be associated with success, and both are crowned by symbols that align the emperor with the gods.

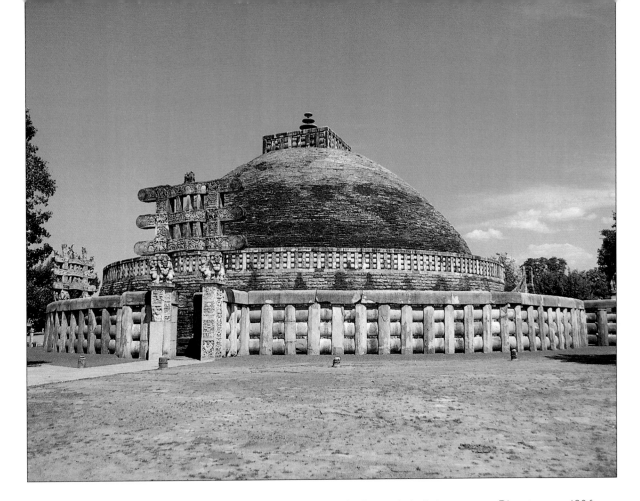

8.K Great Stupa at Sanchi, Madhya Pradesh, India, Shunga and early Andhra periods, 3rd century B.C. Diameter over 120 ft (40 m). The cosmological significance of the stupa's organization is evident in its relationship to the worshiper. On entering one of the four *toraṇas*, one turns left and circumambulates the hemisphere in the direction of the sun (clockwise). In this symbolic passage enclosed by the tall *vedikā*, worshipers leave their worldly time and space and enter the spiritual realm. In so doing, they replicate Shakyamuni Buddha's departure from the world, the *Mahaparinirvana*.

Artistically, the pillars are significant because their capitals constitute the earliest surviving body of Buddhist monumental sculpture. The lion (fig. **8.I**) and bull (fig. **8.J**) capitals seem to continue the two iconographic and stylistic traditions evident nearly two thousand years earlier in the Indus Valley. Four lions joined at the back face outward towards east, west, north, and south. They are rigid and emblematic, their whiskers, manes, and claws stylized in a manner reminiscent of Achaemenid sculpture (cf. fig. 3.39). There are strong similarities to the art of Achaemenid Persia in the general concept of animal capitals as well as in the particular stylizations. The Mauryas apparently borrowed portions of their imperial iconography from the more established empire to the west. In contrast, the bull capital is both iconographically and stylistically South Asian. Like the bull in the Mohenjo-daro seal and the *Nude Male Torso* from Harappa, it is more organically modeled. Massive and fleshy, with a suggestion of underlying bone and muscle structure, it conveys the sense of a living animal.

These capitals demonstrate the Buddhist assimilation of earlier artistic conventions. As in the Near East and Egypt, lions in India are royal animals, and Shakyamuni Buddha himself was referred to as the "lion" of his clan. The bull, as in the Indus Valley seals, denotes fertility and strength.

Both the lion and the bull stand on a circular *abacus*, which surmounts a bell-shaped element in the form of lotus petals (signifying purity). The meaning of the decorations in relief on the sides of the *abaci* has been debated by scholars. But the wheel on the lion's *abacus* is certainly Buddha's Wheel of the Law, which was set in motion during his first sermon. Wheel and lion are vertically aligned and therefore visually linked to denote the power (the lion) of the Buddha's teaching (the Law, or *Dharma*). The *abacus* of the bull capital is decorated with plant and water designs that refer to the fertility of nature. There can be no doubt that this iconography, like the reliefs on Trajan's Column, was intended to proclaim the power and prosperity of the empire. Together with the edicts on the shafts of the pillars, lion and bull also stand for the power of the Buddha's message.

The Shunga Period (c. 185 B.C.–A.D. 30)

The Stupa At the end of Ashoka's reign, India was once again ruled by small republics and local dynasties. One of the latter, the Shungas of central India, enlarged Ashoka's Great Stupa at Sanchi, India's most characteristic Buddhist monument (fig. **8.K**). According to Buddhist texts, when the Buddha died (the *Mahaparinirvana*), he was cremated, and his ashes were divided and enshrined in eight **stupas**, or burial mounds. Emperor Ashoka further divided these relics among sixty-four thousand legendary stupas that have either disappeared or been incorporated into later structures. Stupas thus came to stand for the *Mahaparinirvana*, the last of the four great miracles of Shakyamuni's life. The hemispherical form of the stupa, however, predates Buddhism and, like the monumental pillars, has cosmological significance. Originally, remains or other relics were placed in a hole in the ground, into which a pillar was set, and then earth was mounded around the pillar to prevent plundering. With the development of Buddhism under Ashoka, these mounds evolved into monumental stupas.

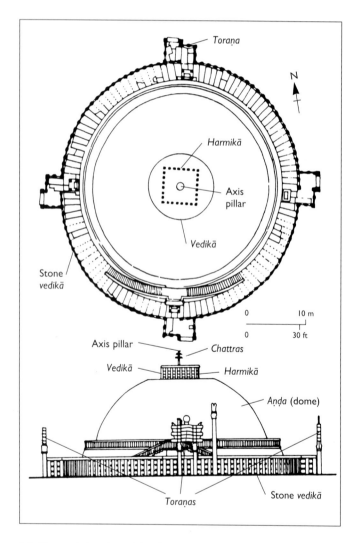

8.L Plan and elevation of the Great Stupa at Sanchi. The outline of the building is a perfect circle, which Buddhists consider an ideal shape. The stupa was designed as a mandala, or cosmic diagram. The square at the center refers to the *harmikā* on the roof, and the small circle inside the square indicates the axis-pillar supporting the *chattras*. The dark outer circle is the *vedikā*, and the four rectangular attachments are the *toranas*, oriented to the cardinal points of the compass and reflecting the identification of the stupa with the cosmos.

The Great Stupa at Sanchi, in Madhya Pradesh (figs. 8.K and 8.L), was begun in brick during the reign of Ashoka, and evolved during the Shunga period. The large hemisphere, or dome, is mainly a product of the first century A.D. This stupa is the largest of three that survive at the Sanchi complex, which is reconstructed in figure **8.M**. The interiors of the stupas were filled with rubble, and presumably contained Shakyamuni's relics.

As is true of Western religious architecture, the stupa creates a transition between one's material and temporal life on earth and the cosmos beyond. The stupa's dome (the **anda**, meaning "egg") symbolizes the dome of heaven. It supports a square platform (the **harmikā**), enclosed by a railing (the **vedikā**), through which a central axis-pillar projects. Attached to the pillar are three umbrella-shaped **chattras**, royal symbols that honor the Buddha. The configuration of the enclosure recalls pre-Buddhist nature worship and the ancient South Asian practice of enclosing a sacred tree with a wooden fence.

Surrounding the stupa is a stone *vedikā* 11 feet (3.4 m) high, based on wooden fences. The *vedikā* is punctuated at the cardinal points by gateways 35 feet (10.2 m) high, called *toranas*. These were added in the first century A.D., and also derived from wooden prototypes. An Ashokan pillar and staircase mark the main (southern) entrance to the sacred compound. The north *torana* (fig. **8.N**) consists of two rectangular posts, on top of which four elephants and riders support three architraves linked by vertical elements. It is completely covered with relief. At the top of the *torana*'s posts, two *Dharmachakra* (Wheels of the Law) support tripartite forms symbolizing the *Triratna*—the Three Jewels of Buddhism: the Buddha himself, the *Dharma* (his Law, or Teaching), and the *Sangha* (the Buddhist monastic community). The architrave sections directly over the gateway sculptures depict Indian folktales, processions, and battles.

The sections that extend beyond the post depict *jatakās* (stories of the Buddha's previous lives as well as his last life as Shakyamuni). There are also many scenes of Buddhist worship and ceremonies, such as one in which Ashoka ritually waters the sacred *bodhi* tree, which stands for the Buddha himself. As is characteristic of early Buddhist art, the Buddha is represented **aniconically**—that is, his presence is indicated only by means of symbols. Instead of being represented in human form, he appears in metonymic form: as something with which he is associated, such as the *bodhi* tree, his throne, his honorific umbrella (related to the *chattras* at the top of a stupa), or a stupa itself. Another sign of Buddha's presence in art is a pair of footprints that refer to his first baby steps. These, in turn, were associated with an earlier tradition in which a god-king encompasses the world in a few strides.

At Sanchi, the *toranas* are decorated with representations of *yakshas* and *yakshīs*, indigenous pre-Buddhist fertility deities, male and female respectively (fig. **8.O**). The *yakshī* on the bracket both swings from and is entwined in a mango tree, which bursts into life at her touch. Such images are the source for the depiction of Queen Maya

8.M Reconstruction drawing of the Sanchi complex.

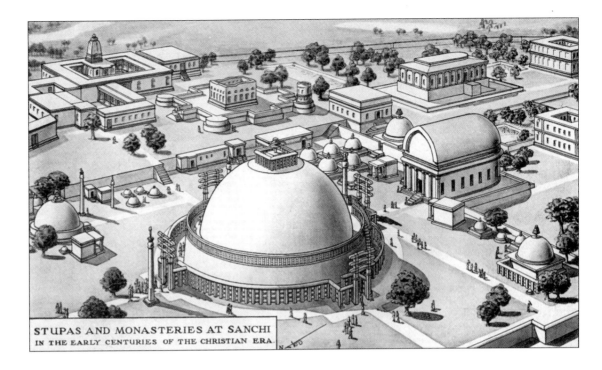

STUPAS AND MONASTERIES AT SANCHI
IN THE EARLY CENTURIES OF THE CHRISTIAN ERA.

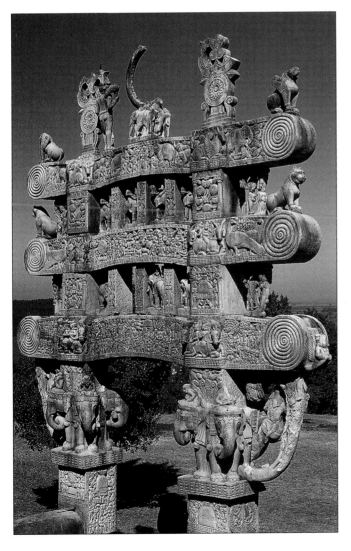

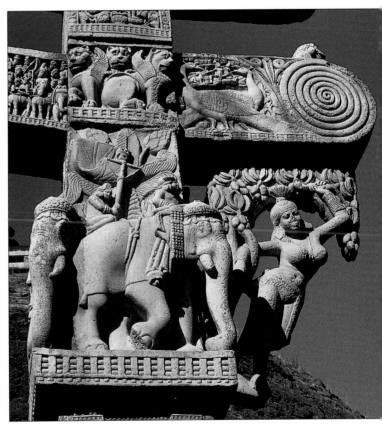

8.N (left) North *toraṇa* at Sanchi, Shunga and early Andhra periods, 1st century B.C.

8.O (above) *Yakshī*—to the right of the elephant—from the east *toraṇa* at Sanchi, Shunga and early Andhra periods, 1st century B.C. The presence of *yakshīs* in Buddhist art reflects assimilation of indigenous Indian motifs into Buddhist iconography.

giving birth to Siddhartha in the Lumbini Grove (cf. fig. 8.G). The form of the *yakshīs* at Sanchi, like the theme itself, is related to the ancient Indian predilection for sensual, organic sculpture. The voluptuous breasts and rounded belly suggest early pregnancy. The seductive pose is called **tribhaṅga**, or "three bends posture." Together with the prominently displayed pubic area, this pose promises auspicious abundance to worshipers.

The Kushan Period (c. A.D. 78/143–3rd century)

During the first century A.D., Central Asian nomads called the Kushans controlled the area now comprising Afghanistan, Pakistan, and northern India. The first extant images of the Buddha in human form date from this period, when Vedic religion still retained enormous popular appeal, partly because of its anthropomorphic gods. As a result, Buddhist artists began to develop an iconography in which buddhas and bodhisattvas were shown in human form.

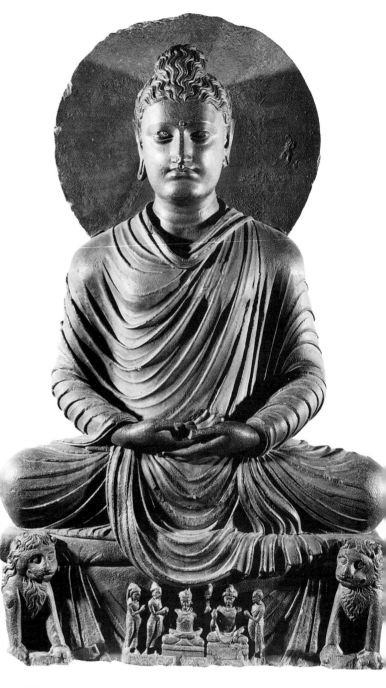

8.Q *Seated Buddha*, from Gandhara, Afghanistan or Pakistan. Kushan period, 2nd century. Grey schist, 3 ft 7½ in (1.1 m) high. Royal Museum of Scotland, Edinburgh.

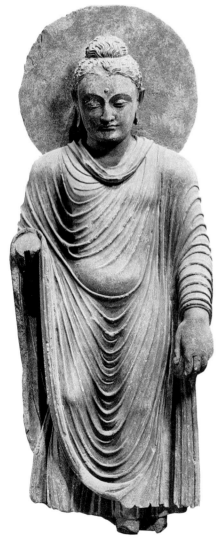

8.P *Standing Buddha*, from Gandhara, Afghanistan or Pakistan, Kushan period, 2nd–3rd century. Grey schist, 3 ft 3 in (98 cm) high. Museum für Indische Kunst, Berlin.

The move toward representing the Buddha as a man in the Kushan period is first reflected in the Gandharan and Mathuran schools of art. The Gandharan region, located in modern Pakistan, was a crossroads of trade routes and hence a cultural melting pot. As a result, Gandharan artists were familiar with styles and motifs from other areas. It seems that both Greek and Roman artists had worked earlier around Gandhara, accounting for Hellenistic elements in Gandharan images of buddhas and bodhisattvas.

The two most typical images of the Buddha in Gandharan sculpture show him standing or sitting, often with a large halo or sun disk behind his head. In figure **8.P** he is shown wearing a monk's robe, whose deeply carved, rhythmically curving folds recall depictions of togas in Roman sculpture. Until recently Gandharan art was seen as strongly Westernized, but the statue's organic quality, with its rounded abdomen, is descended from the indigenous artistic tradition of the *prana*-filled *Nude Male Torso* from Harappa (fig. 8.F).

The standing *Buddha* displays some traditional identifying physical features. Many of these allude to his role as a spiritual ruler, among them the earlobes, elongated from the weight of heavy royal earrings. But the earrings themselves are absent because Siddhartha cast aside his princely jewelry when he set out on his spiritual quest. (Bodhisattvas, in contrast, are shown wearing royal ornaments, since they are not yet buddhas.) The statue's hair conforms to the shape of the head and is formed into the **ushnīsha**, or topknot. This denotes the Buddha's great wisdom and is one of the thirty-two auspicious marks of a buddha or an emperor. On the forehead, the *ūrṇā*, or whorl of hair, is stylized as a small circle. The figure's formal unity derives from repeated curves and circles.

The same emphasis on curvilinear forms characterizes the *Seated Buddha* (fig. **8.Q**). The Buddha's hands rest peacefully on his lap, forming the gesture (**mudrā**) of meditation (**dhyāna**), in which the hands are held palm up, one resting on the other. *Dhyāna mudrā* denotes the intense inner focus through which Shakyamuni attained enlightenment. On either end of the throne is a lion—in keeping with the ancient tradition of lions guarding royal or sacred personages—and also symbolizing Shakyamuni Buddha himself. The face of this seated Buddha, like that of the standing example, is (aside from the fuller lips) reminiscent of beardless Greek and Roman Apollonian types.

Gandharan Buddhist architecture also reflects contemporary religious developments. For example, the second-century stupa at Loriyan Tangai in Gandhara (fig. **8.R**) is more elaborate than the simple hemisphere at Sanchi. Here, a square base supports layered round tiers that end in a small dome. Rising from the dome is an inverted trapezoidal platform that supports a column of *chattras*. In contrast to the relatively plain plaster surface of the Sanchi stupa, the stone masonry at the Gandharan stupa is covered wtih relief sculpture. Hellenistic influence is apparent in specific features such as the Corinthian pilasters and niches formed by round arches.

The degree of Westernization in Gandharan art can be seen by comparison with the indigenous South Asian style prevalent at Mathura, south of Delhi. A *Seated Buddha* (fig. **8.S**) from Mathura, for example, has different proportions: an hourglass figure, with broad shoulders and a thin waist. The figure's taut, *prana*-filled body is fleshier, its physiognomy less Western, and its drapery folds so finely carved that the cloth appears nearly transparent. The hair is not loose and wavy, but instead is pulled tightly into a topknot—the *ushnīsha*—in the shape of a snail-shell.

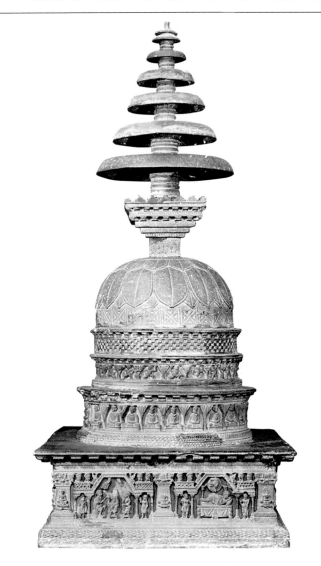

8.R Stupa from Loriyan Tangai, Gandhara, Afghanistan or Pakistan, Kushan period, 2nd century. Grey schist, 145 ft (57.5 m) high.

This representation of the Buddha shows him meditating under the *bodhi* tree at the very moment of his enlightenment. The branches are carved in low relief behind the Buddha's halo, and his facial expression reveals an inner calm. He raises his right hand in the **abhaya mudrā** gesture, which means "have no fear." Compared with Gandharan figures of the Buddha, the Mathuran example communicates more actively with worshipers. Standing behind him are richly dressed attendants with **chaurīs** (fly-whisks), another royal symbol honoring the Buddha. Above are wise celestial beings flying toward Shakyamuni to worship him. Like his Gandharan counterpart, the Mathura Buddha sits on a lion throne, the unusual third lion in the center echoing his own dynamic frontal form.

Having established itself in South Asia, Buddhism spread throughout Southeast Asia and the Far East. During the Gupta period (4th–7th centuries) and its aftermath, Buddhist art in India would undergo remarkable new developments (see "Window on the World" following Chapter 9).

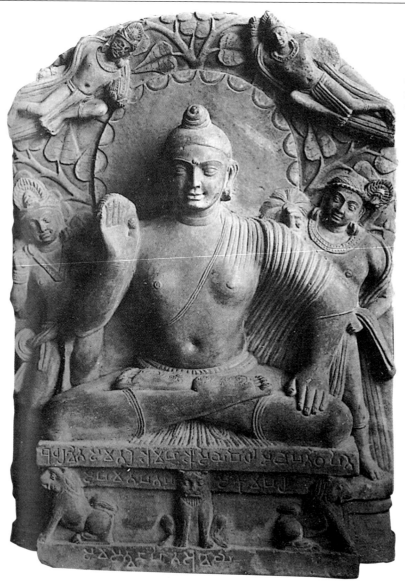

8.S *Seated Buddha,* from the Katra Mound, Mathura, Uttar Pradesh, India, Kushan period, early 2nd century. Spotted red sandstone, 2 ft 3 in (69 cm) high. Government Museum, Mathura.

	Style/Period	Works of Art	Cultural/Historical Developments	
2300 B.C.	INDUS VALLEY CIVILIZATION	Stamp seal (**8.C**), Mohenjo-daro *Dancing Girl* (**8.E**), Mohenjo-daro *Bearded Man* (**8.D**), Mohenjo-daro *Nude Male Torso* (**8.F**), Harappa	Indus Valley Script Etruscan Civilization begins (800–700 B.C.) Urbanization of Indus Valley (800–700 B.C.) Anyan Invasion of Indus Valley (c. 1750 B.C.) The Upanishads are composed (800–600 B.C.)	**Lion capital**
	MAURYA PERIOD 321–185 B.C.	Bull capital (**8.J**) **Bearded** Lion capital (**8.I**) **Man**	Reign of Ashoka (c. 273–232 B.C.) Alexander invades South Asia (326 B.C.)	
	SHUNGA PERIOD 185 B.C.–A.D. 30	Great Stupa (**8.K**), Sanchi *Dream of Queen Maya* (**8.H**), Madhya Pradesh *Yakshī* (**8.0**), Sanchi North *toraṇa* (**8.N**), Sanchi	Birth of Christ (c. 1 B.C.) Augustus becomes first Roman Emperor (27 B.C.)	
A.D. 400	KUSHAN PERIOD c. A.D. 78/143–3rd century	*Seated Buddha* (**8.Q**), Gandhara *Seated Buddha* (**8.S**), Mathura Stupa (**8.R**), Gandhara *Birth of the Buddha* (**8.G**), Gandhara *Standing Buddha* (**8.P**), Gandhara **Seated Buddha**	Height of Roman Empire (98–117 A.D.) Trajan conquers Dacia (101–106 A.D.) Dead Sea Scrolls written (c. 130–168 A.D.)	**Birth of the Buddha**

9

Early Christian and Byzantine Art

A New Religion

Around a.d. 33, during the reign of the Roman emperor Tiberius (a.d. 14–37), Jesus Christ was crucified outside the city of Jerusalem, then part of the vast Roman Empire. The teachings of Christ and his followers led to the establishment of the Christian religion, whose impact on Western art after the fall of the empire cannot be overestimated.

The gradual decline of the Roman Empire and the collapse of its political administration overlapped the development of Christianity, which was a minority religion until the fourth century A.D. In Rome itself, Christianity was first adopted by the urban lower and lower-middle classes, while the aristocracy, for the most part, continued to worship pagan gods. From the second century, however, many educated Romans and some members of the upper classes began to take an interest in the new religion. This encouraged its development and reinforced the emergence of a large, hitherto disenfranchised, segment of society.

For the origins of Christianity we must look to the Near East, which was the site of many religious cults that extended throughout the Mediterranean world, including Rome, during the first century A.D. These persisted into the third century and most combined the Hellenistic influence spread by Alexander the Great with Eastern elements. Mystery cults centered around the Greek Dionysos, the Egyptian Isis, the Phrygian Attis, and many others, while the Persians worshiped Mithras and Zoroaster. Whether an area was under Greek or Roman control, entrenched local customs persisted. Thus, for example, Egypt continued to worship animals and its traditional priesthood still performed traditional rites. In Syria a sacred fish was worshiped by the local population, and was honored in elaborate processions and ceremonies. The west coast of Anatolia was the site of a flourishing Greek culture with a cult of Artemis at Ephesus, of Asklepios and Isis at Pergamon, and of Apollo at Didyma. At Carthage as well, local versions of Greek deities were worshiped.

Dura Europos

In 1922 the little town of Dura Europos, at the edge of the Roman Empire in what is now Syria, was discovered and subsequently excavated. Different types of buildings at Dura Europos reflect the multiplicity of religions around the Mediterranean from the first to the fourth century A.D. Archaeologists found shrines dedicated to Mithras and Zoroaster as well as pagan Roman temples. A Jewish synagogue dating from around 245 A.D. was, despite biblical injunctions against graven images, decorated with painted scenes from the early books of the Old Testament. Some of the figures are identified by Greek inscriptions.

Figure **9.1** shows the west wall of the synagogue. There are three levels of Old Testament scenes and figures

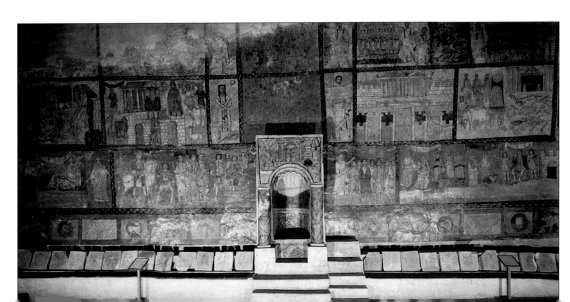

9.1 West wall of Dura Europos synagogue, c. 245. Tempera on plaster (reconstruction). Length of wall approx. 40 ft (12.19 m). National Museum, Damascus, Syria.

arranged horizontally, interrupted by a Torah niche. The Torah was a parchment or leather scroll containing the text of the Pentateuch, the first five books of the Old Testament (Genesis, Exodus, Leviticus, Deuteronomy, and Numbers). Portions of these books were read aloud on the Sabbath during worship in the synagogue. The Pentateuch was of particular importance because it comprises the books of Moses and forms the basis of Jewish teaching.

Below the narrative scenes is a row of more emblematic imagery and panels of painted imitation stone. The detail in figure **9.2** depicts *Moses Giving Water to the Twelve Tribes of Israel*. Each tribe is represented as a single figure with upraised arms, standing at the entrance to a tent. These so-called **orant** figures (from *orare*, meaning "to pray" in Latin) symbolized seeking God and praying to him. Above the well is the *menorah* (the sacred Jewish candelabrum with seven candlesticks) framed by a Corinthian portico. Moses himself is a combination of a bearded Old Testament patriarch and a Roman statesman. He wears a toga, and there is a slight suggestion of *contrapposto* in the folds of drapery defining the bend of his right leg.

In addition to the synagogue, there was a Christian baptistry at Dura Europos, and a private house where Chris-

tians worshiped. By around A.D. 240, the meeting room that had originally held thirty worshipers had expanded to accommodate sixty.

Early Developments in Christianity

Many concepts of Christianity were based in Judaism, which also originated in the Near East. Both were founded on written texts that were believed to be the revealed word of God. They were similar in being monotheistic, and in teaching a code of ethics to their adherents (see Box). As in certain pagan cults, Christianity offered a promise of eternal salvation, but the differences between them were considerable. For example, Christian rituals were not orgiastic, as were the cults of Dionysos, and they did not include animal or blood sacrifices, except in symbolic form. Christ's own sacrifice was re-created in the Last Supper, when the bread stood for his body and red wine for his blood (see Box). This celebration was originally performed by Christ and his followers as part of the Jewish Passover, shortly before his death. He asked his followers to repeat it in his memory, and at first they did so in private dining rooms. It consisted of breaking bread, drinking wine, singing hymns, praying, and reading from the

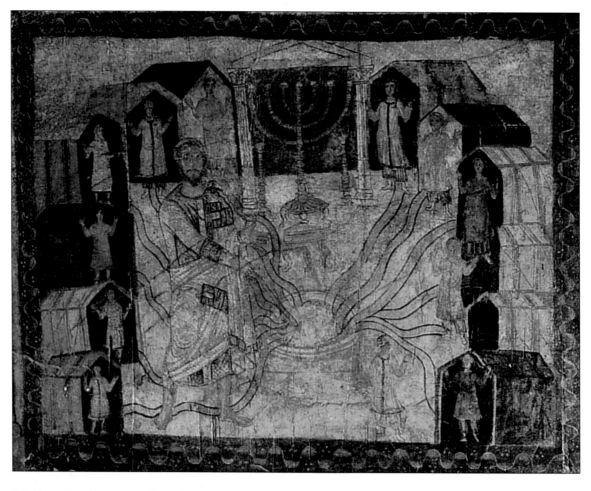

9.2 *Moses Giving Water to the Twelve Tribes of Israel* (detail of fig. 9.1).

Christianity and the Scriptures

Scriptures are literally "what has been written." For Judaism and Christianity, the most authoritative scriptures are collected in the Bible (which is derived from the Greek *biblos*, meaning "book"). The Jewish Bible consists of the Old Testament, to which Christians have added the New Testament. The Apocrypha (Greek for "secret" or "hidden") are Old and New Testament writings whose authenticity is questioned.

Established by the fourth century A.D., the New Testament was organized into three sections: the Gospels and Acts, the Epistles, and the Apocalypse (or Revelation). The four Gospels are essentially biographies of Christ, written in about A.D. 70 to 80 by Saints Matthew, Mark, Luke, and John. The authors are called the four Evangelists (from the Greek *euangelistes*, meaning "bearer of good news"). The Acts relate the works of Christ's twelve apostles in spreading his teachings. The Epistles (or Letters), most of which were written by Saint Paul, contain further doctrine, and advice on how to live as a Christian. The Apocalypse describes the end of the world and Christ's Second Coming as the final judge.

The most important figures in Christian art are the Holy Family, saints, and martyrs. The Holy Family consists of Mary (Christ's mother), Joseph (her husband), and Christ. Theologically, a saint is any holy person, and many were canonized by the Catholic Church; others were canonized by the Eastern Church. Martyr, from the Greek word *martus*, originally meant "witness" and specifically a witness to

Christ's works. Subsequently, martyr came to mean one who dies for a belief—in this case, Christianity. In Western art, saints, martyrs, and members of the Holy Family are usually depicted with a halo—a circle of light around their heads—to indicate their holiness.

An important distinction between Christian and Roman art can be seen in their respective approaches to history. Romans used works of art to record the past—particularly the exploits and triumphs of their rulers. Christian art focused more on the future as determined by the Christian faith. It was important, therefore, for Christians to encompass as much of the past as possible into present and future. One way in which they did this was by a method of historical revision called typology (from the Greek word *tupos*, meaning "example" or "figure"), which paired figures and events from the Old Testament (the Old Dispensation) with those of the New Testament (the New Dispensation). The purpose of typology was to reveal that history before Christ had foreshadowed or prefigured the Christian era. Christ, for example, calls himself greater than Solomon, the Old Testament king known for his wise judgments and temple-building. Christ is referred to as the new Adam, and Mary is the new Eve. Solomon and Adam are thus types for Christ, and Eve is a type for Mary. As Christianity developed, this typological view of history was expanded to include pagan antiquity and contemporary events as well as the Old and New Testaments.

Bible. By the third century A.D., this re-creation of the Last Supper had become the liturgy of the Mass, conducted by a bishop. In the performance of the Mass, also called Holy Communion, the Lord's Supper, or Eucharist (Greek for "thanksgiving"), bread and wine are ritually substituted for the body and blood of Christ. The first detailed description of the Eucharist dates from around A.D. 155, which suggests that by then it was already an established rite. In pagan texts, however, there is very little reference to Christian ritual before A.D. 250.

Christianity, like Judaism, placed greater emphasis on faith than paganism did, and was also more engaged in notions of heresy. The missionary zeal of Christianity was always stronger than in Judaism; among pagans it was practically nonexistent. Many pagan cults were located at specific sites of worship such as sacred caves or islands, while cities had their own gods. Another common theme in paganism that distinguishes it from Christianity was the importance of visibly honoring the gods by various acts and offerings. These were necessary in order to propitiate the gods and appease their anger. In Christianity the notion of divine retribution is primarily concerned with one's fate at the end of the world. Even though certain human transgressions arouse divine anger—a notable example from Christ's life being when he drove the money-changers from the

temple in Jerusalem—Christianity promises salvation to those who repent of their sins.

Finally, Christians differed from the adherents of Near Eastern religions by refusing to worship the Roman emperor as the embodiment of the state. Christian monotheism rejected the Roman and Greek concepts of pantheism, as well as the Near Eastern and Egyptian gods. These attitudes set Christianity at odds with the imperial Roman establishment and made its followers subject to persecution by Rome. In the first century A.D. under Nero (see p. 211) the Christians were blamed for the fires that destroyed large areas of the city. And in the third century, when Goths and Germans invaded the empire, Christians were again blamed and made scapegoats. The worst persecutions occurred in 303, during the reign of Diocletian (see p. 211). As a result of the political liability of being a Christian in imperial Rome, despite its appeal to the lower classes and the fervor of its adherents, Christianity remained an underground movement for nearly the first three hundred years of its existence. Memorial services were conducted in secret underground passages—the catacombs—located on the outskirts of Rome (see Box). Rome was never entirely safe for Christians before A.D. 313, when Emperor Constantine issued the Edict of Milan, granting tolerance to all religions, and especially to Christianity.

Frequently Depicted Scenes from the Life of Christ

Christ's Birth and Childhood

In the *Annunciation*, the Virgin Mary is told by the angel Gabriel that she will give birth to Jesus, the son of God. Often the miraculous conception is indicated by a ray of light, the white dove of the Holy Ghost, or both. When Mary is three months pregnant, she visits her aged, childless cousin Elizabeth (the *Visitation*), and finds her six months pregnant with John the Baptist. The two women are usually shown embracing.

Christ is born in Bethlehem (the *Nativity*), which is celebrated on December 25, at Christmas. The standard iconography shows Mary reclining, Christ swaddled in a manger with an ox and ass, and Joseph sleeping or dozing nearby. In the *Adoration of the Magi*, three wise men, or kings, follow a star from the East to Bethlehem in search of a newborn king. They bring gifts of gold, frankincense, and myrrh and kneel to worship Christ. In the *Presentation in the Temple*, Mary and Joseph bring the infant Christ to be consecrated at the Temple in Jerusalem. They present him to Simeon. God has promised Simeon that he will see the savior before he dies.

King Herod of Jerusalem has been warned that a newborn will overthrow him. Herod decrees the death of all boys under the age of two (the *Massacre of the Innocents*). Alerted to Herod's plans by an angel, Joseph flees with Mary and Christ into Egypt (the *Flight into Egypt*).

At the age of twelve, Christ disputes with the Jewish scholars in the Temple (*Christ Among the Doctors*).

Christ's Ministry and Miracles

John the Baptist baptizes Christ in the River Jordan in the scene of the *Baptism*. The Holy Ghost or God, or both, may be present, usually hovering above Christ.

Christ "calls" his apostles in several scenes; the most commonly represented are the *Calling of Matthew*, the tax collector, and of the fishermen Peter and Andrew. Christ walks on water when the apostles are caught in a storm on the Sea of Galilee. They see Christ walking toward them on the water. Peter leaves the boat and begins to drown, but Christ saves him and then calms the storm.

In the *Resurrection of Lazarus*, Christ restores the deceased Lazarus, brother of Mary and Martha, to life. In the *Marriage at Cana*, Christ is a guest at the celebrations and, because the bridal couple cannot afford wine, he turns the water into wine. When Christ takes three of his apostles, Peter, James,

and John, to Mount Tabor to pray, he manifests his divine nature to them through the *Transfiguration*. Christ appears in a heavenly white light, flanked by Moses and Elijah (the most important Old Testament prophet) and God declares that Christ is his son.

Christ's Passion

Christ enters Jerusalem (the *Entry into Jerusalem*) riding a donkey and followed by his apostles. This event is celebrated on Palm Sunday. Inside Jerusalem, Christ is angered at people transacting business in the Temple. In the *Expulsion of the Money-Changers*, he chases them away.

At the *Last Supper* Christ announces that one of his apostles will betray him. He institutes the Eucharist, declaring that his body is the bread and his blood the wine. This doctrine is referred to as the Transubstantiation. After the Last Supper, as a sign of humility, Christ washes his apostles' feet (the *Washing of the Feet*). Peter objects and is admonished by Christ. In the *Betrayal*, Judas accepts a bribe of thirty pieces of silver to identify Christ to the Romans. He does so in the *Kiss of Judas*, where Christ is arrested by Roman soldiers. Christ is then brought before the high priest Caiaphas and the Roman governor Pontius Pilate. He is condemned to be whipped (the *Flagellation*) and crowned with thorns (the *Mocking of Christ*). He is also tortured and mocked for claiming to be King of the Jews.

In the *Road to Calvary*, Christ carries his Cross to Calvary (Golgotha), where he is put to death (the *Crucifixion*). In the *Deposition*, he is taken down from the Cross and his followers mourn him (the *Lamentation*). When the Virgin Mary alone mourns Christ lying across her lap, the scene is referred to as the *Pietà*.

In the *Entombment*, Christ is placed in his tomb. He is now beyond the confines of natural time and space and enters the part of hell called Limbo (the *Harrowing of Hell*) to lead certain souls to salvation. Three days after his burial, Christ rises from his tomb (the *Resurrection*), which is celebrated at Easter. When Mary Magdalen sees him, she reaches out to determine if he is real. But he repels her, saying "Do not touch me" (*Noli me Tangere*). Later, Christ meets two of the apostles and shares a meal with them (the *Supper at Emmaus*). In the *Ascension*, Christ rises to heaven in the presence of his mother and the apostles. In the *Pentecost*, the apostles are given the gift of tongues—shown in art as divine flames—with which to speak different languages and carry Christ's message throughout the world.

The Catacombs

Christians as well as Jews were relatively safe from Roman persecution when hiding or performing funerary rites in the catacombs, which were underground cemeteries in Rome. The derivation of the term is uncertain, but in Greek *kata* means "down," and in late Latin *cumbere* means "to lie down" (cf. the English "recumbent"). The latter is related to the cubit, an old unit of measurement from the elbow to the tip of the middle finger, i.e. the length of the forearm on which one reclines. Under Hadrian, the Roman aristocracy began to renounce cremation of the dead in favor of inhumation, which was practiced by Christians and Jews. Niches cut out of rock in the catacombs contained the bodies, which were closed in by slabs or tiles. According to Roman law, burial grounds were sacrosanct, so the Romans rarely pursued Christians into the catacombs, where some of the earliest examples of Christian art can be found. After the sixth century the catacombs fell into disuse and were forgotten until their accidental discovery in 1578.

Figure **9.3** shows a fresco depicting *Christ as the Good Shepherd* from the catacomb of Priscilla, dating from the late second or early third century. Christ carries a goat on his shoulders, with a second goat, a sheep, and a tree on either side of him. Each tree is surmounted by a bird. The motif of the Good Shepherd, which had been popular in Roman garden statuary and in the literary bucolic tradition, was assimilated by Early Christian artists as a symbol of compassion. Christ as the Good Shepherd was also incorporated into Christian liturgy, with the priest being paralleled with Christ and the congregation with the flock. The Dura Europos baptistry has an earlier example than figure 9.3 of the Good Shepherd in Christian guise, in which he is typologically paired with Adam and Eve.

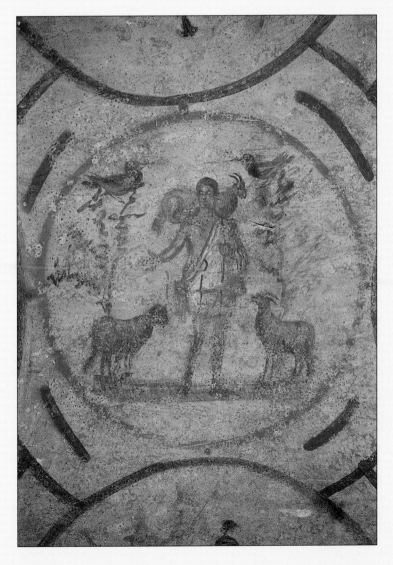

9.3 *Christ as the Good Shepherd*, catacomb of Priscilla, Rome, 2nd–3rd century. Fresco.

Constantine and Christianity

Constantine (see p. 236) followed Diocletian (ruled A.D. 284–305) as emperor of Rome, but not without a struggle. Under Diocletian Rome had been ruled by a Tetrarchy (literally a "government of four") consisting of himself and Maximian (designated as Augusti, or emperors), and two others of lower rank (called Caesars). This arrangement was Diocletian's attempt to defend the weakening borders of the empire from invasions threatened by Persians to the east and Germans to the north. With four leaders, he reasoned, imperial power could be extended outside Rome, and in Rome itself rebellion would be discouraged. But Diocletian's plan failed, for the Tetrarchy actually diluted the centralized administrative power of the emperor, a circumstance that is regarded as a significant factor in Rome's decline.

Although Constantine's edicts and some of his letters survive, the primary source for his assumption of sole power is the biography by Eusebius (A.D. 265–340), which describes Constantine's victory over Maximian's son Maxentius at the Milvian Bridge in Rome. According to Eusebius, Constantine saw two visions before the battle. In one, the Cross appeared against a light with the words "In this sign you conquer." In the other, he was told to place the *Chi-Rho*—the first two letters of Christ's Greek name—on the shields of his soldiers (see Box). After this victory, Constantine issued the Edict of Milan because, according to Eusebius, he recognized the power of the Cross and the Christian God.

Constantine's precise relationship to Christianity is not known, although he clearly took a personal interest in the new religion. In 325, for example, he convened the Council of Nicaea (in modern Turkey), which established the doctrine that Christ and God were equally divine. This was in opposition to the view propagated by Arius of Alexandria and his followers that is referred to as the Arian heresy. Five years later, in 330, Constantine moved his capital from Rome to Byzantium, at least in part because the eastern regions of the Roman Empire were gaining in political importance. It was also there that Christianity had established the firmest foundations by the early years of the fourth century.

Regardless of Constantine's personal view of Christianity, it is clear that he understood its widespread appeal and that he chose to ally himself with it. In this attitude, Constantine can be compared with the Indian emperor Ashoka (see p. 264), who embraced Buddhism several centuries after its inception. Both Constantine and Ashoka took advantage of the artistic possibilities of a powerful new religion, and assimilated them into a new imperial imagery.

The Divergence of East and West

The struggle to establish Christianity as the new official religion of Rome and the resulting controversies reflect the political and religious turmoil of the centuries immediately following the birth of Christ. The title of this chapter is also a reflection of those uncertain times. "Early Christian" is a historical more than a stylistic designation. It refers roughly to the first four centuries A.D. and to Christian works of art made during that period. The term "Byzantine," derived from the city of Byzantium, is used to describe a style that originated in the Eastern Roman Empire, including works made in Italy under Byzantine influence. At first the two terms overlap. However, as Rome and the Western Empire were overrun by northern European tribes and the East rose to prominence under Justinian, the distinction between the Eastern and Western Empires became more pronounced, and Early Christian and Byzantine cultures grew apart.

The geographical separation and political divergence of East and West was paralleled by a schism (split or division) within the Church itself. In Rome and the Western Empire, the pope was the undisputed head of the Church. The Eastern branch of the Church was led by a patriarch, whose power was bestowed on him by the Byzantine emperor (fig. 9.4).

Corresponding to the East–West division were the artistic styles produced by each branch of the Church. In the West, artists worked in the tradition of Hellenistic and Roman antiquity. This led to a proliferation of medieval styles from the seventh to the thirteenth centuries. Eastern artists were more influenced by Greece and the Orient, and remained so. As a result, the Byzantine style persisted in eastern Europe as late as the sixteenth century. Byzan-

---

Christian Symbolism

Christ means the Anointed, Messiah, Savior, Deliverer, and is written in Greek as ΧΡΙΣΤΟΣ. The two letters X and P (*Chi* and *Rho*) are equivalent to the English *Chr* and, as Constantine's symbol, were superimposed and written as

Ichthus, the Greek word for "fish," is an acronym for "Jesus Christ, Son of God, Savior." The *I* is the Greek equivalent of the English *J* (for "Jesus"), *Ch* stands for "Christ," *Th* for *theou* (Greek for "of God"), *U* for [h]*uios* (Greek for "son"), and *S* for *soter* (Greek for "savior"). The *ichthus* and other cryptic signs and symbols were used by Christians to maintain secrecy during the Roman persecutions. Much Early Christian imagery is symbolic in nature and often takes the form of pictorial puzzles known as rebuses. Even after Christianity had become the official religion of Rome and secrecy was no longer necessary, certain images such as the fish, the Cross, the Lamb of God, and the Good Shepherd continued to have symbolic importance in art and liturgy.

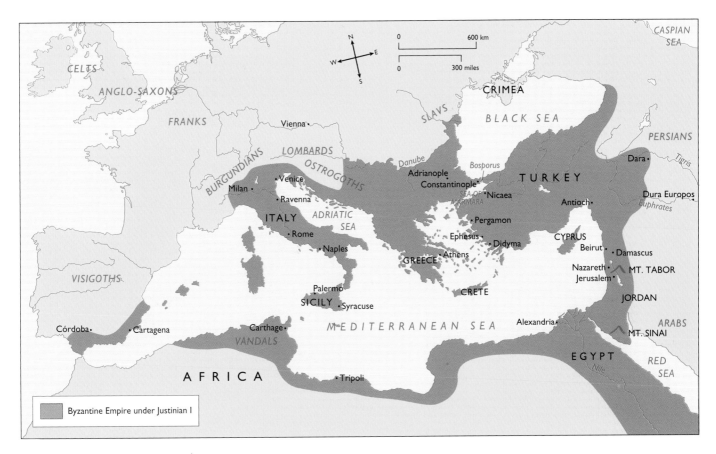

9.4 Map of the Byzantine Empire under Justinian I, A.D. 565.

Early Christian Art

Sarcophagi

tine art also infiltrated the West, especially Italy, and maintained its influence there until the late thirteenth century. Just as republican and imperial Rome had assimilated other cultures, so Christianity and Christian art absorbed aspects of earlier religions and their iconography. Greek and Roman myths were endowed with Christian meaning and interpreted in a Christian light.

A good example of continuing Roman imagery in Early Christian art can be seen in the marble sarcophagus in the Church of S. Maria Antiqua in Rome (fig. **9.5**). The side visible here includes Old and New Testament scenes as well as figures combining Roman with Christian meaning. Reading from left to right, the first character is the Old

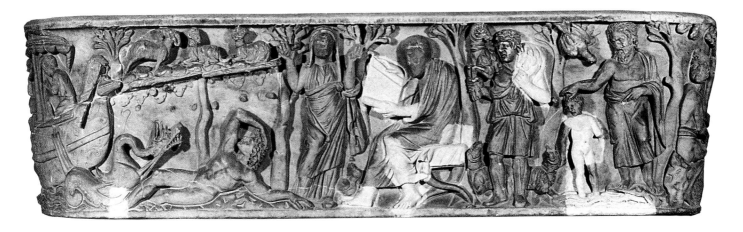

9.5 Early Christian sarcophagus, Santa Maria Antiqua, Rome, 4th century. Marble. Although the Christians continued to decorate their sarcophagi with reliefs, as the Greeks, Etruscans, and Romans had done, they omitted the effigy of the deceased from the cover of the tomb. They also abandoned cremation, because they believed in bodily resurrection.

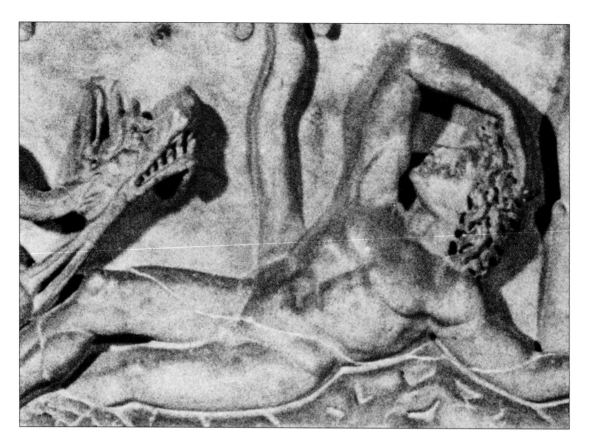

9.6 Jonah as an idealized Classical reclining nude (detail of fig. 9.5).

Testament figure of Jonah, who has emerged from the whale that swallowed him. Jonah's form (fig. **9.6**) is based on the idealized, organic Classical reclining nude, while the whale is represented as a fantastic fish. This story was well suited to a Christian sarcophagus, since Christians interpreted it as a typological prefiguration of the Resurrection of Christ. Just as Jonah spent three days inside the whale, so Christ was entombed for three days before his Resurrection. An Early Christian viewer would have recognized the implications of this iconography as a metaphor for the resurrection of the person buried in the sarcophagus.

To the right of Jonah on the sarcophagus are two Christian transformations of a Greco-Roman poet and his muse. The seated poet wears a Roman toga, but is shown as a Christian poring over a religious text. The muse is also in Classical dress. She stands with her arms raised in a gesture that combines prayer and mourning with a visual reference to Christ's Cross. Spreading out from behind her palms are leafy tree branches, a reminder that the Cross was made of wood. Indeed, trees have replaced columns as architectural dividers between scenes. Because of their relationship to the wood of the Cross, trees were to become a central motif in Christian art.

Next on the right is the Good Shepherd with a sheep on his shoulders. At the far right, a large, bearded John the Baptist stands on the bank of the River Jordan (indicated by wavy lines) and baptizes a small, nude Christ. In the upper left corner of the scene hovers the dove of the Holy Ghost, a traditional element in the iconography of Christ's Baptism. This is another appropriate scene for a sarcophagus because baptism signifies rebirth into the Christian faith, and thus salvation. These themes—baptism as initiation into the faith and hence into a community—were important aspects of the Early Christian movement.

The opposition of the Baptism of Christ on one side of the sarcophagus and Jonah and the whale on the other demonstrates what was to become a traditional typological pairing of left and right in Christian art. This associates the old, or pre-Christian, era with the left, and the new, Christian, era with the right. Such pairing was extended to include standard notions of good and evil, dualities such as light and dark, and so forth. (The negative implications of "left" are contained in the Latin equivalent *sinister*, and survive in the later development of the English word "sinister," which implies a threat of evil.)

Basilicas

The Early Christians worshiped in private homes until the early fourth century. But when Constantine issued the Edict of Milan in A.D. 313, they were free to construct places of worship. From that point on, Christianity was legally protected from persecution, and soon became the official religion of the Roman Empire. New buildings were needed to accommodate the large and ever-growing Christian community. Unlike Greek and Roman temples, whose main purpose was to house the statue of a god, Christian churches were designed so that crowds of believers could gather together for worship. With the active support of Constantine, many churches were constructed in very few years—in Constantinople (the name Constantine had given to Byzantium; it is now Istanbul), in Italy, in the Holy Land, and elsewhere in the Roman Empire. Christian churches were modeled on the Roman basilica (see p. 219) because of the need for space. Such Early Christian basilicas became the basis for church architecture in western Europe.

None of the early Christian basilicas has survived in its original form, but an accurate floor plan of Old Saint Peter's exists (fig. **9.7**), from which a diagram of its nave has been reconstructed (fig. **9.8**; see Box). The architectural design of the Christian basilica conformed to the requirements of Christian ritual and to the role of the altar, where the Mass was performed, as its focal point. The movable communion table used in Christian meeting places before 313 was replaced by a fixed altar that was both visible and accessible to worshipers. Both altar and apse were usually at the eastern end, and the **narthex** (or vestibule) at the western entrance became standard in later churches.

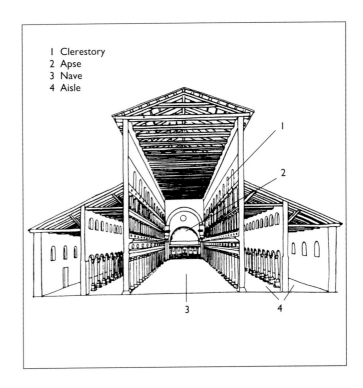

1 Clerestory
2 Apse
3 Nave
4 Aisle

9.8 Reconstruction diagram of the nave of Old Saint Peter's Basilica. Old Saint Peter's is similar to the pagan or secular basilica of pre-Christian Rome in having a long nave flanked by side aisles, clerestory windows on each side, an apse, and a wooden **gable** roof. Unlike pagan basilicas, which typically had an apse at each end, Old Saint Peter's had a single one opposite the entrance. The whole building was demolished in the 16th century when work on the New Saint Peter's began.

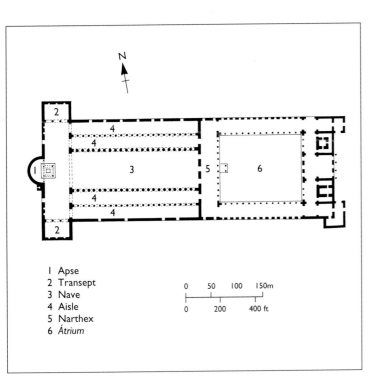

1 Apse
2 Transept
3 Nave
4 Aisle
5 Narthex
6 *Atrium*

0   50   100   150m

0   200   400 ft

9.7 Plan of Old Saint Peter's Basilica, Rome, 333–390. Interior approx. 368 ft (112 m) long. Old Saint Peter's was the largest Constantinian church and became the prototype for later churches. Besides being a place of worship, it was the saint's **martyrium** (a building over the grave of a martyr)—his grave was under a marble canopy in the apse.

Saint Peter

Saint Peter was Christ's first apostle. In Matthew 16:13–20, Christ gives Peter the keys to heaven with the words, "On this rock will I build my Church." That statement became the basis for the pope's authority, although interpretations differ as to whether "rock" refers to Peter or to his faith. The name Peter comes from the Greek *petros* (meaning "rock"), from which comes the English word "petrify," meaning "turn to stone." Rock is also a metaphor for something strong and lasting, as in "solid as a rock" or "Rock of Ages," and here denotes the solid and enduring character of faith. The infinite power of God is also reflected in the phase from the Old Testament Book of Psalms, "God is my rock."

Saint Peter was the first bishop of Rome. Since that office later became the papacy, he is considered to have been the first pope. The basilica of Old Saint Peter's became the prototypical papal church, although it was in fact an exception to the traditional Christian orientation of churches toward the east and was initially built as a pilgrimage site and covered cemetery. During the Renaissance, Saint Peter's was rebuilt by several architects (see Vol. II), and it is still the seat of papal power today.

The altar's location at the eastern end of the basilica served a symbolic as well as a practical function. It generally supported a crucifix with the image of Christ on the Cross (see Box) turned to face the congregation. As Christ's Crucifixion took place in the east (Jerusalem), Christian basilicas and most later churches are oriented with the altar in the east. According to tradition, Christ was crucified facing west, and therefore the cross on the altar usually faces the main western entrance of the church building.

Another symbolic aspect of church design was the new use of the apse. In the Roman basilicas, apses had often contained statues of emperors and were also the location of legal proceedings. In Early Christian apses, therefore, the image of Christ as Judge was particularly appropriate. It referred both to the Roman law courts and to the Christian belief in a Last Judgment when Christ determines the eternal fate of each human soul.

An important new feature in Old Saint Peter's was the addition of a **transept**. This consisted of two transverse spaces, or cross-arms, placed at right angles to the nave, which separated the apse from the nave. The transept provided extra space for the congregation and isolated the clergy from the main body of the church. With the transept, the building forms the shape of a cross, hence the adjective **cruciform** to describe basilicas with this feature.

The altar and apse at Old Saint Peter's were framed by a huge triumphal arch, which was a regular architectural element of Early Christian basilicas. The architects thus transformed the meaning of the Roman triumphal arch from the emperor's triumph to that of Christ.

The exterior of Old Saint Peter's, and of similar churches, was plain brick. The interior, on the other hand, was richly decorated with mosaics, frescoes, and marble columns. The fragmentary mosaic of *Christus-Sol* (Christ as Sun) of around A.D. 250 is from the vault of the necropolis under Old Saint Peter's, and is a good example of the syncretistic character of Early Christian iconography (fig. **9.10**): the vines of Dionysos, generally associated with the ritual drunken orgies of that god's festivals, have become the True Vine of Christ. The latter came to symbolize the Church body, based on Christ's statement: "I am the vine, you are the branches." The pagan sun god, Sol/Apollo, is merged with Christ-as-Sun. The arms of the Cross and rays of light emanate from his head; he holds an orb, symbolizing the world over which he has dominion, and is accompanied by two horses pulling a chariot (indicated by the wheel). Another feature of this image is the implied association of the Roman emperor with a god, but here his pagan apotheosis is superceded by Christian resurrection.

The function of such decorations in Christian buildings was not only to exalt the deity, but also to teach and inspire worshipers. Unlike Classical Greek temples, which were designed to be seen mainly from the exterior, and which were intended to house a god's statue, Early Christian churches were meant to be seen and experienced from both inside and outside.

The Cross

The Cross is the main symbol of the Christian religion (fig. **9.9**). Its principal representations are: (1) the *crux immissa*, known as the **Latin** (or Long) **cross**, whose base arm is longer than the other three (the one most familiar to Western Christians); (2) the *crux quadrata*, or **Greek cross**, with four arms of equal length; (3) the *crux commissa*, known as Saint Anthony's cross or the Tau cross (after the Greek letter); and (4) the *crux decussata* (named after the **decussis**, or Latin numeral ten), known as Saint Andrew's cross. It is generally believed that Christ was crucified on a Latin cross, although some think it was a Tau cross.

Derivations from these types are (5) the Russian cross, (6) the Papal cross, and (7) the Celtic cross. The pre-Christian *crux ansata* (8), or *Ankh* cross—originally an Egyptian hieroglyphic symbol of life (see p. 82)—was also adapted in the Christian era.

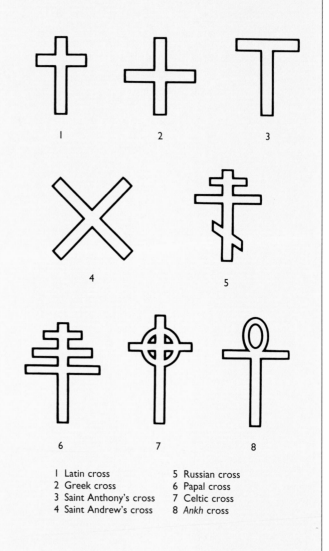

I Latin cross	5 Russian cross
2 Greek cross	6 Papal cross
3 Saint Anthony's cross	7 Celtic cross
4 Saint Andrew's cross	8 *Ankh* cross

9.9 Diagram of crosses.

Centrally Planned Buildings

Another type of structure favored by the Early Christians was the centrally planned building, which could be round or polygonal. It was probably developed from the Roman baths, and associated with the ritual of baptism. Such structures radiated from a central point and were surmounted by a dome. Less suitable for big congregations, these buildings were used mainly as *martyria* (buildings holding the remains of a martyr), baptistries (for performing baptisms), or mausolea (large architectural tombs). Centrally planned churches contained a central altar or a tomb and a cylindrical core with clerestory windows. A circular barrel-vaulted passage, or ambulatory (from the Latin *ambulare*, meaning "to walk"), ran between the central space and the exterior walls.

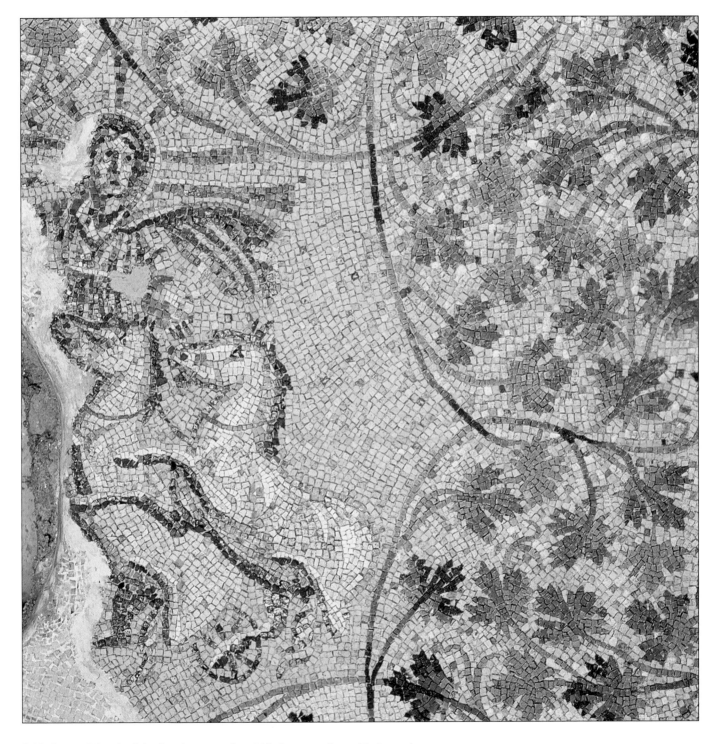

9.10 *Christus-Sol*, under Saint Peter's necropolis, mid-3rd century, Rome. Vault mosaic.

Santa Costanza

The martyrium of Santa Costanza (fig. **9.11**) was built just outside the walls of Rome for Constantine's daughter Constantina, who died in 354. Her sarcophagus was placed opposite the door, so that it was in the visitor's direct line of vision on entering the building. The circular plan includes an inner colonnade of paired columns, separating the central space from the ambulatory and supporting round arches (fig. **9.12**). Composite capitals contain both the Ionic volute and the Corinthian acanthus leaves. The center of the building consists of a tall, cylindrical space surmounted by a dome. Over the ambulatory, the barrel vaults are decorated with mosaics (see Box), again illustrating the syncretistic assimilation of Classical themes by Christian artists. Figure **9.13** shows a detail of the Cupid and Psyche figures, which were reinterpreted by Christian authors as an allegory of the relationship between body (Cupid) and soul (Psyche).

Galla Placidia

The symmetrical cruciform mausoleum of the Empress Galla Placidia (c. 390–450) in Ravenna (see below) was built almost a century after the martyrium of Santa Costanza. Its exterior (fig. **9.14**) is of plain brick, but the four arms are varied by **blind niches** (in which there is only a slight recess in the wall) with round arches, a continuous cornice, and four pediments. Inside each arm is a vault, and the taller central crossing is surmounted by a dome. Spectacular mosaics decorate the inner walls and ceiling, and their iconography, which is heavily imbued with sepulchral themes, attests to the piety of Galla Placidia. Figure **9.15** is a view of a niche showing two apostles in togas who raise their right hands in the manner of Roman senators. Flanking a fountain are two doves symbolizing Christian souls who drink the baptismal water of eternal life. Below, the *Saint Lawrence* mosaic depicts the saint approaching the gridiron over a bed of fiery coals on

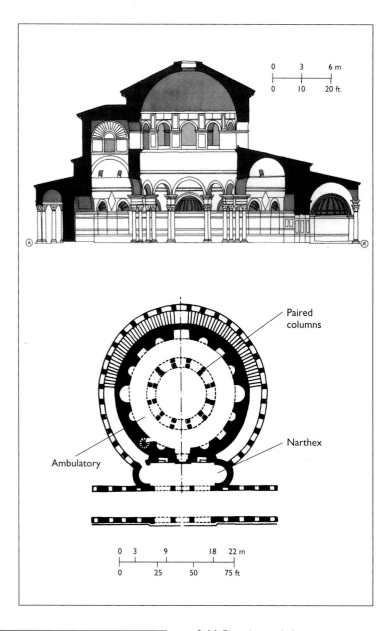

Paired columns

Narthex

Ambulatory

9.11 Elevation and plan (halved) of the martyrium of Santa Costanza, Rome, c. 350.

Mosaic Technique

Unlike Hellenistic mosaic, made by arranging pebbles on the floor, Christian mosaic was made by adapting the Roman method of embedding **tesserae** into wet cement or plaster. *Tesserae* (from the Greek word meaning "squares" or "groupings of four") are more or less regular small squares and rectangles cut from colored stone or glass. Sometimes rounded shapes were used. The gold *tesserae* of the Byzantine style were made by pressing a square of gold leaf between two pieces of cut glass.

The term "mosaic" comes from the same word stem as "museum," a place to house works of art, and "muse," someone—usually a woman—who inspires an artist to create. When we muse about something, we ponder it in order to open our minds to new sources of inspiration. "Music" is also from the same word stem as mosaic.

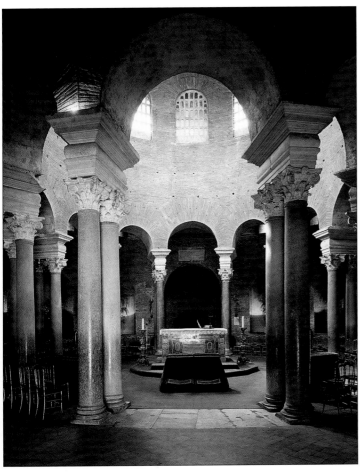

9.12 (above) Interior of Santa Costanza, Rome, c. 350.

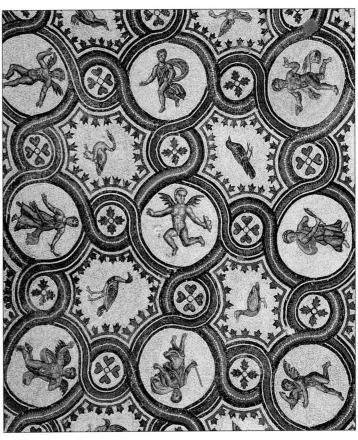

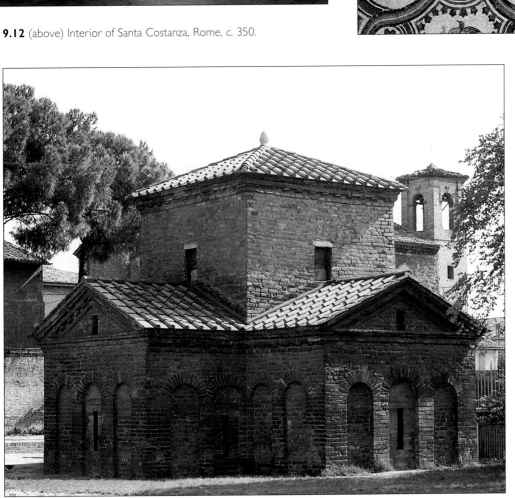

9.13 (above) The ambulatory ceiling of Santa Costanza, Rome, c. 350. Mosaic.

9.14 Exterior of the mausoleum of Galla Placidia, Ravenna, c. 425–426. Galla Placidia was the daughter of Emperor Theodosius I. She was abducted by Alaric the Goth in 410 when his army defeated Rome. Four years later, she married the Goth King Ataulf, who died in 415. Galla Placidia then returned to her Christian family in Constantinople. When her son, Valerian III, was proclaimed emperor, she became regent and remained empress for twenty-five years—from 425 to 450.

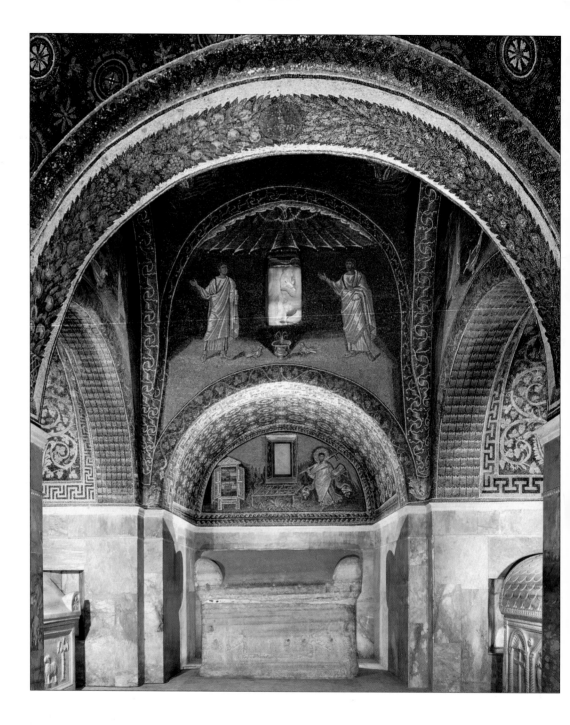

9.15 Interior of the mausoleum of Galla Placidia showing niche with two apostles (above) and the *Saint Lawrence* mosaic (below), Ravenna, c. 425–426.

which he was martyred. The rich, dark blue ceiling represents the dome of heaven, blanketed with brightly lit stars (fig. **9.17**).

Over the entrance is a large lunette (the semicircular wall surface) containing a mosaic of *Christ as the Good Shepherd* (fig. **9.16**). He is surrounded by six sheep, one of which he caresses lightly under the chin. His shepherd's crook has been replaced by a cruciform martyr's staff, which alludes to his own death by crucifixion. Likewise, Christ's robe of purple and gold is a sign of his assimilation of the emperor's royal status, as well as of his future as King of Heaven. He sits on a rock, which is divided into three steps, evoking both the Trinity (the number 3) and the role of Saint Peter (the rock) in establishing the Church. The landscape setting, Christ's *contrapposto*, the shading and foreshortening of the sheep, and their cast shadows indicate the continuation of Hellenistic natural-

ism and its assimilation into Christian art. Figure **9.18** shows a detail of geometric design that reveals the artist's delight in illusionism. But in the course of the next century, these naturalistic and illusionistic qualities would diminish, giving way to a flattening of space and an increase of spirituality in art.

Justinian and the Byzantine Style

During the fifth century, the western part of the Roman Empire was overrun by Germanic tribes from northern Europe. The Ostrogoths occupied the Italian port city of Ravenna until it was recaptured during the reign of the Byzantine emperor Justinian in A.D. 540. Under Justinian, the Eastern Empire rose to political and artistic prominence.

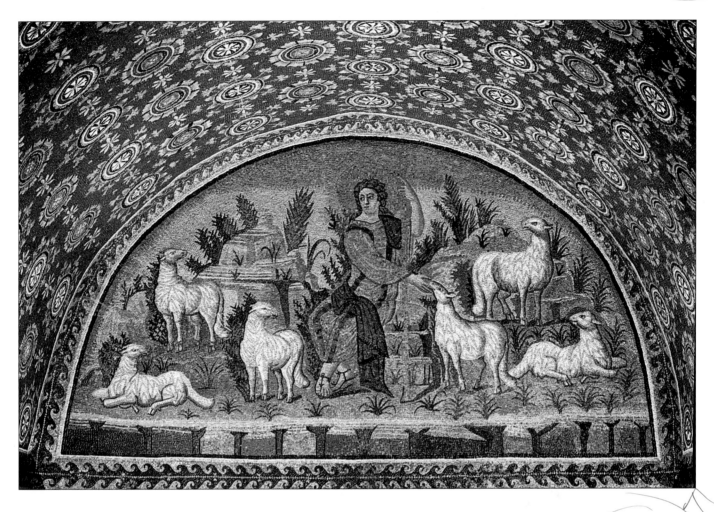

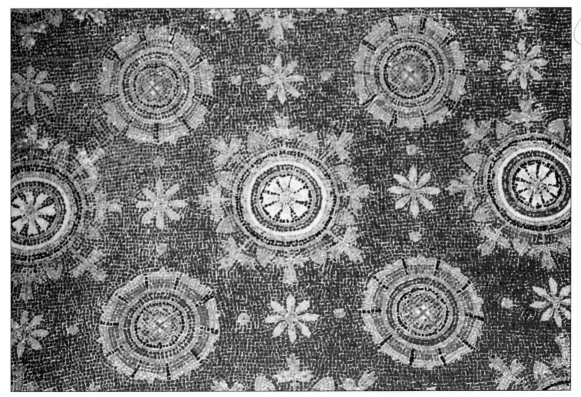

9.16 (above)
Christ as the Good Shepherd,
the mausoleum
of Galla Placidia,
Ravenna,
c. 425–426.
Mosaic.

9.17
Ceiling of the
mausoleum of
Galla Placidia,
Ravenna,
c. 425–426.
Mosaic.

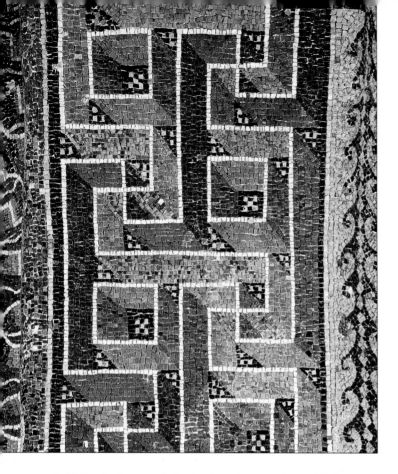

9.18 Detail of geometric border from the mausoleum of Galla Placidia, Ravenna, c. 425–426. Mosaic.

San Vitale

Situated on the Adriatic coast, Ravenna was essential to trade between East and West. Because of its strategic location, it became the Italian center of Justinian's empire and the focus of his artistic patronage in Italy. He strove to restore unity to Christendom and one expression of that effort can be seen in his building programs. Ravenna's most important Justinian church, San Vitale (figs. **9.19** and

9.19 Exterior of San Vitale, Ravenna, 540–547.

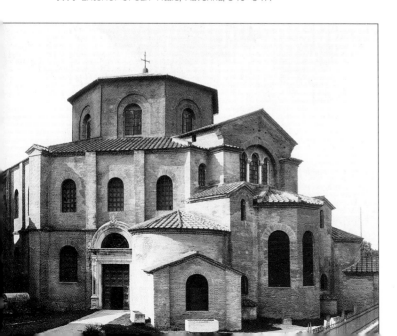

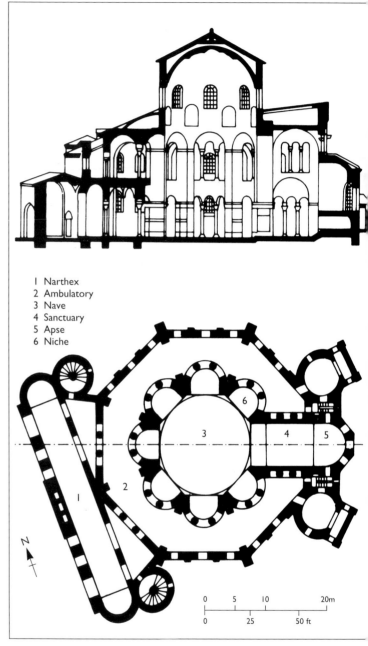

1 Narthex
2 Ambulatory
3 Nave
4 Sanctuary
5 Apse
6 Niche

0 5 10 20m
0 25 50 ft

9.20 Plan and section of San Vitale.

9.19 and **9.20** The domed central core and octagonal plan of San Vitale diverge from the architecture of Western Christendom. Instead of having an east-west orientation along a longitudinal axis with the altar in the east and the entrance in the west, San Vitale is centrally planned. This Eastern style of church architecture is less well suited to the requirements of Christian ritual. The narthex is placed on the western side of San Vitale at an angle to the axis of the apse. The circular central space is equivalent to the nave of Western churches and is ringed by eight large pillars supporting eight arches. Beyond the arches are seven semicircular niches and the cross vault containing the altar. Each niche is surrounded by an ambulatory on the floor level and a **gallery** (reserved for women) on the second story. All three levels—ground, gallery, and clerestory—have arched windows that admit light into the church.

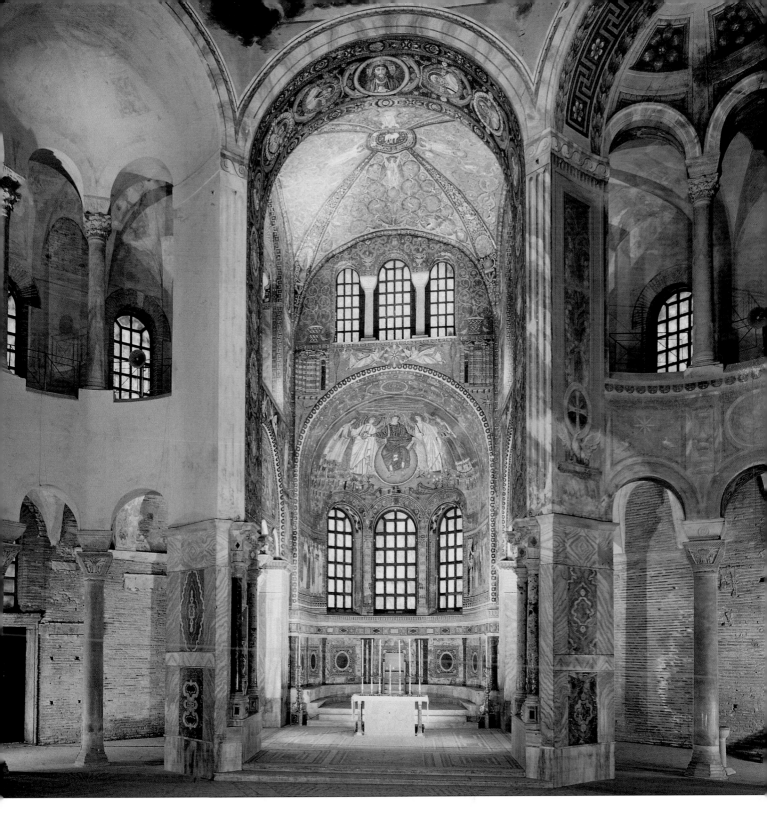

9.21 Interior of San Vitale looking east toward the apse.

9.20), was commissioned by the city's bishop, Ecclesius. Construction continued until its dedication in 547 by Maximian, the Archbishop of Ravenna. San Vitale was named for Saint Vitalis, a Roman slave and Christian martyr who had become the object of a growing cult from the end of the fourth century.

The exterior of San Vitale (fig. 9.19) is faced with plain brick, unbroken except by buttresses and windows, and the interior is richly decorated with mosaics and marble. Looking eastward, toward the apse and the altar, one can see the large rectangular piers that support the main arches and the columns at the base of the smaller arches (fig. 9.21). The interior is suffused with a glow of yellow light, resulting from the prevalence of gold in San Vitale's mosaics, which are among the best examples of Byzantine mural decoration.

The vaulted choir ceiling (fig. **9.22**) creates a natural architectural division into four curved triangles. Each is decorated with elaborate floral and animal designs. At the center, a circular wreath frames a haloed lamb, standing in a star-studded blue sky. It symbolizes Christ as the Lamb of God (both Christ and the Lamb were associated with sacrifice). Four angels in white, Roman-style draperies stand on blue spheres and hold up the ring encircling the Lamb. Directly across from the Lamb, on the arched entrance to the choir, is Christ in another guise. Again framed by a circle, the bust-length figure of Christ is frontal, dark-haired, and bearded. This is his traditional Eastern, or Byzantine, representation. His central position on the arch and his frontality compared with the apostles around him reinforce his triumphal role as leader of the Church.

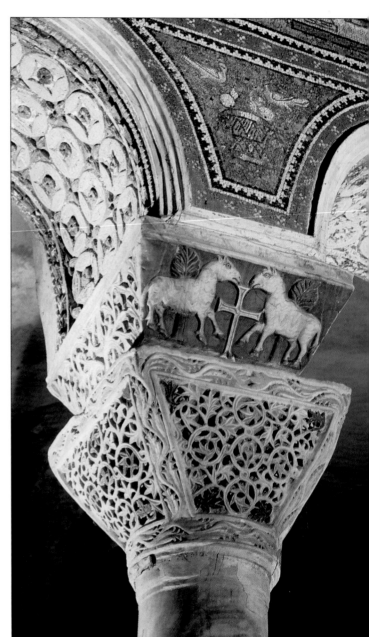

9.23 Detail of a capital, San Vitale, c. 540. Marble.

The capitals no longer conform to the Greek or Roman Orders (fig. **9.23**). Instead, the architect achieved another kind of unity by virtue of geometric repetition. Both parts of the capital are trapezoidal, as is the curved section between the springing of the two arches. The large lower trapezoid is covered with vinescroll, which, because of its symbolic associations, had become a popular Christian motif. Note that the five yellow flowers in the center are arranged to form a Greek cross, which echoes the yellow longitudinal cross in the trapezoid above. The cross is flanked by horses (probably a Near Eastern motif), each in front of a green tree, accentuating the Christian connection between tree and Cross.

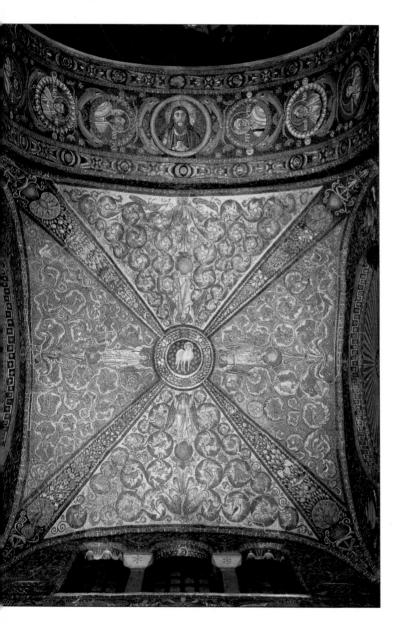

9.22 Ceiling of the choir, San Vitale, c. 547. Mosaic.

The large mosaic (fig. **9.24**) in the apse of San Vitale depicts a young, beardless Christ, based, like the Gandharan Buddhas (see p. 268), on Western Apollonian prototypes. His halo contains an image of the Cross and he wears a royal purple robe. Seated on a globe, Christ is flanked by two angels, and hands a jeweled crown to Saint Vitalis. On the right, the bishop Ecclesius holds up a model of the church. Although there are still traces of Hellenistic and Roman naturalism, for example in the landscaped terrain and hints of shading in figures and draperies, the representation is more conceptual than natural. The draperies do not convey a sense of organic bodily movement in space and the figures are essentially, if not exactly, frontal. The different approach to perspective compared with that of the Roman painters (see p. 250) is evident in the seated pose of Christ: he is not logically supported by the globe and hovers as if in mid-air. In contrast to the Roman extension of space toward a horizon, as if seen through a window or other architectural opening, this Christ seems to advance toward the viewer.

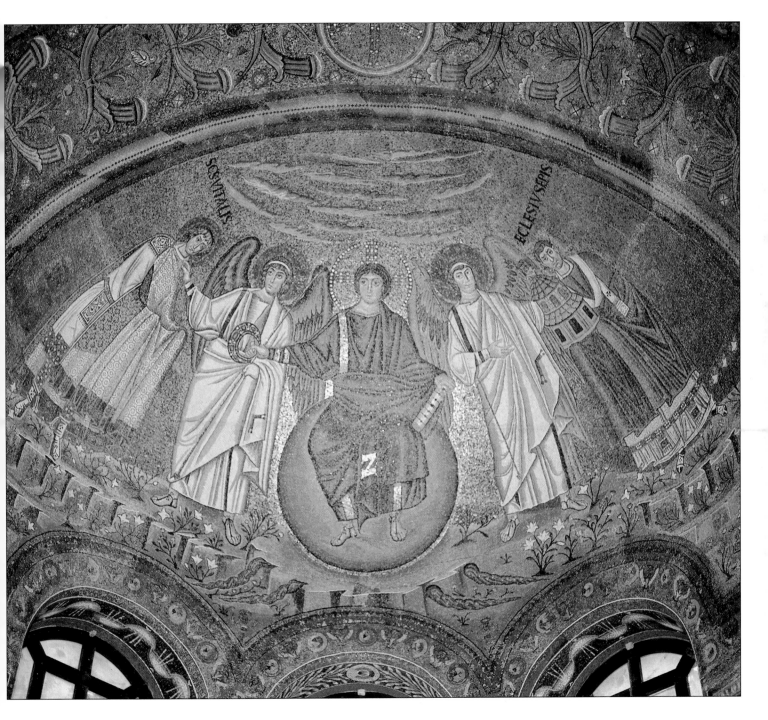

9.24 Apse mosaic, San Vitale, c. 547.

On the two side walls of the apse are mosaics representing the court of Justinian and his empress, Theodora. On the viewer's left, and Christ's right, is Justinian's mosaic (fig. **9.25**). The central figure of the emperor wears the same royal purple as Christ in the apse. On Justinian's left (the viewer's right) the archbishop Maximian wears a gold cloak and holds a jeweled cross. He is identified by an inscription and surrounded by three other members of the clergy. On Justinian's right are two court officials and his military guard, their large green shield decorated with Constantine's *Chi-Rho*. The intention of this mosaic was clearly to depict Justinian as Christ's representative on earth, and to show him as a worthy successor to Constantine—an expression of his power as head of both Church and state.

Opposite Justinian's mosaic, Theodora stands in a niche with her court ladies on the right and two churchmen on the left (figs. **9.26** and **9.27**). Like her husband, she wears

9.25 *Court of Justinian*, apse mosaic, San Vitale, c. 547. 8 ft 8 in × 12 ft (2.64 × 3.65 m). The gold background removes the scene from nature, thereby aiming to transport the viewer into a spiritual realm.

a royal purple robe and her head is framed by a halo. She extends a golden chalice and her gesture is echoed by that of the three Magi bearing gifts, depicted in the embroidery at the bottom of her robe. The figures in this mosaic, like those in Justinian's, stand in vertical, frontal poses. Their diagonal feet indicate that they are not naturally supported by a horizontal, three-dimensional floor. The illusion of movement is created by repetition and elaborate, colorful patterns, rather than by figures turning freely in space. A good example of this typical Byzantine disregard of perspective appears in the baptismal fountain on the abbreviated Corinthian column at the left of the scene. The bowl tilts forward, which in a natural setting would cause the water to spill out. But the water itself forms a foreshortened oval, thereby creating some degree of three-dimensional illusion. In contrast, Theodora's halo is depicted as a flat circle.

The importance of light in Christian art, echoing Christ's self-proclaimed role as "light of the world," is expressed in Byzantine mosaics such as these by the predominance of gold backgrounds and the reflective surfaces of the *tesserae*. The very concept is reminiscent of

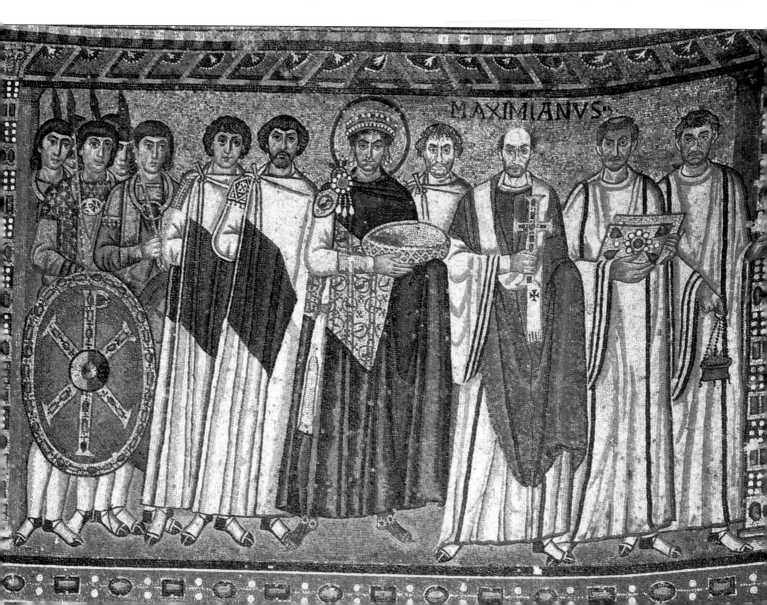

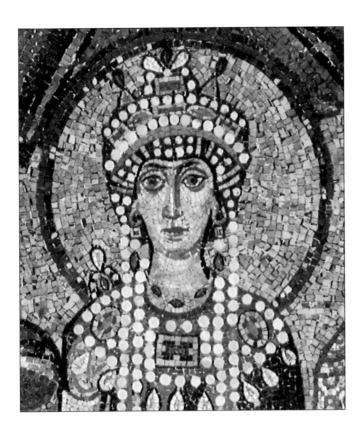

9.27 *Court of Theodora* (detail of figure 9.26). Here there is still an attempt at shading on the side of the nose and under the chin. Removing the image from the illusion of naturalism, however, is the black outline. The tilted, irregular placement of the *tesserae* creates thousands of small shifting planes which reflect the outdoor light entering the church.

9.26 (below) *Court of Theodora*, apse mosaic, San Vitale, c. 547. 8 ft 8 in × 12 ft (2.64 × 3.65 m). Theodora had lived a dissolute life as a courtesan before her notorious romance with Justinian. They were married in 523 and became co-regents of the Eastern Empire four years later. Theodora was a woman of great intelligence. Once in power, she devoted herself to a campaign of moral reform and advised Justinian on political and religious policy.

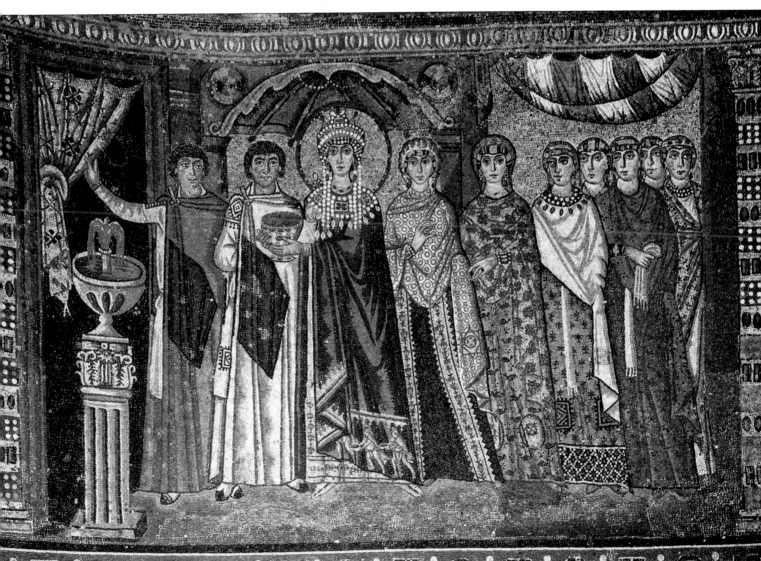

the Eastern sun cults, as well as of Constantine's use of the designation "Sol Invictus" (Invincible Sun) for himself. So when the Byzantine artist depicted Justinian and Theodora with haloes, it was to emphasize their combined roles as imperial leaders on earth and spiritual models in heaven.

The style of Justinian's and Theodora's heads is far removed from the type of Roman portraiture that preserved the features of its subjects. However, the stylistic distinction and positioning of people according to their status has been retained. For example, the prominent position of Theodora's mosaic is a function of her status as co-regent with her husband. But it is subordinate to Justinian's by virtue of being on Christ's left; the emphasis on rank and hierarchy rather than on personality or portraiture reflects the highly structured nature of Byzantine society. The symbolic nature of these images is evident, for Justinian had never been to Ravenna. His mosaic thus served to remind viewers of his earthly and spiritual power, emphasizing his political allegiance to Constantine and his religious devotion to Christ. By juxtaposing the Byzantine emperor with the local archbishop, the artist also alludes to Justinian's support from Ravenna's ecclesiastical hierarchy.

Maximian's Ivory Throne

Despite such monumental expressions of imperial and Church power in architecture and its mosaics, there is very little important Byzantine sculpture. This primarily consists of small reliefs, ivories, church furniture, and ornamentation. The largest Early Christian ivory from Justinian's reign is the sixth-century throne of Maximian (fig. **9.28**), which was restored in 1884, 1919, and 1956. It is a high-backed chair, with a semicircular seat and arms, which may have been a gift from Justinian to the archbishop. Although known as a throne, it was not used as such but was carried as a ritual chair in religious processions, with a silk or velvet cushion probably bearing such jeweled objects as a Gospel book or a Cross.

The wooden core of Maximian's throne is covered with ivory plaques, which are elaborately carved in low relief. On the back of the throne are scenes of Christ's childhood and miracles. Scenes from the life of Joseph, as an Old Testament prefiguration of Christ, decorate the armrests. In the front, below the seat, are the four Evangelists, individually framed and flanking John the Baptist at the center.

The detail in figure **9.29** shows two Evangelists. They are set in niches framed by round arches and columns carved in spiral patterns. The narrow scallop-shell apses, together with the arches, are designed to look like haloes. Each Evangelist carries the characteristic attribute of a book with the Cross on its cover and raises his right hand in the Roman gesture of oratory. Both wear Roman-style togas, whose folds create elaborate curvilinear patterns.

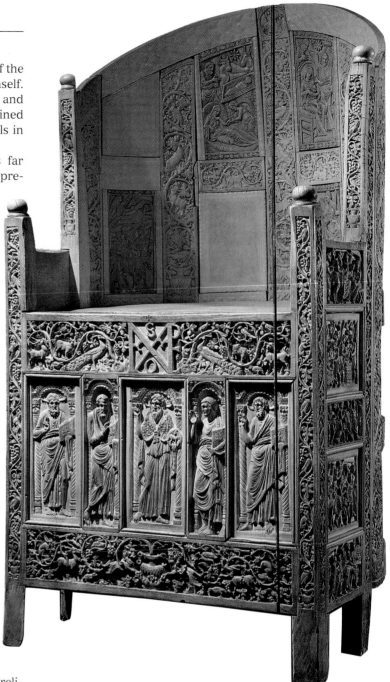

9.28 The throne of Maximian, 545–553. Polished ivory over wooden framework, Museo Arcivescovile, Ravenna. On the front, there are figures of John the Baptist and the four Evangelists (Christ's biographers). The scenes of Joseph on the side—the armrests—"announce" the scenes on the back—the childhood and miracles of Christ. Taken together, the scenes on the throne encompass the time of the Old and New Testaments. It is not known where the throne was made; possibilities include Antioch, Alexandria, Constantinople, and Ravenna itself.

The Evangelist at the right tilts his left foot downward so that it overlaps the ground in a diagonal plane like the feet in the mosaics of Justinian and Theodora. In contrast to the San Vitale mosaics, however, the Evangelists on the ivory throne show the persistence of Hellenism and late antique tradition as it was assimilated into the Early Christian style of Byzantium.

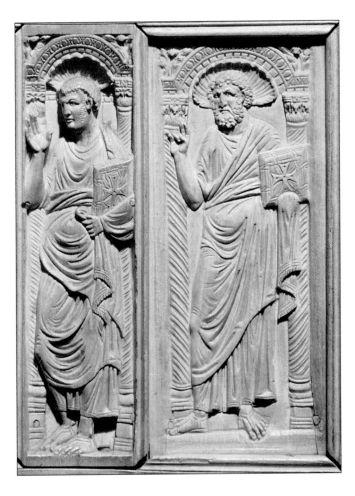

Hagia Sophia

The undisputed architectural masterpiece of Justinian's reign is the basilica of Hagia Sophia (fig. **9.30**) in Constantinople; the name is derived from the Greek for "Holy (*hagia*) Wisdom (*sophia*)." As part of an extensive rebuilding campaign following the suppression of a revolt in 532, Justinian commissioned two Greek mathematicians, Anthemius of Tralles and Isidoros of Miletus, to plan Hagia Sophia. In their design they successfully combined elements of the basilica with enormous rising vaults. The central dome is placed above four arches at right angles to each other and supported by four huge piers. The latter are barely noticeable from the inside because the arches meet at the corners. The piers themselves are supported

9.29 Two Evangelists, from the front of the throne of Maximian (detail of fig. 9.28)

9.30 Exterior of Hagia Sophia, Constantinople (now Istanbul), completed 537. The four tall **minarets**, or slender towers, were added when the Turks captured Constantinople in 1453 and Hagia Sophia was converted into a **mosque**. The Christian mosaics in the interior were largely covered over and replaced by Islamic decorations. Today, Hagia Sophia is a state museum..

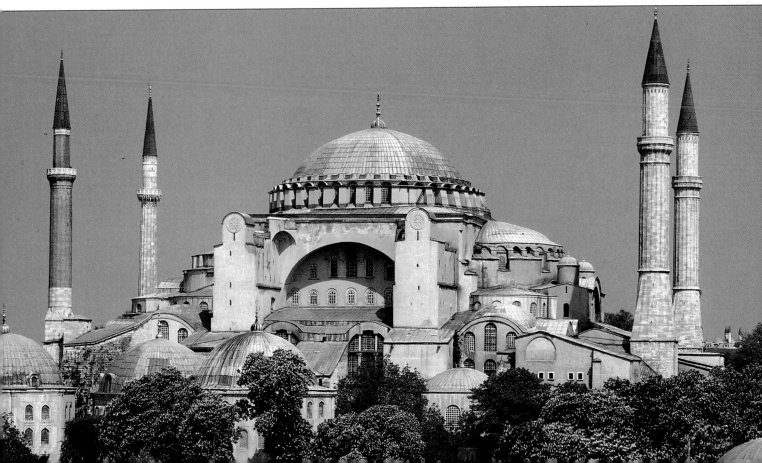

by buttresses, which can be clearly seen both in the plan (fig. **9.31**) and in the exterior view (fig. 9.30).

Whereas in Roman buildings domes were placed on drums, the dome of Hagia Sophia (fig. **9.32)**, like the earlier dome in the mausoleum of Galla Placidia, rests on **pendentives**. These are four triangular segments with concave sides. Their appearance of suspension, or hanging, gives them their name (from the Latin *pendere*, meaning "to hang"). They provide the transition from a square or polygonal plan to the round base of a dome or inter-vening drum, and allow the architect to design larger and lighter domes. Pendentives are the principal Byzantine contribution to monumental architecture.

Hagia Sophia's dome was constructed of a single layer of brick, a relatively thin shell that minimized the weight borne by the pendentives. Nevertheless, the very size of the dome demanded buttressing. The exterior view (fig. 9.30) shows that each of the forty small windows at the base of the dome is flanked by a small buttress, strengthening from the outside the interior juncture of dome and

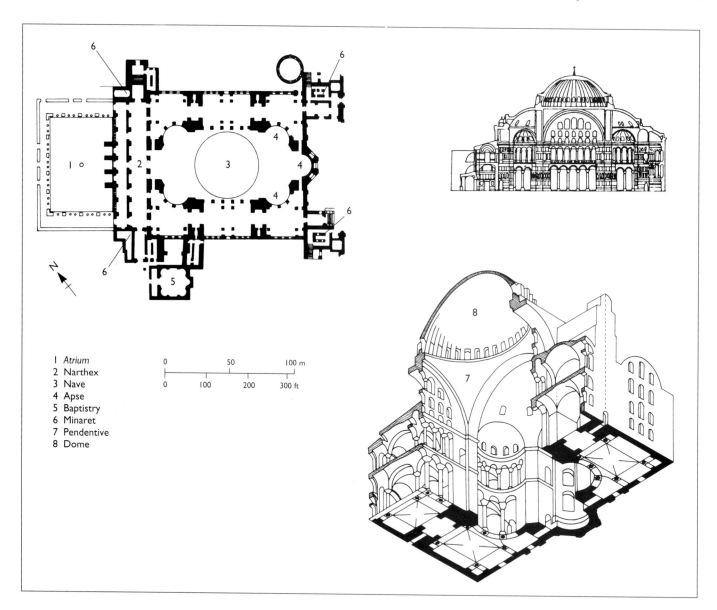

1 Atrium
2 Narthex
3 Nave
4 Apse
5 Baptistry
6 Minaret
7 Pendentive
8 Dome

9.31 Plan, section, and **axonometric projection** of Hagia Sophia. Visitors to Hagia Sophia would enter from the west, through an *atrium* that no longer survives (1 on the plan). The double narthex (2) was covered by a row of nine groin vaults. Passing through the narthex, one stood opposite the apse at the far eastern end. The path from narthex to apse, along a longitudinal axis, is reminiscent of an Early Christian basilica. However, instead of a long symmetrical nave surmounted by a gable roof, Hagia Sophia has a huge central square supporting an enormous dome (8). At the eastern and western ends of the square, two semicircles are topped by smaller half-domes. Surrounding each half-dome are three semicircular apses with open arcades surmounted by even smaller half-domes. Running from east to west along the axis are colonnaded side aisles on the first level and colonnaded galleries on the second level. Both are covered by groin vaults. Were it not for the central square, Hagia Sophia would resemble the typical centrally planned church, albeit on a massive scale. Note the impressive effect created by the open space of the nave, the high central dome, and the smaller half-domes. The central dome is the earliest example of the use of pendentives on such a grand scale.

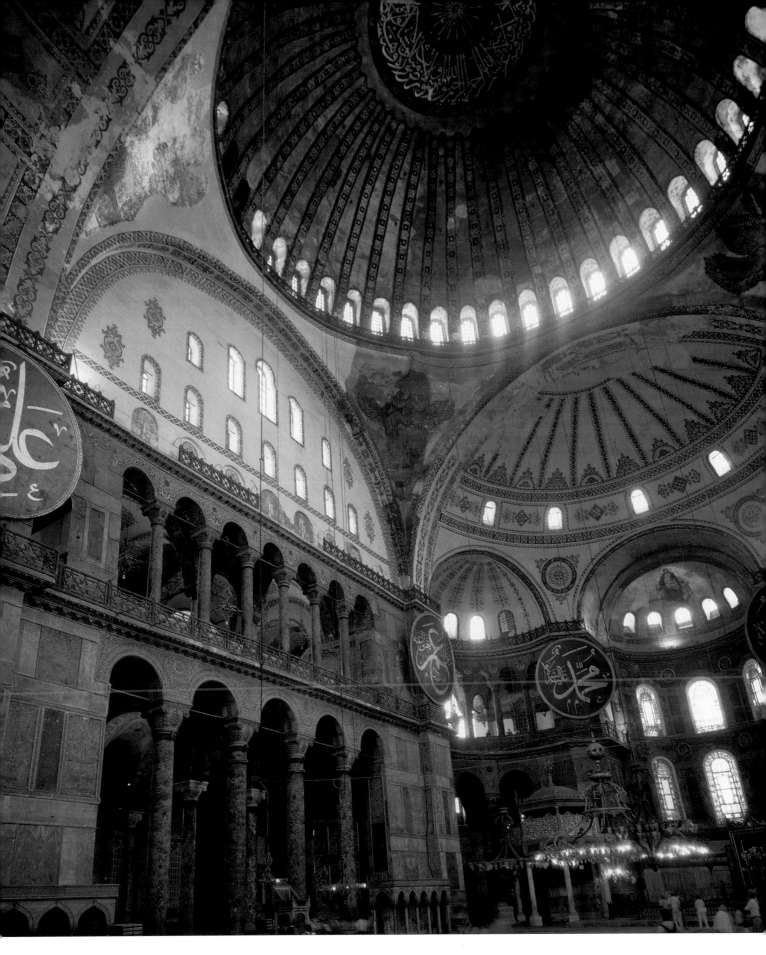

9.32 Interior of Hagia Sophia. The original effect would have been even more dazzling; window space was decreased when Hagia Sophia was rebuilt after earthquake damage. The destroyed mosaics would also have contributed color and reflected light.

Domes, Pendentives, and Squinches

Domes can be erected on circular or square bases. Ancient Roman domes like that of the Pantheon (see fig. 8.30) were usually on round bases. From the Byzantine era onwards, however, it became common to place domes over square or rectangular spaces. This posed the architectural problem of how to create a smooth transition from a cube or rectangle to the round base of the dome or its drum. The two main solutions were the use of structural elements known as pendentives and **squinches**.

Pendentives (figs. **9.33** and **9.35a**) are inwardly curving, triangular sections of vaulting between walls or arches set at right angles to each other. Four pendentives over a cubic space form a circle on which a dome or drum can be placed, as at Hagia Sophia (see fig. 9.32).

Squinches are small single arches (figs. **9.34** and **9.35b**) or a series of concentric corbelled arches (fig. **9.35c**) built across the corners of a square or polygonal space, as at the Great Mosque at Córdoba (cf. fig. 10.8).

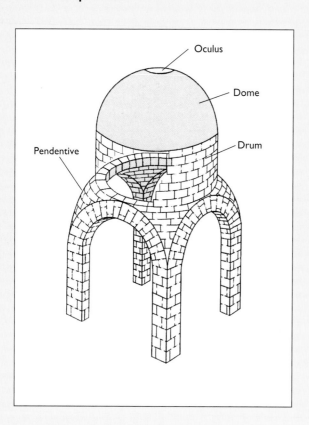

9.33 Dome on pendentives.

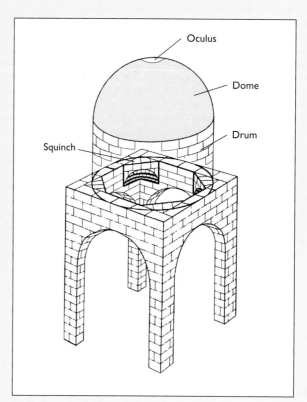

9.34 Dome on squinches.

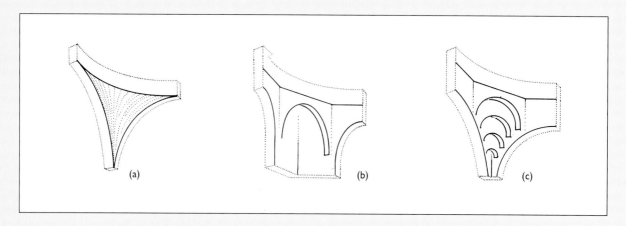

9.35a, b, c   a. Pendentive   b. Single-arch squinch   c. Concentric-arch squinch.

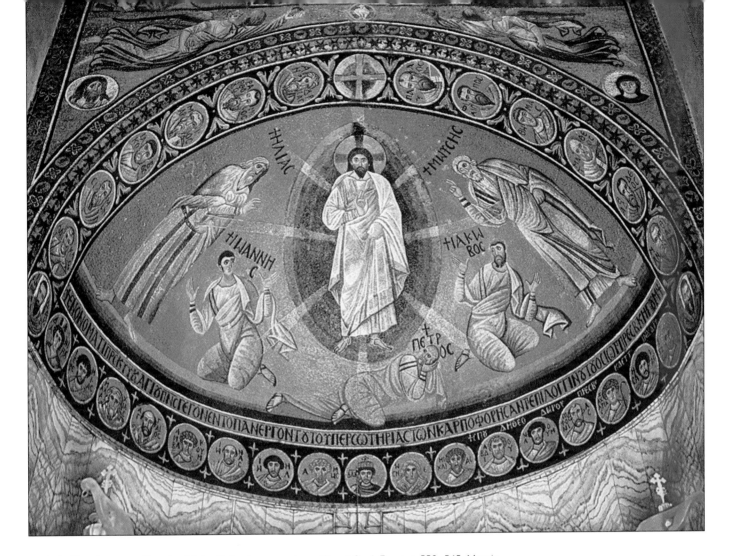

9.36 *The Transfiguration*, Church of Saint Catherine monastery, Mount Sinai, Egypt, c. 550–565. Mosaic.

pendentives, and transferring the dome's outward thrust downward (see Box).

On the north and south sides of the nave there are walls below the arches. As their load-bearing function has been assumed by the four piers, they can be pierced with arcades and windows (fig. 9.32). (Non-supporting walls, which usually have large expanses of windows or other openings, are called **screen walls**.) The extensive use of windows and arcades at Hagia Sophia creates an overwhelming impression of light and space. At the floor level, five arches connect the side aisles with the nave. At the second level, the galleries contain seven arches. The lunettes have two rows of windows, five over seven, and in each of the half-domes, there are five windows. Finally, a series of small windows encircling the bottom edge of the dome permits rays of light to enter from all directions. Although the actual source of light is from the exterior, the shimmering reflections and predominance of gold create the impression that it originates from the interior. Justinian's court historian Procopius expressed this view when he described the dome as a "sphere of gold suspended in the sky."

Hagia Sophia was used for imperial functions, although the imperial churches were located in the palace precinct. It was the personal church of the emperor and his court as well as a place of worship for the whole community. The clergy occupied one half of the central space and the emperor and his attendants the other. Lay people were restricted to the aisles and galleries. Like San Vitale, Hagia Sophia served Justinian's desire to unite Christendom under his leadership, to build churches, and to commission works of art that would express his mission as Christ's representative on earth.

The Expansion of Justinian's Patronage

Justinian's desire to extend his patronage as far afield as possible conformed to his imperial ambition. He commissioned buildings not only in Italy and Constantinople but throughout the Byzantine Empire, including the Balkans, North Africa, and the Near East. Among the most notable examples is the Church of Saint Catherine monastery on Mount Sinai, which has a large apse mosaic of *The Transfiguration* (fig. **9.36**). In this work, virtually all traces of landscape have been eliminated. A bearded, frontal Christ is suspended in a flat plane of gold. He is surrounded by a blue **mandorla** (the almond-shaped aureola) and wears white (a sign of his spiritual "transfigured" state), transmitting rays of white light toward the other figures. In this iconography, Christ is literally represented

31

ΑΠΕΔΟΟΥΔΕΝΠΛΗΝΟΟΥΔΙΚΤΟΕCΓΥΝΑΚΑΥΤΥ
ΕΠΗΝΕΠΟCΠΟΙΗCΩΤΑΡΗΜΑΤΟΠΟΝΗΡΟΥ
ΤΟΥΤΟΟΛΑΜΑΡΤΗCΟΜΕΕΠΑΝΤΙΟΝΤΟΥΘΥ
ΗΝΟΒΑΛΕCΚΑΙΤΩΙΩCΗΦΗΜΕΡΑΝΕΞΗΜΕΡΑC
ΚΑΙΟΥΧΥΠΗΚΟΥCΕΝΑΥΤΗΚΟΘΕΥΔΕΙΝΜΕΤΑΗC
ΤΟΥΧΥΕΙΝΟΝΕCΟΛΑΥΤΗΕΓΕΝΕΤΟΔΕΤΟΙΑΥΤ
ΤΗCΗΜΕΡΑΤΕΙCΗΛΘΕΝΙΩCΗΦΕΙCΤΗΝΟΙΚΙΑΝ
ΠΟΙΕΙΝΤΑΕΡΓΑΑΥΤΟΥΚΑΙΟΥΔΕΙCΤΩΝΕΝΤΗ
ΟΙΚΙΑΗΝΕCΩΠΑCΑΑΥΤΟΝΤΩΝΗΜΑΤΙ
ΚΑΙΕΠΕCΠΑCΑΤΟΑΥΤΟΝΤΩΝΙΜΑΤΙΩΝΛΕΓΟΥCΑΚΑΤΑΚΛΙ
ΤΗΜΕΤΕΜΟΥΚΑΙΑΠΟΛΙΠΩΝΤΑΙΜΑΤΙΑΑΥΤΟΥΕΝΤΑΙCΧΕΡCΙΝ
ΑΥΤΗCΕΦΥΓΕΝΚΑΙΕΞΗΛΘΕΝΕΞΩΑΡΗΟΕ

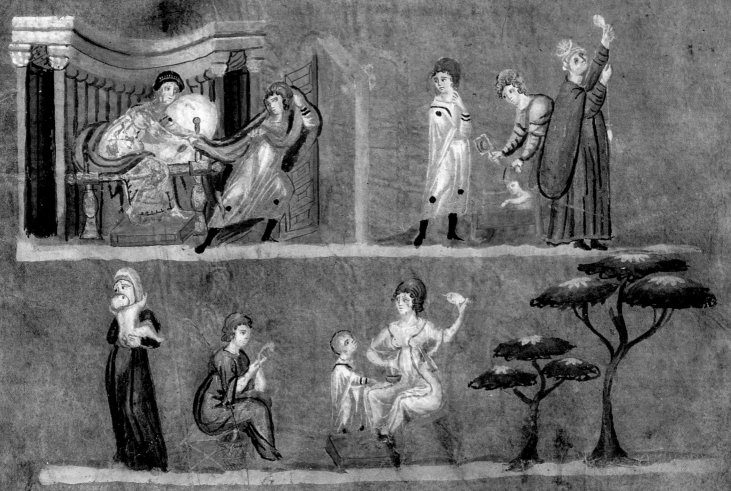

as "the light of the world." Three of his apostles, Peter, James, and John, fall backwards, their awe revealed by their agitated gestures. Moses and Elijah, in contrast, occupy calm, vertical poses, and frame the scene. Compared with the apse mosaic of the *Good Shepherd* in the mausoleum of Galla Placidia (see fig. 9.17), this has a mystical quality that seems to transcend earthly time and space.

The very setting of an image of the Transfiguration on Mount Sinai is imbued with typological meaning, for it was there that Moses had been "transfigured" by light after receiving the Law from God. Christ and the apostles are intended to embody the New Dispensation emerging from, and continuing, the traditions of the Old Dispensation established by Moses and Elijah.

The Development of the Codex

Toward the end of first century, a new method of transmitting "miniature" imagery accompanying written texts came into use. This was the **codex**, which was the ancestor of the modern book. The ancient Egyptians, Greeks, and Romans had used the papyrus scroll (*rotulus*) for texts and their illustrations. On average, a *rotulus* measured some 10 to 11 yards (9 to 10 m) in length when unrolled. The codex was more practical and easier to manage. Its pages were flat sheets of **parchment** and of relatively sturdy **vellum** (calfskin). They were bound together on one side and covered like a book, which made the codex easier to preserve than the *rotulus*. It was also possible to illustrate (or illuminate) the pages with richer colors. The Latin

poet Martial praised the codex, which he called the "book with many folded skins," because it held the complete works of Virgil in a single volume.

The Vienna Genesis

Among the earliest codices to illustrate scenes from the Bible is the Vienna Genesis (its name is derived from its current location, the Nationalbibliothek in Vienna). Originally, the codex had ninety-six folios, of which twenty-four survive; these have forty-eight miniature illustrations. Each sheet is purple, which points to an imperial patron, while the gold and silver script is characteristically Byzantine. Most of the page contains text, relegating the images to the bottom. Usually, as in figure **9.37**, there is more than one event depicted on a page. The narrative is continuous, without frames or dividers between scenes, and it has been suggested that such narratives are related to the continuous spiral of scenes on Trajan's Column (see p. 232).

This page depicts events from the life of Joseph, recorded in Genesis. At the upper left, Potiphar's wife reclines in a colonnaded bedroom. She tries to lure Joseph, who turns to leave. To the right, continuing from the bedroom, Joseph gazes back toward the scene of the temptation he has resisted. An astrologer wearing a starry cape holds up a spindle. Between him and Joseph, Potiphar's wife tends a baby. In the lower register, one woman holds a baby, while two others spin.

Figure **9.38** shows only the illustration below the text. It depicts another event in the story of Joseph. Here he sits in a prison, which is viewed from above. Outside, a few

9.37 (opposite) *Joseph and Potiphar's Wife*, from the Vienna Genesis, early 6th century. Illuminated manuscript, Nationalbibliothek, Vienna. It is not known where the Vienna Genesis was made, although it is believed to have originated in the Near East.

9.38 (right) *Joseph Interpreting Dreams in Prison*, from the Vienna Genesis, early 6th century. Illuminated manuscript, Nationalbibliothek, Vienna.

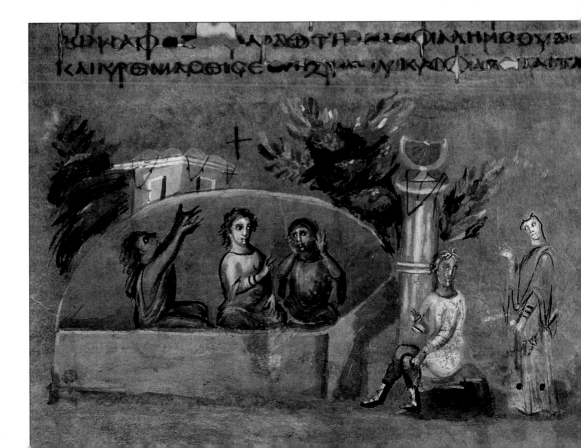

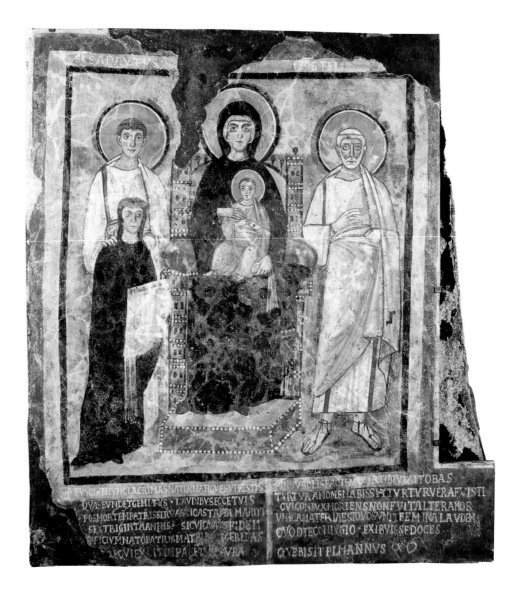

trees show that landscape, in however rudimentary a form, persisted as a way of setting a scene and conveying a sense of place. To the right of the prison, Potiphar's wife talks with the guard, her modest attire disguising her lust for Joseph. Inside the prison, the pharaoh's jailed butler and baker are unhappy because there is no one to interpret their dreams. Joseph informs them that dreams belong to God and asks what they dreamed. The butler reports his dream of a vine with three branches that grew blossoms and grapes, which he pressed into the pharaoh's cup. Joseph informed the butler that in three days the pharaoh would free him to resume his duties. The baker dreamed that he was carrying three white baskets on his head. The top basket was filled with bakemeats for the pharaoh, but birds ate them. Joseph told the baker that in three days the pharaoh would hang him from a tree and birds would eat his flesh. Both interpretations came true: the butler got his job back, and the baker was hanged.

9.39 *Virgin and Child Enthroned with Saints Felix and Augustus*, 528. Fresco. Commodilla catacomb, Rome.

Image and Icon

A comparison of the small detail of the woman holding the infant in the codex (see fig. 9.37) with a sixth-century fresco from a funerary chapel in the Roman catacombs (fig. **9.39**) highlights some significant differences in Early Christian style and meaning. The Vienna Genesis infant is anonymous, and held facing his mother in an ordinary way. His proportions are relatively naturalistic and he, like the woman, turns as if occupying three-dimensional space. Represented in the catacomb fresco, on the other hand, are the *Virgin and Child Enthroned*; the figures here are clearly identifiable and command veneration from Christians. They are flanked by saints, while at the left stands the smaller image of the widow buried in the chapel.

Mary sits regally on a jeweled throne, and is therefore in her aspect as Queen of Heaven. She had been proclaimed *Theotokos* (literally the Bearer of God) in 431 at the Council of Ephesus, and this led to a cult of the Virgin. Evidence of that cult can be seen in her majestic portrayal here. Christ, in such images, is the King of Heaven, seated on the throne that is his mother's lap. Unlike the Vienna Genesis baby, however, Christ is frontal, clothed, and rendered as a *homunculus* (a little man), babylike only in size and setting. His image conforms to the Christian metaphor in which Christ is conceived of as a miraculous baby king. This type of Virgin and Child (notwithstanding

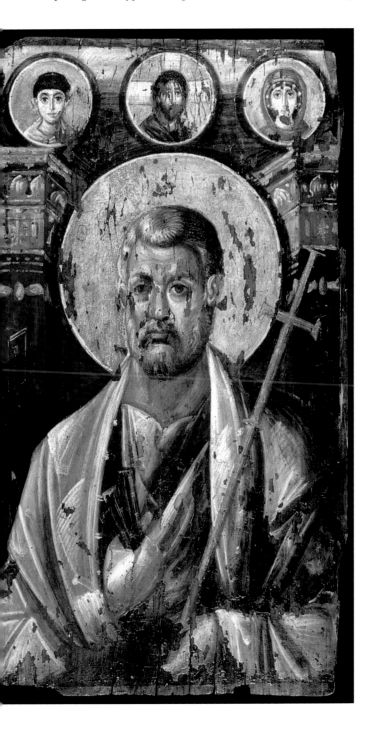

the togas worn by the saints) has an iconic character that is typical of the Byzantine style. Images of this kind invite devotion and prayer through direct confrontation of holy personages by worshipers. The Vienna Genesis figures, in contrast, continue in the Classical tradition of relative naturalism. They invite identification by virtue of shared movement in three-dimensional space and participation in a narrative sequence.

An **icon** (usually a panel painting), as opposed to works with iconic quality, is an image whose purpose is purely devotional. A good example is the icon of Saint Peter from the Justinian monastery of Saint Catherine (fig. 9.40), showing the bearded saint with a halo, a long cross, and his traditional attribute of the keys to heaven. The degree to which Early Christian icons absorbed elements from pagan styles is reflected in the Roman drapery with shaded folds, and the treatment of the face and neck. The halo is flat, but the buildings behind the figure recede in perspective. The three tondos of Christ, Mary, and an unknown saint are reminiscent of Roman examples (cf. fig. 8.64).

Later Byzantine Developments

The Byzantine style continued in both Eastern and Western Christendom for several centuries following the age of Justinian. In the eighth and ninth centuries, the very nature of imagery became a subject of dispute. This is referred to as the Iconoclastic Controversy, in which the virtues and dangers of religious imagery were hotly debated. The Iconoclasts (literally "breakers of images"), centered in Eastern Christendom, followed the biblical injunction against worshiping graven images, and many of them destroyed works of art. They argued that images of holy figures in human form would lead to idolatry—worship of the image itself rather than what it represented. According to the Iconoclasts, it was permissible for religious art to depict designs, patterns, and animal or vegetable forms, but not human figures. The Iconophiles (those in favor of images) were centered in the West. They pointed to the tradition that Saint Luke himself had painted an image of the Virgin and Child. In 726, the Iconoclasts gained the support of Emperor Leo III and in 730 succeeded in having an edict issued against graven images. This was to contribute to the relatively minor role of sculpture in Byzantine art. When the edict was eventually lifted in 843, the Iconophile victory led to a revival of image-making and renewed artistic activity. Mosaics and paintings were now officially encouraged, but sculpture—because of its three-dimensional character—remained unacceptable to the Eastern branch of the Church. Byzantine art and architecture persisted throughout the empire, in Italy, and in Constantinople, in the later phase of the style. Domed churches based on the Greek cross

9.40 *Icon of Saint Peter*, Saint Catherine monastery, Mount Sinai, Egypt.

continued to appeal to Byzantine architects. Their interest in juxtaposing solid geometric forms such as the cube and the hemisphere is also found in metalwork (see Box).

The eleventh-century monastery churches of Hosios Loukas (dedicated to Saint Luke of Stiris) in Greece provide an example of ecclesiastical architecture removed from the centers of imperial power (figs. **9.42** and **9.43**). Although relatively modest in scale, the buildings have more elaborate exteriors than those of San Vitale. Instead of plain brick, the walls are decorated with patterns created by different colored brick and light stone. The greater variety of architectural spaces is also evident in the asymmetrical planes of the exterior walls.

One church is dedicated to the Virgin Theotokos. It is a simple Greek-cross plan with a dome at the center. The extensive interior mosaics have uniform gold backgrounds, and the scenes from Christ's life are far less detailed than the mosaics at San Vitale. The other church,

the Katholikon, has a larger dome rising to a greater height and supported by marble paneled walls. In both churches, the iconography of the mosaics reflects post-Iconoclastic efforts to revive the power of imagery.

The Katholikon is noteworthy for the good state of preservation of its interior decoration. For example, the apse mosaic depicting the *Virgin and Child Enthroned* of around 1020 shows the figures in a gold space, isolated from the natural world (fig. **9.44**). Both are frontal, facing viewers directly and simply. The linear character of their style—despite some shading on the faces and on Mary's draperies—and the flat haloes place them in an otherworldly realm. Echoing the strong black frame of Mary's halo is the Greek inscription flanking it, which means "Mother of God." Christ is represented in typical Byzantine fashion as a homunculus. He sits upright and makes a gesture of blessing, signifying his role as universal God and ruler.

Byzantine Metalwork

The twelfth-century incense burner in the shape of a domed building (fig. **9.41**) shows the elaborate intricacy of late Byzantine metalwork. Its gold and silver material and the high quality of workmanship suggest that it was made for a court, possibly that of Constantinople. The shape is that of a secular building (the crosses are a later addition), its centralized square plan having four domed apses between four triangular sections. The latter have curved, pyramidal roofs. Incense was burned inside the structure, and the scent escaped through the openwork spaces.

The meaning of the iconographic motifs, most in **repoussé**, is not certain. Separating the roof from the walls is a band of rosette and scroll designs in low relief, and animals (including a lion, a griffin, and a centaur) decorate the walls. Figures signifying Courage (an armed man) and Intelligence (a woman pointing to her head) are represented on the double door of one of the apses. Although such personifications are often found in Byzantine court art, their function and meaning in the context of this incense burner are unknown.

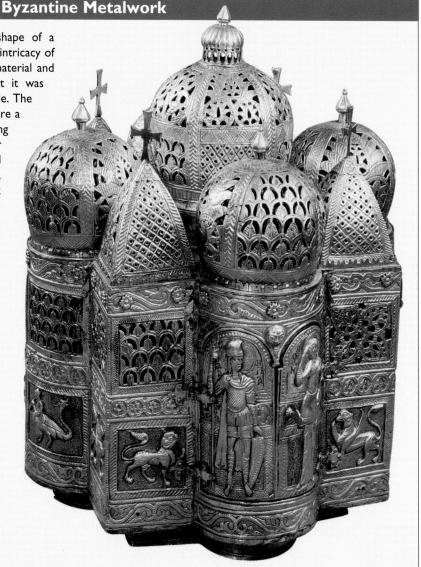

9.41 Incense burner in the shape of a domed building, 12th century. Gilded silver, 14⅛ × 11⅞ in (36 × 30 cm). Procuratoria di San Marco, Venice.

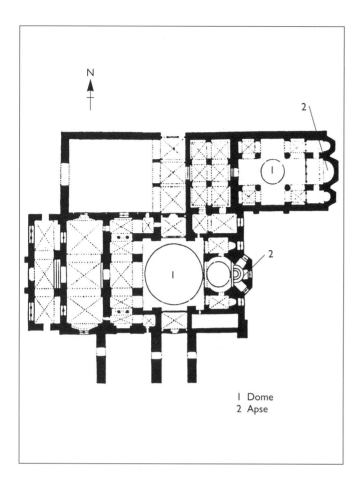

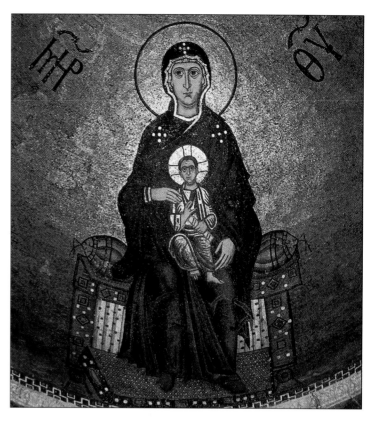

9.44 *Virgin and Child Enthroned*, church of Hosios Loukas, Greece, c. 1020. Apse mosaic.

1 Dome
2 Apse

9.42 Plan of churches of the monastery of Hosios Loukas (after Diehl), Greece, c. 1020.

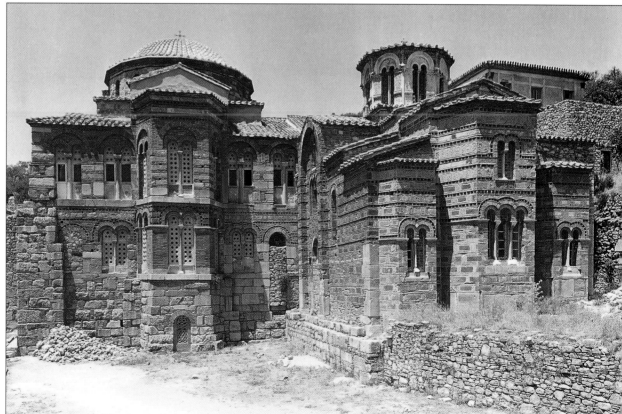

9.43 Monastery churches of Hosios Loukas, Greece, c. 1020.

The *Crucifixion* mosaic contains the figures of Christ on the Cross, the Virgin Mary in blue, and Saint John, the youngest apostle, in pink and green (fig. **9.45**). Supporting the Cross is the abbreviated hill of Calvary with symbols of the sun and moon that refer to the eclipse that occurred when Christ died. These, like Christ-as-baby-king, denote his future as ruler of the universe. The graceful S-shape of Christ's body defies the gravitational pull necessary for death by crucifixion. Also removing Christ from the natural world is the stylized patterning that makes his bone structure visible on the exterior of his body.

The poses and gestures of Mary and John are appropriate to the scene's death content. Mary's hands, for example, cross over each other, which is a visual echo of the Crucifixion itself. With her left hand she grasps the edge of her veil, as if retreating into herself. At the same time, her extended right hand indicates the sacrifice of her son, at whom she gazes sadly, thereby directing the viewer's attention to the central event. Saint John, on the other hand, leans against his right hand, a traditional gesture of mourning seen on Greek grave stelai (cf. fig. 6.68), which continues as a convention of mourning throughout Christian art. Both Mary and John seem to float in a divine space of gold.

In the *Harrowing of Hell* (fig. **9.46**), Christ is centralized as in the *Crucifixion*. He faces the viewer as the new Adam, triumphing over death and leading the original Adam to salvation. Eve, typologically paired with Mary, follows behind Adam. At the left, Kings Solomon and David, Old Testament types for Christ, gesture toward the miracle taking place before them. In contrast to Adam and Eve, their regal status is indicated by their robes and jeweled crowns, and their divine roles as ancestors of Christ by their haloes.

9.45 *Crucifixion*, church of Hosios Loukas, Greece, c. 1020. Mosaic.

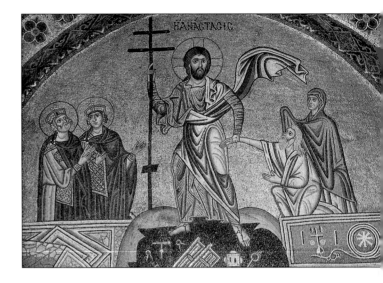

9.46 *Harrowing of Hell*, church of Hosios Loukas, Greece, c. 1020. Mosaic.

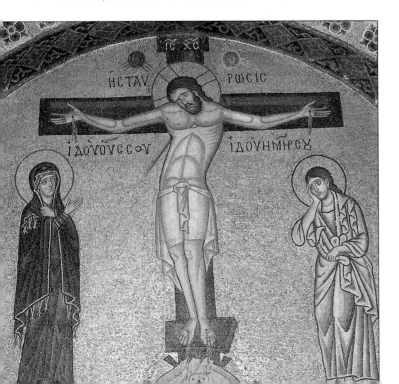

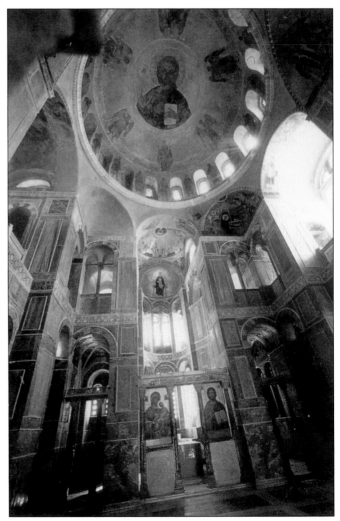

9.47 Central dome and apse, Hosios Loukas Katholikon, Greece, c. 1020.

The late Byzantine image of Christ as *Pantokrator* (literally "Ruler of All") is an expression of post-Iconoclastic efforts to convey the abstract power of Christ. Such an image decorates the interior dome of the Hosios Loukas Katholikon (fig. **9.47**). It shows Christ at the center, hovering over the space below—an all-encompassing power in human form. This particular image was restored after the earthquake of 1593 and is not as well preserved as, for example, the twelfth-century *Pantokrator* mosaic from the abbey church of Monreale outside Palermo, in Sicily (fig. **9.48**). The latter is a powerful image of Christ's dominion over the universe. His huge figure fills the upper part of

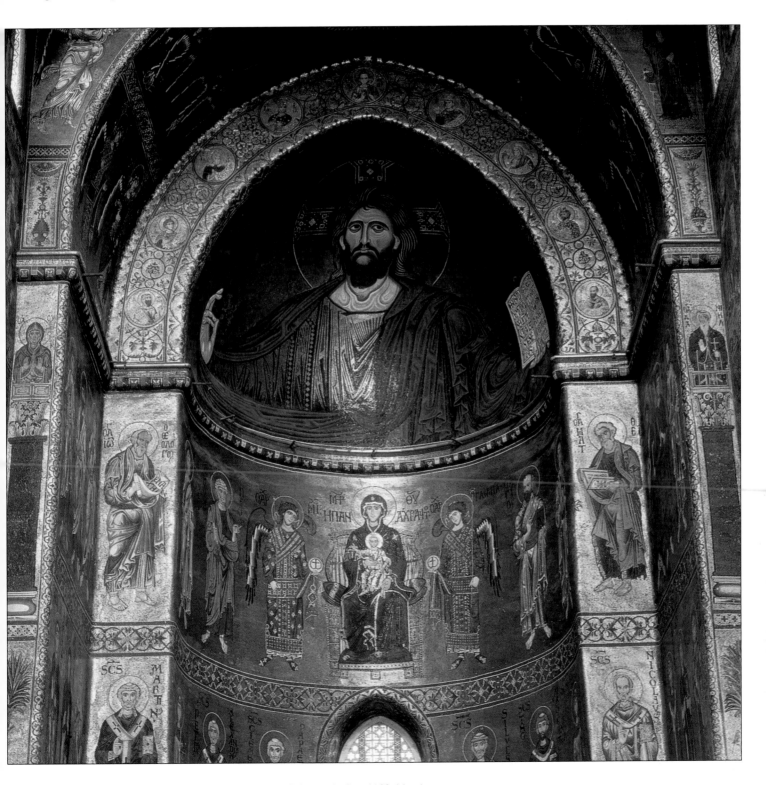

9.48 *Pantokrator*, from the abbey church of Monreale, Palermo, before 1183. Mosaic.

the apse and towers over the enthroned Virgin, his arms and drapery expanding to the sides of the apse. This Christ represents a different order of being from the smaller figures around and below him. The harsh modeling and emphasis on surface patterns—the swirling designs in the face, hair, and neck, as well as the angular drapery folds—enhance the stern character of the *Pantokrator*. The function of such an image is to inspire awe and to command obedience, penance, and faith.

In contrast to the stern, overpowering image of the *Pantokrator*, the thirteenth-century mosaic of *Christ* from Hagia Sophia shows Christ on a somewhat more human level (fig. **9.49**). Compared with the San Vitale mosaics, in which Justinian and Theodora had been portrayed frontally, outlined in black, and devoid of personality, this Christ turns his head slightly and has an individualized,

slightly downcast expression. Although the drapery folds on the left are rendered by dark blue lines, those on the right are somewhat shaded. The background is gold and the halo is entirely flat. The letters *IC* on the left and *XC* on the right stand for "Jesus Christ" (see p. 276).

This depiction of Christ illustrates both the persistence of Byzantine style and its accessibility to change. Although created by an artist in the Eastern Empire and located in the greatest of the Byzantine churches, it contains elements of pre-Christian, Hellenistic, and Roman styles. Shading is evident in the cheeks, neck, and right hand. The edges of Christ's form are also indicated by slight shading rather than by a black outline. The deep eye sockets, the bags under the eyes, the creased forehead, and the downward curve around the mouth convey an air of melancholy.

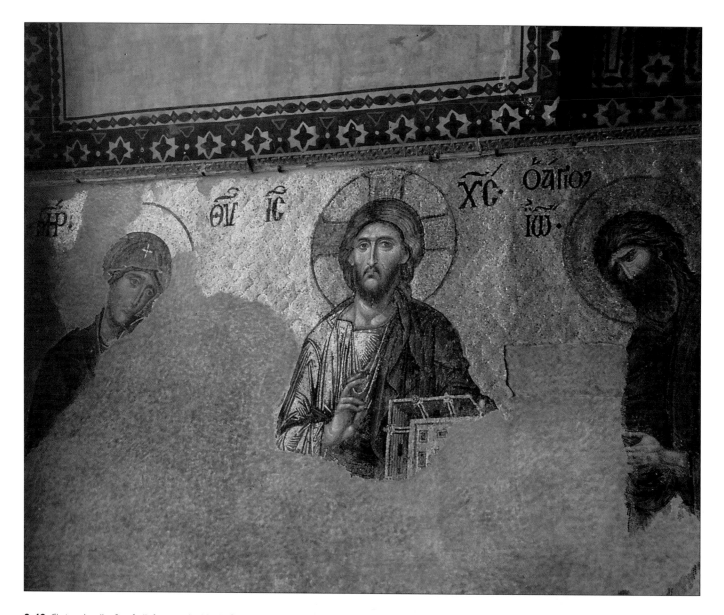

9.49 *Christ*, detail of a **deësis** mosaic, Hagia Sophia, 13th century. *Deësis* refers to an image showing Christ flanked by the Virgin and John the Baptist.

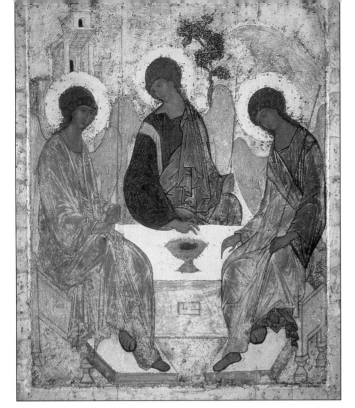

9.50 Andrei Rublev, *Old Testament Trinity*, early 15th century. Panel painting, 55½ × 44½ in (141 × 113 cm). Tretyakov Gallery, Moscow.

The Byzantine style continued in Russia well beyond the thirteenth century, as can be seen in the icons painted by the monk Andrei Rublev (c. 1370–c. 1430). His *Old Testament Trinity* (fig. **9.50**) depicts the three angels who appeared to Sarah and Abraham (the parents of Isaac) in Genesis 18:1–15. This event, which was later read by Christians as a prefiguration of the Trinity (Father, Son, and Holy Ghost), took on a typological meaning. Despite its damaged condition, Rublev's panel is notable for its rich color and elegant, flowing curves.

Most Russian churches were built up from a wooden core, according to a variation on the centrally planned Greek cross. Saint Basil's Cathedral in Moscow (fig. **9.51**) was commissioned by Tsar Ivan IV (Ivan the Terrible, 1534–80). Its plan is an octagon, to which are attached eight chapels, each of which is surmounted by an onion dome and commemorates a military victory. Such domes are designed to protect the interior from the elements, especially snow. The colorful patterns and varied, crystalline shapes on the exterior reflect the sunlight and sparkle in much the same way as the *tesserae* of Byzantine mosaics. Legend has it that Ivan the Terrible so admired the cathedral that he had the architects blinded, thereby ensuring that they would never again design anything so great.

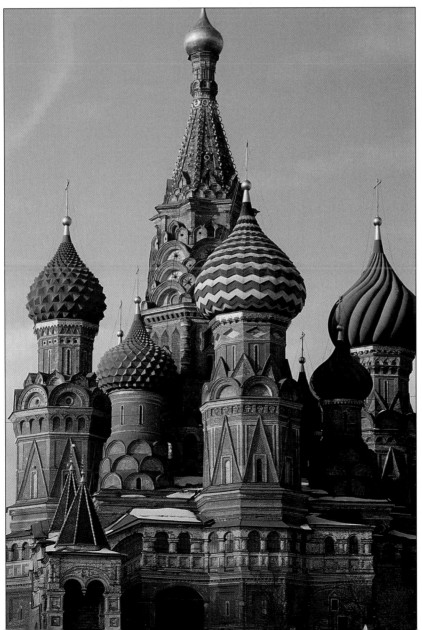

9.51 Barma and Postnik, Saint Basil's Cathedral, Moscow, 1554–60.

Style/Period	Works of Art	Cultural/Historical Developments
EARLY CHRISTIAN 2nd to 3rd Century A.D.	Dura Europos synagogue (**9.1–9.2**) *Christ as the Good Shepherd* (**9.3**), Rome Christus-Sol (**9.10**), Saint Peter's, Rome	Persecution of Christians; catacomb paintings created (2nd c.)
EARLY CHRISTIAN/ BYZANTINE 4th to 5th century	Early Christian sarcophagus (**9.5–9.6**), Santa Maria Antiqua, Rome Old Saint Peter's Basilica (**9.7**), Rome Santa Costanza (**9.12–9.13**), Rome Galla Placidia (**9.14–9.18**), Ravenna	Constantine becomes Roman emperor (306–337) Edict of Milan; Christianity legalized (313) Eusebius made Bishop of Caesarea (c. 313) Constantine moves capital of Roman Empire to Byzantium (330) Books begin to replace scrolls (c. 360) Sack of Rome by Visigoths, led by Alaric (410) Spain overrun by Visigoths (414) Saint Augustine writes *City of God* (426) Celtic church established in Ireland by Saint Patrick (c. 430) Attila becomes ruler of the Huns (433) Flowering of Maya civilization in southern Mexico (late 400s) Sack of Rome by Goths; fall of western Roman Empire (476) Armenian Church secedes from Byzantium and Rome (491) Ostrogoth kingdom established in Italy by Theodoric (c. 493)

Galla Placidia

The Vienna Genesis

San Vitale

Style/Period	Works of Art	Cultural/Historical Developments
EARLY CHRISTIAN/ BYZANTINE 6th–16th century	The Vienna Genesis (**9.37–9.38**) *Virgin and Child Enthroned* (**9.39**), Rome Hagia Sophia (**9.30, 9.32**), Istanbul San Vitale (**9.19, 9.21–9.27**), Ravenna Throne of Maximian (**9.28–9.29**) *The Transfiguration* (**9.36**), Saint Catherine monastery *Icon of Saint Peter* (**9.40**) Saint Catherine monastery Hosios Loukas (**9.43–9.47**), Greece *Pantokrator*, abbey church of Monreale (**9.48**) Incense burner (**9.41**) Deësis mosaic (**9.49**) Rublev, *Old Testament Trinity* (**9.50**) Saint Basil's Cathedral (**9.51**), Moscow	Justinian becomes eastern Roman (Byzantine) emperor (527–565) Saint Benedict founds the Benedictine Order (529) Earliest Chinese roll paintings (c. 535) Plague devastates Europe (542–594) Saint David converts Wales to Christianity (c. 550) Origin of chess in India (c. 550) Lombard kingdom established in northern Italy (568) Birth of Muhammad c. 570 (d. 632) Buddhism firmly established in Japan (c. 575) Block printing of books in China (c. 600) Iconoclastic Controversy between Byzantine emperor and pope (726) Start of the First Crusade (1096) Constantinople becomes Turkish capital (1453) Ivan IV (The Terrible) becomes Tsar of Russia (1530)

Incense burner

Rublev, *Old Testament Trinity*

Developments in Buddhist Art

(1st–7th centuries A.D.)

Rock-Cut Architecture

The Vihara and the Chaitya Hall

Toward the end of the first millennium B.C., in the low cliffs of western India, there developed a new type of monastic architecture (fig. **9.A**). Mountainsides were chiseled out to create caves, which were imitations of free-standing wooden buildings. Most were located near well-traveled trade routes. These caves are of two main types: living spaces for monks called **vihāras**, and large, basilica-like spaces for congregational worship focused on a stupa. The latter are called **chaitya halls**. *Vihāras* generally consist of small, windowless cells surrounding a broad room used by the monastic community for eating, recitation, studying, and other communal activities. From the fifth century A.D., *vihāras* often had small shrines opening off the main space (cf. fig. 9.G) that contained sculptures of the Buddha. Early Buddhist caves provide the only physical record of the appearance of the more perishable wooden structures on which they were modeled. There are approximately a thousand such Buddhist sanctuaries dating from the late second century B.C. to the mid-second century A.D. Some evidence indicates that the caves were furnished inside and out with wooden balconies, doors, rafters, and other architectural elements. The interior walls were decorated with mural paintings and tapestries, illuminated by oil lamps.

The most famous examples of rock-cut architecture in India are located in what is now the state of Maharashtra. In keeping with Buddhist practice, these monastic sites were removed from the center of town but were accessible to travelers as well as to local inhabitants. Inscriptions identify the caves' patrons as lay people, monks and nuns, and kings.

Chaitya halls were remarkably similar in both architectural design and religious purpose to later Christian basilicas. A comparison of the interior of the *chaitya* hall at Karli (figs. **9.B** and **9.C**), which dates from c. 50–70 A.D., with the basilica of Santa Sabina of 423–432 in Rome (fig. **9.D**) highlights the similarities as well as the differences.

Both have a triple entrance and a long, central nave with a semicircular apse at the far end opposite the entrance. The apse is the most sacred area in the *chaitya* hall, as in the basilica. The nave of the *chaitya* hall is pre-

ceded by a shallow space, or **veranda**, which is similar to the narthex of the basilica. Framing the nave of each are rows of columns, which separate the nave from its side aisles. These, in turn, continue around the apse to form an ambulatory. By circumambulating the stupa (inside the apse of the *chaitya* hall), the Buddhist worshiper replicates the circular path of reincarnation in the quest for *nirvana*.

Often, remains or relics of a Christian saint were buried below the apse of the basilica in an underground **crypt**. Similarly, the apse of the *chaitya* hall contains a stupa (see p. 265), the funerary structure originally placed over the

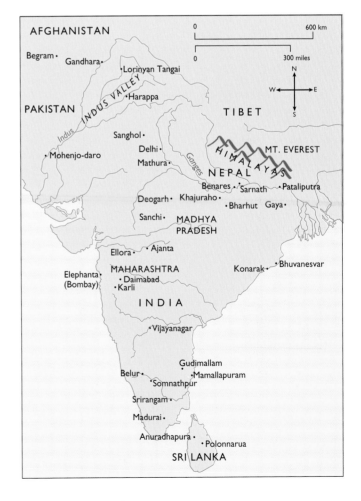

9.A Map of South Asia.

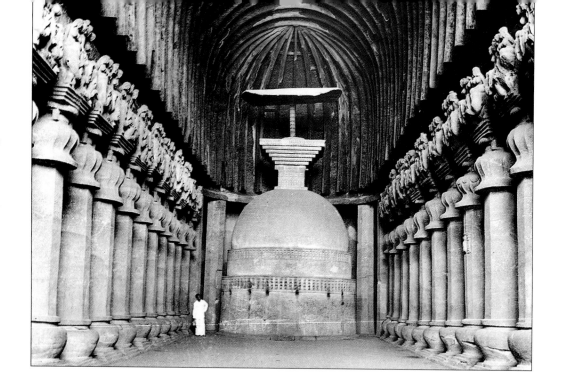

9.B *Chaitya* hall, Karli, Maharashtra, India, c. 50–70 A.D. Granite, nave 45 ft (13.7 m) high. The term *chaitya* originally meant a mound, or sacred place. It came to mean "place of worship" and was applied to the structure that housed a stupa—itself originally a hemispherical mound.

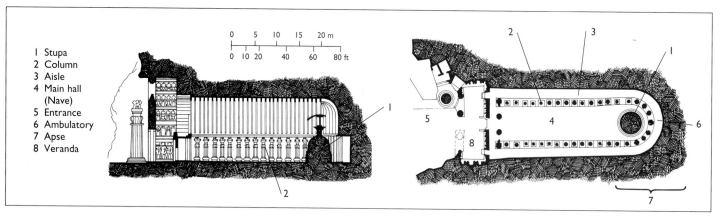

1 Stupa
2 Column
3 Aisle
4 Main hall (Nave)
5 Entrance
6 Ambulatory
7 Apse
8 Veranda

9.C Plan and section of *chaitya* hall, Karli.

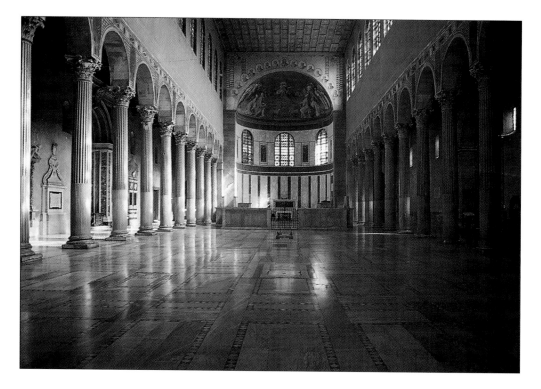

9.D Interior of Santa Sabina, Rome, 423–432.

Gupta Sculpture

The Preaching Buddha from Sarnath

The Gupta Empire, which flourished in the fourth and fifth centuries, dominated the Ganges Valley and extended into the west and south. Its rulers encouraged developments in art and literature that lasted well beyond the period of their political sway. Though the Guptas were proponents of Hinduism, their patronage of the arts fostered the expansion of Buddhist art as well.

A Gupta figure of the *Preaching Buddha* from Sarnath in northern India (fig. **9.F**) exemplifies a new type of Buddha image that emerged in the late fifth century. Its

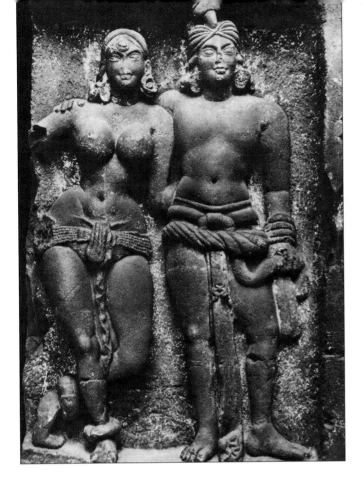

9.E *Mithuna* from the façade of the *chaitya* hall, Karli, Maharashtra, India, c. 50–70 A.D.

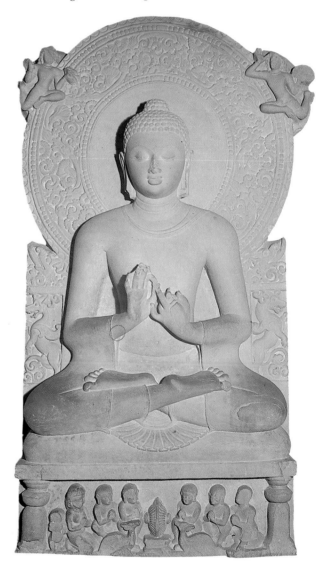

9.F *Preaching Buddha*, from Sarnath, Uttar Pradesh, India, c. 475. Chunar sandstone, 5 ft 3½ in (1.61 m) high. The relief on the base of the throne shows the Wheel of the Law at the center. On either side are three disciples and a deer (referring to the Deer Park Sermon at Sarnath). Carved on the back of the throne are two rearing winged lions (leogryphs), which symbolize royalty. The halo is decorated with lotus motifs and flanked by celestial beings.

remains of Shakyamuni Buddha. And when worshipers enter the *chaitya* hall—as well as the basilica—they are drawn to the spiritual focal point by the formal arrangement of space and mass.

The *chaitya* hall differs from the basilica in several ways. Instead of a flat ceiling, that of the *chaitya* hall is barrel-vaulted. Its designation as "elephant-backed" reflects the association of the form with organic structure. The curved rafters visible in figure 9.B are the original wooden elements used to replicate the prototype, rather than to serve a structural purpose. The columns are thicker than those in Santa Sabina and are composed of a base (in the shape of a water jar), a thick shaft, and a capital, whose bell shape is similar to that on Emperor Ashoka's pillars (see p. 264). Above each bell capital at the Karli *chaitya* hall are two elephants and four riders facing the nave.

Aside from the capitals, there is no sculpture inside the *chaitya* hall at Karli. The veranda, however, is covered with large-scale reliefs; two of the most impressive flank the entrance (fig. **9.E**). They show a royal **mithuna** (loving couple), whose style embodies an ideal of Indian sculpture that would continue for another nine centuries. Although they are made more monumental by the compact space they inhabit, their poses and gestures are casual and relaxed. The woman stands with her left leg bent behind her right, assuming the sensuous **tribhaṅga** (three bends pose) of the Sanchi *Yakshī* (see pp. 266–7). Both the man and the woman convey the impression of specific people, possibly donors.

iconography reflects the evolution of a canon for depictions of Buddhist figures, and is a particularly successful synthesis of iconic and narrative form. The figure is severe and still. The eyelids are lowered, and the legs are folded into a yogic meditation pose. The hands in *Dharmachakra mudrā* symbolize the setting in motion of the Wheel of the Law. In addition to the *ushnīsha*, *ūrnā*, and elongated earlobes (see p. 269) that were already part of the Buddha's iconography in the Kushan period, the Sarnath figure has many elements that evolved later. These include features drawn from nature such as the snail-shell curls, eyebrows "like an archer's bow," and shoulders "like an elephant's trunk." Another canonical detail is the three rings on the neck. In the indigenous tradition of the *prana*-filled *Nude Male Torso* from Harappa (see fig. 8.F) and the *Standing Buddha* from Mathura (see fig. 8.P), this figure radiates a sense of inner energy.

The Ajanta Caves (late 5th century A.D.)

The artistic legacy of the Gupta dynasty is clearly seen in the spectacular Buddhist monastic site at Ajanta (figs. **9.G** and **9.H**). Ajanta is southwest of Sanchi and northeast of Bombay, close to a strategic mountain pass connecting northern and southern India (see fig. 9.A). Altogether there are thirty caves cut into a U-shaped river gorge, out of which *chaitya* halls and **vihāras** were carved in two phases. The earliest dates from the first century B.C. to the first century A.D., and the rest from the second half of the fifth century, when the region was ruled by the Vakataka dynasty.

The two later *chaitya* halls at Ajanta are more elaborate than the earlier one at Karli. The entrance to the *chaitya* hall in Cave 19 (fig. **9.I**) is particularly well preserved. The view illustrated here shows the large lunette-shaped **chaitya arch** window through which light illuminates the cave and hits the stupa. Compared with the interior of the earlier *chaitya* hall at Karli, much more sculpture and certain architectural features—such as the thick columns with "squashed cushion" capitals supporting a cornice and an upper row of carved reliefs—have been added (fig. **9.J**). The walls are covered with small-scale, repeated painted images of enthroned buddhas with their attendant bodhisattvas.

9.G The Ajanta Caves, Maharashtra, India, c. 450–500.

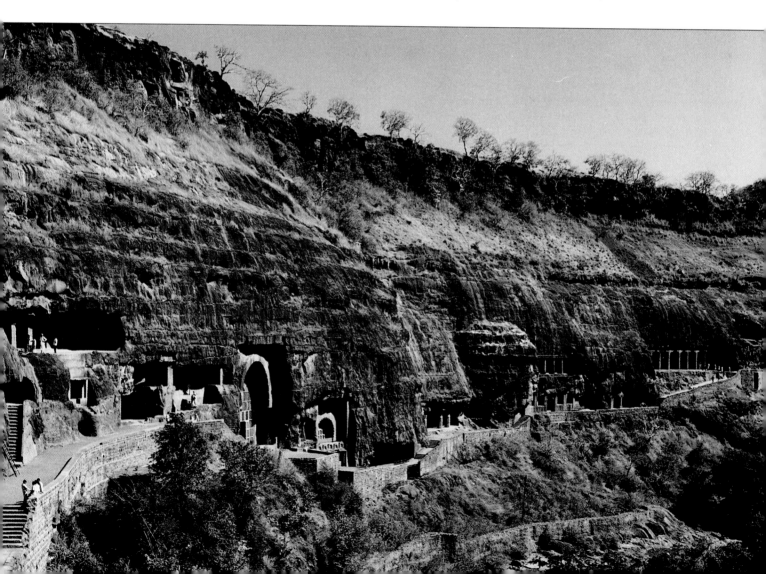

Recent microscopic analysis of the Ajanta murals shows that cave walls were covered with three layers of plaster. The final layer was tinted or painted to create a white ground for the paintings. The paint itself is a kind of tempera (see p. 190), which was probably made by mixing powdered mineral pigments with a gluey binder. Outlines were drawn in reddish brown and forms were filled in with paint. Blue was rarely used, suggesting that its source was an expensive, imported mineral, perhaps lapis lazuli. Black pigment is thought to have been made from soot.

In addition to texts detailing artistic practice, one of the early sources of information on painting technique in India is the Gupta-period commentary on the *Kamasutra*, a Hindu treatise on the art of love. This describes the language of pose and gesture, the expression of mood and feeling, and the rendering of objects three-dimensionally.

The stupa is also decorated with reliefs, and its proportions have grown taller and thinner. A monumental statue of Shakyamuni Buddha stands in a niche framed by pillars supporting a *chaitya* arch. Both the axis-pillar and *chattras* have become more complex.

Some of the greatest examples of monumental Indian painting survive in four of the Ajanta *vihāras* (see Box).

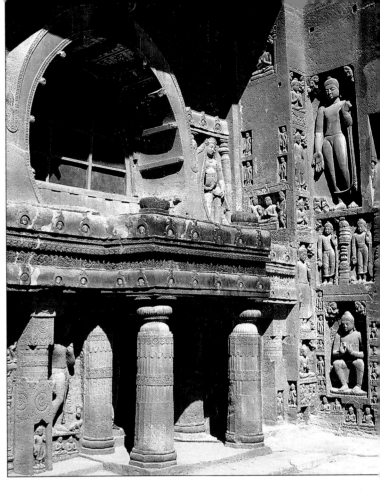

9.I *Chaitya* hall entrance, Ajanta Cave 19, Maharashtra, India, c. 450–500.

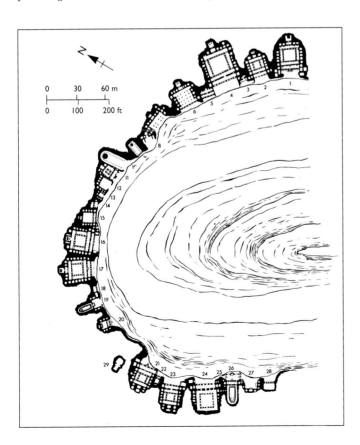

9.H Plan of the Ajanta Cave complex, Maharashtra, India, c. 450–500.

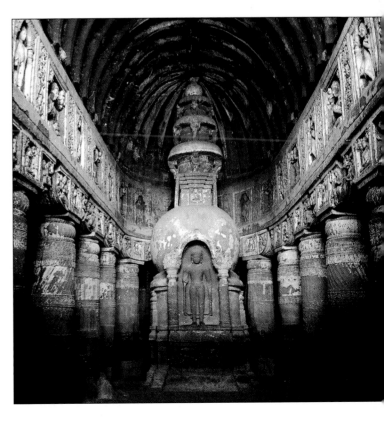

9.J *Chaitya* hall interior, Ajanta Cave 19, Maharashtra, India, c. 450–500.

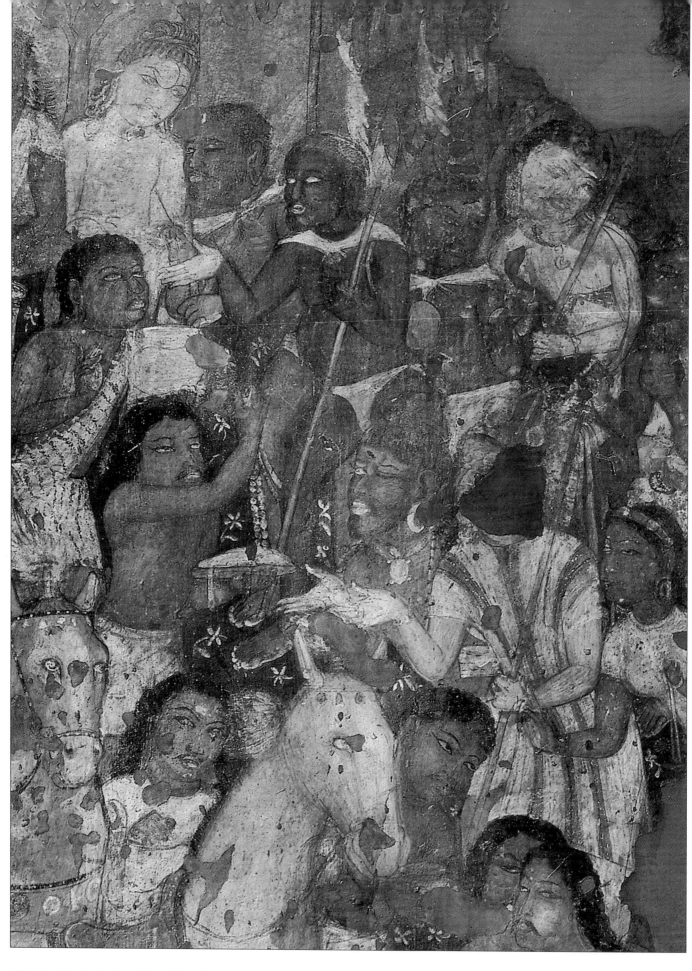

9.K *Prince Distributing Alms*, Ajanta Cave 17, Maharashtra, India, c. 450–500.

Secular paintings from this period are mentioned in texts, but they have not survived. The Ajanta frescoes, like the San Vitale mosaics at Ravenna (see p. 286), constitute monumental religious programs with political significance. Their use of rich colors and displays of opulence were intended to align political power with religious devotion. A large scene showing a *Prince Distributing Alms* (fig. **9.K**) illustrates this combination. Despite the generosity of the prince, motivated as it is by his piety, his elaborate entourage including horses and guards—as well as his rich attire—expresses his love of worldly splendor and his ability to command it.

The famous *Padmapani*, or Lotus Bearer (from *padma*, meaning "lotus," and *pani*, meaning "hand"), is one of a pair flanking the entrance to the shrine at the rear of the *vihāra* in Cave 1 (fig. **9.L**). The detail of the head in figure **9.M** reveals the sensuous naturalism of Indian art also evident in the *Yakshī* at Sanchi (see fig. 8.O). The *Padmapani* in the *tribhaṅga* pose, regally attired and attending the Buddha, is primarily a great emperor serving an even greater lord.

The imposing figure of the *Padmapani* reflects the continuing Indian interest in naturalism, which can be seen in the use of shading to convey organic form—for example, the underside of the chin, the curves of the shoulder and neck, and the natural depressions of the face. In contrast to the Byzantine depiction of spirituality conveyed by flat, vertical planes, frontality, and iconic confrontation with the worshiper, the Ajanta murals convey it by an inner, meditative tranquility.

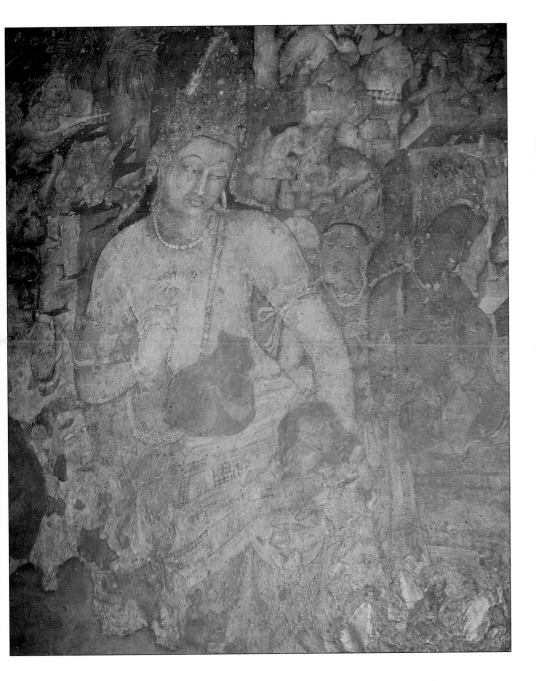

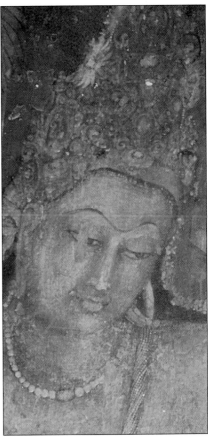

9.L (left) *Padmapani*, Ajanta Cave 1, Maharashtra, India, c. 450–500.

9.M (above) *Padmapani* (detail of head in fig. 9.L).

Even in a devotional scene, such as the *Worship of the Buddha* (fig. **9.N**) from a pillar in Ajanta Cave 10, the figures turn as if in three-dimensional space. The sense of a natural setting is suggested by the floral designs and the fact that the Buddha's throne is set at an oblique angle. Although the halo is flat, the head is rendered in three-quarter view.

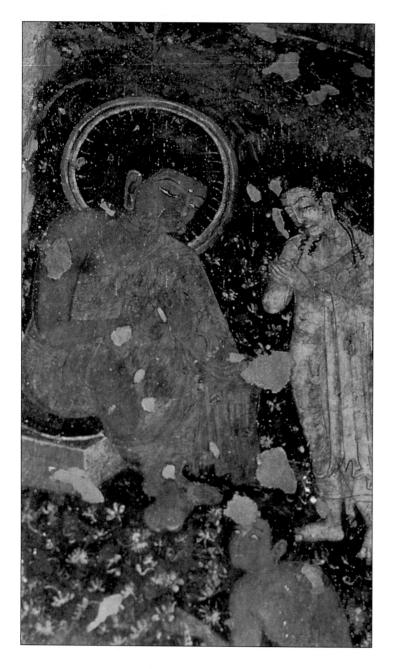

9.N *Worship of the Buddha*, from Ajanta Cave 10, Maharashtra, India, c. 450-500. Photographer: Robert E Fisher.

Buddhist Expansion in China

(2nd–7th centuries A.D.)

Buddhism declined in India, where it would become nearly extinct by the thirteenth century. This was due partly to a revival of Vedic religion, which has a complex association with the development of Hinduism. But Buddhism spread throughout much of the rest of Asia, where it has remained a dominant cultural force. It was transmitted along the Silk Road throughout Central Asia to China (fig. **9.O**) in about the first century A.D., and gained a foothold during the Han Dynasty (c. 206 B.C–A.D. 220). Beginning in the second century A.D., Buddhist texts (*sutras*) were translated from their original Indian languages, Sanskrit and Pali, into Chinese. Only then was Buddhism recognized in China as a school of thought distinct from Daoism. Over the next few centuries, Buddhism brought with it new artistic techniques and styles from Central Asia, India, Iran, and the Mediterranean world. The eclectic nature of Chinese art at this time reflects the continuing exchange of goods and ideas. Contemporary accounts, particularly those of Buddhist pilgrims, vividly describe what the travelers saw.

By the fifth century A.D., under the Northern Wei Dynasty (A.D. 386–535), Buddhist art flourished in China. The early Wei rulers were originally from Central Asia and, to consolidate their position in China, they promoted Daoism and Buddhism rather than Confucianism, the established state doctrine. Like Ashoka and Constantine, they presided over monumental building projects, using religion and religious art in the service of political power.

Their first great artistic program was at Yungang, in Shaanxi Province. Caves were cut into the cliffs and colossal statues carved from the existing rock (fig. **9.P**). At Yungang, the influence of hundreds of Central Asian Buddhist caves—themselves based on Indian *vihāras* and *chaitya* halls—is clear. The monumental stone Buddhas carved from these sandstone cliffs also show traces of the Gandharan style.

The Buddha in figure 9.P bears some resemblance to Gandharan sculpture, particularly in such details as the smooth hair and flowing drapery that covers both shoulders. But the Yungang Buddha is psychologically more remote. All trace of Indian sensuousness has disappeared. The figure retains canonical features such as the *ushnīsha*, elongated earlobes, and monk's robe, but the drapery folds are flatter and more stylized. The combination of the figure's colossal size and impassive gaze seems to elevate this Buddha to a spiritual plane that is beyond human time and place.

In 494, the Wei rulers moved their court southward to Luoyang. There they encountered a different form of Buddhism practiced by the native (Han) Chinese, which offered relief from the cycle of reincarnation through a less difficult route to *nirvana*. Groups known as Paradise Sects promised enlightenment in a resplendent paradise, attainable by anyone through faith, rather than exclusively through the rigors of monastic life. As in India, the popu-

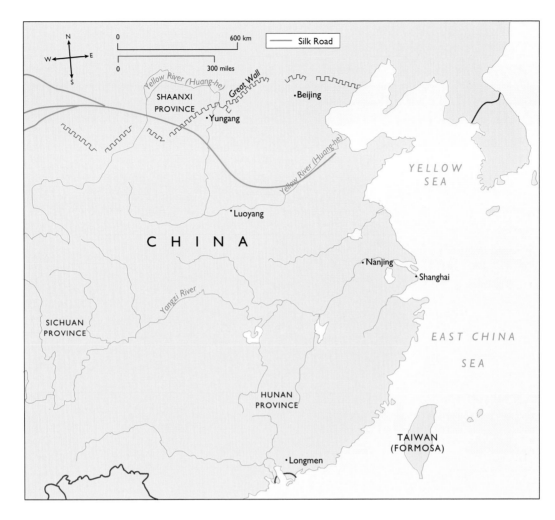

9.0 Map of China.

larity of Shakyamuni Buddha was rivaled by that of buddhas of the Past and Future. The cults of Maitreya and Amitabha, buddhas of the Future, invited believers to be reborn in paradise. These theological changes are noticeable in Buddhist art: for example, some images of Shakyamuni Buddha now appear to relate actively to worshipers. In addition, the number of representations of such buddhas as Maitreya, Amitabha, and Vairochana (the supreme cosmic Buddha) has increased.

When the Wei moved south, they took up a second major artistic program in the caves at Longmen. There the *Buddha with Disciples* (fig. **9.Q**) from the Pinyang Cave is the focal rock-cut image inside the inner chapel. Shakyamuni sits cross-legged on a platform 19 feet (5.7 m) wide. His throne is guarded by the lions of royalty and he is flanked by disciples. He no longer bows his head and lowers his eyelids to convey a state of inward meditation. Instead, in accordance with the *Lotus Sutra* (one of the canonical Buddhist texts) he gazes at worshipers, communicating directly with them. This active connection is reinforced by his enlarged hands: the right is held up in

abhaya mudrā (the "do not fear" gesture), and the left points downward in *bhumisparsha mudrā* ("calling the earth to witness"). The figure's proportions are more elongated than at Yungang.

Shakyamuni's robe is now a Chinese garment. Its cascading folds are stylized as waterfalls and fishtails. In contrast to the relatively three-dimensional treatment of drapery at Yungang, this Buddha's robe is flatter and more linear; it is composed of repeated patterns. Such stylistic differences reflect the assimilation of foreign models into a more purely Chinese style. Similarly, the Longmen Buddha's full-cheeked, square-jawed facial type, with its almond-shaped eyes and smiling, rosebud mouth, is distinctively Chinese. The flat, elaborately carved mandorla that surrounds the throne is filled with flames symbolizing the light of the Buddha's spirit.

The best example of the Longmen style was created under the Tang Dynasty (618–906), when China was again united and the arts flourished. As Buddhism developed in Tang China, the belief that buddhahood could be attained in this world grew in importance. Mystical rituals were

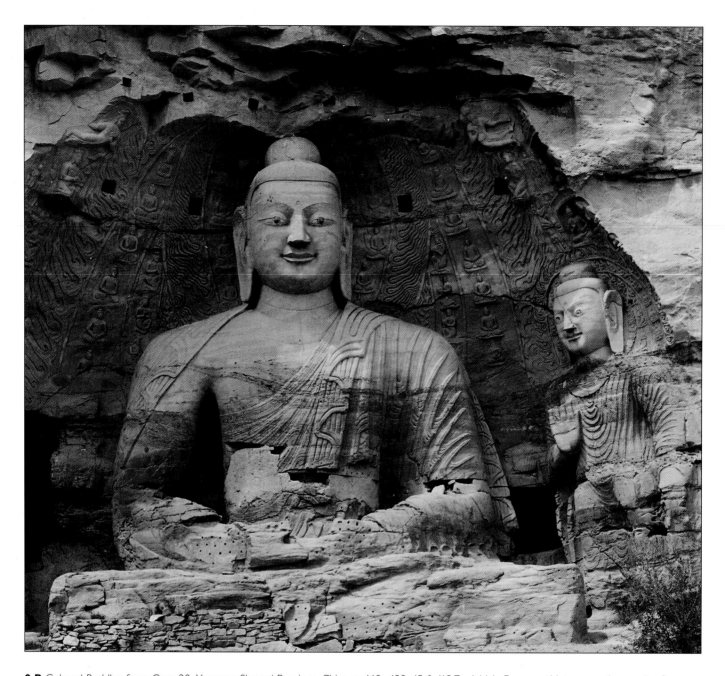

9.P Colossal Buddha, from Cave 20, Yungang, Shaanxi Province, China, c. 460–490. 45 ft (13.7 m) high. For over thirty years, thousands of stoneworkers created such sculptures and carved out cave temples and cells in the Yungang cliffs. The project was proposed to the Wei rulers in A.D. 460 by the monk Tanyao.

intended to connect the earthly, material world with the formless, absolute world, and to guide individuals along the path to spiritual awareness.

Figure **9.R** depicts *Vairochana Buddha*, the embodiment of Shakyamuni's spiritual nature and the most popular of the Five Great Buddhas of Wisdom. The figure's colossal size and simply rendered form enhance the Buddha's otherworldly quality. The original lotus throne, which has

been lost, was conceived of as having one thousand petals, each corresponding to a single Buddhist cosmos with one hundred million Buddhist worlds. Vairochana (meaning "Resplendent") personifies the creativity of Buddhist *Dharma* and the Buddhist view of the universe. In one tradition—Huayen—Vairochana is the Universal Buddha. By association with him, China's emperors legitimized their claim to power.

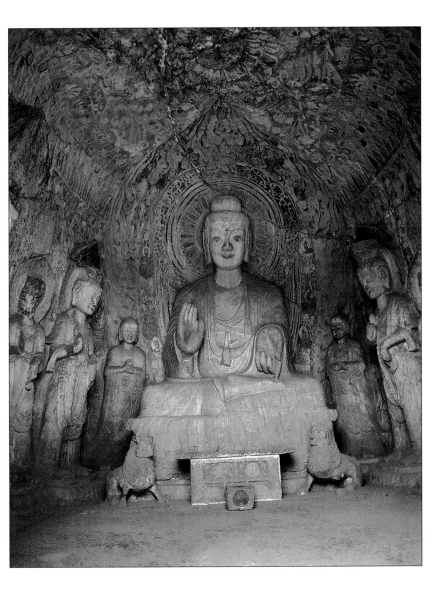

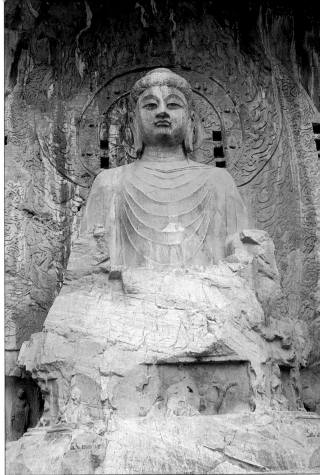

9.Q (left) *Buddha with Disciples*, from the Pinyang Cave, Longmen, Hunan Province, China, early 6th century.

9.R (above) *Vairochana Buddha*, Longmen Caves, Hunan Province, China, 672–675. Natural rock, approx. 49 ft (14.9 m) high.

	Style/Period	Works of Art		Cultural/Historical Developments	
750 B.C. 0 A.D. 700	**BUDDHIST** 8th to 1st century B.C. *Chaitya hall* **BUDDHIST** 1st to 7th century A.D. *Worship of the Buddha*		*Chaitya hall* (**9.B**), Karli *Mithuna* (**9.E**), Karli Santa Sabina (**9.D**), Rome *Preaching Buddha* (**9.F**), Sarnath Colossal Buddha (**9.P**), Yungang Ajanta Caves (**9.G–9.I, 9.J–9.N**), Maharashtra *Buddha with Disciples* (**9.Q**), Longmen *Vairochana Buddha* (**9.R**), Longmen	Legendary founding of Rome by Romulus (c. 750 B.C.) Birth of Siddhartha Gautama, founder of Buddhism, in Nepal c. 563 B.C. (d. 483 B.C.) Birth of Confucius, Chinese philosopher c. 551 B.C. (d. 479) Beginning of Iron Age in China (c. 500 B.C.) Age of Perikles in Athens (460–429 B.C.) Crucifixion of Christ at Jerusalem (c. A.D. 30) Galla Placidia erects mausoleum at Ravenna (c. 425) End of western Roman Empire (476) Building of Hagia Sophia, Constantinople (532–7) Birth of Muhammad, founder of Islam (c. 575)	

Ajanta Caves

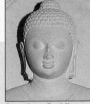

Colossal Buddha

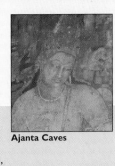

Preaching Buddha

10
The Early Middle Ages

In western Europe, the term "Middle Ages" generally designates the period following the decline of the Roman Empire through the thirteenth or fourteenth centuries. "Early Middle Ages," as used here, covers the period roughly from the seventh to around the end of the tenth century.

As the Roman Empire declined, the Goths invaded much of western Europe and the Visigoths sacked Rome in 410. This hastened the collapse of the Roman imperial hierarchy, as well as of Rome's control of its vast territory. In the early eighth century, Moors (from the Roman province of Mauretania in northwest Africa) conquered Spain, which had also been part of the Roman Empire. The Moors brought with them the new religion of Islam, to which they had been converted in the seventh century by Arab conquerors. Islam grew into a powerful force in parts of Europe, particularly in Spain. It flourished until the thirteenth century, when Christian armies reclaimed the Moorish strongholds—the *Reconquista*, or Reconquest. The last of these was Granada, which fell in 1492, the year that Columbus sailed from Spain in search of a western route to India.

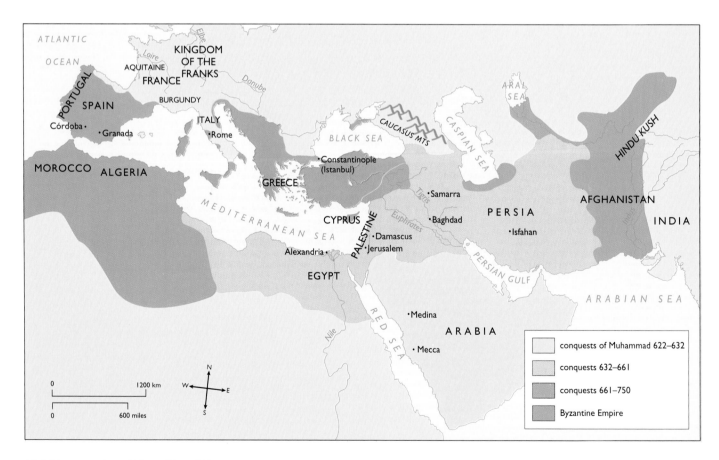

10.1 The expansion of Islam, 622–c. 750.

Islam

One of the world's great religions, Islam literally means "surrender [to God]" (see Box). It was founded by the Prophet Muhammad, who was born in Mecca, in western Arabia, around 570. He and his followers fled to the more hospitable neighboring city of Medina in 622, a watershed event called the *hijra* that marks the starting point of the Islamic calendar. Within two years of Muhammad's death in 632 his successor, the first caliph, or ruler, united Arabia under the new faith. Over the next twenty years, Islamic armies conquered large portions of the Byzantine Empire and the Middle East (fig. **10.1**). Controversy over the succession to the caliphate caused a political and religious schism in 661 that persists today. Islam is thus divided into two sects: Sunni Muslims and Shiite Muslims. As a result of aggressive campaigns of conquest and conversion, a century after its founding Islam stretched from Afghanistan in the east to Portugal, Spain, and southwestern France in the west, where it rivaled Christianity.

The most recent of the world's three monotheistic religions, Islam accepts Moses, Jesus, and others as prophets and forerunners of Muhammad. Like Judaism, Islam discourages the making of images that might be worshiped as idols. Muslim artists thus concentrated their creative energies on the development of nonfigurative forms, not only delighting the eye, but leading the mind to the contemplation of God. They excelled at calligraphy and geometric patterning, as well as at vegetal ornament (see Box).

Architecture

The Dome of the Rock, Jerusalem   The earliest extant Islamic sanctuary is the Dome of the Rock in Jerusalem (fig. 10.4). The structure encloses a rock outcropping that is sacred to Judaism and Christianity as well as to Islam. Its exterior is faced with mosaics and marble. The building, which was inspired by round Christian martyria, is a centrally planned octagon. Stylistically, the architectural ornamentation of the Dome of the Rock is a synthesis of Byzantine, Persian, and other Middle Eastern forms. Figure 10.4 illustrates the richness and complexity of the abstract patterning on the exterior, and the brilliant impression made by the **gilded** dome.

This was precisely the effect desired by Caliph Abd al-Malik, who commissioned it. According to a tenth-century source, he wanted a building that would "dazzle the minds" of Muslims and thereby distract them from the Christian buildings in Jerusalem.[1] This sentiment is a variant of the impulse to compete artistically, using height and size to express achievement and power. In the caliph's view, the splendor of his sanctuary would symbolically "blind" Muslims, preventing them from "seeing" beauty in monuments built by other faiths.

Mosques   Although Muslims may pray anywhere as long as they face Mecca, religious architecture became an important part of Islamic culture. In the earliest days of Islam, the faithful gathered to pray in the courtyard of the Prophet Muhammad's home. From this developed the primary architectural expression of Islam, the **mosque**.

There are two main types of mosque: the *masjid* is used for daily prayer by individuals or small groups, while the larger *jāmi'* is used for congregational worship on Fridays, the Muslim sabbath. Although mosques around the world reflect local architectural traditions, most share certain basic features. These are a **sahn**, or enclosed courtyard (less common in later centuries), and a **qibla**, or prayer wall, oriented toward Mecca. The *qibla* frequently has a **mihrāb** (small niche) set into it. *Jāmi'* mosques also contain a **minbar**, a pulpit from which an *imam* (religious teacher) leads the faithful. By the end of the seventh century, Muslim rulers were beginning to build larger and more elaborate structures. The exterior of a typical mosque

---

Islamic Religion

Islam carries a relatively simple and straightforward message: the unity of the community of Muslims ("those who surrender") and their equality before Allah (God), who is single and absolute, and whose ultimate prophet was Muhammad. The holy book of Islam, the Koran (or Qur'an), is believed to be the word of Allah as revealed to Muhammad in a series of visions. Another text, the Hadith, is a later compilation of traditions. Together, the Koran and the Hadith form the basis of Islamic belief and law. The Five Pillars of the faith are: (1) the affirmation that there is no God but Allah and that Muhammad is his messenger; (2) ritual prayer in the direction of Mecca five times a day; (3) almsgiving; (4) fasting and abstinence during the holy month of Ramadan; and (5) the *hadj*, an annual pilgrimage to Mecca that every devout Muslim strives to make at least once.

Islamic Calligraphy

"Handwriting is jewelry fastened by the hand from the pure gold of the intellect," wrote an early authority on Islamic calligraphy.[2]

Since the Koran was originally revealed to Muhammad in the Arabic language, Muslims must read and recite from it only in Arabic. This has meant that, as Islam spread, Arabic language and Arabic script spread as well. Because of its close association with the sacred text, writing is the most honored art in the Islamic world. It is also the most characteristic, uniting the diverse and far-flung community of believers. Writing adorns not only books, but also ceramics, metal-work, textiles, and buildings (such as the courtyard façade in figure 10.13 and the interior of the dome in figure 10.15). A great many calligraphic styles have developed over the centuries.

There are two main groups of scripts: the earliest, Kufic—similar to Western printed letters and used today mainly for headings and formal inscriptions—and cursive, which evolved from the twelfth century on. Figure **10.2** illustrates a page from a ninth- or tenth-century manuscript of the Koran written in Kufic. It shows the Islamic interest in the linear complexity of texts as well as of designs. The abstract, linear rhythms of Islamic calligraphy lend themselves to a variety of visual effects, from the simple strength of early Kufic script to the intricacies of Sultan Suleyman's imperial emblem (fig. **10.3**).

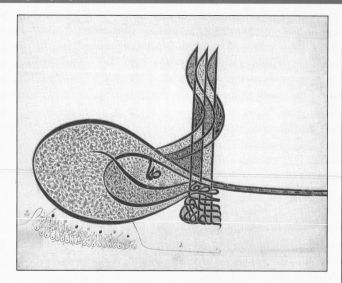

10.3 Illuminated *tugra* of Sultan Suleyman, c. 1555–60. Ink, paint, and gold on paper, 20½ × 25⅜ in (52 × 64.5 cm). Metropolitan Museum of Art, New York. Rogers Fund, 1938 (38.149.1). Photograph © 1986 Metropolitan Museum of Art.

10.2 Page from the Kairouan manuscript of the Koran, written in Kufic, Tunisia, 9th–10th centuries. Ink, gold, and silver on blue dyed parchment, 11⅓ × 14⅞ in (28.73 × 37.62 cm). Arthur M. Sackler Museum. Harvard University Art Museums. Francis H. Burr Memorial Fund.

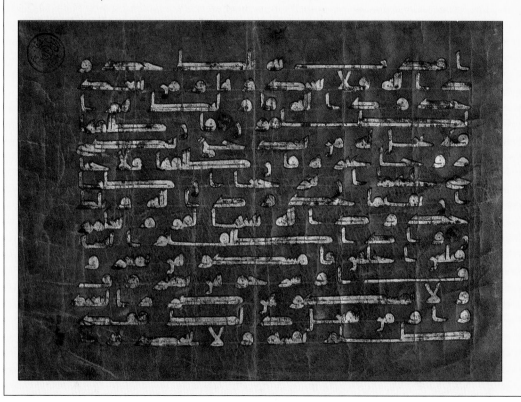

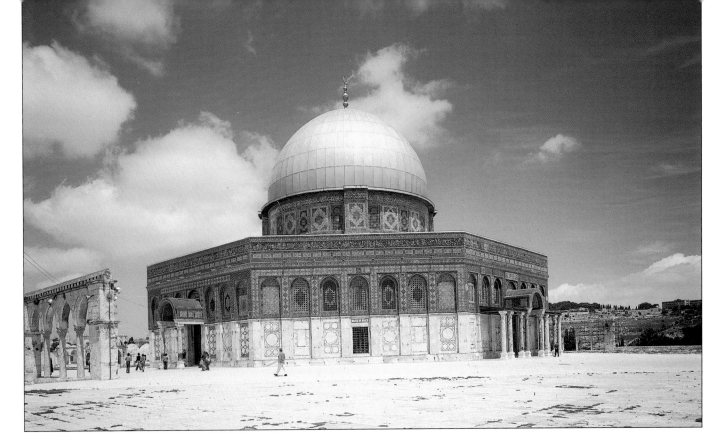

includes one or more tall minarets, such as those added to Hagia Sophia when it was changed from a Christian church to a mosque (cf. fig. 9.30). From these towers, a *muezzin*, or crier, traditionally calls the faithful to prayer at the five prescribed times each day.

As Islam spread to the West and won more converts, new mosques were needed. The biggest of these was located in Samarra, on the banks of the Tigris (fig. **10.5**). Built from 847 to 852 by Caliph al-Mutawakkil, it is now in ruins. Nothing remains of the lavish mosaics and painted

10.4 Dome of the Rock, Jerusalem, late 7th century. Also known as the Mosque of Omar, this was constructed on a 35-acre (140 sq km) plateau in east Jerusalem. Muslims traditionally regard it as the site of Muhammad's ascent to heaven. Jews know the plateau as the Temple Mount—the location of Abraham's sacrifice of Isaac and of the first Jewish temple, built by King Solomon in the 10th century B.C.

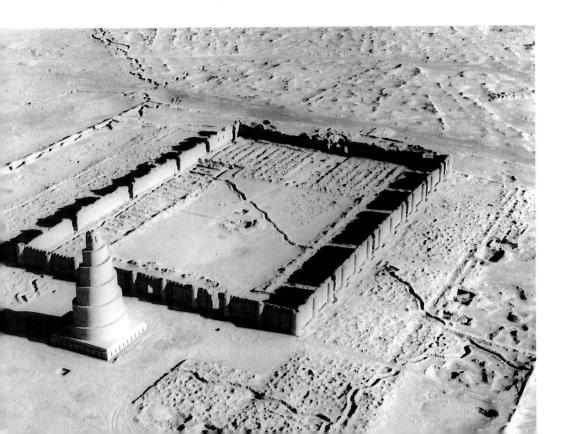

10.5 Great Mosque, Samarra (now in Iraq), 847–852. Approx. 10 acres.

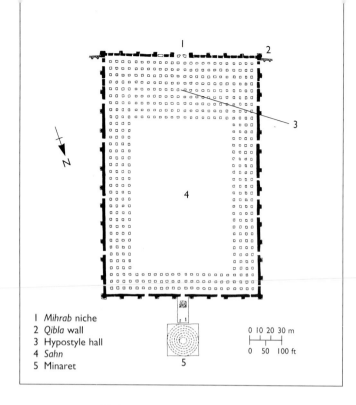

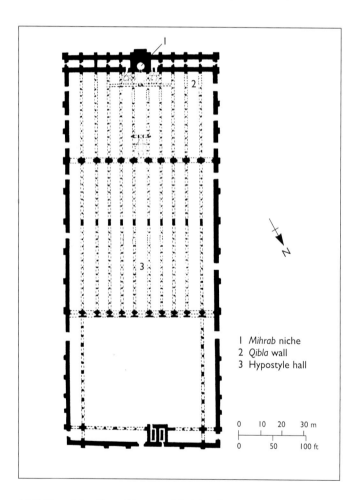

10.6 Plan of the Great Mosque, Samarra, 847–852.

Key:
1 *Mihrab* niche
2 *Qibla* wall
3 Hypostyle hall
4 *Sahn*
5 Minaret

Key:
1 *Mihrab* niche
2 *Qibla* wall
3 Hypostyle hall

10.7 Plan of the Great Mosque, Córdoba, Spain, originally built 786–787. The additions of 832–848 and 961 are shown, but not the final enlargement of 987. The mosque is a rectangular enclosure with its main axis pointing south toward Mecca. Because Spain lies west of Mecca, this orientation is symbolic rather than exact.

plaster that decorated the interior. The plan (fig. **10.6**) shows the location of the 464 supports of the wooden hypostyle roof. These were arranged in rows around a huge, rectangular *sahn*. An unusual feature of this mosque is the single, cone-shaped minaret that rises 60 feet (18.3 m) on the north side. A ramp connects it with the main building, and leading to the top is a spiral stairway. This tower has been related to the ancient Near Eastern ziggurats (see p. 54), although its origins remain a topic of scholarly debate.

The most impressive example of a Western Islamic mosque is the one built by Abd ar-Rahman I at Córdoba. The first Muslim ruler of Spain, he commissioned the mosque in 785 for his capital (fig. **10.7**). After its original construction (on the site of a church), the Great Mosque

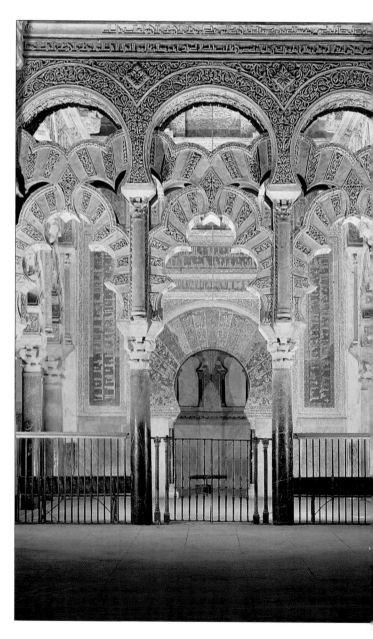

10.8 *Mihrāb* bay, the Great Mosque, Córdoba, c. 961–966.

was enlarged in 832–848, 961, and 987. In the thirteenth century, Christians gained control of the Córboba mosque and turned it into a cathedral, but enough of the original mosque survives to convey the magnificence of its design and ornamentation.

The system of double arches in the original mosque is unique, and it was used in each later addition. Filling the hypostyle interior are numerous columns either salvaged or derived from Roman and Early Christian buildings (fig. **10.9**). These columns were relatively short—under 10 feet (3 m) high. If they had supported the arches and vaults at that height, the interior illumination would have been inadequate. Instead, therefore, the architect constructed a series of double-height, horseshoe-shaped striped arches (using voussoirs of alternating red brick and pale yellow stones) to raise the ceiling height. The second tier of arches springs from posts atop the lower columns and originally supported a tiled wooden roof. (This was replaced by vaulting in the sixteenth century.) The vast numbers of columns have been likened to a forest, and the colored arches create an impression of continual motion that enlivens the dimly lit interior. The multiplication of architectural elements here breaks up the flow of space, creating a sense of mystery.

As part of the second expansion phase in 961, the caliph ruling at Córdoba built a magnificent *mihrāb* in front of the *qibla* wall. To its north is an area reserved for the caliph and his retinue. This consists of three domed chambers entered through three tiers of lobed arches (fig. **10.8**), which crisscross each other to form an interlaced screen.

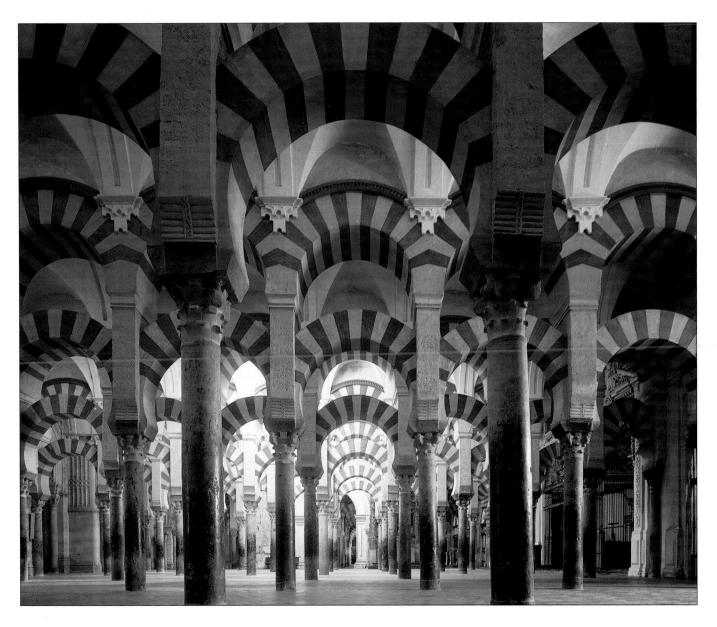

10.9 Arches of the Great Mosque, Córdoba, c. 961–966. Columns 9 ft 9 in (2.97 m) high. The interior space is larger than that of any present Christian church.

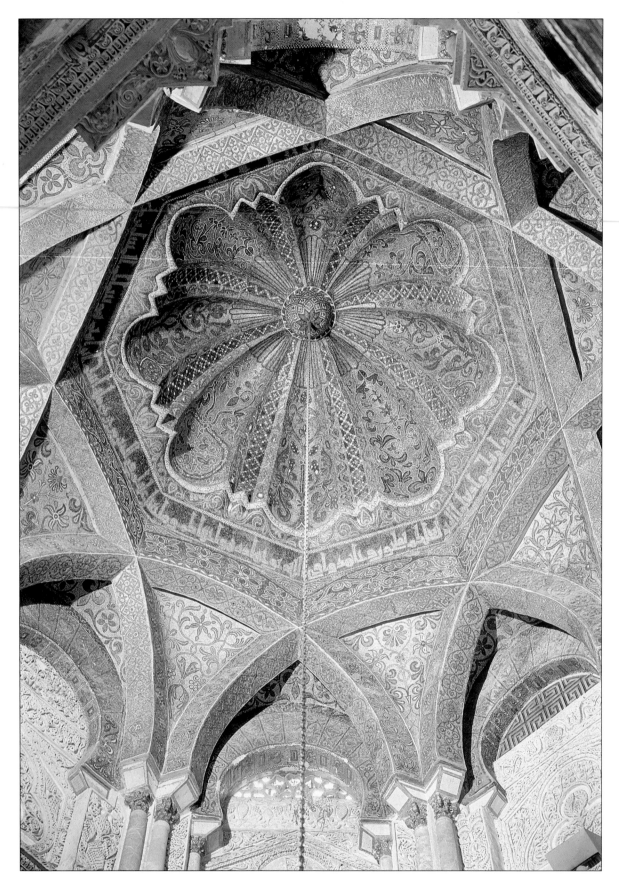

10.10 Dome above the *mihrāb*, the Great Mosque, Córdoba, c. 961–966. Mosaic.

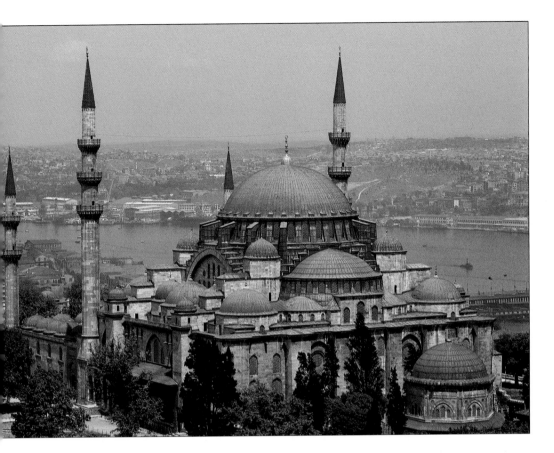

10.11 Sinan the Great, Mosque of Suleyman I, Istanbul, Turkey, begun 1550. Sinan was a Greek who converted to Islam, and at the age of 47 became "Architect of the Empire." As supervisor of building in Istanbul and overseer of all public works, he was referrred to as "Architect in the Abode of Felicity."

The domes themselves are built in intricate geometric patterns—all of them different—on eight intersecting stone arches, or ribs. The central dome (fig. **10.10**) and the *qibla* wall have elaborate, Byzantine-inspired mosaics with gold backgrounds. This synthesis of structure and ornament in the Great Mosque at Córdoba became characteristic of later Islamic architecture.

In 1453, when Constantinople was conquered by the Ottoman Turks from Central Asia, the city was renamed Istanbul. The Ottoman Empire grew rapidly, reached a peak in the sixteenth century, and lasted until 1922. It was under the Ottomans that Hagia Sophia (see p. 293) was transformed from a Byzantine church into a place of worship for Muslims.

The leading Ottoman architect was Sinan the Great (c. 1491–1588), known as Koca (the Architect). His most important work in Istanbul, the mosque of Suleyman I (figs. **10.11** and **10.12**), was part of an imperial complex begun in 1550. By aligning the mosque with the horizon, Sinan used the elevated site to enhance its monumental effect. His notion of an ideal geometric symmetry—particularly a circle inscribed in a square—is clear from the plan. His domes also express the symbolic significance of the circle as a divine shape with God at its center.

The large central dome, preceded by several levels of smaller domes and stepped, buttressed walls, seems to be bubbling up from the interior of the hill. Four minarets

10.12 Plan of the Mosque of Suleyman I and the imperial complex. In addition to the mosque, the vast complex includes seven colleges, a hospital and asylum, baths, two residences, a hostel, kitchens, tombs, a school, fountains, wrestling grounds, shops, and a courtyard. Altogether there are five hundred domes, of which the mosque's is the largest.

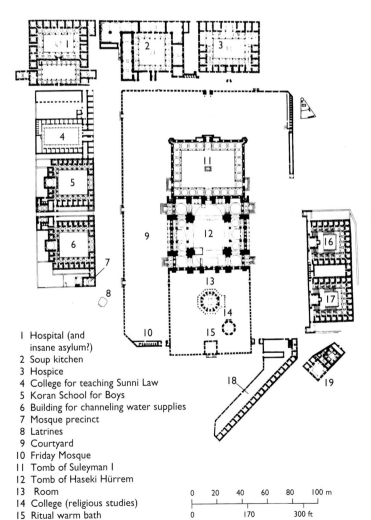

1 Hospital (and insane asylum?)
2 Soup kitchen
3 Hospice
4 College for teaching Sunni Law
5 Koran School for Boys
6 Building for channeling water supplies
7 Mosque precinct
8 Latrines
9 Courtyard
10 Friday Mosque
11 Tomb of Suleyman I
12 Tomb of Haseki Hürrem
13 Room
14 College (religious studies)
15 Ritual warm bath

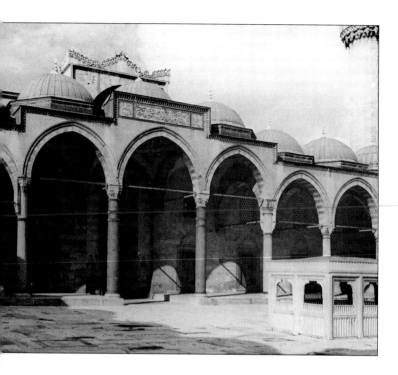

accent the exterior symmetry. The *sahn* (fig. **10.13**) is surrounded by a colonnade of arches, whose sizes correspond to the width of the twenty-four domes they support. The interior of the mosque (fig. **10.15**), despite restoration, shows the influence of Hagia Sophia, with domes resting on pendentives, and many small windows creating an impression of light streaming down from heaven. The *mihrāb*, visible in this view, was decorated with blue, red, and white ceramic tiles arranged to create elaborate floral designs.

The seventeenth-century Luftullah Mosque in Isfahan shows the skill of Muslim artists in creating shimmering, jewel-like surfaces composed of intricate floral and calligraphic tilework (fig. **10.14**). These are reminiscent of knotted carpets, for which Persia (modern Iran)—which became part of the Islamic world in the seventh century—was renowned. Their colorful rhythms reflect influences of nomadic textile traditions, and of the ancient Near Eastern taste for geometric patterns.

10.13 (left) Courtyard (*sahn*) of the Mosque of Suleyman I.

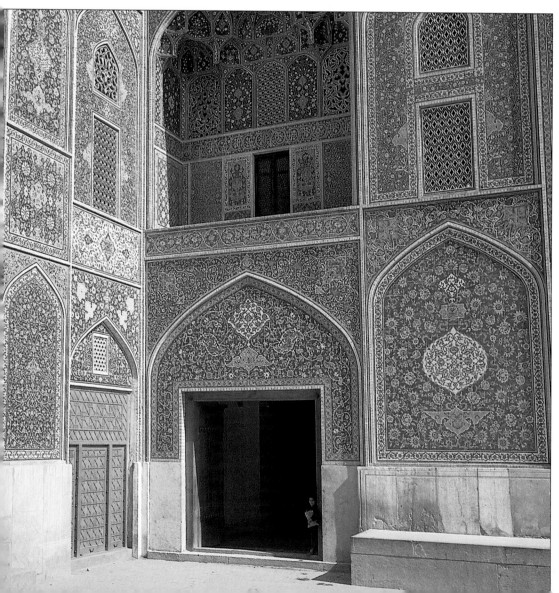

10.14 The Luftullah Mosque, Isfahan, Iran, 1602–16.

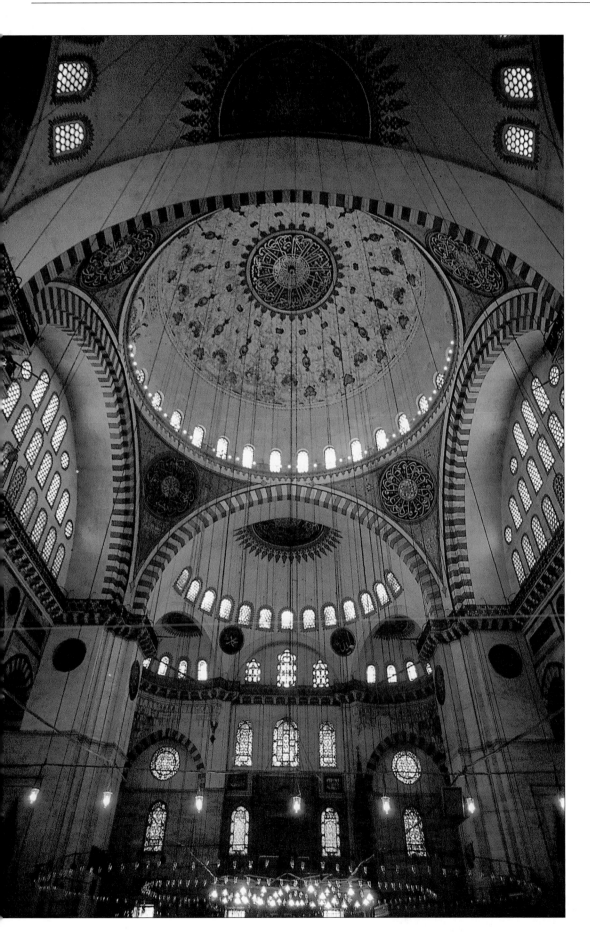

Northern European Art

To all intents and purposes, the early medieval Islamic influence on western Europe and its art was concentrated in the south, for the Frankish ruler Charles Martel had halted the Muslim invasion of Europe at Tours, in central France. The north (fig. **10.16**) became a new focus of political and artistic activity, which was more influenced by Germanic tribes than by either Islam or Hellenistic-Roman tradition. The Germanic Angles and Saxons had invaded the British Isles in the fifth century A.D. and the Franks had invaded Gaul (hence the name France). Because of these continual waves of invasion, no monumental architecture, painting, or sculpture was produced. Instead, a new craft was developed around the metalwork brought by the invaders. Some of it is reminiscent of the nomadic Scythian Animal Style (cf. fig. 3.4).

Anglo-Saxon Metalwork

A good example of Anglo-Saxon metalwork is the seventh-century purse cover from Sutton Hoo in East Anglia on the southeast coast of England (fig. **10.17**). It was part of a purse containing gold coins which was discovered among the treasures of a pagan ship burial. This was a practice in which the deceased was placed in a ship sent out to sea, reflecting the belief that boats carried the dead into the afterlife. The circumstances of the burial suggest that the deceased was a royal personage, for the ship contained an abundance of treasures. The Anglo-Saxon epic *Beowulf* (see Box) describes the lavish burials of kings with armor and other valuable objects.

The purse's decoration is of gold, *cloisonné* **enamel**, and dark red garnets. It has echoes of Early Christian **interlace** designs (cf. fig. 9.23) as well as of the Scythian Animal Style and other ancient Near Eastern motifs. The taste for flat, crowded, interlaced patterns became an undercurrent in western Europe and continued through the Middle Ages. The arrangement of the decorative sections on the purse cover is symmetrical, as is each individual section or pair of sections. At the top, two geometric shapes filled with gold tracery flank a centerpiece containing two fighting animals intertwined in the tracery. This technique, in which animals merge into a design or into each other, had also been characteristic of Scythian gold objects (cf. fig. 3.34). Below, in the center of the purse cover, are two sets of animals. An eagle and a duck face each other and are symmetrically framed by a pair of frontal men flanked by animals in profile, the latter a motif derived from ancient Near Eastern iconography. The merging animal forms suggest that the waves of invaders from the fifth century onwards brought their artistic styles to western Europe.

The Viking Era (A.D. c. 800–1000)

The Vikings were Scandinavian warriors who inhabited Norway, Sweden, and Denmark (Finland and Lapland belonged to different ethnic groups). They were known throughout Europe for their paganism and their ferocious, destructive raids. The best literary sources for Viking society are the sagas (prose narratives dealing with heroic figures and events) of Iceland, which was settled by the Norwegian Harald the Fairhair in the ninth century. The sagas also record the ancient oral traditions of Scandinavia, and present a valuable account of its pre-Christian culture (see Boxes). Inhabited since the Stone Age, Scandinavia was an agricultural society, divided into small communities ruled by kings who were descended from royal families and elected to the throne.

In about 800 the Scandinavians developed sailing ships propelled by oars. This made extensive travel possible, and there is evidence of Viking incursions from Byzantium and the Baltics to northern France, the British Isles, Greenland, and North America. As a result, there are traces of Islamic, Byzantine, and Scythian influence in Viking art. For example, the animal-head post from a ship burial at Oseberg, Norway (fig. **10.18**), is similar in conception to the Scythian lion-head finial from Kul Oba (fig. **10.19**), a site between the Black Sea and the Sea of Azov in Russia. Both works are characterized by a compact monumental form, enhanced by the fiercely bared fangs of the lions. These works combine monumentality with elegant stylization, the finial more related to Achaemenid prototypes and the head post to Anglo-Saxon interlace.

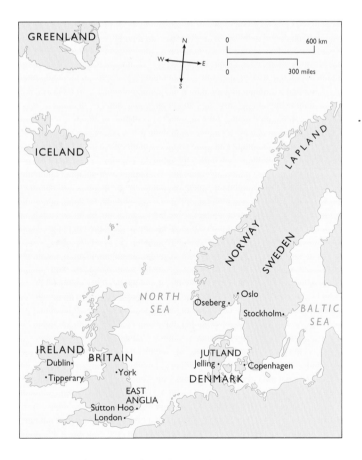

10.16 Map of Northern Europe in the Middle Ages.

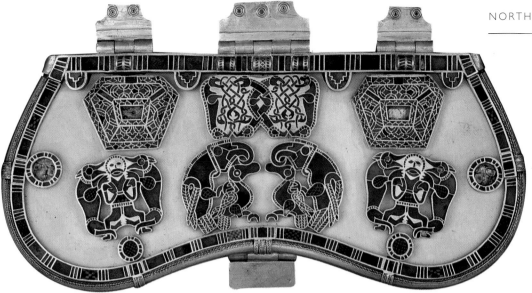

10.17 Sutton Hoo purse cover, from East Anglia, England, c. 630. Gold with garnets and *cloisonné* enamel, originally on ivory or bone (since lost), 8 in (20.3 cm) long. British Museum, London. In the *cloisonné* technique, liquid enamel of different colors is poured into *cloisons*, or compartments, formed by a network of thin metal strips, to create surface decoration. The top of the metal remains exposed.

Beowulf

Beowulf is the earliest surviving European epic composed in the vernacular. Although clearly in the tradition of Germanic folklore, it has a strong sense of Christian morality. The epic is believed to have been written down in the eighth century, but the events it describes take place in the sixth century and the text is known from a late tenth-century manuscript.

Beowulf opens with a miracle that occurred in childhood—in the tradition of the births of Sargon of Akkad (see p. 58) and Moses. The child Scyld Scefing drifts ashore in a boat and starts a new dynasty in Denmark. "Sent from nowhere," according to the text, "the Danes found him floating with gifts a strange king-child." Clearly this image was informed by echoes of Christ as baby-king, as well as of Moses in the bulrushes.

When Scyld Scefing dies, he is given a ship burial like that in which the Sutton Hoo purse cover was discovered. Scyld's burial ship is described as:

> .... ring-prowed ...
> icy and eager   armed for a king.
>   ... From hills and valleys
> rings and bracelets   were borne to the shore.
> No words have sung   of a wealthier grave-ship
> swords and ring-mail   rich for drifting
> through the foaming tide   far from that land.
> ...
> At last they hung   high upon the mast
> a golden banner   then gave him to the sea
> to the mounding waves.... [3]

The epic is divided into two main parts. In the first, the hero Beowulf, a Swedish prince, offers his services to the King of Denmark, whose palace is being ravaged by the monster Grendel. Beowulf destroys Grendel and brings his head to the Danish king. In the second part, Beowulf has become a king. In his old age, he is mortally wounded in a battle with a monster. The epic concludes with a description of Beowulf's funeral rites and burial.

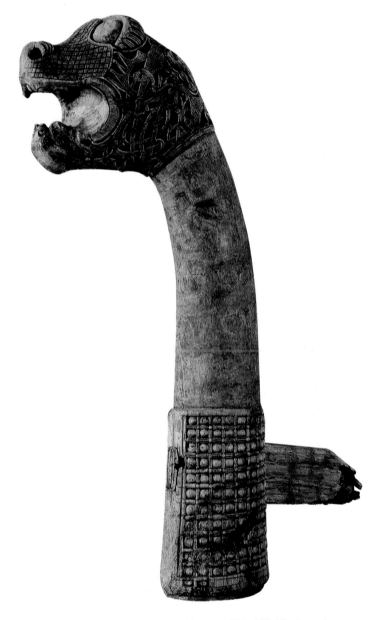

10.18 Animal-head post, Oseberg, Norway, 800–850. Hardwood (probably lime), approx. 23⅝ in (60 cm) high. University Museum of National Antiquities, Oslo.

The Scandinavian Cosmos

For the Scandinavians, as for the ancient Greeks, the beginning of time was primeval chaos (*Ginnungagap*), a dark, formless abyss. An excerpt from *Saemund's Edda* (a myth written down in Scaldic by the thirteenth-century Icelandic author Snorri Sturlson) describes the Norse view of chaos:

> In early times,
> When Ymir lived
> Was sand, nor sea,
> Nor cooling wave;
> No earth was found,
> Nor heaven above;
> One chaos all,
> And nowhere grass.[4]

In Norse myth, the ice-giant Ymir emerged from the frost and iceblocks that filled the abyss. After he was killed, his blood caused the flood that destroyed his race. Only one giant survived and, with his wife, he sailed off in a boat to father a new race of giants, the Jotun. (Note the similarity to the Sumerian flood myth and the Old Testament account of Noah.)

Unlike the ancient Greeks, who believed that the anthropomorphic Olympians had destroyed the primitive Giants, the Scandinavian giants continued to exist. They were in continual conflict with the gods, but they also made alliances with them, and occasionally intermarried. In Greek mythology, the cosmic battle between the Giants and the Olympians had already taken place, but in Scandinavia the cosmic battle (*Ragnarok*, or "Twilight of the Gods") between these forces was set in the future, as is the Christian Apocalypse. Whereas in the Judeo-Christian traditions there had been a paradise (the Garden of Eden), in Norse myth peace and prosperity would come only after *Ragnarok*.

The Norse universe was polytheistic. It had been ordered by the chief god, Odin, who scheduled the seasons and established the positions of the sun and moon. He divided the world into three areas:

- **Asgard** The dwelling of the gods and location of Valhalla, where Odin presided over the dead warrior elite preparing for *Ragnarok*.

- **Midgard** Middle Earth, inhabited by people. The gods created Midgard from the dead body of Ymir. His flesh became the earth, his blood the sea, his hair the trees and plants. His skull was emptied and turned upside down to form the dome of heaven, and his brains were scattered and became clouds.

- **Utgard** Outer Earth, home of the Jotun. At the axis of the world was the tree Yggdrasil, where gods held daily council. (There are comparable tree cults elsewhere—for example, in India and Crete.)

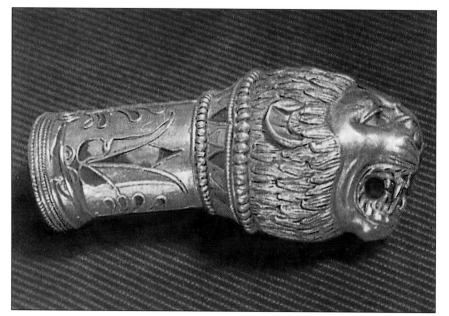

10.19 Lion-head finial, Kul Oba, Russia. Gold and bronze.

have been a member of Harald Bluetooth's court (see below). The combination of geometric design with natural elements such as foliage and a bird suggests familiarity with Anglo-Saxon metalwork.

Rune Stones and Picture Stones

More specifically native to Scandinavia than interlace are forms of inscription on upright boulders known as **rune stones** and **picture stones**. The earliest runes (letters of the runic alphabet) are from the third century, when the Vikings arrived in the north. Runes were also used by Germanic tribes, Goths, and Anglo-Saxons. In the Viking era, there were sixteen stick-shaped letters in the alphabet. The runic inscriptions on stones could be memorials, or records of voyages, battles, and even daily activities. Only an initiated few could read the rune stones, which were intended to preserve the mythical, literary, and cultural history of Scandinavia.

Although the function of these objects is unknown, it is likely, given their leonine character, that they were guardians.

The pure interlace motif appears on a tenth-century axe from Denmark (fig. **10.20**). Its gold neck and silver inlay indicate the high status of the owner, who is thought to

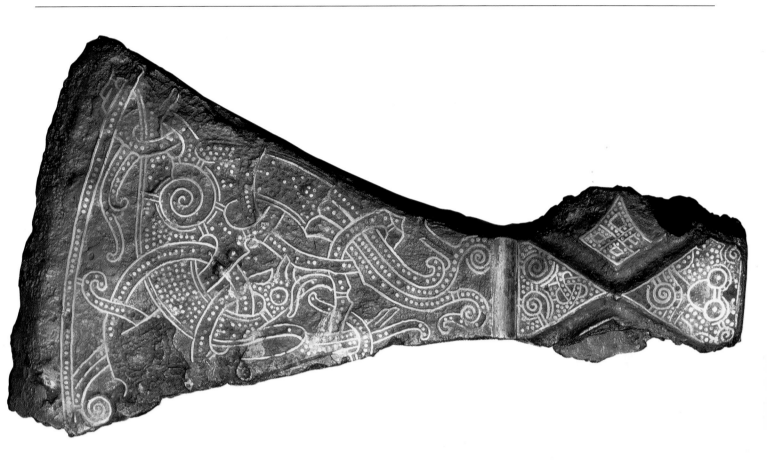

10.20 Axe from Mammen, Jutland, Denmark, Late Viking, c. 950–975. Silver inlay and gold, 6⅞ in (17. 5 cm) long. National Museum, Copenhagen.

The Norse Pantheon

GODS	Attributes and Qualities
The Aesir	
Odin	God of wisdom, created the first human couple, god of Vikings and royal families, stole poetry from the Jotun and gave it to the human race, gave people the secret of writing and the runes. He was also a shaman, and the ruler of Valhalla.
Thor	God of the peasants, a giant gourmand, protector of the cosmos (comparable to Indra, Zeus, and Jupiter), wields a hammer.
Frigg	Wife of Odin. Fertility.
Baldr	Son of Odin and Frigg.
Heimdall	Son of nine giant mothers. Guardian of the world at the end of the rainbow, originator of social classes.
Loki	Fire god, troublemaker, trickster. Offspring of the Jotun and Odin's bloodbrother. At *Ragnarok*, he sides with the Jotun.

The Vanir	
Njoro	Fertility.
Frey	Phallic fertility god, brother of Freyja.
Freyja	Fertility and war, fosters romance, leads the Valkyries.
Divine Groups	
Jotun	Primeval giants.
Volur	Wise women who know the history of the world.
Norns	Fates, female powers who sit under the tree Yggdrasil.
Valkyries	Beautiful immortal virgins with gold and silver armor who decide which warriors will be admitted to Valhalla after their death. They ride magnificent horses which are personifications of the clouds.
Elves	Fertility gods. Keepers of the ancestor cults.
Dwarves	Smith gods who inhabit the underground.

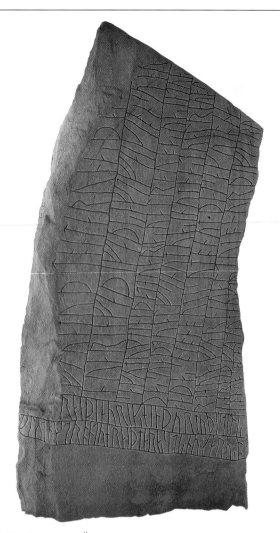

10.21 The Rök stone, Östergötland, Sweden, early 9th century.

The early ninth-century rune stone at Rök, in Sweden, has the first known runic inscription of an oral narrative in Scandinavia, a memorial dedicated by a Viking chieftain to his dead son (fig. **10.21**). The inscription on the side shown here praises Tjodrek (the Ostragoth king Theodoric the Great, d. 520) as a brave king of sea-fighters.

The typically phallic shape of Viking picture stones harks back to Neolithic beliefs that upright stones serve a fertility function in association with the earth. The runic inscription at the side of the example in figure **10.23** says that the stone was "raised for his brother Hjoruv," and the image on the face of the stone confirms its memorial function. At the top, a warrior (presumably Hjoruv) rides Odin's eight-legged horse, Sleipnir, into Valhalla. Above are two more warriors (denoting battle), one falling and the other already dead. Welcoming Hjoruv into Valhalla by extending a drinking horn is a Valkyrie with long hair and a long skirt; a dog follows behind her. Above the dog, another Valkyrie offers a horn to a man with an axe. The shape over these two figures echoes the shape of the stone, and represents the halls of Valhalla. On the lower half of the stone is a Viking ship filled with warriors and a sail decorated with a pattern of diamond shapes. This

undoubtedly refers to the tradition of ship burials described in *Beowulf* and to the belief that the deceased sail into the afterlife. The scenes are framed with interlace, which also separates the upper and lower halves of the image.

Around 965, Denmark became Christian. Prior to that time, the Viking raids on northwestern Europe had been successful. But in 934 the Germans invaded Denmark and brought Christian missionaries with them. Some thirty years later, the Danish king Harald Bluetooth (d. c. 987) converted to Christianity, and raised a huge rune stone at Jelling to commemorate the event (fig. **10.22**). Its surface is covered with interlace designs that flow into the arms of the image of Christ, who stands upright, faces front, and wears a short tunic. This representation is a good example of the integration of Christian imagery with pagan interlace.

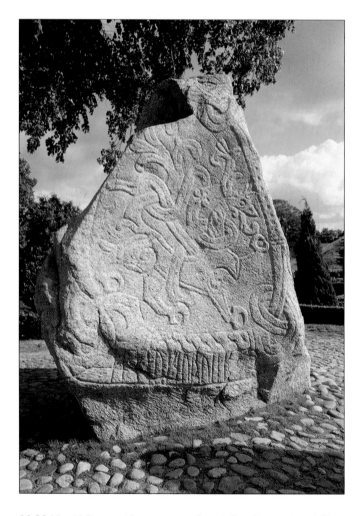

10.22 Harald Bluetooth's rune stone, from Jelling, Denmark, c. 965. According to a contemporary chronicler, a priest at Harald's court lifted a hot iron with his bare hands. When he was miraculously unharmed, he persuaded the king to become a Christian. The inscription visible toward the bottom of the stone states that "King Harald had these memorials made to Gorm his father and to Thyre his mother. That Harald who won fame for himself, all Denmark and Norway and made the Danes Christian."

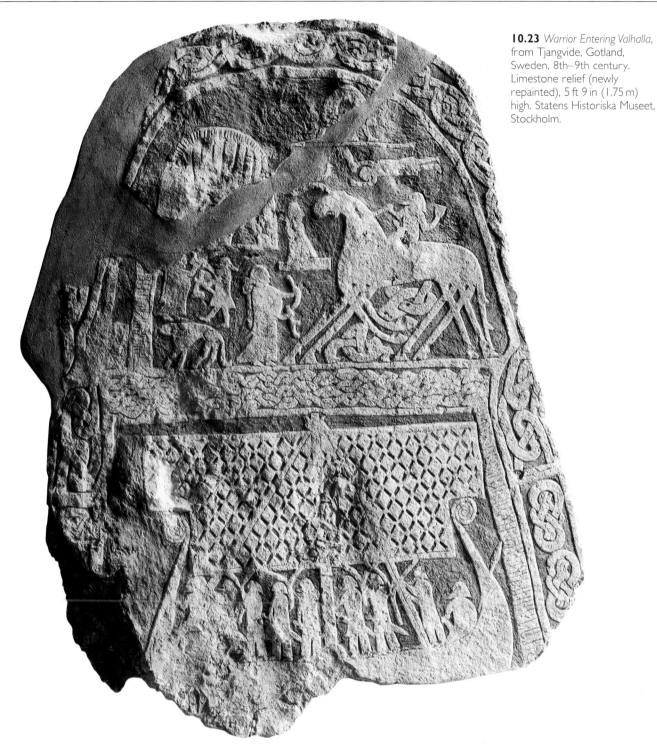

10.23 *Warrior Entering Valhalla*, from Tjangvide, Gotland, Sweden, 8th–9th century. Limestone relief (newly repainted), 5 ft 9 in (1.75 m) high. Statens Historiska Museet, Stockholm.

Hiberno-Saxon Art

Because of its remote position, Ireland had escaped occupation by the Romans in the first and second centuries A.D. and invasion by the Germanic hordes in the fifth century. Saint Patrick (c. 387–463) introduced Christianity into Ireland in the first half of the fifth century, and for the following 250 years Irish monasteries provided a haven for European scholars, becoming centers of learning where Classical and theological studies were pursued. In the Early Middle Ages, missionaries from Ireland were partly responsible for the spread of the Christian faith in mainland Europe. Among them was the Irish abbot Saint Columba, who established an outpost on the island of Iona in southwest Scotland from 563 to 597. Together with twelve close followers, he brought Christianity to the neighboring islands and converted all of Scotland.

During this period there was a flowering of Christian art in Ireland and various other islands off the coasts of northern Britain. Its style has been given a number of labels, including Insular and Hiberno-Saxon (*Hibernia* is Latin for "Ireland").

Stone Crosses

From the early seventh century to around 800, pagan interlace patterns were incorporated into Christian art. They were carved in relief on the large stone crosses that still dot the Irish countryside. Three types of interlace adorn the vertical and arms of a cross in Tipperary (fig. **10.24**). At the bottom, a single row of scrolls is repeated in the broken circle. The pedestal design has largely worn away with time. Generally, these Irish monumental crosses mark graves or sacred places on roads.

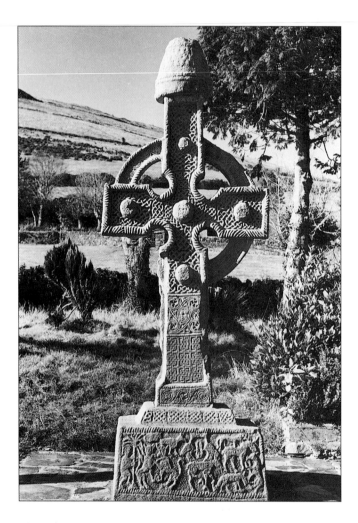

10.24 Celtic cross, Ahenny, Tipperary, Ireland, late 8th century. Granite. The use of interlace designs for stone carving was probably derived from their previous use in metalwork, as in the Sutton Hoo purse cover (fig. 10.17).

Manuscript Illumination

Another typical use of the pagan interlace in Christian iconography occurs in illuminated manuscripts (see Box) produced by monks in Irish and English monasteries (see p. 299). The main impetus of their style may have originated in Ireland, and from there it infiltrated England and other parts of western Europe.

Manuscript Illumination

Illuminated **manuscripts** are hand-decorated pages of text. Great numbers of these texts were needed because of the importance of the Bible, and especially the Gospels, for the study and spread of Christianity. Most were made during the Middle Ages in western Europe, before the invention of the printing press. (The Chinese are thought to have used movable type from the eleventh century A.D., but printing was not known in Europe before the fifteenth century.) Medieval manuscripts were copied in monastery **scriptoria** (Latin for "writing places"). Medieval scribes had to know Latin, have good penmanship, excellent eyesight, and the ability to read the writing of other scribes whose manuscripts they were copying.

It is not known what tools the scribes had for illuminating the manuscripts, although it is obvious that compasses and rulers were used for the geometric designs. The magnifying glass had not yet been invented. The scribes' pigments consisted of minerals and animal or vegetable extracts. These were mixed with water and bound with egg whites to thicken the consistency. The paint was applied to vellum (as in the early codex), which is high-quality calfskin parchment, specially prepared and dried for manuscripts.

The page in figure **10.25** of the *Lion Symbol of St. John* from the Book of Durrow is a relatively early example of medieval manuscript illumination from the second half of the seventh century. The lion is in profile, its mouth open and teeth bared as if growling or roaring. Note the dense patterning of the surface of its body with red and green diamond shapes. They are accentuated by a yellow outline that merges into stylized muscle, yellow and red feet, and green and brown striations toward the end of the tail. These colors, as well as the dot pattern on the face, are repeated in the interlace inside the border.

The artist has created a strict unity of color and form on this page. In the border, for example, the reds are reserved for the upper and lower sections, thereby repeating the horizontal of the lion's body as well as its color arrangement. The edges are crisp and clear, the colors contrasting, and the surfaces flat like those of the Sutton Hoo cover (fig. 10.17). Design-driven optical illusions are created in the interlace, as if a ribbon has been threaded and re-threaded through itself. This kind of illusory maze-like play was to become more complex in the course of the Middle Ages. Such early medieval illuminated manuscripts from northern Europe create a world of images that seems totally independent of the humanistic tastes of Greco-Roman tradition.

Perhaps the most famous Early Medieval Hiberno-Saxon illuminated manuscript is the Book of Kells, which dates from the late eighth or early ninth century. Its text consists of the four Gospels, written in Latin in 680 pages. The color and form of the manuscript illuminations have

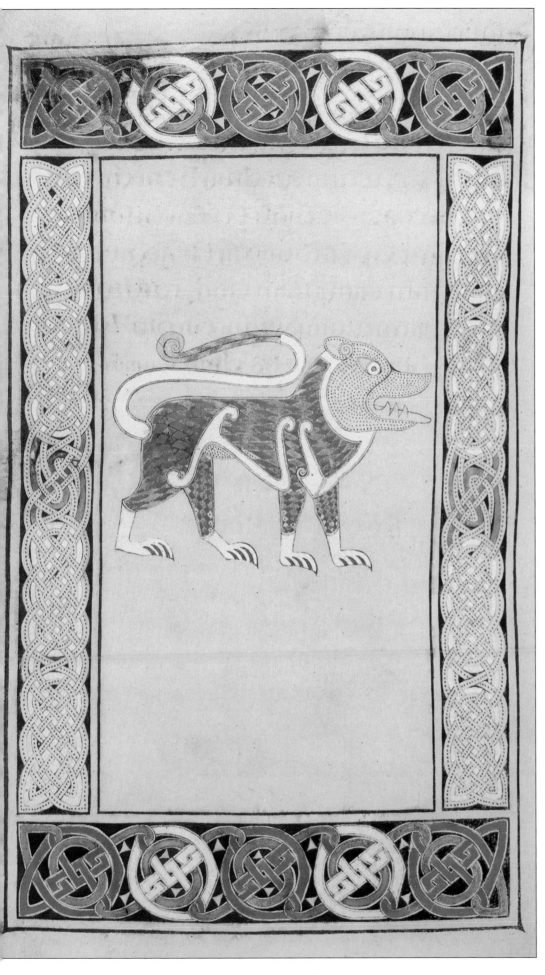

10.25 *Lion Symbol of Saint John*, from the Book of Durrow, fol. 191v, c. 650–700. Illuminated manuscript on vellum, 9⅔ × 5¾ in (24.5 × 14.5 cm). Library of Trinity College, Dublin, Ireland. This manuscript originally came from either Ireland or Northumbria in England. It represents Saint John the Evangelist as a lion surrounded by a rectangular border filled with interlace. Later, Saint John's symbol was changed to an eagle.

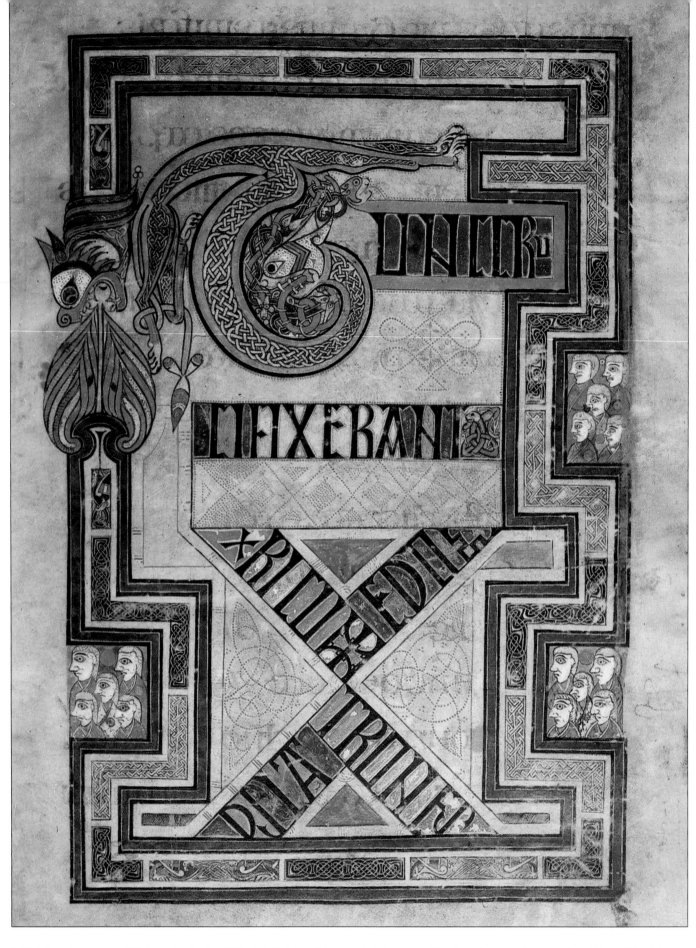

10.26 *Tunc Crucifixerant XPI*, from the Book of Kells, fol. 124r, late 8th or early 9th century. Illuminated manuscript on vellum, 9½ × 13 in (24 × 33 cm). Library of Trinity College, Dublin, Ireland. This is a page from the Gospel of Matthew (27:38). The scribe has written "Tunc crucifixerant XPI cum eo duo latrones" ("Then they crucified Christ and, with him, two thieves").

become more complex, with animal and human figures incorporated into the design of the letters. In the *T* of *Tunc* on the folio illustrated in figure **10.26**, for example, the two arms of the letter stretch into the legs and claws of a lion, or dragon. Its head is part of the left border, and its gaping jaws eject a series of colorful ribbonlike forms—probably a stylized representation of flames. The inside of the curve of the *T* contains more interlacing—notably fish-like creatures with prominent eyes. The large white fish emerging from the lower curl of the *T* bites the thick red interlace. This in turn metamorphoses into the ears of the little green fish on the upper right. Human forms have also been added to the repertory. Three sets of small human heads appear in rectangular spaces, two on the right of the folio and one on the left. Such delight in intricate detail was to continue in border imagery throughout the Middle Ages.

In addition to the obvious visual pleasure these designs gave their artists as well as their viewers, their purpose was to illuminate the "Word of God." The fish is an early symbol of Christ (see p. 276), so its presence on a page of text describing the Crucifixion symbolizes Christ's role as the Savior. The illumination of Christ with two thieves on the lower half of the page is fitted within a large *Chi* (written as *X*), the beginning of Christ's Greek name and also a visual reference to the Cross (see p. 280). The interlacing that characterizes these manuscripts is thus echoed in the formal assimilation of iconography into text.

Carolingian Period

The era of the Book of Kells corresponds to an important historical landmark in western Europe. On December 25, 800, the pope crowned Charlemagne (Charles the Great) Roman Emperor at Saint Peter's in Rome. When Charlemagne came to power, he ruled a large part of western Europe, including France, Germany, Switzerland, Belgium, Holland, northern Spain, and Italy to the south of Rome. This territory was to be the subject of extensive political and religious controversy between the popes in Rome and the German emperors right up until the nineteenth century. It was named the Holy Roman Empire in the thirteenth century, and lasted as such for over six hundred years (fig. **10.27**). Charlemagne was also King of the Franks from 771 to 814.

Charlemagne created a cultural revival intended to enhance his imperial image in the tradition of ancient Rome. The term used to describe the period—Carolingian—derives from the name of Charlemagne's grandfather, Charles Martel ("Carolus" is Latin for "Charles"). Under Charlemagne, monasteries expanded the network of learning throughout Europe in which Latin, as the language of the manuscript texts, had been kept alive. Besides the Latin language, Charlemagne wanted to revive other aspects of the Roman past, and he was responsible for the reinstatement of the political organization of ancient

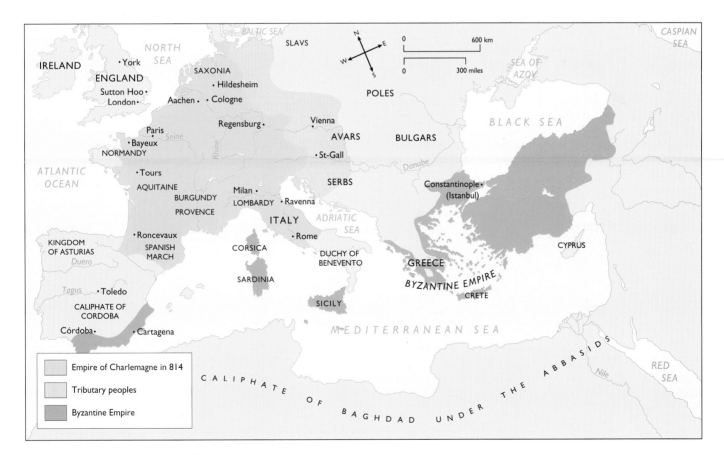

10.27 Map of the Holy Roman Empire under Charlemagne, 814.

Rome, the establishment of a unified code of laws, the creation of libraries, and educational reform.

In his pursuit of the last of these, Charlemagne hired the English scholar Alcuin of York, in Northumbria, and invited him to his court at Aachen. Alcuin organized cathedral and monastic schools to emphasize Latin learning, culture, and language. He adopted from Aelius Donatus, who had taught Latin grammar and rhetoric in Rome, a curriculum and a grammar book that set the standard in western European schools until the end of the Middle Ages. The curriculum was divided into two sets of disciplines based on the Seven Liberal Arts. The *trivium* consisted of Grammar, Rhetoric, and Dialectic, and the *quadrivium* of Geometry, Arithmetic, Astronomy, and Music.

The Palace Chapel

In the last decade of the eighth century, Charlemagne moved his capital and his court to Aachen (Aix-la-Chapelle in French), 45 miles (72 km) southwest of Cologne, near the

modern Belgian–Dutch border. There he constructed a palace, together with offices, workshops, and other buildings. Of particular architectural importance was the Palace Chapel, which doubled as Charlemagne's personal chapel and a place of worship for the imperial court (figs. **10.28**, **10.29**, and **10.30**).

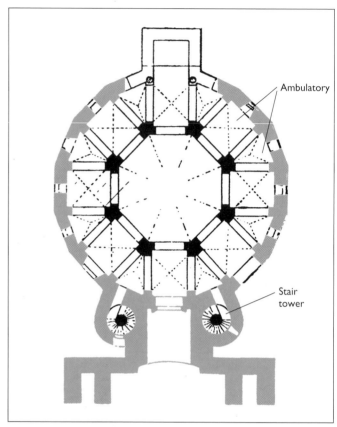

10.29 Plan (restored) of Charlemagne's Palace Chapel.

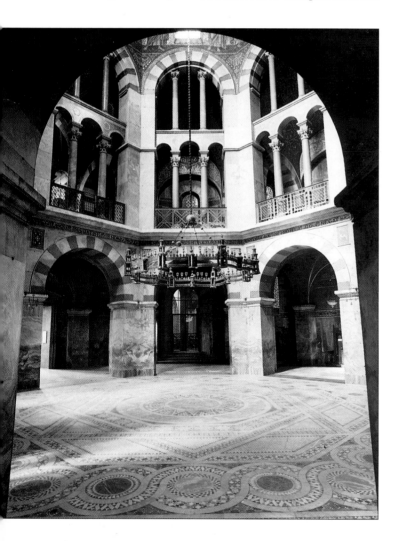

10.28 Odo of Metz, interior of Charlemagne's Palace Chapel, Aachen, 792–805.

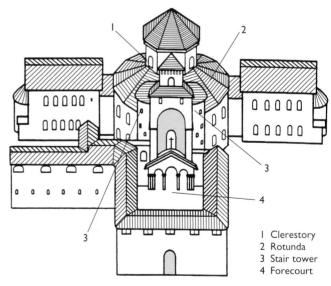

1 Clerestory
2 Rotunda
3 Stair tower
4 Forecourt

10.30 Reconstruction drawing of Charlemagne's Palace Chapel.

The Palace Chapel has certain features in common with the Church of San Vitale in Ravenna (see p. 286). Both are large, sturdy, centrally planned buildings; San Vitale is octagonal, and the Palace Chapel has a sixteen-sided outer wall and an octagonal central core surrounded by an ambulatory supporting a gallery. The gallery opens onto the central area through a series of arches, which allowed Charlemagne and his entourage to watch the celebration of the Mass. At the third level, the central core rises to a clerestory. To the front of the Palace Chapel, a square entrance flanked by round towers was added, with tower stairs leading to a throne room at the level of the gallery. Originally the chapel also had a walled courtyard around the entrance. From here visitors could catch a glimpse of the emperor at a window in the second level of the façade. This appearance of the ruler, visible through a window, was an ancient royal tradition dating back to ancient Egypt.

Like Justinian, Charlemagne used the arts to enhance his political image. His architect, Odo of Metz, revived the massive piers and round arches of ancient Rome, which reinforced Charlemagne's claim to the Holy Roman Empire. As in the Colosseum (cf. fig. 8.23), the supports of the Palace Chapel decrease in size as they rise, creating a sense of greater weight at ground level. In the gallery, triple arches are aligned with single round arches, and two central columns with Corinthian capitals stand between each set of piers. The result is a combination of the Justinian central plan with the monumental symmetry and order of the Roman buildings.

Manuscripts

Because education was an important aspect of Charlemagne's Roman revival, manuscripts played a significant role in his efforts to bring back the learning and culture of Roman anti-quity. Charlemagne's court at

Aachen was the hub of his empire, but manuscripts were portable and thus an important form of artistic and educational communication.

A comparison of three manuscript illuminations made during Charlemagne's reign reflects the evolution of his Roman revival. The page of *Christ Blessing* was commissioned by Charlemagne and his wife Hildegarde in 781 from Godescalc, the court scribe (fig. **10.31**). Its dependence on Byzantine icons is clear in the enthroned Christ holding a book in his left hand and raising his right in a gesture of blessing. Christ is frontal, his head is framed by a flat halo including a cross, and the folds and edges of his stylized drapery are depicted as black lines. Despite some shading in the face, the slightly oblique footstool, and traces of landscape at the top of the scene, Christ's frontality and overall patterning flatten the space. Symmetrical interlaced designs above, below, and at the sides of the throne reflect the influence of Hiberno-Saxon art.

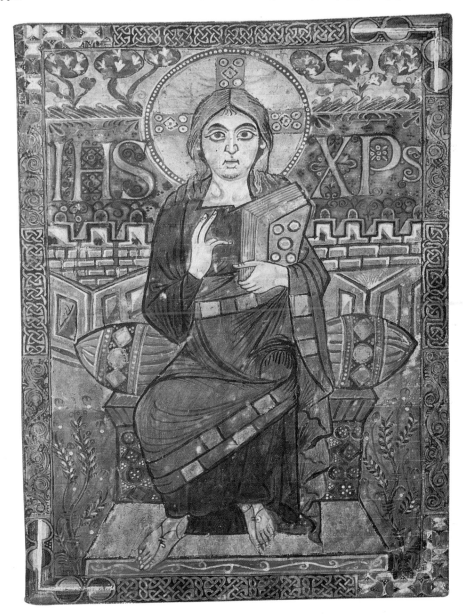

10.31 Court School of Charlemagne, *Christ Blessing*, from the Godescalc Gospels, Lat. 1203, fol. 3r, 781–783. Text written in gold and silver on vellum. 12 × 8¼ in (30.5 × 21 cm). Bibliothèque Nationale, Paris.

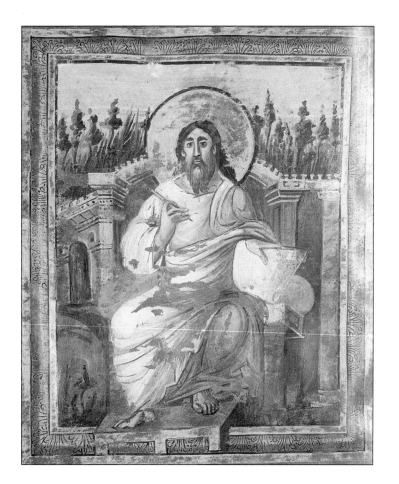

10.32 *Saint John*, from the Coronation Gospels, fol. 178v, late 8th century. Parchment, 12¾ × 10 in (32.4 × 24.9 cm). Kunsthistorisches Museum, Vienna. Tradition has it that this codex (manuscript book) was discovered in Charlemagne's tomb and opened in the year 1000 by Otto III. It gained its name through the practice of German emperors who swore their coronation oaths on it.

The depiction of *Saint John* in figure **10.32**, from the Coronation Gospels, demonstrates both a new interest in naturalism and the persistence of medieval style. The saint is seated in an architectural niche within a landscape. His pen is poised, and his drapery combines surface pattern with an indication of organic form. Shading defines the body contours, especially the face, with the head slightly inclined, although the halo remains flat. The position of the footstool—both inside and outside the frame—reveals the artist's struggle to reconcile the early medieval and Greco-Roman traditions.

The four Evangelists from a Carolingian Gospel book illustrated in figure **10.33** include the saints' symbols set in a landscape indicated by rolling hills. The oblique writing desks and stools define space, while the draperies define the forms and natural movement of the figures. This artist probably came from Constantinople, where the Hellenistic traditions had persisted most strongly (see Box).

10.33 *Four Evangelists*, from a Carolingian Gospel book, Palace Chapel school, Aachen, early 9th century.

Revelation and the Four Symbols of the Evangelists

The Book of Revelation, written by Saint John the Divine, is the last book of the New Testament. It opens as follows: "The Revelation of Jesus Christ, which God gave unto him, to show unto his servants things which must shortly come to pass; and he sent and signified it by his angel unto his servant John: who bare record of the word of God, and of the testimony of Jesus Christ, and of all things that he saw."

While John was on the Greek island of Patmos, Christ is said to have appeared to him and told him to convey his message to the world. The Book of Revelation is believed to be John's account of Christ's word and all that he is shown in heaven. It is a visionary work imbued with scripture, literary tradition, the early efforts to establish Christianity, and influences from Judaism and Greco-Roman thought.

In Christian art, the four Evangelists are often represented as four symbols, which are taken from chapters 4 and 5 of Saint John's vision (see fig. 12.10). They are a lion, a bull, a man, and an eagle. The lion came to stand for Saint Mark, the bull for Saint Luke, the man for Saint Matthew, and the eagle for Saint John.

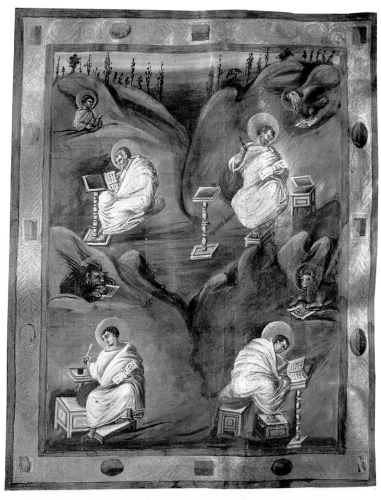

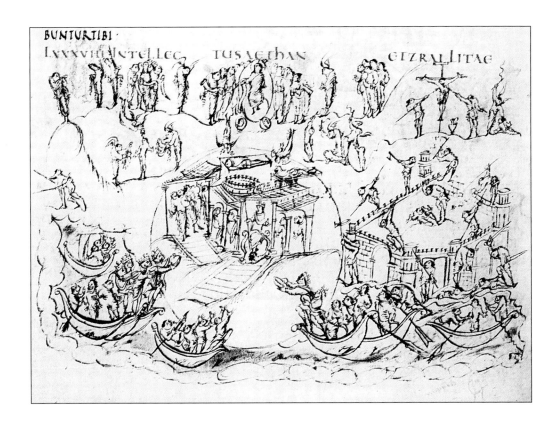

10.34 Rheims school, illustration to Psalm 88, from the Utrecht Psalter, Ms. 32, fol. 51v, c. 820. 12⅞ × 9⅞ in (32.7 × 25.1 cm). University Library, Utrecht.

The Carolingian prayerbook known as the Utrecht Psalter of c. 825–850 introduced a new correspondence between word and image. The manuscripts produced at Charlemagne's court had reflected the belief that biblical texts did not lend themselves to illustration. But the Utrecht Psalter, which was produced in Reims, in northern France, reflects a different view. The psalter itself consisted of the Old Testament Book of Psalms, but was illustrated with line drawings in red-brown ink interspersed among the written text. Rather than illustrating a straightforward narrative, these drawings capture the essence of a particular set of metaphorical images. For example, the drawing that accompanies Psalm 88 (fig. **10.34**) includes scenes of the Last Judgment and the Crucifixion in the top half, while the lower half denotes the sufferings of earthly life, with two figures in boats reaching out in supplication, and, at the right, a castle on top of which soldiers are killing enemies. These scenes reflect the troubled words of the psalm, for example, verse 7: "Thy wrath lieth hard upon me, and thou has afflicted me with all thy waves"; and verse 9: "Mine eye mourneth by reason of affliction: Lord, I have called daily upon thee, I have stretched out my hands unto thee."

Monasteries

Of all the institutions in western Europe during the Middle Ages, the monastery was particularly important to Charlemagne's plan for controlling conquered territory and directing reforms in art and education (see Box). Each monastery included a school, and this created a network through which artists and scholars could communicate with each other. The monastery was also a religious and administrative center, and performed an economic function through its agricultural production.

Charlemagne decided that monasteries should follow the Benedictine Rule, a series of regulations which had been devised by Saint Benedict of Nursia some two

---

Monasticism: Chastity, Obedience, and Poverty

Monasticism is a way of religious life in which the individual takes vows of chastity, obedience, and poverty and serves God in relative seclusion. Monasticism began in the pre-Christian era among Middle Eastern Jews. The first Christian monks date from the third century. Some chose to live as hermits, isolating themselves individually from society and devoting themselves to prayer. Others withdrew into communal groups that formed the basis of the monastic tradition.

Many monks became expert in a particular art or craft, and the monasteries played an important role in medieval cultural life and education. Works of literature, science, and philosophy, in addition to religious texts, have survived in copies handwritten in the *scriptoria* of the monasteries.

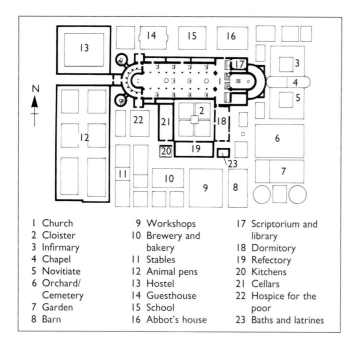

1 Church	9 Workshops	17 Scriptorium and
2 Cloister	10 Brewery and	library
3 Infirmary	bakery	18 Dormitory
4 Chapel	11 Stables	19 Refectory
5 Novitiate	12 Animal pens	20 Kitchens
6 Orchard/	13 Hostel	21 Cellars
Cemetery	14 Guesthouse	22 Hospice for the
7 Garden	15 School	poor
8 Barn	16 Abbot's house	23 Baths and latrines

10.35 Plan of the monastery of Saint Gall, Switzerland, c. 820. This plan has been drawn from a tracing on five pieces of parchment, itself taken from an earlier document, from which scholars have been able to draw various conclusions about monastic life and architectural practice during the Carolingian period.

10.36 Reconstruction model of the monastery of Saint Gall, Switzerland, c. 820. The design of the monastery placed the church at the center and the buildings adjacent to it in approximate order of importance. The library and scriptorium were attached to the church, not far from the main altar. To the north were the abbot's house (connected to the transept by a private passage), guesthouse, and a school. The latter fulfilled Charlemagne's mandate that monasteries should provide education even for those not intending to take holy orders.

hundred years earlier, in the sixth century. According to Benedict's Rule, monks should live communally under the supervision of an abbot, devoting themselves to a strict routine of work, study, and prayer. In 816–817, Charlemagne convened a council of abbots at Aachen to discuss the Rule and draw up a standard plan for Benedictine abbeys (fig. **10.35**). The council sent this plan to the abbot who was rebuilding the Saint Gall monastery in Switzerland.

Figure **10.36** is a model constructed from the plan. About a hundred people were to form a self-sufficient community—almost a small town—occupying an area some 500 by 700 feet (150 × 210 m). Entrance to the monastery was from the west, through a passage between a hostel and stables. From there a gate led to a semicircular arcade flanked by two cylindrical towers, and into the vestibule at the western end of a church. This combination of towers with an entrance, chapels, and galleries at the west of a Carolingian church is known as **westwork** (from the German *Westwerk*). The church is designed along the lines of a basilica: at the eastern end are a transept, choir, apse, and altar (approached by seven steps); another apse was located at the west. The nave and aisles are screened off from each other. They contain additional altars to make it possible for each priest to say Mass every day.

To the east of the church was a novitiate (a building to house novices, or trainees) and an infirmary. Next to the infirmary stood the physicians' houses and a medicinal herb garden. Conveniently close was the cemetery, which doubled as an orchard. To the south, in the sunniest spot, was a square cloister surrounded by a covered portico

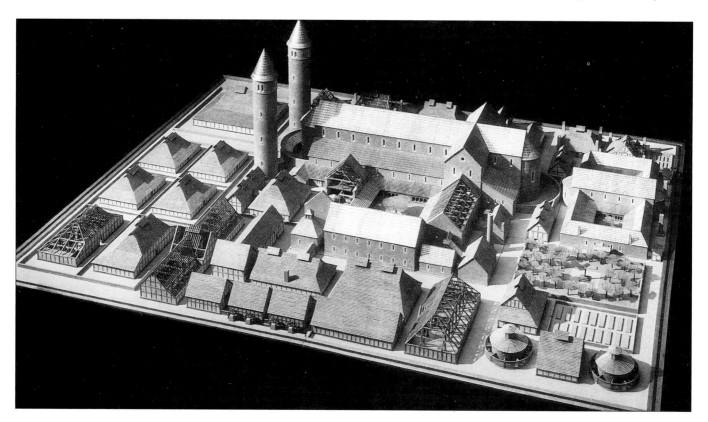

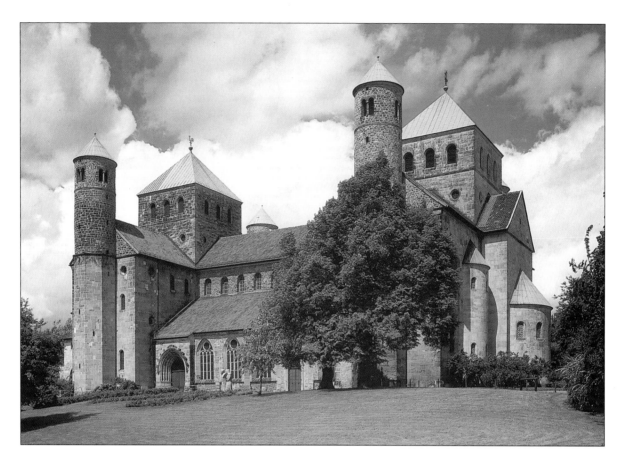

10.37 Restored abbey church of Saint Michael's, Hildesheim, c. 1001–1031. The building was destroyed during World War II.

where the monks could walk. The cloister was flanked by the dormitory, with a bath house and lavatory, a **refectory** (dining hall), and a cellar. Outbuildings included a bakery, a brewhouse, and barns for farm animals. The plan of St. Gall lays out the entire ideal monastery in meticulous, practical detail, right down to the shed for pregnant mares and foals.

Charlemagne's grandsons were ineffective rulers and, by the end of the ninth century, Europe again fell prey to invaders. The Vikings took over Normandy (in northern France), and the Saxons resumed their control of Germany. The Saxon emperor Otto I the Great (936–973) was crowned by the pope in 962. He continued Charlemagne's revival of Classical antiquity as a way of reinforcing his own imperial position.

Ottonian Period

"Ottonian" refers to the three rulers named Otto who stabilized the Holy Roman Empire after the disruptions following Charlemagne's death. Their empire included only Germany and parts of northern Italy, and was therefore smaller than Charlemagne's. The major architectural work of this period was the Benedictine abbey church of Saint Michael's at Hildesheim (figs. **10.37**, **10.38**, and **10.39**). It was commissioned by Bernward, Bishop of Hildesheim (c. 960–1022), who had been the tutor of Otto III. Both visited Rome, where they studied ancient ruins.

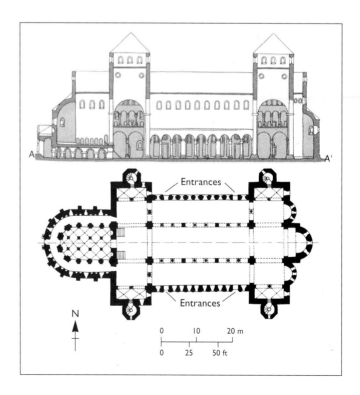

10.38 Section and plan of Saint Michael's.

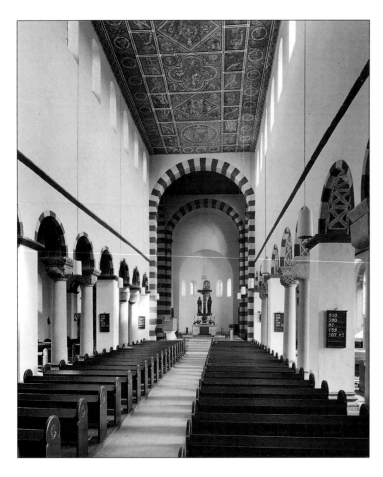

10.39 Restored interior of Saint Michael's, looking west.

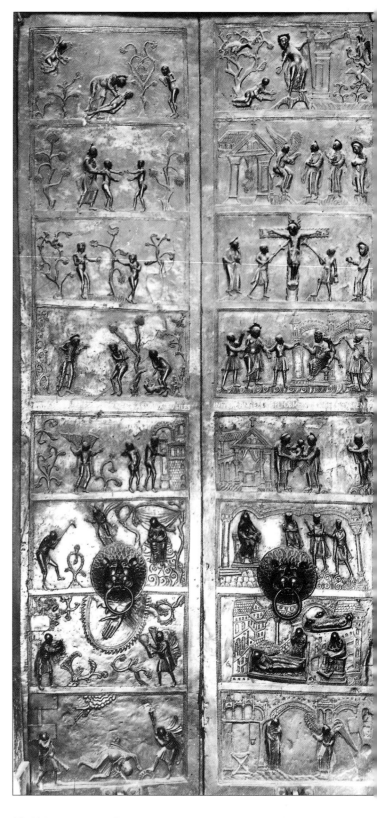

10.40 Bronze doors, Saint Michael's, completed 1015. 16 ft 6 in (5.02 m) high. According to a contemporary biographer, Bishop Bernward was himself an expert goldsmith and bronze caster. He stayed with Otto II at his Roman palace, which was near the church of Santa Sabina (see fig. 9D). The bronze doors of Santa Sabina are believed to have inspired those of Saint Michael's.

The massive quality of Charlemagne's Palace Chapel also characterizes Saint Michael's. Although symmetry is maintained, the architectural variety—towers, round arches, sloping roofs, cylindrical and cubic forms—gives it a formal energy, reflected in the plan of the exterior section (fig. 10.38). The entrances are untypically located at the side aisles; note the triple eastern apses, the large western apse, and circular towers. The restored nave walls (fig. 10.39) are two stories high. The lower level is composed of an arcade, which is unusual in the alternation of a single pier with pairs of columns. Piercing the relatively plain upper story are small windows with round arches, which are the main source of interior illumination.

Saint Michael's bridges the gap between Carolingian architecture and the apparent simplicity of the new Romanesque style (see Chapter 11). Its plan was partly derived from Saint Gall, which, in turn, was related to the basilica. Through their contacts with Rome, Bernward and Otto III assimilated Classical architectural features.

The metalwork at Hildesheim also shows the impact of Roman influence on Bernward and Otto. An impressive surviving example, commissioned before 1015, is the pair of bronze doors originally at the entrance (fig. **10.40**), the first large-scale works cast in one piece since antiquity. The emphasis on typology is apparent in the left-right

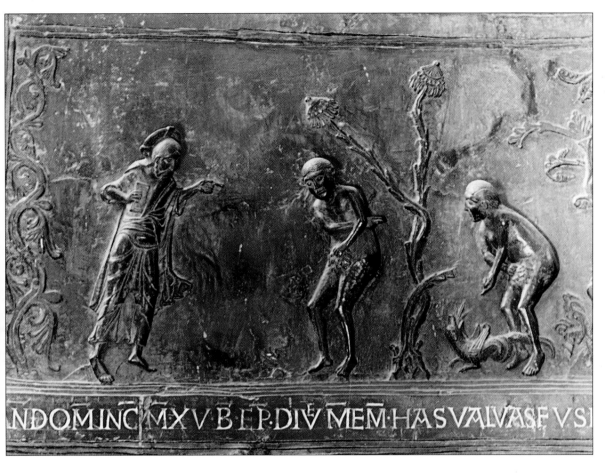

10.41 *Adam and Eve Reproached by God*, from the bronze doors of Saint Michael's (detail of fig. 10.40), approx. 23 × 43 in (58.3 × 109.3 cm).

pairing of Old and New Testament scenes, which the medieval viewer would have understood as meaning that the former prefigured the latter (see p. 273). The horizontal scenes are depicted in relatively high relief, and the thin, lively figures are well within the tradition of Byzantine and Carolingian style.

In the scene of *Adam and Eve Reproached by God* (fig. **10.41**), the tree forms, especially at the far left, resemble Hiberno-Saxon interlace motifs. The serpent is a version of the fantastic creatures that populate works in the traditional Animal Style. But there is also a new dramatic character, which is combined with fluid, linear rhythms; for example, the juxtaposition of figure with void. The hierarchy of pose and gesture is clearly delineated: God's superiority is denoted by his taller form, his admonishing gesture, and the fact that he is clothed. Adam cowers before God and covers his nakedness. The diagonal of his back is reinforced by the tree branch above him. He points to Eve behind him, cowering even more than he as she points to the serpent at her feet. The narrative direction starts with God and ends with the serpent (in the Bible, God condemns him to crawl forever on the ground): formal "uprightness" is thus an echo of moral "rightness." Furthermore, the intended left-to-right reading of the

scene is a reversal of the biblical text, in which the serpent tempted Eve, who tempted Adam, who angered God.

About five years after the completion of the doors, Bernward commissioned a monumental bronze Paschal candlestick, which was used on Easter Sunday to celebrate Christ's Resurrection (fig. **10.42**). The spiral narrative design was clearly derived from that of Trajan's Column (see p. 232), its reliefs illustrating the life of Christ. The commemorative character of the Roman column has thus been assimilated into a Christian context as an expression of Christ's triumph over death.

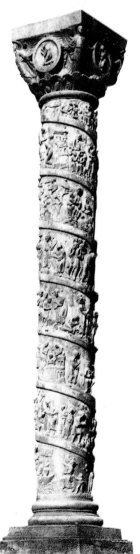

10.42 Paschal candlestick, Saint Michael's, Hildesheim, c. 1022. Bronze, 12 ft 5½ in (3.81 m) high.

Ottonian manuscript illuminations also reflect a change from the Carolingian style. The two-dimensional, iconic image of *Saint Luke* in Otto III's Gospel book (fig. **10.43**), compared with the landscape setting of the *Four Evangelists* from the Gospel book of the Aachen court (fig. 10.33), is an example. Saint Luke sits on a rainbow inside a green mandorla suspended in a gold space. Instead of natural landscape, the Ottonian manuscript depicts an abbreviated rocky platform beneath Christ. This is flanked by two lambs drinking from water that flows from the rocks, but there is no rational relationship between these forms. Both the water and the lambs are suspended, like the saint, in gold. Their significance here is wholly symbolic, for the rocks denote the church building and the drinking lambs (cf. Christ as the Lamb of God) refer to rebirth through baptism. Whereas the Evangelists prepare to write, Saint Luke exuberantly holds up a decorative array of circular clouds containing angels and prophets. Directly over his own halo is the most prominent cloud

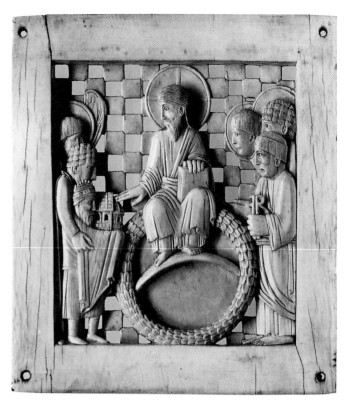

10.44 *Christ Enthroned with Saints and Emperor Otto I*, Ottonian, 962–973, from Milan or Richenau. Ivory, 5 × 4½ in (12.7 × 11.4 cm).

with his symbol, the bull. Framing the scene are two columns with non-Classical, stylized cabbage-leaf capitals. These support an arch decorated with fanciful interlace that is more three-dimensional than Hiberno-Saxon and Viking examples.

Ottonian ivories also reflect the change from Carolingian Classicism. This is evident, for example, in the plaque for the dedication of Magdeburg Cathedral (fig. **10.44**). It shows a frontal Christ seated on a stylized wreath, with his feet resting on a curved platform. He turns to Otto, who presents him with a model of the cathedral Church of Saint Mauritius (a third-century Roman general martyred in Africa). Saint Peter stands at the right, identified by his attribute, the key. The figures on this ivory lack the three-dimensional, organic qualities of Charlemagne's Classical revival. Instead they are short, stubby, and rather block-like. Surface patterns on the draperies, as well as in the background, have replaced natural form.

Like the Ottonian abbey of Saint Michael's and the illumination of *Saint Luke* from the Gospel book of Otto III, the ivory is stylistically transitional. It reflects the waning of naturalism at the end of the Carolingian period, and the trend toward the more iconic imagery which will become characteristic of the Romanesque style.

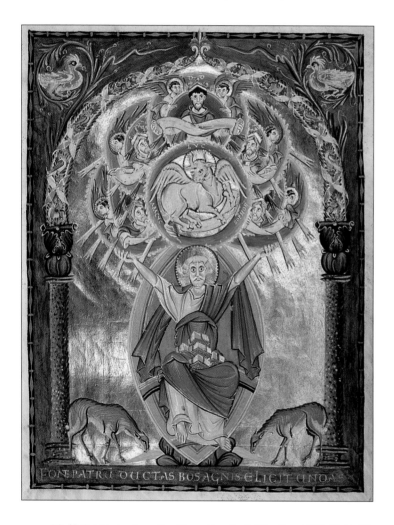

10.43 *Saint Luke*, from the Gospel book of Otto III, c. 1000. 13 × 9⅜ in (33 × 23.8 cm). Bayerische Staatsbibliothek, Munich.

	Style/Period	Works of Art	Cultural/Historical Developments
300	EARLY MIDDLE AGES 4th century		Dedication of the city of Constantinople (300) Visigoths sack Rome (410)
400	EARLY MIDDLE AGES 5th century		Founding of Constantinople University (425) Last Roman legions leave Britain (476) End of western Roman Empire (476)
500	EARLY MIDDLE AGES 6th century	 **Sutton Hoo purse cover**	Founding of Essex and Middlesex, kingdoms of Anglo-Saxon England (527) Building of Hagia Sophia, Constantinople (532–7) Building of Church of S. Vitale, Ravenna (540–7) Golden era of Byzantine art (c. 550) Saint Columba (c. 521–597) settles on Isle of Iona and begins conversion of the Picts (c. 560) Birth of Muhammad, founder of Islam (c. 570) Development of Gregorian chant as part of religious services (late 500s) Golden age of Celtic culture (600–800)
600	EARLY MIDDLE AGES 7th century	Sutton Hoo purse cover (**10.17**), East Anglia Book of Durrow (**10.25**) Dome of the Rock (**10.4**), Jerusalem	Saint Augustine establishes the archiepiscopal See of Canterbury (602) Founding of Monastery of Saint Gall (612) Death of Muhammad (632) The Venerable Bede, English writer and historian (673–735)
700	EARLY MIDDLE AGES 8th century	Celtic cross (**10.24**), Tipperary Coronation Gospels (**10.32**) Evangelistary of Godescalc (**10.31**) Charlemagne's Palace Chapel (**10.28**), Aachen *Warrior Entering Valhalla* (**10.23**), Tjangvide Book of Kells (**10.26**) **Book of Kells**	 **Book of Durrow** Writing of *Beowulf*, English epic (early 700s) Moors conquer North Africa and Spain (711–15) Byzantine Emperor Leo III bans images in churches and provokes Iconoclastic Controversy (726) Victory of Charles Martel over Muslims at Battle of Tours (732) Charlemagne (742–814) crowned Holy Roman Emperor at Rome; consolidates most of Europe into a single kingdom (800) Charlemagne establishes Carolingian schools; study of Latin texts encouraged (c. 800)
800	EARLY MIDDLE AGES 9th century	Great Mosque (**10.8–10.10**), Córdoba Animal-head post (**10.18**), Oseberg Utrecht Psalter (**10.34**), Reims Monastery of Saint Gall (**10.35–10.36**), Switzerland Gospel book (**10.33**), Palace Chapel school, Aachen Rök stone (**10.21**), Östergötland Great Mosque (**10.5**), Samarra	Danish Vikings discover Iceland and invade England (c. 866)
900	EARLY MIDDLE AGES 10th century	*Christ Enthroned with Saints and Emperor Otto I* (**10.44**) Bluetooth's rune stone (**10.22**), Jelling Axe, Mammen, Jutland (**10.20**)	Period of Ottonian rule (919–1024) Completion of Koran (935) Beginning of Ottonian architecture (936)
1000	MIDDLE AGES 11th century	Gospel book of Otto III (**10.43**) Saint Michael's (**10.37, 10.39–10.41**), Hildesheim Paschal candlestick (**10.42**), Saint Michael's, Hildesheim Kufic Koran (**10.2**), Tunisia	Great Schism between Rome and Constantinople (1054)
1200	MIDDLE AGES 12th century		Omar Khayyam writes *Rubaiyat* (c. 1100) **Gospel book of Otto III**
	MIDDLE AGES 13th century	**Saint Michael's**	Saint Thomas Aquinas (1225–1274) writes *Summa theologiae* (1265–73) Giotto di Bondone born (c. 1267)
	BYZANTINE 15th century		Ottomans capture Constantinople, which becomes Turkish capital (1453)
1500–1650	ISLAMIC 16–17th century	Mosque of Suleyman I (**10.11, 10.13, 10.15**), Istanbul Illuminated *tugra* of Sultan Suleyman (**10.3**) Luftullah Mosque (**10.14**), Isfahan	

Mesoamerica

(1500 B.C.–A.D. 1500)

While the arts and cultures so far considered flourished in Europe, Africa, Australia, and the Far East, civilizations also rose and fell in the Americas. The Americas were isolated from the rest of the world by vast oceans, and to date there is scant archaeological evidence of contact. However, there are intriguing formal and conceptual similarities, as well as significant differences, between the cultures of the Americas and other civilizations contemporary with them.

The origins of the Native Americans have been traced to the arrival of Paleolithic peoples from Siberia to Alaska over a land mass (now the Bering Strait) that connected them during the last Ice Age. During the Paleolithic era, migrations to the south from the far north (Alaska and Canada) led to settlements in North and South America. By around 9000 B.C. human culture had spread to the

southernmost tip of South America. It was not until 1492 that Columbus sailed for India and proved that the world was round by discovering the American continents between Europe and Asia. With their subsequent conquest by Spain in the sixteenth century, many American civilizations were destroyed. The European invaders (particularly the Spanish) devastated some of these cultures to such an extent that scholars now divide their history into pre-Columbian and post-conquest periods.

The arts of three major civilizations from Mesoamerica—the land mass connecting North and South America—are outlined here. These are Olmec, Teotihuacán, and Maya. Mesoamerica stretches from northern Mexico to Nicaragua, and includes the Yucatán, Belize, Guatemala, Honduras, and El Salvador (figs. **10.A, 10.B**). The archaeology of the region is in a state of flux,

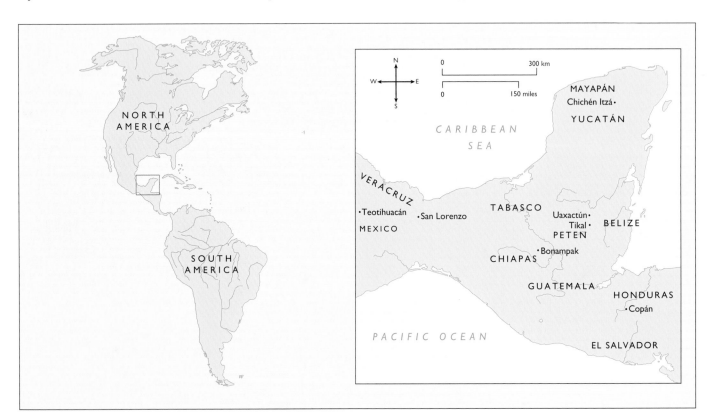

10.A Map of Mesoamerica in relation to North and South America.   **10.B** Map of Mesoamerica.

although advances have been made in deciphering Mesoamerican writing systems since the 1960s. Nevertheless it remains difficult to understand the complex nature of these civilizations.

The history of the region has been divided into three major phases: the Preclassic (or Formative), c. 2000 B.C. to A.D. 250/300; the Classic, c. 300 to 900; and the Postclassic, 900 to 1500. As elsewhere, a period of hunting and gathering (c. 11,000–7500 B.C.) preceded the development of agriculture, monumental stone architecture, and the organization of villages into social and political hierarchies. Examples of pottery, as well as figurines that probably served a fertility function, survive from around 1800 B.C. By late Preclassic there is evidence of urbanization; temples were constructed on pyramidal platforms, and stone monuments containing portraits and inscriptions were carved.

Although Mesoamerica produced culturally distinctive civilizations and correspondingly distinct styles of art and architecture, certain important similarities appear in all of them. These include the development of (base 20) mathematics, an understanding of astronomy, hieroglyphic writing, books made of fig-bark paper or deerskin, and a complex calendar. The religions were polytheistic, requiring offerings to the gods, bloodletting rituals, and human sacrifice. One of the most intriguing Mesoamerican practices was a ritual ball-game, which was played on a large rectangular court. As in modern soccer, players were not supposed to touch the ball with their hands. The movements of the ball were symbolic, apparently conceived of in relation to the sun and moon. Often, captives were forced to play and losers could be sacrificed to the gods.

Olmec (c. 1200–900 B.C.)

The Olmec civilization, located in present-day Mexico, dates from Early to Middle Preclassic and had a lasting influence on the entire region. As in other areas of Mesoamerica, by around 900 B.C. Olmec society was stratified into a class of commoners and an elite. The elite maintained a flourishing trade in exotic goods that were symbols of authority and status, especially jade, obsidian, and iron pyrites (used for mirrors). Most of the population were farmers who supported the priests and rulers with labor and goods.

Monumental stone sculptures of basalt such as the *Jaguar Deity* (fig. **10.C**) were produced at San Lorenzo, in Veracruz, the oldest known Olmec site. The solid, blocklike forms remain characteristic of Mesoamerican art well into the Late Classic period. Merging with the features of a jaguar—an animal indigenous to Mesoamerica and important in its mythology—is the physiognomy of a human child. The hands and feet are pawlike, but the pose and upright posture are human. Such combinations of human with animal elements are first seen in Olmec sculpture and continue in later Mesoamerican art.

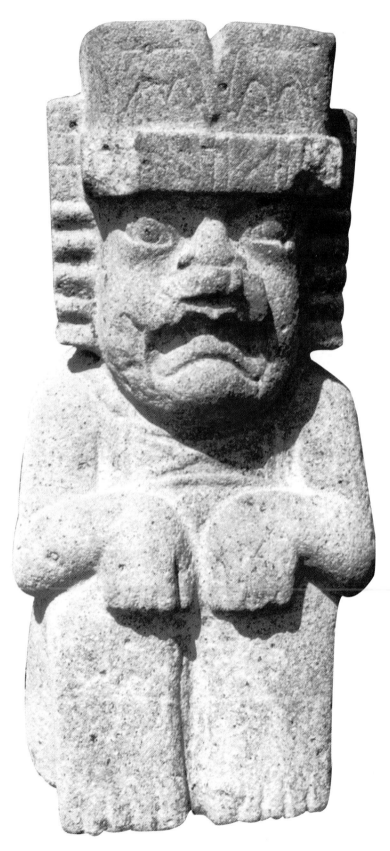

10.C *Jaguar Deity*, San Lorenzo, Veracruz, Mexico, Olmec, Early Preclassic, 1200–900 B.C. Basalt, 35½ in (90 cm) high. Because this figure seems to be shedding tears, it is believed to be an aspect of a rain god. Elsewhere in Mesoamerica, the jaguar is the god of the Underworld.

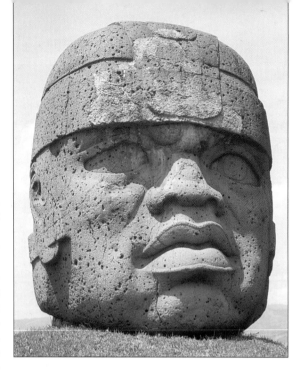

10.D Colossal head, from San Lorenzo, Veracruz, Mexico, Olmec, before 400 B.C. Basalt, 70⅞ in (180 cm) high. Museo Regional de Veracruz, Jalapa, Mexico.

The colossal basalt head in figure **10.D** is one of nine that have been found at San Lorenzo. These heads, weighing between 5 and 20 tons, representing males, are probably portraits of individual rulers. The fleshy, organic faces usually have broad, flat noses and thick lips; also characteristic is the tight, domed headdress with earflaps and a strap under the chin. Most of these colossal heads were defaced and buried, probably to mark the death of the ruler and prepare for his successor. Similar sculptures are found at La Venta, a site that flourished from around 900 to 400 B.C., along with monumental public architecture and elaborate tombs containing jade offerings.

Although the platform in figure **10.E** is a Late Preclassic example from the Chicanel culture, it derives from earlier Olmec prototypes. It is composed of rectangular tiers that decrease in size towards the platform at the top. A central stairway set in each side provided access to a thatched temple originally supported by the platform. Flanking the stairs are stone "masks" of sky serpents and the jaguar god of the underworld. Structures such as this one reflect the influence of the Olmec throughout Mesoamerica. Following the decline of the Olmec, the great center at Teotihuacán in the Valley of Mexico reached its peak during the Classic period.

Teotihuacán

(flourished c. 350–650)

By A.D. 200, Teotihuacán had become a commercial city-state specializing in the manufacture of stone tools (especially of obsidian) and pottery. Between c. 350 and 650, Teotihuacán was the biggest and most influential city anywhere in the Americas. It spread over an area of 8 square miles (20.7 sq km) and supported a population of as many as two hundred thousand. The later Aztec culture dominated the region at the time of the Spanish conquest and attached mythical importance to the great ruins of Teotihuacán (an Aztec name, as are the names of many of the gods) (see Box).

The most significant architecture at Teotihuacán was the ceremonial complex (fig. **10.F**) aligned with the Avenue of the Dead, which was 3 miles (4.8 km) long. The largest structure, called the Pyramid of the Sun by the Aztecs, was to the east of the avenue, near its center (figs. **10.G** and **10.H**). A stairway on the west side led to a platform at the top. This supported a two-room temple that has since disappeared. The slightly smaller Pyramid of the Moon (see

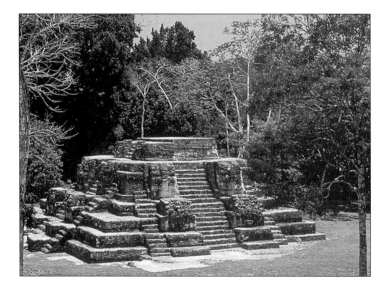

10.E Pyramid E-VII-sub, north side, Uaxactún, Chicanel, Late Preclassic. 26 ft 4 in (8 m) high.

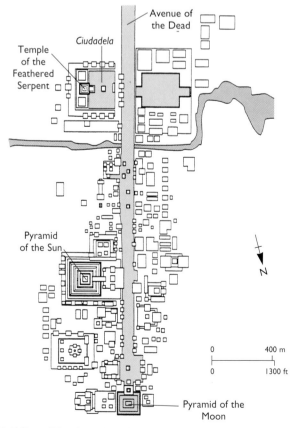

10.F Plan of Teotihuacán.

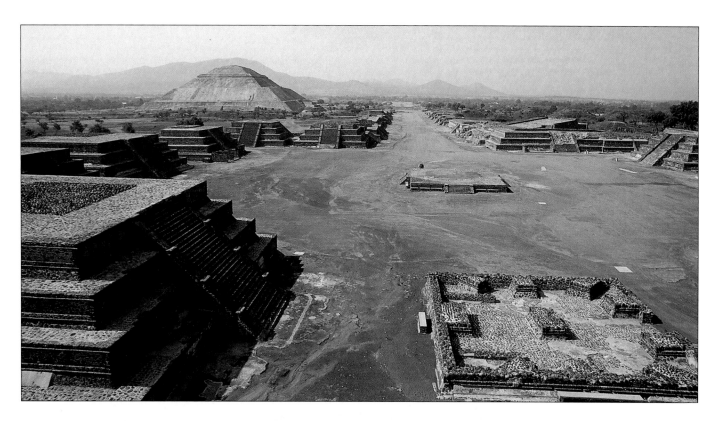

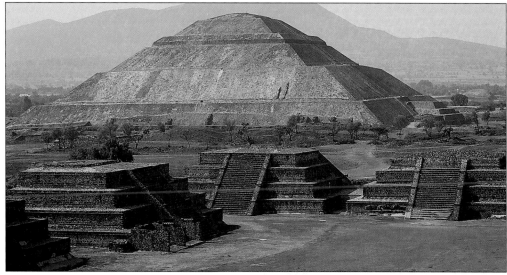

10.G (above) View of Teotihuacán.

10.H The Pyramid of the Sun as seen from the Pyramid of the Moon, Teotihuacán. Square base over 700 ft (213 m) per side; over 210 ft (64 m) high; 1,700,400 cubic yards (1.3 million cubic meters) volume. The Moon Pyramid is somewhat smaller with a height of 130 feet (39.6 m) and a base of 400 × 500 feet (122 × 152 m).

The Aztecs

When the Spaniard Hernando Cortés arrived in 1519 in what is today Mexico City, he found the dazzling capital of the Aztec Empire. It was built on a series of islands in the Valley of Mexico. The city of Tenochtitlán, with its stone walls, towers, and temples, impressed the Spanish invaders. It had been established in the fourteenth century by the Aztecs (who called themselves the Mexica—hence Mexico). In the fifteenth century, the Aztecs conquered more territory and expanded their empire. They amassed great wealth and created lavish works of art. However, their blood-letting rituals demanded human sacrifice on a vast scale.

The subjugated enemies of the Aztecs joined forces with Cortés and facilitated his destruction of their empire. His soldiers destroyed Tenochtitlán, and he sent enormous quantities of plundered objects to the Spanish queen. The spoils were subsequently melted down for their gold and silver. As a result, very little Aztec art survives, but Aztec names persist at important Mesoamerican sites.

fig. 10.F) was located at the north end of the avenue. Toward the southern end was the *Ciudadela*, or citadel, a square large enough for crowds of sixty thousand, functioning as the religious and political center of Teotihuacán.

Surrounding the *Ciudadela* were temple platforms constructed in **talud-tablero** style (fig. **10.I**). This style is typical of Teotihuacán architecture: the *tablero* is the framed vertical element built above a sloping base, or *talud*. The platform façades were faced with painted stucco. The cores of the platforms were reinforced with stone piers and filled with rubble embedded in clay.

Excavations at the *Ciudadela* have revealed dramatic monumental painted reliefs on the façade of a temple platform dedicated to the Feathered Serpent (called Quetzalcoatl by the Aztecs). The detail in figure **10.J** shows massive, blocklike serpent heads with bared fangs, surrounded by a circle of feathers. They alternate with heads of Tlaloc, the rain god. Both are carved frontally, and their fixed gazes are reinforced by their wide, round eyes. The stylized geometry of these figures is characteristic of figural imagery at Teotihuacán, but the exact meaning of their iconography is not known.

That Tlaloc may have served an apotropaic function is suggested by his role—like that of the Gorgoneion—as a shield device. As such, he appears on a stele found at the Classic Maya site of Tikal and carved with the representation of a warrior in Teotihuacán costume (fig. **10.K**). Dressed in full regalia with an elaborate feathered helmet and a shell necklace, he carries a shield decorated with the face of Tlaloc. The warrior is depicted with his head in profile and his torso slightly turned. But his shield is frontal, like the gods on the temple of Quetzalcoatl in the *Ciudadela*, and the image of Tlaloc therefore confronts viewers with a direct, and symbolically protective, gaze.

Around 750, the architectural complex along the Avenue of the Dead was burned and the thriving city of Teotihuacán fell into decline. Its culture was kept alive, however, particularly through Aztec legends, and continued to influence the art and architecture of Mesoamerica for centuries.

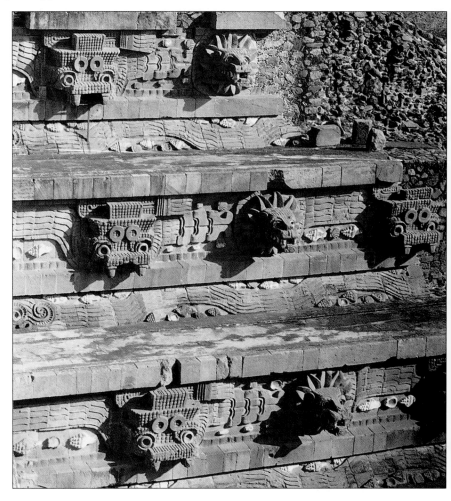

10.J Detail of heads from the façade of the Temple of Quetzalcoatl, Teotihuacán, before 300 A.D. Painted relief.

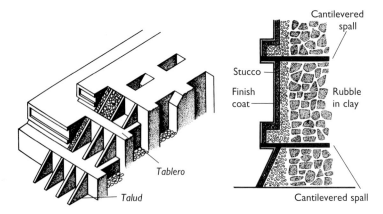

10.I Diagrams of a *talud-tablero* platform.

Maya (c. 1100 B.C.–A.D. 1500)

Maya civilization originated in the southern part of Mesoamerica and lasted until its destruction in the sixteenth century. It occupied eastern Mexico (particularly the Yucatán, Tabasco, and Chiapas), Belize, Guatemala, and the west of Honduras and El Salvador.

Maya culture developed not only the most complex writing system in Mesoamerica, but a sophisticated knowledge of mathematics and methods of observing celestial phenomena, recorded in books made from strips of bark paper (see Box). The Maya created many important political and religious centers, each populated by an aristocratic class of rulers, priests, and nobles, supported by a far more numerous class of farmers and artisans.

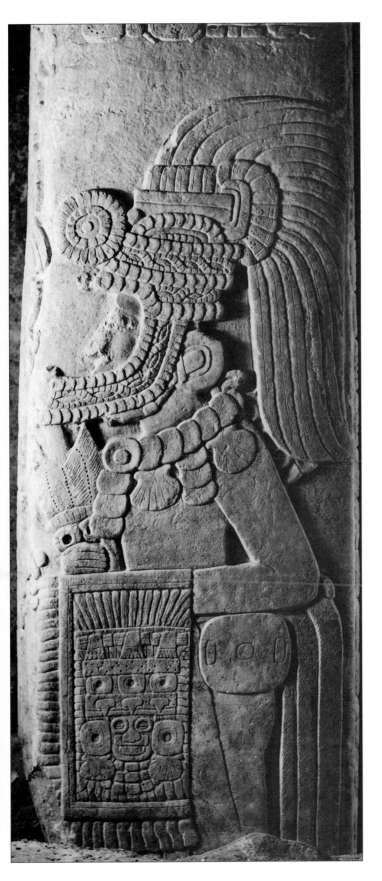

The Maya Calendar

Several calendrical systems were developed by the Maya, all of them intimately related to seasonal change and astronomical phenomena. They were used in the service of religious rituals, ceremonies, and festivals. One of the most intriguing creations is the calendar round of fifty-two years, which developed in the Late Preclassic period (300 B.C–A.D. 250). At the end of a fifty-two-year cycle, the ceremony of the New Fire was celebrated. Fires in domestic hearths were extinguished and, at sunrise, priests rekindled a new fire and brought it to each home.

Two time cycles within the calendar round have been identified. The 260-day count, which is still used by some contemporary Maya, is based on a sequence of thirteen periods, each of twenty days. Each day has specific omens that prophesy future events. The other cycle is the 365-day year, consisting of eighteen months, also twenty days long. Five unlucky days are added at the end to round out the total.

The so-called "long count" was developed after the calendar round, although precisely when is not known. It was perfected by the Maya, and its use extended to other Mesoamerican cultures. The long count differed from the calendar round in being based on a 360-day period whose cycles range from twenty to 144,000 days.

The jade plaque known as the Leiden Plate (fig. **10.L**) shows, on the front, an Early Classic Maya ruler from Tikal as he steps on the back of a defeated enemy, a typical iconographic motif in Maya stelai. The reverse shows glyphs indicating a long count date corresponding to September 17, 320, probably the day on which this particular ruler assumed power.

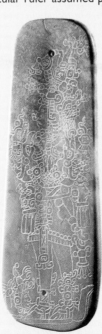
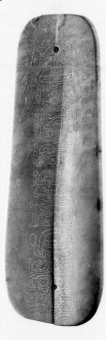

10.L The Leiden Plate. Jade, 8½ in (21.6 cm) high. Rijksmuseum voor Volkenkunde, Leiden.

10.K Detail of warrior in Teotihuacán costume, from side of stele 31, Tikal, Guatemala, Maya. University Museum, Philadelphia.

Maya Religion

The Maya believed in cycles of creation and destruction, ages of development, and an apocalyptic end of the world. They conceived of the universe as having three tiers: sky, earth, and underworld. The earth was a square or rectangle resting on the back of a crocodile. The four corners of the world were oriented to the cardinal directions and associated with specific colors. East was red like the sunrise, and west, where the sun sets, was black. North was white, and south was yellow. Supporting the Maya sky—conceived of as a two-headed serpent—was the great Tree of Life at the center of the world. When Maya died, they went to the underworld, or "place of night" (*Xibalba*), which had nine levels.

The *Popol Vuh*, a Late Postclassic epic history of the Quiche Maya (an important nation that flourished just before the Spanish conquest), relates the story of Hero Twins who defeat the Xibalbans in a ball-game. The heroes ascend to heaven and become the sun and the planet Venus. In so doing, they are a model for Maya rulers who likewise hope to escape eternal night. The epic is known from a manuscript discovered in the nineteenth century.

Maya religion was polytheistic and each god was made more complex by having multiple aspects. Hunabku was the omnipotent god who controlled the universe. The chief god Itzamna ("Lizard House") was depicted as an old man who invented writing; he was the god of science and knowledge. His wife, Ix Chel ("Lady Rainbow"), was the goddess of weaving, medicine, childbirth, and the moon. Together, Itzamna and Ix Chel gave birth to all the other gods in the Maya pantheon.

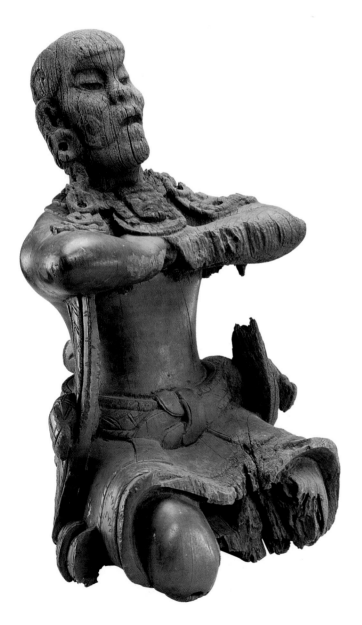

Hereditary rulers were theocratic, that is, their claim to power rested on establishing a connection with the gods (see Box). The *Maya Lord* (fig. **10.M**), a wood carving from Tabasco, kneels in a ritual pose, wearing a skirt and an elaborate necklace. The Maya shared the pervasive Mesoamerican belief that the gods had given people their own blood when they created them. The gods thus had to be repaid in kind with human blood, and elaborate rites were performed in which rulers let their own blood slightly as a sign of their identification with the gods. The fate of their captives, however, was not so benign. Typically, four men would each hold a limb of the captive, while a fifth cut out the heart.

Classic Maya

Copán (early 5th century–c. 820) One of the best-preserved Classic Maya sites is Copán, in western Honduras. The reconstruction drawing (fig. **10.N**) is based on the Late Classic period. It shows the temple pyramids with their stairways on the acropolis at the right, and the plaza with carved stelai at the left. Copán artists used durable green volcanic tufa for architectural monuments and their sculptural decorations, which included elaborate portraits of Maya kings. The ballcourt at Copán (fig. **10.O**) is the finest surviving example of Classic architecture. It was dedicated in A.D. 738 by a king known as Eighteen Rabbit, who also presided over the construction of a large palace.

10.M *Maya Lord*, from Tabasco, Mexico, 6th century. Wood with hematite pigment, 14 in (35.5 cm) high. Metropolitan Museum of Art, New York. Michael C. Rockefeller Memorial Collection. Bequest of Nelson A. Rockefeller, 1979 (1979.206.1063). Photograph © 1980 Metropolitan Museum of Art.

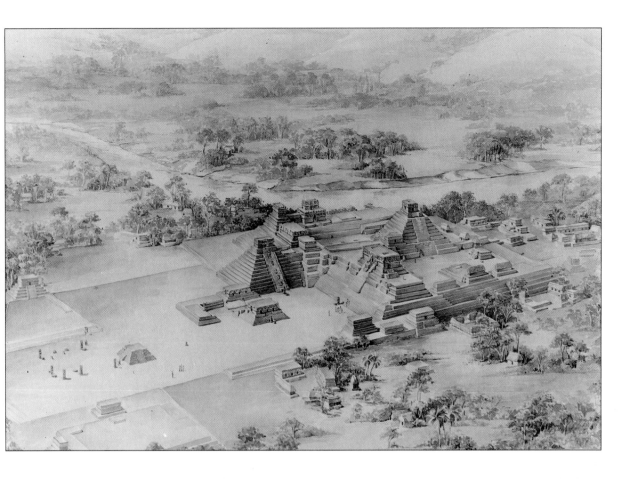

10.N Tatiana Proskouriakoff, reconstruction drawing of the site of Copán, Honduras. Maya, Late Classic.

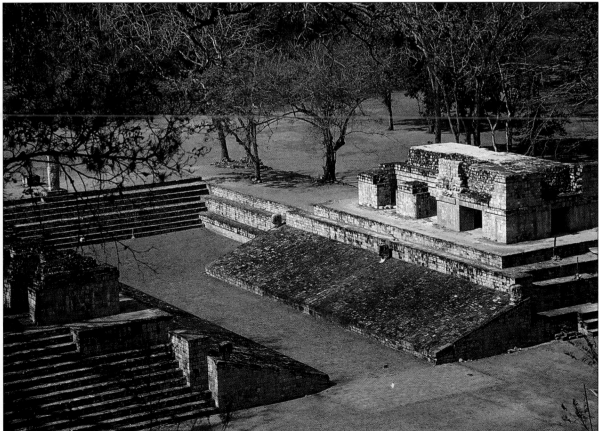

10.O Ballcourt, Copán, Honduras. Maya, Late Classic, c. 800.

Also at Copán, archaeologists have discovered a scribal palace of the Classic period decorated with sculptures of the monkey-man god represented as a scribe (fig. **10.P**). Scribes were members of the elite, along with the rulers and the aristocrats. The example illustrated here shows a scribe sitting cross-legged, like the Egyptian scribe (cf. fig. 4.23), and listening attentively. His necklace is similar to that worn by the *Maya Lord* (fig. 10.M), while his combination of human and animal features is reminiscent of the Olmec *Jaguar Deity* (fig. 10.C).

Tikal: Temple I At Tikal, in the Petén region of modern-day Guatemala, Temple I (the Temple of the Jaguar) is one of six structures that reflect the increasing height of Maya temple pyramids (fig. **10.Q**). In its heyday Tikal was one of the largest Classic Maya city-states. It had an elevated ceremonial complex consisting of rulers' tombs surmounted by temples, open squares, and ballcourts. Temple I has nine layers supporting a temple, accessible by a staircase on the long side, and faces Temple II on the other side of an open square. The temple has two rooms with corbeled vaults and is crowned by a **roof comb** (the crestlike feature, originally decorated with painted sculpture). Beneath Temple I, archaeologists found the tomb of a ruler nicknamed "Au Cacao," which means "Lord Chocolate" (ruled c. 682–727); he was buried with jewelry, food and drink, and bone tubes incised with representations of the gods.

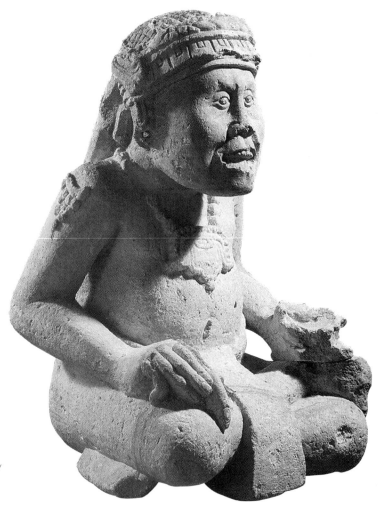

10.P (right) Monkey-man scribal god, from Copán, Honduras. Maya, Late Classic. Maya scribes wrote with brush or feather pens, which they dipped into small pots made from conch shells. The writing liquid itself was either black or red paint. Museo Municipal, Copán, Honduras.

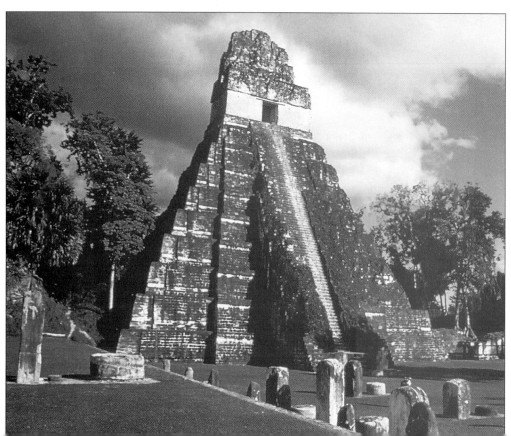

10.Q Temple I, Tikal, Guatemala. Maya, before A.D. 800. Approx. 157 ft (48 m) high.

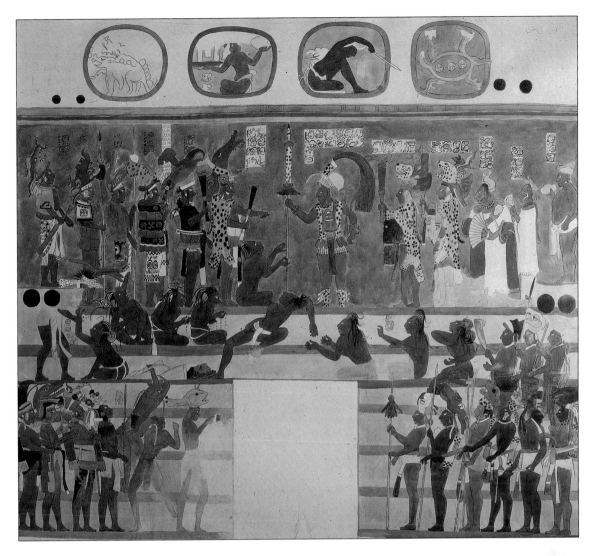

10.R Reconstruction of mural painting from Bonampak, Chiapas, Mexico, Maya, Classic, c. 790. Peabody Museum of Archaeology and Ethnology, Harvard University.

Bonampak: Mural Painting   In 1946, at the Classic Maya site of Bonampak (in Chiapas, Mexico), a remarkable group of murals dating to the late eighth century was discovered. These depict narratives of battles, victory celebrations, and the torture and sacrifice of prisoners. The recopied mural in figure **10.R** illustrates the Mayan treatment of captured prisoners. The scene is set on a stepped pyramid with King Chaan-muan at the center of the top step (fig. **10.S**). He wears a jaguar-skin jacket and is flanked by masked and costumed members of the nobility. Standing at the right is his principal wife wearing a white robe and holding a fan. Between the top step and the attendants at the bottom are nearly nude captives awaiting death. Some stare in shock at their hands, which drip blood. A dead captive lies below the ruler's staff, while a decapitated trophy head is beside his right foot.

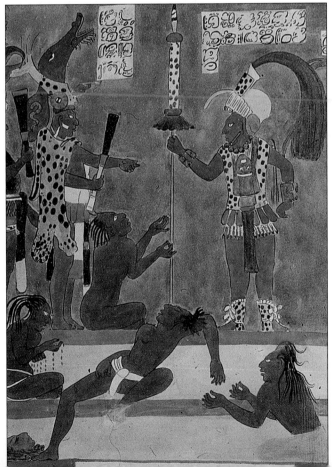

10.S Mural painting, Bonampak (detail of fig. 10.R).

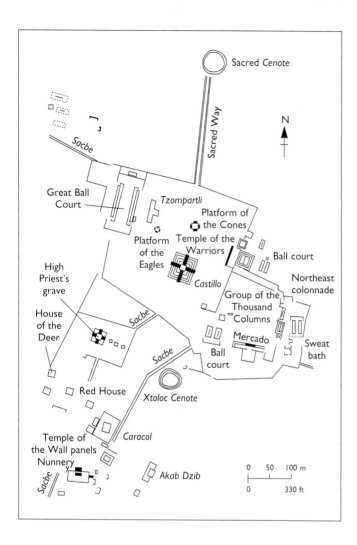

Postclassic Maya: Chichén Itzá

A Postclassic Maya people, the Itzá, flourished in northern Mexico. In their central city of Chichén Itzá (fig. **10.T**), a more cosmopolitan Maya style assimilated forms from central Mexico, as did Maya social and religious institutions. The many frescoes at Chichén Itzá—on the walls of the ballcourt, and in the Temples of the Jaguars and the Warriors—are unfortunately in very poor condition. But architecture here clearly reflects the continuing development of new forms. The view in figure **10.U** shows the *Caracol*, a circular temple, in the foreground, and in the distance the Temple of Kukulcan (called the *Castillo*) at the left and the Temple of the Warriors farther away at the right. Kukulcan—literally the Feathered (*kukul*) Serpent (*can*)—is mentioned in Maya records as the founder of Chichén Itzá's capital. The Temple of Kukulcan has corbeled vaulting, as at Temple I at Tikal, but unlike most Classic Maya temples it has multiple doorways and larger rooms. An earlier stage of the temple is encased by the terraced platform. Inside this buried temple, there is a room containing a red throne in the shape of a jaguar, with jade eyes and shell fangs.

The so-called *Chacmool* (fig. **10.V**) reclines at the top of the steps leading to the Temple of the Warriors. It turns its head abruptly, as if to stare toward the main open square. At the same time, it holds a plate which is believed to have been for receiving the hearts cut from sacrificial captives.

Chichén Itzá declined in the thirteenth century, and the center of Maya civilization in the north shifted to a new capital at Mayapan. Today, despite the Spanish conquest in the sixteenth century, aspects of traditional Maya culture still survive in Mesoamerica.

10.T (above) Plan of the site of Chichén Itzá, Mexico.

10.U View of Chichén Itzá showing the *Caracol* with the Temple of the Warriors (left) and the *Castillo* (right) in the distance.

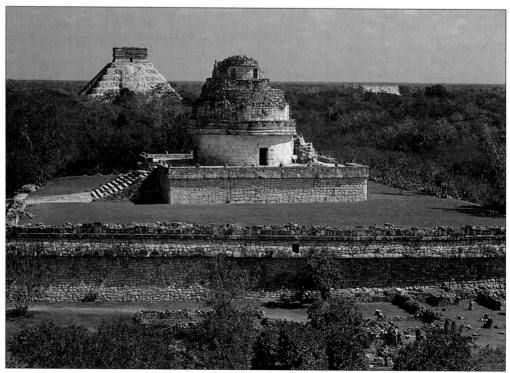

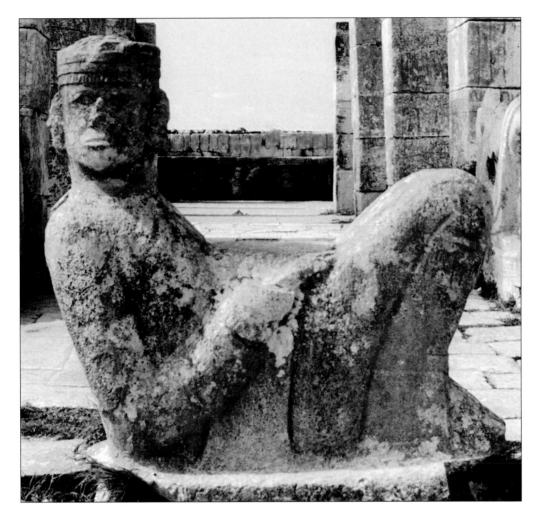

10.V *Chacmool*, Chichén Itzá. 3 ft 6 in (1.1 m) high.

	Style/Period	Works of Art		Cultural/Historical Developments	
1200 B.C.	OLMEC c. 1200–900 B.C.	*Jaguar Deity* (**10.C**), San Lorenzo Colossal head (**10.D**), San Lorenzo Pyramid (**10.E**), Uaxactún		Geometric Period in Greece (c. 1000–700 B.C.)	
A.D. 350	TEOTIHUACÁN c. A.D. 350–650	Warrior in Teotihuacán costume (**10.K**), Tikal The Leiden Plate (**10.L**) Teotihuacán (**10.G**) Pyramid of the Sun (**10.H**), Teotihuacán Temple of Quetzalcoatl (**10.J**), Teotihuacán	**Colossal head**	Sack of Rome by Visigoths (410) Reign of Justinian (6th century)	
1500	MAYA c. 1100 B.C.–A.D. 1500	*Maya Lord* (**10.M**), Tabasco Copán (**10.N**) Ballcourt (**10.0**), Copán Monkey-man scribal god (**10.P**), Copán Temple I (**10.Q**), Tikal Mural painting (**10.R–10.S**), Bonampak Chichén Itzá (**10.T–10.U**) *Chacmool* (**10.V**), Chichén Itzá	**Mural detail, Bonampak** **Monkey-man scribal god**	Julius Caesar becomes dictator (49 B.C.) Death of Christ (c. 30 A.D.) Beginning of Gothic Style in France (12th century) The Renaissance in Italy (1300–1550) Columbus sets sail on new route to India (1492)	**Jaguar Deity**

11

Romanesque Art

The term "Romanesque" (or "Roman-like") refers to a broad range of styles, embracing many regional variants, that flourished in western Europe in the eleventh and twelfth centuries. It is a stylistic rather than a historical term, intended to describe medieval art that shares certain characteristics with ancient Roman architectural style. Similar features include round arches, stone vaults, thick walls, and exterior relief sculpture. As Europe at this time was a patchwork of regions, rather than of nations with centralized political administrations, scholars tend to identify the various styles by the name of the relevant region, for example "Norman" (from Normandy).

Reflecting the relative stability and prosperity of the Christian Church, there was an enormous surge in building activity, especially of cathedrals, churches, and monasteries. Monasteries owned significant tracts of land, which enhanced their political and economic power in Romanesque Europe. This contributed to the widespread revival of architectural sculpture and the ornamentation of Christian buildings. As the most innovative Romanesque works were created in France, most of the buildings and works of art discussed in this chapter are French, with a few representative examples from Italy, Spain, and Norway.

Historical Background

During the late ninth century A.D., the Muslims continued their expansion in the south and, from the east, the Magyars (an eastern European tribe whose language is related to Finnish) advanced in search of a permanent home. From the north came the Vikings, who occupied Normandy, in northwest France. By the second half of the eleventh century, the threat of invasion had decreased, largely because many pagans had been assimilated and converted to Christianity. The Magyars had settled in present-day Hungary. The Vikings had also become Christians and their leaders were recognized as dukes by the French king. In 1066 William of Normandy (better known as William the Conqueror) invaded England,

becoming its first Norman king and establishing feudalism as the pervasive social system in England (see Box). In the early twelfth century, the Normans, who were descended from the Vikings, expelled the Arabs from Sicily, and wrested control of much of southern Italy from the Byzantines. Muslim dominance of Spain had declined and the Christians, maintaining their resistance from the mountains in the north, were poised to recapture most of the Iberian peninsula (modern Spain and Portugal).

The social structure of western Europe was based on the feudal system, with the economic and political core centered in manorial estates. Kings, dukes, and counts, to whom lesser barons and lords owed their allegiance, ruled

Feudalism

Feudalism (from the Latin word *foedus*, meaning "oath") was the prevailing socio-economic system of the Middle Ages. Under the feudal system, the nobility had hereditary tenure of the land. In theory, all land belonged to the emperor, who granted the use of certain portions of it to a king in return for an oath of loyalty and other obligations. The king, in turn, granted the use of land (including the right to levy taxes and administer justice locally) to a nobleman. He granted an even smaller portion to a local lord, for whom unpaid serfs, or peasants, worked the land. At each level of dependency, the vassal owed his loyalty to his lord and had to render military service on demand. In practice, however, these obligations were fulfilled only when the king or lord had the power to enforce them.

The principal unit of feudalism was the manor. In exchange for their services, the serfs were allowed to cultivate a part of the lord's land for their own benefit. Feudalism and serfdom declined from the thirteenth century onward, partly because of a growing cash economy, and partly because of peasant revolts. In France, however, these social systems lingered on until the Revolution of 1789. In Russia and certain other European countries feudalism continued well into the nineteenth century.

The Crusades

The Crusades were a series of military expeditions from western Christendom, originally undertaken in the name of the Cross (*crux* in Latin), to recapture the holy places in Syria and Palestine from the Muslims.

The First Crusade began in 1095 and ended with the capture of Jerusalem in 1099. The Second (1147–9), Third (1189–92), and Fourth (1202–4) Crusades met with varying degrees of success. Many rulers and nationalities participated in these early crusades, including the kings of England and France and the emperor of Germany. Several other expeditions to the Near East took place in the thirteenth century, but in 1291 Acre (near Haifa in modern Israel), the last Frankish foothold in the Near East, fell to the Muslims, and the original impetus behind the Crusades waned. Later Crusades were launched in other regions against non-Christians (for example, the Moors in Spain and the Slavs), heretics, and excommunicated Christian rulers. In 1464 Pope Pius II failed to win support for a last attempt at a Crusade to the Near East.

An assortment of spiritual benefits and material motives encouraged men (and in one case children—in the Children's Crusade of 1212) to undertake these long and arduous journeys. Spiritual benefits included the remission of time that one's soul would spend in purgatory and the promise of becoming a martyr if one were killed. Material motives included the territorial ambitions of feudal princes, the first stirrings of Western colonialism, and the desire of Italian cities (especially Venice) to secure trading bases in the Levant.

The territorial gains of the early Crusades soon disappeared. More lasting results were seen in a widening division between western and eastern Christendom and the formation of orders of knighthood (notably the Knights of Saint John of Jerusalem and the Knights Templar), consisting of soldiers who took monastic vows and devoted themselves to military service against non-Christians.

---

these manors. But there was no centralized political order, and the main unifying authority remained with the pope in Rome. The Church played a vital role in the social and economic structures of secular life, owning a large amount of landed property—close to a third in France—and claiming the same temporal authority as the kings and nobles.

Despite conflicts between social classes engendered by feudalism and the manorial system, however, a degree of military and political equilibrium was achieved. This led to economic growth, especially in Italy, where Mediterranean trade routes were opened and several seaports (such as Naples, Pisa, Genoa, and Venice) became centers of renewed commercial activity. Manufacturing and banking flourished, and new groups of craftsmen and merchants arose. Cities and towns that had declined during the Early Middle Ages revived, and new ones were founded. Gradually, towns began to assert their independence from their lords and the Church. They demanded, and received, charters setting out their legal rights and obligations. Some even established republican governments.

Pilgrimage Roads

By the first half of the eleventh century, Christianity was in the ascendant in western Europe. The spirit of religious vitality affected almost all aspects of life and manifested itself particularly in the Crusades—a series of military campaigns undertaken from 1095 and lasting into the fifteenth century to recover the Holy Land from the Muslims (see Box).

Earlier in the Middle Ages, it was only penitent Christians who had made pilgrimages to atone for their sins (fig. **11.1**). From the eleventh century, however, it became customary for devout Christians generally to make pilgrimages, particularly to churches containing sacred relics (see Box). These might be the physical remains of saints or remnants of their clothing.

The two most sacred pilgrimage sites were Jerusalem and Rome. Jerusalem had been the site of Solomon's Temple and the Holy Sepulcher (see Box), of Christ's Entry and Last Supper (see p. 274), of the events leading to his death, and of some of the miracles that followed. Rome was the center of Christendom in the West. It contained the papal residence, and the tombs of Saints Peter and Paul. But journeys to these cities, especially Jerusalem, could be dangerous. A third choice, which became popular in the eleventh century, was the shrine of Saint James (Santiago in Spanish) at Compostela, Galicia (a region of northwest Spain).

The shrine of Santiago also became associated with Charlemagne, and therefore had a particular attraction for the French. Two generations earlier, Charlemagne's grandfather, Charles Martel, had ended the Muslim invasion of France at the Battle of Poitiers in 732. This association took on mythic proportions and was based on Charlemagne's military campaign against the Muslims in Spain. According to tradition, Charlemagne dreamed of a star-filled road in the sky (the Milky Way). Saint James appeared in the dream, explaining that the stars pointed the way to his tomb and telling Charlemagne to follow them. In the popular French imagination, Charlemagne was the first pilgrim to Compostela. Further enhancing the significance of Charlemagne's dream was its twofold connection with important Christian events: the Vision of Constantine (see pp. 372–3) and the angels' instruction to the shepherds to follow the star to Bethlehem.

Pilgrims, Relics, and the *Liber Sancti Jacobi* (the *Book of St. James*)

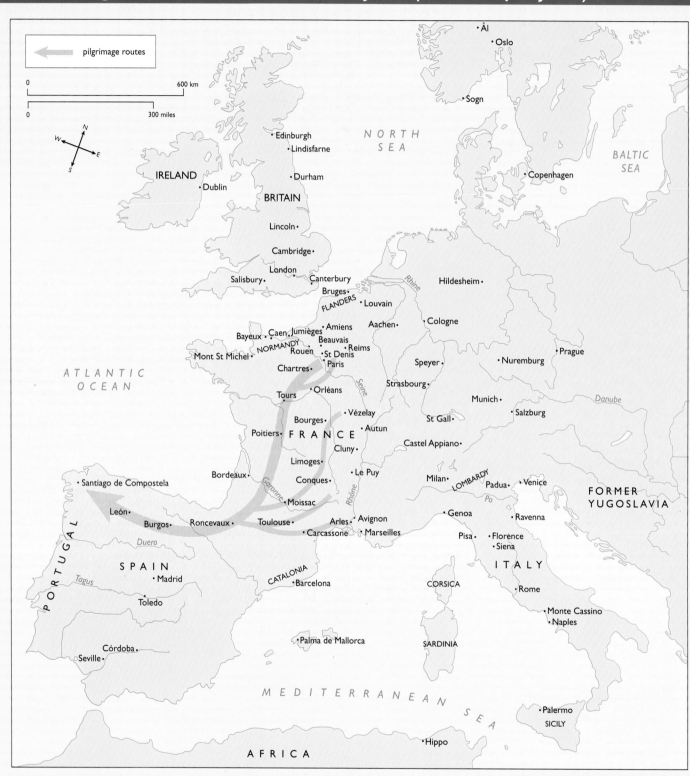

11.1 Map of Romanesque and Gothic sites in western Europe, including pilgrimage routes to Santiago de Compostela.

In the sense applied by the Church, the term "relics" refers to a personal memorial of a holy person. Often relics were parts of the person—such as hair, bones, and fingernails. Such relics are believed to have miraculous powers, including that of healing. But in order to benefit from the relic, one must travel to it—that is, make a pilgrimage. The pilgrim then has to see the relic, and ideally to touch it. If the relic itself could not be touched because of its fragility, then a **reliquary**, or container for relics (see p. 367), could act as a substitute. In some cases, as at the Church of Sainte-Foy, pilgrims viewed the reliquary through an elaborate choir screen, which separated the ordinary worshiper from the most sacred space. Having absorbed the sacred into his own being, the pilgrim returns home.

In A.D. 42, James was beheaded by King Herod, becoming the first of Christ's apostles to be martyred. His remains were believed to have been "translated" (miraculously relocated) from Herod's Judea to Spain. This miracle is celebrated on December 30 in the liturgical calendar of the Roman Church.

The *Liber Sancti Jacobi* was a twelfth-century guide in five books for pilgrims to the shrine of Santiago de Compostela. Book I contains hymns and liturgical texts related to Saint James. Book II describes his miracles, and Book III glorifies his cult. Book IV purports to be a history of the events celebrated in the *Song of Roland*. The actual guide, Book V, describes the pilgrimage roads and the regions they traverse. For those who travel via Le Puy, a visit to Conques is regarded as essential. At the church, according to the guide, "Many benefits have been granted there to the healthy no less than to the sick. In front of the portals of the basilica there is an excellent stream, more marvelous than what one is able to tell."[1]

Once in Compostela, the pilgrims are introduced to the town and its cathedral, told how to behave, and how they should be welcomed. The final destination of every pilgrim to Compostela is, of course, the richly decorated reliquary of Saint James.

Solomon's Temple and the Holy Sepulcher

Solomon, the son of David and Bathsheba, was King of Israel from around 970 to 930 B.C. He was known for his great wisdom and his political centralization of Israel over tribal factions. The temple traditionally associated with him was originally located on the present site of the Dome of the Rock in Jerusalem (cf. fig. 10.4). It was seen as an expression of his own power and of Israel's international status. According to Josephus (see p. 236), Solomon and Herod enlarged an existing temple whose plan resembled that of the Tabernacle. This was a portable sanctuary some 105 by 75 feet (32 × 23 m), which had been built by Moses and was designed to be taken apart and reassembled as travel required.

The plan also had elements in common with temples built in other Mediterranean cultures. Solomon's Temple had an open courtyard, an interior holy area, and an inner sanctuary (the "holy of holies"). The inner sanctuary contained the Ark of the Covenant, a rectangular wooden chest covered with gold. It signified the presence of God to the Hebrews and was thus their most holy symbol. One entered the Temple through an eastern portico flanked by two hollow bronze columns.

Reflecting the political sway of King Solomon and the relative peace and prosperity of his reign was the international character of the skilled laborers sent by King Hiram of Tyre, in Phoenicia, and the opulent imported materials they used to construct the Temple. The walls were lined with Lebanese cedar. Gold lined the inner sanctuary and covered the olive-wood doors separating the sanctuary from the nave and the nave from the portico. The altar in the nave was also gold, whereas that in the courtyard was bronze, a reflection of the more sacred status accorded the inner altar. In 587/6 B.C. Jerusalem fell and Solomon's Temple was destroyed by Nebuchadnezzar (see p. 69), King of Babylon. The Ark of the Covenant disappeared and was never recovered.

The Holy Sepulcher refers to the rock cave in Jerusalem, which was believed to have been the location of Christ's burial and resurrection. According to the Legend of the True Cross (see p. 372), Saint Helena found the tomb, and had a church built on the site in the fourth century. In 614 this was destroyed by the Persians. A second church constructed in 626 was also destroyed, followed by a third structure around 1050. The Crusaders built a large church around 1130 which covered other sacred Christian sites, including Calvary. The present church dates to the nineteenth century.

In the typological system of reading history, the Christians paired both David and Solomon with Christ as exemplars of wise kingship, and Saint Helena with Mary. The Temple and the Holy Sepulcher were typologically paired with church buildings and Jerusalem with Christian cities throughout Christendom.

Another link between Charlemagne and the effort to oust the Muslims from Spain was incorporated into the French medieval epic poem, the *Chanson de Roland* ("Song of Roland"). In reality, Charlemagne's troops returned to France, but a contingent led by Roland stayed behind, and everyone was killed by a surprise attack. This minor skirmish was exaggerated by the poet and proliferated into numerous mythic episodes of chivalry. The encounter became a symbol of the struggle between Islam and Christianity.

Inspired by these events, as well as by the need to see and touch the relics, pilgrims traveled to Compostela. They followed four main routes across France, through the Pyrenees, and then westward. Along these roads, an extensive network of churches, hospices (or lodging places), and monasteries was constructed. The design and location of such buildings were a direct response to the ever-growing crowds of pilgrims. As we saw in the description of Saint Gall (see p. 344), monasteries were organized to accommodate the Rules of their founders and of the subsequent orders that were established. Similarly, church plans were designed so that worshipers (especially the monks) could follow the strict routines of the relevant order.

Romanesque Pilgrimage Churches

In addition to accommodating the Rule of an order, Romanesque architects had to construct churches big enough for the influx of pilgrims. At the same time, churches had to be structurally sound and adequately illuminated. The availability of materials often presented problems because of the great increase in building activity. More subjective considerations, such as esthetic appeal, also had to be taken into account. These might be influenced by the wishes of a local religious order or a wealthy patron.

11.2 Aerial view of Sainte-Foy, Conques, Auvergne, France, c. 1050–1120. Apart from two 19th-century towers on the west façade, Sainte-Foy stands today as it did in the 12th century. It has a relatively short nave, side aisles built to the full height of the nave (so that there is no clerestory lighting), and a transept. The belfry, or bell tower, rises above the roof of the **crossing**.

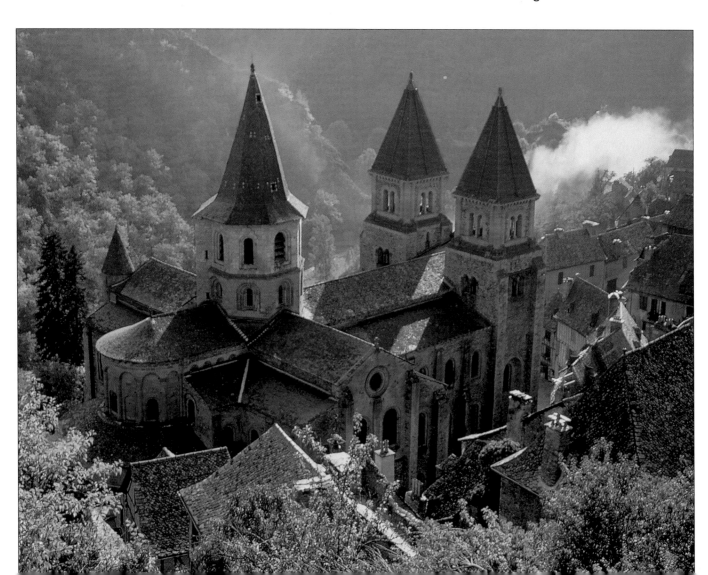

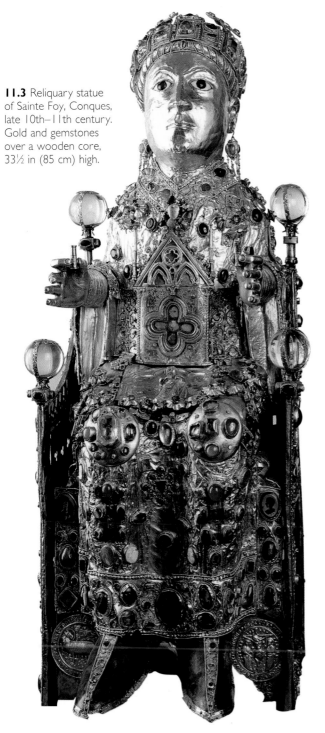

11.3 Reliquary statue of Sainte Foy, Conques, late 10th–11th century. Gold and gemstones over a wooden core, 33½ in (85 cm) high.

elaborate gold reliquary statue (fig. **11.3**), the head of which is believed to have been formed around the saint's skull. The figure is made of gold repoussé, with several sheets of gold placed over a wooden core for stability. The saint sits frontally as if enthroned, wearing a Roman helmet and a rich, gold robe covered with gems and Roman cameos.

The builders of Sainte-Foy, and indeed of all pilgrimage churches, had to solve the problem of accommodating large crowds without interfering with the duties of the clergy. The plan in figure **11.4** shows how the traditional Latin-cross basilica was modified by extending the side aisles around the transept and the apse to form an ambulatory. This permitted the lay visitors to circulate freely, leaving the monks undisturbed access to the main altar in the choir. Three smaller apses, or **radiating chapels**, protrude from the main apse, and two chapels of unequal size have been added at the east side of the transept arms. Essentially such architectural arrangements accommodated two social and temporal systems. One was based on the social world of the laity, while the other provided an architectural space for those whose daily lives followed another "order" of business and a liturgical schedule. The Benedictines, for example, devoted as many as eight to ten hours per day to performing services.

Sainte-Foy at Conques

Communication along the pilgrimage routes must have been constant, with pilgrims, masons, and other craftsmen continually moving back and forth. It is thus not surprising that many Romanesque churches had similar features. The earliest surviving example of a pilgrimage church (fig. **11.2**) is dedicated to Sainte Foy, a third-century virgin martyr known in English as Saint Faith. She was martyred in 303 while still a child, because she refused to worship pagan gods. The church, which belonged to the Benedictine order (see p. 343), was erected over her tomb, and stands today in Conques, a remote village on the pilgrimage route from Le Puy in southeastern France.

The single most important attraction for pilgrims to this church was the saint's relics. They were contained in an

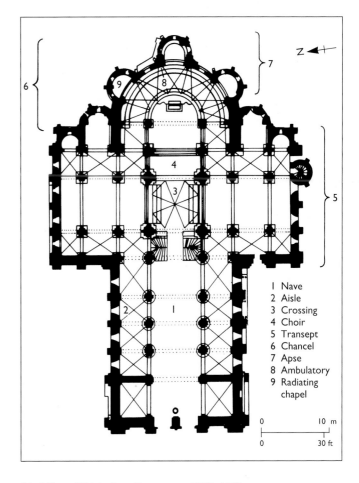

1 Nave
2 Aisle
3 Crossing
4 Choir
5 Transept
6 Chancel
7 Apse
8 Ambulatory
9 Radiating chapel

0 ____ 10 m
0 ____ 30 ft

11.4 Plan of Sainte-Foy, Conques, c. 1050–1120.

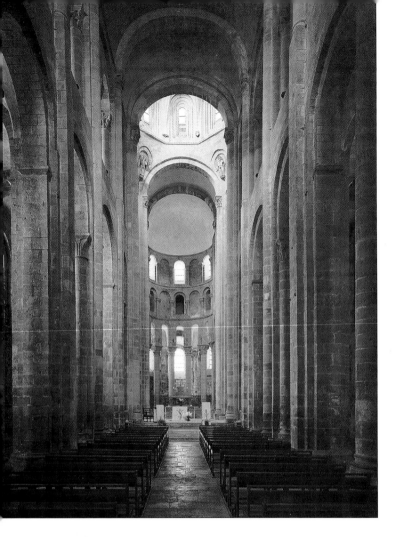

11.5 Tribune and nave vaults, Sainte-Foy, Conques, c. 1050–1120. Romanesque builders solved the problem of supporting the extra weight of the stone by constructing a second-story gallery, or tribune, over the side aisles as an **abutment**. Structurally, the gallery diverted the thrust from the side walls back onto the piers of the nave. It also provided an extra interior space for the pilgrims.

An important new architectural development in Romanesque churches was the replacement of wooden roofs by stone barrel vaults (fig. **11.5**), which not only lessened the risk of fire but improved the acoustics (music, particularly Gregorian chant, was an integral feature of the Christian liturgy). The stone vaults required extra support, or buttressing, to counteract the lateral thrust, or sideways force, they exerted against the walls. At Sainte-Foy **transverse ribs** cross the underside of the **quadrant**, i.e. the half-barrel vaults of the nave. They are supported by **cluster piers**, each of which is reinforced by four engaged half-columns. The piers accent the corners of the groin-vaulted wall sections, or **bays**, of the side aisles.

Romanesque churches were also often provided with sculpture, painting, and wall hangings, through which an illiterate general population could "read" the Bible stories and events portrayed in other texts. Tapestries, most of which are now lost, often hung along the aisles, adding color and warmth to the church interiors.

Most pilgrimage churches had images carved in relief at the main entrance. The area immediately around the doorways, or **portals**, would have contained the first images

encountered and the reliefs were therefore intended to attract the attention of the worshiper approaching the church. The general layout of medieval church portals is fairly consistent (fig. **11.6**); what varies from building to building is the **program**, or arrangement and meaning, of the subjects depicted on each section.

At Conques, the relief sculpture on the western portal (fig. **11.7**) is confined to the **tympanum** and the lintel. The scene is the *Last Judgment* (figs. **11.8** and **11.9**), in which Christ the Judge determines whether souls will spend eternity in heaven or hell. It conforms to the iconographic norm in its overall arrangement. The figures on Christ's right (the viewer's left) and on his level are saints and churchmen. Above them, angels hold scrolls that form arches. Below, also on Christ's right, are figures framed by semicircular arches. Christ's left hand is lowered, toward hell. His gesture directs the viewer's attention to the damned souls falling and being tortured by devils. In the center of hell, on the viewer's right, is the crowned figure of Satan. He and his company of devils, together with the damned, are entwined by snakes. They are symmetrically opposite the figures under semicircular arches on the left side of the lintel. Note that the saved souls on Christ's right are neatly arranged under framing devices, whereas the damned, on Christ's left, appear jumbled and disordered.

At the center of the lintel, directly below Christ, the traditional right–left Christian symbolism is maintained. Two individual scenes are divided by a vertical. On Christ's right, angels welcome saved souls into heaven. On his left, a grotesque devil with spiked hair and a long nose brandishes a club at a damned soul. The latter bends over as if to enter the gaping jaws of a monster, which pokes its

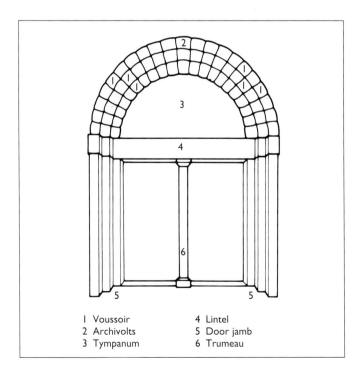

1 Voussoir	4 Lintel
2 Archivolts	5 Door jamb
3 Tympanum	6 Trumeau

11.6 Diagram of a Romanesque portal.

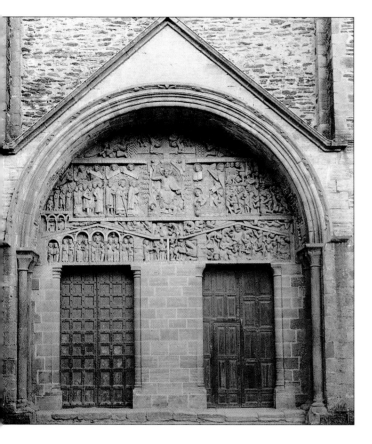

11.7 West portal with tympanum, Sainte-Foy, Conques, c. 1130. Stone, approx. 12 × 22 ft (3.66 × 6.71 m).

11.8 *Last Judgment*, tympanum of west portal, Sainte-Foy, Conques. Christ is both the central and largest figure. He is surrounded by a **mandorla**, an oval of light (an eastern motif), and his halo contains the Cross. He raises his right hand, reminding the viewer that the souls on his right will be received in heaven—a visual rendition of the advantages of being "on the right hand of God."

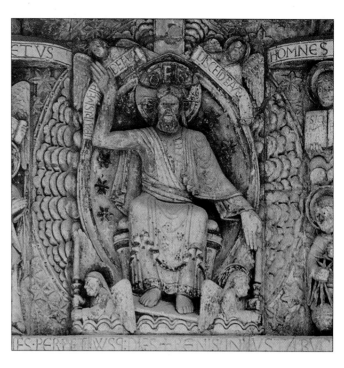

11.9 *Christ the Judge*, tympanum of west portal (detail of fig. 11.8), Sainte-Foy, Conques.

head through a doorway. This image thus conflates the Christian metaphors of the "gate of hell" and the "jaws of death."

Images of heaven and hell vary as Christian art develops. The basic arrangement of the *Last Judgment*, however, is fairly constant. It is intended to act as a reminder of the passage of time, and of the belief that the unrighteous will be condemned to 'eternal punishment, but the righteous will enter eternal life' (Matthew 25:46).

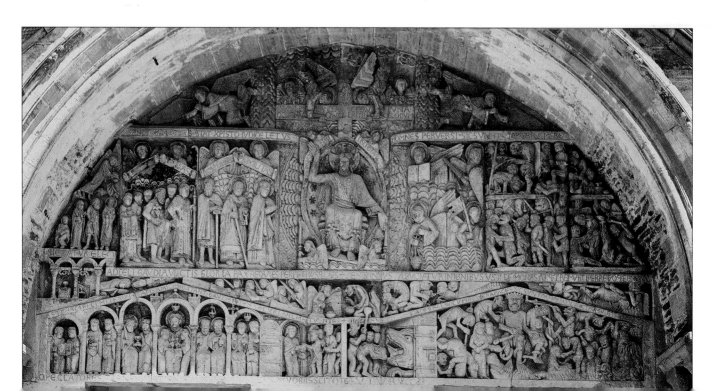

Saint-Pierre at Moissac

To the southwest of Conques, on the route to Santiago de Compostela, the medieval pilgrim would probably pause at Moissac. Figure **11.10** shows the plan of the abbey and church of Saint-Pierre, which were founded in the seventh century, but destroyed and rebuilt several times later. The Romanesque sections that survive are the cloister, the remains of the lower walls of the church, the south porch, and a tower. The most important Romanesque sculptures are on the south porch entrance (fig. **11.11** and 3 on the plan) and in the cloister (5 on the plan).

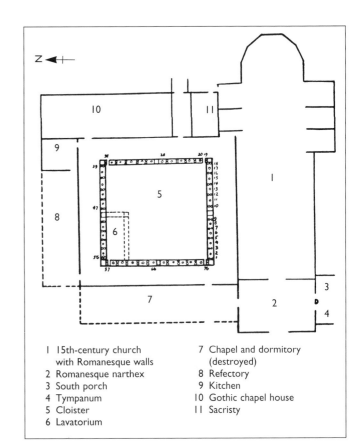

11.10 Plan of the abbey and church of Saint-Pierre, Moissac, France.

11.11 South porch, Saint-Pierre, Moissac, c. 1115–35. 16 ft 6 in (5.5 m) diam. According to local tradition, a dream sent by God inspired Clovis, King of the Franks, to found the abbey at Moissac. This is consistent with the visionary character of the tympanum's iconography.

1 15th-century church with Romanesque walls
2 Romanesque narthex
3 South porch
4 Tympanum
5 Cloister
6 Lavatorium
7 Chapel and dormitory (destroyed)
8 Refectory
9 Kitchen
10 Gothic chapel house
11 Sacristy

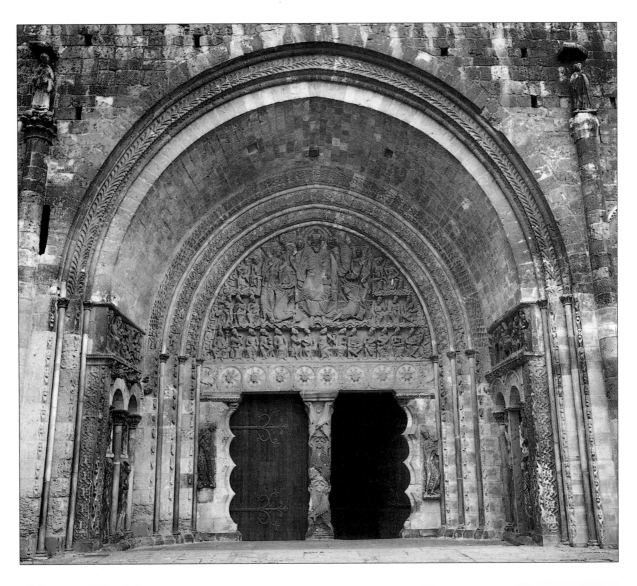

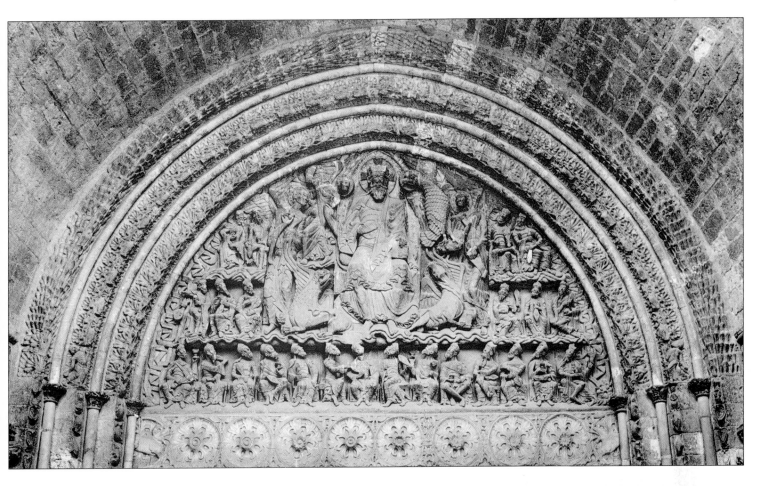

11.12 (above) Tympanum of south porch, Saint-Pierre, Moissac, c. 1115–35. The imagery carved here is derived from Revelations 4:2–7: "... and behold, a throne was set in heaven and one sat on the throne.... And round about the throne were four and twenty seats; and upon the seats I saw four and twenty elders sitting, clothed in white raiment; and they had on their heads crowns of gold.... And before the throne there was a sea [the wavy lines] of glass like unto crystal; and in the midst of the throne, and round about the throne, were four beasts full of eyes before and behind.... And the first beast was like a lion, and the second beast like a calf, and the third beast had a face as a man, and the fourth beast was like a flying eagle."

11.13 *Christ*, tympanum of south porch (detail of fig. 11.12), Saint-Pierre, Moissac.

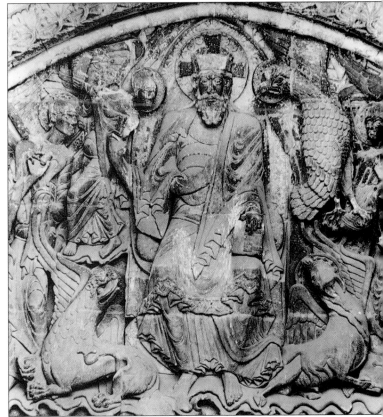

The tympanum over the south portals is filled with reliefs depicting the *Second Coming of Christ* (fig. **11.12**), based on the book of Revelation (see p. 342). The artist has eliminated the theological connection between the Second Coming and the Last Judgment—hence there is no representation of the damned and the saved, as at Conques. Instead, he has focused on Christ in Glory, with images derived from Saint John's apocalyptic vision. The tympanum is framed by floral motifs on the archivolts and by ten rosettes in the lintel.

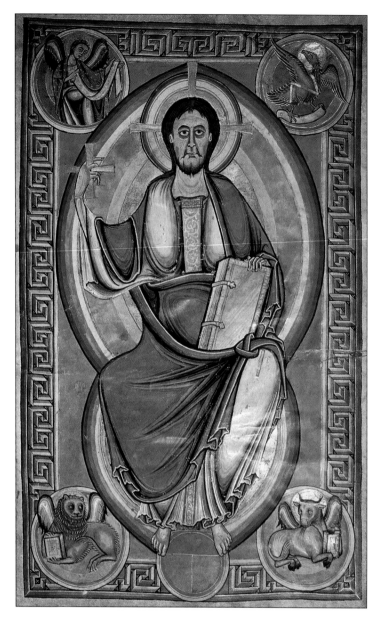

11.14 *Christ in Majesty*, from the Stavelot Bible, 1093–97. Parchment, 22½ × 14½ in (57.5 × 37 cm). British Library, London.

The figure of Christ at Moissac (fig. **11.13**) is larger than that at Sainte-Foy in relation to the available space. He is rendered frontally, his presence commanding the scene, and in this respect the figure can be compared with the page depicting Christ in Majesty from the Stavelot Bible (fig. **11.14**) (see Box), in which the monumental proportions of Christ are barely contained within the page of the manuscript. His mandorla overlaps the inner edges of the meander pattern. The four tondos at the corners of the page contain representations of the Evangelists' symbols. The two lower ones—the icon of Saint Mark and the bull of Saint Luke—gaze at each other and hold a book, referring to their roles as biographers of Christ.

One of the best examples of a Romanesque reliquary is the Stavelot Triptych (fig. **11.15**). It was probably commissioned in the twelfth century by Abbot Wibald of the imperial Benedictine abbey at Stavelot, in the region of the Meuse River in Belgium. The Stavelot reliquary contained relics believed to be of Christ's Cross—referred to as the True Cross to distinguish it from the crosses on which the two thieves were crucified.

It is the earliest known reliquary illustrating scenes from the popular medieval Legend of the True Cross. Each scene is composed of enamel on gold, and is set in a circular frame. Here there are six scenes, three on each wing of the triptych. The wings are framed by Corinthian columns supporting round arches. In the central panel are two additional triptychs. The larger depicts the Cross with standing figures of Constantine and his mother, Saint Helena, who went to search for the True Cross. Two archangels occupy the space above the arms of the Cross. On the inside of the open wings are four Byzantine saints: Theodore and Demetrius at the right, and George and Procopius at the left. When closed (not illustrated here), the four Evangelists are visible on the outside of the wings.

The smaller triptych shows an *Annunciation* when closed, but here we see a *Crucifixion* flanked by the Virgin and the apostle John. Sun and moon fill the spaces over the Cross. A recess inside the Crucifixion enamel contained a Byzantine parchment. On it was an inscription identifying the contents of a small, silk pouch as fragments of the True Cross, the Holy Sepulcher, and the Virgin's dress. The pouch also contained the head of a nail, which was probably believed to have been a relic of one of the nails used in the Crucifixion.

The six scenes on the wings are divided into three Constantine scenes (on the left), and three Helena scenes (on the right). They focus on that part of the legend dealing with Constantine's conversion to Christianity and with Helena's discovery of the True Cross. On the left, reading from the bottom, is the Vision of Constantine (fig. **11.16**), his Victory over Maxentius, and his Baptism. On the right, the lowest scene shows Helena in Jerusalem, searching for the Cross. (According to the legend, Constantine was so impressed with the power of the Cross that he sent his mother to Jerusalem to find it.) Here Helena questions the Jews about the location of the Cross. In the middle scene, she is on Calvary as three crosses are excavated from the ground. At the top, the miracle of the True Cross is enacted. To discover which of the three crosses was Christ's, Helena had each in turn held over the body of a dead boy, whose funeral procession happened by. The True Cross restored him to life.

Taken as a whole, the message of these scenes to the medieval pilgrim was, of course, the power of the Cross and its role in establishing Christianity as the official religion of Rome. The Vision of Constantine, here represented as a

The Stavelot Reliquary Triptych

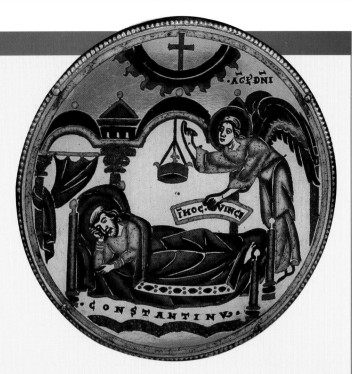

dream, was the miracle that set in motion this sequence of events. An angel leans over Constantine's bed, points to a cross in the sky, and carries the inscription "In this sign you conquer."

The pairing of the Constantine and Helena events also pairs Rome (on the left) with Jerusalem (on the right). In so doing, the artist evokes the two most important pilgrimage sites and identifies Stavelot with them. When pilgrims traveled to Stavelot, they reinforced their identification with these sites. They would also have associated Constantine with Charlemagne, and known of the typological relationships of these two emperors with Christ, and of Saint Helena with the Virgin.

11.15 (below) The Stavelot Triptych, open, Mosan c. 1156–58. Gold, *cloisonné* enamel, 19 1/16 in (48.4 cm) high, 26 in (66 cm) wide, when open. The Pierpont Morgan Library, New York.

11.16 (right) The Vision of Constantine (detail of fig. 11.15, left wing).

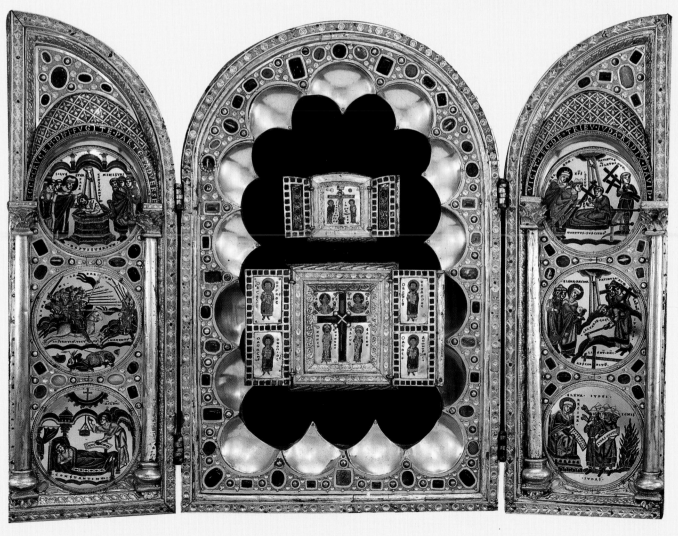

In the tympanum at Moissac, the four symbols of the Evangelists and the twenty-four elders (fig. **11.17**) focus their gaze on Christ. In the Stavelot illumination, on the other hand, the bull and lion seem to cower beneath Christ, while the eagle gazes upwards, away from Christ, as does the lion, with a wistful, slightly apprehensive air. Only the angel looks directly at Christ, drawing the viewer's attention directly to him. At Moissac, this effect is multiplied through the tympanum figures, all of whom twist themselves and tilt their heads in order to see Christ, as if riveted by his power. The detail of the elder (fig. **11.18**) shows not only the tilted head but the taste for elongated proportions and flat patterns in the Romanesque sculptural style. The beard is rendered as layers of very slightly curved, parallel lines, which are crossed by a diagonal layer of mustache. This pattern is repeated in the long strands of hair and short curls emerging from below the crown.

The **trumeau** figures at Moissac are even more elongated than the elders, necessitated by the thin, vertical architectural rectangle in which they are located. The relief of *Saint Paul* (fig. **11.19**) is lengthened from the

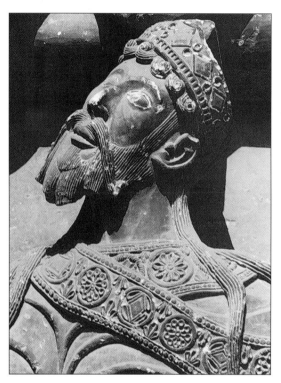

11.18 An elder, tympanum of south porch (detail of fig. 11.12), Saint-Pierre, Moissac.

waist down, creating an unexpected shift in proportion. The flat drapery folds, despite suggesting the forms of the legs, do not really flow in relation to the body. The diagonal feet, like those in the Justinian mosaics at Ravenna (see p. 286), reinforce the illogical quality of the figure's support. In this case, the saint seems rather like a wooden puppet, hanging as if attached to the trumeau from behind.

The figure of *Abbot Durand* (figs. **11.20** and **11.21**) on the cloister pier is carved in even flatter relief than *Saint Paul*. Here the figure is symmetrical, and tightly enclosed by the arch and its colonnettes. He is perfectly unified with his frame—his halo, hat, and the curve of his crook echo the round arch, and the crook's staff and the edge of his drapery conform to the outlines of the pier. His head sinks into his shoulders, thereby eliminating his neck and flattening the space. Reinforcing this two-dimensional effect is the verticality of the feet, which make no pretense of naturally supporting the figure.

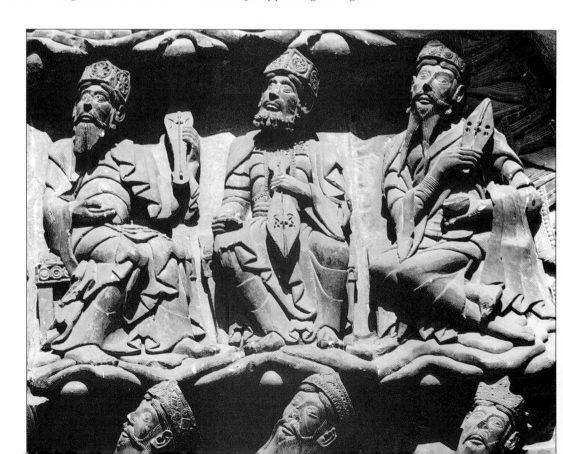

11.17 The elders, tympanum of south porch (detail of fig. 11.12), Saint-Pierre, Moissac.

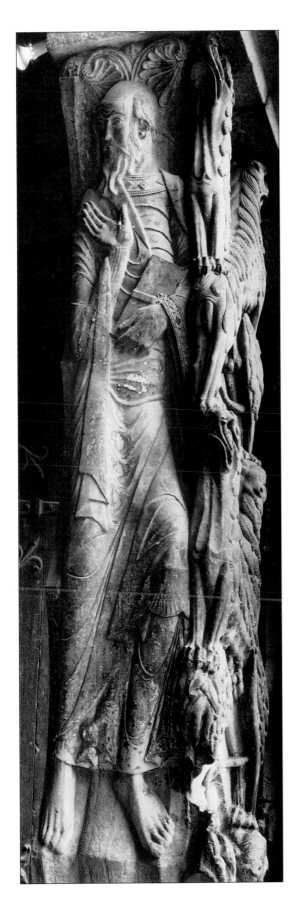

11.19 *Saint Paul*, trumeau of Saint-Pierre, Moissac.

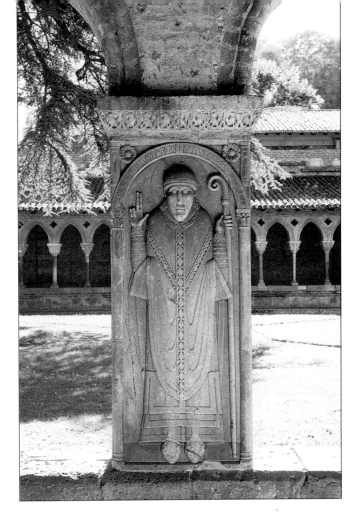

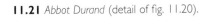

11.20 Cloister pier with relief of *Abbot Durand*, Saint-Pierre, Moissac, 1047–72. Durand was Bishop of Toulouse and Abbot of Saint-Pierre, which prospered under his administration. He consecrated a church in the abbey complex in 1063, and he commissioned several churches throughout the region under his authority.

11.21 *Abbot Durand* (detail of fig. 11.20).

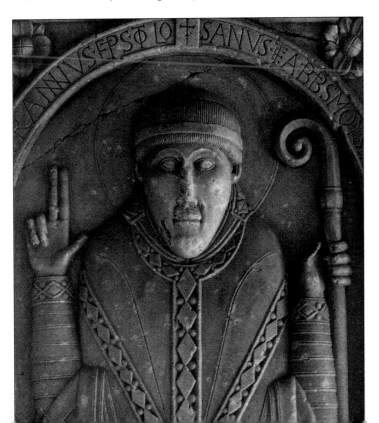

A similar flattened treatment of space characterizes Romanesque manuscript illumination. The Saint Matthew in figure **11.22** resembles the relief of *Abbot Durand* in its frontality, relative symmetry, and setting. Matthew's feet are flat, and contained in a patterned semicircle that echoes his halo and the round arch above it. The intertwined human, animal, and floral forms on the initial L are typical Romanesque manuscript motifs. Also typical is the contrast between the animation inherent in the initial and the more static, iconic quality of the saint. The illuminator's imagination had more freedom of expression in marginal areas than in the central image. Here, the interlaced forms are reminiscent of Viking and Anglo-Saxon metalwork, and possibly also of Islamic design.

A capital from the Moissac cloister (fig. **11.23**) can be related to interlace of the kind illustrated in figure **11.24**. The latter is a detail of a page showing an initial T from a folio in the sacramentary of Saint-Sauveur de Figeac (see frontispiece). In both, there is a sense of energy conveyed by the forms intertwining: despite being geometric, the design borders on figuration. The sense of transition between nature and abstraction is enhanced by the interlaces emerging from the mouths of birds. The illumination resembles the northern (Anglo-Saxon and Viking) tradition, whereas the capital is reminiscent of the tighter weave found in Islamic mosque decoration and carpets.

Capitals decorated with geometric designs had been in use from the Early Christian period. They assimilated Islamic and Anglo-Saxon motifs into non-figural sculpture decoration in churches—a lasting effect of the Iconoclastic Controversy. But during the revival of monumental figurative sculpture in Romanesque churches, capitals offered artists a new surface for narrative scenes and individual figures, as well as for geometric patterns.

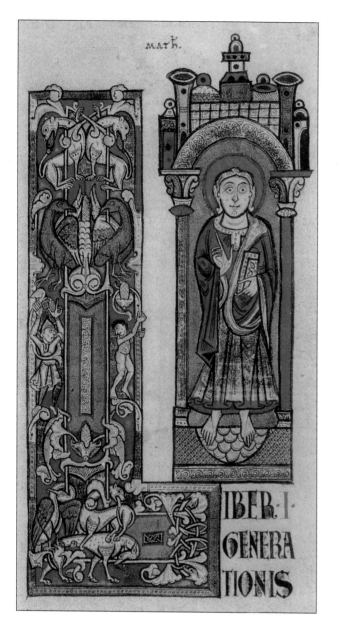

11.22 (above) Initial L and Saint Matthew, region of Agen-Moissac, c. 1100. 7½ × 4 in (19 × 10.2 cm). Ms. Lat.254, fol.10. Bibliothèque Nationale, Paris.

11.23 (right) Capital, north gallery of the cloister, Saint-Pierre, Moissac, c. 1100.

11.24 (far right) Detail of an initial from the sacramentary of Saint-Sauveur de Figeac, 11th century. Ms. Lat. 2293, fol. 19v. Bibliothèque Nationale, Paris.

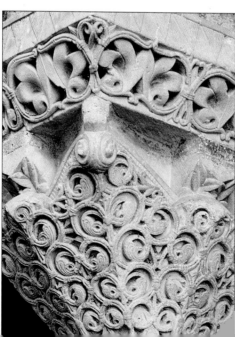

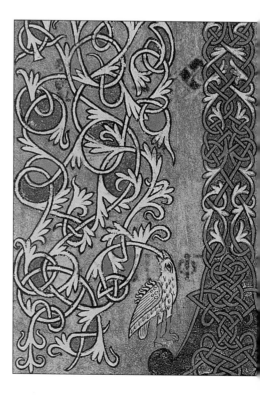

Developments at Autun

The new developments in capital decoration are reflected at Autun Cathedral in Burgundy. Its sculptural decoration was carved by Gislebertus, who signed his name on the tympanum. The capital representing the *Flight into Egypt* (fig. **11.25**) shows the Holy Family fleeing the edict of King Herod, which decreed the death of all male children under the age of two. Joseph leads a lively, high-stepping donkey carrying Mary and Christ out of Bethlehem into Egypt. The capital exemplifies a taste for elegant surface design characteristic of Romanesque sculpture. Decorative foliage is relegated to the background and design-filled circles support the figures. Open and closed circle designs are repeated in the borders of the draperies, on Joseph's hat, on the haloes, and in the donkey's trappings. Also typical are the repeated curves representing folds, which are carved into the draperies more for their patterned effect than to define organic quality. On Joseph's tunic, the surface curves enhance the impression of backward motion, as if the cloth had been blown by a sudden gust of wind. The Romanesque artist's disregard of gravity is evident in the figure of Christ. He faces front, with his right hand resting on a sphere held by Mary. He is suspended between her knees, with no indication of support for his weight.

A similar taste for flat patterns and weightlessness characterizes the monumental tympanum at Autun (fig. **11.26**). It depicts a large, imposing figure of Christ

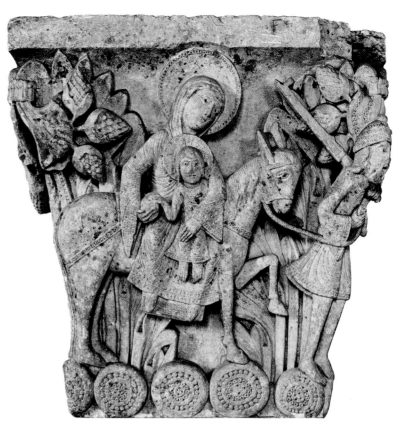

11.25 Gislebertus, capital depicting the *Flight into Egypt*, Cathedral of Saint-Lazare, Autun, Burgundy, France, c. 1130. Gislebertus was the only sculptor to inscribe his name on the tympanum of a Romanesque church. Little is known about him, but his distinctive artistic personality influenced other sculptors considerably.

11.26 Gislebertus, *Last Judgment*, tympanum of west portal, Cathedral of Saint-Lazare, Autun, Burgundy, c. 1120–35.

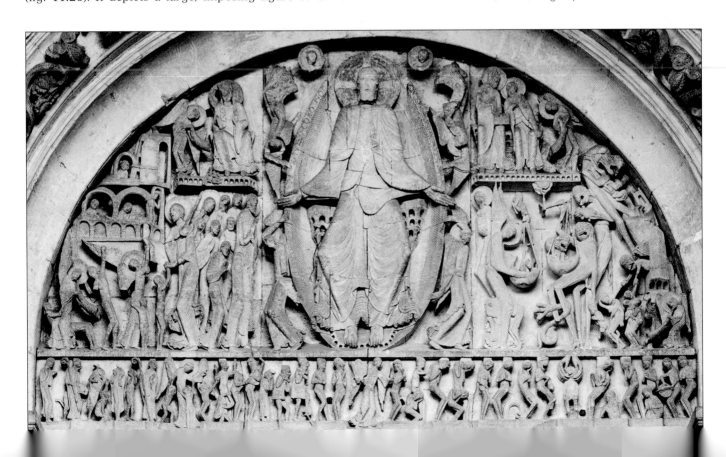

appearing in majestic light at the Last Judgment. Surrounded by a mandorla supported by four angels, Christ sits frontally on a throne and spreads out his arms in a broad, gesture proclaiming his divine presence. His drapery forms a pattern of flattened curves that correspond to the curved arms. Zigzags repeat the animated poses of the other figures as well as the diagonals of Christ's legs. On either side of Christ are two tiers of angels and souls—the saved at his right, and the damned at his left. Christ's left hand indicates the weighing of the souls on the lower tier (fig. **11.27**). The archangel Michael bends at the left of the scale and weighs a soul in human form, while two little souls huddle under his robe for protection. To the right of the scale, two grotesque devils weigh a tiny monstrous creature, clearly one of the damned. At the extreme right, several more damned souls fall downward, denoting their future in hell. In this detail, Gislebertus plays on the theme of physical weight and weightlessness as a metaphor for spirituality and salvation. The irony of his image is that the saved human soul seems to weigh more, for he pulls down the scale, and the damned soul weighs less. Since the damned are destined to "go down," their lesser "substance" is shown by the scale. The saved, on the other hand, "go up," but actually weigh more because of their greater spiritual substance.

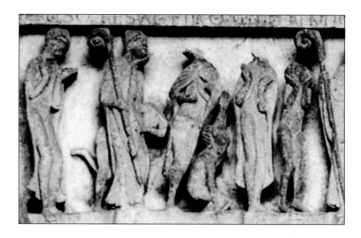

11.28 Gislebertus, *Last Judgment* (detail of fig. 11.26, showing two pilgrims).

On the lowest horizontal tier, at the far left, there are two pilgrims (fig. **11.28**), identifiable from their walking sticks and traveling bags with scallop-shells. The latter were signs of pilgrimage, and also of resurrection. Here, represented on the tympanum of a church on the pilgrimage road, the shells refer to the belief that pilgrimage is a route to salvation.

The Stave Church of Norway and Stone Interlace

In Norway, the translation of early medieval manuscript interlace into monumental stone relief sculpture became characteristic of later Romanesque churches. A good example is on the twelfth-century west portal of Ål Cathedral (fig. **11.29**), where several elements of early medieval manuscript art are combined. The elaborate curvilinear interlace merges into floral and leaf designs, and is also transformed into animal forms. But rather than being relegated to capital and border designs, this assumes a conspicuous position on the door jamb.

The derivation of such interlace from wood carving is evident in the head post from the Oseberg ship burial (see p. 330). In Norway, the custom of building wooden churches (while stone was being adopted elsewhere) persisted into the thirteenth century. A few such stave churches survive—for example, that at Borgund (fig. **11.30**). The walls are supported by a timber frame on a foundation of boulders. The frame supports a tall structure containing the nave, and occasionally an apse. Projecting from the sides are sloping gables, whose surfaces resemble thatching. The points of the gables, like the prows of Viking ships, were decorated with animal heads, usually dragons. Above each door stood a cross, and at the top of the building was a turret and a spire. The elaborate wood carvings around the portals were similar to stone examples (cf. fig. 11.29).

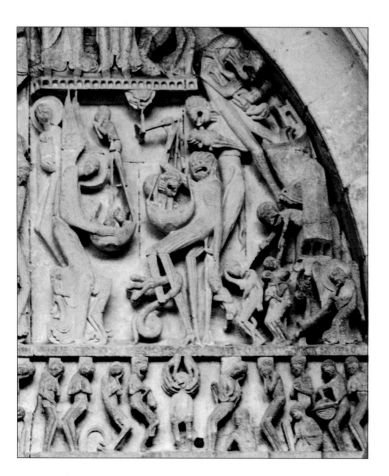

11.27 Gislebertus, *Last Judgment* (detail of fig. 11.26, showing the weighing of souls).

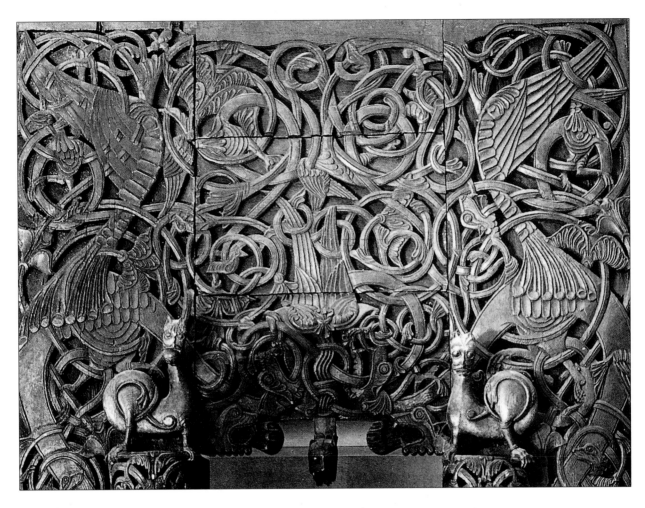

11.29 Decorative detail of interlace sculpture, right jamb of west portal, Ål Cathedral, Norway, 12th century.

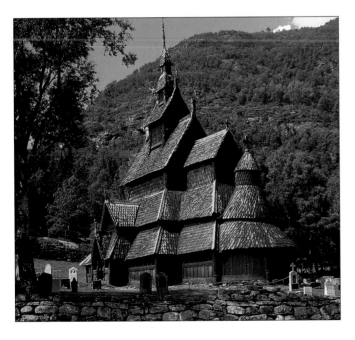

11.30 Borgund stave church, Sogne, Norway, second half of 12th century.

The Italian Romanesque Cathedral Complex at Pisa

The diversity of Romanesque architecture is evident not only in the contrasts between the stave churches of the north and French pilgrimage churches but also in those of Italy, where Romanesque buildings were influenced by the Classical tradition. These rarely had façade towers or westwork, which were common in France and Germany. The paradigm for Italian Romanesque churches was the Early Christian basilica.

In 1062 the Republic of Pisa, a port on the west coast of Tuscany, defeated the Muslim naval force of Sicily, an island south of Italy. To celebrate their victory, the Pisans used the booty taken from enemy boats to start a fund for a new cathedral. Dedicated to the Virgin, the cathedral was begun the following year, consecrated in 1118, and eventually completed in 1272. In 1153, Pisa celebrated another victory at sea—this time against the Christian Republic of Amalfi, also in the south—by starting the construction of a baptistry opposite the cathedral façade. These two buildings are part of an extraordinary architectural complex, including the famous "leaning tower" (built 1174–1271), and a thirteenth-century burial ground (the Campo Santo; fig. **11.31**).

The cathedral itself (fig. **11.32**) is an amalgam of diverse influences. The entire exterior is of white marble, the material favored in ancient Rome. The cruciform plan (see fig. 11.31) is based on that of the Early Christian basilica with transept arms—each containing an apse at the end— double side aisles, and a flat, wooden roof. Arcades separating the nave from the aisles are formed of round arches resting on columns with Corinthian and Byzantine capitals (fig. **11.33**). The apse mosaic is also in the Byzantine style. Islamic features occur in the elliptical dome over the crossing, the interior arch at the end of the nave, and the bronze griffin (now lost), which was looted by the Crusaders and adorned the pinnacle of the façade.

The façade differs from many French examples in the absence of a tympanum illustrating the Last Judgment. Instead it has three entrances, each of which is flanked by a blind round arch, and is surmounted by four stories of freestanding columns forming arcaded galleries. The arcades continue around the building and create a dynamic surface pattern that unifies the whole. Similar arcades encircle the lower level of the baptistry wall; the upper stories and round dome are later.

11.31 Plan of Pisa Cathedral and surrounding complex.

11.32 View of the baptistry, cathedral, and campanile, Pisa, 1053–1272.

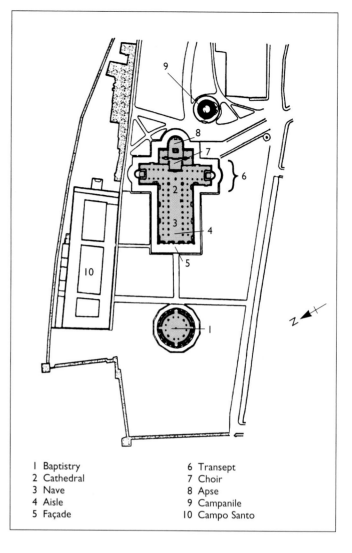

1 Baptistry	6 Transept
2 Cathedral	7 Choir
3 Nave	8 Apse
4 Aisle	9 Campanile
5 Façade	10 Campo Santo

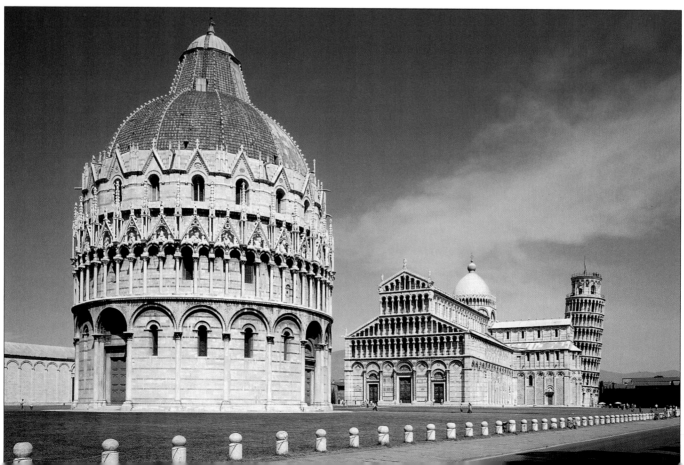

Six stories of arcaded galleries are repeated on the cylindrical "leaning tower"—the **campanile** (bell tower) of the cathedral (fig. **11.34**). This feature was characteristic of Italian churches influenced by Byzantine tradition, in contrast to northern Romanesques churches where westwork was preferred. At Pisa, as elsewhere, the round arches are of Roman inspiration, and their repetition contributes to the sense of unity that pervades the entire complex. The tower leans because it was originally built on a soft foundation; efforts to compensate for the tilt have so far proved unsuccessful. It is now some 13 feet (4 m) out of plumb (or off its vertical axis). Recently, a new and firmer foundation has halted the gradual movement, which would eventually have caused the campanile to topple over.

The Romanesque style of architecture at Pisa spread south from northern Italy and the former Yugoslavia to Sardinia. In Tuscany, elements of the style—especially the interior and exterior surface patterns formed by alternating green and white marble—would remain characteristic for several centuries.

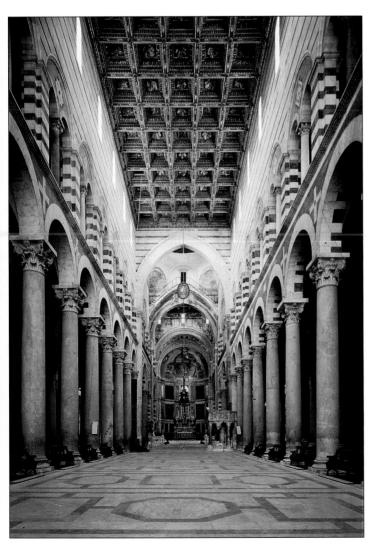

11.33 Nave of Pisa Cathedral.

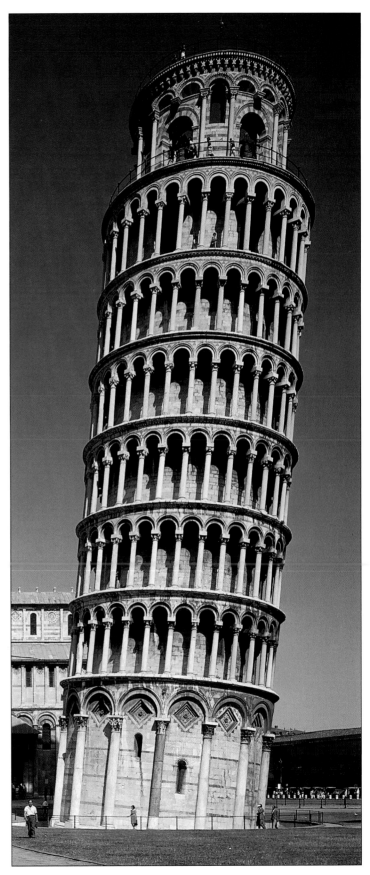

11.34 Campanile of Pisa Cathedral, 1174–1271.

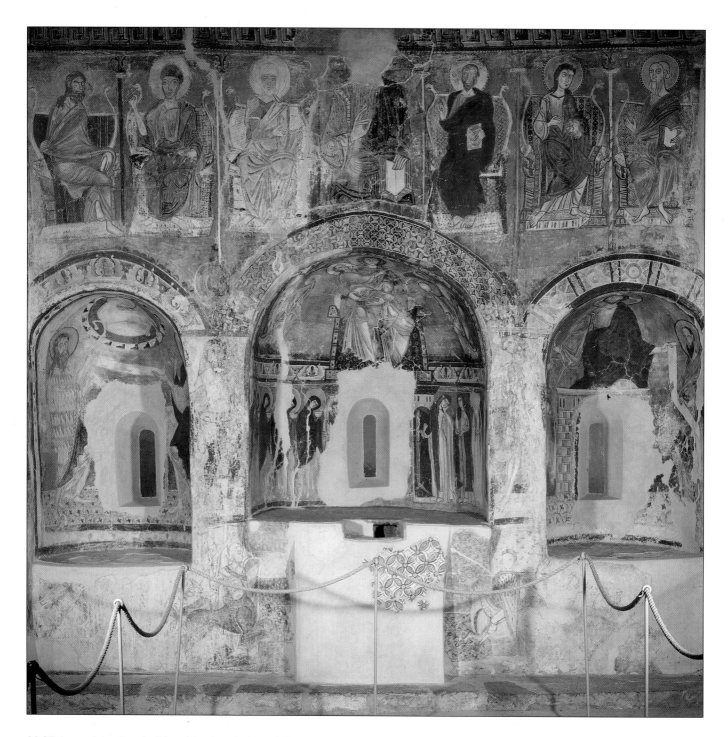

11.35 Apse of the chapel of Castel Appiano, Italy, c. 1200.

Mural Painting

In contrast to those of the Early Middle Ages, Romanesque churches and chapels contain some well-preserved monumental mural paintings. These had both a decorative and a didactic function. Usually, several painters would work on a particular series of murals. The program was generally planned by the principal artist, often in conjunction with a member of the clergy or other patron. A preliminary drawing, in *buon fresco,* was made to prepare outlines and certain details, and compasses were used for repeated curvilinear designs. The painting itself was usually *fresco secco,* possibly redampened so the plaster would absorb the paint. Sometimes, however, tempera was applied as well. Generally the darker areas were painted before the highlights. In the final stage, the forms would be outlined in black or brown. As in Byzantine

mosaics, this technique emphasized the figures, but decreased the realistic relation of figures to three-dimensional space.

The frescoes in the chapel of Castel Appiano in northern Italy (fig. **11.35**), although damaged, are characteristic in their use of rich colors—blues, greens, browns, and yellows. In the semidome of the central apse, Mary and Christ are enthroned between two angels (fig. **11.36**). The scene is framed by a floral border, interrupted by the base of the

11.36 *Mary and Christ with Two Angels* (detail of fig. 11.35). Fresco.

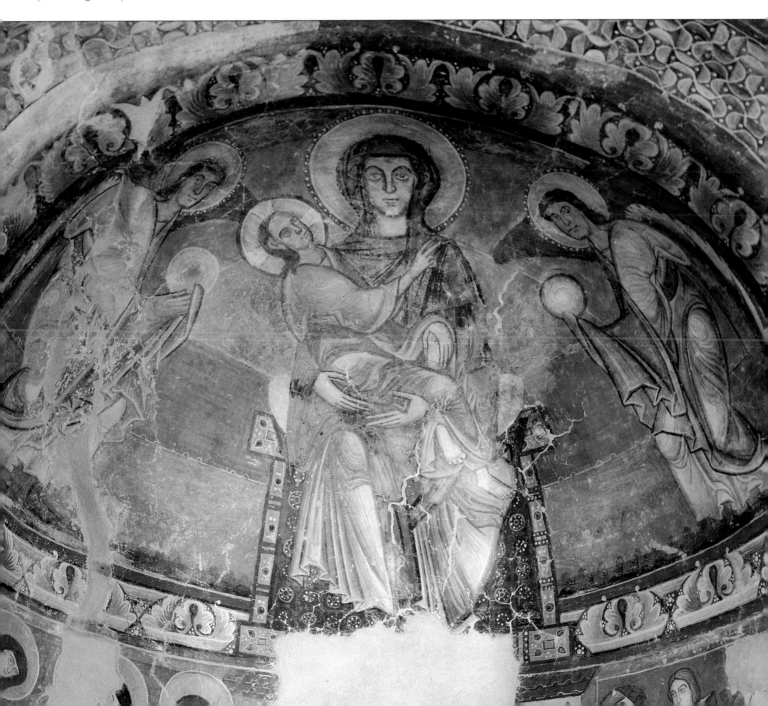

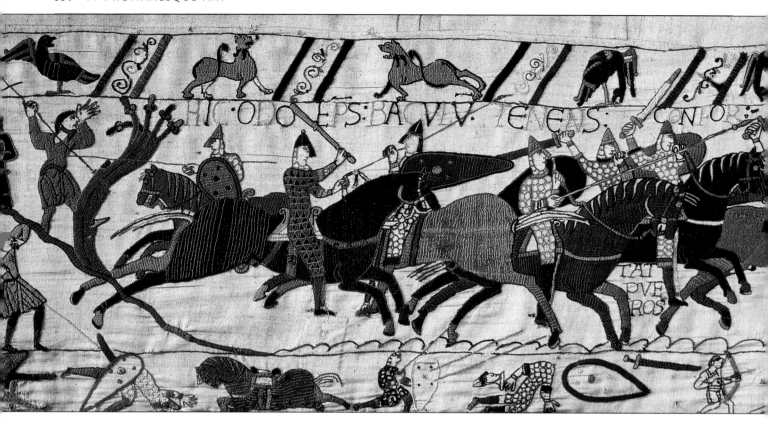

11.37 Detail of battle scene showing Bishop Odo with a mace, from the Bayeux "Tapestry," c. 1070–80. Wool embroidery on linen, 20 in (50.8 cm) high. Musée de l'Evêché, Bayeux. Note how the smooth texture of the linen contrasts with the rough texture of the raised woolen threads. Single threads were used for waves, ropes, strands of hair on the horses' foreheads, and the outlines of each section of color.

throne, whose jeweled golden surface suggests Byzantine influence. A formal unity is created, as the background green repeats the shape of the border, while the blue repeats the pointed oval of the apse itself. Mary is frontal, staring directly at the viewer. Her draperies echo the background blue and green, and her flat halo repeats the color and beaded designs of the throne. This painting shares certain stylistic features with the capital shown in figure 11.25: although differing in proportions, Christ is a small man held in Mary's lap. His right hand extends upwards in a gesture of benediction, and the draperies reflect a taste for elegant, curvilinear surface patterns.

The Bayeux "Tapestry"

One of the most intriguing Romanesque works of art is the so-called Bayeux "Tapestry," which depicts the Norman invasion of England in 1066 (figs. **11.37**, **11.38**, and **11.39**). It is over 230 feet (70 m) long, and contains 626 human figures, 731 animals, 376 boats, and 70 buildings and trees. Such an undertaking probably involved several artists, technicians, and a general designer working together with a historian. Although invariably called a tapestry, the work is actually an embroidery, made by stitching colored wool onto bleached linen. We have no records of who the artists were, but most medieval embroidery was done by women, especially at the courts.

The "Tapestry" was created for the cathedral of Bayeux in Normandy, near the northern coast of France. It was probably commissioned by Bishop Odo of Bayeux, half-brother of William the Conqueror. The events it depicts unfold from left to right and are accompanied by Latin inscriptions. The detail in figure 11.37 shows William the Conqueror leading a group of Norman nobles, including Odo, on galloping horses against the English. This scene takes place on Saturday morning, October 14, 1066, when William's army departed from Hastings to fight Harold, the Saxon king of England.

All the riders are helmeted and armed. Their chain mail is indicated by circular patterns within the outlines of the armor. Odo holds a mace, while the nobles carry banners, shields, and lances. The weapons, held on a diagonal, increase the illusion of forward movement, as Odo seems to clash with an enemy riding against him. The ground is indicated by a wavy line on a horizontal plane, but, aside from the overlapping of certain groups of figures, there is little attempt to depict three-dimensional space. Above and below the narrative events are borders containing human figures (note the decapitated figure below), natural and fantastic animals, and stylized plant forms.

The Viking longboats from William's fleet (fig. 11.38) reflect the Scandinavian origins of the Normans. Ready to set sail for England, they are propelled by oars and a sail. The man at the far left steers the boat by means of the fixed, rotating rudder characteristic of Viking ships. The prows are decorated with carved dragon heads. Two shields are attached to the bow, and these are believed to have been antiramming devices.

Figure 11.39 shows several craftsmen putting finishing touches on the boats. Above, the figure on the left holds an adze, and the one on the right drills holes into which the oars will be inserted. The two figures below are using axes of the type illustrated in figure 10.20. Note that their feet are visible beneath the ship, a rudimentary attempt to create a sense of three-dimensional space.

Unlike the other Romanesque works of art discussed in this chapter, the Bayeux "Tapestry" is secular in subject. The events depicted in it are primarily historical, and are shown from the Norman point of view. While the Latin embroidery helps to explain the images, much of the narrative is transmitted through the pictures themselves, and many of the details remain puzzling.

The sculptural decoration of Romanesque architecture, like mural and manuscript painting, continues the medieval taste for flat space, inorganic figures, and lively, decorative stylization. Beginning in the late twelfth century, Gothic architects would expand the scale of the cathedrals and a new trend toward naturalism would develop in painting and sculpture. But Gothic architecture did not emerge suddenly, or without precedent—like Athena from the head of Zeus. The precursors of Gothic style can be found in Romanesque buildings as early as the late eleventh century, particularly in northern France and in England. Examples of this early evolution within Romanesque of what would come to typify Gothic are discussed in the next chapter.

11.38 Detail of Viking Ships from the Bayeux "Tapestry."

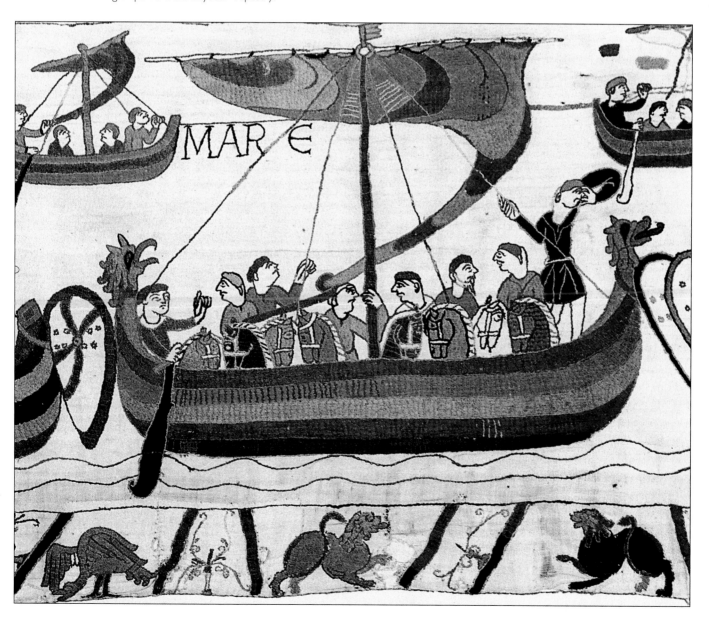

11.39 Detail of craftsmen from the Bayeux "Tapestry." (Figs. 11.37–11.39 by special permission of the City of Bayeux.)

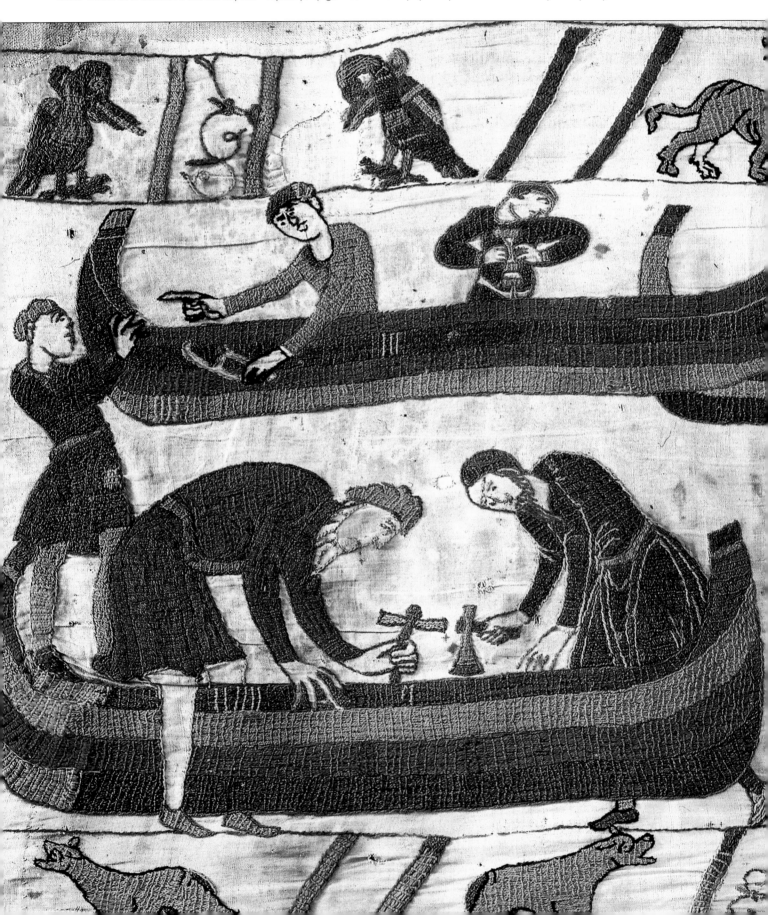

	Style/Period	Works of Art	Cultural/Historical Developments
900	ROMANESQUE 10th century		First canonization of saints (993)
1000	ROMANESQUE 11th century **Sacramentary, Saint-Sauveur de Figeac**	Sacramentary, Saint-Sauveur de Figeac (11.24) Church of Sainte-Foy (11.2–11.3, 11.5, 11.7–11.9), Conques Pisa Cathedral (11.32–11.33) Bayeux "Tapestry" (11.37–11.39) **Bayeux "Tapestry"**	Leif Ericson reported to have discovered America (Nova Scotia) (1000) The Chinese discover gunpowder (1000) Normans under William the Conqueror invade England (1066) Appearance of Halley's comet (1066) Excommunication of married priests (1074) Building of Church of Santiago de Compostela, Spain, begins (1075) Building of Tower of London begins (1078) Peter Abelard, French theologian and philosopher, born 1079 (d. 1142) Church of San Marco, Venice, completed (1094) First Crusade; Crusaders take Jerusalem (1095–99)

1100	ROMANESQUE
	12th century
	
	Gislebertus, *Flight into Egypt*
		Stavelot Bible (11.14)
		New Testament initial L and Saint Matthew (11.22), Agen-Moissac
		    Church of Saint-Pierre (11.11–11.13, 11.17–11.21, 11.23), Moissac
		    Interlace sculpture (11.29), Ål Cathedral, Ål, Norway
		    Gislebertus, *Last Judgment* (11.26–11.28), Cathedral of Saint-Lazare, Autun
		    Gislebertus, *Flight into Egypt* (11.25), Cathedral of Saint-Lazare, Autun
		    Stavelot Triptych (11.15–11.16)
		    Pisa Cathedral Campanile (11.34)
		    Borgund stave church (11.30), Sogne
			La Chanson de Roland, French heroic poem written, (c. 1100)
			First appearance of Gothic architecture (early 1100s)
			Carmelite Order founded
			Building of Nôtre-Dame, Paris (1163–1235)
			Founding of Oxford University (1167)
			Murder of Thomas à Becket at Canterbury (1170)
			Construction of Chartres Cathedral begins (1194)

1200 **1300**	ROMANESQUE 13th century	Chapel of Castel Appiano (11.35–11.36) **Castel Appiano**	Founding of University of Paris (the Sorbonne) (1200) Francis of Assisi founds Franciscan Order (1209) King John signs Magna Carta, limiting absolute powers of the monarchy (1215) First Lateran Council of bishops establishes confession, relic worship, and transubstantiation as Catholic doctrines (1215) Genghis Khan, Mongol ruler, crosses Asia and Russia and threatens Europe (1206–23) Founding of Dominican Order (1216)

12

Gothic Art

Gothic cathedrals are among the greatest and most elaborate monuments in stone. The term "Gothic" is applied primarily to the architecture, and also to the painting and sculpture, produced in western Europe from about the middle of the twelfth century in France to the sixteenth century in some parts of Europe. The term was first used by Italians in the sixteenth century to denigrate the art preceding their own Renaissance style (see Vol. II). Literally, "Gothic" refers to the Germanic tribes who invaded Greece and Italy, and sacked Rome in A.D. 410 (see p. 212). The Goths were blamed for destroying what remained of the Classical style. In fact, however, the origins of Gothic art had nothing to do with what had happened several hundred years earlier. By the nineteenth century, when scholars realized the source of the confusion, it was too late. Gothic remains the accepted name of the style discussed in this chapter.

The Origins of the Gothic Style in France

The time and place in which the Gothic style emerged can be identified with unusual precision, given the dynamic character of art historical development. It dates from 1137–44, and originated in the Ile-de-France, the region in northern France that was the personal domain of the French royal family. The credit for its invention goes to one remarkable man, Abbot Suger of the French royal monastery at Saint-Denis, which is about 6 miles (10 km) north of Paris.

Abbot Suger was born in 1084 and educated in the monastery school of Saint-Denis along with the future French king Louis VI. Suger later became a close political and religious adviser to both Louis VI and Louis VII, and remained a successful mediator between the Church and the royal family. While Louis VII was away on the Second Crusade (1147–9), Suger was appointed regent of France.

In 1122 Suger was named Abbot of Saint-Denis, which had a special place in French history. Not only was Denis,

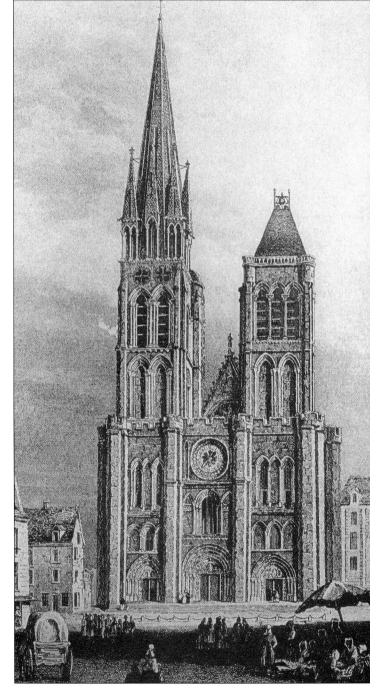

12.1 West façade, Saint-Denis, near Paris, dedicated 1140. After an engraving by A. and E. Rourgue, before the 19th-century restoration.

the first bishop of Paris and the patron saint of France, buried there, but it was also the burial place of the French royal family. Suger conceived a plan to rebuild and enlarge the eighth-century Carolingian church of Saint-Denis. He intended to make it the spiritual center of France, and searched for a new kind of architecture to reinforce the divine right of the king's authority and enhance the spirituality of his church. The rebuilding program did not start until 1137, and in the meantime Suger made extensive preparations. He studied the biblical account of the construction of Solomon's Temple (see p. 365) and immersed himself in what he thought were the writings of Saint Denis. Scholars now believe that Suger was reading the works of Dionysius, a sixth-century mystic theologian.

Regardless of the identity of the original source, Suger was inspired by the author's emphasis on the mathematical harmony that should exist between the parts of a building and the miraculous, even mystical, effect of light. This was elaborated into a theory based on musical ratios; the result was a system that expressed complex symbolism based on mathematical ratios. The fact that these theories about light and the mathematical symbolism of architecture could be attributed to Saint Denis made them all the more appealing to Abbot Suger. In his preoccupation with light, Suger was thinking in a traditional Christian framework, for the formal qualities of light had been associated with Christ and divinity since the Early Christian period. In his reconstruction of the church, Suger rearranged the elements of medieval architecture to express the relationship between light and God's presence in a distinctive way. None of the individual architectural devices that Suger and his builders used was new; it was the way in which he synthesized elements of existing styles that was revolutionary. Alone among great art patrons of this time, Suger wrote an extensive memoir of the work he commissioned and his reasons for commissioning it. *The Book of Suger, Abbot of Saint-Denis* describes the beginning of work on Saint-Denis as follows:

> The first work on this church which we began under the inspiration of God [was this]: because of the age of the old walls and their impending ruin in some places, we summoned the best painters I could find from different regions, and reverently caused these [walls] to be repaired and becomingly painted with gold and precious colors. I completed this all the more gladly because I had wished to do it, if ever I should have an opportunity, even while I was a pupil in school.[1]

Early Gothic Architecture: Saint-Denis

Suger's additions to Saint-Denis consisted of a new narthex and west façade with twin towers and three portals (fig. **12.1**). Most of the original sculptural decoration on the portals has since been lost. On the interior, Suger retained the basic elements of the Romanesque pilgrimage choir that had made it possible for large crowds of pilgrims to visit the church without disturbing the clergy. A semicircular ambulatory in the apse permitted the lay public to circulate freely, while the clergy remained in the radiating chapels. But Suger combined these elements in an original way (figs. **12.2** and **12.3**).

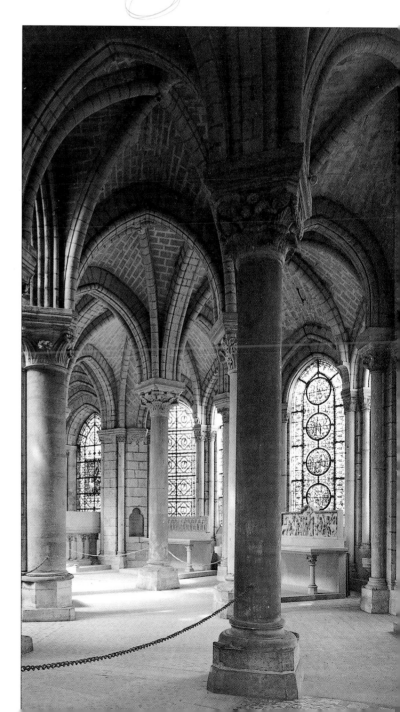

12.2 Interior of Saint-Denis. Each chapel bay has a pair of large stained-glass windows, delicate columns, and pointed vaults. The ambulatory and chapels have become a series of large windows supported by a masonry frame. Suger described the new effect as "a circular string of chapels, by virtue of which the whole [sanctuary] would shine with the miraculous and uninterrupted light of the most luminous windows …''

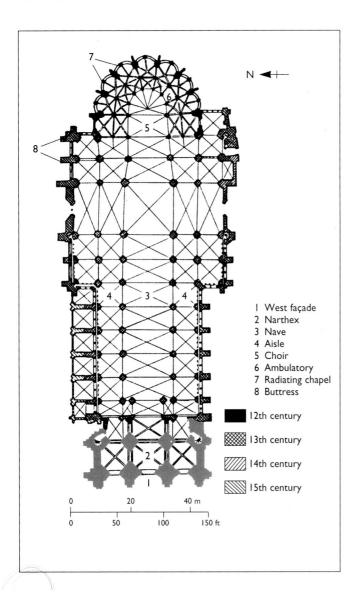

1 West façade
2 Narthex
3 Nave
4 Aisle
5 Choir
6 Ambulatory
7 Radiating chapel
8 Buttress

■ 12th century
▨ 13th century
▨ 14th century
▨ 15th century

0   20   40 m
0   50   100   150 ft

12.3 Plan of Saint-Denis, 1140–44. The chapels are connected shallow bays, which form a second ambulatory parallel to the first. This arrangement creates seven wedge-shaped compartments radiating out from the apse. Each wedge is a trapezoidal unit (in the area of the traditional ambulatory), and a pentagonal unit (in the radiating chapel). The old nave and the choir were rebuilt in the High Gothic style between 1231 and 1281.

Under Suger's revision, the arrangement of the chapels is a formal echo of the ambulatory, which creates a new sense of architectural unity. Suger's **chevet** (the east end of the church, comprising the choir, ambulatory, and apse) also emphasized the integration of light with lightness, because the entire area was covered with **ribbed vaults** (fig. **12.4**) supported by pointed arches. The Romanesque builders, in contrast, had restricted the lighter vaulting to the ambulatory. The arches, in turn, were supported by slender columns, which further enhanced the impression of lightness. On the exterior, thin buttresses were placed between the chapels (fig. 12.3) to strengthen the walls. Suger's new architectural approach attracted immediate

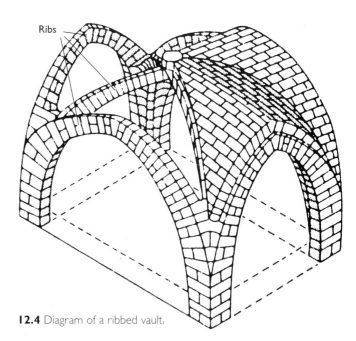

Ribs

12.4 Diagram of a ribbed vault.

attention, because the effect was so different from the dark interiors and thick, massive walls of Romanesque architecture. He describes the effect of his changes on the interior light in the verses of the consecration inscription:

> Once the new rear part is joined to the part in front,
> The church shines with its middle part brightened.
> For bright is that which is brightly coupled with the bright,
> And bright is the noble edifice which is pervaded by the new light;
> Which stands enlarged in our time,
> I, who was Suger, being the leader while it was being accomplished.[2]

The new style was particularly popular in northern and central France, where royal influence was strongest. From the 1230s to 1250, French architects built over eighty cathedrals. Notwithstanding the close association of Gothic with France (it was soon dubbed *opus francigenum*, or "French work"), the style migrated north to England and south to Spain. There was also an Italian Gothic period, although Italy was the region that welcomed the style least and rejected it soonest.

Elements of Gothic Architecture

Rib Vaults

In Gothic architecture, the rib vault (fig. 12.4) supersedes the earlier barrel vaults typical of Romanesque. The advantage of the rib vault is that it requires less buttressing, whereas the barrel vault exerts pressure along its entire length and thus needs strong buttressing. Since the weight of the rib vault is concentrated only at the corners of the bay, the structure can be buttressed at intervals, freeing up more space for windows. The ribs could be built before the intervening space (usually triangular or rectangular) was

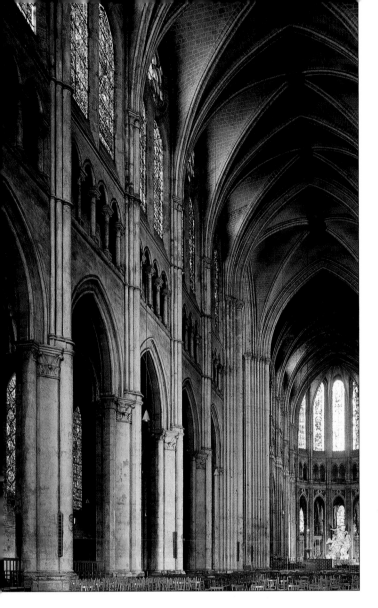

12.5 View of piers in the nave arcade, Chartres Cathedral, France, 13th century. The compound piers along the two sides of the nave are massive columnar supports to which clusters of colonnettes, or pilaster shafts, are attached. The clusters usually correspond to arches or vault ribs above them.

filled in. Adding ribs also enabled Gothic builders to reinforce rib vaults and to distribute their weight more efficiently. Because of the weight-bearing capacity of the ribs, the vault's surfaces (the **web** or infilling) could be made of lighter material.

Piers

As the vaults became more complex, so did their supports. One such support is the cluster, or **compound** pier (fig. **12.5**). Although compound piers had been used in Romanesque buildings, they became a standard Gothic feature. The ribs of the vaults formed a series of lines which were continued down to the floor by colonnettes resting on compound piers.

With this system of support, the Gothic builders created a vertical unity leading the observer's gaze to the clerestory windows, the architectural source of interior

light. The pier supports, with their attached colonnettes branching off into arches and vaults, have been likened to the upward growth of a tree.

Flying Buttresses

In Romanesque architecture thick walls performed the function of buttressing. This decreased the amount of available window space, limiting the interior light. In the Gothic period, builders developed the flying buttress, an exterior structure composed of thin half-arches, or flyers. This supported the wall at the point where the thrust of an interior arch or vault was greatest (fig. **12.6**).

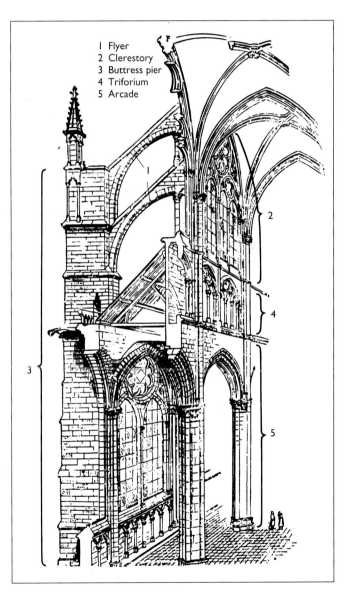

1 Flyer
2 Clerestory
3 Buttress pier
4 Triforium
5 Arcade

12.6 Section diagram of a Gothic cathedral (after E. Viollet-le-Duc). The **elevation** of the Gothic cathedral illustrates the flyers, which transfer interior thrusts to a pier of the exterior buttress. Since the wall spaces between the buttresses were no longer necessary for structural support, they could be pierced by large windows to achieve the desired increase in light.

Pointed Arches

The pointed arch, which is a characteristic and essential feature of Gothic architecture, can be thought of as the intersection of two arcs of non-concentric circles. Examples are found in Romanesque, but in a much more tentative form. The piers channel the downward thrust of the pointed arch, minimizing the lateral, or sideways, thrust against the wall. Unlike round arches, pointed arches can theoretically be raised to any height regardless of the distance between their supports. The pointed arch is thus a more flexible building element, with more potential for increased height. Dynamically and visually, the thrust is far more vertical than that of a round arch.

The Skeleton

The features described above combined to form what is called a "skeletal" structure. The main architectural supports (buttresses, piers, ribs) form a "skeleton" to which non-supporting elements, such as walls, are attached. The Gothic builders had, in effect, invented a structure that biologists would describe as exo-skeletal. An exo-skeletal creature is one, such as a crab or a lobster, whose skeleton is on the outside of its body.

Stained-Glass Windows

Finally, the light that had so inspired Abbot Suger required an architectural solution. That solution was Suger's special use of the stained-glass window. Suger was not seeking natural daylight, but rather light that had been filtered through colored fragments of glass (see Box). Light and color were diffused throughout the interior of the cathedral, producing a different kind of radiance than had been achieved in Early Christian and Byzantine buildings (Chapter 9). The predominant colors of Gothic stained glass tend to be blue and red in contrast to the golds that characterize most Byzantine mosaics.

Romanesque Precursors of Gothic

Among other buildings that show elements of Gothic style evolving from Romanesque precursors is the abbey church of Saint-Etienne at Caen, in Normandy (figs. **12.8**, **12.9**, and **12.10**). It was begun in 1067 by William the Conqueror (see p. 362); the nave was completed in 1087. The organization of the façade (fig. 12.8) into three distinct

Stained-Glass Windows

Stained glass is translucent colored glass cut to form a window design. Compositions are made from pieces of colored glass formed by mixing metallic oxides with molten glass or fusing colored glass with clear glass. The artist cuts the individual pieces as closely as possible to the shape of the face or other individual feature to be represented. The pieces are then fitted to a model drawn on wood or paper, and details are added in black enamel.

The dark pigments are hardened and fused with the glass through firing, or baking in a kiln. The pieces of fired glass are then arranged on the model and joined by strips of lead. Figure **12.7** is a detail of a stained-glass window from Chartres Cathedral. Jeroboam, an Old Testament king, is shown praying before two golden calves. The red background is broken up, seemingly at random, into numerous sections. In the figures, however, the lead is arranged to conform either to an outline or to a logical location within the forms. Lead strips frame the head of the first calf and outline Jeroboam's crown. Once the pieces of stained glass are joined together, the units are framed by an iron **armature** and fastened within the **tracery**, or ornamental stonework, of the window.

Stained-glass windows were made occasionally for Early Christian and Byzantine churches and more often in the Romanesque period. In the Gothic period, stained glass became an integral part of religious architecture and a more prominent artistic medium.

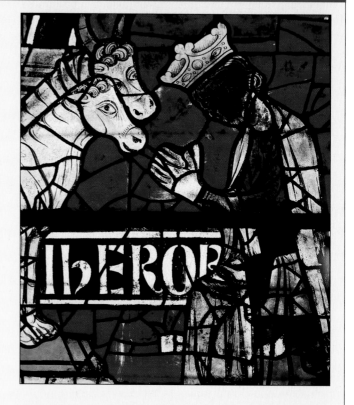

12.7 *Jeroboam Worshiping Golden Calves*, detail of a **lancet** under the north **rose window** (see fig. 12.31), Chartres Cathedral, early 13th century.

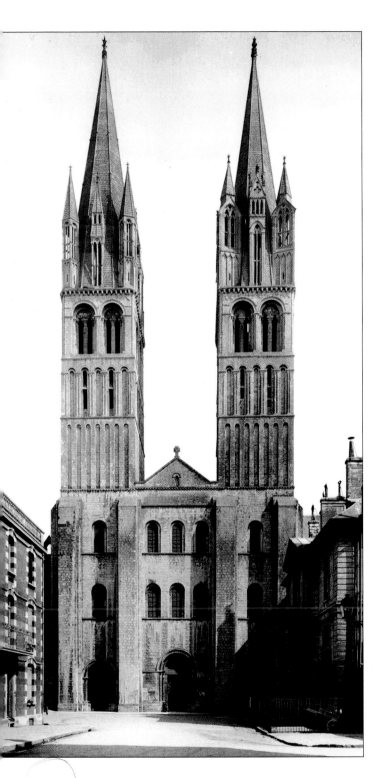

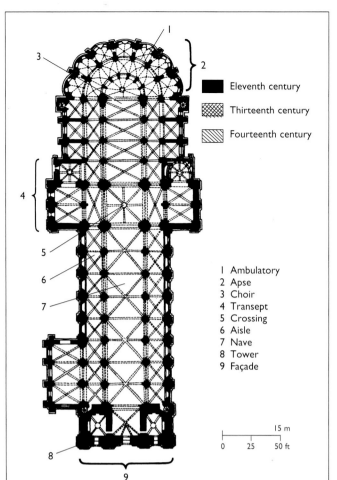

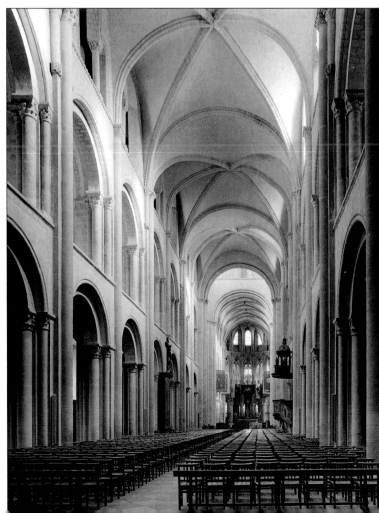

12.8 (above) West façade, Saint-Etienne, Caen, Normandy, France, 1067–87.

12.9 (above right) Plan of Saint-Etienne, Caen.

12.10 (right) Nave, Saint-Etienne, Caen. The vaults date from c. 1115–20.

Eleventh century
Thirteenth century
Fourteenth century

1 Ambulatory
2 Apse
3 Choir
4 Transept
5 Crossing
6 Aisle
7 Nave
8 Tower
9 Façade

15 m

0   25   50 ft

sections—a central rectangle surmounted by a gable and flanked by towers—became characteristic of Gothic façades. (The spires date from the Gothic period.)

A few years after the completion of Saint-Etienne's nave, the first European cathedral with rib vaults and pointed arches was planned at Durham, in the northeast of England (figs. **12.11**, **12.12**, and **12.13**). Construction began in 1093 under the supervision of its French bishop, William of Calais. The nave was finished in 1130, and the view in figure 12.13 shows some of the advantages of combining the pointed arch with a second transverse rib. This divided the vault into six sections and allowed for increased height, while relieving the massiveness of the Romanesque walls. It also made larger clerestory windows possible, which opened up the wall space and admitted more light.

The esthetic effect of these structural developments was an impression of upward movement toward the source of light. This is consistent with the symbolic role of light as a divine presence in Christian churches since the fourth century. The success of the vaulting at Durham led the builders of Saint-Etienne at Caen to change the original flat roof into sexpartite (six-part) vaulting. This, like the three-part façade, influenced Early Gothic architecture in the Ile-de-France.

The Age of Cathedrals

Chartres

By the time that the choir and west façade of Saint-Denis were completed, in about 1144, and even before Abbot Suger turned his attention to the rest of the church, other towns in northern France had been competing to build cathedrals in the new Gothic style. A cathedral is, by definition, the seat of a bishop (from the Greek word *kathedra*, meaning "seat" or "throne") and belongs to the city or town in which it is located. In contrast to churches such as Sainte-Foy (see p. 367), which were often built in rural areas, cathedrals required a more urban setting. Also consistent with increased urbanization in the twelfth century was the development of cathedral schools and universities. Their growing educational importance encroached on the relatively isolated monasteries that had proliferated in the earlier Middle Ages.

12.11 Exterior of Durham Cathedral, England, from the north, begun 1093.

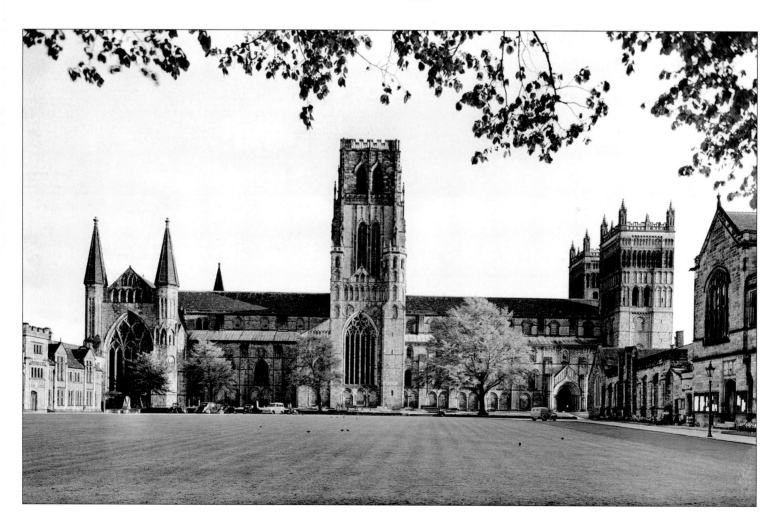

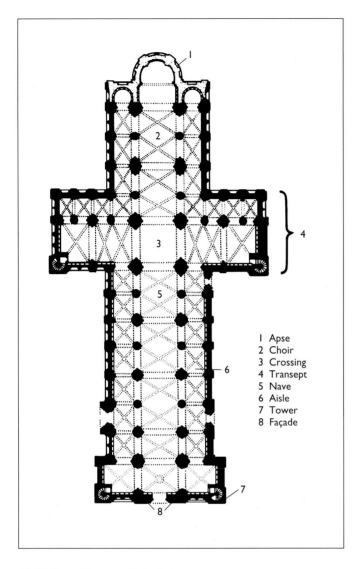

12.12 Plan of Durham Cathedral.

1 Apse
2 Choir
3 Crossing
4 Transept
5 Nave
6 Aisle
7 Tower
8 Façade

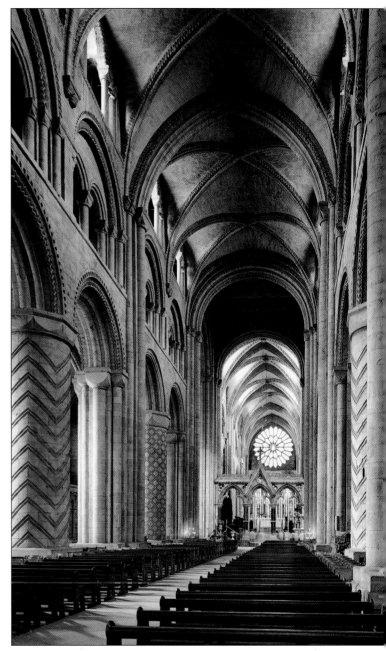

12.13 Nave, Durham Cathedral.

The construction of a cathedral was the largest economic enterprise of the Gothic era. It had a significant effect on neighboring communities, as well as on the city or town itself. Jobs were created for hundreds of masons, carpenters, sculptors, stonecutters, and other craftsmen. When a cathedral was finished, it attracted thousands of pilgrims and other visitors, and this continual traffic stimulated the local economy. Cathedrals also provided a focus for community activities, secular as well as religious. Above all, they generated an enormous sense of civic pride among the townspeople.

The cult of the Virgin Mary expanded during the Gothic period. Most of the great French cathedrals were dedicated to "Notre Dame," i.e. "Our Lady," or the Virgin. To avoid confusion, therefore, it is customary to refer to the cathedrals by the towns in which they are located. At Chartres, the Virgin Mary played a particularly significant role as the embodiment of the church building and the Bride of Christ. Her strong link to Chartres was reflected

in the tradition that a pagan statue of a virgin and child worshiped in a nearby cave had prefigured the coming of Christ and the Virgin Birth. One effect of this legend was the preeminence of Chartres in Mary's cult.

The town of Chartres is approximately 40 miles (64 km) southwest of Paris. Its cathedral (cf. fig. 12.17) combines the best preserved early Gothic architecture with High Gothic, as well as demonstrating the transitional developments in between. For a town like Chartres, with only about 10,000 inhabitants in the thirteenth century, the building of a cathedral dominated the economy just as the structure itself dominated the landscape. At Chartres, the

Guilds

Medieval **guilds**, or gilds, were associations formed for the aid and protection of their members and the pursuit of common religious or economic goals. The earliest form of economic guild was the Guild Merchant, which was responsible for organizing and supervising trade in the towns. Efforts by merchants to exclude craftsmen from the guilds led in the twelfth and thirteenth centuries to the formation of the craft guilds. These comprised all practitioners of a single craft or profession in a town. Craftsmen had to be members of the guild before they could ply their trade.

The functions of the craft guilds included regulating wages and prices, overseeing working conditions, and maintaining high standards of workmanship. Their effect, especially early on, was to ensure an adequate supply of trained workers and to enhance the status of craftsmen. They also provided charity to members in need, and pensions to their widows.

The guilds had three grades of membership—masters, journeymen (or paid assistants, *compagnons* in French), and apprentices. A precise set of rules governed the terms of apprenticeship and advancement to other grades. For promotion to the rank of master, a craftsman had to present to his guild a piece of work to be judged by masters. This is the origin of the term "masterpiece."

construction continued off and on from around 1134 to 1220. The most intensive work, however, followed a fire in 1194, when the nave and choir had to be rebuilt.

The bishop and chapter (governing body) of the cathedral were in charge of contracting out the work. The funds, however, came from a much broader cross-section of medieval French society. The church itself usually contributed by setting aside revenues from its estates. At Chartres, the canons (resident clergy) agreed in 1194 to give up their stipends (salaries) for three years so that the rebuilding program could begin. When the royal family or members of the nobility had a connection with a particular project, they also helped. At Chartres, Blanche, the mother of Louis IX, donated funds for the entire north transept façade, including the sculptures and windows. The Duke of Brittany contributed to the southern transept.

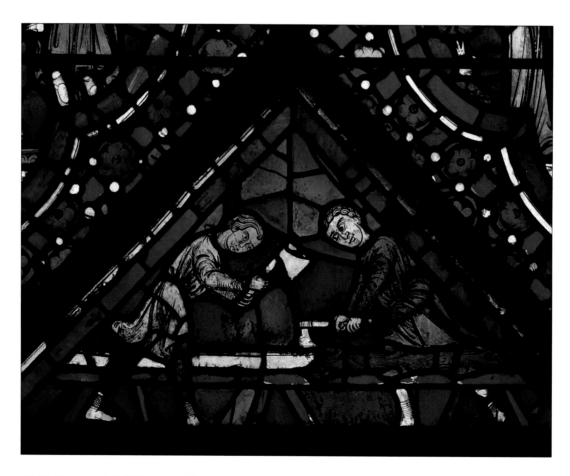

12.14 Carpenters' Guild Signature Window, detail of a stained-glass window, Chartres Cathedral, early 13th century. This signature scene depicts two carpenters at work on a plank of wood lying across three saw horses.

Saint Augustine and *The City of God*

Saint Augustine (354–430), Bishop of Hippo in North Africa, and later a Doctor of the Church, had an immense impact on the development of Christian thought. His mother was a Christian, and his father a pagan, and he himself embraced several philosophies before his baptism as a Christian in 387. He fought heresy and wrote prodigiously; his two best-known works are the *Confessions*, an autobiographical account up to the time of his conversion, and *The City of God* (*Civitas Dei*) (in 22 books), written between 413 and 426. The latter opens with a reply to the pagans, who sacked Rome under the leadership of Alaric the Goth in 410.

One of Augustine's main historical themes is the opposition of the Christian world to the non-Christian world. He contrasted the City of God, the Heavenly City, with the Earthly City, and transience with permanence:

> Most glorious is and will be the City of God, both in this fleeting age of ours, wherein she lives by faith, a stranger among infidels, and in the days when she shall be established in her eternal home.[3]

It is likely that Augustine had been influenced by Plato's *Republic* (see p. 139), and the work of other Classical philosophers, as well as by Old Testament references to the City of Jerusalem. These are essentially architectural metaphors which extend through Christianity from its very beginnings. In a sense, every Christian church—especially the cathedrals—was seen as a typological parallel to Solomon's Temple, and as a metaphor for the City of Jerusalem and the Heavenly City of God.

Other wealthy families of the region gave windows, and their donations were recorded by depicting their coats of arms in the stained glass.

Guilds (see Box) representing specific groups of craftsmen and tradesmen donated windows illustrating their professional activities (fig. **12.14**). Pilgrims and less wealthy local inhabitants gave money in proportion to their means, often by buying what were believed to be holy relics or in gratitude for answers to prayers. These donations went toward general costs rather than to a designated use. There were thus economic and social distinctions not only in the size and nature of the contributions, but also in the degree to which they were publicly recognized.

Workers and Master Builders

Chartres was one of over eighty cathedrals and large abbeys constructed in the region around Paris in the thirteenth century. Each one was an enormous undertaking fraught with problems, including fires and poor weather. To make matters worse, funds often ran out in the course of a building project, which meant that work came to a halt. Without banks there was no system for building up capital or long-term financial planning. It also took three to six months for mortar to set, depending on the weather. And whenever work stoppages did occur, the workers were dismissed and moved on to other cathedrals that would hire them. As a result, the workforce often lacked continuity, which is reflected in stylistic variations of the finished building.

Supervising the construction of every cathedral was the master builder, usually a literate, well-traveled man who had been to school and apprenticed to an older master at the age of thirteen. Typically he would be well paid, and acquainted with both the clergy and the nobles helping to finance the project. He would also understand the iconographic significance of the artistic program. A sign of the high status of the master builder was the custom of inscribing his name in the labyrinth design on the cathedral floor. In some cases, he was even buried along with royal patrons and bishops in a cathedral he had built. The social position of the master builder was sufficiently high that it became a convention to criticize his vanity, for he was conceived of as building the City of God on earth (see Box). We have seen in Chapter 1, from the story of the Tower of Babel, that the theme of architectural vanity is an ancient one; it is also explored in the classic play entitled *The Master Builder*, by the nineteenth-century Norwegian author, Henrik Ibsen (1828–1906).

In the Gothic period, master builders worked from templates, which were birchwood replicas of numbered stones. Corresponding numbers were marked on the vaults and elevations to indicate the location of each stone. Each master builder designed his own template, which he took with him if he had to stop work on one cathedral and move on to another. The next master could then continue the work from his predecessor's drawings.

Stones were cut at a quarry and brought by a carter to the building site. There, a foreman sorted the stones according to size and shape, and assigned them to groups of eight to twelve workers. At Chartres there were over four hundred workers to be supervised, and some two hundred stones were carted from a quarry 7½ miles (12 km) away from the site. As there were no power tools, stones had to be individually cut and dressed. They were raised up by huge cranes (of which there were four at Chartres) and by small cranes, or winches, which were powered by the workers themselves. At Chartres, some 45 tons of stone were raised in an average day. Scaffolds also had to be built because of the great heights involved, and workers had to learn how to protect themselves from accidents.

Since technology was limited, the accuracy of the master builder was crucial. His instruments were rudimentary; they consisted of a compass, a square, straightedges (rules), measuring rods, and proportional dividers. His template was organized according to geometric principles, which accounts for the overall formal unity of the cathedrals. Geometry was easy to replicate, so that even if several master builders worked at a particular cathedral,

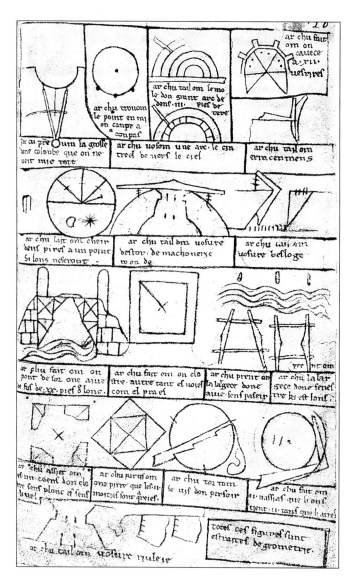

12.15 Geometric architectural diagrams from the sketchbook of Villard de Honnecourt, c. 1225, from R. Willis. Bibliothèque Nationale, Paris.

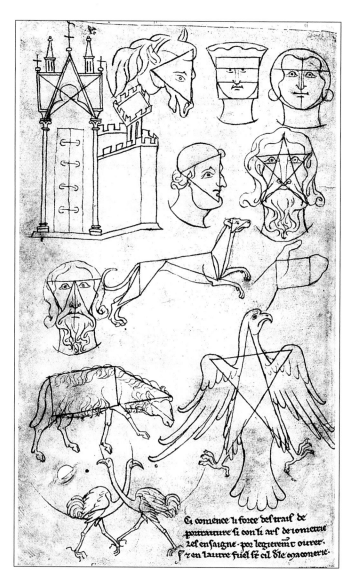

12.16 Geometric analysis of human and animal figures from the sketchbook of Villard de Honnecourt, c. 1225, from R. Willis. Bibliothèque Nationale, Paris.

the completed building was a unified structure. Figures **12.15** and **12.16** illustrate pages from the only surviving sketchbook made around 1225 by a master builder known as Villard de Honnecourt. They show the geometric basis by which both architecture and human and animal forms were conceived and designed.

The Exterior Architecture of Chartres

Chartres (fig. **12.17**) was constructed on an elevated site to enhance its visibility. The vertical plane of its towers seems to reach toward the sky, while the horizontal of the side walls (fig. **12.18**) carries one's gaze east toward the apse (fig. **12.19**). The view in figure 12.17 shows the west façade, whose towers illustrate the dynamic, changing nature of Gothic style. The southern tower, on the right, dates from before 1194, and reflects the transition from

Late Romanesque to Early Gothic. The northern tower, begun in 1507, which is taller, thinner, and more elaborate than the southern tower, is Late Gothic. Its greater height reflects advances in structural technology, as well as Suger's theological emphasis on verticality and light as expressions of God's presence.

The tripartite organization of Chartres' west façade is characteristic of most Gothic cathedrals. Like the Romanesque church of Saint-Etienne at Caen (fig. 12.8), it is divided into three sections. Towers with a belfry flank the central rectangle, which is further subdivided. The three portals consist of the same elements as the Romanesque abbey church at Conques (cf. fig. 11.7); above each portal is a tall, arched, stained-glass lancet window. Inscribed in the rectangle over the lancets is the round rose window, a feature of almost all Gothic cathedral entrance walls. Above the rose window, a gallery of niche

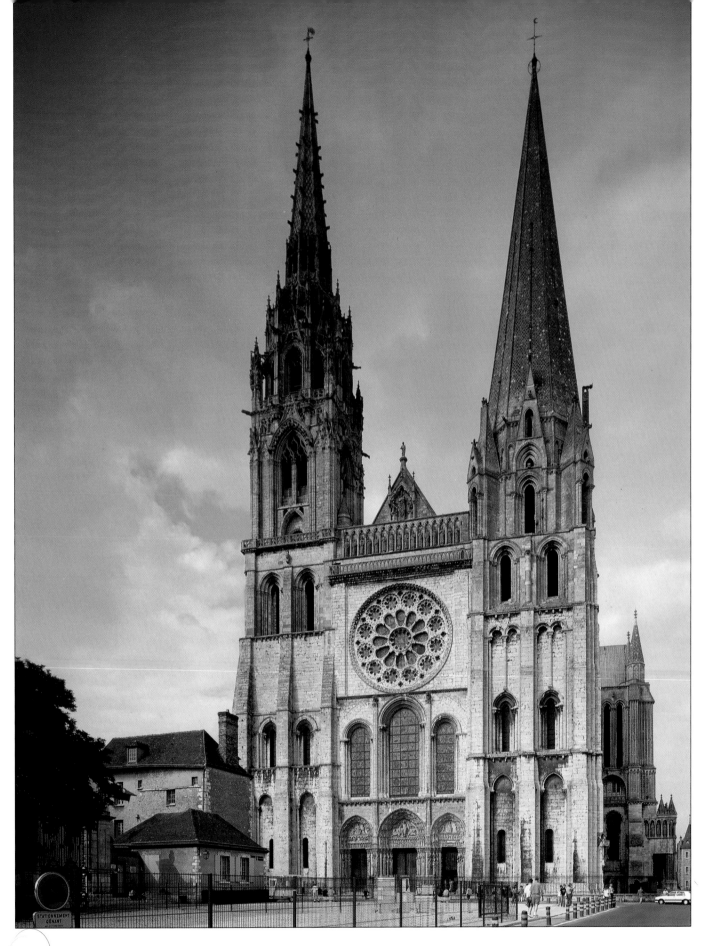

12.17 West façade, Chartres Cathedral, c. 1140–50. Symmetry in the Classical sense was not a requirement of the Gothic designers. Gothic cathedrals are structurally, but not formally, symmetrical. That is, a tower is opposite a tower, but the towers need not be identical in size or shape.

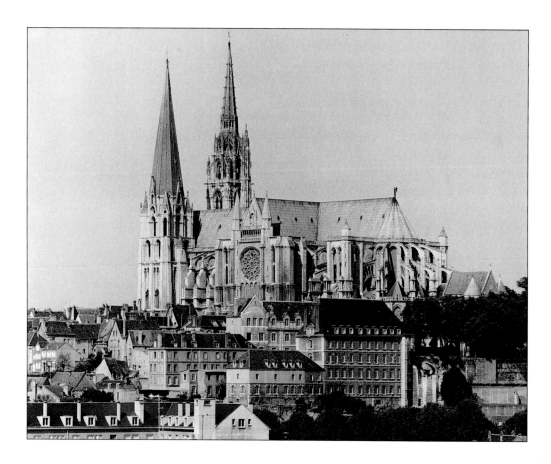

12.18 South wall of Chartres Cathedral.

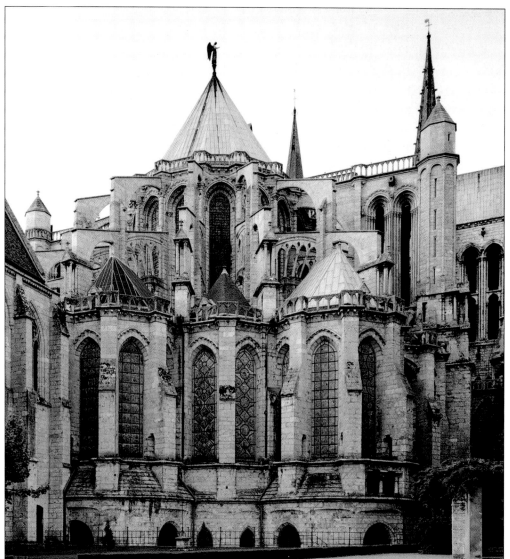

12.19 Apse of Chartres Cathedral, with radiating chapels and flying buttresses. Visible in this view are three projecting, semicircular radiating chapels, the flying buttresses above them, and, at the top, the curved end of the roof.

figures representing Old Testament kings stretches between the two towers. Finally, the gallery is surmounted by a triangular gable with a niche containing a statue of the Virgin with the infant Christ. The repetition of triple elements, portals, lancets, three horizontal divisions, and the triangular gable, all suggest a numerical association with the Trinity (the Father, Son, and Holy Ghost), a central tenet of Church dogma.

In the rose window, too, there is a symbolic Christian significance in the arrangement of the geometric shapes. Three groups of twelve elements surround the small central circle. These refer to Christ's twelve apostles. The very fact that the rose window is a circle could symbolize Christ, God, and the universal aspect of the Church itself.

Proceeding counter-clockwise around the southern tower, the visitor confronts the view in figure 12.18. This is one of two long, horizontal sides of the cathedral, parts of which are labeled in figure **12.20**. Visible in the photograph are the roof (10 in fig. **12.21**), the buttresses (8) between the tower and the transept entrance, and the flying buttresses, or flyers (9), over the buttresses and, at the east end, behind the apse. This transept, which is on the south, has five lancet windows, a larger rose window than that of the west façade, and a similar gallery and triangular gable with niche statues.

Continuing east to the end of the cathedral, turning around and facing west, the visitor sees the view of the apse in figure 12.19.

Exterior Sculpture

On the exterior of Chartres there are so many sculptural details that it would take several volumes to consider them thoroughly. We shall therefore concentrate on a few of the most characteristic examples on the west and south sides of the cathedral.

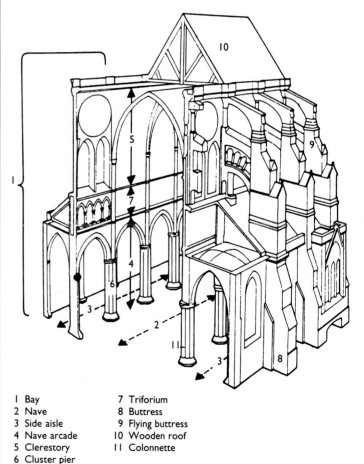

1 Tower
2 Nave
3 Side aisle
4 Crossing
5 North transept
6 South transept
7 Choir
8 Apse
9 Radiating chapel
10 Buttress
11 West façade

0   20   40 m
0   50 ft   100   150 ft

1 Bay
2 Nave
3 Side aisle
4 Nave arcade
5 Clerestory
6 Cluster pier
7 Triforium
8 Buttress
9 Flying buttress
10 Wooden roof
11 Colonnette

12.20 Plan of Chartres Cathedral. Although the plan is quite symmetrical, the number of steps leading to each of the three entrances increases from west to north, and from north to south. This increase parallels the building sequence, for Gothic architecture became more detailed and complex as the style developed.

12.21 Perspective diagram and cross-section of Chartres Cathedral.

Royal Portal (west façade) There are three portals, together known as the Royal Portal, on the western entrance of Chartres (fig. **12.22**), the central portal being slightly larger than the other two. This triple arrangement was derived from the Roman triumphal arch (see p. 233), which marked an entryway into a city. The derivation of the cathedral portal from the Roman arch highlights the symbolic parallel between the interior of the church and the heavenly city of Jerusalem (see p. 274). Throughout the Middle Ages, entering a church was thought of as an earthly prefiguration of one's ultimate entry into heaven.

The sculptural decorations at Chartres, like those on Romanesque churches and cathedrals, had a didactic function. They were part of an iconographic program intended to convey particular messages. It is not known who the author of the program was, but it is possible that theologians at Chartres' cathedral school were involved in planning it.

In the most general sense, these portals remind the observer of the typological view of history (see p. 273), which was characteristic of Christian thought from its beginnings. The right, or southern, portal contains scenes of Christ's Nativity and childhood on a double lintel. An enthroned Virgin holding the Christ Child occupies the tympanum, which is surrounded by the Seven Liberal Arts in the archivolts. The Liberal Arts as depicted here correspond to the *trivium* (Grammar, Rhetoric, and Dialectic) and the *quadrivium* (Arithmetic, Geometry, Astronomy, and Music) adopted from Donatus by Alcuin of York under Charlemagne (see p. 339). This curriculum reflects the importance of learning and the high status of the cathedral school, as well as Mary's designation as one who "perfectly possessed" the Liberal Arts. On the left, or northern, tympanum and lintel are scenes of the Ascension. The archivolts contain the signs of the zodiac and symbols of the seasonal labors of the twelve calendar months.

The central portal juxtaposes Old Testament kings and queens on the door jambs with the apocalyptic vision of St. John the Divine above the door. The door jamb statues, dating to around 1140–50, are the oldest surviving

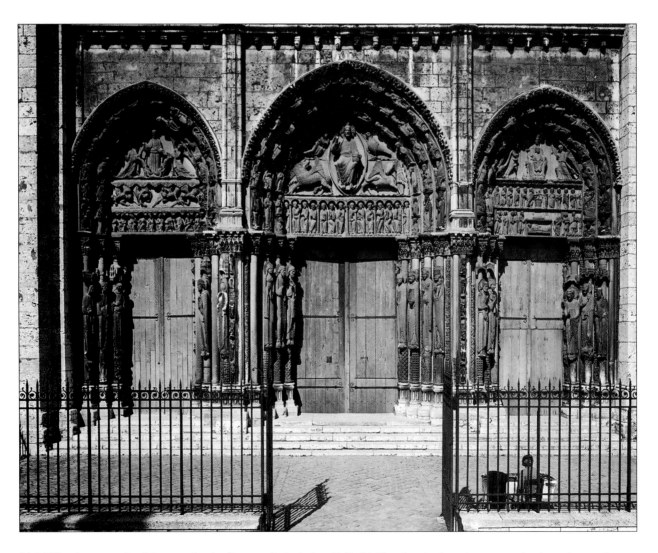

12.22 The three portals of the west façade, Chartres Cathedral, c. 1140–50. The door jamb sculptures are slender, columnar figures of Old Testament kings and queens, hence the name "Royal Portal."

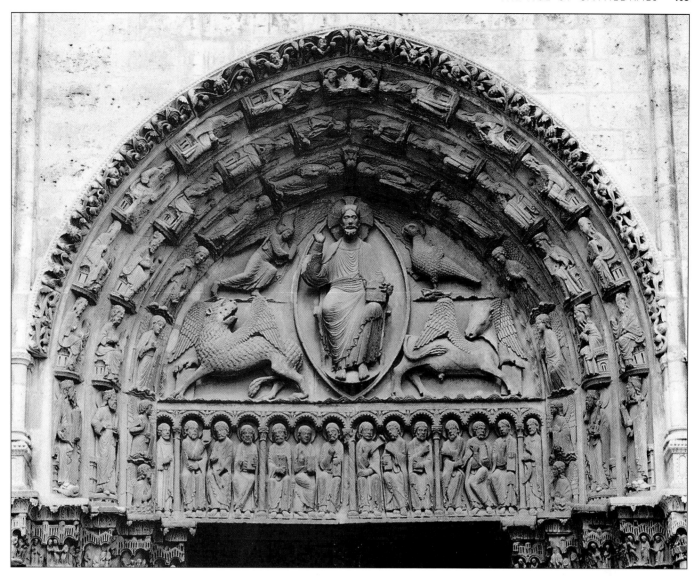

12.23 Tympanum, lintel, and archivolts of the central portal, west façade, Chartres Cathedral, c. 1145–70. The scene on the tympanum represents the *Second Coming of Christ*, with the four apocalyptic symbols of the Evangelists: the eagle stands for John, the angel for Matthew, the lion for Mark, and the bull for Luke. The surface patterns on all of the tympanum figures are stylized—for example, Christ's drapery folds, and the wings, drapery, and fur of the Evangelists' symbols. Christ is frontal, directly facing the visitors to the cathedral, as if reminding them of their future destiny.

examples of Early Gothic sculptural style. Each figure is slim and vertical, reflecting the shape of the colonnette behind. Separating each statue and each colonnette is a space decorated with floral relief patterns, which acts as a framing device.

As in Byzantine mosaics of the early Christian period, the Old Testament kings and queens are frontal. Their arms are contained within their vertical planes and their haloes are flat. Their feet slant downward on a diagonal, indicating that they are not naturally supported. As in the trumeau figure of *Saint Paul* at Moissac (see fig. 11.19), the drapery folds reveal the artist's delight in surface patterns. The repeated zigzags along the hems and circles at the elbows, along with the hair and beards, are stylizations. Compared with the Romanesque figures at Moissac, however, the kings and queens on the door jambs at Chartres

are more independent of their columns. Figures and columns are vertically aligned, but they are no longer merged in a manner reminiscent of early medieval interlace. Instead, they project forward from the column.

The New Testament event represented over the central door (fig. **12.23**) is the *Second Coming of Christ* as described by John the Divine in the book of Revelation. On the tympanum, a seated Christ is surrounded by an oval mandorla, and the four apocalyptic symbols of the Evangelists. Beneath the tympanum on the lintel, the twelve apostles are arranged in four groups of three. Each group is separated by a colonnette supporting round arches that resemble haloes. At either end of the lintel stands a single prophet, holding a scroll. Of the three archivolts, the outer two contain the twenty-four elders of the Apocalypse described by John the Divine. The inner archivolt contains twelve angels; the two in the center hold a crown over Christ's head, proclaiming his role as King of Heaven.

In contrast to the treatment of the same subject on the tympanum at the church of Saint-Pierre at Moissac (fig. 11.12), the program at Chartres separates each group of figures into a discrete architectural element. This creates a greater sense of order and logic, and reduces the sense of crowding. It is thus easier to read this tympanum than its Romanesque predecessor. The resulting clarity is enhanced by the deeper relief and the minimal floral designs—here framing the outer archivolt. By now the influence of Islamic patterning, as well as of interlace, on monumental stone buildings in France has virtually disappeared.

Considered as an iconographic totality, the Royal Portal of Chartres offers the visitor a Christian view of history. The beginning and end of Christ's earthly life are placed over the right and left doors, respectively. The Old Testament kings and queens on the door jambs are typological precursors of Christ and Mary, while the *Second Coming of Christ*, as envisioned by Saint John, dominates the central portal.

A comparison of the door jamb statues from the Royal Portal (figs. **12.24** and **12.25**) with those on the south door jambs reveals the stylistic changes that occurred from Early Gothic to the beginning of High Gothic.

The South Façade The saints on the left portal of the south transept (fig. **12.26**) conform less strictly than the figures on the Royal Portal to their colonnettes, and their

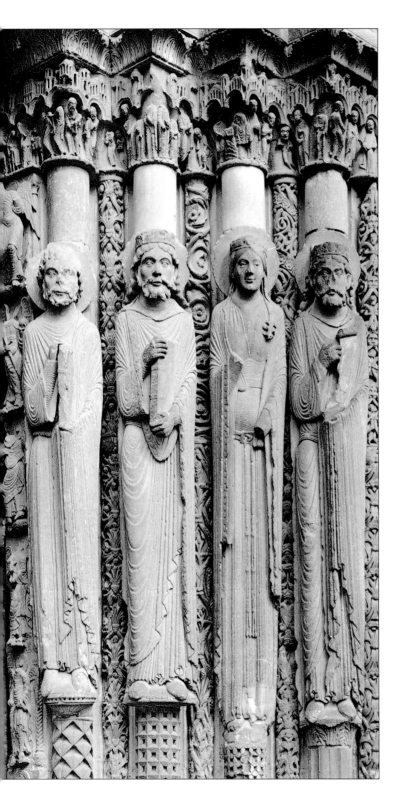

12.24 (above) Door jamb statues, west façade, Chartres Cathedral, c. 1145–70.

12.25 (right) Stylized drapery (detail of fig. 12.24).

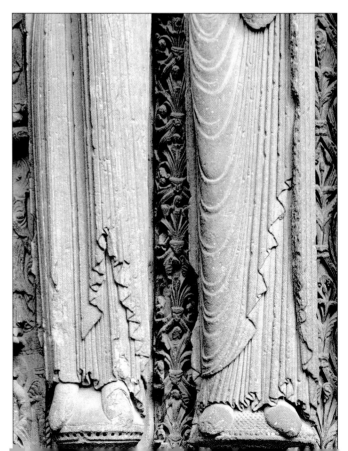

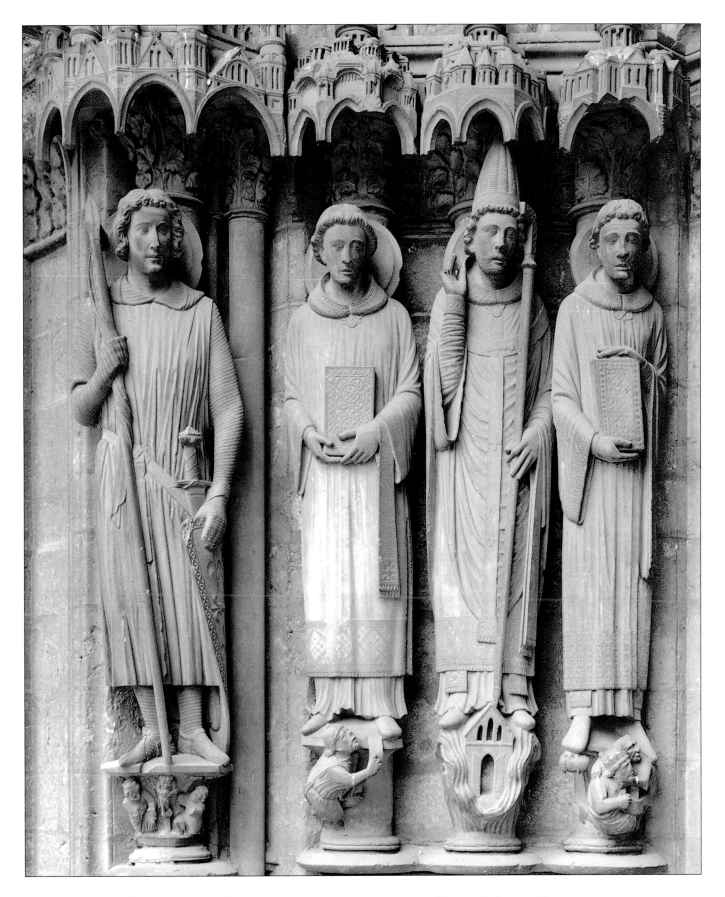

12.26 *Saints Theodore, Stephen, Clement, and Lawrence*, door jamb statues, south transept, Chartres Cathedral, 13th century.

feet rest naturally on a horizontal plane. They are no longer strictly frontal. They have facial expressions, and are of different heights. The heads turn slightly, and there is more variety in their poses, gestures, and costumes. In the figure of *Saint Theodore* at the far left, for example, the right hip swings out slightly in response to the relaxation of the stance. The diagonal of the belt, apparently weighed down at the saint's left by a heavy sword, conveys a slight suggestion of movement in three-dimensional space.

This general increase in the sense of depth is enhanced by the more deeply carved folds and facial features, as well as by the projecting, crownlike architectural elements over the figures' heads. The proportions of the figures have also changed in comparison to those on the west door jambs. They are no longer as tall and thin as the figures on the west door jambs. Instead, they are wider, and seem as if they might step down from their supports into the real world of the observer. Such changes from Early to High Gothic reflect a new, fledgling interest in human form and emotion that would continue to develop into Late Gothic.

Between the two doors of the central portal is the trumeau, also a feature of Romanesque cathedrals. It is decorated with a statue of the *Teaching Christ* (fig. **12.27**). He stands on a lion and a dragon, associated with the beasts and monsters of the Apocalypse, which denote Satan and Antichrist (see Box). Still frontal and strictly vertical, Christ's pose makes him seem more aloof than the door jamb saints. At the same time, however, he is shown teaching rather than judging, and is thus potentially more accessible to the viewer.

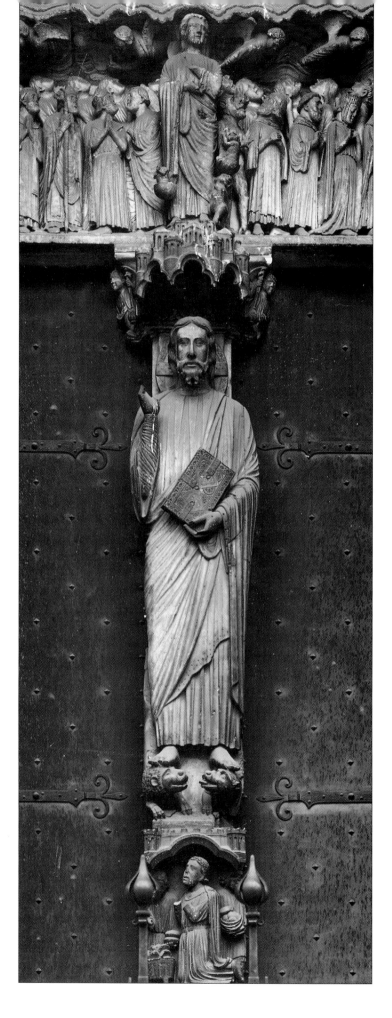

12.27 *Teaching Christ*, trumeau, south transept, Chartres Cathedral, 13th century. Christ's earthly role as a teacher is reflected by the book in his left hand, and his divinity by his gesture of blessing. The act of standing on Satan and Antichrist symbolizes Christ's triumph over the forces of evil.

Antichrist

The notion of Antichrist, mentioned in the First Epistle of Saint John (2:18 and 22), is about the end of time, and is apocalyptic in nature. It developed in Europe along with the spread of Christianity, and became a powerful force in the Western imagination. Antichrist is not Satan, but an incarnation of evil, a "Final Enemy," and a "Last Emperor," who takes over from Satan at the end of the world and presides over killing, torture, and universal destruction. Many traditional myths and legends were absorbed into the Antichrist, who was used for political as well as for religious purposes.

The image of Antichrist appealed to visionary writers, and was frequently illustrated in Christian art. Antichrist iconography was derived from the apocalyptic beasts and monsters described in the book of Revelation. Early Christian allusions to his appearance mention huge stature, bloodshot eyes, white eyelashes, pointed hair, gigantic teeth, sickle-

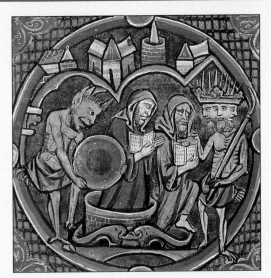

12.28 *Antichrist as a Three-headed Tyrant,* from the Halley Manuscript, fol. 127r, 1527. British Library, London.

shaped fingers, and a double skull. When he walked, according to one account, he left green footprints.

Around 950, one Brother Adso wrote a biography of Antichrist, which attracted an enormous popular following. In Adso's version, Antichrist was born in Babylon, educated in magic, and capable of performing miracles. He rebuilt the Temple of Jerusalem, circumcised himself, and claimed to be the son of God. A twelfth-century liturgical *Play of Antichrist* portrayed the fate of Christianity as depending on the German emperor and warned against the weakness of the French. Various reform movements within the Church similarly took advantage of Antichrist propaganda.

The first woman mystic who significantly influenced Antichrist imagery was the German abbess Hildegard of Bingen (1098–1179). Among her writings is the *Liber scivias* (*The Book of Knowing the Ways of Light*), in which she detailed twenty-six visions, including an account of Antichrist's birth from Mother Church, and his subsequent destruction (fig. **12.29**). She writes that he was born of a licentious woman, and emerged from her body with a black head covered with dung. He had fiery eyes, donkey's ears, a lion's mouth and nostrils, and gnashing teeth. When he tried to climb to heaven, a clap of thunder forced him to his death.

In the thirteenth century, so-called Moralized Bibles (sets of paired Old and New Testament events given allegorical meanings) contained many allusions to Antichrist. He was often represented as a three-headed tyrant (fig. **12.28**), which was a reference to his claim to be God and the Trinity. In 1242, a widely quoted verse reflected fears of a Mongol invasion: "When twelve hundred years and fifty After the birth from the dear Virgin are completed, Then will be born demon-filled Antichrist."[4]

Frederick II (1194–1250), Holy Roman Emperor and King of Germany and Sicily, was among those accused of being Antichrist. Considered a threat to papal territorial expansion, he was excommunicated and, in 1239, Pope Gregory IX likened him to the apocalyptic sea monster of the book of Revelation (13:1–3). Frederick replied in similar terms, whereupon the pope called him the "Final Enemy." Other targets of Antichrist propaganda in Western history have included the Jews and Muslims, the Roman emperor Nero, the Russian tsar Peter the Great, Napoleon, and Mussolini.

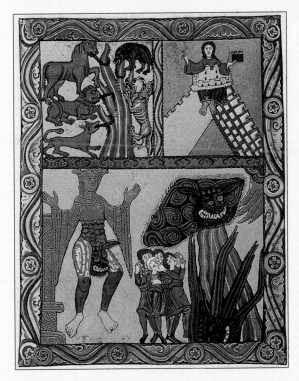

12.29 Hildegard of Bingen, *Antichrist's Birth and Destruction, Liber scivias* 3.11, Codex I, from Eibington Abbey, late 12th century. This is a modern copy of the lost original.

Interior

The overwhelming sensation on entering Chartres Cathedral from the western entrance is one of height. Its nave is the earliest example of High Gothic architectural style. The view in figure **12.30** shows the nave from the Royal Portal entrance, looking down toward the curved apse at the east end of the building. The ceiling vaults of the nave rise nearly 120 feet (37 m) and are only about 45 feet (14 m) wide.

The new height achieved by Gothic builders was made possible by the buttressing system, whose effect can be seen in the clerestory (see fig. 12.21). The latter is supported at two points by flyers, allowing more space to be used for windows. In each bay, the clerestory windows consist of two lancets under a small round window. At the far end, in the apse, the clerestory lancets are taller, but there are no round windows.

Proceeding down the nave, from west to east, one arrives at the crossing (see fig. 12.20) and the two transept entrances. Figure **12.31** shows the north rose window illuminated by outside light filtering through the stained glass. Dominating the interior entrance walls, these window arrangements are like colossal paintings in light. Their intensity varies according to weather conditions and time of day. At the center of the rose window, a small circle contains an image of Mary and the infant Christ, surrounded by twelve even smaller circles.

12.30 Nave, Chartres Cathedral, looking east. The three stories of Gothic elevation rise on either side of the nave. The lowest story, or nave arcade, is defined by a series of large arches on heavy piers. These separate the nave from the side aisles (fig. 12.20). The second story, or **triforium**, is a narrow passageway above the side aisle. At the top is the clerestory, whose windows are the main source of light in the nave.

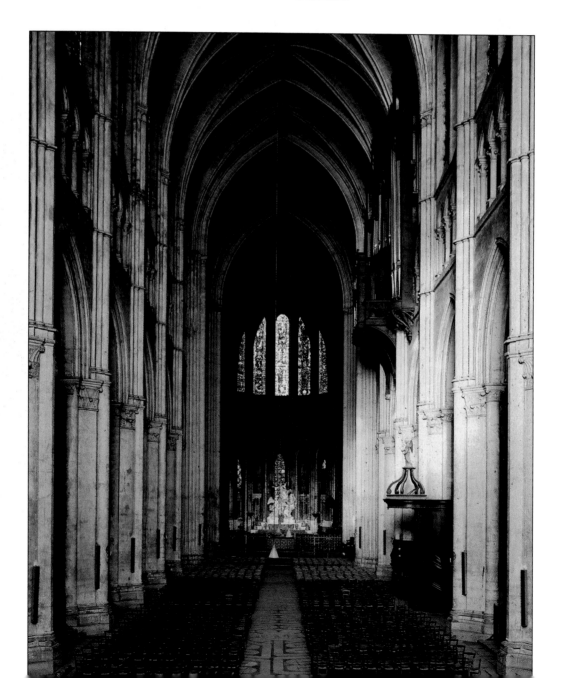

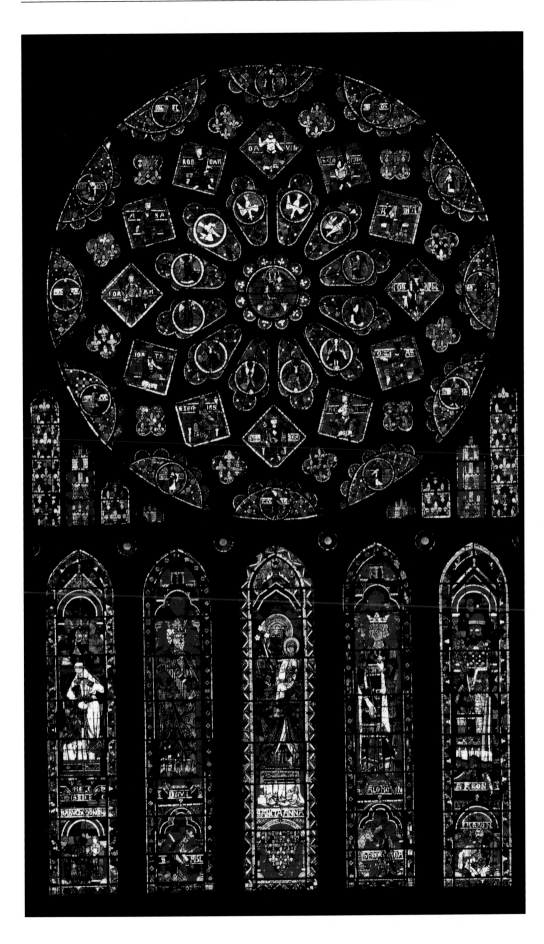

12.31 Rose window and lancets, north transept, Chartres Cathedral, 13th century. Note that the north windows are larger and more elaborate than the earlier west façade windows. The north lancets are taller and thinner than those on the west. The north rose window is larger, and has a greater variety of geometric shapes within it. Additional windows have also been inserted betweeen the lancets and rose window. The rose window measures over 42 feet (12.8 m) in diameter. The windows between the rose window and lancets are decorated with royal coats of arms, which proclaim the divine right of French kings. They also serve as a signature recording the donation of the north transept by Blanche, the queen mother.

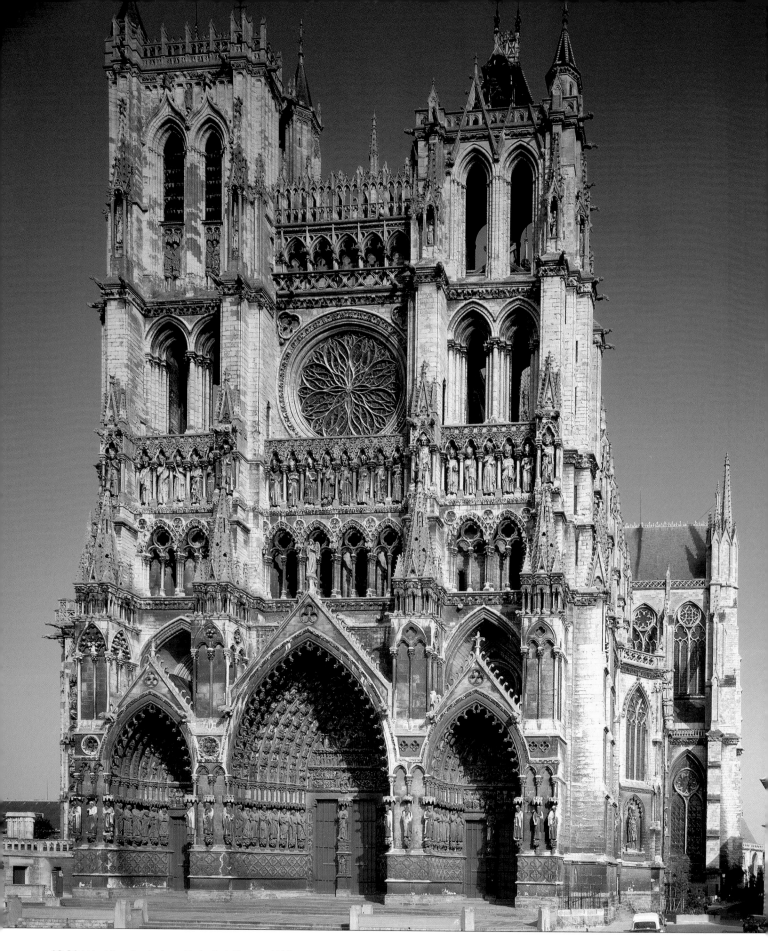

12.32 West façade, Amiens Cathedral, France, 1220–69. Three architects worked on this cathedral: Robert de Luzarches, Thomas de Cormont, and Regnault de Cormont.

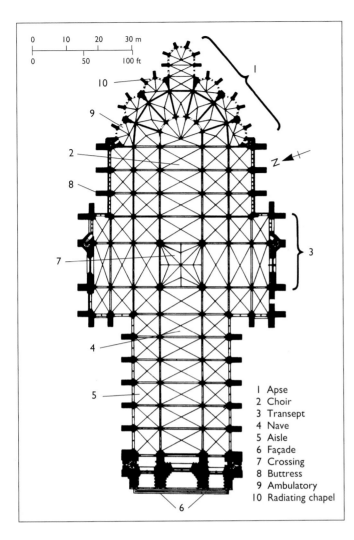

1 Apse
2 Choir
3 Transept
4 Nave
5 Aisle
6 Façade
7 Crossing
8 Buttress
9 Ambulatory
10 Radiating chapel

12.33 (above) Plan of Amiens Cathedral.

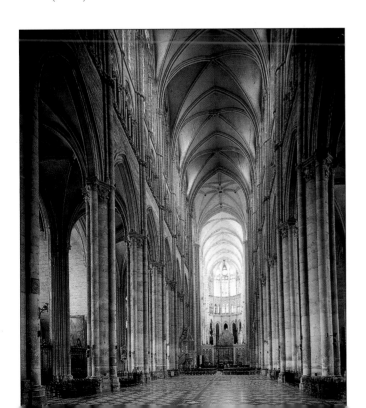

Each series of geometric shapes around the center of the rose window numbers twelve—an implicit reference to the twelve apostles who followed Christ during his lifetime. The first series after the tiny circles contains four doves and eight angels. Twelve Old Testament kings, typological precursors of Christ, occupy the squares. The twelve quatrefoils contain gold lilies on a blue field, symbols of the French kings. The outer semicircles represent twelve Old Testament prophets, who are types for the New Testament apostles.

The central lancet depicts Saint Anne with the infant Virgin Mary. At the left are the high priest Melchizedek and King David, and on the right are King Solomon and the priest Aaron—all Old Testament figures. In these windows, as in the west façade sculptures, the lower images act as visual and symbolic supports for the upper images: the New Dispensation is built on the Old. Here, the additional genealogical link between Christ and Saint Anne is arranged vertically, with Mary as an infant in the lancet below and as the Virgin Mother above, at the center of the rose window.

Wherever possible and appropriate, Gothic artists integrated Christian dogma into the cathedrals. Such buildings were designed to be a supreme monument to the glory of God as well as a unified expression of the skills of the architects, sculptors, artists, and other craftsmen who contributed to it.

Later Developments of the French Gothic Style

Chartres, completed in 1220, set the standard for other great French cathedrals built in the High Gothic style. Height and luminosity were the criteria by which they were measured. The cathedral at Reims, northeast of Paris, was the next to be built, from 1211 to about 1290. Its nave was 125 feet (38.1 m) high. Amiens, also to the north, was begun in 1220, and its nave reached a height of 144 feet (43.89 m). Each was wider than the last, but the ratio of height to width continued to increase.

Amiens

The High Gothic cathedral at Amiens (fig. **12.32**), like Chartres, was built on the site of a church that had burned down. Because it was conceived from the start as a Gothic structure, the plan (fig. **12.33**) is more unified than that of Chartres. Transept entrances and the towers, for example, are symmetrical. There is also a new integration of parts with the whole in the construction of the nave (fig. **12.34**).

12.34 Nave, Amiens Cathedral, 1220–69.

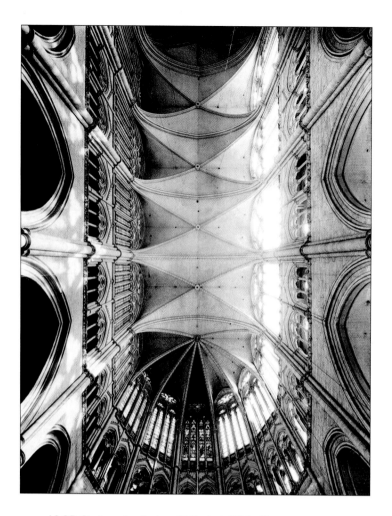

12.35 Choir vaults, Amiens Cathedral, 1220–69.

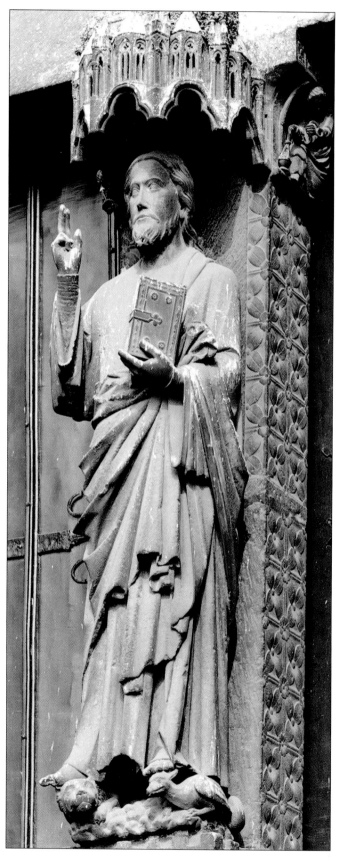

12.36 *Beau Dieu*, central portal, west façade, Amiens Cathedral, c. 1225–30.

Each feature is now in the service of height, and the elements of the wall work together to carry one's gaze upwards in a soaring thrust toward the vaults and the source of light through the clerestory windows. The view of the choir vaults in figure **12.35** shows the "uplifting" effect of light and lightness on the delicate, upper story colonnettes and on the webbing of the vaults.

Two trumeau statues at Amiens exemplify certain developments in Gothic sculptural decoration: the *Beau Dieu* ("Beautiful God": fig. **12.36**) and the *Vierge dorée* ("Gilded Virgin": fig. **12.37**). The *Beau Dieu* is carved in deeper relief than the *Teaching Christ* from Chartres (fig. 12.27), and the right arm is more extended. The hemline is no longer horizontal, but appears to rise up in the middle, which creates more open space and fluid drapery movement. As at Chartres, Christ stands on apocalyptic monsters—here, a lion and a basilisk (a legendary serpent having a deadly glance and poisonous breath), again denoting Satan and Antichrist.

The *Vierge dorée* was carved about twenty years after the *Beau Dieu*, and seems even more independent of its architectural background. Whereas the trumeau figures of Christ have an iconic character, the Virgin is represented

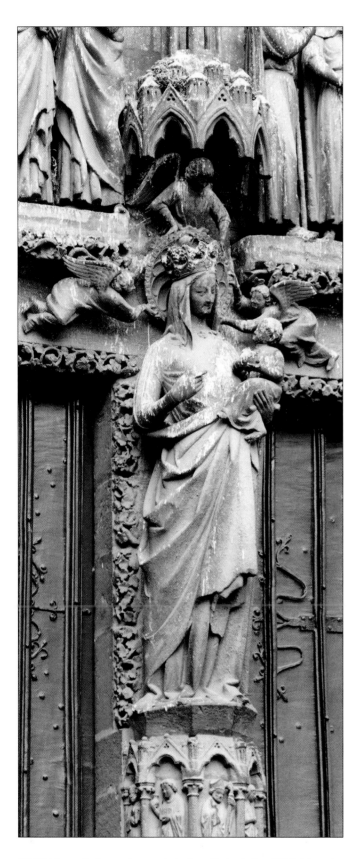

12.37 *Vierge dorée*, south portal, Amiens Cathedral, c. 1250. Note the implicit references to Christ's crucifixion (the arrangement of the angels holding the halo) and to the doctrine of the Trinity (the number of angels).

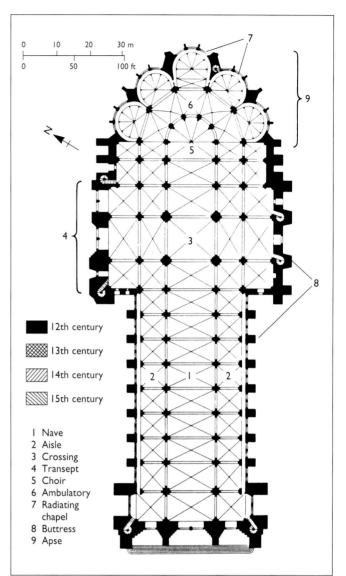

12.38 Plan of Reims Cathedral (after W. Blaser).

Scale: 0 10 20 30 m / 0 50 100 ft

- ▉ 12th century
- ▓ 13th century
- ▨ 14th century
- ▧ 15th century

1 Nave
2 Aisle
3 Crossing
4 Transept
5 Choir
6 Ambulatory
7 Radiating chapel
8 Buttress
9 Apse

in more human terms. Although she is the Queen of Heaven by virtue of her crown, she turns to gaze not at the viewer, but at her infant. She holds him on her left arm, while the diagonal drapery folds convey the impression that a shift in her stance helps support his weight. The statue is unusual in combining monumental form on the exterior of a cathedral with an intimate depiction of the mother-child relationship.

Reims

At Reims, the west façade (fig. **12.39**) and interior view of the nave (fig. **12.40**) show the extent to which cathedral designs were becoming progressively elongated, with an increasingly vertical thrust. The proportions of the arches at Reims are taller and thinner than those at Chartres, and the plan (fig. **12.38**) is longer and thinner. The radiating

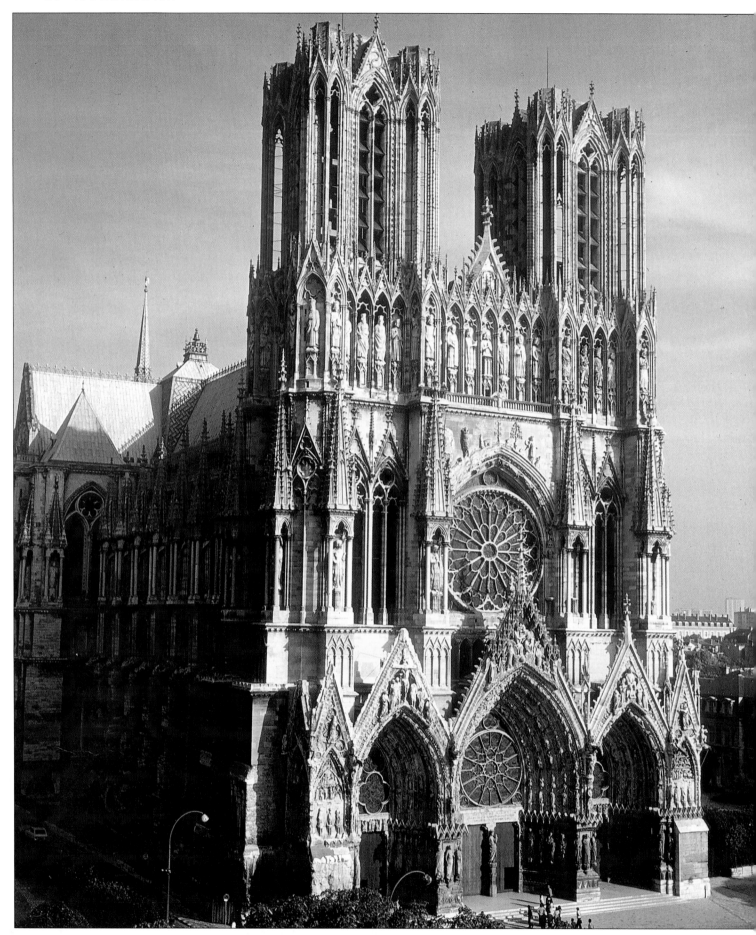

12.39 (opposite) West façade, Reims Cathedral, France, begun 1211. The window space has been dramatically increased at Reims, as a result of continual improvements in the buttressing system. The tympanums on the façade, for example, are filled with glass rather than stone. At Reims the portals are no longer recessed into the façade, but are built outward from it.

12.40 (right) Nave, Reims Cathedral, 1211– c. 1290. 125 ft (38.1 m) high.

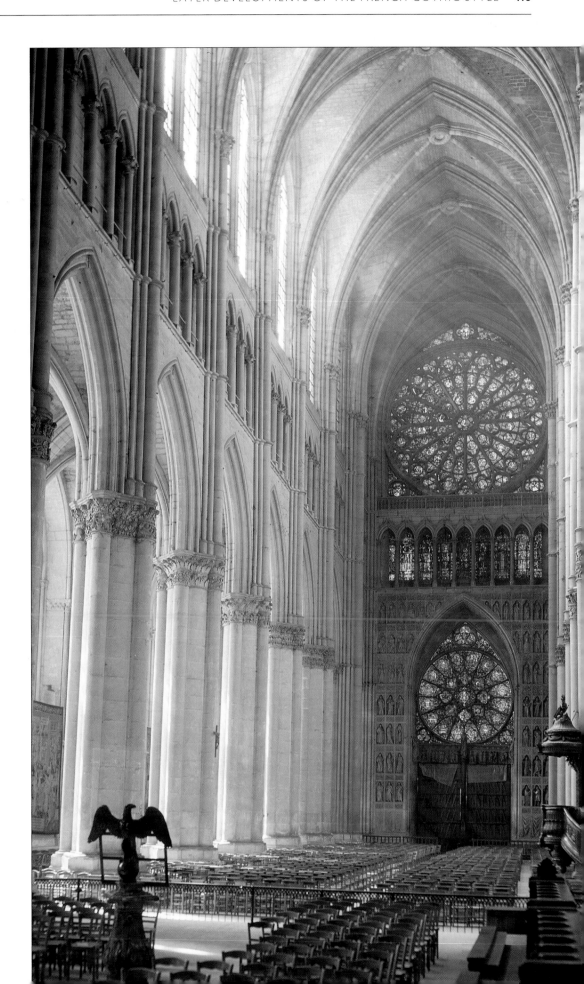

chapels are deeper than at Chartres, and the transepts are somewhat stubby, appearing to merge into the choir with little or no break. Because Amiens was designed slightly later than Reims, however, its height is both absolutely and proportionately greater, and its nave proportionately narrower than at Reims.

The exterior surfaces at Reims are filled with greater numbers of sculptures than at either Chartres or Amiens. In contrast to the increased verticality of the architecture, the sculptures have become more naturalistic, as can be seen in the door jamb statues on the west façade at Reims (fig. **12.41**). Rather than being vertically aligned and facing the viewer as at Chartres, the Reims figures turn to face each other, thereby interacting in a dramatic narrative and engaging the spaces between them. The drapery folds reflect human anatomy, poses, and gestures in a more pronounced way than even at the south transept of Chartres. This is one of the earliest examples in the monumental Christian art of western Europe of an interest in the relationship between drapery and the human form it covers.

Gothic Architecture and Scholasticism

This heading was the title of a small book published in 1951 by the art historian Erwin Panofsky. He showed the way in which Scholasticism influenced the Gothic style in terms of its clear, hierarchical systems. Among the examples he used to show this connection was an illustration from a thirteenth-century manuscript (fig. **12.42**). At the upper left, the king sits on a throne and is enclosed by a tripartite Gothic arch. He is the largest figure on the page, and his frame is the most elaborate architectural

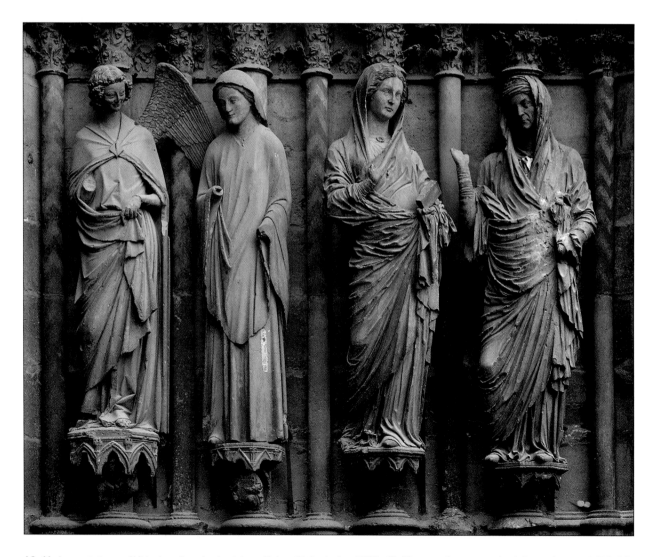

12.41 *Annunciation and Visitation*, door jamb statues, Reims Cathedral, c. 1225–45. The two figures on the left are the angel Gabriel and Mary. They enact the scene of the Annunciation, in which Gabriel announces Christ's birth to Mary. On the right, in the Visitation scene, Mary visits her cousin Elizabeth and tells her that she is three months pregnant. Elizabeth informs Mary that she herself is six months pregnant. Her son will be John the Baptist, Christ's second cousin and childhood playmate.

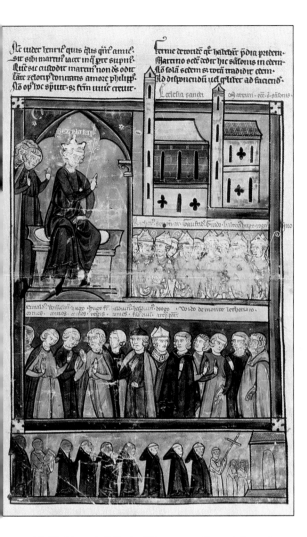

12.42 (above) Philip I of France granting privileges to the priory of Saint Martin-des-Champs, France. c. 1250. Book illumination, ms. 1359, fol. 6. Bibliothèque Nationale, Paris.

12.43 (right) Scene from the *Life of Saint Denis*, completed 1317. Book illumination, ms. fr. 2091, vol. II, fol. 125. Bibliothèque Nationale, Paris. This manuscript was commissioned during the reign of Philip IV (the Fair). It contains twenty-seven illuminations of the life of Saint Denis. In this scene, the saint asks two others (Saints Antonin and Saintin) to write his biography.

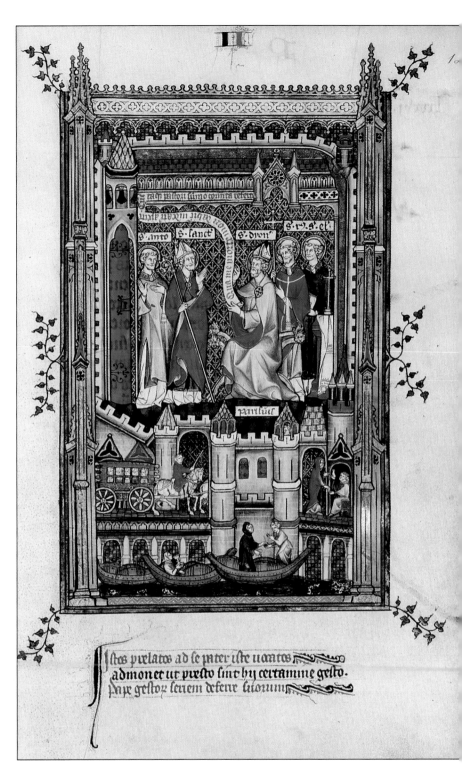

element. His greater verticality and his higher placement are consistent with his position as ruler. Interior is separated from exterior, which appears in the buildings to the right. Other figures, including members of the clergy, are arranged in three horizontal rows.

The same organizing principle can be seen in an illustration from the early fourteenth-century manuscript of the *Life of Saint Denis* (fig. **12.43**). Its elaborate frame is Late Gothic, and the vines make it a metaphor of the Church itself by reference to Christ's "I am the vine" (see p. 280). At the top, Saint Denis, the largest figure, sits on a lion throne, which connects him typologically with King Solomon, and his Church with Solomon's Temple. The abbreviated cathedral entrance over the saint's head emphasizes his position as Archbishop of France. His scroll winds around and forms a lintel-like horizontal under the clerestory windows.

The scene below depicts the everyday life of the Earthly City, in this case fourteenth-century Paris. A coach enters the city gate on the upper left, a doctor checks his patient's urine sample on the right, and in one of the boats a wine taster and two men complete a commercial transaction. Travel, medicine, and trade are among the transient activities of daily life, while the saints above are engaged in the loftier pursuit of preserving the name and memory of St. Denis through his image and biography.

Scholasticism was a philosophical method combined with theology. It was designed to explain spiritual truth by a kind of inquiry based on analogy. Above all, it was an effort to reconcile faith and reason. The foundations of Scholasticism were set down by Saint Augustine's juxtaposition of the Earthly and Heavenly Cities of Jerusalem (see p. 397). He argued that, although understanding can precede faith, faith leads to understanding. His esthetic argument, that beauty is symmetry, and the harmonious relation of parts to the whole, is consistent with the visual and structural order of Gothic.

At the end of the eleventh century, Anselm (c. 1033–1109), the Archbishop of Canterbury (see below), established a program based on Augustine's precepts. In the 1130s, the theologian Peter Abelard (1079–1142) published *Yes and No*, a treatise applying the dialectic method to theology, arguing from reason (*ratio*) on the one hand, and for and against an issue (*quaestio*) on the other. About this time, the writings of Aristotle (see p. 139) were revived in western Europe. By the thirteenth century, his logical system had been absorbed into Scholasticism.

The work that summed up Scholasticism at its peak was the *Summae Theologiae* of Thomas Aquinas (c. 1225–74). Influenced by Aristotelean logic, Aquinas discussed doctrine according to a system of argument, counter-argument, and solution. The synthetic character of this system established the relationship between faith and reason. It concluded that, far from being at odds, the one actually complements the other.

The architectural solutions which became typical of the Gothic cathedral are, in a sense, parallel to Scholastic logic. The sculptures and stained glass constitute an illustrated Bible. According to Panofsky, the Scholastic clarification of faith by intellectual demonstration parallels the articulation of the cathedral. For him, Amiens best illustrates a "final" solution in creating a uniformity of divergent features.

What began with Suger's desire for transparency in architecture led to the philosophical pursuit of a new totality. At Amiens, the three-part nave (counting its two side aisles) corresponds to the three-part transept (the two entrances and the section crossing the nave). The expansion of the nave into the five-part choir creates a logical transition to the semicircular ambulatory in the apse. And the curve of the ambulatory leads one naturally into the radiating chapels. The symmetrical towers repeat the symmetry of the transepts further east, and stand as equals on either side of the western entrance. Here, therefore, by the process of philosophical debate (*disputatio*), the Gothic architects finally arrived at *concordantia* (the harmonious reconciliation of seemingly contradictory elements).

Taking a specific architectural detail and applying its solution to Scholasticism, Panofsky cites the example of the rose window. At Saint-Denis (fig. 12.1), he argues, the window is too small; at Amiens (fig. 12.32) it is crowded by the surrounding elements. But at Reims (fig. 12.38) a sol-

ution has been found. There the architect has opened up the west façade wall and set the rose window inside the pointed arch of another huge window. As a result, the rose window is more logically connected to the west wall. Instead of being a round window in a rectangular wall as at Saint-Denis, Chartres, and Amiens, it is now a window in a window in a wall.

The new window—with the pointed arch—serves a transitional purpose, because it shares a structure with the wall, and colored glass with the rose window. Whether viewed from the exterior (fig. 12.38) or from the interior (fig. 12.39), the esthetic effect is striking in the grand vertical sweep of the wall. This is then unified by the repeated rose window inscribed in the pointed arch window over the door. (Note that in the exterior view, the rose window is repeated in each of the three tympanums.) The east-to-west view of the nave (fig. 12.39) accentuates the larger size of the upper rose window compared with the lower. Although such an arrangement would appear to defy structural logic, it works because the eye is immediately drawn upwards. This effect has a theological, as well as an architectural, purpose. It synthesizes the traditional association of height and greatness with the belief that spiritual perfection is attained in the light of the Heavenly City.

Sainte-Chapelle

The transcendent quality of Gothic light is nowhere more evident than in the reliquary chapel of Sainte-Chapelle in Paris (fig. **12.44**). It was commissioned by King Louis IX (who was canonized in 1297) and epitomizes the *rayonnant* style. Here the walls literally become glass, as the stone supports diminish. There is no transept, which allows the tall, thin colonnettes to rise uninterruptedly from a short, dimly lit first story. This clear distinction between the lower darkness and the upper light is an architectural mirror of traditional Christian juxtapositions associating darkness with the lower regions of hell, the Earthly City, and the pre-Christian era of the Old Testament. Light, in this context, evokes the Heavenly City, and the enlightened teachings of the New Testament. The same parallelism between Old and New Testaments determined the iconography of the scenes represented in the stained-glass windows. These metaphors are reinforced by the ceiling vaults, which are painted blue, and decorated with gold stars in the form of fleurs-de-lis—the emblem of the French kings.

12.44 Nave, Sainte-Chapelle, Paris, 1243–48. 32 × 99.5 ft (9.75 × 30.3 m). Thomas de Cormont, who also worked on Amiens Cathedral, designed Sainte Chapelle. It was the chapel of the French kings, located on the Ile-de-la-Cité, and attached to the palace.

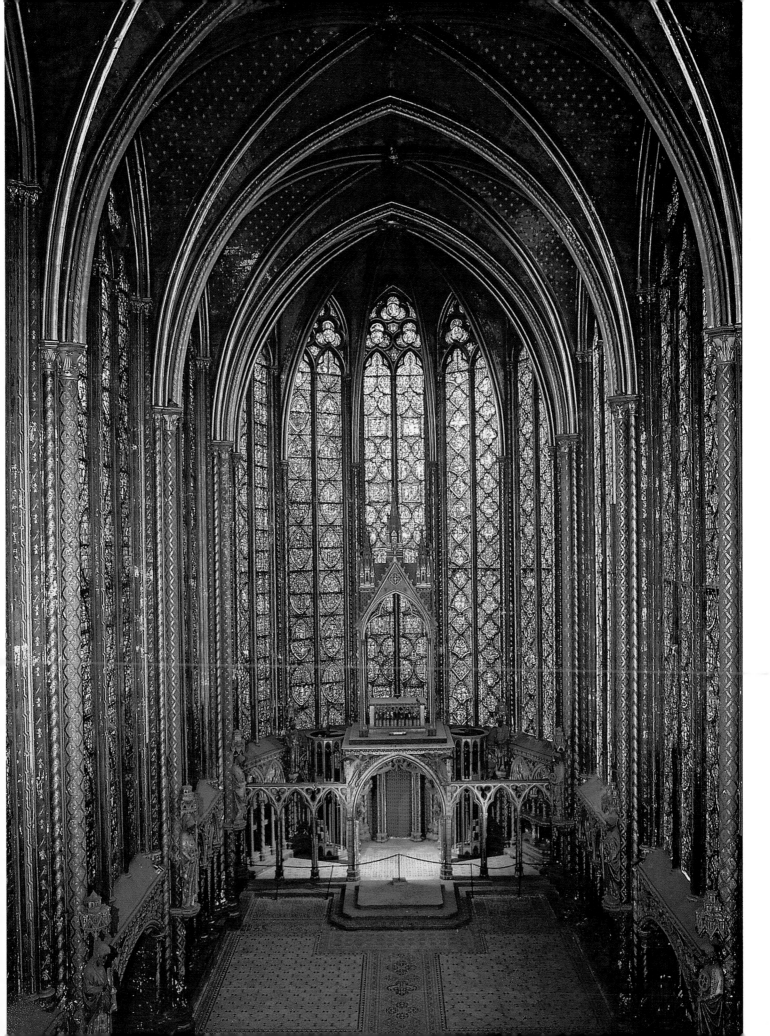

The original impetus behind the construction of Sainte-Chapelle is also based in tradition. Louis IX obtained from Byzantium crucifixion relics believed to be of the True Cross, the Crown of Thorns, the lance, sponge, and a nail. At the time of their arrival, Louis went to the gates of Paris to receive them. (This was in imitation of the last event in the Legend of the True Cross—see p. 372—when the Cross is restored to Jerusalem and the townspeople welcome it at the city gate.) The relics were placed in the large, Gothic-style gold and glass reliquary in the apse.

English Gothic

Within a generation of the new choir at Saint-Denis, the Gothic style had spread beyond France to other countries in western Europe. Among the first to adopt the new style was England. Since its defeat by the Normans in 1066, there had been commercial, cultural, and political contacts between the two countries.

Canterbury Cathedral

The Gothic style in England begins with the choir of Canterbury Cathedral (figs. **12.45–12.50**), in the county of Kent, in southeastern England. It was originally built in the Norman style, which developed in England after the conquest of 1066. In 1174 a fire destroyed the choir, and

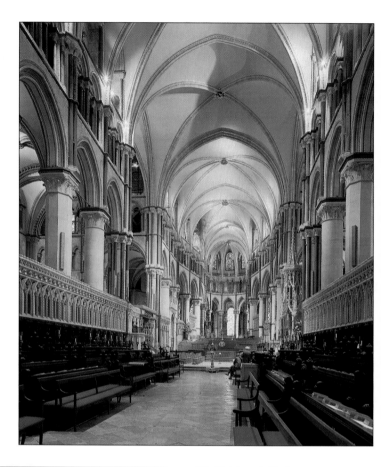

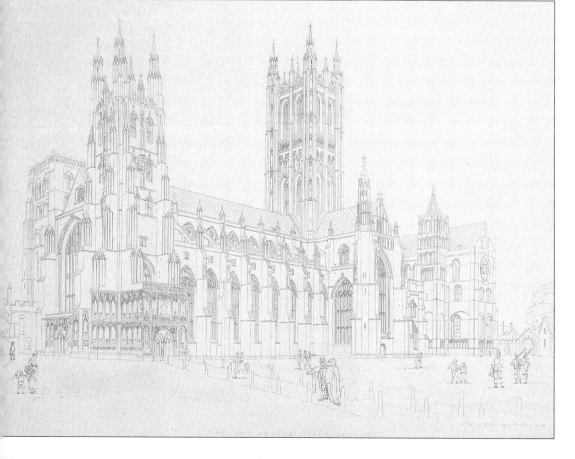

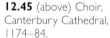

12.45 (above) Choir, Canterbury Cathedral, 1174–84.

12.46 J. Buckler, View of Canterbury Cathedral, Kent, England, in 1804. Consecrated in 1130. The Bell Tower—called the Bell Harry Tower—was added in the 15th century. Victoria and Albert Museum, London.

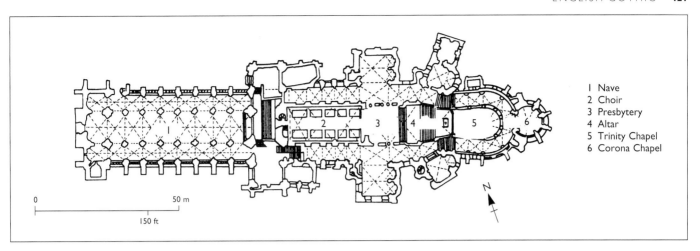

1 Nave
2 Choir
3 Presbytery
4 Altar
5 Trinity Chapel
6 Corona Chapel

0   50 m
150 ft

12.47 (above) Plan of Canterbury Cathedral.

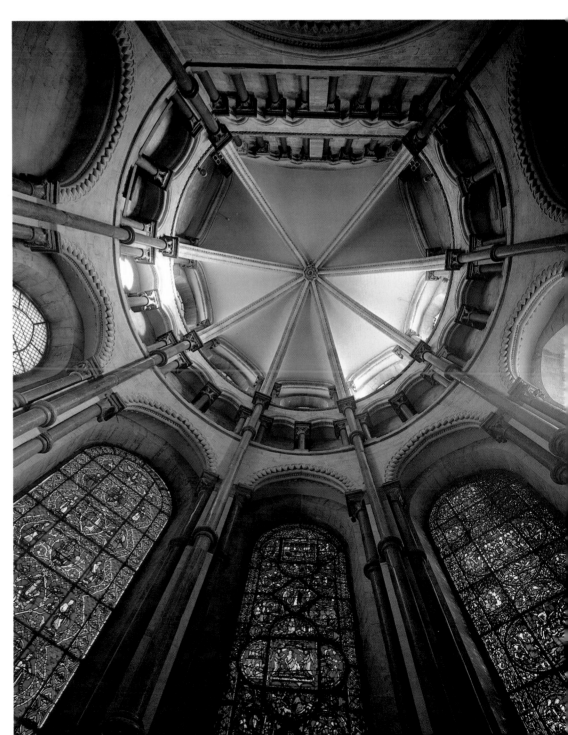

12.48 Vault, Corona Chapel, Canterbury Cathedral.

architects were summoned from France and England to advise on reconstruction. The French architect William of Sens began the new work with stone imported from Caen; five years into the project, he died of a 50-foot fall from the scaffolding, and an English William took over.

In the reconstruction of the choir, a Gothic superstructure was erected over the crypt, which was inside the remaining Norman walls. A monk of Canterbury, one Gervase, described the new Gothic elements and their effect. He noted that the number of piers had increased (by six), as had their length (by nearly 12 feet (3.7 m)), drawing attention also to the more elaborately carved capitals, the use of marble and different-colored stone, and the sexpartite arched-rib vaulting held in place by a keystone. The decorations observed by Gervase remained typical of English Gothic, and were derived from the taste for Anglo-Saxon interlace (cf. the lower arches in fig. 12.48).

William the Englishman added two shrines—the Trinity and Corona Chapels—for Thomas à Becket (see Box), whose cult attracted pilgrims to Canterbury (see Box). These additions made the plan more elongated and more complex than French Gothic cathedrals (fig. 12.47). The view of the ceiling of the Corona Chapel (fig. 12.48) shows the crownlike, octagonal organization of the vaults, and the variations in the supports. Also distinguishing Canterbury from French Gothic and increasing its complexity is the use of round as well as pointed arches within the same structure.

The stained glass in Canterbury Cathedral, on the other hand, is similar in style to French examples. Figures are

Thomas à Becket

Thomas à Becket (c. 1118–70) was a close friend of King Henry II of England. He was appointed Chancellor in 1155, and allied himself with Henry against the Church. Once elected Archbishop of Canterbury (in 1162), however, Becket changed his allegiance, now siding with the Church in matters of taxation and legal jurisdiction. The conflict between the secular and ecclesiastical courts escalated and enraged the king. Henry is recorded as having declared in a fit of anger: "Is there no one who will rid me of this low-born priest?"

Four knights obliged. They rode to Canterbury and found the Archbishop praying before the altar in the west transept of the cathedral. They killed him, and afterward Henry reportedly did penance for the murder. In 1173 Becket was canonized and became the object of a pilgrimage cult. The Corona Chapel (fig. 12.48) was built as a reliquary to house his scalp, which was severed from his head by the assassin's blow. In 1220, Saint Thomas' remains were transferred to the Trinity Chapel.

elongated, outlined in black, and occupy a relatively flat space. The details illustrated here have typological content, and also refer to the theme of pilgrimage. In *The Return of the Messengers from the Promised Land* (fig. 12.49), two men shoulder a huge bunch of grapes, and walk with a pilgrim's stick. The weight, centrality, and

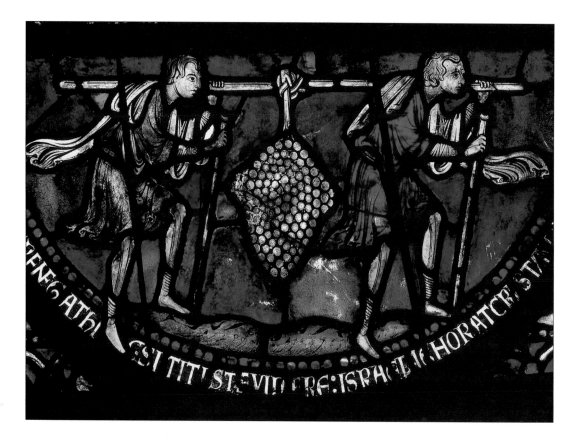

12.49 *The Return of the Messengers from the Promised Land*, detail of window, Corona Chapel, Canterbury Cathedral.

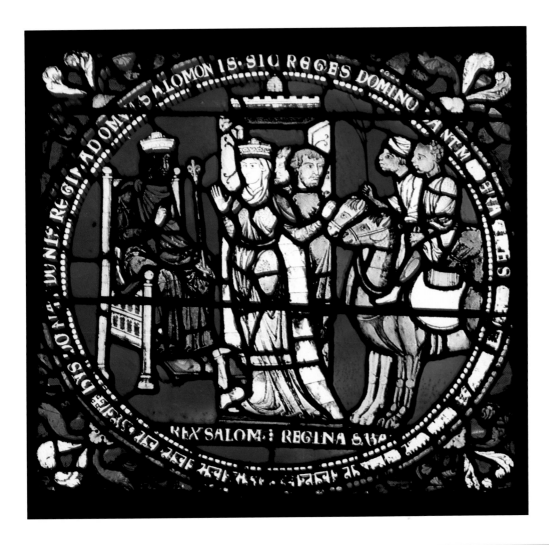

12.50 *Solomon and the Queen of Sheba*, detail of window, Canterbury Cathedral, late 12th century.

The *Canterbury Tales* (c. 1387)

The pilgrimage to Canterbury became the subject of one of the canonical works of English literature, Geoffrey Chaucer's *Canterbury Tales*. Chaucer (c. 1340–1400) held several offices at the English court, and in April 1388 decided to make a pilgrimage to Saint Thomas à Becket's shrine. The *Canterbury Tales* is a work of some 17,000 lines in prose and verse, predominantly rhyming couplets. The General Prologue describes thirty-one pilgrims, including Chaucer, gathered at the Tabard Inn at Southwark, the main entry to London from the south. The innkeeper, who is joining them, offers a free meal to whoever tells the best tale on return. If each person tells two tales, he proposes, the way will seem shorter. They take him up on his offer, and recount tales ranging from versions of myths and fables, to popular stories of the time. Several are harshly satirical and criticize the corruption of both the Church and society.

The *Prologue* is a vivid description of contemporary life. This is reflected in the broad spectrum of society represented by the pilgrims. They include a knight and a reeve (a bailiff or steward of a manor), a cook and a carpenter, a prioress and a pardoner (seller of indulgences). The most colorful character is the Wife of Bath, who extols the pleasures of the flesh, condemns celibacy, and enjoys her good fortune in having survived five husbands. Her tale, which is based on a medieval romance, reflects her philosophy. A convicted rapist is given one year to discover what women most want. An old hag offers him the answer in exchange for granting her one wish. He agrees, and she demands that he marry her. When they are in bed, she asks if he prefers her ugly and faithful, or beautiful and unfaithful. He leaves the decision to her, and she rewards him by becoming both beautiful and faithful.

slightly cruciform shape evoke the Crucifixion, while the grapes refer to the Eucharist.

Solomon and the Queen of Sheba (fig. 12.50) was an iconographic type for the Adoration of the Magi. Both Sheba and the three kings travel from east to west, Sheba to visit Solomon and the Magi to see Christ. This journey is symbolically replicated when one enters the cathedral and proceeds along the nave to the main altar supporting a crucifix. Solomon was a type for Christ, who calls himself "the new Solomon" in the Gospel of Matthew. When the pilgrim traveled to Canterbury, it was to worship the relics of Thomas à Becket as Sheba had bowed before Solomon and the Magi had knelt before Christ.

Salisbury Cathedral

English Gothic, as in the different-colored stone and elongated plan at Canterbury, was typically more varied than French Gothic. Salisbury Cathedral (fig. **12.51**) was built from 1220 onward in a relatively homogeneous style. It has a cloister (7 in fig. **12.52**), a feature of monastic communities that the English adopted as part of their cathedral plans. In contrast to French cathedrals, Salisbury has a double transept and a square apse. Its chapter house (8 in fig. 12.52) is octagonal, which also distinguishes English

12.51 Salisbury Cathedral, England, begun 1220. The magnificent tower and spire were added in the 14th century.

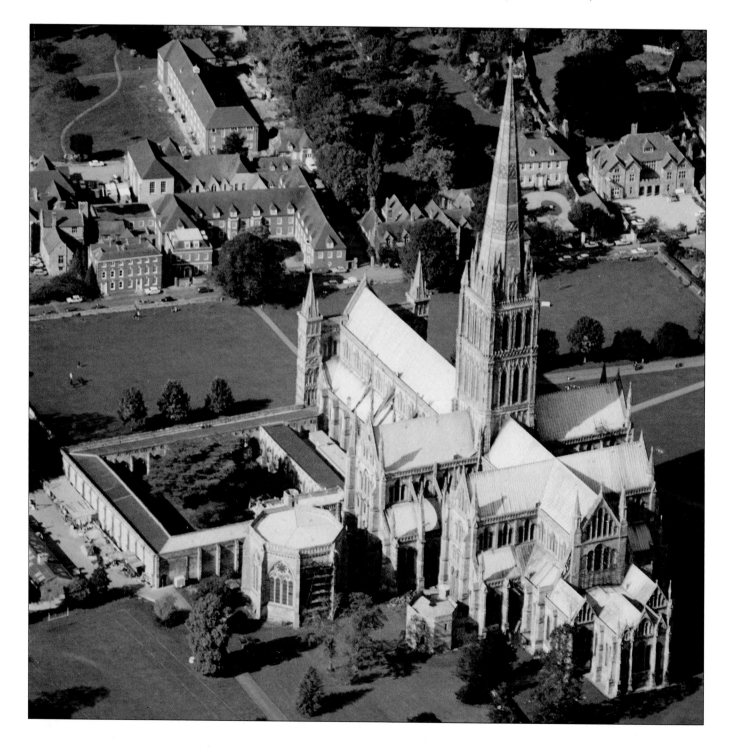

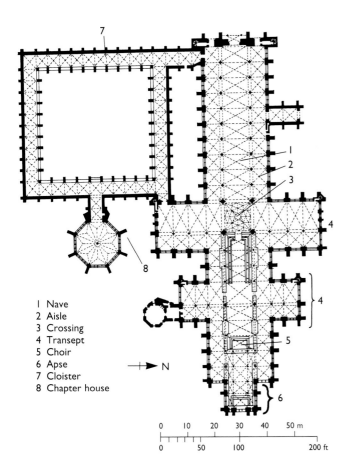

1 Nave
2 Aisle
3 Crossing
4 Transept
5 Choir
6 Apse
7 Cloister
8 Chapter house

→ N

0   10   20   30   40   50 m

0   50   100   200 ft

from French Gothic. Characteristic of English cathedrals, Salisbury is set in a cathedral close, a precinct of lawns and trees. Whereas French cathedrals usually rise directly from the streets and squares of a town, emphasizing their verticality, Salisbury is integrated into the natural land-scape, with horizontal planar thrusts. It has fewer stained-glass windows and therefore less need for exterior buttressing. The view of the ceiling (fig. **12.53**) shows the fanning out of the central pier into a vault that reverses the shape of the fan. The fan ribs join those of the vault and resemble the spokes of an inverted umbrella.

12.52 Plan of Salisbury Cathedral. The large square is a cloister attached to the south side of the cathedral. Apart from the cloister and a small porch on the north side of the nave, the plan is relatively symmetrical. The double transept and the square apse differ from the corresponding parts of a typical French Gothic cathedral.

12.53 Vault, chapter house, Salisbury Cathedral, 1263–84.

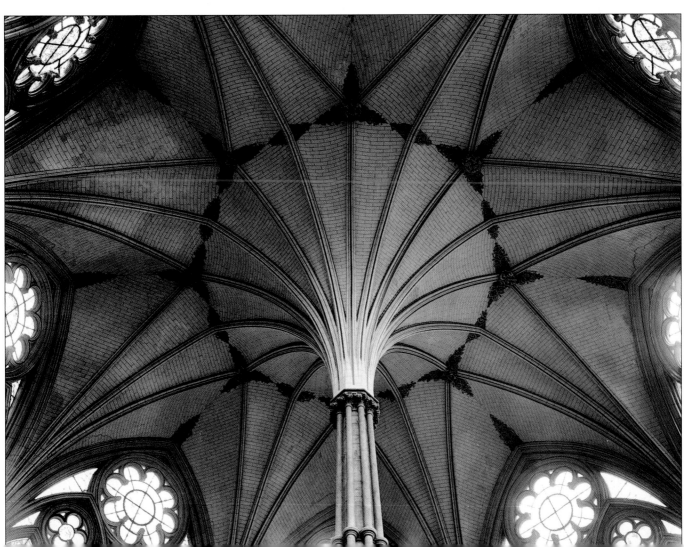

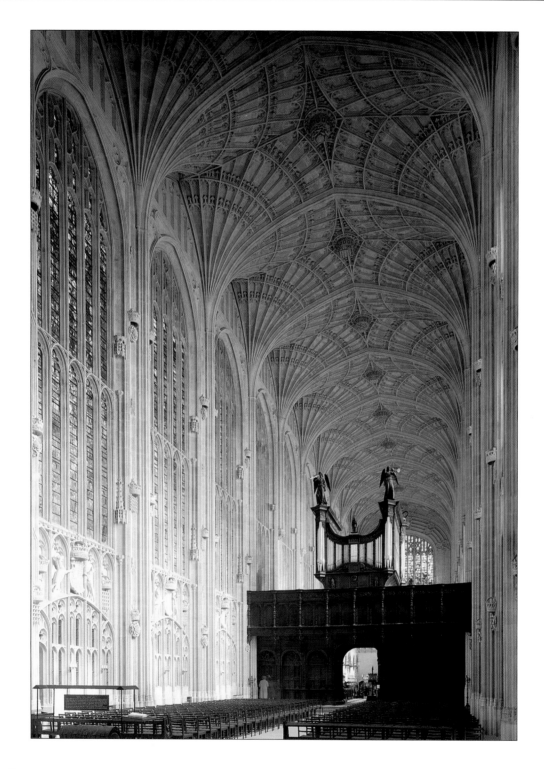

King's College Chapel, Cambridge

Fan vaulting became characteristic of English Gothic, one of the most spectacular examples being the chapel at King's College, Cambridge (fig. **12.54**). Its tall, unbroken supports exemplify the late Perpendicular style. The college was founded by Henry VI, in 1440, and he was probably involved in the plan of the chapel, assisted by the resident master mason, Reginald Ely. As at Sainte-Chapelle, the weight of the walls is supported by external

12.54 King's College Chapel, Cambridge, England. The chapel was founded in 1441, and its vaulting was designed by John Wastrell in 1508–15.

buttresses, which are masked by chapels on either side. William Wordsworth's sonnet "Tax not the royal saint with vain expense," written in 1822, was inspired by King's College Chapel and refers to the elegance and cost of such work.

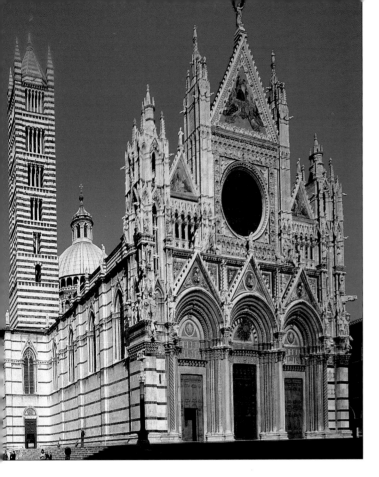

The Spread of Gothic

In Italy, the Gothic style was a continuation of Italian Romanesque, but it was also influenced by French Gothic. A good example of early Italian Gothic is the façade of Siena Cathedral, which dates to around 1284–99 (fig. **12.55**). It was designed by Giovanni Pisano (active c. 1265–1314), whose father, Nicola, is discussed in the next chapter. Although retaining the dark marble stripes of Italian Romanesque (see p. 381), the general organization of the façade is Gothic. There are three portals surmounted by sharply pointed arches, which recur in the triangular gables. A rose window dominates the center of the façade. In contrast to the French examples, however, most of the relief sculpture is on the tympanums. Other sculptures, on the gables and around the doors, are freestanding.

The largest Italian Gothic cathedral is in the northern city of Milan (fig. **12.56**). Begun in 1386, it is also one of the later examples of the style: the choir and transepts were not completed until 1450. The huge, imposing form looms over the square, combining massive size with delicate surface patterns. It is likely that the final structure reflects the debates between local Milanese architects and experts

12.55 (above) Siena Cathedral, Tuscany, Italy, 1284–99.

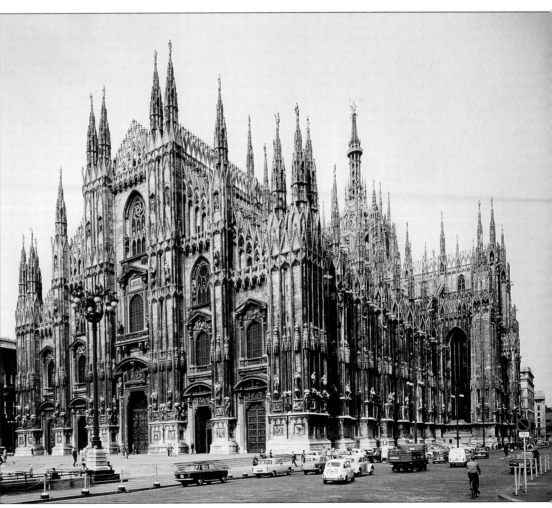

12.56 Milan Cathedral, Milan, Italy, begun 1386.

from France and Germany who advised on the project. The lacy effect of traceries, multiple windows, and thin, vertical spires is far more elaborate than the façade of the earlier, and more purely Italian, Siena Cathedral.

In 1306, the enormous cathedral of Palma on the Spanish island of Mallorca was begun (fig. **12.57**). Here it is shown from the southeast, where it towers over the edge of the sea. It is one of many buildings inspired by the ouster of Muslims from major cities in southern Europe just before the middle of the thirteenth century. The cathedral is noteworthy for its huge buttresses, as well as the Islamic influence evident on the entrance arch.

Among the most notable examples of the Gothic style in eastern Europe is Prague Cathedral, commissioned in 1344 by Emperor Charles IV. The original designs were made by a Frenchman who died in 1356, and work was resumed by Peter Parler (1333–99), a member of a family of master masons active in southern Germany. The view illustrated here (fig. **12.58**) shows the vertical emphasis of the pinnacled buttresses around the apse and the radiating chapels.

In terms of secular architecture, the Doges' (Senators') Palace on the Piazza San Marco is characteristic of Venetian Gothic (fig. **12.59**). The first two stories of the façade consist of a lower portico surmounted by an open loggia. These create a striking pattern of light and dark formed by the slightly pointed arches and the lobed windows. The upper story façade is a more solid wall, faced with a pink and white surface pattern that lightens its effect. Above this is a row of delicate pinnacles that repeat the lacy, curvilinear patterns of the lower levels. Because Venice had been for centuries an important seaport on the east coast of Italy, its architecture reflects the cosmopolitan character of the city.

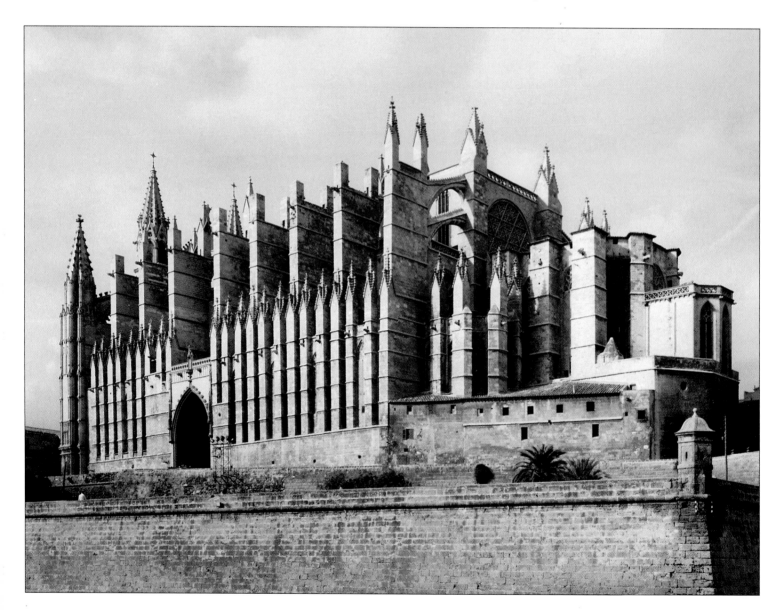

12.57 Southeast view of Palma de Mallorca Cathedral, island of Mallorca, begun 1306.

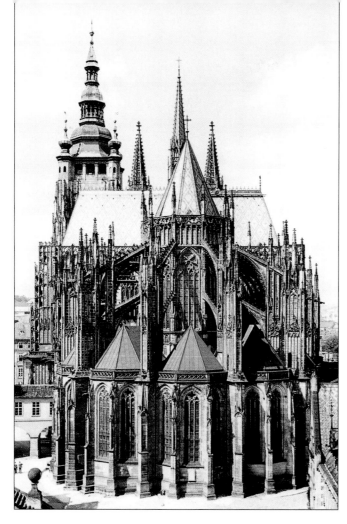

12.58 Apse, Prague Cathedral, Czech Republic.

12.59 (below) Doges' Palace, Venice, Italy. The façade dates from the 1420s.

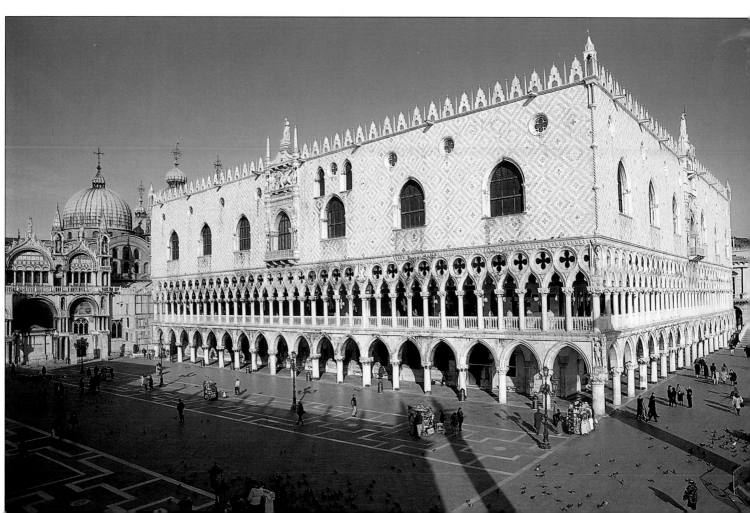

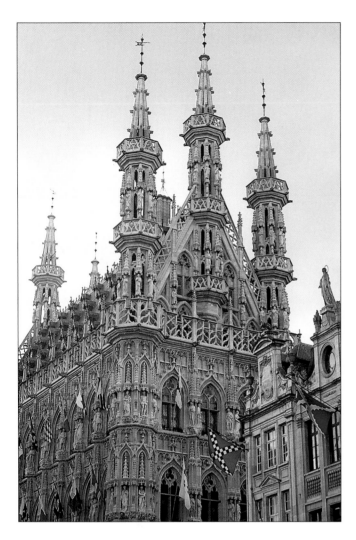

12.60 (above) Town Hall, Louvain, Belgium, 1448.

12.61 Aerial view of Saint Patrick's Cathedral, New York, 1858–79, spires 1888.

Belgium, which was in the diocese of Cologne, in Germany, was well known for its town halls and guild halls. These reflected the commercial successes, especially of the cloth industry, in the fifteenth century. The Town Hall at Louvain (known in Flemish as Leuven), which dates to 1448, is another example of secular Gothic architecture. It has an elaborate façade with three towers, one at each side and a third over the central gable (fig. **12.60**).

In the nineteenth-century Neo-Gothic style (see Vol. II, Chapter 22), aspects of Gothic were revived, especially in England and America. Figure **12.61** is an aerial view of Saint Patrick's Cathedral in New York City, designed by James Renwick and William Bodrigue. It was built from 1858 to 1879, and the spires were completed in 1888. The basic elements of Gothic—a cruciform plan, a west–east orientation, pointed arches, and architectural layout—are retained. Nor has its imposing verticality been overshadowed by the much taller skyscrapers that were built subsequently.

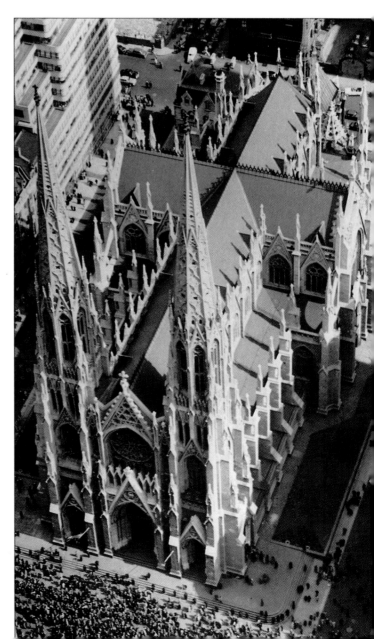

	Style/Period	Works of Art	Cultural/Historical Developments
1000	GOTHIC 11th century	Saint-Etienne (**12.8–12.10**), Caen Durham Cathedral (**12.11, 12.13**) **Saint-Etienne**	Edward the Confessor begins building Westminster Abbey (1052) Permanent separation of Roman and Eastern churches (1054) Normans under William the Conqueror invade England (1066) Beginnings of secular music (c. 1100) **Durham Cathedral**
1100	GOTHIC 12th century	Canterbury Cathedral (**12.45–12.46,** **12.48–12.50**) Saint-Denis (**12.1–12.2**), Paris Chartres Cathedral (**12.5, 12.17–12.19,** **12.22–12.27, 12.30–12.31**)	Suger named Abbot of Saint-Denis (1122) Birth of Moses Maimonides, Jewish religious philosopher, 1134 (d. 1204) Game of chess introduced into England (c. 1150) University of Paris founded (1150) First silver florins minted at Florence (1189)
1200	GOTHIC 13th century **Sainte-Chapelle**	Carpenters' Guild Signature Window (**12.14**), Chartres *Jeroboam Worshiping Golden Calves* (**12.7**), Chartres Reims Cathedral (**12.39–12.41**) Salisbury Cathedral (**12.51, 12.53**) Amiens Cathedral (**12.32, 12.34–12.37**) Sketchbook of Villard de Honnecourt (**12.15–12.16**) Hildegard of Bingen, *Antichrist's Birth and* *Destruction* (**12.29**) *Antichrist as a Three-headed Tyrant* (**12.28**) Sainte-Chapelle (**12.44**), Paris Philip I granting privileges, Saint Martin-des- Champs (**12.42**) Pisano, Siena Cathedral (**12.55**), Siena	King John signs Magna Carta (1215) Dominican Order founded (1216) Death of Francis of Assisi (1226) Kublai Khan ruler of the Mongols (1260–94) Arabic numerals introduced into Europe (late 1200s) Dante Alighieri, Italian poet, author of *The Divine Comedy* (1265–1321) Jacopo da Voragine (c. 1228–98) publishes *The Golden* *Legend*, a collection of apocryphal religious stories (1266–83) Marco Polo travels from Venice to China (1271–95) Thomas Aquinas writes *Summa Theologica* (1273) Rise of Florence as a leading commercial center (c. 1280) Fall of Acre; end of Christian rule in the East (1291)
1300	GOTHIC 14th century	Palma de Mallorca Cathedral (**12.57**) Scenes from the *Life of Saint Denis* (**12.43**) Prague Cathedral (**12.58**) Milan Cathedral (**12.56**)	
1400	GOTHIC 15th century	Doges' Palace (**12.59**), Venice King's College Chapel (**12.54**), Cambridge Town Hall (**12.60**), Louvain	
1800	GOTHIC 19th century	Saint Patrick's Cathedral (**12.61**), New York	**Doges' Palace** **Milan Cathedral**

Buddhist and Hindu Developments in East Asia

6th–13th Century

In 1210 the Mongols, Central Asian nomads who were feared in Europe as the Antichrist (see p. 407), began their conquest of China. Leading the so-called Mongol hordes was Jenghiz Khan. Fifty years later, his sons ruled a vast territory. By 1279, his grandson Kublai Khan had founded the Yuan Dynasty and become its first emperor. This conquest resulted in a unification of China, which would be ruled by khans until 1368. Under Mongol control, China continued to trade with western Europe, exporting silk cloth, ceramics, and carpets. These rela-

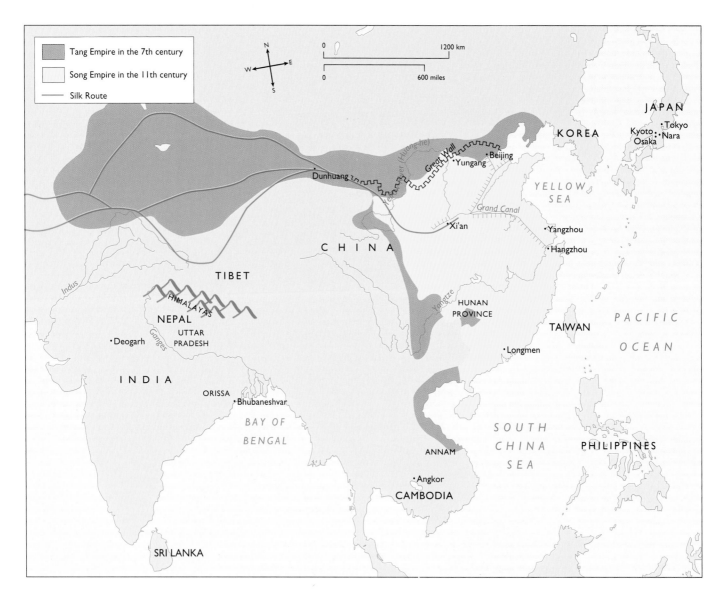

12.A Map of East Asia.

tively transportable items exposed Europeans to Far Eastern art forms and motifs that occasionally appear in Western art.

The Venetian merchant Marco Polo (c. 1254–1324) wrote an account of his travels in Asia; although its authenticity has been doubted, the Western image of the Far East during the thirteenth century was long based on this source.

Buddhist Paradise Sects

The Buddhist Paradise sects responsible for the change in the representation of the Buddha between the period of the Yungang Caves (see p. 316) and those at Longmen (see p. 317) fostered a new imagery in painting. Spectacular examples of paradise iconography from the eighth century have been found in caves at Dunhuang. Nearly one thousand miles (1600 km) west of Yungang, the Dunhuang oasis was the easternmost stop on the Silk Route in Central Asia.

Buddha Preaching the Law (fig. **12.B**) from Cave 17 at Dunhuang shows the rich, bright colors used to express the wealth of Amitabha's Great Western Paradise. The Buddha sits cross-legged under an elaborate canopy on a lotus throne, which symbolizes *nirvana*, his blue hair contrasting sharply with the bright orange of his robe. Four elegantly attired bodhisattvas sit at the corners of his throne. Behind the Buddha, to the left and right, are two sets of three monks, who appear to turn in space. Their

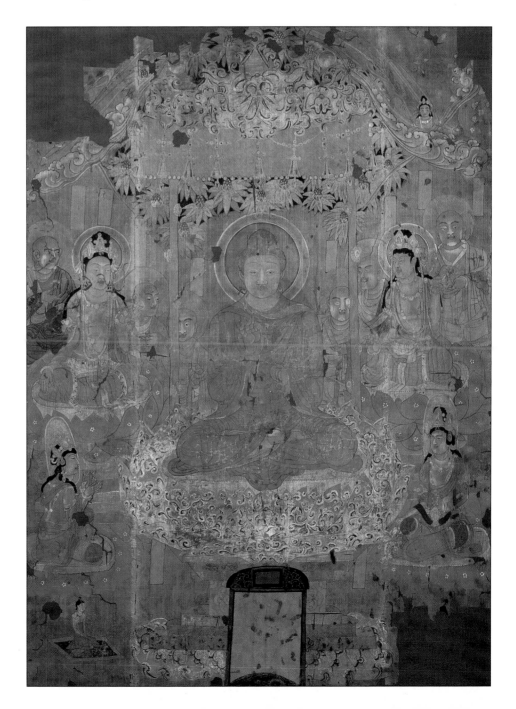

12.B *Buddha (Shakyamuni or Amitabha) Preaching the Law*, Cave 17, Dunhuang Province, China, early 8th century. Ink and colors on silk, 11 ft 6 in (3.5 m) high. British Museum, London. Both this Buddha image and the one in figure 12.C were part of an important cache of manuscripts and art hidden by the monks of Dunhuang in the 11th century. It was discovered in 1907–8 by Sir Aurel Stein, an English archaeologist, who sent as much of the hoard as he could to the British Museum in London. Many such banners were apparently produced in monastery workshops. They were sold to pilgrims as offerings to be laid in Dunhuang's famous Caves of the Thousand Buddhas. The blank space at the bottom of each image was intended for its donor's customized dedication inscription.

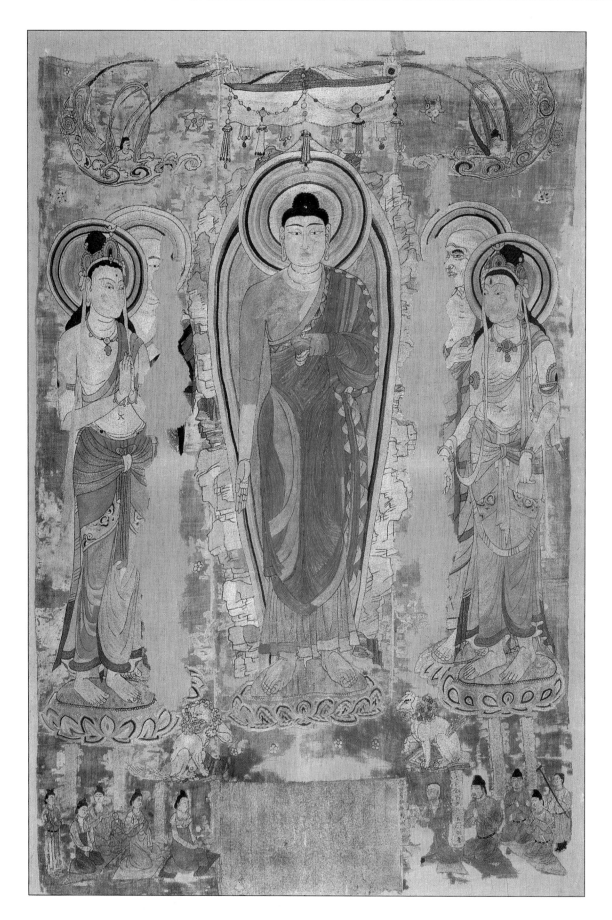

12.C *Shakyamuni Buddha Preaching on Vulture Peak*, Cave 17, Dunhuang Province, China, 8th century. Silk embroidery, 20 ft (6.09 m) high. British Museum, London. This large image, created entirely of fine stitches in silk thread, demonstrates the high level of skill attained by Chinese embroiderers in rendering three-dimensional forms.

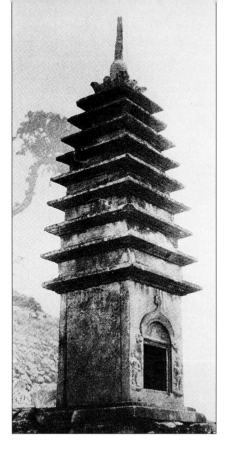

12.D Pagoda, Yunshusu, Mount Fang, Hopei, China, early 8th century.

small size indicates their lesser status, and they reinforce the Buddha's central position and iconic quality by focusing their gaze on him. The tiny female donor in the lower left corner had a male counterpart on the right, but all that remains is his hat.

Among the doctrines related to the Paradise sects was Tiantai, according to which everyone could achieve buddhahood. This belief derived from the *Lotus Sutra*'s doctrine that faith, rather than deeds, could lead to salvation. The silk embroidery of *Shakyamuni Buddha Preaching on Vulture Peak* (fig. **12.C**) depicts the Buddha propounding the Tiantai Law, as described in the *Lotus Sutra*. He stands under a canopy on a small lotus throne, surrounded by a mandorla, against a backdrop of rocks representing the Vulture Peak. Two bodhisattvas stand on either side of him, with a pair of small lion guardians below. At the bottom of the image are tiny figures of donors.

The Pagoda

The interiors of many of the Yungang and Dunhuang caves contained multistoried towers. These became the characteristic Buddhist structure of the Far East (China, Korea, and Japan; also known as East Asia). Beginning in the seventh century, **pagodas**—as they were called by the Portuguese living in India—were a synthesis of Indian stupas and Chinese military watchtowers. Like stupas, pagodas have a reliquary function, and a setting that leaves enough space for worshipers to circumambulate them, although later Far Eastern pagodas can actually be entered. The pagoda was conceived in sections, which

were stacked one on top of the other and tapered toward the top. Each section was a cube, with an eavelike cornice projecting over it. A pyramidal form at the top was surmounted by a vertical element symbolizing the axis-pillar of the World Mountain. Inside the caves, these spires merged into the roof.

The pagoda developed from an interior tower-like structure into an exterior, freestanding one made of wood, brick, or stone in several variations on the basic form. Some types were extremely elaborate. The individual tiers ranged from two to fifteen in number, although seven was standard. An early eighth-century pagoda with nine tiers is illustrated in figure **12.D**, while the mid-eleventh-century example in figure **12.E** has thirteen.

12.E Pagoda, Kaifeng, Hunan Province, China, mid-11th century.

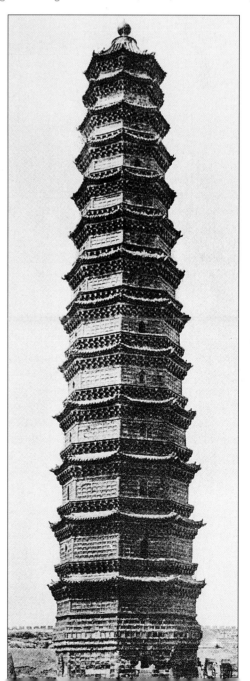

Very little early Chinese architecture survives, but its descendants are found elsewhere in the Far East. From early on, the pagoda was assimilated throughout East Asia into Buddhist architectural complexes, especially monasteries. Besides signifying the spiritual force of Buddhism, the pagoda was also believed to represent the passage of time. Relics embodied the past, the structure itself the present, and its height the future aspirations of faith. Like the towers of Gothic cathedrals, pagodas were the tallest part of Buddhist monasteries and were thus visible from afar. In each case, the vertical plane functions as a visual statement of presence, power, and piety.

The Buddhist Monastery: Horyu-ji

Buddhism reached Japan from China through images and *sutras* sent by the Korean kingdom of Paekche in the middle of the sixth century. Chinese culture was of great interest in Japan at the time. The imported religion flourished under the patronage of Japan's first great leader, Prince Shotoku (574–622). He founded what became the monastery of Horyu-ji (*ji* meaning "temple") in Nara (which from 710 to 784 was the capital of Japan), 25 miles (40 km) east of Osaka.

Horyu-ji's five-tiered pagoda (*Goju-no-to*), dating from the late seventh century, is a good example of a pagoda in a monastic community (fig. **12.F**). The gently sloping hills on the outskirts

of Nara provide a natural enclosure for the monastery complex (fig. **12.G**), which not only is the earliest surviving Buddhist architectural group in Japan, but also includes the oldest wooden temple in the world. In addition to the pagoda, the small complex consisted of a **kondō** (the Golden Hall; fig. **12.H**), a cloister, temples, living quarters for the monks, and a gate. The complex was arranged on an east–west axis that ran from the gate, between the *kondō* and the pagoda, to a refectory (now destroyed). The pagoda faces the *kondō*, creating a balance of asymmetrical structures.

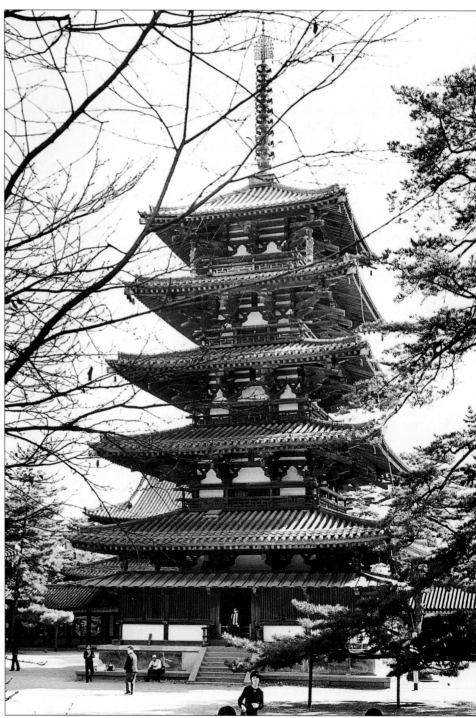

12.F Five-storied pagoda, *Goju-no-to*, monastery of Horyu-ji, Nara, Japan, late 7th century.

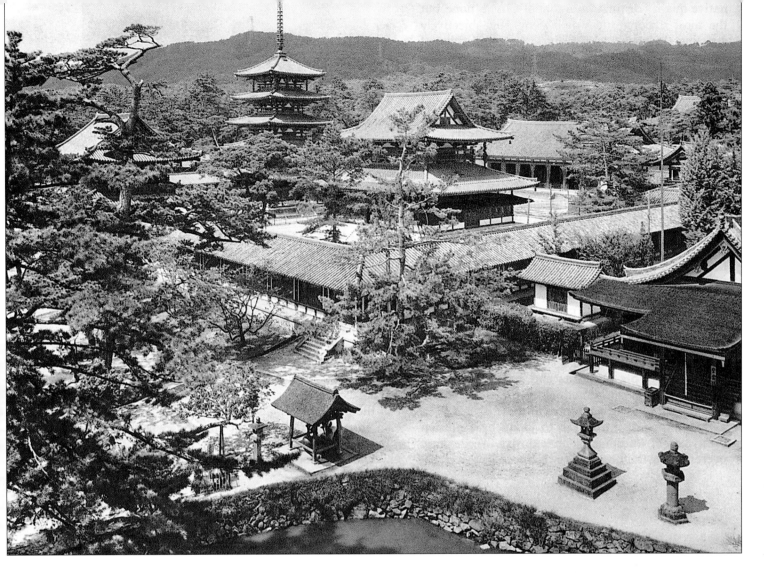

12.G (above) View of the monastery of Horyu-ji, Nara, late 7th century. Prince Shotoku's original temple complex was burned in 670 and rebuilt nearby as the monastery of Horyu-ji.

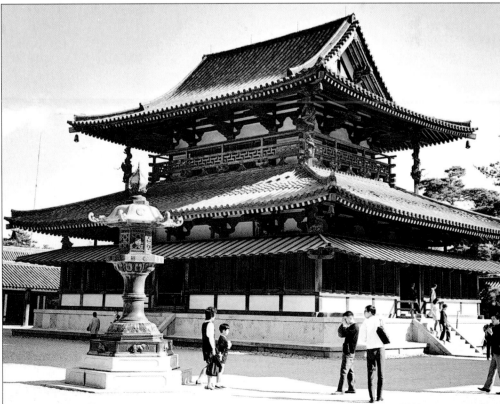

12.H *Kondō* (Golden Hall), Horyu-ji, Nara, late 7th century.

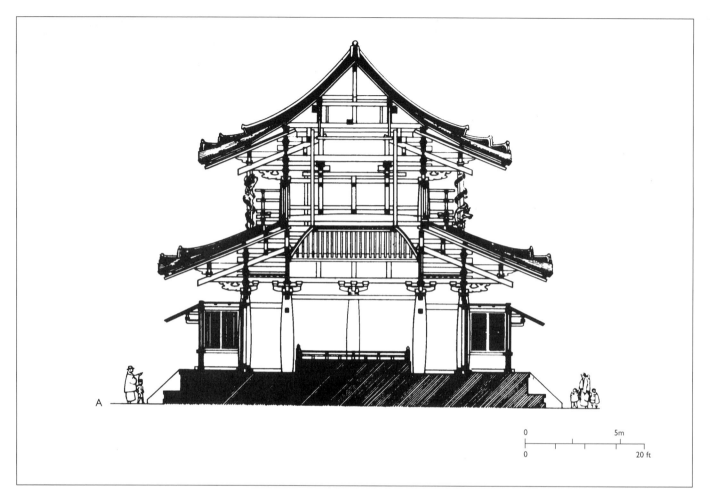

12.I Diagram section of the Horyu-ji *kondō*.

The *kondō* (fig. 12.H), also derived from a Chinese building type, is supported by a stone plinth oriented to the cardinal points of the compass. Stairs at the center of each side lead to double doors. The basic elevation is post-and-lintel, with the lintel inserted into the upper part of the post (figs. **12.I** and **12.J**). The points where post and lintel join are reinforced by brackets decorated with carvings. Such brackets channeled the thrust of the tile roof through the wooden posts and into the main foundation supports, and remained a strong design element in later Japanese architecture. By making the inner posts taller than those at the ends, it was possible to create a curved roof supported by the extended (**cantilevered**) lintels.

The Hindu Temple

The roots of Hinduism (see Box) predated Buddhism in South Asia by some fifteen hundred years, and the newer faith borrowed many ideas and artistic motifs from the older one. Hinduism also spread to other regions, particularly to Southeast Asia, although to a lesser degree than Buddhism.

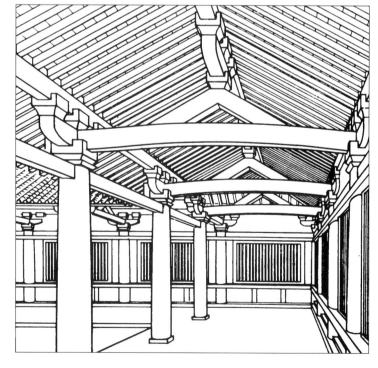

12.J Drawing of part of the Horyu-ji *kondō*. Gallery, showing post-and-lintel construction.

Hinduism

Hinduism is the only major religion without a founder, being based on an accumulation of sacred and devotional texts, myths, rituals, and practices. Its origins lie somewhere in the second millennium B.C., following the Aryan invasion of the Indian subcontinent (see p. 262). Hindus conceive of the universe as cyclical, destroyed by fire, and dissolving into the ocean at the end of each cosmic age, to be reborn again and again. This universe is conceived of as an egg, separated into three regions where gods, humans, and demons—the forces of order on the one hand, and of chaos on the other—battle for control. Hinduism recognizes this cosmic struggle as a necessary, even desirable, search for balance between opposing forces.

The Hindu gods appear in many manifestations, and in art the varied iconography of a single deity represents its different aspects. Often, like Vishnu (see fig. 12.M), the gods are represented with multiple limbs and heads as a sign of their superhuman powers. Each deity is believed to embody a truth that transcends its physical guise, and images are a conduit for bringing the divine world into contact with the human. By making sculptures of the gods beautiful—following certain canons of proportion and form, clothing and anointing the figures, and so forth—deities can be induced to inhabit their representations. Priests chant in Sanskrit, the sacred language of Hinduism, pray, and make offerings to attract the gods.

The Hindu pantheon is vast and includes deities assimilated from indigenous nature cults (such as *Yakshas* and *Yakshis*), as well as from early Aryan religion. The abode of the gods is Mount Meru, the central World Mountain whose axis links earth to heaven. A trio of male gods is responsible for the great cycles of cosmic time: Brahma (the Creator), Vishnu (the Preserver), and Shiva (the Destroyer). Each has a powerful female energy, his *shakti*. While Hindus identify themselves as either Vaishnavite or Shaivite (devotees of Vishnu or Shiva respectively), they honor multiple deities.

Embodying the multiplicity that is characteristic of Hinduism, Shiva is both destructive and creative. He is associated with male sexual energy and procreation (worshiped in the form of a *lingam*, or phallus, or in anthropomorphic guise astride his bull Nandi), as well as with asceticism and sacred texts (in the form of a meditating yogi with matted hair, clad in an animal skin). He is the three-eyed lord of the beasts and of the battlefield (symbolized by his trident), and patron god of the arts. His consort is Uma, daughter of the Himalaya Mountains. Their elephant-headed, pot-bellied son Ganesh is popularly worshiped as the remover of obstacles.

Vishnu keeps the universe in equilibrium. According to the creation myth illustrated in figure 12.M, he dreams the plan of the universe at the beginning of each cycle of existence—hence, we are living Vishnu's dream, and what we perceive as reality is actually illusion. Vishnu has ten *avatars*, or manifestations, among them a fish, tortoise, boar, man-lion, a dwarf who encompasses the universe in three strides, and Rama, the hero of the *Ramayana* epic. (Hanuman, a monkey-general who helps Rama, is a popular god.) Vishnu's best-loved *avatar* is Krishna, the blue-skinned, flute-playing erotic trickster god. In each of these forms, Vishnu saves the world from destruction by demons. To upstage Buddhism, its younger rival, Hinduism, incorporated the Buddha as another *avatar* of Vishnu.

Among Hinduism's many important female deities are Sarasvati (goddess of learning), and Lakshmi (goddess of fortune). The holy rivers Ganga (Ganges) and Yamuna (Jumna) are worshiped as fertility goddesses. Collectively, Hindu goddesses may be thought of as embodying aspects of Devi, the Great Mother. Like Shiva, Devi is both creative and destructive: she is a voluptuous, maternal nurturer and she is also Kali, the skeletal, bloodthirsty hag who eats children; she is both a subservient consort of a male god and Durga, the super-warrior whose strength combines that of the male gods to defeat an otherwise invincible Buffalo Demon. Devi is also worshiped in the ancient form of the Sapta Matrikas, the Seven Mothers. She is closely associated with nature and fertility, and is sometimes represented as a *yoni* (female sex organ) encircling a *lingam*, thus symbolizing the conjunction of female and male energies. Outside mainstream Hinduism, goddess worship is a powerful force in esoteric Tantric sects (Buddhist as well as Hindu), whose practices may include ritual sexual intercourse and offering sacrificial animal blood to the goddess.

One of the central Hindu beliefs is reincarnation leading to *nirvana*, the ultimate release from the cycle of rebirth, when the soul unites with the cosmos. Each incarnation is a stage in the long journey toward liberation from this illusory world, and progress toward *nirvana* depends on karma, the quality of behavior in a current or previous life. While in the world, everyone is ruled by *Dharma*, the law, in addition to which each hereditary social class (*varnas*, or caste) has its own code of conduct. Society is divided into an elite, ritually pure Brahmin caste, whose men are traditionally priests; a warrior and ruler Kshatriya caste; an artisan and merchant Vaishya caste; and a peasant Shudra caste. Those beneath caste, considered ritually polluted, were known as Untouchables until they were renamed Harijans (Children of God) by Mahatma Gandhi (1869–1948) in an attempt to improve their social status. While hereditary caste is no longer all-important in the lives of Hindus, one must still be born Hindu in order to be Hindu.

The earliest sacred structures on the Indian subcontinent may have been *vedikās* (railings; see p. 266) that surrounded trees and stones to mark places of spiritual significance. As Vedic religion developed, Brahmin priests constructed temporary, open-air fire altars according to a strict geometric system. Hindu temple architecture evolved from these two traditions. (While fire altars are rarely built today, the ancient practice of worshiping at very simple outdoor shrines continues.)

The highly sophisticated mathematics of Hindu temples was codified in texts called *Shilpa shastras*, in which temples were conceptualized as both anthropomorphic forms and as *mandalas* (cosmic diagrams connecting the human world with the celestial). The temples are believed to concentrate divine energy and anchor sacred space along a world axis.

Basically Hindu temples, like Greek temples, are houses for deities. Images abound, and worship takes place throughout temple precincts. A temple's main cult image is contained within its inner sanctuary, or **garbha griha** (literally "womb chamber"), which is a small, windowless, cube-shaped *cella*. This dark, intimate space is typically perfumed by incense and lit by the glow of oil lamps. Priests and worshipers perform *puja*, or devotions. The protective, womb-like function of the Hindu temple is reflected by the thickness of the ceiling and the *cella* walls.

Hindu worship is not congregational in the Western sense. Instead, priests perform elaborate sacred rites on behalf of their communities. *Puja* at a temple begins with the sunrise, when a priest opens the chamber of the "womb" and salutes the door guardians. In a ritual involving all the senses, he sounds a bell and claps to expel negative spirits, arouse the deity or deities, and announce his presence. He then chants hymns and *mantras* (ritual sacred formulae), accompanied by *mudras* (symbolic hand gestures). Vessels are readied for the cleansing and dressing of images, which are anointed, draped with garlands, and offered specially prepared food. When the priest has completed his ceremonial duties, he circumambulates the statue clockwise, bows, and leaves the sanctuary.

For Hindus, the temple was one stop on a long journey that was a metaphor of the quest for spiritual perfection. In the course of this journey, worshipers progress from a large to a small space, from natural light to a dark interior, and from the illusory complexities of the material world to spiritual simplicity.

These beliefs are reflected in the concepts underlying temple construction. First, a sacred site is chosen—a grove for its links to early tree cults, a river for its life-giving water, or a mountain by association with Mount Meru (see p. 439). Several years are then dedicated to purifying the ground and ridding it of evil and impure spirits. Sacred cows graze on the site in order to enhance its fertility. The ground plan is thought of as a mandala, which maps divine space. This is a geometric "picture" of the pantheon and a miniature manifestation of the cosmos, in which the temple represents Mount Meru. After its plan has been laid out, a temple's proportions are arranged according to a unit of measurement deemed to be in alignment with cosmic harmony. Finally, foundation stones are placed in the ground and construction begins (see Box).

The materials of which Hindu temples are built, like the Hindu social structure, were conceived of hierarchically in the early *Shilpa shastras*. Some recommended stone and wood for the higher classes of society, while others related materials to gender. Generally, however, most Hindu temples were of stone and the color of the stone was associated with a particular caste—white being reserved for Brahmins. Either stone was quarried, and bricks baked, near a building site, or the materials were floated to the

The Hindu Artist

For Hindus, art is an expression that transcends the individual artist. The creation of religious art is both a hereditary vocation and an act of devotion, an offering to the gods. Hindu artistic activity centers around temples, much as the cathedral towns of medieval Europe were a focus of Christian artistic production. Some Hindu artists were organized into guilds, which tended to be composed of family groups, and within which skills were passed from one generation to the next. The guilds set ethical and artistic standards, as well as rules regulating the lives of their members. They set prices and arranged contracts. Duties were strictly divided by rank, including those of the chief architect (*sutradhara*), the general overseer, the head stonemason, and head image-maker (sculptor). Each supervised a particular group of workers. Brahmins, who were expert in art theory and iconography, were in charge of quality and content. The Vaishyas under them were regarded as skilled laborers.

Artists and their families who lived and worked at temple sites were so numerous that thriving communities grew up around them. Since temples were the intellectual as well as spiritual centers of their communities, schools were established, and festivals were held in their vicinity.

The financing of Hindu temple construction was primarily in the hands of royal patrons. It was supported by donations of money, cattle (sacred to Hindus), objects of value, land grants, and services from others. Contributions to temples were partly motivated by the donor's hope of accumulating good *karma*, and of receiving divine assistance. Since Hindu temples amassed considerable wealth, which included land, they became major employers and landlords. In southern India, there are vast temple complexes that were once cities-within-cities, employing hundreds of specialized artists.

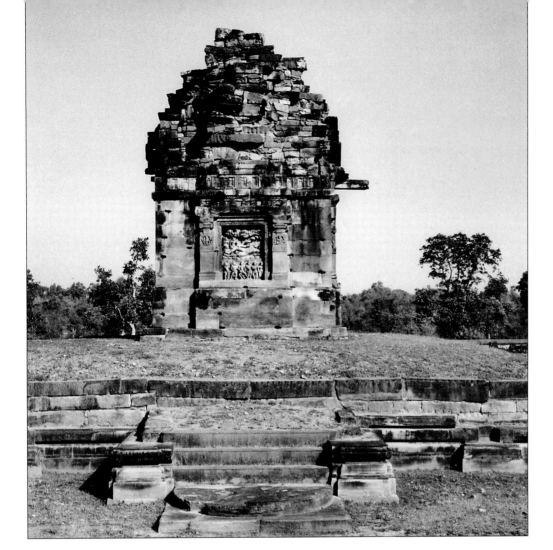

site on barges or brought on wood rollers by elephants. Stone blocks were shaped by masons, and hauled up onto the structure by a pulley system. They were then held in place with iron clamps. In what remained basically a post-and-lintel elevation system, Hindu temples had projecting lintels made possible by the strength of the clamps. The main supporting elements were stone columns, and doors were of wood. Window bars were stone copies of wooden prototypes. Hindu temple architecture is characterized by a wealth of regional variations on two general temple types—the northern and southern—differing primarily in the forms of their towers.

The Vishnu Temple
(6th century)

The early sixth-century temple of Vishnu at Deogarh, in Uttar Pradesh (figs. **12.K** and **12.L**), exemplifies early northern-style Hindu temples. This relatively simple, one-chambered structure was crowned by a *shikhara* (northern-style tower), most of which is now in ruins. Its cubic *garbha griha* (sanctuary) stood on a raised plinth, and was accessible by a stairway on each side. The dark corner rectangles on the plan mark lesser shrines dedicated to different gods. The temple's relief sculpture, with its rounded, rhythmically swaying forms, embodies the classic Gupta style. In the view shown here, one of the framed panels containing reliefs is visible.

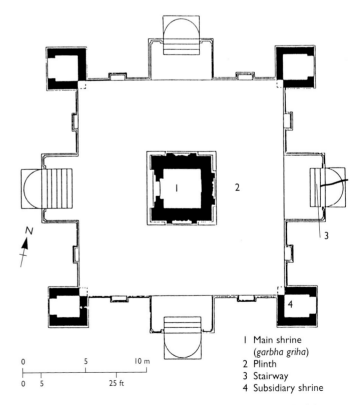

1 Main shrine
  (*garbha griha*)
2 Plinth
3 Stairway
4 Subsidiary shrine

12.L Plan of temple of Vishnu, Deogarh, Uttar Pradesh, early 6th century.

The relief panel of *Vishnu Sleeping on Ananta* (fig. **12.M**), on the south side, depicts the origin of the universe and the forces of evil within it. The large reclining figure of Vishnu, whose four arms reflect his powers, dominates the image. Crowned and jeweled, he dreams the universe into existence as he sleeps on Ananta, the Endless Serpent encircling the world, whose cobra-hood frames the god's head. Holding Vishnu's foot is his wife Lakshmi, the goddess of fortune. As his *shakti*, she represents his female nature, which energizes his male self to conceive of, and give birth to, the universe. Time is set in motion when a lotus flower emerges from Vishnu's navel. Among the gods at the top of the relief, the first deity, the four-headed Brahma, sits on the lotus. Holding the tools of a builder, he will construct the world. The four figures below Vishnu to the right represent the god's weapons and prepare to do battle against two demons, Madhu and Kaitabha, at the left. The demons were born from Vishnu's ear, and tried to destroy Brahma, but Vishnu killed them instead.

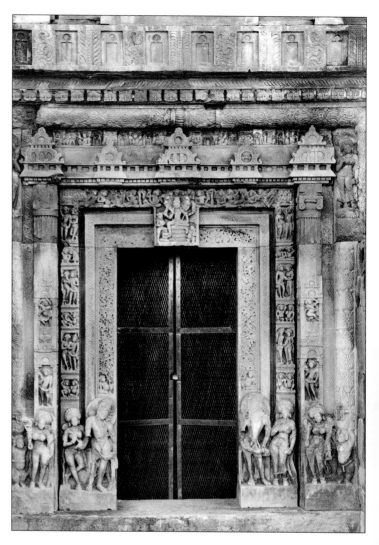

12.N West doorway, temple of Vishnu, Deogarh, Uttar Pradesh, 6th century.

The doorway at the west of the temple that leads to the *garbha griha* (fig. **12.N**) is framed by a series of elements. The lintels and door jambs are decorated with reliefs of foliage and various theological guardians. Within the upper corners, the river goddesses Ganga and Yamuna bless the sanctuary by pouring their waters over the threshold. Set in a square panel over the doorway is Vishnu enthroned on Ananta's coils. Here, as in the large relief on the south, Lakshmi strokes his foot to stimulate his cosmic dream.

The Orissan Temple
(8th–13th century)

By the eighth century, Hindu temples had become extremely complex structures. They varied according to period, region, patronage, and cult affiliation. From the eighth to the thirteenth century, Orissa, in eastern India, was a center of architectural development with a relatively

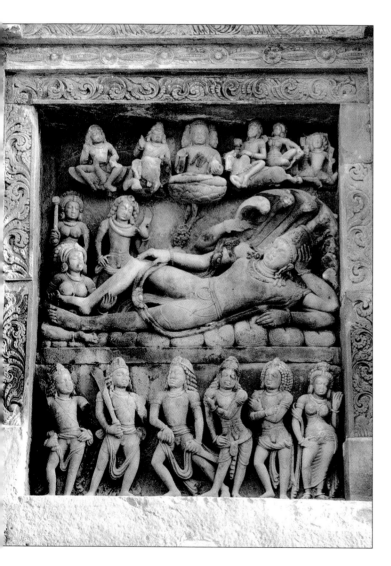

12.M *Vishnu Sleeping on Ananta*, relief panel, south side, temple of Vishnu, Deogarh, Uttar Pradesh, early 6th century.

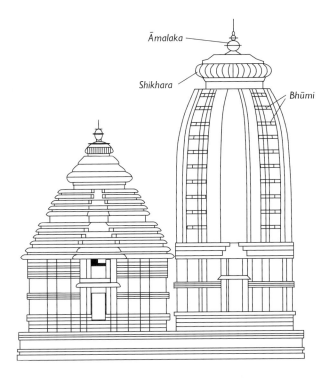

Āmalaka

Shikhara

Bhūmi

12.O Elevation of a typical Orissan temple.

consistent evolution of style. Figure **12.O** is a diagram of the elevation of a typical Orissan temple, which shows the extent to which architectural style had become elaborated.

The Temple of Shiva The mid-tenth-century Mukteshvar temple of Shiva at Bhubaneshvar (figs. **12.P** and **12.Q**) illustrates the Orissan version of northern-style temple architecture. This is the only one of India's famed "temple-cities" to survive. It originally had some seven thousand temples, of which about five hundred still exist, as do some of the *Shilpa shastras* on which they were based (see p. 440). This view of the exterior shows the towering superstructure that rises over the *garbha griha*. The tower consists of a lobed *shikhara*, surmounted by an *āmalaka* (finial in the shape of a notched ring). An assembly hall (**mandapa**) has also been added. The projecting veranda was used for meditation and reading, as well as for dancing and ceremonies. The slightly convex outline of the exterior, which has been referred to as "expanding form," is an architectural expression of *prana* (see p. 261). This small temple's vertical and horizontal planes are unified by the carved detail covering its surface. The repetition of stacked ridges (**bhūmi**) on the superstructure is complemented by a rich variety of organic and abstract forms designed to welcome Shiva.

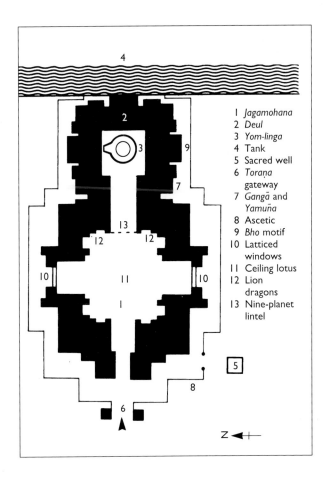

1 *Jagamohana*
2 *Deul*
3 *Yom-linga*
4 Tank
5 Sacred well
6 *Toraṇa* gateway
7 *Gaṅgā* and *Yamuṇa*
8 Ascetic
9 *Bho* motif
10 Latticed windows
11 Ceiling lotus
12 Lion dragons
13 Nine-planet lintel

12.P Mukteshvar temple of Shiva, Bhubaneshvar, Orissa, India, c. 950. Sandstone. The temple compound is entered through a *torana* (gateway) on the right. Inside the *garbha griha* at the heart of the temple, the focus of worship is a Shiva *lingam* inside a *yoni* (see Box). At the far left is a sacred water tank used for ritual bathing.

12.Q Plan of Mukteshvar temple of Shiva, Bhubaneshvar, Orissa, India, c. 950.

The meaning of these forms is associated with the Hindu concept of the temple as a manifestation of Mount Meru; the very term for the towers, "shikhara," means "mountain peak." The term "bhūmi," meaning "earth" (in the sense of "soil"), has similar symbolic connections with landscape. The crowning āmalaka symbolizes the spiritual heights achieved when one transcends the reincarnation cycle. As an elaboration of the ancient Indian axis-pillar, this finial was placed directly over the garbha griha, so that the most sacred and highest points of the temple were in alignment.

Synthesis of Buddhism and Hinduism at Angkor

Both Hinduism and Buddhism spread from India to Southeast Asia, and were assimilated into the local belief systems. Under the Khmer Empire (sixth to thirteenth century) in Cambodia, the main local contribution to the imported religions was the cult of the Devaraja (god king), in which Hinduism and Buddhism merged. The royal Khmer capital was the city of Angkor, founded by the late ninth-century king, Indravarman. His rule was notable for the development of an irrigation system that made rice the economic backbone of Cambodia during the Khmer period. Under the patronage of Indravarman, characteristic Khmer architectural features were first established. These included temple complexes consisting of several buildings united in an axial plan. Relatively modest at first, these royal temple complexes grew in size and splendor as each Devaraja sought to outdo his predecessor.

Angkor Wat
(12th century)

In the twelfth century, Khmer architecture culminated in the massive complex of interconnected waterways, roadways, terraces, monastic buildings, and shrines called Angkor Wat (wat meaning "temple"). These were built in gray-black sandstone, under the patronage of Suryavarman II (ruled c. 1113–50), and dedicated to Vishnu. The temple's central icon depicted Suryavarman in the guise of Vishnu. The plan of the central complex (fig. **12.R**) shows the characteristic rectangle arranged in an east–west orientation, and concentric colonnaded galleries. An inner rectangle (fig. **12.S**), three stories high, has five towered shrines and connecting colonnades accessible by stairways. At the focal point of this complex is the central temple, which stands for Mount Meru. Thus the entire conception is a two- and three-dimensional mandala of the cosmos. At the same time, the temple had a mortuary significance and was designed as a memorial to its patron. This is reflected in the frequent representations of the death god Yama in the relief sculptures covering the walls. In addition, the temple's unconventional orientation toward the west reinforces its association with death.

The main roadway leading to Angkor Wat (fig. **12.T**) is flanked by balustrades in the shape of giant water serpents, which are cosmic fertility symbols. The drawing in

0   50   100 m
100   200 ft

12.R Plan of the central complex at Angkor Wat, Cambodia, c. 1113–50.

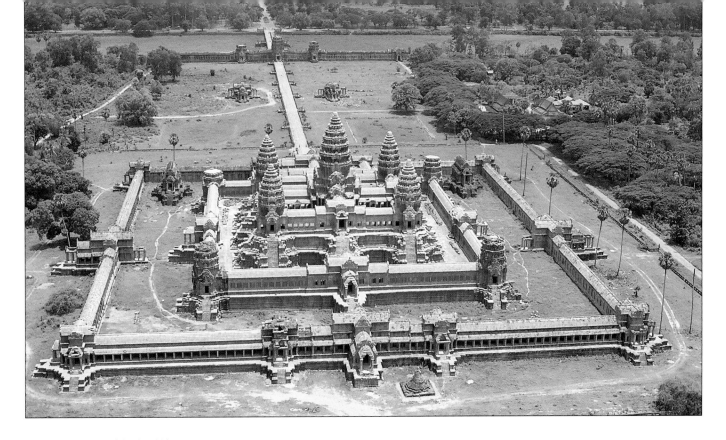

12.S Aerial view of Angkor Wat.

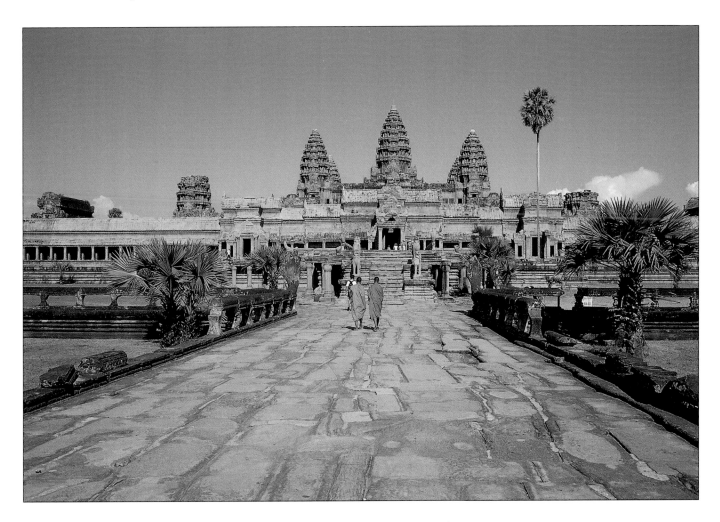

12.T Roadway approaching Angkor Wat.

Bibliothèque Nationale, Paris

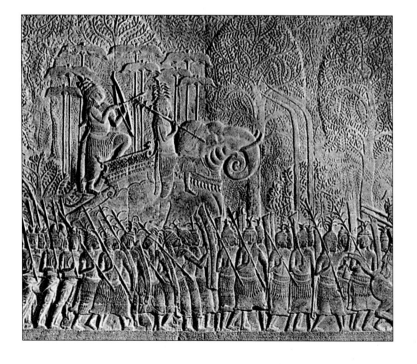

12.U (above) Drawing of towers, Angkor Wat. Bibliothèque Nationale, Paris.

12.V *Army on the March*, Angkor Wat. Sandstone, first half of 12th century.

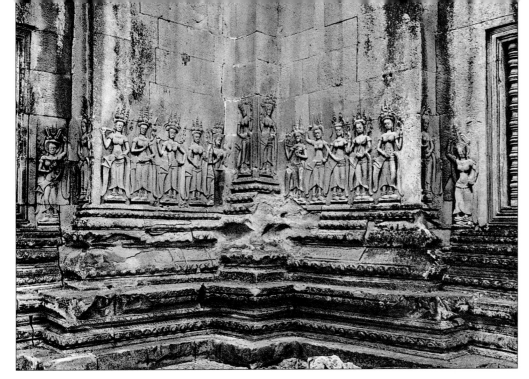

12.W *Apsarases*, exterior wall of a gallery, Angkor Wat.

figure **12.U** shows the elaborate surface decoration of the tall towers, with their flamelike motifs, and the supporting stone columns. As in Hindu temples, the towers at Angkor are tiered, overlaying a basic vertical plane with repeated horizontal bands. This repetition is broken only at the peaks, which, as in India, stand for the highest spiritual state of being.

Angkor Wat is covered with nearly 13,000 square feet (1200 sq m) of intricate relief sculpture. As on the towers, the low relief depicting an *Army on the March* (fig. **12.V**) is characterized by repetitive detail, which can be hypnotic in effect. The elephant-drawn chariot creates a formal counterpoint, its curves and diagonals combined with expansive forms.

An isocephalic frieze of celestial *Apsarases* (fig. **12.W**)— courtesans and dancers, probably water nymphs—adorns the exterior wall of a gallery. They provide a visual transition from the carved moldings to the plain wall, and thus are integrated with the architecture. The *Apsarases* are portrayed dancing on short, horizontal platforms that repeat the projections of the molding. Each figure faces outward and appears to sway with the music. They seem to greet visitors with seductive grace, while also referring to the spiritual heights symbolized by the peaks of the towers. This synthesis of the spiritual with the erotic is characteristic of much Hindu sculpture, particularly at transition points. The detail of the frieze (fig. **12.X**) shows one of the dancers, whose jewelry is carved in low relief patterns

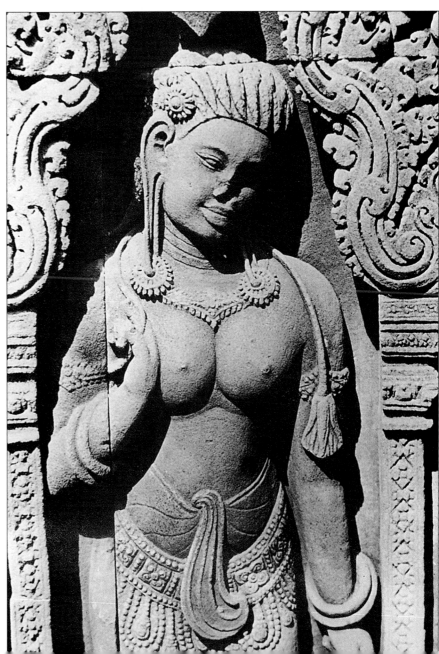

12.X "Water Nymph," detail of frieze, Angkor Wat.

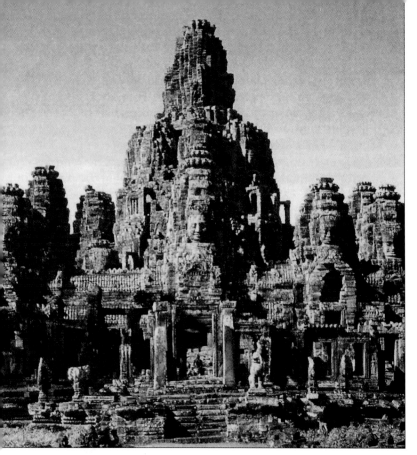

12.Y Bayon temple, Angkor Thom, Cambodia, c. 1200.

that contrast with her voluptuous breasts and ample proportions. Echoing her S-shape pose are the framing arch and her belt. The combination of physical sensuousness with an otherworldly inward gaze is typical of Hindu esthetics.

Angkor Thom
(13th century)

Angkor was abandoned after being sacked by a neighboring ruler. By the beginning of the thirteenth century, the Buddhist Khmer king Jayavarman VII (ruled 1181–1218) had planned a new capital and sacred precinct at the nearby Angkor Thom, meaning "Great Angkor" (fig. **12.Y**). There, the city walls have huge gateways with towers, on which monumental images of the Devaraja's face are carved (fig. **12.Z**). The most important temple at Angkor Thom, the Bayon, was Buddhist, and also incorporates local ancestor cults. As at Angkor Wat, the Angkor Thom temple was intended to replicate the cosmic center, and to identify it as the king's power base. The height of the large central tower (see fig. 12.Y) is equal to its depth below ground, uniting the subterranean realm with earth and sky. Similarly, the wide moat around the complex was identified with the cosmic ocean. Jayavarman VII's huge face over the entrance proclaims his union with the mountain, and his symbolic role as "King of the Mountain"—specifically the King of Mount Meru.

The Buddhist era at Angkor was short-lived. With the death of Jayavarman VII, and the subsequent decline of Angkor's importance, Hinduism was revived in Cambodia.

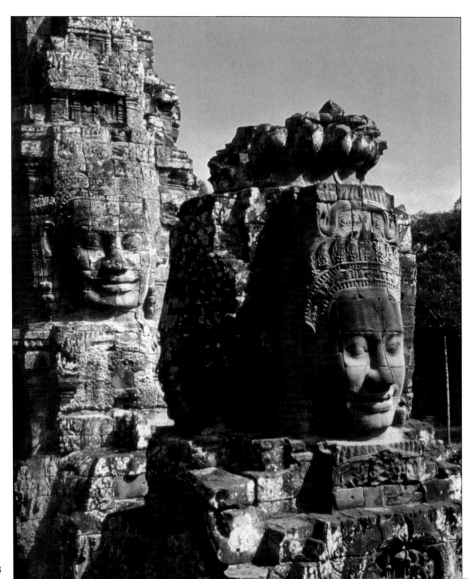

12.Z Towers with monumental faces of Devaraja, Bayon, Angkor Thom.

13

Precursors of the Renaissance

Thirteenth-Century Italy

During the eleventh and twelfth centuries, Italy continued to be accessible to Byzantine influences, particularly through its eastern port cities, Venice and Ravenna. Around the turn of the thirteenth century, however, momentous developments in Italy, inspired by imperial Roman traditions, laid the foundations for a major shift in western European art.

The name given to the period of Italian history from the thirteenth through the sixteenth centuries is "Renaissance"—the French word for "rebirth," or *rinascimento* in Italian. Dating the beginning of Renaissance style remains an issue of debate, and some would consider the works in this chapter to be late Gothic. But the term "Renaissance" denotes a self-conscious revival of interest in ancient Greek and Roman texts and culture which is reflected in the work of most of the artists discussed here. Italy was the logical place for such a revival, since the model of imperial Rome was part of its own history and territory.

Nicola Pisano

Around 1260 the late Gothic sculptor Nicola Pisano (c. 1220–84) carved the marble pulpit (fig. **13.1**) for the Baptistry in Pisa. The relief of the *Nativity* (fig. **13.2**) provides a good example of the Roman heritage in Italian medieval art. It is crowded with figures, including, from left to right at the bottom, a bearded Joseph, two midwives washing the infant in a basin, and sheep and goats. The largest figure, showing the influence of Etruscan and Roman tomb effigies, is Mary, whose monumentality and central position evoke her connections with the earth goddesses of antiquity. Despite the Christian subject and symbolism, the forms are reminiscent of imperial Roman reliefs. Most clearly related to the Roman past is the artist's rendition of draperies, which identify the organic, three-dimensional movements of figures in space.

Furthermore, the pulpit as a whole shows a fusion of Gothic arrangement (the combination of columns with Corinthian capitals and trilobed arches) with the round

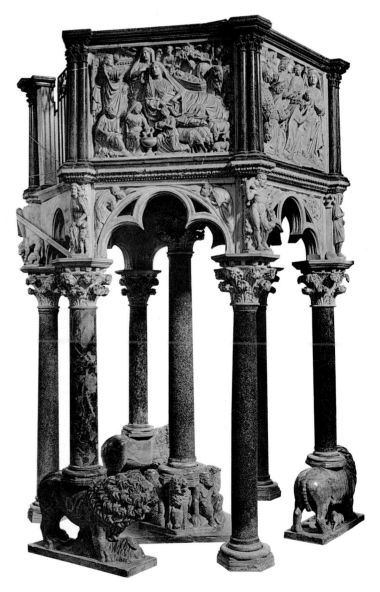

13.1 Nicola Pisano, pulpit, Pisa Baptistry, 1259–60. Marble, 15 ft (4.6 m) high. Nicola probably came from southern Italy and trained at the court of Frederick II. When Frederick died in about 1250, Nicola went north to Tuscany. He and his son Giovanni settled in Pisa, where they worked mainly in marble.

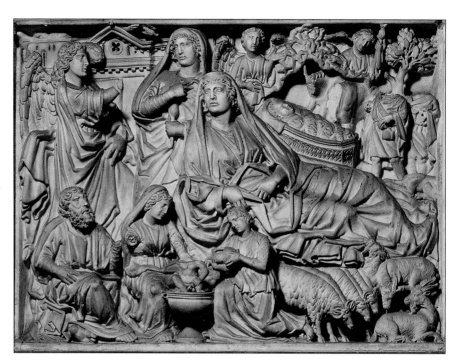

13.2 Nicola Pisano, relief of the *Nativity* (detail of fig. 13.1). Marble, approx. 34 in (86.4 cm) high.

arches of the Roman (and Romanesque) styles. Every other column rests on a lion, which recalls typological parallels between the Old and New Testaments. In that context, the lions refer to Solomon's throne, and here denote the foundation on which the teachings of Christ are built.

Both the conception and execution of the pulpit reflect the cultural and stylistic crosscurrents to which Nicola Pisano had been exposed at the court of the Holy Roman Emperor, Frederick II. During the first half of the thirteenth century, Frederick controlled territories in southern Italy, and his patronage brought French and German artists, as well as Italians, to his court at Capua, just north of Naples. There, imported and local elements were combined with Frederick's personal taste for ancient Roman styles. Like many rulers before and after him, Frederick used the revival of Classical antiquity for his own political purposes, relating his accomplishments to those of imperial Rome.

Cimabue

Byzantine influence remained strong in Italy, as can be seen in the monumental *Madonna Enthroned* (fig. **13.4**) by Cimabue (c. 1240–1302). The gold background, the flecks of gold in Mary's drapery, and the long, thin figures are characteristic of Byzantine style. The elaborate throne has no visible support at the back, but seems instead to rise upward, denying the material reality of its weight. As in Byzantine and medieval art, the Christ Child is depicted with the proportions and gestures of an adult (see p. 302). Four elderly men at the foot of the throne hold scrolls, attributes of Old Testament prophets. Mary and Christ are thus represented according to the typological reading of history and embody the New Dispensation in fulfillment of Old Testament prophecy.

Fourteenth-Century Italy

Cimabue is generally thought of as the last great painter working in the Byzantine tradition. The rise of humanism in the fourteenth century reflected, but also significantly extended, the High Gothic interest in nature. Humanists began to collect Classical texts, establishing major libraries of Greek and Roman authors. Artists began to study the forms of antiquity by observing Roman ruins. And gradually a new synthesis emerged, in which nature—including human character and human form—became the ideal pursued during the Renaissance.

Awareness of the Classical revival began to be reflected in the works of several Italian writers such as Dante, Petrarch, and Boccaccio, who discussed art and artists in a new way.

Literacy among the general population increased dramatically, and works of literature dealt more and more with art and artists, bringing their achievements to a wider public. Another important feature of the Renaissance in Italy was a new attitude to individual fame. While most medieval artists remained anonymous, those of the Renaissance frequently signed their works. The very fact that the names of many more Italian artists of the thirteenth and fourteenth centuries are documented than in the Early Christian and medieval periods in Europe attests to the artists' intention to record their identity and to preserve it for posterity.

Giotto

In painting, the individual who most exemplified, and in large part created, the new developments was Giotto di Bondone (c. 1267–1337). He was born in the Mugello Valley near Florence, and lived mainly in that city, which was to be the center of the new Renaissance culture. His fame was such that he was summoned all over Italy, and possibly also to France, on various commissions.

Boccaccio, an ardent admirer of ancient Rome, described Giotto as having brought the art of painting out of medieval darkness into daylight. He also compared Giotto with the Greek Classical painter Apelles as a master of clarity and illusionism. Petrarch, who was an avid collector of Classical texts and had written extensively about the benefits of nature, owned a painting by Giotto. In his will, he bequeathed the work to his lord. "The beauty of this painting," wrote Petrarch around 1361, "the ignorant

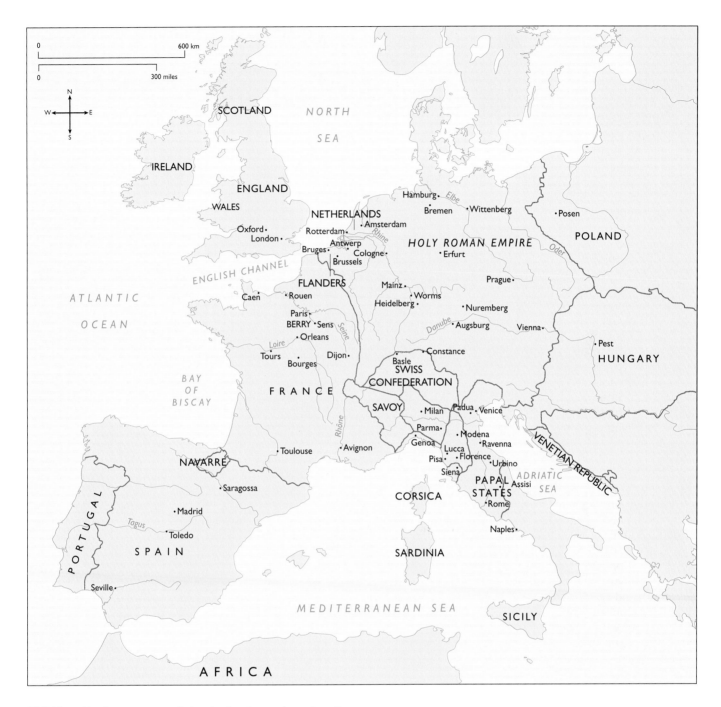

13.3 Map of leading art centers during the Renaissance in western Europe.

cannot comprehend, but masters of the art marvel at it."[1] Petrarch thus shared Boccaccio's view that Giotto appealed to the intellectually and artistically enlightened. Ignorance, by implication, was associated with the "darkness" of the Middle Ages.

Giotto became the subject of a growing number of anecdotes about artists that became popular from the fourteenth century onward. The anecdotal tradition is itself indicative of the Classical revival and derives from accounts of Classical Greek painters who were renowned for their illusionistic skill. These survive primarily in Pliny

the Elder's *Natural History* (see p. 213), which was an important source on ancient art and artists during the Renaissance.

In Dante's *Purgatory* (see Box), Giotto and Cimabue are juxtaposed as a lesson in the transience of earthly fame:

O empty glory of human powers! How short the time
its green endures at its peak, if it be not
overtaken by crude ages! Cimabue thought to hold
the field in painting, and now Giotto has the cry,
so that the fame of the former is obscured.[2]

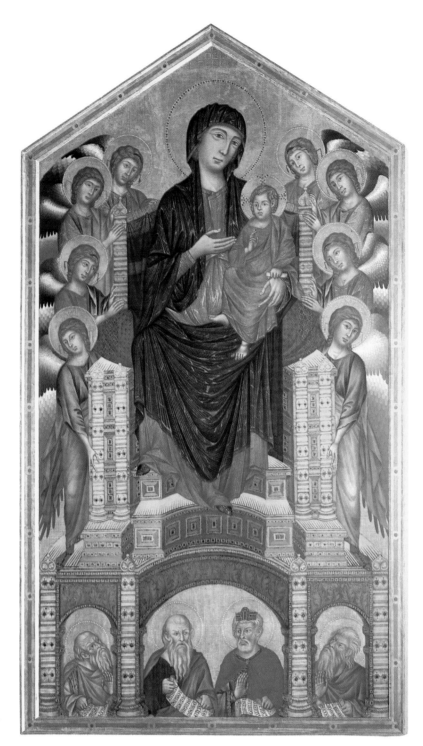

13.4 Cimabue, *Madonna Enthroned*, c. 1280–90. Tempera on wood, 12 ft 7 in × 7 ft 4 in (3.84 × 2.24 m). Galleria degli Uffizi, Florence.

Dante: The Poet of Heaven and Hell

The Florentine poet Dante Alighieri (1265–1321) wrote *The Divine Comedy*, a long poem divided into three parts: *Inferno* (Hell), *Purgatorio* (Purgatory), and *Paradiso* (Paradise). Dante describes a week's journey in the year 1300 down through the circles of hell to Satan's realm. From there he climbs up the mountain of purgatory, with its seven terraces, and finally ascends the spheres of heaven.

The Roman poet Virgil, author of *The Aeneid*, guides Dante through hell and purgatory. The very fact that Dante chooses Virgil as his guide is evidence of the growing interest in Roman antiquity. But because Virgil lived in a pre-Christian

era, according to Dante he cannot continue past purgatory into paradise. Instead, it is Beatrice, Dante's deceased beloved, who guides him through heaven and presents him to the Virgin Mary.

Long valued for its literary and spiritual qualities, Dante's poem is equally important for its insights into medieval and early Renaissance history. In the course of his journey, Dante encounters many historical figures to whom he metes out various punishments or rewards, according to his opinion of them.

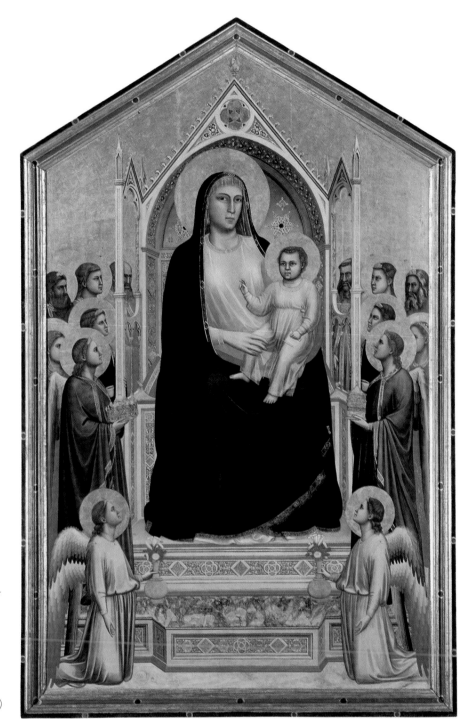

13.5 Giotto, *Madonna Enthroned* (Ognissanti Madonna), c. 1310. Tempera on wood, 10 ft 8 in × 6 ft 8 in (3.25 × 2.03 m). Galleria degli Uffizi, Florence. Despite Giotto's fame, few of his works are undisputed. This is the only panel painting unanimously attributed to him. It was commissioned for the Church of Ognissanti (All Saints) in Florence.

In the fifteenth century, the sculptor and goldsmith Lorenzo Ghiberti (see Vol II, chapter 14) would record the popular anecdote that inspired Dante's lines. He described Giotto as a boy tending sheep: Giotto was drawing the image of a sheep on a rock, when Cimabue happened by. Instantly recognizing the artistic genius of the young shepherd, the older artist obtained permission from Giotto's father to train his son as a painter. This account exemplifies the conventional recognition story, in which inborn talent reveals itself in childhood. The necessary corollary is discovery and encouragement by an older practitioner of the same art. According to Ghiberti, Giotto was skilled in all the arts, abandoned the Byzantine style, and revived the genius of Classical antiquity.

Filippo Villani, writing at the turn of the fifteenth century on the history of Florence, commented on the role of art in the development of the Renaissance. In Villani's opinion, Cimabue had laid the foundations of the new style, and Giotto "is not only celebrated enough to be compared with the painters of Antiquity, but is even to be preferred to them in skill and genius—[he] restored painting to its pristine dignity and high reputation. For pictures formed by his brush follow nature's outlines so closely that they seem to the observer to live and breathe."[3]

A comparison of Giotto's *Madonna Enthroned* (fig. **13.5**) of c. 1300 with Cimabue's (see fig. 13.4) illustrates their different approaches to space and to the relationship between space and form. Both pictures are tempera on panel (see Box) and were intended as altarpieces (see Box). Giotto's is surrounded by an architectural frame that cuts off parts of the angels around the throne, while Cimabue's has no such framework. Both have elaborate thrones (Giotto's with Gothic pointed arches), Byzantine gold backgrounds, and flat, round haloes that do not turn illusionistically with the heads. Whereas Cimabue's throne rises in an irrational, unknown space (there is no floor), Giotto's is on a horizontal support approached by steps. In contrast to Cimabue's long, thin, elegant figures, Giotto's are bulky, with draperies that correspond convincingly to organic form and obey the law of gravity. Giotto has thus created an illusion of three-dimensional space—his figures seem to turn and move as in nature.

Tempera: Painstaking Preparation and Delicate Detail

Examples of the use of tempera are found as early as ancient Egyptian times. From the medieval period through the fifteenth century, however, it was the preferred medium for wooden panel paintings, especially in Italy, lending itself to precise details and clear edges.

For large panels, such as those illustrated in figures 13.4 and 13.5, elaborate preparations were required before painting could begin. Generally, a carpenter made the panel from poplar, which was glued and braced on the back with strips of wood. He also made and attached the frame. Apprentices then prepared the panel, under the artist's supervision, by sanding the wood until it was smooth. They sealed it with several layers of size, a glutinous material used to fill in the pores of the panel and to make a stable surface for later layers. Strips of linen reinforced the wood to prevent warping. The last step in the preparation of the panel was the addition of several layers of **gesso**, a water-based paint thickened with chalk and size. Once each layer of gesso had dried, the surface was again sanded, smoothed, and scraped. The gesso thus became the support for the artwork.

At this point, painting could begin. Using a brush, the artist lightly outlined the figures and forms in charcoal before reinforcing the outline with ink. The decorative gold designs, haloes, and gold background were applied next, and were polished so that they would glow in the dark churches.

Apprentices made the paint by grinding pigments from mineral or vegetable extracts to a paste and suspending them in a mixture of water and egg. The artist then applied the paint with small brushes made of animal hair. Once the artist had completed the finishing touches, the painting was left to dry—a year was the recommended time—and then it was varnished.

Altarpieces

An altarpiece is a devotional panel painting (usually tempera on wood), which was originally located behind an altar, visible only to the clergy. After the church's Lateran Council of 1215, however, the altarpiece was moved to the front of the altar in order to engage viewers in the sacred drama of the Mass. From the twelfth century onward, altarpieces became more common and increasingly elaborate. They typically had a fixed base (the **predella**), surmounted by one or more large panel paintings. In most cases the large panels contain the more iconic images—such as an enthroned Virgin and Christ, or individual saints—and the predellas contain narrative scenes related to the larger figures.

Taking as examples the illustrations in this chapter, figures 13.4 and 13.5 would have been central altarpiece panels. Figure 13.14 is a reconstruction of the front of Duccio's *Maestà*, the original of which replaced a small, undistinguished early thirteenth-century panel painting. Duccio's large panel of the *Enthroned Virgin and Christ* surrounded by saints and angels rests on a predella with scenes of Christ's early life—from the *Annunciation* at the left to *Christ among the Doctors* at the right, and individual figures between the narrative scenes. Above is a row of saints under round arches surmounted by scenes from Mary's life—starting with the *Annunciation* of her death and ending with her *Burial*. The upper sections of the pinnacles are lost.

Simone Martini's *Saint Louis* altarpiece (fig. 13.23) shows the saint crowning his brother Robert in the larger panel. Small scenes on the predella depict events from the saint's life.

Originally, wings (side panels) would usually have been attached with hinges. These wings would then "close" the altarpiece when it was not on display or being used for a service. The Ghent altarpiece (see Vol. II) is particularly elaborate. Figure 14.72 shows the altarpiece closed so that the paintings on the outside of the wings are visible.

Whereas Cimabue uses lines of gold to emphasize Mary's drapery folds, Giotto's folds are rendered by shading. Giotto's V-shaped folds between Mary's knees identify both their solidity and the void between them, while the curving folds above the waist impart a suggestion of *contrapposto* and also direct the viewer's attention to Christ.

A comparison of the two figures of Christ reveals at once that Giotto was more interested in the reality of childhood than Cimabue. The latter's Christ retains aspects of the medieval homunculus (see p. 302). He has a small head and thin proportions, and he is not logically supported on Mary's lap. Giotto's Christ, on the other hand, has chubby proportions and rolls of baby fat around his neck and wrists; he sits firmly on the horizontal surface of Mary's leg. Although Giotto's Christ is depicted in a regal and frontal position, his right hand raised in a gesture of blessing, his proportions are more natural than those of Cimabue's Christ.

It was precisely in the rendition of nature that Giotto seemed to his contemporaries to have surpassed Cimabue and to have revived the forms of antiquity, heralding the emergence of a new generation of artists. Giotto's success also exemplifies the benefits of the master–apprentice relationship in medieval and Renaissance artistic training (see Boxes).

The Arena Chapel

The best preserved examples of Giotto's work are the paintings in the Arena Chapel in Padua, a small town about 25 miles (40 km) southwest of Venice. In the second half of the thirteenth century, under a republican form of government, a group of Paduan lawyers developed an interest in Roman law, which led to an enthusiasm for Classical thought and literature. Roman theater was revived, along with Classical poetry and rhetoric. As the site of an old and distinguished university, Padua was a natural center for a humanist revival, which acknowledged

Cennino Cennini: *Il libro dell'arte* (*The Craftsman's Handbook*)

Cennino Cennini was born around 1370 in Colle, near Florence, but worked in Padua. He had learned painting from students of Giotto, and proclaimed his descent from the master. His handbook, written at the turn of the century, mediates between the medieval and Renaissance approaches to training and style. He traces the art of painting to Adam and Eve, who turned to agriculture and crafts after the Fall. One of these crafts was painting, "which calls for imagination," according to Cennino, "and skill of hand, in order to discover things not seen, hiding themselves under the shadow of natural objects, and to fix them with the hand, presenting to plain sight what does not actually exist. And it justly deserves to be enthroned next to theory, and to be crowned with poetry."[4]

Cennino recommends that artists apprentice themselves to a good master. He describes the preparation of pigments, techniques of drawing, and the ideal lifestyle of the artist. Above all, he prescribes constant drawing from nature, which, he says, is the best model of all. In this sentiment, Cennino departs from medieval practice and states what would become a Renaissance ideal in art.

Training in the Master's Workshop

In the Middle Ages and Renaissance, artists learned their trade by undertaking a prolonged period of technical training in the shop of a master artist. Young men became apprentices in their early teens, either because they had already shown talent or because their families wanted them to be artists. Artists usually came from the middle classes, often from families of artists. Quite a few married into such families and went into business with their relatives.

The term of apprenticeship varied. Cennino Cennini recommended six years. Apprentices began learning their trade at the most menial level. They mixed paints, prepared pigments and the painting surface, and occasionally worked on less important border areas or painted the minor figures of a master's composition. By the time an apprentice was ready to start his own shop, he had a thorough grounding in techniques and media. He would probably also have assimilated elements of his master's style.

Renaissance artists were an influential professional group, and the increased demand for art was the result of growth in the sources of patronage. During the Middle Ages, most of the patronage had been ecclesiastic (i.e. from the Church authorities). In the Renaissance, art was also commissioned by civic or corporate groups, and even by wealthy individuals. The commissions were generally sealed by legal contract between artist and patron, and these contracts have become an important documentary source for modern art historians.

the primacy of individual intellect, character, and talent. Giotto, more than any other artist, transformed these qualities into painting.

The Arena Chapel (named after the old Roman arena adjacent to it) was founded by Enrico Scrovegni, Padua's wealthiest citizen—hence its designation as the Scrovegni Chapel. Having inherited a fortune from his father Reginaldo Scrovegni, whom Dante had consigned to the seventh circle of hell for usury (money-lending), Enrico commissioned the chapel and its decoration as an act of atonement. The building itself is a simple, barrel-vaulted, rectangular structure, faced on the exterior with brick and plain pilasters. The interior is decorated with one of the most remarkable fresco cycles in Western art (fig. **13.6**). Architectural elements are kept to a minimum: the south wall has six windows while the north wall is solid, making it an ideal surface for fresco painting (see Box). The west wall, which has one window divided into three lancets, is covered with an enormous *Last Judgment* (see fig. 13.10).

On the north and south walls, three levels of rectangular scenes illustrate the lives of Mary, her parents Anna and Joachim, and Christ. Below the narrative scenes on the north and south walls are Virtues and Vices (see Box), disposed according to traditional left–right symbolism. As the viewer enters the chapel, the Virtues are on the right and the Vices on the left. Facing the observer is the chancel arch, containing *Gabriel's Mission* at the top, two other events from Christ's life (the *Betrayal of Judas* on the left, and the *Visitation* on the right), and two illusionistic chapels.

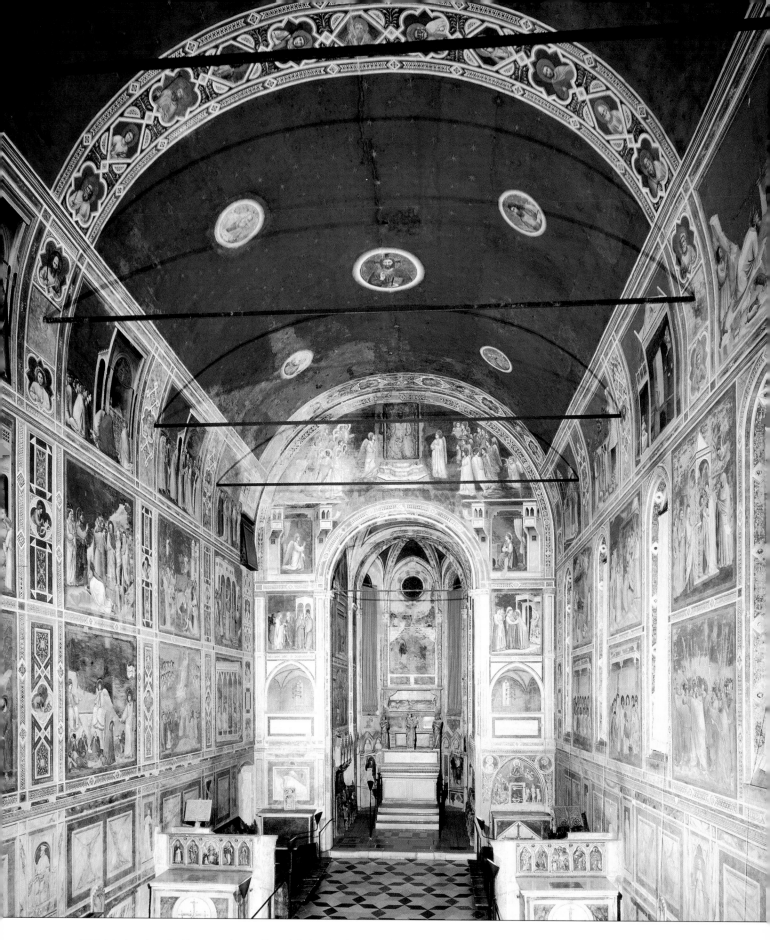

13.6 Interior view, looking east, Arena Chapel, Padua. At the top of the round chancel arch, which is reminiscent of Roman triumphal arches, there is a tempera panel set into the plaster wall, depicting God the Father enthroned. He summons the angel Gabriel and entrusts him with the Annunciation of Christ's birth to Mary.

Fresco: A Medium for Speed and Confidence

From the thirteenth to the sixteenth centuries, there was a significant increase in the number of monumental fresco cycles, especially in Italy.

Fresco cycles were typically located on plaster walls in churches or private palaces, and large scaffolds were erected for such projects. First, the wall was covered with a coarse plaster, called the **arriccio**, which was rough enough to hold the final layer of plaster. When the first layer had dried, the artist found his bearings by establishing the exact center of the surface to be painted, and by locating the vertical and horizontal axes. He blocked out the composition with charcoal, and made a brush drawing in red ocher pigment mixed with water. These drawings are called *sinopie* (*sinopia* in the singular) after Sinope, a town on the Black Sea known for the red color of its earth.

Once the artist had completed the *sinopia*, he added the final layer of smooth plaster, or *intonaco*, to the walls one patch at a time. The artist applied the colors to the *intonaco* while it was still damp and able to absorb them. Thus when the plaster dried and hardened, the colors became integrated with it. Each patch was what the artist planned to paint in a single day—hence the term *giornata*, the Italian word for a day's work. Because each *giornata* had to be painted in a day, fresco technique encouraged advance planning, speed of execution, broad brushstrokes, and monumental forms. Sometimes small details were added in tempera, and certain colors, such as blue, were applied *secco* (dry). These have been largely lost or turned black by chemical reaction.

Virtues and Deadly Sins

The seven Christian Virtues and Vices, or Deadly Sins, are commonly personified in Christian art. The seven Virtues are divided into four Cardinal Virtues—Prudence, Temperance, Fortitude, and Justice—and three Theological Virtues—Faith, Hope, and Charity.

The seven Vices vary slightly, but generally consist of Pride, Covetousness, Lust, Envy, Gluttony, Anger, and Sloth.

Immediately below *Gabriel's Mission*, separated into two images on either side of the arch, is the *Annunciation* (fig. **13.7**). The setting is a rectangular architectural space with balconies that seem to project outward. Equally illusionistic are the curtains, which appear to hang outside the architecture and swing in toward the windows.

Illusion is an important aspect of theater, and in the Arena Chapel the space in which the sacred drama unfolds has been compared with a stage. In the *Annunciation*, for example, the painted space is three-dimensional but narrow, and the architecture—like a stage set—is small in relation to the figures. Gabriel and Mary face each other across the span of the actual arch, while the viewer observes them as if through the "fourth wall" of a stage.

The combination of Classical restraint and psychological insight in Giotto's frescoes may be related to the contemporary revival of Roman theater in Padua. Although

13.7 Giotto, *Annunciation*, Arena Chapel, Padua, c. 1305. Fresco.

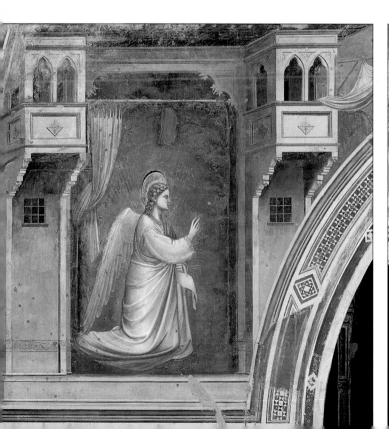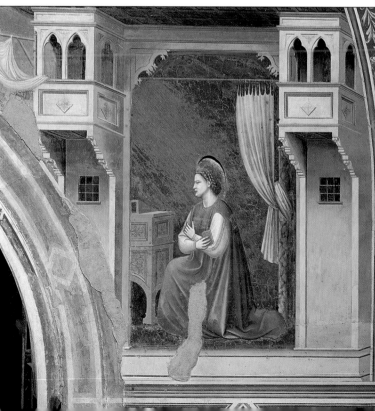

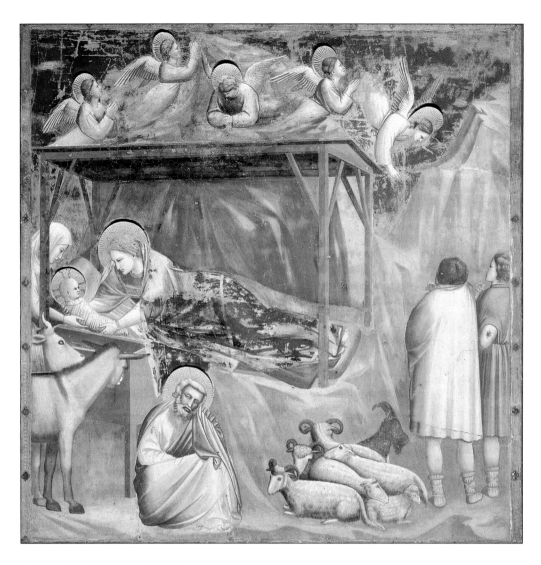

13.8 Giotto, *Nativity*, Arena Chapel, Padua, c. 1305. Fresco.

there is no documentary evidence for it, the pictures themselves suggest that, in creating the most dramatic fresco cycles of his generation, Giotto was influenced by this revival, as well as by the traditional Christian mystery plays performed in front of churches. This combination of influences may also explain Giotto's dramatic depictions of pose and gesture.

In the *Annunciation*, both Mary and Gabriel are rendered as solid, sculpturesque figures, their poses identified mainly by their drapery folds. Gabriel raises his right hand in a gesture of greeting. Mary holds a book, signifying that Gabriel has interrupted her reading, a conventional detail in Annunciation scenes which is from the Apocrypha (see p. 8). As Gabriel makes his announcement, diagonal rays of light enter Mary's room. The lack of a logical or natural source for this light emphasizes that it is divine light, emanating from heaven. As such, it is prophetic of the symbolic light, or en*light*enment, that Christ will bring to the world. Equally prophetic is Mary's gesture, for her crossed arms refer forward in time to Christ's Crucifixion. According to Christian doctrine, this is the means by which salvation is achieved.

A comparison of the Arena Chapel *Nativity* (fig. **13.8**) with Nicola Pisano's *Nativity* on the Pisa pulpit (see fig.

13.2) illustrates Giotto's reduction of form and content to its dramatic essence. In Giotto's fresco, as in Nicola's sculpture, two events are merged into a single space. Nicola combines the *Nativity* with the *Washing of the Infant Christ*, and the shepherds arrive in Bethlehem at the upper right. Giotto combines the *Annunciation to the Shepherds* at the right with the *Nativity* at the left. Both artists use simple, massive draperies that naturally outline human form and monumentalize the figures. But Nicola's composition is more crowded, and the dramatic relationships between figures do not have the power of Giotto's version.

Giotto's shepherds, for example, are rendered in back view, and stand riveted to the angels' announcement. In the *Nativity*, the human figures are reduced to four: Mary, Christ, Joseph, and a midwife. A single foreshortened angel above the shed gazes down at the scene, interrupting the left-to-right flow of the other angels toward the shepherds and focusing the viewer's attention onto the Nativity.

A sculpturesque Joseph dozes in the foreground, withdrawing from the intimate relationship between mother and infant. Giotto accentuates this by the power of a gaze that excludes a third party. Nicola's Mary, on the other

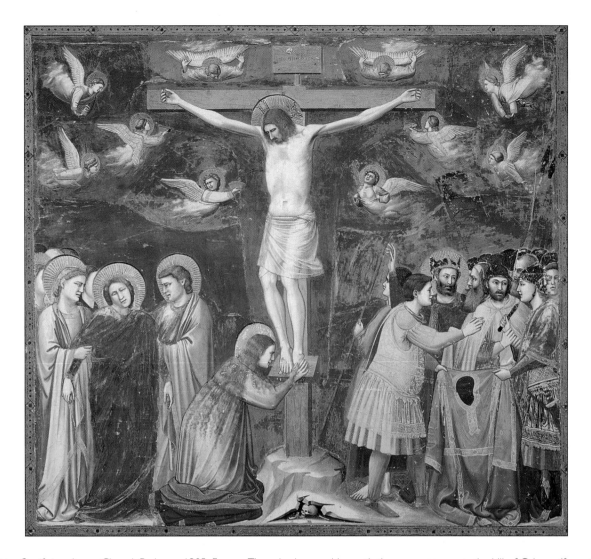

13.9 Giotto, *Crucifixion*, Arena Chapel, Padua, c. 1305. Fresco. The raised ground beneath the cross represents the hill of Calvary (from the Latin *calvaria*, meaning "skull"). According to tradition, Christ was crucified on the Hill of Skulls outside Jerusalem. The skull that appears in the opening of the rock is Adam's—a reminder of the tradition that Christ was crucified on the site of Adam's burial. Both that tradition and its visual reference here are typological in character, for Christ was considered the new Adam and the redeemer of Adam's sins.

hand, stares forward while Christ lies in the manger behind her. Rather than emphasize the dramatic impact of the mother's first view of her son, Nicola monumentalizes Mary as an individual maternal image and, in the *Nativity*, relegates Christ to the background. In the *Washing of Christ*, the same Mary towers over Christ, but does not exchange a glance with him.

Giotto reinforces his perception of the mother–child relationship in the depiction of the animals. Among the sheep, he repeats the theme of protection and physical closeness. In the ox and ass at the manger, he plays on the Christian meaning of their glances and merges it with the emotional significance of the gaze. The ass looks down and fails to see the importance of the event before him. He thus becomes a symbol of ignorance and sin. The ox, however, stares at the gaze of Mary and Christ, recognizing its importance in Christian terms and also replicating the role of the outsider looking in, like the viewer, on a dramatic confrontation.

In contrast to the *Annunciation*, the *Crucifixion* (fig. **13.9**) takes place outdoors, on a narrow, rocky, horizontal ground. Christ hangs heavily from the Cross, his neck and

shoulders forced below the level of his hands. His arms are elongated, his muscles are stretched, and his rib-cage is visible beneath his flesh. Transparent drapery reveals the form of his body. Family and friends are gathered to Christ's right. Mary, dressed in blue, slumps in a faint, her weight supported by Saint John and an unidentified woman. Forming a diagonal bridge from Mary and John to the Cross is the kneeling figure of Mary Magdalen, traditionally understood to have been a prostitute before she became one of Christ's most devoted followers. In this painting, she wears her hair long, an iconographic convention denoting her penance.

In contrast to the formal and psychological link between Christ and his followers on his right (our left), there is a void immediately to the left of the Cross. The symbolic distance between Christ and his executioners is reinforced by the diagonal bulk of the Roman soldier leaning to the right. The group of soldiers haggles over Christ's cloak, which one soldier prepares to divide up with a knife. (See Matthew 27:35: "they divided his clothes among them by casting lots.") Framing the head of a Roman soldier in the background is a halo, which sets him apart from

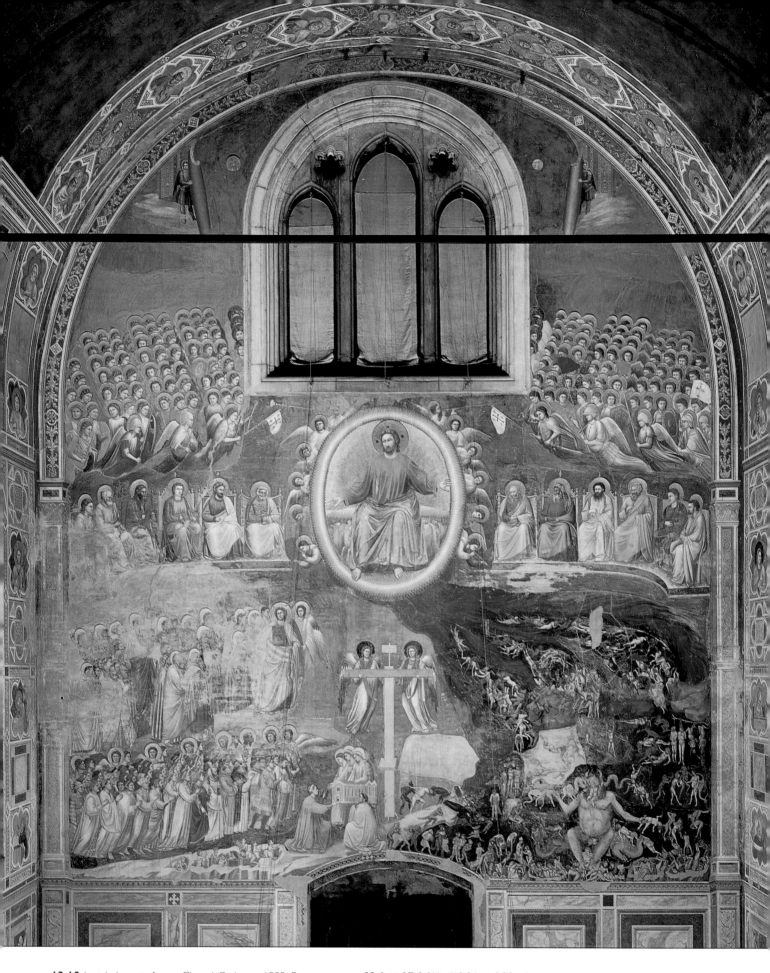

13.10 *Last Judgment*, Arena Chapel, Padua, c. 1305. Fresco, approx. 33 ft × 27 ft ¾ in (10.06 × 8.38 m).

the others and identifies him as Longinus, who converted to Christianity and became a martyr.

The sky is filled with two symmetrical groups of mourning angels. Like a Greek chorus, they echo and enhance the human emotions of Christ's followers. The spatial positions of the angels are indicated by varying degrees of foreshortening, the two above the arms of the Cross being the most radically foreshortened. Two angels extend cups to catch Christ's blood flowing from his **stigmata**, or wounds. The greater formal activity and melodrama of the angels act as a foil to the restraint of the human figures.

Chronologically, the last scene in the chapel is the *Last Judgment* (fig. **13.10**), which fulfills the Christian prophecy of Christ's Second Coming. The finality of that event corresponds to its location on the west wall of the Arena Chapel, where it is the last image to confront viewers on their way out. The fresco occupies the entire wall, adding a monumental dimension to its impact. The host of heaven, consisting of military angels, is assembled on either side of the window. Above the angels, two figures roll up the sky, to reveal the golden vaults of heaven, again evoking the image of a theater, as if stagehands were rolling up a curtain at the end of a play.

Immediately below the window, Christ sits in a circle of light, surrounded by angels. Seated on a curved horizontal platform on either side of Christ are the twelve apostles. Christ's right hand summons the saved souls, while his left rejects the damned. He inclines his head to the lower left of the fresco (his right), where two levels of saved souls rise upward. At the head of the upper group stands the Virgin Mary, who appears in her role as intercessor with Christ on behalf of humanity.

Giotto's hell, conventionally placed below heaven and on Christ's left, is the most medieval aspect of the Arena Chapel frescoes. It is surrounded by flames emanating from the circle around Christ. In contrast to the orderly rows of saved souls, those in hell are disordered—as in the Romanesque example from Conques (fig. 11.8). The elaborate visual descriptions of the tortures inflicted on the damned by the blue and red devils, and their contorted poses, are reminiscent of medieval border figures, whether on manuscripts or church sculptures.

The large, blue-gray Satan in the depths of hell is typical of the medieval taste for monstrous forms merging with each other. Satan swallows one soul while the serpentine creatures who emerge from his ears bite into other souls, an image of oral aggression that appears in many medieval manuscripts. Dragons on either side of Satan's rear also swallow souls, and, from the ear of one of the dragons, rises a ratlike creature biting into a soul, who falls back in despair. The falling and tumbling figures emphasize the Christian conception of hell as disordered, violent, and located among the lowest realms of the universe.

Directly under Christ, two angels hold the Cross, which divides the lower section of the fresco into the areas populated by the saved and the damned. Giotto's reputation for humor is exemplified in the little soul behind the Cross who is trying to sneak over to the side of the saved. Toward the bottom of hell, a mitered bishop is approached by a damned soul holding a bag of money, possibly hoping to buy an indulgence. Besides being a criticism of corruption in the Church, this detail may be an implied reference to Reginaldo Scrovegni's financial sin, for which his son tried to atone through his patronage of the Arena Chapel. Nor surprisingly, Enrico is placed on the side of the saved (fig. **13.11**). As he kneels, his drapery falls on the ground in soft folds, suggesting the weight of the fabric. Such portrayal of the donor within a work of art was to become characteristic of the Renaissance.

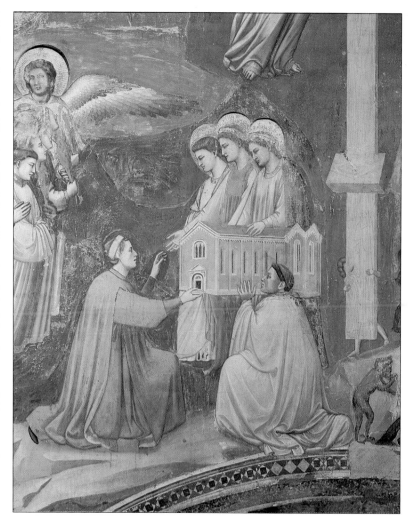

13.11 Giotto, *Last Judgment* (detail of fig. 13.10), Arena Chapel, Padua, c. 1305. Enrico Scrovegni, assisted by a monk, lifts up a model of the Arena Chapel and presents it to three female saints. Scrovegni holds the model and faces the exterior of the entrance wall, the interior of which contains the *Last Judgment*. The monk's cloak looks as if it is falling out of the picture plane over the doorway arch, another illustration of the Classical taste for illusionism.

Saint Francis was the son of a rich merchant in the Umbrian town of Assisi. As a young man, Francis made a pilgrimage to Rome, where he felt a sudden sense of identification with a beggar and traded clothes with him. For the first time in his life of privilege, Francis experienced poverty and realized its spiritual potential. He then renounced his father's wealth and dedicated his life to poverty. In 1224, while he was praying and meditating on the mountain of La Verna, he looked into the rising sun and saw a vision of Christ on the Cross. Christ's arms were the outstretched wings of a seraph (a type of angel). Scars corresponding to the wounds of the crucified Christ are then believed to have appeared on Saint Francis's body (a phenomenon known as "stigmatization"). In 1209 Francis received the pope's permission to found an order of friars, the Franciscan Order. He established a strict, simple Rule, insisting that his followers—the Friars Minor—live by the work of their own hands, or by begging. They were forbidden to accept money or property in exchange for services. Pope Innocent III approved the Rule in 1209–10, and Francis traveled to Spain, eastern Europe, and Egypt to spread his message.

Around 1212, a noblewoman of Assisi, Clare, decided to follow the Rule of Saint Francis. When other women joined her, Francis established a separate community with Clare as its abbess. Her followers became known as the Poor Clares. The power of the Franciscan movement attests to its wide appeal and, in the course of the thirteenth century, Franciscan churches proliferated. So-called "Daughter houses," established by the Poor Clares, also sprang up throughout Europe.

Partly because of the large number of Saint Francis' followers, and partly because of conflict over the rigors of his Rule, the Franciscans split into two factions. The Spiritualists adhered to strict interpretation of the Rule, whereas the Conventualists took a more flexible position.

After Saint Francis received the stigmata, he wrote his most famous work, *The Canticle of Brother Sun*. It is a long hymn in praise of the divine presence he believed resided in nature:

> Praised be You, my Lord, with all your creatures,
>   especially Sir Brother Sun,
> Who is the day and through whom You give us light.
> And he is beautiful and radiant with great splendor;
>   and bears a likeness of You, Most High One.
> Praised be You, my Lord, through Sister Moon and
>   the stars,
> In heaven You formed them clear and precious and
>   beautiful.[5]

This hymn reflects the role of Saint Francis in the new emphasis on nature that developed in the later Gothic period, and that would characterize much of the Renaissance. Saint Francis' Rule heralded a shift from monastic isolation to greater involvement—largely through preaching—with urban populations, especially the poor.

On July 6, 1228, two years after his death, Francis was canonized by Pope Gregory IX. His remains are in the thirteenth-century basilica of San Francesco in Assisi, which is the center of his cult.

Before leaving the Arena Chapel, we consider the Virtue of *Justice* (fig. **13.12**), which illustrates the contemporary Italian concern with government. Two forms of government prevailed in Italy as the Renaissance dawned. Popes and princes ruled the relatively authoritarian states, while republics and communes were more democratic. Although the latter were, in practice, more often oligarchies (governments controlled by a few aristocrats) than democracies in the modern sense, the concept of a republican government was based on the Classical ideal.

Giotto's *Saint Francis*

Although Giotto's acknowledged masterpiece is the Arena Chapel in Padua, he himself was a citizen of Florence. In that city he later decorated two surviving chapels in the medieval Franciscan church of Santa Croce. These were the family chapels of two leading banking families, the

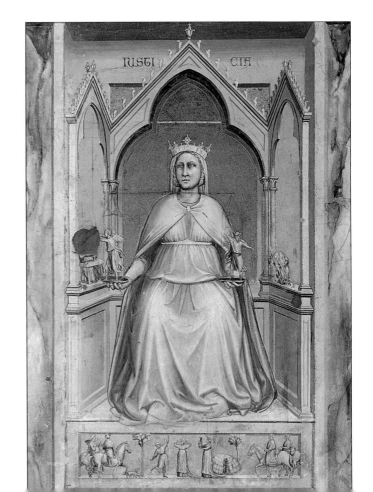

13.12 Giotto, *Justice*, Arena Chapel, Padua, c. 1305. Fresco. Justice is personified as an enthroned queen in a Gothic architectural setting. She holds a Nike in her right hand, as did Phidias' Athena in the Parthenon *naos*, indicating that justice brings victory. Justice also leads to good government and a well-run state, with all the benefits that this implies. Painted as an imitation relief in the rectangle at the bottom of the picture are images of dancing, travel (men on horseback), and agriculture.

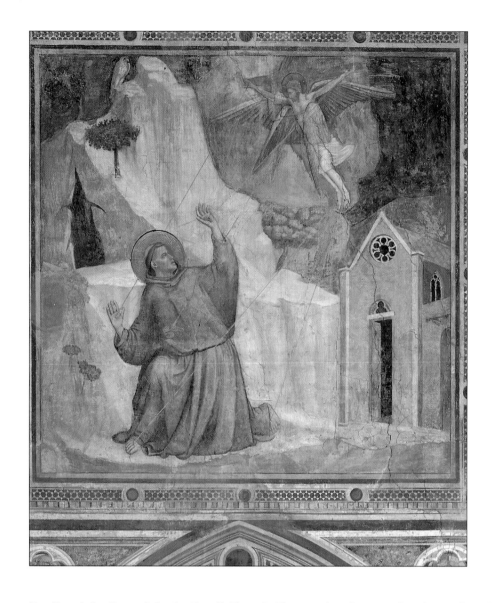

13.13 Giotto, *Stigmatization of Saint Francis*, exterior of the Bardi Chapel, Sta. Croce, Florence, after 1317. Fresco.

Bardi and the Peruzzi. In the Bardi Chapel, Giotto painted scenes from the life of Saint Francis (see Box), whose cult was one of the most prominent in Italy. Because of his insistence on poverty, the issue of decorating Franciscan churches became controversial. Likewise, the role of rich patrons in commissioning works of art depicting the lives of saints highlighted the contrast between wealthy patrons and the message of the works they commissioned.

Saint Francis pursued poverty in imitation of Christ, with whom he identified, particularly in receiving the wounds that Christ had suffered on the Cross. Giotto depicted the *Stigmatization of Saint Francis* (fig. **13.13**) in a fresco on the outer wall of the Bardi Chapel. The scene takes place in a rocky, mountainous landscape dotted with a few trees. A church stands at the right. As in the Arena Chapel, landscape and architecture are subordinate to the human figures, and reinforce them. The cubic mass of Saint Francis from the waist down is mirrored in the building and the base of the mountain. The diagonal of the torso repeats the slanting triangle of the mountaintop. Despite the mystical content of the event, Giotto represents Saint Francis as a solid, three-dimensional figure and conveys a sense of physical reaction to the experience of religious transport. He is shown as if "taken aback" by the force of light rays emanating from his vision.

By virtue of the fresco's location on the chapel's outside wall the scene is the first to be encountered by visitors. Its purpose must have been at least partly to proclaim the spiritual sentiments of the Bardi family, whose commercial acumen and wealth were well known.

Duccio's *Maestà*

The leading early fourteenth-century artists in Siena, Florence's rival city, worked in a style that was influenced by Byzantine tradition. Siena was ruled by a group known as the Nine, which was in charge of public commissions. The Nine were particularly devoted to the Virgin, for they believed her intercession had been responsible for a major thirteenth-century military victory over Florence. Her cult was a significant feature of Sienese culture, and she was the city's patron saint. Siena called itself "the Virgin's ancient city" (*vetusta civitas virginis*).

In 1308, the Nine commissioned the prominent Sienese painter Duccio di Buoninsegna (active 1278–1318) to create a new altarpiece for the high altar of their cathedral. It was to honor the Virgin, whose image is the largest in the entire work. The completed altarpiece was two-sided, and originally consisted of between fifty-four and fifty-eight panels, fifteen of which have been lost; most of

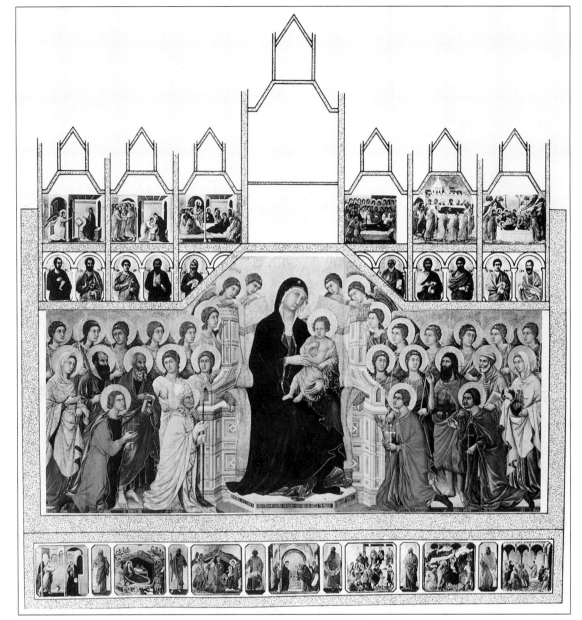

13.14a John White, photo montage of Duccio's *Maestà* (front), 1308–11. This is Duccio's only signed work (signed on the base of the throne). According to the commission contract, which was signed October 9, 1308, Duccio would receive 16 *soldi* for every day that he worked on the altarpiece. For those days that he did not work, he was docked from a monthly stipend of 10 *lire*.

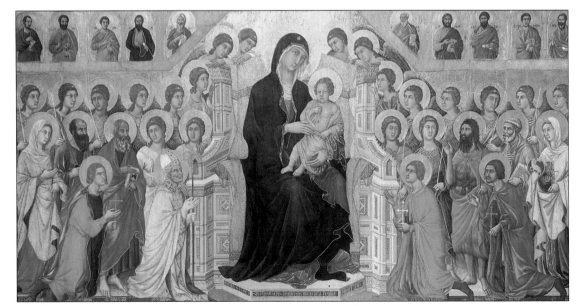

13.14b Duccio, *Maestà*, from Siena Cathedral, 1308–11. Tempera and gold on panel, 7 ft × 13 ft 6¼ in (2.13 × 4.12 m). Museo dell'Opera del Duoma, Siena.

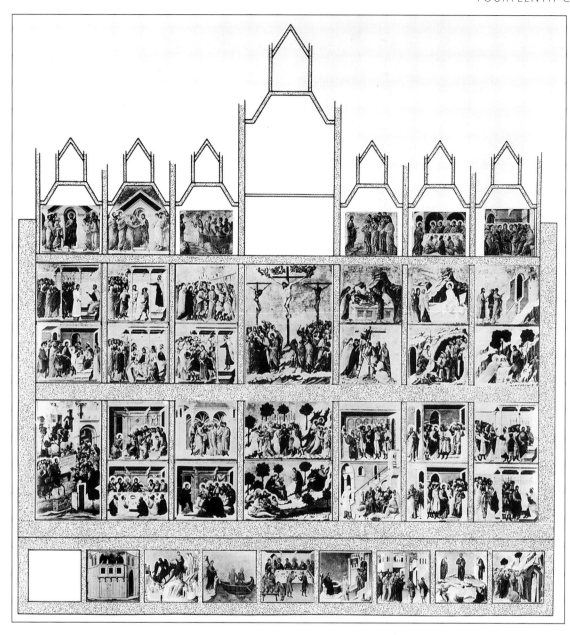

13.15 John White, photo montage of Duccio's *Maestà* (back), 1308–11.

the dismantled panels are now in museums elsewhere (e.g. the National Gallery of Art, Washington, and National Gallery, London). In its original state, Duccio's *Maestà* was about as high as the monumental altarpieces by Cimabue and Giotto discussed above, but was considerably wider (about 13 feet/4 m). Its former appearance has been reconstructed in photo montage by the art historian John White. The front (fig. **13.14**) exalts the Virgin in her aspect as Queen of Heaven—*maestà* means "majesty." She occupies the large, horizontal panel, the sides of her throne opening up as if to welcome the viewer. Surrounding her are saints, angels, and the apostles of Christ. Above is a row of saints, each standing under a round arch. The lower sections of the pinnacles contain scenes of her last days, beginning on the left with the *Annunciation of the Death of the Virgin* and ending with the *Burial of the Virgin* on the right. At the bottom are predella panels with scenes of Christ's early life, from left to right: the *Annunciation of*

his birth, the *Nativity, Adoration of the Magi, Presentation in the Temple, Massacre of the Innocents, Flight into Egypt*, and *Christ among the Doctors*. Standing by each of these events is the Old Testament prophet interpreted as having foretold it.

The four registers on the reconstructed back of the *Maestà* (fig. **13.15**) depict Christ's Passion in thirty-two scenes. The largest, at the center, is the *Crucifixion*. The six pinnacle scenes illustrate Christ's miraculous appearances after his death, and on the predellas are scenes of his ministry.

The iconography of the altarpiece covers the full range of the Virgin's majesty and of her maternity. She is not only the heavenly mother of Christ, but of the saints and apostles, and of the citizens of Siena as their patron. In 1311, when Duccio completed the *Maestà*, it was carried in a triumphal procession, accompanied by pipes and drums, from his studio to the cathedral.

The *Kiss of Judas*

Duccio and Giotto exemplify two significant currents in early fourteenth-century Italian painting. Duccio was more closely tied to the Byzantine tradition, whereas Giotto was steeped in the humanist revival of Classical antiquity. These relationships can be clarified by comparing three examples of the *Kiss of Judas*: a Byzantine mosaic (fig. **13.16**), Duccio's panel below the Crucifixion in the *Maestà* (fig. **13.17**), and the Arena Chapel fresco (fig. **13.18**). All three represent the moment when Judas identifies Christ to the Romans with a kiss. In the mosaic and in Duccio's panel, Christ is nearly frontal, and Judas leans over in a sweeping curved plane to embrace him. Their heads connect, but in neither case do Judas' lips actually touch Christ's face. Both scenes are set outdoors, against a gold sky. The figures in the mosaic face the viewer, and are only minimally engaged with each other. They are outlined in black, and their diagonal feet accentuate the two-dimensionality of their space. As the largest figure, Christ stands out as the most significant; he also has a jeweled halo and wears the purple robe of royalty, denoting his future role as King of Heaven.

Duccio's panel is more densely packed with figures than the mosaic. This, together with the landscape background, conveys an illusion of greater depth. The more subtle shading of the drapery folds also gives the figures a greater sense of three-dimensional form. In the mosaic, the apostles at the right wear Roman-style togas, and stand in vertical planes. The only sign of emotion at the arrest of their leader is the slight agitation of their tilted heads. In the Duccio, however, the apostles break away from the central crowd, and rush off to the right. Their long, curvilinear planes have the quality of a graceful dance movement performed in unison. At the left, Saint Peter also turns from Christ, but, in a rage, he cuts off the ear of Malchus, the servant of the High Priest.

Giotto's version of the *Kiss of Judas* (fig. 13.18) lives up to his reputation among humanist authors for having reintroduced naturalism to painting. The sky, for example, is no longer gold, but rather a natural blue. (It is likely that Giotto knew the Ravenna mosaics in the mausoleum of Galla Placidia, where the skies are also blue.) The fresco is virtually devoid of landscape forms that might distract viewers from the central event. Nor do any of Giotto's figures face the picture plane. All are focused on the dramatic confrontation between Christ and Judas. These two, in turn, are locked in each other's gaze, surrounded ominously by the black helmets framing their heads. Over Christ's head, the two hands holding stakes accentuate the rage of the mob against him; none of the stakes is vertical,

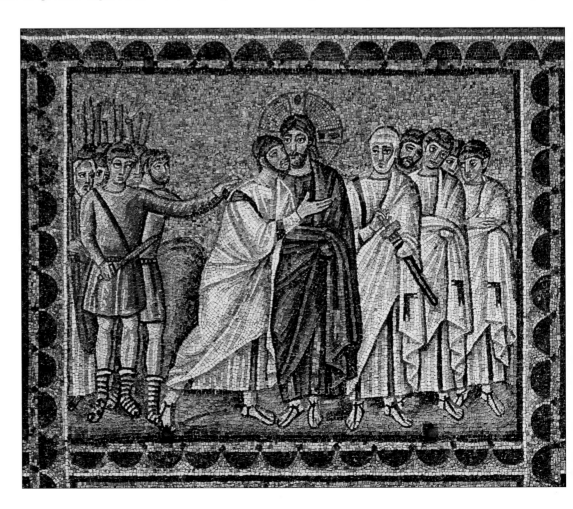

13.16 *Kiss of Judas*, Sant'Apollinare Nuovo, Ravenna, early 6th century. Mosaic.

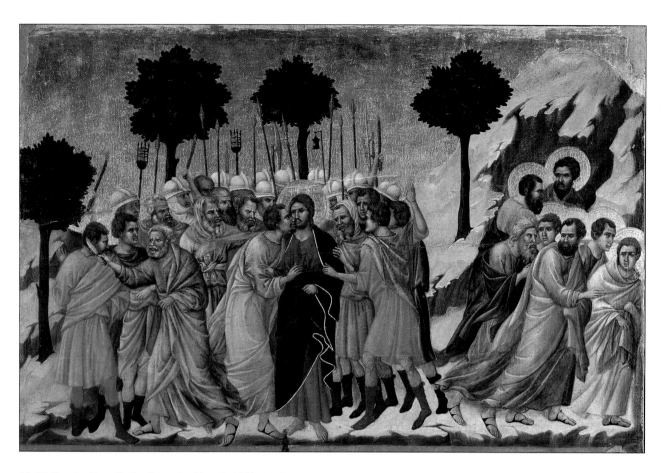

13.17 Duccio, *Kiss of Judas*, from the *Maestà*, 1308–11. Tempera on panel. Museo dell'Opera del Duomo, Siena.

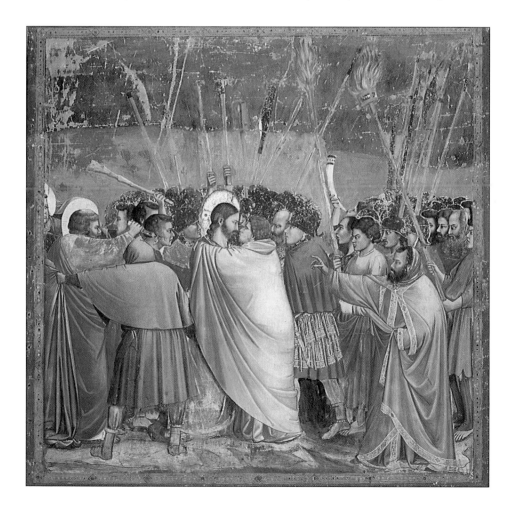

13.18 Giotto, *Kiss of Judas*, Arena Chapel, Padua, c. 1305. Fresco.

as in the Duccio, those behind Christ seeming to radiate from an unseen point. In this convergence of forms, therefore, Giotto signals the violence of Christ's death, and also his ultimate triumph.

Giotto is the first Western artist since ancient Rome to have depicted figures in back view. In the *Kiss of Judas*, he places three figures as if in different stages of a turn: the pointing man at the right is in three-quarter view; Judas turns farther to the right as his yellow cloak envelops Christ; and the hooded man in gray is seen directly from the rear. Together, these three create a sense of movement from right to left across the picture plane, counteracting the left–right flow of the narrative. Another countermotion can be seen in the figure of Saint Peter, who raises his hand behind the head of the hooded man, and vigorously cuts off the ear of Malchus. Saint Peter does not, as in Duccio's scene, turn away from Christ. The thrust of his blow interacts with the gesture of the hooded figure, whose very presence conveys an air of foreboding. His facelessness, characteristic of the executioner, alludes to Christ's imminent death on the Cross.

Ambrogio Lorenzetti and the *Effects of Good Government*

Some twenty-seven years after the triumphal procession for Duccio's *Maestà*, the innovative Sienese artist Ambrogio Lorenzetti (active 1319–47) painted *Allegories of Good and Bad Government* for the Palazzo Pubblico (Town Hall) of Siena. Figure **13.19**, like Giotto's *Justice* (fig. 13.12), illustrates the effects of good government on a city—in this case Siena. In contrast to the *Maestà*, Ambrogio's *Allegory* is secular, and reflects the new humanist interest in republican government. He depicts a broad civic panorama with remarkable realism. In the foreground (from left to right), women wearing the latest fashions dance and sing in celebration of the joys of good government; people ride on horseback among the buildings, whose open archways reveal a school, a cobbler's shop, and a tavern; farmers are shown entering the city to sell their produce. On top of the central building in the background, workers carry baskets and lay masonry. In this imagery, Lorenzetti suggests that both agricultural prosperity and architectural construction are among the advantages of good government.

Just outside the city walls, people ride off to the country. Below, a group of peasants tills the soil, and the cultivated landscape visible in the distance draws the viewer into an almost unprecedented degree of spatial depth. Floating above this tranquil scene, an allegorical figure of Security holds a scroll with an inscription reminding viewers that peace reigns under her aegis. And should one fail to read the inscription, she provides a pictorial message in the form of a gallows. Swinging from the rope is a criminal executed for violating the laws of good government. Accompanying Ambrogio's vision of prosperity and tranquility, therefore, is a clear warning of the consequences of social disruption.

Just behind the left foot of Security, Ambrogio has included the statue of the legendary she-wolf who nursed Romulus and Remus. Projecting from the city's wall, she seems to survey the surrounding countryside. At the

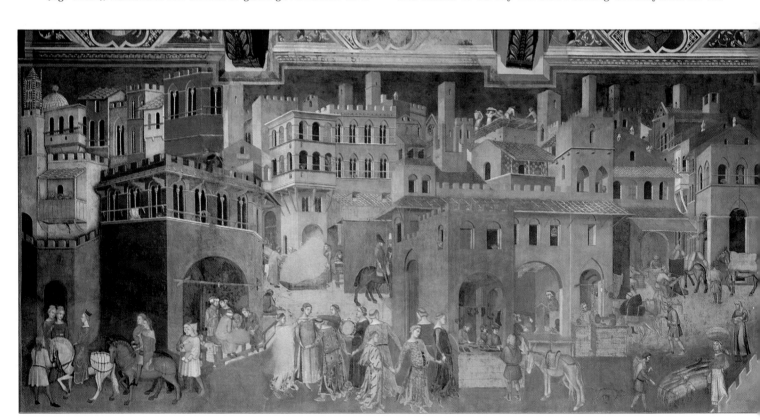

same time, the wolf makes explicit the link between ancient Rome and Siena.

Stylistically, Ambrogio's *Allegories* fall between Giotto and Duccio. Although the *Allegory of Bad Government* is severely damaged, certain details are clear. That in figure **13.20** shows two soldiers attacking a woman, rendered in a graceful S-curve. Above are the feet of two hanged criminals, echoing the exemplary gallows of Security. Despite its violence, the scene lacks the dramatic power that characterizes Giotto's work. On the other hand, Ambrogio's figures are closer to Giotto's than to Duccio's in their sense of mass and volume. Nor are their draperies trimmed with gold as Duccio's often are.

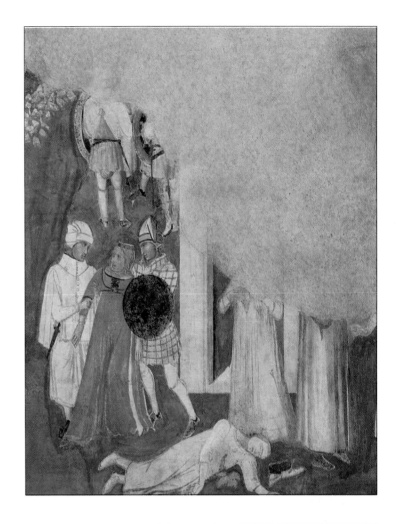

13.19 (opposite and below) Ambrogio Lorenzetti, *Effects of Good Government in the City and the Country*, from the *Allegory of Good Government*, 1338–39. Fresco, entire wall 46 ft (14 m) long. Sala della Pace, Palazzo Pubblico, Siena. Ambrogio was the younger of two artist brothers who were active in the first half of the 14th century. Both were born and worked in Siena, and they are believed to have died from the Black Death, since nothing is heard of them after 1348. Ambrogio also worked in Florence, where he was exposed to Giotto's style. The *Allegory of Good Government*, which has considerable documentary value as well as artistic merit, is considered his greatest surviving work.

13.20 (right) Ambrogio Lorenzetti, detail showing soldiers attacking a woman, from the *Allegory of Bad Government*, 1338–39. Fresco. Palazzo Pubblico, Siena.

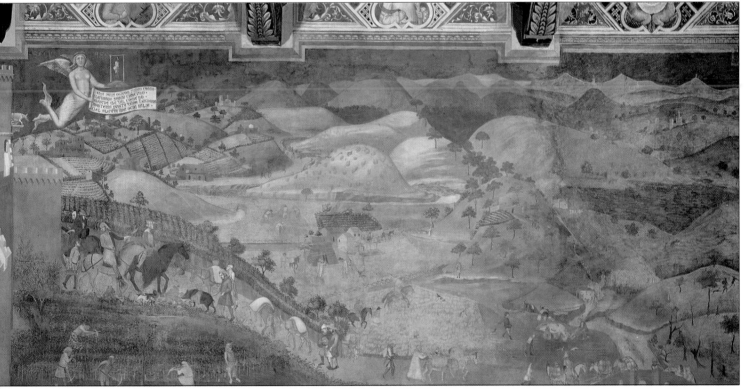

The Black Death

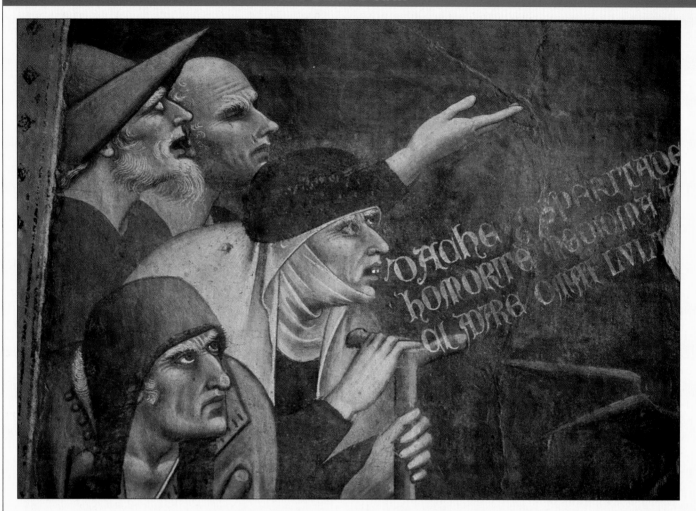

13.21 Andrea Orcagna, detail showing figures invoking Death, from the *Triumph of Death*, c. 1360. Fresco. Museo dell'Opera di Santa Croce, Florence.

The bubonic plague of 1348 killed some 25 million people. It was carried by a bacillus in fleas that lodged in the fur of common rodents. The effects of the Black Death were described by Boccaccio in the preface of the *Decameron*, a collection of 100 stories set in fourteenth-century Italy:

> 1348. The mortal pestilence then arrived in the excellent city of Florence.... It carried off uncounted numbers of inhabitants, and kept moving ... in its early stages both men, and women too, acquired certain swellings, either in the groin or under the armpits. Some of these swellings reached the size of a common apple ... people called them plague-boils ... the deadly swellings began to reach ... every part of the body. Then ... began to change into black or livid blotches ... almost everyone died within the third day ... even to handle the clothing or other things touched by the sick seemed to carry with it that same disease....

> Some persons advised that a moderate manner of living, and the avoidance of all excesses, greatly strengthened resistance to this danger.... Others ... affirmed that heavy drinking and enjoyment ... were the most effective medicine for this great evil....

> The city was full of corpses ... there was not enough blessed burial ground ... they made huge trenches in every churchyard, in which they stacked hundreds of bodies in layers like goods stowed in the hold of a ship, covering them with a bit of earth until the bodies reached the very top.[6]

There was, as Boccaccio observed, a general air of penance on the one hand, and a "seize the day" mentality on the other. As a result of the disasters that swept Europe during the first half of the fourteenth century, artists became drawn to such subjects as the Triumph of Death. Andrea di Cione—known as Orcagna (active c. 1343–68)—painted a monumental fresco in the church of Santa Croce in Florence in which he combined the theme with depictions of hell and the Last Judgment. Although the work survives only in fragments, its message of impending doom remains clear.

The detail in figure **13.21** shows two cripples and two blind men invoking Death. The anxious gesture of one of the sightless men contrasts with the wide-eyed stares of the cripples, whose hands are needed for their crutches. The inscription reads: "Since prosperity has departed, Death, the cure of all pain, come and give us our last supper." In another fragment of Orcagna's *Triumph of Death* (fig. **13.22**), two men gaze at an eclipse of the sun. Since contemporary documents related the eclipse of 1333 to subsequent flooding, it is likely that this detail associates those events with both the Old Testament Flood and the apocalyptic "day of wrath" (Revelation 6:12–17).

13.22 Andrea Orcagna, detail showing two men watching an eclipse of the sun, from the *Triumph of Death*, c. 1360. Fresco. Museo dell'Opera di Santa Croce, Florence.

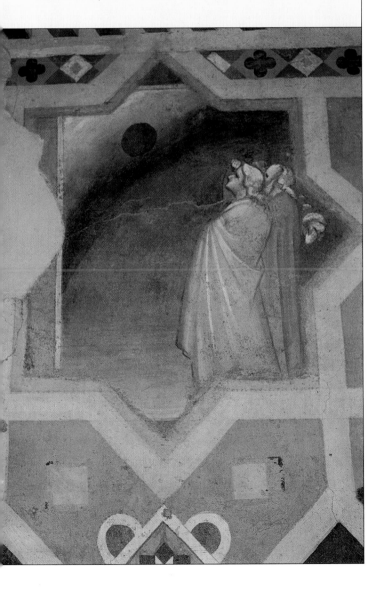

Ambrogio Lorenzetti's monumental secular paintings were the first of their kind in Western art since Christianity had become the official religion of Rome. They reflected the shift that had occurred in patronage, which was no longer exclusively tied to the Church—even in Siena where the Virgin's cult was at its strongest. As Lorenzetti's work reveals, the new cultural and intellectual concerns of the early fourteenth century had resulted in a revolutionary development in style. Giotto had created a new approach to painted space, influenced as he was by the sculpture of Nicola Pisano and his son Giovanni, and by discoveries of Classical texts. For the first time since Greco-Roman antiquity, human figures occupy three-dimensional settings. Backgrounds are no longer gold but rather defined by natural blue skies or landscape. Architecture is set at an oblique angle to the picture plane, creating an illusion of spatial recession.

A series of disasters in western Europe disrupted the activities of the next generations of fourteenth-century artists. In 1304 a fire destroyed much of Florence; eight years later, the city was under siege by the Emperor of Luxemburg, who had sacked the Tuscan countryside. In 1329, there was famine, an eclipse followed by a flood in 1333, and a smallpox epidemic in 1335 that killed thousands of children. In the early 1340s, both the Bardi and Peruzzi banks failed, and in 1348 the bubonic plague—referred to as the Black Death—devastated Europe (see Box). In Florence and Siena, between 50 and 70 percent of the residents died, resulting in population shifts, economic depression, and radical changes in artistic patronage and style.

Contemporary sermons document the resurgence of religious fervor following the Black Death. In the visual arts there was a revival of certain aspects of the Byzantine style. The increasingly humanistic style of the first half of the century yielded to a more pessimistic view of the world, with greater emphasis on death and damnation. The innovations of Giotto and other early fourteenth-century artists remained in abeyance, and were revived by the first generation of Italian painters, sculptors, and architects of the fifteenth century.

The International Gothic Style

An entirely different mood characterized works commissioned by the courts in fourteenth-century Italy and France. Their wealth made it possible to import artists from different regions and to pay them well. The resulting convergence of styles, generally known as International Gothic, continued into the fifteenth century; the best fourteenth-century examples were executed under French patronage.

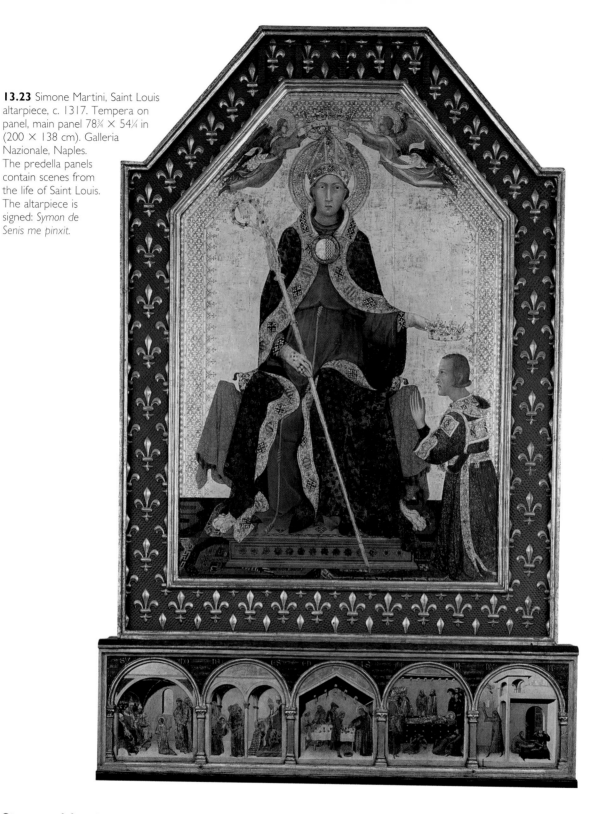

13.23 Simone Martini, Saint Louis altarpiece, c. 1317. Tempera on panel, main panel 78¾ × 54¼ in (200 × 138 cm). Galleria Nazionale, Naples. The predella panels contain scenes from the life of Saint Louis. The altarpiece is signed: *Symon de Senis me pinxit.*

Simone Martini

In the Angevin court at Naples (in southern Italy), French taste predominated, even in the work of Italian artists. King Robert of Anjou was the younger brother of Louis of Toulouse, who had joined the Franciscan order of the Friars Minor. When elected to the rank of bishop in 1296, Louis renounced the throne in favor of Robert, and died a year later. Amid rumors that he had usurped the throne, Robert commissioned the Sienese artist Simone Martini to paint the altarpiece illustrated in figure

13.23. The date of the commission, 1317, coincided with Louis' canonization.

The enthroned Franciscan saint is dressed in embroidered velvet robes, and wears a bishop's miter. He is set against a rich gold background with a raised gold halo and border inside the frame. In keeping with courtly tastes, especially that of Naples, the drapery was originally decorated with real jewels embedded in the panel. Simone Martini's attraction to such taste is further evident in the fluid, curvilinear robes, the jeweled crozier (bishop's staff) and crowns, the long, thin hands, and pale, delicate faces of his figures. Two angels crown Saint Louis as he bestows the earthly crown on his brother. Through his large size, central position, and frontality, Louis is endowed with an imposing, iconic presence, whereas Robert is portrayed in miniature, and in three-quarter view. It is clear that Simone (and presumably his patron) intended the viewer to perceive the saint as the more important figure and his ecclesiastic office as more powerful than that of the earthly ruler. The gold fleurs-de-lis on the blue background of the frame identify the scene with the French royal family, which reinforces the legitimacy of Robert's claim to the throne.

Claus Sluter

Toward the end of the fourteenth century, France was ruled by Charles V. Two of his brothers—Philip the Bold (1342–1404) and Jean, Duc de Berry (1340–1416)—presided over lavish courts, which were enriched by their ambitious patronage. The sumptuousness of the works produced for them shows the degree to which the courts were far removed from the real world, with France and other areas of Europe suffering continual upheaval from the ravages of the Hundred Years' War.

Philip's court was located at Dijon, in the Burgundy region of central France. His wife, Margaret of Flanders

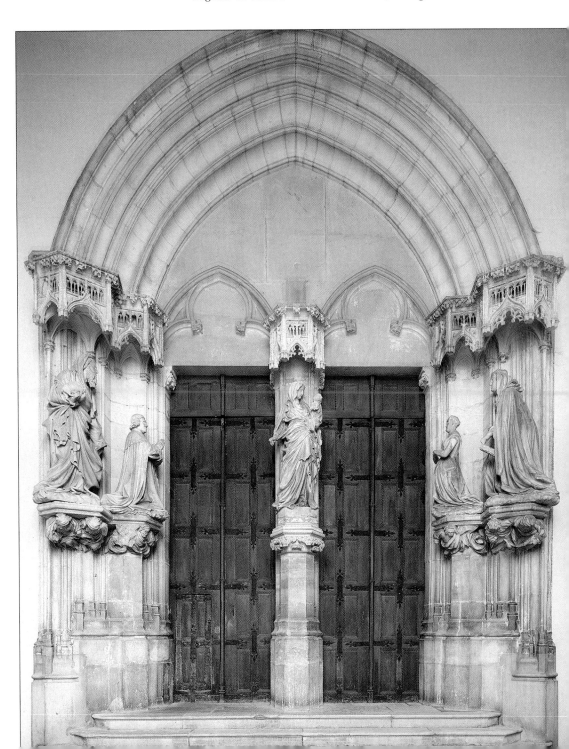

13.24 Claus Sluter, Portal, Chartreuse de Champmol, Dijon, 1385–93. The sculptor Claus Sluter was born in Haarlem, the Netherlands. After he went to the court of Philip the Bold, he was quickly promoted to the position of *imagier* and *valet de chambre*.

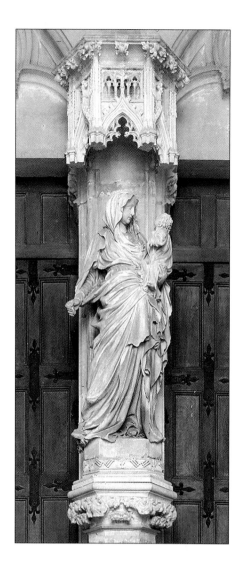

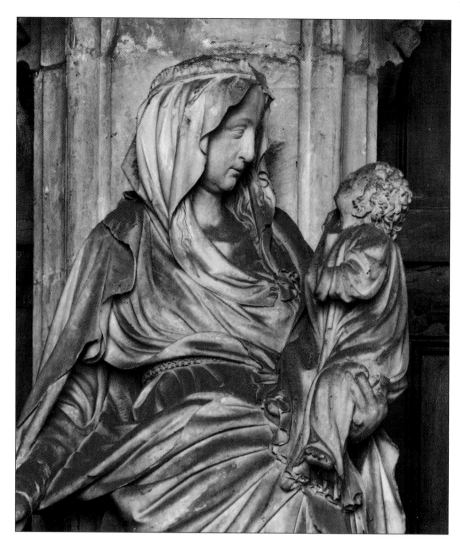

13.25 (above left) Claus Sluter, *Virgin Mary*, central trumeau of portal, Chartreuse de Champmol, Dijon, 1385–93.

13.26 (above right) Claus Sluter (detail of fig. 13.25).

(modern Holland, Belgium, and parts of France), provided a link with the North. Reflecting the international character of his court and his patronage, Philip commissioned an architect from Paris and a sculptor from the Netherlands to design a Carthusian monastery—the Chartreuse de Champmol—near his Dijon palace. This building was to house the family tombs. Philip's competition with the king is suggested by the fact that his architect had worked for Charles in Paris, and that the monastery's portal followed Charles' lead in placing portrait sculptures of living people on the door jambs—a site formerly reserved for Old Testament kings, queens, and prophets, and for Christian saints.

Philip's sculptor, Claus Sluter (active 1379–1406), placed a figure of the *Virgin Mary* on the trumeau of the portal (figs. **13.24**, **13.25**, and **13.26**). She is crowned, but her character is primarily maternal. Although the architectural feature above her is entirely Gothic and Sluter worked in an essentially Gothic tradition, a comparison of his *Virgin* with the thirteenth-century *Vierge dorée* at Amiens (see fig. 12.37) shows the degree to which he has transformed the representation of human figures. His *Virgin* turns more freely in space, and gazes on a Christ who is more child-

like than his Gothic predecessors. Christ's floppy head and chubby proportions articulated by the drapery folds indicate that Sluter was a careful observer of children. He has represented the physical and psychological character of this infant Christ with a new, naturalistic accuracy, while Mary is animated by the sweep of her billowing draperies. The arrangement of the folds emphasizes her spatial flexibility, and creates a sense of dynamic energy.

Mary's gaze, focused as it is on Christ, is repeated by the door jamb figures. Philip (on the left) and Margaret (on the right) are represented kneeling in prayer toward the Virgin. They adore the Queen of Heaven as she adores the child. Leaning over the noble pair and interceding on their behalf are saints, John the Baptist and Catherine. Sluter contrasts the rhythmic orchestration of deeply carved, elegant drapery curves with the fixed, arrested concentration of the door jamb figures on Mary and Christ.

Two years after completing the portal, Sluter set to work on the Well of Moses, a monumental fountain for the Chartreuse (figs. **13.27** and **13.28**). It was set on a hexagonal base with an Old Testament figure on each side. Six small angels stand on colonnettes located between the life-size figures. They lean over in the compressed space under the edge of the basin, and spread out their wings to form an arch over each large figure. Their crossed arms allude to the Crucifixion, which was originally represented by a great Cross (now lost). It was set in stone that was carved

in imitation of Mount Golgotha. This was supported by the "Well," just as the Old Testament was seen as the foundation of the New. Christ was thus the "fountain of life"— the *fons vitae*—and he faced east, in the same direction as David (fig. 13.27), the ancestor of Christ, represented as both prophet (the scroll) and king (his crown). Philip the Bold's identification with David is accentuated by the design of the crown, which is ringed with fleurs-de-lis. To the right of David is Jeremiah, who prophesied that the New Covenant would replace the Old. To David's left is

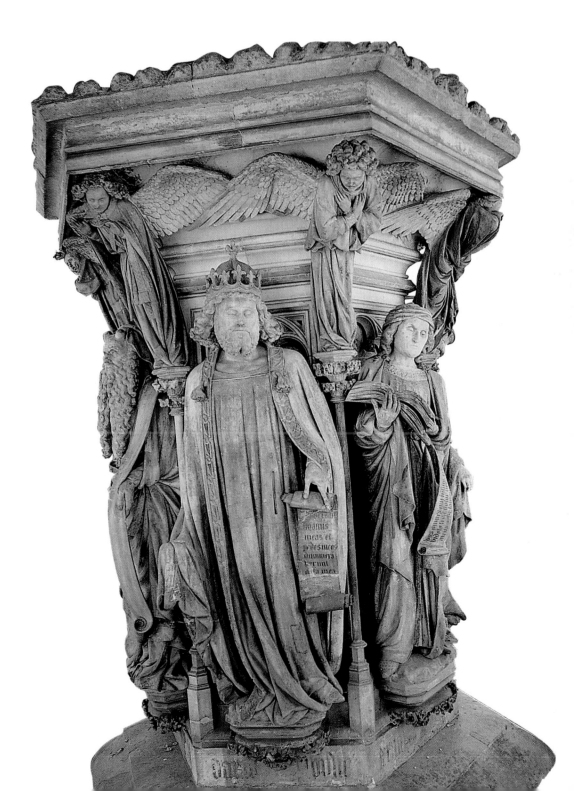

13.27 Claus Sluter, Well of Moses, Chartreuse de Champmol, Dijon, begun 1395. Painted stone, interior diameter of basin 23 ft 6 in × 23 ft 7 in (7.16 × 7.19 m). David's right hand rests on his harp, and he holds a scroll in his left hand. The inscription on the scroll is from Psalms 22:16–17: "they pierced my hands and my feet. I may tell all my bones" (*foderunt manus meas et pedes meos, numerarunt ossa mea*).

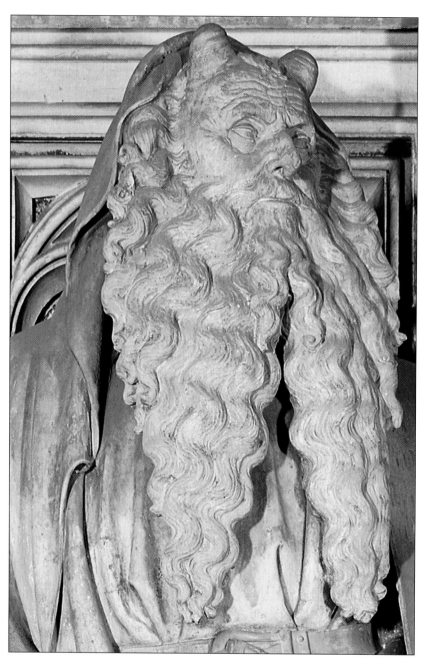

13.28 Claus Sluter, head of Moses (detail of fig. 13.27).

Sinai with the Tables of the Law. These ushered in a new social and religious order. Moses, therefore, stands as a prefiguration of the new Christian order signified in the great Crucifix over the fountain. And it is to that event that the inscription of Moses' scroll refers: "the whole assembly of the congregation of Israel shall kill it [the lamb] in the evening" (Exodus 12:6).

The Limbourg Brothers

In northern Europe, manuscript illumination was the primary medium of painting at the turn of the century. The illuminated manuscripts of the Limbourg brothers were among the most impressive works of art produced at the court of Jean, Duc de Berry. Jean was an ardent patron, who collected jewels and books, tapestries and goldwork, and led a life of immense luxury. The three Limbourg brothers—Paul, Herman, and Jean—came from the Netherlands, first to the Burgundy court and then to Berry. They made Books of Hours, which are prayer books organized according to the liturgical calendar. The most famous of these is the *Très Riches Heures du Duc de Berry* (the *Very Rich Hours of the Duke of Berry*).

Books of Hours were made for lay people, and most were commissioned by the aristocracy and upper middle class. They were expensive heirlooms, prized by their owners and passed down from one generation to the next. Ever since the fourth century, the illuminated manuscripts accompanying Books of Hours had been sources of learning and esthetic pleasure. The contents of these books vary, but generally include the prayers to be said at the eight canonical hours of the day. In the fourteenth century, Books of Hours had become best sellers, and, for the first time in the Christian era, they were even more popular outside clerical circles than the Bible. Most were produced in France, England, and the Netherlands, while Italy, Spain, and Germany were more likely to import them. Their significance for the rise of literacy in the fourteenth century is problematic, although it is clear that literacy did increase in the later Middle Ages. Strictly speaking, one did not have to be able to read to enjoy Books of Hours: merely gazing on their illuminations was considered a form of prayer, and, in any case, their owners would have known their contents by heart. The primary function of these images was to evoke identification through prayer as a route to salvation.

The manuscript page of the *Annunciation* from the *Très Riches Heures* (fig. **13.29**) shows Mary interrupted at her *prie-dieu* (a type of prayer desk) by Gabriel's arrival. He

Moses, who transmitted the Old Testament Law to the Hebrews; the other figures on the fountain are the prophets Zechariah, Daniel, and Isaiah.

The detail of Moses (fig. 13.28) shows a powerful, thoughtful patriarch. His lined face, strong nose, and slight frown give the sculpture a portrait-like quality. But the features are overwhelmed by the swirling energy of the beard, and the stunted horns emerging from his head. These became an iconographic convention in representations of Moses, when the word *cornuta*, meaning "rays of light," was misread as "horns." They make manifest the radiance of Moses on descending from Mount

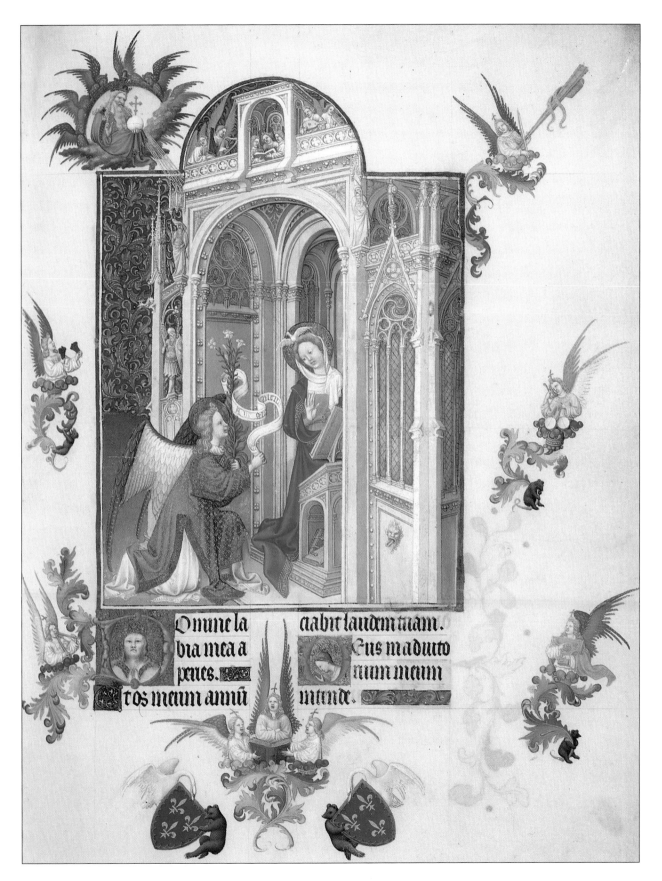

13.29 Limbourg Brothers, *Annunciation*, from the *Très Riches Heures du Duc de Berry*, 1413–16. Illumination. Musée Condé, Chantilly, France.

carries three lilies, signifying the passion and purity of the Virgin, and a scroll with the inscription *"Ave gratia plena"* ("Hail [Mary] full of grace"). The scene takes place in a Gothic chapel (despite the round arch) decorated with delicate stone tracery, and set against a sumptuous, blue brocade backdrop. An angelic choir makes music on the chapel roof, and at the left are statues of two prophets. In the upper left, outside the frame, God the Father appears in a winged circle of light. He holds an orb with a cross, and sends down to Mary the impregnating rays of his light. Decorating the rest of the border are musician angels (those beneath the text are singing angels) intertwined with elegant, curvilinear foliate forms. Jean de Berry's two coats of arms are held by his emblems, the swan and the bear, and serve as the signature of his patronage.

The manuscript page illustrating the month of *February* (fig. **13.30**) is the first snowscape in Western art. In the semicircle above are the zodiac signs that correspond to the time of year. The detailed observation of nature in this scene is typical of the Limbourg brothers' work, and reflects a new focus on the representation of everyday life.

In the distance, a man drives his donkey to town. In the middle ground, a man cuts wood for fire. The foreground is a specific depiction of a farm in winter. Four beehives are neatly lined up on a low platform. A woman rushes toward the house, and blows warm breath on her cold hands. The sheep huddle together for warmth in their fold, and birds search for food under the snow. Smoke rises from the chimney of the farmhouse. Inside the house, the peasant couple lift their clothing to get the full benefit of the fire, but they immodestly expose themselves. The mistress of the house is more discreet: she turns from the peasants and gingerly raises her own skirt, exposing only her lower leg and a slip.

Such representation of observed detail, whether to reveal social distinctions or to depict nature, entered the vocabulary of painting in the course of the fourteenth century. The art of the courts seems to have avoided the effects of the disasters that swept western Europe in the first half of the century. The International Gothic style persisted into the fifteenth century, but the major innovations in art from 1400 resume the developments introduced by Giotto.

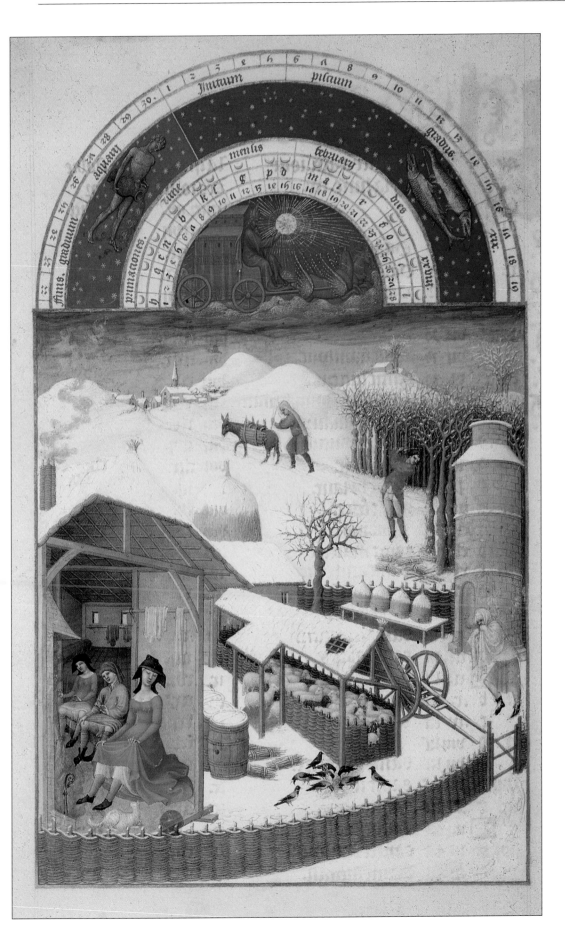

13.30 Limbourg Brothers, *February*, from the *Très Riches Heures du Duc de Berry*, 1413–16. Illumination, 8¾ × 5⁵⁄₁₆ in (22.2 × 13.5 cm). Musée Condé, Chantilly.

Style/Period	Works of Art	Cultural/Historical Developments
PRECURSORS OF THE RENAISSANCE Mid-13th to 14th century 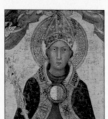 **Martini, Saint Louis altarpiece** 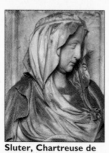 **Sluter, Chartreuse de Champmol Portal**	*Kiss of Judas* (**13.16**), Sant'Apollinare Nuovo Pisano, *Nativity* (**13.1**), Pisa Baptistry Cimabue, *Madonna Enthroned* (**13.4**) Giotto, *Kiss of Judas* (**13.18**), Arena Chapel Giotto, Frescoes (**13.7–13.12**), Arena Chapel Duccio, *Kiss of Judas* (**13.17**), *Maestà* altarpiece Giotto, *Madonna Enthroned* (**13.5**) Martini, Saint Louis altarpiece (**13.23**) Giotto, *Stigmatization of Saint Francis* (**13.13**), Bardi Chapel Lorenzetti, *Allegory of Good Government* (**13.19**), Palazzo Pubblico, Siena Lorenzetti, *Allegory of Bad Government* (**13.20**), Palazzo Pubblico, Siena Orcagna, *Triumph of Death* (**13.21–13.22**) Sluter, Chartreuse de Champmol Portal (**13.24–13.26**), Dijon Sluter, *Well of Moses* (**13.27–13.28**) 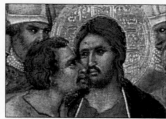 **Duccio,** *Kiss of Judas*	Invention of the glass mirror (1278) Rise of Florence as a leading commercial center (c. 1280) The "Pied Piper of Hamelin" (1284) End of the Crusades; Knights of Saint John of Jerusalem settle in Malta (1291) Building of Palazzo Vecchio, Florence (1299–1301) 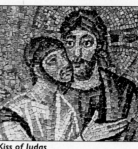 *Kiss of Judas* Birth of Italian poet Petrarch 1304 (d. 1374) Dante writes *The Divine Comedy* (1307–21) Papal seat moves to Avignon (1309) Birth of John Wycliffe, English church reformer (1328) Bankruptcy of Bardi and Peruzzi banking houses of Florence (1345) The Black Death ravages Europe (1347–51) Giovanni Boccaccio writes the *Decameron* (1353) The Aztecs build their capital at Tenochtitlán, Mexico (1364) Development of the steel crossbow (c. 1370) Peasants' Revolt in England (1381) Chaucer writes *The Canterbury Tales* (1387–1400) Birth of Johann Gutenberg, inventor of printing in Europe (1396)
EARLY RENAISSANCE 15th century	Limbourg Brothers, *Très Riches Heures du Duc de Berry* (**13.29–13.30**)	The invention of scientific perspective (c. 1400) Rise to power of the Medicis in Florence (1400) The English defeat the French at Agincourt (1415) 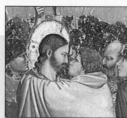 **Giotto,** *Kiss of Judas*

1250

1400

Glossary

Abacus: the flat slab that forms the topmost unit of a Doric **column** and on which the **architrave** rests (see p. 160).

Abhaya: see **mudrā**.

Abstract: in painting and sculpture, having a generalized or essential form with only a symbolic resemblance to natural objects.

Abutment: the part of a building intended to receive and counteract the thrust, or pressure, exerted by **vaults** and **arches**.

Academy: (a) the gymnasium near Athens where Plato taught; (b) from the eighteenth century, the cultural and artistic establishment and the standards that they represent.

Acanthus: a Mediterranean plant with prickly leaves, supposedly the source of foliage-like ornamentation on Corinthian **columns**.

Achromatic: free of color.

Aedicule: (a) a small building used as a shrine; (b) a **niche** designed to hold a statue. Both types are formed by two **columns** or **pilasters** supporting a **gable** or **pediment**.

Agora: the open space in an ancient Greek town used as a marketplace or for general meetings.

Aisle: a passageway flanking a central area (e.g. the corridors flanking the **nave** of a **basilica** or **cathedral**).

Alabaster: a dense variety of fine-textured gypsum, usually white and translucent, but sometimes gray, red, yellow, or banded, used for carving on a small scale.

Allegory: the expression (artistic, oral, or written) of a generalized moral statement or truth by means of symbolic actions or figures.

Altar: (a) any structure used as a place of sacrifice or worship; (b) a tablelike structure used in a Christian church to celebrate the **Eucharist**.

Altarpiece: a painted or sculpted work of art designed to stand above and behind an **altar**.

Āmalaka: a **finial** in the shape of a notched ring (derived from a fruit) atop a northern-style Hindu temple's **shikhara** (fig. **12.P**).

Ambulatory: a **vaulted** passageway, usually surrounding the **apse** or **choir** of a church (fig. **11.4**).

Amphitheater: an oval or circular space surrounded by rising tiers of seats, as used by the ancient Greeks and Romans for plays and other spectacles (fig. **6.63**).

Amphora: an ancient Greek two-handled vessel for storing grain, honey, oil, or wine (fig. **6.8**).

Analogous hues: **hues** containing a common color, though in different proportions.

Anda: the **dome** of a Buddhist **stupa**, its egg-shape symbolizing the arc of the heavens (figs. **8.K–L**).

Aniconic: depicting a figure, usually a deity, symbolically instead of anthropomorphically.

Annular: ring-shaped, as in an annular **barrel vault**.

Apocalypse: (a) a name for the last book of the New Testament, generally known as the Revelation of Saint John the Divine; (b) a prophetic revelation.

Apostle: in Christian terminology, one of the twelve followers, or disciples, chosen by Christ to spread his Gospel; also used more loosely to include early missionaries such as Saint Paul.

Apotropaion: an object or device designed to avert, or turn aside, evil.

Apsaras (pl. **Apsarases**): celestial dancers seen in South and Southeast Asian religious art (figs. **12.W–X**).

Apse: a projecting part of a building (especially a church), usually semicircular and topped by a half-**dome** or **vault**.

Aqueduct: a manmade conduit for transporting water (fig. **8.25**).

Arcade: a **gallery** formed by a series of **arches** with supporting **columns** or **piers** (fig. **12.5**), either freestanding or blind (i.e. attached to a wall).

Arch: a curved architectural member, generally consisting of wedge-shaped blocks (**voussoirs**), which is used to span an opening; it transmits the downward pressure laterally (see p. 213).

Archaeometry: a branch of archaeology that dates objects through the use of various techniques such as amino-acid and **radiocarbon dating**.

Architrave: the lowest unit of an **entablature**, resting directly on the **capital** of a **column**.

Archivolt: the ornamental band or **molding** surrounding the **tympanum** of a Romanesque or Gothic church.

Arena: the central area in a Roman **amphitheater** where gladiatorial spectacles took place.

Armature: (a) a metal framework for a **stained-glass** window; (b) a fixed, inner framework supporting a sculpture made of a more flexible material.

Arriccio: the rough first coat of plaster in a **fresco**.

Asymmetrical: characterized by asymmetry, or lack of **balance**, in the arrangement of parts or components.

Atrium: (a) an open courtyard leading to, or within, a house or other building, usually surrounded on three or more sides by a **colonnade**; (b) in a modern building, a rectangular space off which other rooms open.

Attic: in Classical architecture, a low story placed above the main **entablature**.

Attribute: an object closely identified with, and thought of as belonging to, a specific individual —particularly, in art, a deity or saint.

Axis: an imaginary straight line passing through the center of a figure, form, or structure and about which that figure is imagined to rotate.

Axonometric projection: the depiction on a single **plane** of a **three-dimensional** object by placing it at an angle to the **picture plane** so that three faces are visible (fig. **9.31**).

Balance: an esthetically pleasing equilibrium in the combination or arrangement of elements.

Balustrade: a series of balusters, or upright **pillars**, supporting a rail (as along the edge of a balcony or bridge).

Baptistry: a building, usually round or polygonal, used for Christian baptismal services.

Barrel (or tunnel) vault: a semicylindrical **vault**, with parallel **abutments** and an identical **cross-section** throughout, covering an oblong space (see p. 213).

Base: (a) that on which something rests; (b) the lowest part of a wall or **column** considered as a separate architectural feature.

Basilica: (a) in Roman architecture, an oblong building used for tribunals and other public functions (see p. 219); (b) in Christian architecture, an early church with similar features to the Roman prototype (fig. **9.7**).

Bas-relief: see **low relief**.

Bay: a unit of space in a building, usually defined by **piers**, **vaults** or other elements in a structural system (fig. **12.2**).

Bhūmi (literally "earth"): the stacked ridges that horizontally segment a northern-style Hindu temple's **shikhara** (fig. **12.P**).

Bhūmisparsha: see **mudrā**.

Binder, binding medium: a substance used in paint and other **media** to bind particles of **pigment** together and enable them to adhere to the **support**.

Black-figure: describing a style of Greek pottery painting of the sixth century B.C., in which the decoration is black on a red background.

Bodhisattva: one of many enlightened Buddhist deities who delay their own nirvana in order to help mortals attain enlightenment.

Book of Hours: a prayer book, intended for lay use, containing the devotions, or acts of worship, for the hours of the Roman Catholic Church (i.e. the times appointed for prayer, such as Matins and Vespers).

Broken pediment: a **pediment** in which the **cornice** is discontinuous or interrupted by another element.

Bronze: a metal alloy composed of copper mixed with tin.

Buon fresco: see **fresco**.

Bust: a sculptural or pictorial representation of the upper part of the human figure, including the head and neck (and sometimes part of the shoulders and chest).

Buttress: an external architectural support that counteracts the lateral thrust of an **arch** or wall.

Caduceus: the symbol of a herald or physician, consisting of a staff with two snakes twined around it and two wings at the top.

Calligraphy: handwriting designed to be beautiful; **calligraphic** writing or drawing can be expressive as well as beautiful.

Campanile: Italian for bell tower, usually freestanding, but built near a church.

Canon: a set of rules, principles, or standards used to establish scales or **proportions**.

Canopic: relating to the city of Canopus in ancient Egypt; used to denote a vessel in which ancient Egyptians preserved the viscera of the dead.

Cantilever: a long, low architectural support that enables a **cantilevered** element such as an eave or a **cornice** to project horizontally without vertical support at the far end.

Capital: the decorated top of a **column** or **pilaster**, providing a transition from the **shaft** to the **entablature**.

Cartonnage: layers of linen or papyrus glued together and usually coated with **stucco**.

Cartouche: an oval or **scroll**-shaped design or ornament, usually containing an inscription, a heraldic device, or (as in Egypt) a ruler's name.

Caryatid: a supporting **column** in **post-and-lintel** construction carved to represent a human or animal figure.

Casting: a process in which liquefied material, usually metal, is formed by being poured into a mold; the mold is removed when the material has solidified, leaving a **cast** object in the shape of the mold.

Castrum (pl. **castra**): an ancient Roman fortress; a Roman encampment.

Catacomb: an underground complex of passageways and **vaults**, such as those used by Jews and early Christians to bury their dead.

Cathedral: the principal church of a diocese (the ecclesiastical district supervised by a bishop).

Cella: the main inner room of a temple, often containing the cult image of the deity.

Centering: the temporary wooden framework used in the construction of **arches**, **vaults**, and **domes**.

Ceramics: (a) the art of making objects from clay or other substances (such as **enamel** and porcelain) that require **firing** at high temperatures; (b) the objects themselves.

Chaitya arch: a splayed, horseshoe-shaped curve derived from the profile of a **barrel-vaulted chaitya hall**; used to frame doors, windows, and gables, and as a decorative motif in early South Asian architecture.

Chaitya hall: a U-shaped Buddhist structural or rock-cut chamber for congregational worship centered on a **stupa** (figs. **9.B–C, I–J**).

Chancel: that part of a Christian church, reserved for the clergy and choir, in which the **altar** is placed.

Chapter house: a meeting place for the discussion of business in a **cathedral** or **monastery**.

Chattra: a royal parasol crowning the **dome** (**anda**) of a Buddhist **stupa**, symbolically honoring the Buddha (fig. **8.L**).

Chaurī: a royal fly-whisk, symbolically honoring the Buddha (fig. **8.S**).

Chevet: French term for the east end of a Gothic church, comprising the **choir**, **ambulatory**, and **radiating chapels**.

Choir: part of a Christian church, near the **altar**, set aside for those chanting the services (fig. **11.4**); usually part of the **chancel**.

Chroma: see **intensity**.

Chromatic: colored or pertaining to color.

Chryselephantine: consisting of, or decorated with, gold and ivory.

Circumambulate: to walk around something, especially an object of worship or veneration.

Circus: in ancient Rome, an oblong space, surrounded by seats, used for chariot races, games, and other spectacles.

Cire-perdue: see **lost-wax bronze casting**.

Citadel: a fortress or other fortified area placed in an elevated or commanding position (fig. **3.3**).

Clerestory: the upper part of the main outer wall of a building (especially a church), located above an adjoining roof and admitting light through a row of windows (fig. **9.8**).

Cloisonné: a multicolored surface made by pouring **enamels** into compartments outlined by bent wire fillets, or strips.

Cloister: in a **monastery**, a covered passage or **ambulatory**, usually with one side walled and the other open to a courtyard.

Close: an enclosed space, or precinct, usually next to a building such as a **cathedral** or castle.

Cluster (or **compound**) **pier**: a **pier** composed of a group, or cluster, of **engaged column** shafts, often used in Gothic architecture (fig. **12.5**).

Codex (pl. **codices**): sheets of **parchment** or **vellum** bound together—the precursor of the modern book.

Coffer, coffering: a recessed geometrical panel in a ceiling (fig. **8.32**).

Colonnade: a series of **columns** set at regular intervals, usually supporting **arches** or an **entablature**.

Colonnette: a small, slender **column**, usually grouped with others to form **cluster piers**.

Color wheel: a circular, two-dimensional model illustrating the relationships of the various **hues** (fig. **1.18**).

Column: a cylindrical support, usually with three parts—**base**, **shaft**, and **capital** (see p. 160).

Complementary colors: **hues** that lie directly opposite each other on the **color wheel**.

Compluvium (pl. **compluvia**): a square opening in the roof of a Roman **atrium** through which rain fell into an **impluvium**.

Composition: the arrangement of **formal elements** in a work of art.

Compound pier: see **cluster pier**.

Conceptual art: art in which the idea is more important than the **form** or style.

Cone mosaic: a decorated surface decorated by pressing pieces (usually colored and of conical shape) of stone or baked clay into damp plaster.

Content: the themes or ideas in a work of art, as distinct from its **form**.

Contour: a line representing the outline of a figure or form.

Contrapposto (or **counterpoise**): a stance of the human body in which one leg bears the weight, while the other is relaxed, creating an **asymmetry** in the hip-shoulder axis (fig. **6.26**).

Contrast: an abrupt change, such as that created by the juxtaposition of dissimilar colors, objects, etc.

Convention: a custom, practice, or principle that is generally recognized and accepted.

Corbelling: brick or masonry courses, each projecting beyond, and supported by, the one below it; the meeting of two corbels would create an **arch** or **vault**.

Corinthian: see **Order**.

Cornice: the projecting horizontal unit, usually molded, that surmounts an **arch** or wall; the topmost member of a Classical **entablature** (see p. 160).

Counterpoise: see **contrapposto**.

Crenellated: having a series of indentations, like those in a battlement.

Cromlech: a prehistoric monument consisting of a circle of **monoliths**.

Cross-hatching: pattern of superimposed parallel lines (**hatching**) on a two-dimensional surface used to create shadows and suggest **three-dimensionality** (fig. **1.16**).

Cross-section: a diagram showing a building cut by a vertical **plane**, usually at right angles to an **axis** (fig. **8.31**).

Cross-vault: see **groin vault**.

Crossing: the area in a Christian church where the **transepts** intersect the **nave**.

Cruciform: shaped or arranged like a cross (fig. **9.7**).

Crypt: a chamber or **vault** beneath the main body of a church.

Cuneiform: a form of writing consisting of wedge-shaped characters, used in ancient Mesopotamia (fig. **3.11**).

Cupola: a small, domed structure crowning a roof or **dome**, usually added to provide interior lighting.

Curvilinear: composed of, or bounded by, curved lines.

Cyclopaean masonry: stone construction using large, irregular blocks without mortar.

Cylinder seal: a small cylinder of stone or other material engraved in intaglio on its outer surface and used (especially in Mesopotamia) to roll an impression on wet clay.

Decussis: the Latin numeral ten (or X).

Deësis: a tripartite **icon** in the Byzantine tradition, usually showing Christ enthroned between the Virgin Mary and Saint John the Baptist.

Dendrochronology: a science using the annual rings of trees to determine the chronological order and dates of historical events.

Dharmachakra: see **mudrā**.

Dhyāna: see **mudrā**.

Diorite: a type of dark (black or gray) crystalline rock.

Diptych: a writing tablet or work of art consisting of two panels side by side and connected by hinges.

Dolmen: a prehistoric structure consisting of two or more **megaliths** capped with a horizontal slab.

Dome: a **vaulted** (frequently hemispherical) roof or ceiling, erected on a circular **base**, which may be envisaged as the result of rotating an **arch** through 180 degrees about a central **axis**.

Doric: see **Order**.

Dressed stone: blocks of stone that have been cut and shaped to fit in a particular place for a particular purpose.

Drum: (a) one of the cylindrical blocks of stone from which the **shaft** of a **column** is made; (b) the circular or polygonal wall of a building surmounted by a **dome** or **cupola**.

Earthenware: pottery that has either been air-dried or **fired** at a relatively low temperature.

Echinus: in the **Doric Order**, the rounded **molding** between the **necking** and the **abacus** (see p. 160).

Egg-and-dart: a decorative **molding** consisting of alternating oval (egg) and downward pointing (dart) elements.

Elevation: an architectural diagram showing the exterior (or, less often, interior) surface of a building as if projected onto a vertical **plane**.

Enamel: a vitreous coating applied by heat-fusion to the surface of metal, glass, or pottery. See also **cloisonné**.

Encaustic: a painting technique in which **pigment** is mixed with a **binder** of hot wax and fixed by heat after application (see p. 148).

Engaged (half-) column: a **column**, decorative in purpose, which is attached to a supporting wall.

Entablature: the portion of a Classical architectural **order** above the **capital** of a **column** (see p. 160).

Entasis: the slight bulging of a **Doric column**, which is at its greatest about one third of the distance from the **base**.

Esthetic: the theory and vocabulary of an individual artistic style.

Esthetics: the philosophy and science of art and artistic phenomena.

Eucharist: (a) the Christian sacrament of Holy Communion, commemorating the Last Supper; (b) the consecrated bread and wine used at the sacrament.

Evil eye: a malicious glance which, in superstitious belief, is thought to be capable of causing material harm.

Façade: the front or "face" of a building.

Facing: an outer covering or sheathing.

Faïence: **earthenware** or pottery decorated with brightly colored **glazes** (originally from Faenza, a city in northern Italy).

Fantasy: imagery that is derived solely from the imagination.

Figurative: representing the likeness of a recognizable human (or animal) figure.

Finial: a small decorative element at the top of an architectural member such as a **gable** or pinnacle, or of a smaller object such as a **bronze** vessel.

Fire (verb): to prepare (especially **ceramics**) by baking in a kiln or otherwise applying heat.

Flutes, fluting: a series of vertical grooves used to decorate the **shafts** of **columns** in Classical architecture.

Flying buttress, or **flyer**: a **buttress** in the form of a strut or open half-**arch**.

Foreground: the area of a picture, usually at the bottom of the **picture plane**, that appears nearest to the viewer.

Foreshortening: the use of **perspective** to represent a single object extending back in space at an angle to the **picture plane**.

Form: the overall plan or structure of a work of art (see p. 17).

Formal analysis: analysis of a work of art to determine how its integral parts, or **formal elements**, are combined to produce the overall style and effect.

Formal elements: the elements of style (line, shape, color, etc.) used by an artist in the **composition** of a work of art.

Formalism: the doctrine or practice of strict adherence to **stylized** shapes or other external forms.

Forum: the civic center of an ancient Roman city, containing temple, marketplace, and official buildings.

Fresco: a technique (also known as *buon fresco*) of painting on the plaster surface of a wall or ceiling while it is still damp, so that the **pigments** become fused with the plaster as it dries.

Fresco secco: a variant technique of **fresco** painting in which the paint is applied to dry plaster; this is often combined with *buon fresco*, or "true" fresco painting.

Frieze: (a) the central section of the **entablature** in the Classical **Orders**; (b) any horizontal decorative band.

Gable (or **pitched**) **roof**: a roof formed by the intersection of two **planes** sloping down from a central beam.

Gallery: the second story of a church, placed over the side **aisles** and below the **clerestory**.

Garbha griha (literally "womb chamber"): a small, cubical **sanctuary** that is the sacred core of a Hindu temple.

Geometric: (a) based on mathematical shapes such as the circle, square, or rectangle; (b) a style of Greek pottery made between c. 900 and 700 B.C., characterized by geometric decoration.

Gesso: a white coating made of chalk, plaster, and size that is spread over a surface to make it more receptive to paint.

Gilding: a decorative coating made of gold leaf or simulated gold; objects to which gilding has been applied are **gilded** or **gilt**.

Glaze: (a) in oil painting, a layer of translucent paint or varnish, sometimes applied over another color or ground, so that light passing through it is reflected back by the lower surface and modified by the glaze; (b) in pottery, a material applied in a thin layer that, when **fired**, fuses with the surface to produce a glossy, non-porous effect (see p. 71).

Glyptic art: the art of carving or engraving, especially on small objects such as seals or precious stones.

Gospel: one of the first four books of the New Testament, which recount the life of Christ.

Greek cross: a cross in which all four arms are of equal length.

Groin (or **cross-**) **vault**: the ceiling configuration formed by the intersection of two **barrel vaults**.

Ground plan: a plan of the ground floor of a building, seen from above (as distinguished from an **elevation**).

Guild: an organization of craftsmen, such as those that flourished in the Middle Ages and Renaissance (see p. 396).

Half-column: see **engaged column**.

Halo: a circle or disk of golden light surrounding the head of a holy figure.

Harmikā: a square platform surmounting the **dome** of a Buddhist **stupa** (figs. **8.K–L**).

Hatching: close parallel lines used in drawings and prints to create the effect of shadow on **three-dimensional** forms. See also **cross-hatching**.

Hierarchical scale: the representation of more important figures as larger than less important ones.

Hieroglyphic: written in a script (especially in ancient Egypt) whose characters are pictorial representations of objects.

Highlight: in painting, an area of high **value** color.

High relief: **relief** sculpture in which the figures project substantially (e.g. more than half of their natural depth) from the background surface.

Hue: a pure color with a specific wavelength (see p. 20).

Hydria: an ancient Greek or Roman water jar.

Hypostyle: a hall with a roof supported by rows of **columns**.

Icon: a sacred image representing Christ, the Virgin Mary, or some other holy person.

Iconography: the analysis of works of art through the study of the meanings of symbols and images in the context of the contemporary culture.

Iconology: the study of the meaning or content of a larger **program** to which individual works of art belong.

Idealized, idealization: the representation of objects and figures according to ideal standards of beauty rather than to real life.

Ideograph: a written symbol standing for a concept, usually formed by combining **pictographs**.

Illuminated manuscript: see **manuscript**.

Illusionism, illusionistic: a type of art in which the objects are intended to appear real.

Impluvium (pl. *impluvia*): a basin or cistern in the **atrium** of a Roman house to collect rainwater falling through the *compluvium* (fig. **8.4**).

Incise: to cut designs or letters into a hard surface with a sharp instrument.

Incised relief: see **sunken relief**.

Inlay: to decorate a surface by inserting pieces of a different material (e.g. to inlay a panel with contrasting wood).

Insula (pl. *insulae*): an ancient Roman building or group of buildings standing together and forming an apartment block (fig. **8.5**).

Intensity: the degree of purity of a color; also known as **chroma** or **saturation**.

Interlace: a form of decoration composed of strips or ribbons that are intertwined, usually symmetrically about a longitudinal **axis**.

Ionic: see **Order**.

Isocephaly, isocephalic: the horizontal alignment of the heads of all the figures in a composition.

Isometric projection: an architectural diagram combining a **ground plan** of a building with a view from an exterior point above and slightly to one side (fig. **12.21**).

Ithyphallic: an image having an erect or prominent phallus.

Jambs: the upright surfaces forming the sides of a doorway or window, often decorated with sculptures in Romanesque and Gothic churches (fig. **12.22**).

Jātaka: a tale recounting an incident in one of the Buddha's lives, frequently depicted in Buddhist art.

Keystone: the wedge-shaped stone at the center of an **arch**, **rib**, or **vault**, which is inserted last, locking the other stones into place.

Kiln: an oven used to bake (or **fire**) clay.

Kondō: the main hall of a Japanese Buddhist temple, where religious images are kept (fig. **12.H**).

Kore (pl. *korai*): Greek word for maiden; an Archaic Greek statue of a standing female, usually clothed (fig. **6.21**).

Kouros (pl. *kouroi*): Greek word for young man; an Archaic Greek statue of a standing nude youth (fig. **6.19**).

Krater: a wide-mouthed bowl for mixing wine and water in ancient Greece (fig. **6.8**).

Kufic: an early form of Arabic script in which letters are relatively uncursive; used later for headings and formal inscriptions.

Kylix: an ancient Greek drinking cup with a wide, shallow bowl (fig. **6.8**).

Lamassu (pl.): in Assyrian art, figures of bulls or lions with wings and human heads (fig. **3.30**).

Lancet: a tall narrow, arched window without **tracery**.

Landscape: a pictorial representation of natural scenery.

Lantern: the structure crowning a **dome** or tower, often used to admit light to the interior.

Lapis lazuli: a semiprecious blue stone; used to prepare the blue **pigment** known as ultramarine.

Lares and **penates**: (a) in ancient Rome, the tutelary gods of the household; (b) figuratively, one's most valued household possessions.

Latin cross: a cross in which the vertical arm is longer than the horizontal arm, through the midpoint of which it passes (fig. **9.9**).

Leaf-and-dart: a decorative design consisting of alternating leaf- and dart-shaped elements.

Lekythos (or *lecythus*): an ancient Greek vessel with a long, narrow neck, used primarily for pouring oil (fig. **6.8**).

Linear: a style in which lines are used to depict figures with precise, fully indicated outlines.

Lintel: the horizontal cross-beam spanning an opening in the **post-and-lintel** system.

Load-bearing construction: a system of construction in which solid forms are superimposed on one another to form a tapering structure.

Loggia: a roofed **gallery** open on one or more sides, often with **arches** or **columns**.

Longitudinal section: an architectural diagram giving an inside view of a building intersected by a vertical **plane** from front to back.

Lost-wax bronze casting (also called *cire-perdue*): a technique for **casting bronze** and other metals (see p. 154).

Low relief (also known as **bas-relief**): **relief** sculpture in which figures and forms project only slightly from the background **plane**.

Lunette: (a) a semicircular area formed by the intersection of a wall and a **vault**; (b) a painting, **relief** sculpture, or window of the same shape.

Machtkunst: art used in the service of a military or other authority; literally, "power art" in German (fig. **3.17**).

Magus (pl. **magi**): in the New Testament, one of the three Wise Men who traveled from the East to pay homage to the infant Christ.

Mandala: a cosmic diagram in Asian art.

Maṇḍapa: a northern-style Hindu temple's assembly hall (fig. **12.P**).

Mandorla: an oval or almond-shaped aureola, or radiance, surrounding the body of a holy person.

Manuscript: a handwritten book produced in the Middle Ages or Renaissance. If it has painted illustrations, it is known as an **illuminated manuscript**.

Martyrium: a church or other structure built over the tomb or relics of a martyr.

Mastaba: a rectangular burial monument in ancient Egypt.

Mausoleum (pl. **mausolea**): an elaborate tomb (named for Mausolos, a fourth-century-B.C. ruler commemorated by a magnificent tomb at Halikarnassos).

Meander pattern: a fret or key pattern originating in the Greek **Geometric** period (fig. **6.5**).

Medium (pl. **media**): (a) the material with which an artist works (e.g. watercolor on paper); (b) the liquid substance in which **pigment** is suspended, such as oil or water.

Megalith: a large, undressed stone used in the construction of prehistoric monuments (see p. 41).

Megaron: Greek for "large room"; used principally to denote a rectangular hall, usually supported by **columns** and fronted by a porch, traditional in ancient Greece since Mycenaean times (figs. **5.22–3**).

Menhir: a prehistoric **monolith** standing alone or grouped with other stones.

Metonym: an allusion to a subject through the representation of something related to it or a part of it.

Metope: the square area, often decorated with **relief** sculpture, between the **triglyphs** of a **Doric frieze** (see p. 160).

Mezzanine: in architecture, an intermediate, low-ceilinged story between two main stories.

Mihrāb: a niche, often highly ornamented, in the center of a **qibla** wall, toward which prayer is directed in an Islamic **mosque** (fig. **10.8**).

Minaret: a tall, slender tower attached to a **mosque**, from which the *muezzin* calls the Muslim faithful to prayer (fig. **10.14**).

Minbar: a **pulpit** from which a Muslim (Islamic) *imam* addresses a congregation in a *jāmi* **mosque**.

Mithuna: a loving couple, symbolizing unity, in ancient South Asian art.

Modeling: (a) in two-dimensional art, the use of **value** to suggest light and shadow, and thus create the effect of mass and weight; (b) in sculpture, the creation of form by manipulating a pliable material such as clay.

Molding: a continuous contoured surface, either recessed or projecting, used for decorative effect on an architectural surface.

Monastery: a religious establishment housing a community of people living in accordance with religious vows (see p. 343).

Monochromatic: having a color scheme based on shades of black and white, or on **values** of a single **hue**.

Monolith: a large block of stone that is all in one piece (i.e. not composed of smaller blocks), used in **megalithic** structures.

Monumental: being, or appearing to be, larger than lifesize.

Mosaic: the use of small pieces of glass, stone, or tile (**tesserae**), or pebbles, to create an image on a flat surface such as a floor, wall, or ceiling (see p. 282).

Mosque: an Islamic (Muslim) house of worship of two main types: the *masjid*, used for daily prayer by individuals or small groups; and the *jāmi*, used for large-scale congregational prayer on the Friday sabbath and holidays.

Motif: a recurrent element or theme in a work of art.

Mudrā: a symbolic hand gesture, usually made by a deity, in Hindu or Buddhist art. Common Buddhist *mudrās* include: **abhaya mudrā** (right hand raised, palm outward and vertical), meaning "fear not"; **dhyāna mudrā** (hands in lap, one resting on the other, palms up, thumbtips touching), signifying meditation; **dharmachakra mudrā** (hands at chest level, palms out, thumb and forefinger of each forming a circle), representing the beginning of Buddhist teaching; and **bhūmisparsha mudrā** (left hand in lap, right hand reaching down, palm in and vertical, to ground level), symbolizing Shakyamuni Buddha's calling the earth to bear witness at the moment of his enlightenment (fig. **8.Q**).

Mural: a painting on a wall, usually on a large scale and in **fresco**.

Naos: the inner **sanctuary** of an ancient Greek temple.

Narthex: a porch or vestibule in early Christian churches (fig. **9.7**).

Naturalism, naturalistic: a style of art seeking to represent objects as they actually appear in nature.

Nave: in **basilicas** and churches, the long, narrow central area used to house the congregation.

Necking: a groove or **molding** at the top of a **column** or **pilaster** forming the transition from **shaft** to **capital**.

Necropolis (pl. **necropoleis**): an ancient or prehistoric burial ground (literally "City of the Dead").

Nemes: a headcloth worn by the pharaohs of ancient Egypt (fig. **4.45**).

Neutral: lacking color; white, gray or black.

Niche: a hollow or recess in a wall or other architectural element, often containing a statue; a blind niche is a very shallow recess.

Nike: a winged statue representing Nike, the goddess of victory.

Nonrepresentational (or **nonfigurative**): not representing any known object in nature.

Obelisk: a tall, four-sided stone, usually **monolithic**, that tapers toward the top and is capped by a **pyramidion** (fig. **4.33**).

Oculus: a round opening in a wall or at the apex of a **dome**.

Oenochoe: an ancient Greek wine jug.

Opisthodomos (or **opisthodome**): a back chamber, especially the part of the **naos** of a temple furthest from the entrance (fig. **6.37**).

Orant: standing with outstretched arms as if in prayer (fig. **9.2**).

Orchestra: in an ancient Greek theater, a circular space used by the chorus.

Order: one of the architectural systems (Corinthian, Ionic, Doric) used by the Greeks and Romans to decorate and define the **post-and-lintel** system of construction (see p. 160).

Organic: having the quality of living matter.

Pagoda: a multistoried Buddhist **reliquary** tower, tapering toward the top and characterized by projecting eaves (figs. **12.D-F**).

Papyrus: (a) a plant found in ancient Egypt and neighboring countries; (b) a paperlike writing material made from the pith of the plant.

Parapet: (a) a wall or rampart to protect soldiers; (b) a low wall or railing built for the safety of people at the edge of a balcony, roof, or other steep place (fig. **12.23**).

Parchment: a paperlike material made from bleached and stretched animal hides, used in the Middle Ages for **manuscripts**.

Patina: (a) the colored surface, often green, that forms on **bronze** and copper either naturally (as a result of oxidation) or artificially (through treatment with acid); (b) in general, the surface appearance of old objects.

Patron: the person or group that commissions a work of art from an artist.

Pedestal: the **base** of a **column**, statue, vase, or other upright work of art.

Pediment: (a) in Classical architecture, the triangular section at the end of a **gable roof**, often decorated with sculpture; (b) a triangular feature placed as a decoration over doors and windows.

Pendentive: in a domed building, an inwardly curving triangular section of the **vaulting** that provides a transition from the round **base** of the **dome** to the supporting **piers** (fig. **9.33**).

Peplos: in ancient Greece, a woolen outer garment worn by women, wrapped in folds about the body (fig. **6.21**).

Peripteral: surrounded by a row of **columns** or **peristyle**.

Peristyle: a **colonnade** surrounding a structure (fig. **8.4**); in Roman houses, the courtyard surrounded by **columns**.

Perspective: the illusion of depth in a two-dimensional work of art.

Pictograph: a written symbol derived from a **representational** image.

Picture plane: the flat surface of a drawing or painting.

Picture stone: in Viking art, an upright boulder with images **incised** on it (see p. 332).

Piece-molding: a complex technique for shaping pottery, metal, or glass objects between an inner core and an outer mold; especially suited to elaborate decoration.

Pier: a vertical support used to bear loads in an **arched** or **vaulted** structure (fig. **12.5**).

Pigment: a powdered substance that is used to give color to paints, inks, and dyes.

Pilaster: a flattened, rectangular version of a **column**, sometimes **load-bearing**, but often purely decorative.

Pillar: a large vertical architectural element, usually freestanding and **load-bearing**.

Pitched roof: see **gable roof**.

Plane: a surface on which a straight line joining any two of its points lies on that surface; in general, a flat surface.

Plinth: (a) in Classical architecture, a square slab immediately below the circular **base** of a **column**; (b) a square block serving as a base for a statue, vase, etc.

Podium: (a) the masonry forming the **base** of a temple; (b) a raised platform or **pedestal**.

Polychrome: consisting of several colors.

Polyptych: a painting or **relief**, usually an **altarpiece**, composed of more than three sections.

Portal: the doorway of a church and the architectural composition surrounding it.

Portico: (a) a **colonnade**; (b) a porch with a roof supported by **columns**, usually at the entrance to a building.

Portrait: a visual representation of a specific person, a likeness.

Portraiture: the art of making portraits.

Post-and-lintel construction: an architectural system in which upright members, or posts, support horizontal members, or **lintels** (see p. 45).

Postament: (a) a **pedestal** or base; (b) a frame of **molding** for a **relief**.

Prana: the fullness of life-giving breath that appears to animate some South and Southeast Asian sculpture.

Predella: the lower part of an **altarpiece**, often decorated with small scenes that are related to the subject of the main panel (figs. **13.14** and **13.23**).

Primary color: the pure **hues**—blue, red, yellow—from which all other colors can in theory be mixed.

Program: the arrangement of a series of images into a coherent whole.

Pronaos: the vestibule of a Greek temple in front of the *cella* or *naos*.

Proportion: the relation of one part to another, and of parts to the whole, in respect of size, height, and width.

Propylaeum (pl. **propylaea**): (a) an entrance to a temple or other enclosure; (b) the entry gate at the western end of the Acropolis, in Athens.

Protome (or **protoma**): a representation of the head and neck of an animal, often used as an architectural feature.

Provenience: origin, derivation; the act of coming from a particular source.

Psalter: a copy of the Book of Psalms in the Old Testament, often illuminated.

Pseudo-peripteral: appearing to have a **peristyle**, though some of the **columns** may be **engaged columns** or **pilasters**.

Pulpit: in church architecture, an elevated stand, surrounded by a **parapet** and often richly decorated, from which the preacher addresses the congregation.

Pylon: a pair of truncated, pyramidal towers flanking the entrance to an Egyptian temple.

Pyramidion: a small pyramid, as at the top of an **obelisk**.

Qibla: a wall inside the prayer hall of an Islamic **mosque** that is oriented toward Mecca and is therefore the focus of worship.

Quadrant (or **half-barrel**) **vaulting**: vaulting whose arc is one quarter of a circle, or 90 degrees (fig. **11.5**).

Radiating chapels: chapels placed around the **ambulatory** (and sometimes the **transepts**) of a medieval church.

Radiocarbon dating: a method of dating prehistoric objects based on the rate of degeneration of radioactive carbon in organic materials.

Realism, realistic: attempting to portray objects from everyday life as they actually are; not to be confused with the nineteenth-century movement called Realism.

Rebus: the representation of words and syllables by pictures or symbols, the names of which sound the same as the intended words or syllables.

Rectilinear: consisting of, bounded by, or moving in, a straight line or lines.

Red-figure: describing a style of Greek pottery painting of the sixth or fifth century B.C., in which the decoration is red on a black background.

Refectory: a dining hall in a **monastery** or other similar institution.

Register: a range or row, especially when one of a series.

Relief: (a) a mode of sculpture in which an image is developed outward (**high or low relief**) or inward (**sunken relief**) from a basic **plane**; (b) a printmaking process in which the areas not to be printed are carved away, leaving the desired image projecting from the plate.

Reliquary: a casket or container for sacred relics.

Repoussé: in metalwork, decorated with patterns in **relief** made by hammering on the reverse side (fig. **11.3**).

Representational: representing natural objects in recognizable form.

Rib: an **arched** diagonal element in a **vault** system that defines and supports a **ribbed vault**.

Ribbed vault: a **vault** constructed of **arched** diagonal **ribs**, with a **web** of lighter masonry in between.

Romanticize: to glamorize or portray in a romantic, as opposed to a **realistic**, manner.

Roof comb: an ornamental architectural crest on top of a Maya temple.

Rose window: a large, circular window decorated with **stained glass** and **tracery** (fig. **12.31**).

Rotunda: a circular building, usually covered by a **dome**.

Rune stone: in Viking art, an upright boulder with characters of the runic alphabet inscribed on it (fig. **10.22**).

Sahn: an enclosed courtyard in an Islamic **mosque**, used for prayer when the interior is full.

Sanctuary: (a) the most holy part of a place of worship, the inner sanctum; (b) the part of a Christian church containing the **altar**.

Sarcophagus: a stone coffin, sometimes decorated with a **relief** sculpture.

Sarsen: a large, sandstone block used in prehistoric monuments.

Saturation: see **intensity**.

Satyr: an ancient woodland deity with the legs, tail, and horns of a goat (or horse), and the head and torso of a man.

Schematic: diagrammatic and generalized rather than specifically relating to an individual object.

Screen wall: a nonsupporting wall, often pierced by windows.

Scriptorium: the room (or rooms) in a **monastery** in which **manuscripts** were produced.

Scroll: (a) a length of writing material, such as **papyrus** or **parchment**, rolled up into a cylinder; (b) a curved **molding** resembling a scroll (e.g. the **volute** of an **Ionic** or **Corinthian capital**).

Sculpture in the round: freestanding sculptural figures carved or modeled in **three dimensions**.

Secondary colors: **hues** produced by combining two **primary colors**.

Section: a diagrammatic representation of a building intersected by a vertical **plane**.

Serapaeum: a building or shrine sacred to the Egyptian god Serapis (see p. 216).

Serekh: a rectangular outline containing the name of a king in the Early Dynastic period of ancient Egypt.

Seriation: a technique for determining a chronology by studying a particular type or style and analyzing the increase or decrease in its popularity.

Shading: decreases in the **value** or **intensity** of colors to imitate the fall of shadow when light strikes an object.

Shaft: the vertical, cylindrical part of a **column** that supports the **entablature** (see p. 160).

Shikhara: (literally "mountain peak"), a northern-style Hindu temple tower surmounting a *garbha griha*, typically curved inward toward the top, with vertical lobes and horizontal segments (*bhūmi*), and crowned by *āmalaka*.

Sibyl: a prophetess of the ancient, pre-Christian world.

Skene: in a Greek theater, the stone structure behind the **orchestra** that served as a backdrop or stage wall.

Slip: in **ceramics**, a mixture of clay and water used (a) as a decorative finish or (b) to attach different parts of an object (e.g. handles to the body of a vessel) (see p. 144).

Spacer: a small peg or ball used to separate metal, pottery, or glass objects from other objects during processes such as **casting**, **firing**, and mold-blowing.

Spandrel: the triangular area between (a) the side of an **arch** and the right angle that encloses it, or (b) two adjacent arches.

Sphinx: in ancient Egypt, a creature with the body of a lion and the head of a human, an animal, or bird (fig. **4.18**).

Spolia: materials taken from an earlier building for re-use in a new one.

Springing: (a) the architectural member of an **arch** that is the first to curve inward from the vertical; (b) the point at which this curvature begins.

Squinch: a small single **arch**, or a series of concentric **corbeled** arches, set diagonally across the upper inside corner of a square building to facilitate the transition to a round **dome** or other circular superstructure (figs. **9.34** and **9.35**).

Stained glass: windows composed of pieces of colored glass held in place by strips of lead (see p. 392).

Stele: an upright stone slab or **pillar**, usually carved or inscribed for commemorative purposes.

Stereobate: a substructure or foundation of masonry visible above ground level (see p. 160).

Stigmata (pl.): marks resembling the wounds on the crucified body of Christ (from "stigma," a mark or scar).

Still life: a picture consisting principally of inanimate objects such as fruit, flowers, or pottery.

Stratigraphy: a technique for determining a chronology by studying the relative locations of layers of material in an archaeological site.

Stucco: (a) a type of cement used to coat the walls of a building; (b) a fine plaster used for **moldings** and other architectural decorations.

Stupa: in Buddhist architecture, a **dome**-shaped or rounded structure made of brick, earth, or stone, containing the relic of a Buddha or other honored individual (figs. **8.K-L**).

Style: in the visual arts, a manner of execution that is characteristic of an individual, a school, a period, or some other identifiable group.

Stylization: the distortion of a **representational** image to conform to certain artistic **conventions** or to emphasize particular qualities.

Stylobate: the top step of a **stereobate**, forming a foundation for a **column**, **peristyle**, temple, or other structure (see p. 160).

Stylus: a pointed instrument used in antiquity for writing on clay, wax, **papyrus**, and **parchment**.

Sunken (or **incised**) **relief**: a style of **relief** sculpture in which the image is recessed into the surface.

Support: in painting, the surface to which the **pigment** is applied.

Symmetry: the esthetic balance that is achieved when parts of an object are arranged about a real or imaginary central line, or **axis**, so that the parts on one side correspond in some respect (shape, size, color) with those on the other.

Symposium: (a) a drinking party; (b) a social gathering at which there is a free exchange of ideas.

Synthesis: the combination of parts or elements to form a coherent, more complex whole.

Taberna: part of a Roman building fronting on a street and serving as a shop.

Talud-tablero: an architectural style typical of Teotihuacán sacred structures in which paired elements—a sloping **base** (the *talud*) supporting a vertical *tablero* (often decorated with sculpture or painting)—are stacked, sometimes to great heights (fig. **10.I**).

Tectonic: of, or pertaining to, building or construction.

Tell: an archaeological term for a mound composed of the remains of successive settlements in the Near East.

Tempera: a fast-drying, water-based painting **medium** made with egg yolk, often used in **fresco** and panel painting (see p. 454).

Tenon: a projecting member in a block of stone or other building material that fits into a groove or hole to form a joint.

Terracotta: (a) an **earthenware** material, with or without a **glaze**; (b) an object made of this material.

Tessera (pl. **tesserae**): a small piece of colored glass, marble, or stone used in a **mosaic**.

Texture: the visual or tactile surface quality of an object.

Tholos: (a) a circular tomb of beehive shape approached by a long, horizontal passage; (b) in Classical times, a round building modeled on ancient tombs.

Three-dimensional: having height, width, and depth.

Thrust: the lateral force exerted by an **arch**, **dome**, or **vault**, which must be counteracted by some form of **buttressing**.

Tondo: (a) a circular painting; (b) a medallion with **relief** sculpture.

Toraṇa: a ritual gateway in Buddhist architecture (figs. **8.K-L** and **12.P**).

Trabeated: constructed according to the **post-and-lintel** method.

Tracery: a decorative, **interlaced** design (as in the stonework in Gothic windows).

Transept: a cross arm in a Christian church, placed at right angles to the **nave**.

Transverse rib: a **rib** in a **vault** that crosses the **nave** or **aisle** at right angles to the **axis** of the building.

Travertine: a hard limestone used as a building material by the Etruscans and Romans.

Tribhaṅga: in Buddhist art, the "three bends posture," in which the head, chest, and lower portion of the body are angled instead of being aligned vertically (fig. **8.O**).

Tribune: (a) the **apse** of a **basilica** or basilican church; (b) a **gallery** in a Romanesque or Gothic church.

Triforium: in Gothic architecture, part of the **nave** wall above the **arcade** and below the **clerestory**.

Triglyph: in a **Doric frieze**, the rectangular area between the **metopes**, decorated with three vertical grooves (glyphs).

Trilithon: an ancient monument consisting of two vertical **megaliths** supporting a third as a **lintel**.

Triptych: an **altarpiece** or painting consisting of one central panel and two wings.

Trompe l'oeil: **illusionistic** painting that "deceives the eye" with its appearance of reality.

Trumeau: in Romanesque and Gothic architecture, the central post supporting the **lintel** in a double doorway.

Tufa: a porous, volcanic rock that hardens on exposure to air, used as a building material.

Tumulus (pl. **tumuli**): an artificial mound, typically found over a grave.

Tunnel vault: see **barrel vault**.

Tympanum: a **lunette** over the doorway of a church, often decorated with sculpture (fig. **11.7**).

Type: a person or object serving as a prefiguration or symbolic representation, usually of something in the future (see p. 273).

Typology: the Christian theory of **types**, in which characters and events in the New Testament (i.e. after the birth of Christ) are prefigured by counterparts in the Old Testament.

Underpainting: a preliminary painting, subsequently covered by the final layer(s) of paint.

Uraeus (pl. **uraei**): a **stylized** representation of an asp, often included on the headdress of ancient rulers.

Ūrṇā: in Buddhist art, a whorl of hair or protuberance between the eyebrows of a Buddha or other honored individual (fig. **8.P**).

Ushṇīsha: a **conventional** identifying topknot of hair on an image of Shakyamuni Buddha, symbolic of his wisdom (fig. **8.P**).

Value: the degree of lightness (high value) or darkness (low value) in a **hue** (fig. **1.19**).

Vault, vaulting: a roof or ceiling of masonry constructed on the **arch** principle (see p. 213); see also **barrel vault, groin vault, quadrant vaulting, ribbed vault**.

Vedikā: a railing marking off sacred space in South Asian architecture, often found surrounding a Buddhist **stupa** or encircling the **axis**-pillar atop its **dome** (*aṇḍa*) (figs. **8.K–L**).

Vehicle: the liquid in which **pigments** are suspended and which, as it dries, binds the color to the surface of the painting.

Vellum: a cream-colored, smooth surface for painting or writing, prepared from calfskin.

Veranda: a **pillared** porch preceding an interior chamber, common in Hindu temples and Buddhist **chaitya halls** (figs. **9.B–C**).

Verisimilitude: the quality of appearing real or truthful.

Vihāra: Buddhist monks' living quarters, either an individual cell or a space for communal activity (fig. **9.G**).

Villa: (a) in antiquity and the Renaissance, a large country house; (b) in modern times, a detached house in the country or suburbs.

Visible spectrum: the colors, visible to the human eye, that are produced when white light is dispersed by a prism.

Vitreous: related to, derived from, or consisting of, glass.

Volute: in the Ionic **order**, the spiral **scroll** motif decorating the **capital** (see p. 160).

Voussoir: one of the individual, wedge-shaped blocks of stone that make up an **arch** (see p. 213).

Wattle and daub: a technique of wall construction using woven branches or twigs plastered with clay or mud.

Web: in Gothic architecture, the portion of a **ribbed vault** between the **ribs**.

Westwork: from the German *Westwerk*, the western front of a church, containing an entrance and vestibule below, a chapel or **gallery** above, and flanked by two towers.

White-ground: describing a style of Greek pottery painting of the fifth century B.C., in which the decoration is usually black on a white background.

Yaksha, Yakshī: indigenous South Asian fertiliy deities, respectively male and female, later assimilated into Buddhist art.

Ziggurat: a trapezoidal stepped structure representing a mountain in ancient Mesopotamia (fig. **3.20**).

Suggestions for Further Reading

General

Adams, Laurie. *Art on Trial*. New York: Walker & Co., 1976.
—. *Art and Psychoanalysis*. New York: HarperCollins, 1993.
—. *Methodologies of Art: An Introduction*. New York: HarperCollins, 1996.
Arntzen, Etta, and Robert Rainwater. *Guide to the Literature of Art History*. Chicago, American Library Association/Art Book Company, 1980.
Barasch, Moshe. *Theories of Art: From Plato to Winckelmann*. New York: New York University Press, 1985.
—. *Modern Theories of Art, I: From Winckelmann to Baudelaire*. New York: New York University Press, 1990.
Baxandall, Michael. *Patterns of Intention: On the Historical Explanation of Pictures*. New Haven: Yale University Press, 1985.
Bois, Yve-Alain. *Painting as Model*. Cambridge, MA: MIT Press, 1990.
Broude, Norma, and Mary D. Garrard, eds. *Feminism and Art History: Questioning the Litany*. New York: Harper & Row, 1982.
—, eds. *The Expanding Discourse: Feminism and Art History*. New York: HarperCollins, 1992.
Bryson, Norman, ed. *Vision and Painting: The Logic of the Gaze*. New Haven: Yale University Press, 1983.
—, *Vision and Painting*. New Haven: Yale University Press, 1987.
—, et al., eds. *Visual Theory: Painting and Interpretation*. New York: Cambridge University Press, 1991.
Cahn, Walter. *Masterpieces: Chapters of the History of an Idea*. Princeton: Princeton University Press, 1979.
Chadwick, Whitney. *Women, Art, and Society*. New York: Thames & Hudson, 1990.
Chicago, Judy, and Miriam Schapiro. *Anonymous Was a Woman*. Valencia, CA: Feminist Art Program, California Institute of the Arts, 1974.
Chilvers, Ian, and Harold Osborne, eds. *The Oxford Dictionary of Art*. New York: Oxford University Press, 1988.
Clark, Kenneth M. *The Nude: A Study in Ideal Form*. Garden City, NY: Doubleday, 1959.
Clark, Toby. *Art and Propaganda in the Twentieth Century*. New York: Harry N. Abrams, 1997.
Ehresmann, Donald L. *Architecture: A Bibliograph Guide to Basic Reference Works, Histories and Handbooks*. Littleton, CO: Libraries Unlimited, 1984.
—. *Fine Arts: A Bibliographical Guide to Basic Reference Works, Histories and Handbooks*. 3rd ed. Littleton, CO: Libraries Unlimited, 1990.
Eliade, Mircea. *A History of Religious Ideas*. 2 vols. Trans. W.R. Trask. Chicago: University of Chicago Press, 1978.
Elsen, Albert E. *The Purposes of Art*. 4th ed. New York: Holt, Rinehart & Winston, 1981.
Encyclopedia of World Art. 14 vols., with index and supplements. New York: McGraw-Hill, 1959–68.
Fine, Elsa Honig. *Women and Art*. Montclair, NJ: Allanheld & Schram, 1978.
Flynn, Tom. *The Body in Three Dimensions*. New York: Harry N. Abrams, 1998.
Freedberg, David. *The Power of Images*. Chicago: University of Chicago Press, 1989.
Gilbert, Rita. *Living with Art*. 5th ed. New York: McGraw-Hill, 1998.

Gombrich, Ernst. *Art and Illusion*. New York: Pantheon, 1972.
—. *The Image and the Eye*. Ithaca, NY: Cornell University Press, 1982.
—. *Meditations on a Hobby Horse*. London: Phaidon, 1963.
—. *Shadows: The Depiction of Cast Shadows in Western Art*. London: National Gallery, 1995.
Hall, James. *Subjects and Symbols in Art*. 2nd ed. New York: HarperCollins, 1979.
—. *Illustrated Dictionary of Symbols in Eastern and Western Art*. New York: HarperCollins, 1994.
Harris, Ann S., and Linda Nochlin. *Women Artists, 1550–1950*. Los Angeles: County Museum of Art; New York: Knopf, 1977.
Harrison, Charles, and Paul Woods, eds. *Art in Theory, 1900–1990*. Cambridge, MA: Blackwell, 1993.
Hauser, Arnold. *The Philosophy of Art History*. Cleveland: World Publishing Company, 1963.
—. *The Social History of Art*. 4 vols. New York: Vintage Books, 1958.
Hedges, Elaine, and Ingrid Wendt. *In Her Own Image: Women Working in the Arts*. New York: McGraw-Hill, 1980.
Heller, Nancy G. *Women Artists: An Illustrated History*. Rev. ed. New York: Abbeville, 1991.
Hess, Thomas B., and Elizabeth Baker, eds. *Art and Sexual Politics*. New York: Macmillan, 1973.
Hins, Berthold. *Art in the Third Reich*. Trans. Robert Kimber and Rita Kimber. Oxford: Basil Blackwell, 1979.
Holt, Elizabeth G. *A Documentary History of Art*. 2 vols. Garden City: Doubleday, 1981.
Kemp, Martin. *The Science of Art: Optical Themes in Western Art from Brunelleschi to Seurat*. New Haven: Yale University Press, 1989.
Kleinbauer, Walter E., and Thomas P. Slavens. *Research Guide to Western Art History*. Chicago: American Library Association, 1982.
Kleinbauer, Walter E. *Modern Perspectives in Western Art History: An Anthology of Twentieth-Century Writings on the Visual Arts*. Reprint of 1971 ed. Toronto: University of Toronto Press, 1989.
Kostof, Spiro. *The Architect: Chapters in the History of the Profession*. New York: Oxford University Press, 1977.
—. *A History of Architecture: Settings and Rituals*. New York: Oxford University Press, 1985.
Kris, Ernst, and Otto Kurz. *Legend, Myth, and Magic in the Image of the Artists*. New Haven: Yale University Press, 1979.
Kultermann, Udo. *The History of Art History*. New York: Abaris Books, 1993.
Lever, Jill, and John Harris. *Illustrated Dictionary of Architecture, 800–1914*. Boston: Faber & Faber, 1993.
Levine, Lawrence. *Highbrow, Lowbrow: The Emergence of Cultural Hierarchy in America*. Cambridge, MA: Harvard University Press, 1988.
Mayer, Ralph. *The HarperCollins Dictionary of Art Terms & Techniques*. 2nd ed. New York: HarperCollins, 1991.
—. *The Artists' Handbook of Materials and Techniques*. 5th ed. New York: Viking, 1991.
McCoubrey, John W. *American Art, 1700–1960: Sources and Documents*. Englewood Cliffs, NJ: Prentice-Hall, 1965.
Munsterberg, Hugo. *A History of Women Artists*. New York: Clarkson N. Potter, 1975.

Murray, Peter, and Linda Murray. *A Dictionary of Art and Artists*. 5th ed. New York: Penguin, 1988.
Nochlin, Linda. *Women, Art, and Power and Other Essays*. New York: Harper & Row, 1988.
Ocvirk, Otto G., Robert E. Stinson, Philip R. Wigg, and Robert O. Bone. *Art Fundamentals: Theory and Practice*. 8th ed. New York: McGraw-Hill, 1998.
Panofsky, Erwin. *Meaning in the Visual Arts*. Garden City, NY: Doubleday, 1955.
—. *Idea: A Concept in Art Theory*. Columbia: University of South Carolina Press, 1968.
—. *Perspective as Symbolic Form*. New York: Zone Books, 1991.
Parker, Roszika, and Griselda Pollock. *Old Mistresses: Women, Art and Ideology*. New York: Pantheon Books, 1981.
Penny, Nicholas. *The Materials of Sculpture*. New Haven: Yale University Press, 1993.
Peterson, Karen, and J.J. Wilson. *Women Artists*. New York: Harper & Row, 1976.
Pollock, Griselda. *Vision and Difference: Feminity, Feminism and the Histories of Art*. London: Routledge and Kegan Paul, 1988.
Praz, Mario, *Mnemosyne*. Princeton: Princeton University Press, 1967.
Pultz, John. *The Body and the Lens*. New York: Harry N. Abrams, 1995.
Reid, Jane D., ed. *The Oxford Guide to Classical Mythology in the Arts, 1330–1990*. 2 vols. New York: Oxford University Press, 1993.
Roth, Leland M. *Understanding Architecture: Its Elements, History and Meaning*. New York: HarperCollins, 1993.
Saxl, Fritz. *A Heritage of Images*. Harmondsworth: Penguin, 1970.
Schiller, Gertrud. *Iconography of Christian Art*. 2 vols. Greenwich, CT: New York Graphic Society, 1971.
Sporre, Dennis J. *The Creative Impulse: An Introduction to the Arts*. 4th ed. Upper Saddle River, NJ: Prentice-Hall, 1996.
Stephenson, Jonathan. *The Materials and Techniques of Painting*. New York: Watson-Guptill, 1989.
Summerson, John. *The Classical Language of Architecture*. Cambridge, MA: MIT Press, 1963.
Trachtenberg, Marvin, and Isabelle Hyman. *Architecture, from Pre-History to Post-Modernism*. New York: Abrams, 1986.
Van Keuren, Frances. *Guide to Research in Classical Art and Mythology*. Chicago: American Library Association, 1991.
Verhelst, Wilbert. *Sculpture: Tools, Materials, and Techniques*. Englewood Cliffs, NJ: Prentice-Hall, 1973.
Watkin, David. *The Rise of Architectural History*. Chicago: University of Chicago Press, 1980.
Westermann, Mariet. *A Worldly Art*. New York: Harry N. Abrams, 1996.
Williams, Raymond. *Culture and Society, 1870–1950*. New York: Harper & Row, 1966.
—. *The Sociology of Culture*. New York: Schocken Books, 1982.
Winternitz, Emanuel. *Musical Instruments and their Symbolism in Western Art*. London: Faber and Faber, 1967.
Wittkower, Rudolf. *Allegory and the Migration of Symbols*. London: Thames & Hudson, 1977.
—, and Margot Wittkower. *Born Under Saturn*. New York: Norton, 1969.
Wodehouse, Lawrence, and Marian Moffet. *A History of Western Architecture*. Mountain View, CA: Mayfield Publishing, 1989.

Wolff, Janet. *The Social Production of Art.* 2nd ed. New York: New York University Press, 1993.

Wölfflin, Heinrich. *Classic Art.* London, 1952.

—. *Principles of Art History: The Problem of the Development of Style in Later Art.* 7th ed. New York: Dover, 1950.

—. *The Sense of Form in Art.* New York: Chelsea, 1958.

Wollheim, Richard. *Art and its Objects.* New York: Cambridge University Press, 1980.

—. *Painting as an Art.* Princeton: Princeton University Press, 1984.

Wren, Linnea H., and David J. Wren, eds. *Perspectives on Western Art, Vol. 1.* New York: Harper & Row, 1987.

—. *Perspectives on Western Art, Vol. 2.* New York: HarperCollins, 1994.

Yates, Frances A. *The Art of Memory.* London: Routledge & Kegan Paul, 1966.

The Art of Prehistory

Amiet, Pierre, ed. *Art in the Ancient World: A Handbook of Styles and Forms.* New York: Rizzoli, 1981.

Bandi, Hans-Georg, and Henri Breuil. *The Art of the Stone Age: Forty Thousand Years of Rock Art.* 2nd ed. London: Methuen, 1970.

Bataille, Georges, *Lascaux: Prehistoric Painting, or the Birth of Art.* Lausanne: Skira, 1980.

Breuil, Henri. *Four Hundred Centuries of Cave Art.* Reprint of 1952 ed. New York: Hacker, 1979.

Castelden, Rodney. *The Making of Stonehenge.* London: Routledge, 1993.

Chauvet, Jean-Marie, Eliette Brunel Deschamps, and Christian Hilaire. *Dawn of Art: The Chauvet Cave.* New York: Harry N. Abrams, 1996.

Chippindale, Christopher. *Stonehenge Complete.* London: Thames & Hudson, 1983.

Clottes, Jean, and Jean Courtin. *The Cave beneath the Sea: Paleolithic Images at Cosquer.* New York: Harry N. Abrams, 1996.

Finegan, Jack. *Light from the Ancient Past.* 2 vols. 2nd ed. Princeton: Princeton University Press, 1974.

Gimbutas, Maria. *The Gods and Goddesses of Old Europe. 7000–3500 B.C.: Myths, Legends, and Cult Images.* Berkeley: University of California Press, 1974.

Graziosi, Paolo. *Paleolithic Art.* New York: McGraw-Hill, 1960.

James, Edwin O. *From Cave to Cathedral: Temples and Shrines of Prehistoric, Classical and Early Christian Times.* London: Thames & Hudson, 1965.

Leroi-Gourhan, André. *The Dawn of European Art: An Introduction to Paleolithic Cave Painting.* Cambridge: Cambridge University Press, 1982.

—. *Treasures of Prehistoric Art.* New York: Harry N. Abrams, 1967.

Powell, Thomas G.E. *Prehistoric Art.* New York: Praeger, 1966.

Ruspoli, Mario. *The Cave of Lascaux: The Final Photographs.* New York: Harry N. Abrams, 1987.

Sieveking, Ann. *The Cave Artists.* London: Thames & Hudson, 1979.

Sandars, Nancy K. *Prehistoric Art in Europe.* 2nd ed. Pelican History of Art. New Haven: Yale University Press, 1985.

Twohig, Elizabeth Shee. *The Megalithic Art of Western Europe.* New York: Oxford University Press, 1981.

Wainwright, Geoffrey. *The Henge Monuments: Ceremony and Society in Prehistoric Britain.* London: Thames & Hudson, 1990.

The Art of the Ancient Near East

Akurgal, Ekrem. *Art of the Hittites.* New York: Harry N. Abrams, 1962.

Bottero, Jean. *Mesopotamia: Writing, Reasoning, and the Gods.* Trans. Z. Bahrani. Chicago: University of Chicago Press, 1992.

Collon, Dominique. *First Impressions: Cylinder Seals in the Ancient Near East.* London: British Museum Press, 1987.

Crawford, Harriet. *Sumer and the Sumerians.* New York: Cambridge University Press, 1991.

Ferrier, Ronald W., ed. *The Arts of Persia.* New Haven: Yale University Press, 1989.

Frankfort, Henri. *The Art and Architecture of the Ancient Orient.* Rev. ed. Pelican History of Art. Baltimore: Penguin, 1971.

Ghirshman, Roman. *The Arts of Ancient Iran from its Origins to the Time of Alexander the Great.* Trans. Stuart Gilbert and James Emmons. New York: Golden Press, 1962.

Gilgamesh, trans. James Gardner and John Maier. New York: Knopf, 1984.

Groenewegen-Frankfort, Henriette A. *Arrest and Movement: An Essay on Space and Time in Representational Art of the Ancient Near East.* Cambridge, MA: Belknap Press, 1987.

—, and Bernard Ashmole. *Art of the Ancient World.* New York: Harry N. Abrams, 1975.

Harper, Prudence, Joan Arz, and Françoise Tallon, eds. *The Royal City of Susa: Ancient Near Eastern Treasures in the Louvre.* New York: Metropolitan Museum of Art, 1992.

Kramer, Samuel N. *History Begins at Sumer.* New York: Doubleday, 1959.

—. *The Sumerians: Their History, Culture, and Character.* Chicago: University of Chicago Press, 1963.

Leick, Gwendolyn. *A Dictionary of Ancient Near Eastern Architecture.* New York: Routledge, 1988.

Lloyd, Seton. *The Archaeology of Mesopotamia: From the Old Stone Age to the Persian Conquest.* London: Thames & Hudson, 1978.

—, and Hans W. Müller. *Ancient Architecture: Mesopotamia, Egypt, Crete.* New York: Electa/Rizzoli, 1986.

Mellaart, James. *Çatal Hüyük: A Neolithic Town in Anatolia.* New York: McGraw-Hill, 1967.

—. *The Earliest Civilizations of the Near East.* New York: McGraw-Hill, 1965.

Moortgat, Anton. *The Art of Ancient Mesopotamia.* New York: Phaidon, 1969.

Moscati, Sabatino, ed. *The Phoenicians.* New York: Abbeville, 1988.

Muscarella, Oscar W. *Bronze and Iron.* New York: Metropolitan Museum of Art, 1988.

Oates, John. *Babylon.* Rev. ed. London: Thames & Hudson, 1986.

Oppenheim, A. Leo. *Ancient Mesopotamia: Portrait of a Dead Civilization.* Rev. ed. Chicago: University of Chicago Press, 1977.

Parrot, André. *The Arts of Assyria.* Trans. Stuart Gilbert and James Emmons. New York: Golden Press, 1961.

—. *Sumer: The Dawn of Art.* Trans. Stuart Gilbert and James Emmons. New York: Golden Press, 1961.

Porada, Edith, and Robert H. Dyson. *The Art of Ancient Iran: Pre-Islamic Cultures.* Rev. ed. New York: Greystone Press, 1967.

Reade, Julian. *Mesopotamia.* London: British Museum Press, 1991.

Roux, Georges. *Ancient Iraq.* 3rd ed. London: Penguin, 1992.

Saggs, Henry W.F. *The Greatness That Was Babylon.* New York: Praeger, 1968.

Woolley, Charles L. *The Art of the Middle East, including Persia, Mesopotamia, and Palestine.* New York: Crown, 1961.

—. *The Development of Sumerian Art.* Westport, CT: Greenwood Press, 1981.

The Art of Ancient Egypt

Aldred, Cyril. *Akhenaten and Nefertiti.* New York: Viking Press, 1973.

—. *Egyptian Art in the Days of the Pharaohs, 3100–320 B.C.* New York: Oxford University Press, 1980.

Andrews, Carol. *Ancient Egyptian Jewelry.* New York: Harry N. Abrams, 1991.

Badawy, Alexander. *A History of Egyptian Architecture.* 3 vols. Berkeley: University of California Press, 1954–68.

Brier, Bob. *Egyptian Mummies.* New York: Morrow, 1994.

Davis, Whitney. *The Canonical Tradition in Ancient Egyptian Art.* New York: Cambridge University Press, 1989.

Doxiadis, Euphrosyne. *The Mysterious Fayum Portraits: Faces from Ancient Egypt.* New York: Harry N. Abrams, 1995.

Edwards, I.E.S. *The Pyramids of Egypt.* Rev. ed. Harmondsworth: Penguin, 1991.

The Egyptian Book of the Dead: The Book of Going Forth by Day: Being the Papyrus of Ani (Royal Scribe of the Divine Offerings). Trans. Raymond O. Faulkner. San Francisco: Chronicle, 1994.

Gardiner, Alan H. *Egypt of the Pharaohs.* Oxford: Oxford University Press, 1978.

Hayes, William C. *The Scepter of Egypt.* 2 vols. New York: Harper & Row, 1953–9.

James, Thomas Garnet Henry. *Egyptian Painting.* London: British Museum Press, 1985.

—, and W.V. Davies. *Egyptian Sculpture.* Cambridge, MA: Harvard University Press, 1983.

Lange, Curt, and Max Hirmer. *Egypt: Architecture, Sculpture, and Painting in Three Thousand Years.* 4th ed. London: Phaidon, 1968.

Lurker, Manfred. *The Gods and Symbols of Ancient Egypt.* Trans. Barbara Cummings. London: Thames & Hudson, 1982.

Mahdy, Christine, ed. *The World of the Pharaohs: A Complete Guide to Ancient Egypt.* London: Thames & Hudson, 1990.

Martin, Geoffrey T. *The Hidden Tombs of Memphis: New Discoveries from the Time of Tutankhamun and Rameses the Great.* London: Thames & Hudson, 1991.

Panofsky, Erwin. *Tomb Sculpture: Four Lectures on its Changing Aspects from Ancient Egypt to Bernini.* Introduction by Martin Kemp. New York: Harry N. Abrams, 1992.

Priese, Karl-Heinz. *The Gold of Meroë.* New York: Metropolitan Museum of Art, 1993.

Redford, Donald B. *Akhenaten: The Heretic King.* Princeton: Princeton University Press, 1984.

Reeves, Nicholas. *The Complete Tutankhamun.* London: Thames & Hudson, 1990.

Schaefer, Heinrich. *Principles of Egyptian Art.* Oxford: Clarendon Press, 1986.

Smith, William Stevenson, and W. Kelly Simpson. *The Art and Architecture of Ancient Egypt.* Rev. ed. New York: Viking, 1981.

Strouhal, Eugen. *Life of the Ancient Egyptians.* Norman: University of Oklahoma Press, 1992.

Taylor, John H. *Egypt and Nubia*. London: British Museum Press, 1991.

Walker, Susan, and Morris Bierbrier. *Ancient Faces: Mummy Portraits from Roman Egypt*. London: British Museum Press, 1997.

Wilkinson, Charles K. *Egyptian Wall Paintings: The Metropolitan Museum of Art's Collection of Facsimiles*. New York: Metropolitan Museum of Art, 1983.

Wilkinson, Richard H. *Reading Egyptian Art: A Hieroglyphic Guide to Ancient Egyptian Painting and Sculpture*. New York: Thames & Hudson, 1992.

Woldering, Irmgard. *Gods, Men, and Pharaohs: The Glory of Egyptian Art*. New York: Harry N. Abrams, 1967.

Wolf, Walther. *The Origins of Western Art: Egypt, Mesopotamia, the Aegean*. New York: Universe Books, 1989.

Aegean Art

Barber, R.L.N. *The Cyclades in the Bronze Age*. Iowa City: University of Iowa Press, 1987.

Boardman, John. *Pre-Classical: From Crete to Archaic Greece*. Baltimore: Penguin, 1967.

Chadwick, John. *The Mycenaean World*. Cambridge: Cambridge University Press, 1976.

Doumas, Christos. *The Wall-paintings of Thera*. Trans. Alex Doumas. Athens: Thera Foundation, 1992.

Getz-Preziosi, Pat. *Sculptors of the Cyclades*. Ann Arbor: University of Michigan Press, 1987.

Graham, J. *The Palaces of Crete*. Rev. ed. Princeton: Princeton University Press, 1987.

Hampe, Roland, and Erika Simon. *The Birth of Greek Art from the Mycenaean to the Archaic Period*. New York: Oxford University Press, 1981.

Higgins, Reynold A. *Minoan and Mycenaean Art*. Rev. ed. Oxford: Oxford University Press, 1981.

Hood, Sinclair. *The Arts in Prehistoric Greece*. Pelican History of Art. Harmondsworth: Penguin, 1978.

—. *The Minoans: The Story of Bronze Age Crete*. New York: Praeger, 1981.

Hurwit, Jeffrey M. *The Art and Culture of Early Greece, 1100–480 B.C.* Ithaca, NY: Cornell University Press, 1985.

Immerwahr, Sara A. *Aegean Painting in the Bronze Age*. University Park: Pennsylvania State University Press, 1990.

Jenkins, Ian. *The Parthenon Friezes*. Austin: University of Texas Press, 1994.

Marinatos, Spyridon N., and Max Hirmer. *Crete and Mycenae*. New York: Harry N. Abrams, 1960.

McDonald, William. *Progress into the Past: The Rediscovery of Mycenaean Civilization*. 2nd ed. Bloomington: Indiana University Press, 1990.

Morg, Catherine. *Athletes and Oracles: The Transformation of Olympia and Delphi in the Eighth Century B.C.* Cambridge: Cambridge University Press, 1990.

Morgan, Lyvia. *The Miniature Wall Paintings of Thera: A Study in Aegean Culture and Iconography*. Cambridge: Cambridge University Press, 1988.

Mylonas, George E. *Mycenae and the Mycenaean Age*. Princeton: Princeton University Press, 1966.

Nilsson, Martin P. *Minoan Mycenaean Religion*. 2nd rev. ed. Lund: Gleerup, 1968.

Palmer, Leonard R. *Mycenaeans and Minoans*. 2nd rev. ed. Westport, CT: Greenwood Press, 1980.

Renfrew, Colin. *The Emergence of Civilization: The Cyclades and the Aegean in the Third Millennium B.C.* London: Methuen, 1972.

Willetts, Ronald F. *The Civilization of Ancient Crete*. Berkeley: University of California Press, 1978.

The Art of Ancient Greece

Arafat, Karim W. *Classical Zeus: A Study in Art and Literature*. Oxford: Clarendon Press, 1990.

Ashmole, Bernard. *Architect and Sculptor in Classical Greece*. New York: New York University Press, 1972.

Beazley, John D. *Attic Red-figure Vase-painters*. 3 vols. First published 1963. Reprint. New York: Hacker, 1984.

—. *The Development of the Attic Black-figure*. Rev. ed. Berkeley: University of California Press, 1986.

Biers, William. *The Archaeology of Greece: An Introduction*. Rev. ed. Ithaca, NY: Cornell University Press, 1987.

Boardman, John. *Athenian Black-figure Vases*. New York: Oxford University Press, 1974.

—. *Greek Art*. New rev. ed. New York: Thames & Hudson, 1985.

—. *The Parthenon and its Sculptures*. Austin: University of Texas Press, 1985.

—. *Greek Sculpture: The Archaic Period: A Handbook*. New York: Thames & Hudson, 1985.

—. *Greek Sculpture: The Classical Period: A Handbook*. New York: Thames & Hudson, 1985.

—. *Athenian Red-Figure Vases: The Classical Period: A Handbook*. New York: Thames & Hudson, 1989.

—. *Athenian Red-Figure Vases: The Archaic Period: A Handbook*. New York: Thames & Hudson, 1991.

Brilliant, Richard. *Arts of the Ancient Greeks*. New York: McGraw-Hill, 1973.

Camp, John M. *The Athenian Agora: Excavations in the Heart of Classical Athens*. New York: Thames & Hudson, 1986.

Carpenter, Rhys. *The Architects of the Parthenon*. Baltimore: Penguin, 1970.

—. *The Esthetic Basis of Greek Art*. Bloomington: Indiana University Press, 1959.

—. *Greek Sculpture*. Chicago: University of Chicago Press, 1960.

Carpenter, Thomas H. *Art and Myth in Ancient Greece: A Handbook*. New York: Thames & Hudson, 1991.

Chitham, Robert. *The Classical Orders of Architecture*. New York: Rizzoli, 1985.

Cook, Robert M. *Greek Art: Its Development, Character, and Influence*. New York: Farrer, Straus & Giroux, 1973.

Coulton, J.J. *Ancient Greek Architects at Work: Problems of Structure and Design*. Ithaca, NY: Cornell University Press, 1977.

Dinsmoor, William B. *The Architecture of Ancient Greece*. 3rd ed. New York: Norton, 1975.

Francis, Eric David. *Image and Idea in Fifth-century Greece: Art and Literature after the Persian Wars*. London: Routledge, 1990.

Havelock, Christine M. *Hellenistic Art*. Greenwich, CT: New York Graphic Society, 1973.

Kampen, Natalie Boymel. *Sexuality in Ancient Art*. Cambridge: Cambridge University Press, 1996.

Koloski-Ostrow, Ann Olga, and Claire L. Lyons, eds. *Naked Truths: Women, Sexuality, and Gender in Classical Art and Archaeology*. London: Routledge, 1997.

Kraay, Colin., and M. Hirmer. *Greek Coins*. New York: Harry N. Abrams, 1966.

Lawrence, Arnold W. *Greek Architecture*. 4th ed. Pelican History of Art. Harmondsworth: Penguin, 1983.

Onians, John. *Art and Thought in the Hellenistic Age*. London: Thames & Hudson, 1979.

—. *Bearers of Meaning: The Classical Orders in Antiquity, the Middle Ages, and the Renaissance*. Princeton: Princeton University Press, 1988.

Papaionnou, Kostas. *The Art of Greece*. New York: Harry N. Abrams, 1989.

Pedley, John Griffiths. *Greek Art and Archaeology*. 2nd ed. New York: Harry N. Abrams, 1998.

Pollitt, Jerome J. *The Ancient View of Greek Art: Criticism, History, and Terminology*. New Haven: Yale University Press, 1974.

—. *Art and Experience in Classical Greece*. Cambridge: Cambridge University Press, 1972.

—. *Art in the Hellenistic Age*. Cambridge: Cambridge University Press, 1986.

—. *The Art of Greece, 1400–31 B.C.: Sources and Documents*. Englewood Cliffs, NJ: Prentice-Hall, 1965.

Richter, Gisela M.A. *Archaic Greek Art against its Historical Background*. New York: Oxford University Press, 1949.

—. *A Handbook of Greek Art*. 6th ed. London: Phaidon, 1969.

—. *Kouroi*. 3rd ed. New York: Phaidon, 1970.

—. *The Sculpture and Sculptors of the Greeks*. 4th ed., rev. New Haven: Yale University Press, 1970.

Ridgway, Brunilde Sismondo. *The Archaic Style in Greek Sculpture*. Princeton: Princeton University Press, 1977.

—. *Fifth-century Styles in Greek Sculpture*. Princeton: Princeton University Press, 1981.

—. *The Severe Style in Greek Sculpture*. Princeton: Princeton University Press, 1970.

Robertson, Charles M. *A History of Greek Art*. 2 vols. Cambridge: Cambridge University Press, 1975.

Roes, Anna. *Greek Geometric Art: Its Symbolism and its Origin*. London: Oxford University Press, 1933.

Schefold, Karl. *Myth and Legend in Early Greek Art*. New York: Harry N. Abrams, 1966.

—. *Gods and Heroes in Late Archaic Greek Art*. New York: Cambridge University Press, 1992.

Schmidt, Evamaria. *The Great Altar of Pergamon*. Trans. Lena Jack. Leipzig: VEB Edition Leipzig, 1962.

Scully, Vincent. *The Earth, the Temple, and the Gods: Greek Sacred Architecture*. Rev. ed. New Haven: Yale University Press, 1979.

Smith, R. R. R. *Hellenistic Sculpture*. New York: Thames & Hudson, 1991.

Stewart, Andrew. *Greek Sculpture: An Exploration*. New Haven: Yale University Press, 1990.

—. *Art, Desire, and the Body in Ancient Greece*. Cambridge: Cambridge University Press, 1997.

Stobart, John C. *The Glory that was Greece*. 4th ed. New York: Praeger, 1971.

Vermeule, Emily: *Aspects of Death in Ancient Greek Art and Poetry*. Berkeley: University of California Press, 1979.

—. *Greece in the Bronze Age*. Chicago: University of Chicago Press, 1972.

Webster, Thomas B.L. *The Art of Greece: The Age of Hellenism*. New York: Crown, 1966.

Whitley, James. *Style and Society in Dark Age Greece: The Changing Face of a Pre-literate Society, 1100–700 B.C.* Cambridge: Cambridge University Press, 1991.

The Art of the Etruscans

Bloch, Raymond. *Etruscan Art*. Greenwich, CT: New York Graphic Society, 1965.

Boethius, Axel, and John B. Ward-Perkins. *Etruscan and Early Roman Architecture*. Pelican History of Art. Baltimore: Penguin, 1970.

Bonfante, Larissa. *Etruscan: Reading the Past*. Berkeley: University of California Press/British Museum, 1990.

—, ed. *Etruscan Life and Afterlife: A Handbook of Etruscan Studies*. Detroit: Wayne State University Press, 1986.

Brendel, Otto J. *Etruscan Art*. ed. E.H. Richardson. Harmondsworth: Penguin, 1978.

Buranelli, Francesco. *The Etruscans: Legacy of a Lost Civilization from the Vatican Museums*. Memphis, TN: Lithograph, 1992.

de Grummond, Nancy T., ed. *A Guide to Etruscan Mirrors*. Florida: Tallahassee, 1982.

Harris, William Vernon. *Rome in Etruria and Umbria*. Oxford: Clarendon Press, 1971.

Macnamara, Ellen. *Everyday Life of the Etruscans*. Cambridge, MA: Harvard University Press, 1991.

Mansuelli, Guido Achille. *The Art of Etruria and Early Rome*. New York: Crown, 1965.

Pallottino, M. *Etruscan Painting*. Geneva: Skira, 1953.

Richardson, Emeline H. *The Etruscans: Their Art and Civilization*. Chicago: University of Chicago Press, 1964.

Spivey, Nigel, and Simon Stoddart. *Etruscan Italy: An Archaeological History*. London: Batsford, 1992.

Sprenger, Maja, Gilda Bartoloni, and Max Hirmer. *The Etruscans: Their History, Art, and Architecture*. New York: Harry N. Abrams, 1983.

Steingräber, Stephen, ed. *Etruscan Painting: Catalogue Raisonné of Etruscan Wall Paintings*. New York: Johnson Reprint, 1986.

Ward-Perkins, John B. *Roman Architecture*. New York: Harry N. Abrams, 1977.

The Art of Ancient Rome

Andreae, Bernard. *The Art of Rome*. Trans. R.E. Wolf. New York: Harry N. Abrams, 1977.

Bianchi Bandinelli, Ranuccio. *The Centre of Power: Roman Art to A.D. 200*. Trans. P. Green. London: Thames & Hudson, 1970.

—. *Rome: The Late Empire: Roman Art A.D. 200–400*. Trans. P. Green. New York: Braziller, 1971.

Brendel, Otto J. *Prolegomena to the Study of Roman Art*. New Haven: Yale University Press, 1979.

Brilliant, Richard. *Pompeii A.D. 79*. New York: Clarkson N. Potter Inc. (Museum of Natural History Publications), 1979.

—. *Roman Art from the Republic to Constantine*. London: Phaidon, 1974.

D'Ambra, Eve. *Roman Art*. New York: Cambridge University Press, 1999.

Feder, Theodore. *Great Treasures of Pompeii and Herculaneum*. New York: Abbeville Press, 1978.

Goldscheider, Ludwig. *Roman Portraits*. London: Phaidon, 1940.

Guilland, Jacqueline, and Maurice Guilland. *Frescoes in the Time of Pompeii*. New York: Potter, 1990.

Hanfmann, George M.A. *Roman Art*. Greenwich, CT: New York Graphic Society, 1964.

Heintze, Helga von. *Roman Art*. New York: Universe, 1990.

Jenkyns, Richard., ed. *The Legacy of Rome: A New Appraisal*. New York: Oxford University Press, 1992.

Krautheimer, Richard. *Rome: Profile of a City, 312–1308*. Princeton: Princeton University Press, 1980.

Ling, Roger. *Roman Painting*. New York: Cambridge University Press, 1991.

MacDonald, William L. *The Pantheon: Design, Meaning, and Progeny*. Cambridge, MA: Harvard University Press, 1976.

—. *The Architecture of the Roman Empire*. New Haven: Yale University Press, 1982.

Menig, Martin, ed. *Handbook of Roman Art*. Ithaca, NY: Cornell University Press, 1983.

Pollitt, Jerome J. *The Art of Rome c. 753 B.C.–A.D. 337: Sources and Documents*. New York: Cambridge University Press, 1983.

Ramage, Nancy H., and Andrew Ramage. *Roman Art: Romulus to Constantine*. 2nd ed. Upper Saddle River, NJ: Prentice-Hall, 1996.

—. *Roman Art: Romulus to Constantine*. New York: Harry N. Abrams, 1991.

—. *The Cambridge Illustrated History of Roman Art*. Cambridge: Cambridge University Press, 1991.

Robertson, Donald S. *Greek and Roman Architecture*. 2nd ed. Cambridge: Cambridge University Press, 1969.

Sear, Frank. *Roman Architecture*. Ithaca, NY: Cornell University Press, 1982.

Strong, Donald E. *Roman Imperial Sculptures: An Introduction to the Commemorative and Decorative Sculpture of the Roman Empire down to the Death of Constantine*. London: Tiranti, 1961.

—. *Roman Art*. Pelican History of Art. Baltimore: Penguin, 1976.

Vermeule, Cornelius. *European Art and the Classical Past*. Cambridge, MA: Harvard University Press, 1964.

Vitruvius. *The Ten Books of Architecture*. Trans. M.H. Morgan. Reprint of 1914 edition. New York: Dover, 1960.

Ward-Perkins, John B. *Roman Architecture*. New York: Harry N. Abrams, 1977.

—. *Roman Imperial Architecture*. Harmondsworth: Penguin, 1981.

Wells, Colin. *The Roman Empire*. Stanford: Stanford University Press, 1984.

Wheeler, Mortimer. *Roman Art and Architecture*. New York: Praeger, 1964.

Wilkinson, Lancelot Patrick. *The Roman Experience*. New York: Knopf, 1974.

Zanker, Paul. *The Power of Images in the Age of Augustus*. Ann Arbor: University of Michigan Press, 1988.

Early Christian and Byzantine Art

Age of Spirituality: Late Antique and Early Christian Art, Third to Seventh Century. New York: Metropolitan Museum of Art, 1979.

Beckwith, John. *The Art of Constantinople: An Introduction to Byzantine Art (330–1453)*. New York: Phaidon, 1968.

—. *Early Christian and Byzantine Art*. Baltimore: Penguin, 1979.

Boyd, Susan A. *Byzantine Art*. Chicago: University of Chicago Press, 1979

Christe, Yves. *Art of the Christian World, A.D. 200–1500: A Handbook of Styles and Forms*. New York: Rizzoli, 1982.

Demus, Otto. *Byzantine Art and the West*. New York: New York University Press, 1970.

—. *Byzantine Mosaic Decoration: Aspects of Monumental Art in Byzantium*. New Rochelle: Caratzas, 1976.

Ferguson, George W. *Signs and Symbols of Christian Art*. New York: Oxford University Press, 1967.

Gough, Michael. *Origins of Christian Art*. London: Thames & Hudson, 1973.

Grabar, André. *The Beginnings of Christian Art, 200–395*. Trans. Stuart Gilbert and James Emmons. London: Thames & Hudson, 1967.

—. *Byzantium: Byzantine Art in the Middle Ages*. Trans. B. Forster. London: Methuen, 1969.

—. *Christian Iconography: A Study of its Origins*. Princeton: Princeton University Press, 1968.

—. *The Golden Age of Justinian, from the Death of Theodosius to the Rise of Islam*. Trans. Stuart Gilbert and James Emmons. New York: Braziller, 1971.

Kitzinger, Ernst. *Byzantine Art in the Making: Main Lines of Stylistic Development in Mediterranean Art, 3rd–7th Century*. Cambridge, MA: Harvard University Press, 1978.

Krautheimer, Richard. *Early Christian and Byzantine Architecture*. 4th ed. Pelican History of Art. Baltimore: Penguin, 1986.

—. *Studies in Early Christian, Medieval, and Renaissance Art*. New York: New York University Press, 1969.

Lane Fox, Robin. *Pagans and Christians*. Harmondsworth: Viking, 1986.

Lowrie, Walter. *Art in the Early Church*. New York: Norton, 1969.

Mainstone, Rowland J. *Hagia Sophia: Architecture, Structure and Liturgy of Justinian's Great Church*. London: Thames & Hudson, 1988.

Mango, Cyril. *Art of the Byzantine Empire, 312–1453: Sources and Documents*. Englewood Cliffs, NJ: Prentice-Hall, 1972.

—. *Byzantine Architecture*. New York: Electa/Rizzoli, 1985.

Manicelli, Fabrizio. *Catacombs and Basilicas: The Early Christians in Rome*. Florence: Scala, 1981.

Mathew, Gervase. *Byzantine Aesthetics*. London: John Murray, 1963.

Mathews, Thomas. *Byzantium: From Antiquity to the Renaissance*. New York: Harry N. Abrams, 1998.

Morey, Charles Rufus. *Early Christian Art*. 2nd ed. Princeton: Princeton University Press, 1953.

Oakshott, Walter. *The Mosaics of Rome: From the Third to the Fourteenth Century*. London: Thames & Hudson, 1967.

Rice, David T. *The Appreciation of Byzantine Art*. Oxford: Oxford University Press, 1972.

Schapiro, Meyer. *Late Antique, Early Christian, and Medieval Art*. New York: Braziller, 1979.

Stevenson, James. *The Catacombs: Rediscovered Monuments of Early Christianity*. London: Thames & Hudson, 1978.

Volbach, Wolfgang, and Max Hirmer. *Early Christian Art*. New York: Harry N. Abrams, 1962.

von Simson, Otto G. *Sacred Fortress: Byzantine Art and Statecraft in Ravenna*. Princeton: Princeton University Press, 1987.

Weitzmann, Kurt. *Art in the Medieval West and its Contacts with Byzantium*. London: Variorum, 1982.

—. *Studies in Classical and Byzantine Manuscript Illustration*. Chicago: University of Chicago Press, 1971.

—, et al. *The Icon*. New York: Knopf, 1982.

The Early Middle Ages

Alexander, Jonathan J.G. *Medieval Illuminators and their Methods of Work*. New Haven: Yale University Press, 1992.

Atil, Esin. *Art of the Arab World*. Washington, D.C.: Smithsonian Institution, 1975.

Backes, Magnus, and Regine Dölling. *Art of the Dark Ages*. Trans. F. Garvie. New York: Harry N. Abrams, 1971.

Backhouse, Janet, ed. *The Lindisfarne Gospels*. Oxford: Phaidon, 1981.

—, D.H. Turner, and Leslie Webster. *The Golden Age of Anglo-Saxon Art, 966–1066*. Bloomington: Indiana University Press, 1984.

Barasch, Moshe. *Gestures of Despair in Medieval and Early Renaissance Art*. New York: New York University Press, 1976.

Basing, Patricia. *Trades and Crafts in Medieval Manuscripts*. London: The British Library, 1990.

Beckwith, John. *Early Medieval Art: Carolingian, Ottonian, Romanesque*. New York: Oxford University Press, 1974.

Blair, Sheila S., and Jonathan M. Brown. *The Art and Architecture of Islam, 1250–1800*. New Haven: Yale University Press, 1994.

Braunfels, Werner. *Monasteries of Western Europe*. London: Thames & Hudson, 1972.

Brown, Peter. *The Book of Kells*. New York: Knopf, 1980.

Calkins, Robert G. *Illuminated Books of the Middle Ages*. Ithaca, NY: Cornell University Press, 1983.

Conant, Kenneth J. *Carolingian and Romanesque Architecture, 800–1200*. 3rd ed. Pelican History of Art. Harmondsworth: Penguin, 1973.

Davis-Weyer, Caecilia. *Early Medieval Art, 300–1150: Sources and Documents*. Reprint of 1971 ed. Toronto: University of Toronto Press, 1986.

Dodwell, Charles Reginald. *Pictorial Art of the West, 800–1200*. Pelican History of Art. New Haven: Yale University Press, 1993.

Ettinghausen, Richard. *Arab Painting*. Geneva: Skira, 1962.

—, and Oleg Grabar. *The Art and Architecture of Islam, 650–1250*. New York: Viking Penguin, 1987.

Fernie, Eric. *The Architecture of the Anglo-Saxons*. London: Batsford, 1983.

Finlay, Ian. *Celtic Art: An Introduction*. London: Faber & Faber, 1973.

Frishman, Martin, and Hasan-Uddin Khan. *The Mosque: History, Architectural Development and Regional Diversity*. London: Thames & Hudson, 1994.

Grabar, André, and Carl Nordenfalk. *Early Medieval Painting*. Geneva: Skira, 1957.

Grabar, Oleg. *The Formation of Islamic Art*. New York: Yale University Press, 1973.

Grant, Michael. *The Dawn of the Middle Ages*. New York: Bonanza Books, 1981.

Green, Miranda Aldhouse. *Celtic Art*. New York: Sterling Publishing Company, 1997.

Grube, Ernest J. *Architecture of the Islamic World: Its History and Social Meaning*. Ed. George Mitchell. New York: Morrow, 1978.

Henderson, George. *Early Medieval*. Harmondsworth: Penguin, 1972.

—. *From Durrow to Kells: The Insular Gospel-books, 650–800*. London: Thames & Hudson, 1987.

Henry, Françoise, ed. *Irish Art in the Early Christian Period, to 800 A.D.* Ithaca, NY: Cornell University Press, 1965.

—. *Irish Art during the Viking Invasions, 800–1020*. Ithaca, NY: Cornell University Press, 1967.

Hinks, Roger P. *Carolingian Art*. Ann Arbor: University of Michigan Press, 1962.

—. *The Carolingian Renaissance*. New York: Braziller, 1970.

Horn, Walter W., and Ernest Born. *Plan of Saint Gall: A Study of the Architecture and Economy of and Life in a Paradigmatic Carolingian Monastery*. 3 vols. Berkeley: University of California Press, 1979.

Hubert, Jean. *The Carolingian Renaissance*. New York: Braziller, 1970.

—, Jean Porcher, and W.F. Volbach. *Europe of the Invasions*. New York: Braziller, 1969.

Irwin, Robert. *Islamic Art in Context*. New York: Harry N. Abrams, 1997.

Kendrick, Thomas D. *Anglo-Saxon Art to A.D. 900*. New York: Barnes & Noble, 1972.

Kidson, Peter. *The Medieval World*. New York: McGraw-Hill, 1967.

Kitzinger, Ernst. *Early Medieval Art in the British Museum*. Rev. ed. Bloomington: Indiana University Press, 1983.

Laing, Lloyd. *Art of the Celts*. New York: Thames & Hudson, 1992.

Lasko, Peter. *Ars Sacra, 800–1200*. Pelican History of Art. Harmondsworth: Penguin, 1972.

Martindale, Andrew. *The Rise of the Artist in the Middle Ages and Early Renaissance*. New York: McGraw-Hill, 1972.

Megaw, Ruth, and Vincent Megaw. *Celtic Art: From Its Beginnings to the Book of Kells*. London: Thames & Hudson, 1989.

Mütherich, Florentine, and Joachim E. Gaehde. *Carolingian Painting*. New York: Braziller, 1976.

Nordenfalk, Carl. *Celtic and Anglo-Saxon Painting: Book Illumination in the British Isles, 600–800*. New York: Braziller, 1977.

—. *Early Medieval Book Illumination*. New York: Rizzoli, 1988.

Pacht, Otto. *The Rise of Pictorial Narrative in 12th-Century England*. Oxford: Clarendon Press, 1962.

—. *Book Illumination in the Middle Ages: An Introduction*. London: Miller, 1986.

Panofsky, Erwin. *Tomb Sculpture*. New York: Harry N. Abrams, c. 1954.

Papadopoulo, Alexandre. *Islam and Muslim Art*. Trans. R. Wolf. New York: Harry N. Abrams, 1979.

Pevsner, Nikolaus. *An Outline of European Architecture*. 7th ed. Baltimore: Penguin, 1970.

—. *Islamic Art*. London: Thames & Hudson, 1975.

Richardson, Hilary, and John Scarry. *An Introduction to Irish High Crosses*. Dublin: Mercier, 1990.

Rickert, Margaret. *Painting in Britain: The Middle Ages*. Pelican History of Art. Harmondsworth: Penguin, 1965.

Saalman, Howard. *Medieval Architecture*. New York: Braziller, 1962.

Schimmel, Annemarie. *Calligraphy and Islamic Culture*. New York: New York University Press, 1983.

Snyder, James. *Medieval Art: Painting, Sculpture, Architecture, 4th–14th Century*. New York: Harry N. Abrams, 1989.

Stokstad, Marilyn. *Medieval Art*. New York: Harper & Row, 1986.

Tasker, Edward G. *Encyclopedia of Medieval Church Art*. London: Batsford, 1993.

Verzone, Paola. *The Art of Europe: The Dark Ages from Theodora to Charlemagne*. New York: Crown, 1968.

Ward, Rachel. *Islamic Metalwork*. New York: Thames & Hudson, 1993.

Wilson, David M. *Anglo-Saxon Art: From the Seventh Century to the Norman Conquest*. London: Thames & Hudson, 1984.

—, and Ole Klindt-Jensen. *Viking Art*. 2nd ed. Minneapolis: University of Minnesota Press, 1980.

Wormald, Francis. *Collected Writings*, Vol. I, *Studies in Medieval Art from the Sixth to the Twelfth Centuries*. New York: Oxford University Press, 1984.

Zarnecki, George. *Art of the Medieval World*. New York: Harry N. Abrams, 1975.

Romanesque Art

Busch, Harald, and Bernd Lohse. *Romanesque Sculpture*. London: Batsford, 1962.

Cahn, Walter. *Romanesque Bible Illumination*. Ithaca, NY: Cornell University Press, 1982.

Clapham, Alfred W. *Romanesque Architecture in Western Europe*. Oxford: Clarendon Press, 1959.

Demus, Otto. *Romanesque Mural Painting*. New York: Harry N. Abrams, 1971.

Evans, Joan. *Art in Medieval France, 987–1498*. New York: Oxford University Press, 1952.

Focillon, Henri. *The Art of the West in the Middle Ages*. Ed. J. Bony, trans. D. King. 2 vols. New York: Phaidon, 1963.

Forsyth, Ilene H. *The Throne of Wisdom: Wood Sculptures of the Madonna in Romanesque France*. Princeton: Princeton University Press, 1972.

Gibbs-Smith, Charles H. *The Bayeux Tapestry*. London: Phaidon, 1973.

Grabar, André, and Carl Nordenfalk. *Romanesque Painting*. New York: Skira, 1958.

Grape, Wolfgang. *The Bayeux Tapestry: Monument to a Norman Triumph*. New York: Prestel, 1994.

Hearn, Millard F. *Romanesque Sculpture in the 11th and 12th Centuries*. Ithaca, NY: Cornell University Press, 1981.

—. *Romanesque Sculpture: The Revival of Monumental Stone Sculpture*. Ithaca, NY: Cornell University Press, 1981.

Holt, Elizabeth G. *A Documentary History of Art*. 3 vols. Princeton: Princeton University Press, 1982.

Jacobs, Michael. *Northern Spain: The Road to Santiago de Compostela*. San Francisco: Chronicle, 1991.

Kennedy, Hugh. *Crusader Castles*. Cambridge: Cambridge University Press, 1994.

Kubach, Hans E. *Romanesque Architecture*. New York: Electa/Rizzoli, 1988.

Kunstler, Gustav. *Romanesque Art in Europe*. Greenwich, CT: New York Graphic Society, 1969.

Little, Bryan D.G. *Architecture in Norman Britain*. London: Batsford, 1985.

Male, Emile. *Religious Art in France, the Twelfth Century: A Study of the Origins of Medieval Iconography*. Bollingen Series, 90:1. Princeton: Princeton University Press, 1978.

—. *Art and Artists in the Middle Ages*. Redding Ridge, CT: Black Swan Books, 1986.

Nichols, S. *Romanesque Signs: Early Medieval Narrative and Iconography*. New Haven: Yale University Press, 1983.

Petzold, Andreas. *Romanesque Art*. New York: Harry N. Abrams, 1995.

Platt, Colin. *The Architecture of Medieval Britain: A Social History*. New Haven: Yale University Press, 1990.

Radding, Charles M., and William W. Clark. *Medieval Architecture, Medieval Learning: Builders and Masters in the Age of Romanesque and Gothic*. New Haven: Yale University Press, 1992.

Saxl, Fritz. *English Sculptures of the 12th Century.* ed. Hanns Swarzenski. London: Faber & Faber, 1954.

Schapiro, Meyer. *Romanesque Art: Selected Papers.* New York: Braziller, 1976.

—. *The Romanesque Sculpture of Moissac.* New York: Braziller, 1985.

Stoddard, Whitney S. *Art and Architecture in Medieval France.* New York: Harper & Row, 1972.

Swarzenski, Hanns. *Monuments of Romanesque Art: The Art of Church Treasuries in North-Western Europe.* 2nd ed. Chicago: University of Chicago Press, 1967.

Tate, Robert B., and Marcia Tate. *The Pilgrim Route to Santiago.* Oxford: Phaidon, 1987.

The Year 1200. 2 vols. New York: Metropolitan Museum of Art, 1970.

Thompson, Daniel V. *The Materials and Techniques of Medieval Painting.* New York: Dover, 1957.

Zarnecki, George. *Romanesque Art.* New York: Universe Books, 1971.

—, Janet Holt, and Tristram Holland. *English Romanesque Art, 1066–1200.* London: Weidenfeld & Nicolson, 1984.

Gothic Art

Alexander, Jonathan J.G., and P. Binski, eds. *Age of Chivalry: Art in Plantagenet England.* London: Royal Academy of Arts, 1987.

Andrews, Francis B. *The Medieval Builder and his Methods.* New York: Barnes & Noble, 1993.

Armi, C. Edson. *The "Headmaster" of Chartres and the Origins of "Gothic" Sculpture.* University Park: Pennsylvania State University Press, 1994.

Aubert, Marcel. *The Art of the High Gothic Era.* New York: Crown, 1965.

—. *Gothic Cathedrals of France and their Treasures.* New York: N. Kay, 1959.

Blum, Pamela Z. *Early Gothic Saint-Denis: Restorations and Survivals.* Berkeley: University of California Press, 1992.

Bony, Jean. *The English Decorated Style: Gothic Architecture Transformed, 1250–1350.* Ithaca, NY: Cornell University Press, 1979.

—. *French Gothic Architecture of the Twelfth and Thirteenth Centuries.* Berkeley: University of California Press, 1983.

Bowie, Theodore, ed. *The Sketchbook of Villard de Honnecourt.* Reprint of 1968 ed. Westport, CT: Greenwood Press, 1982.

Branner, Robert. *St. Louis and the Court Style in Gothic Architecture.* London: Zwemmer, 1965.

—. *Chartres Cathedral.* New York: Norton, 1969.

Brieger, Peter H. *English Art, 1216–1307.* Oxford: Clarendon Press, 1957.

Camille, Michael. *Gothic Art: Glorious Visions.* New York: Harry N. Abrams, 1996.

—. *The Gothic Idol: Ideology and Image Making in Medieval Art.* New York: Cambridge University Press, 1989.

Erlande-Brandenburg, Alain. *Gothic Art.* New York: Harry N. Abrams, 1989.

Favier, Jean. *The World of Chartres.* Trans. F. Garvie. New York: Harry N. Abrams, 1990.

Frankl, Paul. *Gothic Architecture.* Pelican History of Art. Harmondsworth: Penguin, 1962.

Frisch, Teresa G. *Gothic Art, 1140–c.1450: Sources and Documents.* Reprint of 1971 ed. Toronto: University of Toronto Press, 1987.

Gerson, Paula, ed. *Abbot Suger and Saint-Denis: A Symposium.* New York: Metropolitan Museum of Art, 1986.

Grodecki, Louis. *Gothic Architecture.* New York: Harry N. Abrams, 1977.

—, and Catherine Brisac. *Gothic Stained Glass, 1200–1300.* Ithaca, NY: Cornell University Press, 1985.

Jantzen, Hans. *High Gothic: The Classical Cathedrals of Chartres, Reims, Amiens.* Reprint of 1962 ed. Princeton: Princeton University Press, 1984.

Henderson, George D.S. *Chartres.* Baltimore: Penguin, 1968.

—. *Gothic.* Baltimore: Penguin, 1967.

Katzenellenbogen, Adolf. *The Sculptural Programs of Chartres Cathedral.* Baltimore: Johns Hopkins University Press, 1959.

Lord, Carla. *French Royal Patronage of Art in the Fourteenth Century: An Annotated Bibliography.* Boston: G.K. Hall, 1985.

Male, Emile. *The Gothic Image: Religious Art in the 12th Century.* Rev. ed. Princeton: Princeton University Press, 1978.

—. *Religious Art in France: The 13th Century—A Study of Medieval Iconography and its Sources.* Princeton: Princeton University Press, 1984.

—. *Religious Art in France: The Late Middle Ages—A Study of Medieval Iconography and its Sources.* Princeton: Princeton University Press, 1986.

Martindale, Andrew. *Gothic Art.* New York: Praeger, 1967.

Meulen, Jan van der. *Chartres: Sources and Literary Interpretation: A Critical Bibliography.* Boston: G.K. Hall, 1989.

Panofsky, Erwin, and Gerda Panofsky-Soergel. eds. *Abbot Suger on the Abbey Church of Saint-Denis and its Art Treasures.* Princeton: Princeton University Press, 1979.

—. *Gothic Architecture and Scholasticism.* Latrobe, PA: Archabbey Press, 1951.

Pevsner, Nikolaus, and Priscilla Metcalf. *The Cathedrals of England.* 2 vols. Harmondsworth: Viking, 1985.

Pope-Hennessy, John. *Italian Gothic Sculpture.* 2nd ed. New York: Phaidon, 1970.

Sandler, Lucy. *Gothic Manuscripts, 1285–1385.* Survey of Manuscripts Illuminated in the British Isles. London: Miller, 1986.

Sauerlander, Willibald. *Gothic Sculpture in France, 1140–1270.* New York: Harry N. Abrams, 1972.

von Simson, Otto G. *The Gothic Cathedral: Origins of Gothic Architecture and the Medieval Concept of Order.* 3rd ed. Princeton: Princeton University Press, 1988.

Swaan, Wim. *The Gothic Cathedral.* New York: Park Lane, 1969.

Voelkle, William. *The Stavelot Triptych: Mosan Art and the Legend of the True Cross.* New York: The Pierpont Morgan Library, 1980.

Watson, Percy. *Building the Medieval Cathedrals.* Cambridge: Cambridge University Press, 1976.

Wieck, Roger S. *Time Sanctified: The Book of Hours in Medieval Art and Life.* New York: Braziller, 1988.

Williamson, Paul. *Gothic Sculpture, 1140–1300.* New Haven: Yale University Press, 1995.

Wilson, Christopher. *The Gothic Cathedral: The Architecture of the Great Church, 1130–1530.* New York: Thames & Hudson, 1992.

Precursors of the Renaissance

Art and Politics in Late Medieval and Early Renaissance Italy, 1250–1500. South Bend, IN: University of Notre Dame Press, 1990.

Barasch, Moshe. *Giotto and the Language of Gesture.* Cambridge: Cambridge University Press, 1987.

Baxandall, Michael. *Giotto and the Orators.* Oxford: Oxford University Press, 1971.

Barolsky, Paul. *Giotto's Father and the Family of Vasari's Lives.* University Park, PA: Pennsylvania State University Press, 1992.

Bomford, David. *Art in the Making: Italian Painting before 1400.* London: National Gallery, 1989.

Borsook, Eve. *The Mural Painters of Tuscany.* London: Phaidon, 1960.

—, and Fiorelli Superbi Gioffredi. *Italian Altarpieces 1250–1550: Function and Design.* Oxford: Clarendon Press, 1994.

Burckhardt, Jakob C. *The Civilization of the Renaissance in Italy.* Trans. S.G.C. Middlemore. 3rd rev. ed. London: Phaidon, 1950.

Campbell, Lorne. *Renaissance Portraits: European Portrait-Painting in the 14th, 15th, and 16th Centuries.* New Haven: Yale University Press, 1990.

Cennini, Cennino. *The Craftsman's Handbook (Il Libro dell'Arte).* Trans. Daniel V. Thompson, Jr. New York: Dover, 1954.

Chiellini, Monica. *Cimabue.* Trans. Lisa Pelletti. Florence: Scala, 1988.

Cole, Bruce. *Giotto and Florentine Painting, 1280–1375.* New York: Harper & Row, 1975.

—. *The Renaissance Artist at Work.* New York: Harper & Row, 1983.

—. *Sienese Painting: From its Origins to the 15th Century.* Bloomington: Indiana University Press, 1985.

Davis, Howard McP. *Gravity in the Paintings of Giotto.* 1971. Reprinted in Schneider, 1974.

Martindale, Andrew. *The Rise of the Artist.* New York: McGraw-Hill, 1972.

—. *Simone Martini.* New York: New York University Press, 1988.

Meiss, Millard. *Painting in Florence and Siena after the Black Death.* New York: Harper & Row, 1951.

—. *French Painting in the Time of Jean de Berry: The Late Fourteenth Century and the Patronage of the Duke.* New York: Braziller, 1967.

—. *The "Belles Heures" of Jean, Duke of Berry.* New York: Braziller, 1974.

Moskowitz, Anita. *The Sculpture of Andrea and Nino Pisano.* Cambridge: Cambridge University Press, 1986.

Schneider, Laurie M., ed., *Giotto in Perspective.* Englewood Cliffs, NJ: Prentice-Hall, 1974.

Smart, Alastair. *The Dawn of Italian Painting, c. 1250–1400.* Ithaca, NY: Cornell University Press, 1978.

Stubblebine, James H., ed. *Giotto: The Arena Chapel Frescoes.* New York: Norton, 1969.

—. *Assisi and the Rise of Vernacular Art.* New York: Harper & Row, 1985.

—. *Ducento Painting: An Annotated Bibliography.* Boston: G.K. Hall, 1985.

Vasari, Giorgio. *The Lives of the Most Eminent Painters, Sculptors, and Architects.* Trans. Gaston du C. de Vere. New York: Harry N. Abrams, 1979.

White, John. *The Birth and Rebirth of Pictorial Space.* 2nd ed. Boston: Boston Book and Art Shop, 1967.

—. *Duccio: Tuscan Art and the Medieval Workshop.* New York: Thames & Hudson, 1979.

Far Eastern Art (General)

Bussagli, Mario. *Oriental Architecture.* 2 vols. New York: Electa/Rizzoli, 1989.

Frankfort, Henri. *Art and Architecture of the Ancient Orient.* 4th ed. Pelican History of Art. Harmondsworth: Penguin, 1970.

Frederic, Louis. *The Temples and Sculpture of Southeast Asia.* London: Thames & Hudson, 1965.

Lee, Sherman E. *A History of Far Eastern Art.* 5th ed. New York: Harry N. Abrams, 1994.

Martynov, Anatolii I. *Ancient Art of Northern Asia.* Urbana: University of Illinois Press, 1991.

Buddhist Art

Bechert, Heinz, and Richard Gombrich. *The World of Buddhism.* New York: Facts on File, 1984.

Fisher, Robert E. *Buddhist Art and Architecture.* New York: Thames & Hudson, 1983.

Rowland, Benjamin. *The Evolution of the Buddha Image.* New York: Asia Society, 1968.

Seckel, Dietrich. *Art of Buddhism.* New York: Crown, 1964.

Zwalf, W., ed. *Buddhism: Art and Faith.* London: British Museum Press, 1985.

Chinese Art

The Arts of China. 3 vols. Tokyo: Kodansha International, 1968–70.

Barnhart, Richard M., James Cahill, Wu Hung, Yang Xin, Nie Chongzheng, and Lang Shaojun. *Three Thousand Years of Chinese Painting.* New Haven: Yale University Press, 1997.

Confucius. *Analects,* ed. Bradley Smith and Wan-go Weng in *China: A History in Art.* New York: Doubleday, n.d.

Laozi, *Daode jing,* ed. Wing-tsit Chan in *A Source Book in Chinese Philosophy.* Princeton: Princeton University Press, 1963.

Loehr, Max. *The Great Painters of China.* New York: Harper & Row, 1980.

Rawson, Jessica, ed. *The British Museum Book of Chinese Art.* New York: Thames & Hudson, 1993.

Sickman, Lawrence, and Alexander Soper. *Art and Architecture of China.* Pelican History of Art. Harmondsworth: Penguin, 1972.

Speiser, Werner. *The Art of China: Spirit and Society.* New York: Crown, 1961.

Treasures from the Bronze Age of China. New York: Metropolitan Museum of Art, 1980.

Tregear, Mary. *Chinese Art.* New York: Oxford University Press, 1980.

Vainker, S.J. *Chinese Pottery and Porcelain: From Prehistory to the Present.* London: British Museum Press, 1991.

Indian Art

Basham, Arthur Llewellyn. *The Wonder that was India.* 3rd ed. London: Sidgwick & Jackson, 1985.

Brown, Percy. *Indian Architecture (Buddhist and Hindu Periods).* 3rd ed. Bombay: D.B. Taraporevala Sons and Co., 1976.

Coomaraswamy, Ananda K. *History of Indian and Indonesian Art.* New York: Dover, 1985.

Craven, Roy C. *Indian Art: A Concise History.* New York: Thames & Hudson, 1985.

Dallapiccola, Anna L. *The Stupa: Its Religious, Historical, and Architectural Significance.* Wiesbaden: Steiner, 1980.

Goetz, Hermann. *The Art of India: Five Thousand Years of Indian Art.* 2nd ed. New York: Crown, 1964.

Harle, James C. *The Art and Architecture of the Indian Subcontinent.* Pelican History of Art. Harmondsworth: Penguin, 1987.

Huntington, Susan L., and John C. Huntington. *The Art of Ancient India: Buddhist, Hindu, Jain.* New York: Weatherhill, 1985.

Lannoy, Richard. *The Speaking Tree: A Study of Indian Culture and Society.* Oxford: Oxford University Press, 1971.

Meister, Michael, and M.A. Dhaky, eds. *Encyclopaedia of Indian Temple Architecture.* Philadelphia: University of Pennsylvania Press, 1983.

Michell, George. *The Hindu Temple: An Introduction to its Meaning and Forms.* Chicago: Chicago University Press, 1988.

—. *The Penguin Guide to the Monuments of India.* 2 vols. New York: Viking, 1989.

Rowland, Benjamin. *Art and Architecture of India: Buddhist, Hindu, Jain.* Pelican History of Art. Harmondsworth: Penguin, 1977.

Sivaramamurti, Calambur. *The Art of India.* New York: Harry N. Abrams, 1977.

Soundara Rajan, K.V. *Indian Temple Styles.* New Delhi: Munshiram Manoharlal, 1972.

Volwahsen, Andreas. *Living Architecture: India.* London: Macdonald, 1970.

Weiner, Sheila L. *Ajanta: Its Place in Buddhist Art.* Berkeley: University of California Press, 1977.

Zimmer, Heinrich. *Myths and Symbols in Indian Art and Civilization.* New York: Harper & Brothers, 1962.

Japanese Art

Akiyama, Terukazu. *Japanese Painting.* Treasures of Asia. Geneva: Skira, 1961.

Mason, Penelope. *History of Japanese Art.* New York: Harry N. Abrams, 1993.

Paine, Robert T., and Alexander Soper. *Art and Architecture of Japan.* 3rd ed. Pelican History of Art. Harmondsworth: Penguin, 1981.

Stanley-Baker, Joan. *Japanese Art.* New York: Thames & Hudson, 1984.

Yoshikawa, Itsuji. *Major Themes in Japanese Art.* Trans. Armins Nikovskis. New York: Weatherhill, 1976.

Mesoamerican and South Pacific Art

Blocker, Harry Gene. *The Aesthetics of Primitive Art.* Lantham, MD: University Press of America, 1994.

Caruana, Wally. *Aboriginal Art.* New York: Thames & Hudson, 1993.

Coe, Michael D. *The Maya.* 5th ed. New York: Thames & Hudson, 1993.

Coote, Jeremy, and Anthony Shelton, eds. *Anthropology: Art and Aesthetics.* New York: Oxford University Press, 1992.

Corbin, George A. *Native Arts of North America, Africa, and the South Pacific.* New York: Harper & Row, 1988.

Kubler, George. *The Art and Architecture of Ancient America.* 3rd ed. Pelican History of Art. New Haven: Yale University Press, 1990.

Mexico, Splendors of Thirty Centuries. New York: Metropolitan Museum of Art, 1990.

Miller, Mary Ellen. *The Art of Mesoamerica from Olmec to Aztec.* New York: Thames & Hudson, 1986.

Pasztory, Esther. *Pre-Columbian Art.* New York: Cambridge University Press, 1990.

Spinden, Herbert J. *A Study of Maya Art: Its Subject Matter and Historical Development.* New York: Dover, 1975.

Stone-Miller, Rebecca. *The Art of the Andes from Chavuin to Inca.* New York: Thames & Hudson, 1986.

Townsend, Richard. *The Ancient Americas: Art from Sacred Landscapes.* Chicago: Art Institute of Chicago, 1992.

Notes

Chapter 1

1. Cited by Martha Joukowsky, *A Complete Manual of Field Archaeology*, Englewood Cliffs, NJ, 1980, p. 1.

Chapter 2

1. James McNeill Whistler, "The Ten O'Clock" lecture, Princes Hall, London, 1885.
2. Abbé H. Breuil, *Four Hundred Centuries of Cave Art*, New York, 1979.
3. Jennifer Isaacs, *Australian Dreaming*, Sydney and New York, 1980, p. 69.

Chapter 3

1. Cited by Diane Wolkstein and Samuel Noah Kramer, *Inanna: Queen of Heaven and Earth*, New York, 1983, p. 105.
2. Quotes from the *Epic of Gilgamesh* are from James Gardner and John Maier, *Gilgamesh*, New York, 1984, p. 57.
3. Cited by Spiro Kostof, *A History of Architecture*, New York, 1985, p. 60.
4. Cited by Linnea H. Wren and David J. Wren, eds., *Perspectives on Western Art*, vol. I, New York, 1987, p. 13.
5. Cited by Spiro Kostof, *A History of Architecture*, New York, 1985, pp. 133–34.

Chapter 4

1. Cited by Miriam Lichtheim, *Ancient Egyptian Literature*, vol. I, Berkeley, 1975, pp. 205–6.
2. T. G. H. James, *An Introduction to Ancient Egypt*, New York, 1979.
3. Cited by Miriam Lichtheim, *Ancient Egyptian Literature*, vol. I, Berkeley, 1975, pp. 43–4.
4. Herodotus, *History of Greece*, vol. II, trans. A. D. Godley, Loeb Edition, Cambridge, MA, 1982, p. 124.

Chapter 6

1. Plutarch, *Lives*, vol. III, trans. Bernadotte Perrin, Loeb Edition, Cambridge, MA, 1984, p. 36.

2. Cited by John Onians, *Art and Thought in the Hellenistic Age*, London, 1979, p. 46.

Chapter 7A ("Window")

1. *Treasures from the Bronze Age of China*, Metropolitan Museum of Art, New York, 1980, p. 45.
2. Florian Coulmas, *The Writing Systems of the World*, Oxford, 1989; Georges Jean, *Writing: The Story of Alphabets and Scripts*, London, 1992; Andrew Robinson, *The Story of Writing*, London, 1995.
3. *A Source Book in Chinese Philosophy*, translated and compiled by Wing-tsit Chan, Princeton, 1963, p. 30.
4. Cited by Bradley Smith and Wan-go Weng, *China: A History in Art*, London, 1973, p. 44.

Chapter 8

1. Virgil, the *Aeneid*, Bk. VI., ll. 847–53, trans. Robert Fitzgerald, New York, 1983.
2. Cited by William L. Macdonald, *The Architecture of the Roman Empire*, New Haven and London, 1982, pp. 31–32.
3. Josephus, *Jewish Wars* VII, pp. 5, 132. Cited in J. J. Pollitt, *The Art of Rome c. 753 B.C.–A.D. 337: Sources and Documents*, Cambridge, 1996, p. 159.
4. Marcus Aurelius, *Meditations V*, pp. 1, 2. Cited in J. J. Pollitt, *The Art of Rome c. 753 B.C.–A.D. 337: Sources and Documents*, Cambridge, 1996, p. 185.
5. The *Odyssey*, Bk. X, II, trans. A. T. Murray, Loeb Edition, vol. I, Cambridge, MA, 1984, pp. 120–26.

Chapter 10

1. Robert Irwin, *Islamic Art in Context: Art, Architecture, and the Literary World* (Perspectives Series), New York, p. 254.
2. Franz Rosenthal, "Abu Haiyun al-Tawhidi on Permanship," *Ars Islamica*, 13–14 (1948), p. 18. Cited in *Calligraphy in the Arts of the Muslim World* by Anthony Welch, Texas, 1979.
3. *Beowulf*, trans. Frederick Rebsamen, New York, 1991, p. 2.

4. Cited by H. A. Guerber, *Myths of the Norsemen*, New York, 1992, p. 3.

Chapter 11

1. William Melczer, *The Pilgrim's Guide to Santiago de Compostela*, New York, 1993, pp. 103–4.

Chapter 12

1. Cited by Erwin Panofsky, *The Book of Suger, Abbot of Saint Denis*, Princeton, 1979, p. 43.
2. Cited by Erwin Panofsky, *ibid*, p. 51.
3. Saint Augustine, *The City of God (Civitas Dei)*, Book 6, trans. George E. McCracken, Loeb Edition, Cambridge, Massachusetts, p. 11.
4. Cited by Bernard McGinn, *Antichrist*, New York, 1994, p. 15.

Chapter 13

1. Cited by Laurie M. Schneider, ed., *Giotto in Perspective*, Englewood Cliffs, NJ, 1974, p. 29.
2. Dante, *Purgatory*, vol. II, lines 91–95, in Millard Meiss, *Painting in Florence and Siena after the Black Death*, Princeton, 1951, p. 5.
3. Cited by Laurie M. Schneider, ed., *Giotto in Perspective*, Englewood Cliffs, NJ, 1974, p. 38.
4. Cited by Elizabeth Holt, *A Documentary History of Art*, New York, 1957, p. 137.
5. Cited by Linnea H. Wren and David J. Wren, eds., *Perspectives on Western Art*, New York, 1987, p. 270.
6. Cited by Linnea H. Wren and David J. Wren, eds., *ibid*, p. 274–77.

Acknowledgments

Many of the line drawings in this book have been specially drawn by Taurus Graphics, Kidlington. Calmann & King Ltd. are grateful to all who have allowed their plans and diagrams to be reproduced. Every effort has been made to contact the copyright holders, but should there be any errors or omissions, they would be pleased to insert the appropriate acknowledgement in any subsequent edition of this publication.

2.8   From Abbé H. Breuil, *Quatre Cents Siècles d'Art*. Montignac: Centre d'Études et de Documentation Préhistorique, 1979.

2.23   From Spiro Kostof, *A History of Architecture: Settings and Rituals*. Oxford: Oxford University Press, 1985. © 1985. Drawings by Richard Tobias.

3.9   From Lois Fichner-Rathus, *Understanding Art*. Upper Saddle River, NJ: Prentice-Hall, Inc., 1986. © 1986. Reprinted by permission of Prentice-Hall, Inc., Upper Saddle River, NJ.

3.28, 3.29 From Henri Frankfort, *Art & Architecture of the Ancient Orient*. London: Yale University Press, Pelican History of Art Series, 1970.

4.4, 4.5 From Quirke and Spencer, eds., *British Museum Book of Ancient Egypt*. London: British Museum Press, 1992.

4.18   From W. Stevenson Smith, *The Art and Architecture of Ancient Egypt*. London: Yale University Press, Pelican History of Art series, 1981.

4.31   From Phipps and Wink, *Invitation to the Gallery*. New York: McGraw-Hill, 1987.

4.32   From Richard Tansey and Fred Kleiner, *Gardner's Art Through the Ages*, 10e. Fort Worth: Harcourt Brace College Publishers, 1996.

5.5   From Reynold A. Higgins: *The Archaeology of Minoan Crete*. Henry Z. Walck, Random House, Inc., 1973.

5.16   From Christos Doumas, *Thera*. London: Thames & Hudson Ltd, 1983.

5.22   Fondazione Giorgio Cini, Istituto di Storia dell'Arte, Venice.

5.29   Drawn by P. P. Platt after Piet de Jong, from Reynold A. Higgins, *Minoan & Mycenaean Art*. London: Thames & Hudson Ltd, 1983.

6.29   From Boardman et al, *The Oxford History of Classical Art*. Oxford: Oxford University Press, 1997.

6.35   From John Boardman, *Greek Sculpture: The Classical Period*. London: Thames & Hudson Ltd, 1985.

6.36   From John Griffiths Pedley, *Greek Art and Architecture*. New York: Simon & Schuster, 1993.

6.39, 6.40 From John Boardman, *Greek Sculpture: The Classical Period*. London: Thames & Hudson Ltd, 1985.

6.37, 6.41, 6.42, 6.49, 6.64 From Leland M. Roth: *Understanding Architecture*, Boulder, CO: Westview Press, 1994.

6.54   From B. F. Cook, *The Elgin Marbles*. London: British Museum Press, 1984.

7.2   From Emeline Hill Richardson, *The Etruscans: Their Art and Civilization*. Chicago: University of Chicago Press, 1964.

7.8b   Museo Archeologico, Florence, Italy.

7.12   From Mario Moretti, *Cerveteri*. Instituto Geografico De Agostins, Navaro, 1984.

7.B   From *Treasures from the Bronze Age of China*. New York: Metropolitan Museum of Art, 1980.

8.11, 8.13, 8.14, 8.18 From Leland M. Roth: *Understanding Architecture*. Boulder, CO: Westview Press, 1994.

8.24   From Frank Sear, *Roman Architecture*. London: B. T. Batsford Ltd, 1982.

8.58   From A. Maiuri, *La Villa dei Misteri*. New York: George Braziller, Inc., 1961 (originally published in Rome, 1931).

8.M   From Percy Brown, *Indian Architecture (Buddhist and Hindu Periods)*. Bombay: D. B. Taraporevala Sons & Co. Private Ltd, 1971.

9.7   From Leland M. Roth, *Understanding Architecture*. Boulder, CO: Westview Press, 1994.

9.8   From Lois Fichner-Rathus, *Understanding Art*. Upper Saddle River, NJ: Prentice-Hall, Inc. © 1986. Reprinted by permission of Prentice-Hall, Inc., Upper Saddle River, NJ.

9.11   From Richard Tansey and Fred Kleiner, *Gardner's Art Through the Ages*, 10e. Fort Worth: Harcourt Brace College Publishers, 1996.

9.35   From Spiro Kostof, *A History of Architecture: Settings and Rituals*. Oxford: Oxford University Press, 1985. © 1985. Drawings by Richard Tobias.

9.C   British Architectural Library: Royal Institute of British Architects, London.

9.H   From Robert E. Fisher, *Buddhist Art and Architecture*. London: Thames & Hudson Ltd, 1993.

10.6, 10.38 From Richard Tansey and Fred Kleiner, *Gardner's Art Through the Ages*, 10e. Fort Worth: Harcourt Brace College Publishers, 1996.

10.12   From Godfrey Goodwin, *History of Ottoman Architecture*. London: Thames & Hudson Ltd, 1971. By permission of Mrs G. T. M. Goodwin.

10.I   From George Kubler, *Art and Architecture of Ancient America,* 3rd ed. London: Yale University Press, 1984.

10.T   Drawing by Jean Blackburn from Michael D. Coe, *The Maya*, 5th ed. London: Thames & Hudson Inc., 1993.

11.10   From Meyer Schapiro: *The Sculpture of Moissac*. New York: George Braziller, Inc., 1985.

12.4   From Lois Fichner-Rathus, *Understanding Art*. Upper Saddle River, NJ: Prentice-Hall, Inc., 1986. © 1986. Reprinted by permission of Prentice-Hall, Inc., Upper Saddle River, NJ.

12.6   From *Dictionnaire raisonné de l'architecture française*. Paris, 1859–68.

12.9, 12.33 From Richard Tansey and Fred Kleiner, *Gardner's Art Through the Ages*, 10e. Fort Worth: Harcourt Brace College Publishers, 1996.

12.52   From Leland M. Roth: *Understanding Architecture*. Boulder, CO: Westview Press, 1994.

12.I, 12.J From Laurence Sickman and Alexander Soper, *The Art and Architecture of China*. London: Yale University Press, Penguin History of Art series, 1971.

12.L   From Susan Huntington, *Art of Ancient India*. New York: Weatherhill Inc., 1993.

12.Q   From *Traveler's Key to Northern India*. New York: Alfred A. Knopf Inc., 1983.

12.U   From Freeman and Warner, *Angkor: The Hidden Glories*. Paris: Bibliothèque Nationale de France, 1990.

Picture Credits

Calmann & King Ltd., the picture researcher, and the author wish to thank the institutions and individuals who have kindly provided photographic material or artwork for use in this book. Museums and galleries are given in the captions; other sources are listed below.

1.1 Rijksmuseum Vincent Van Gogh, Amsterdam/Bridgeman Art Library, London and New York
1.2 © Daniel Schwartz/Lookat, Zurich
1.3 A. F. Kersting, London
1.4 The Museum of Modern Art, New York. Given anonymously. Photo: © 1999 The Museum of Modern Art, New York/ © ADAGP, Paris and DACS, London, 1999
1.5 Los Angeles County Museum of Art, CA, USA/Bridgeman Art Library, London and New York/© ADAGP, Paris and DACS, London, 1999
1.7 Kunsthistorisches Museum, Vienna/ Bridgeman Art Library, London and New York
1.8 Photo: © Board of Trustees, National Gallery of Art, Washington, D.C.
1.9 Musée d'Orsay, Paris/Peter Willi/ Bridgeman Art Library, London and New York
1.10 Gemäldegalerie, Berlin/Artothek, Peissenberg
1.11 The Museum of Modern Art, New York. Purchase. Photo: © 1999 The Museum of Modern Art, New York/© DACS 1999
1.14 Detail from *Children's Page*, 1943/© 1999 Estate of Alexander Calder/Artists Rights Society (ARS), New York
1.23, 1.25, 1.26, 1.27 The Museum of Modern Art, New York. Purchase. Photo: © 1999 The Museum of Modern Art, New York/ © DACS 1999
1.24 The Museum of Modern Art, New York. Gift of Nelly van Doesburg. Photo: © 1999 The Museum of Modern Art, New York/ © DACS 1999
2.1 Naturhistorisches Museum, Vienna/Ali Meyer/Bridgeman Art Library, London and New York
2.2 © Cliché: Musée d'Aquitaine, Bordeaux/Photo: Jean-Michel Arnaud
2.3 Photo: © RMN, Paris
2.4, 2.7 Photo: Jean Vertut, Issy-les-Moulineaux
2.5 Museo Arqueológico Nacional de Madrid/Institut Amatller d'Art Hispànic, Barcelona
2.6 Robert Harding Picture Library, London/© Robert Frerck
2.9a Jean Dominique Lajoux, Paris
2.9b From Abbé Breuil: *Four Hundred Centuries of Cave Art*, opp. p. 167/By permission of the Syndics of the Cambridge University Library
2.10 AKG Photo/AKG London
2.11 Robert Harding Picture Library, London
2.12 Soit © Arch. Phot., Paris/soit © CNMHS/Photo: Mario Ruspoli
2.14 Photo: J. Collina-Girard/Ministère de la Culture, France
2.15, 2.16, 2.17 Cliché: J. Clottes/Ministère de la Culture et de la Communication, Direction du Patrimoine, Sous Direction de l'Archéologie
2.19 George Chaloupka Collection, Darwin

2.20 Ron Ryan/Coo-ee Picture Library, Elwood, Victoria
2.22 Powerstock/Zefa, London
2.24, 2.25, 2.26 J. Allan Cash Ltd, London
2.27, 2.32 © Skyscan Balloon Photography, Cheltenham, UK
2.31 © English Heritage Photograph Library, London
3.2 Jericho Excavation Fund, B.S.A.J.
3.3, 3.4 James Mellaart, London
3.5 © Bildarchiv Preussischer Kulturbesitz, Berlin, Vorderasiatisches Museum, 1998
3.6, 3.7 The State Antiquities Organization, Baghdad, Republic of Iraq
3.10 © Roger-Viollet/Frank Spooner Pictures, London
3.11, 3.25, 3.26, 3.27 © British Museum, London
3.12, 3.13 Courtesy of The Oriental Institute of the University of Chicago
3.14, 3.15, 3.21 University of Pennsylvania Museum (neg# T4-29c.2) (neg# T4-848c.2) (neg# S4-140070, Ur, Iraq, Libation scene stone) (neg# S4–142807) (neg# S8–61926)
3.16 Scala, Florence
3.17 Photo: © RMN, Paris/Photo: H. Lewandowski
3.18 Courtesy of Museum of Fine Arts, Boston (26.289). Francis Bartlett Fund
3.19 Photo: © RMN, Paris
3.22 Gallimard, Paris
3.23 J. Allan Cash Ltd, London
3.30 Giraudon, Paris
3.31 © Bildarchiv Preussischer Kulturbesitz, Berlin, Vorderasiatisches Museum, 1998/Photo: Jürgen Liepe
3.32 Photo: © RMN, Paris/Photo: Gérard Blot
3.34 Boltin Picture Library, Croton-on-Hudson, New York
3.36 Powerstock/Zefa, London
3.37, 3.38 E. Boudot-Lamotte
3.39 The Metropolitan Museum of Art, New York. Fletcher Fund, 1954 (54.3.3). Photo: © 1982 The Metropolitan Museum of Art
4.2, 4.3, 4.46 Werner Forman Archive/The Egyptian Museum, Cairo
4.6 British Museum/E.T. Archive, London
4.9, 4.10, 4.38, 4.39, 4.40, 4.47, 4.49, 4.52, 4.53 © British Museum, London
4.13 Carolyn Clarke/Spectrum Picture Library, London
4.18 Werner Forman Archive, London
4.20, 4.41 Hirmer Fotoarchiv, Munich
4.21 Harvard-Museum Expedition, courtesy of Museum of Fine Arts, Boston
4.22, 4.51 Peter Clayton, Hemel Hempstead
4.23 Photo: © RMN, Paris/Photo: H. Lewandowski
4.24, 4.25 Museum Expedition, courtesy of Museum of Fine Arts, Boston. © 1998 Museum of Fine Arts, Boston. All rights reserved
4.26, 4.35 Robert Partridge. The Ancient Egypt Picture Library, Knutsford, Cheshire, UK
4.27 The Metropolitan Museum of Art, New York. Gift of Edward S. Harkness, 1914 (14.3.17). Photo: © 1993 The Metropolitan Museum of Art
4.28 The Metropolitan Museum of Art, New York. Purchase, Edward S. Harkness Gift, 1926 (26.7.1394). Photo: © 1983 The Metropolitan Museum of Art

4.29 Harvard University-Museum of Fine Arts Expedition, courtesy of Museum of Fine Arts, Boston
4.30 The Metropolitan Museum of Art, New York. Levi Hale Willard Bequest, 1890 (90.35.1). Photo: © The Metropolitan Museum of Art
4.36 The Metropolitan Museum of Art, New York. Museum Excavations, 1927–28 (28.3.18). Photo: © The Metropolitan Museum of Art
4.37 Douglas Dickins, London
4.42 © Bildarchiv Preussischer Kulturbesitz, Berlin, Ägyptisches Museum, 1998/Photo: Margarete Büsing
4.43 © Bildarchiv Preussischer Kulturbesitz, Berlin, Ägyptisches Museum und Papyrussammlung, 1998/Photo: Margarete Büsing
4.44, 4.45 Scala, Florence
4.48 Courtesy of Dr Timothy Kendall, Museum of Fine Arts, Boston
4.50 Egyptian Expedition of The Metropolitan Museum of Art, New York. Rogers Fund, 1930 (30.4.21). Photo: © 1978 The Metropolitan Museum of Art
4.54 Courtesy of W. V. Davies, London
4.55 By permission of the Syndics of the Cambridge University Library
5.2, 5.3, 5.12, 5.28 Photo by Studio Kontos, Athens/© Studio Kontos
5.4, 5.26 Hirmer Fotoarchiv, Munich
5.6 Sonia Halliday Photographs, Weston Turville, UK/Photo by FHC Birch
5.7, 5.21, 5.25, 5.32, 5.33 Peter Clayton, Hemel Hempstead, UK
5.8, 5.10 Ronald Sheridan/Ancient Art & Architecture Collection, London
5.9 National Archaeological Museum, Athens/ Scala, Florence
5.11 Archaeological Museum, Heraklion, Crete/Giraudon, Paris/Bridgeman Art Library, London and New York
5.13 Hirmer Fotoarchiv/from Marinatos and Hirmer, *Crete and Mycenae*, Pl. VII, opp. p. 22, by permission of the syndics of Cambridge University Library
5.14, 5.24 Scala, Florence
5.15, 5.17, 5.18, 5.19, 5.20 Courtesy of Idryma Theras-Petros M. Nomikos (Thera Foundation), Athens
5.16 Courtesy of Dr Christina Televantou, Athens
5.23 From George E. Mylonas, *Mycenae Rich in Gold*, fig. 80, pp. 102–3. Photo courtesy of Ekdotike Athenon, S.A.
5.27 The Conway Library, Courtauld Institute of Art, London
5.31 © Photoarchive, Archaeological Receipts Fund, Athens
6.2, 6.6, 6.7, 6.17, 6.21b Photo by Studio Kontos, Athens/© Studio Kontos
6.4, 6.10, 6.11, 6.51c, I, 6.52, 6.53, 6.56 © British Museum, London
6.5 National Archaeological Museum, Athens/ Scala, Florence
6.9 Vatican Museums and Galleries, Vatican City, Italy/Bridgeman Art Library, London and New York
6.12, 6.21a, 6.22, 6.24, 6.27, 6.44, 6.51r, 6.55, 6.56, 6.66, 6.71, 6.75 Hirmer Fotoarchiv, Munich
6.13 Photo: Christa Koppermann/Studio Koppermann, Gauting, Munich

Index